Controlling
the Dangerous Classes

A History of Criminal Justice in America

SECOND EDITION

Randall G. Shelden

University of Nevada–Las Vegas

Foreword by Michael Hallett

PEARSON

Boston • New York • San Francisco
Mexico City • Montreal • Toronto • London • Madrid • Munich • Paris
Hong Kong • Singapore • Tokyo • Cape Town • Sydney

Senior Acquisitions Editor: *Dave Repetto*
Series Editorial Assistant: *Jack Cashman*
Senior Marketing Manager: *Kelly May*
Production Editor: *Pat Torelli*
Editorial-Production Service: *Valerie A. Heffernan, S4Carlisle Publishing Services*
Composition Buyer: *Linda Cox*
Manufacturing Buyer: *Debbie Rossi*
Electronic Composition: *S4Carlisle Publishing Services*
Cover Administrator: *Linda Knowles*
Cover Designer: *Susan Paradise*

For related titles and support materials, visit our online catalog at www.ablongman.com.

Between the time website information is gathered and then published, it is not unusual for some sites to have closed. Also, the transcription of URLs can result in typographical errors. The publisher would appreciate notification where these errors occur so that they may be corrected in subsequent editions.

Library of Congress Cataloging-in-Publication Data

Shelden, Randall G.,
   Controlling the dangerous classes : a history of criminal justice in America / Randall
G. Shelden.—2nd ed.
      p.   cm.
   Includes bibliographical references and index.
   ISBN-13: 978-0-205-57189-5
   ISBN-10: 0-205-57189-1
   1. Criminal justice, Administration of—United States—History. 2. Crime—Government policy—United States. 3. Prisons—United States—History. 4. Juvenile justice, Administration of—United States—History. I. Title.
   HV9950.S54 2008
   364.973—dc22   2007022301

Printed in the United States of America

Contents

Foreword by Michael Hallett   ix

Preface   xiii

1 *Perpetuating the Class System: The Development of Criminal Law*   *20*

Introduction: Nature and Functions of Criminal Law   *20*

Criminal Law in Ancient Times   *21*
  Emergence of Criminal Law in Athens   22
  Criminal Law in Rome   22
  Acephalous or Non-state Societies and Law   23

Criminal Law in Medieval Times   *24*

Emergence of Criminal Law in England   *25*
  Criminal Law as an Ideological System of Legitimate Control   28
  Emergence of the Concept of Crime   29
  Two Case Studies: The Law of Theft and the Law of Vagrancy   30

Emergence of Criminal Law in America   *34*
  Racism and the Law   36
  An Illustrative Case: The Tramp Acts   41

Controlling the Dangerous Classes: Drug Laws as an Example   *42*
  Crack versus Powder Cocaine   49
  The Impact of the Drug Laws Passed in the 1980s   56

Whose Interest Does the Law Serve? **58**

Notes **62**

2 *The Development of the Police Institution:*
Controlling the Dangerous Classes **66**

Early Police Systems **66**

The Emergence of the Police Institution in England **68**
    The Metropolitan Police of London 70
    Sir Robert Peel 72

The Development of the Police Institution in the United States **74**

An Illustrative Case: Buffalo, New York **76**
    The Rise and Growth of Private Policing 79

The Growth of the Police Institution in the 20th Century **81**
    The Progressive Era 82
    Police Reforms During the Progressive Era 85
    New Developments in Private Policing 86
    Policing the Ghetto in the 1960s 88
    Police Corruption: A Continuing Problem 89

Still Controlling the Dangerous Classes:
The "War on Drugs" **98**

Notes **101**

3 *Processing the Dangerous Classes:*
The American Court System **102**

Introduction **102**

The Development of the Modern Court System:
The Colonial System **105**
    Elite Dominance of the Legal Profession in Colonial America 106
    Processing Criminal Cases: The Justice of the Peace in Colonial
    America 107
    Upholding Morality 108
    Hunting for Witches and Religious Dissidents 109

After the Revolution: The Federal System and the
Supreme Court **111**
    Post-Civil War Changes in the Court System 114

The Jail: Managing the Rabble **116**

The 1960s: The Warren Court and the Reaffirmation of the
Right to Counsel   *118*

Traditional vs. Radical-Criminal Trials   *122*
    The Traditional Criminal Trial   122
    Challenging the System: Radical-Criminal Trials   122
    The St. Patrick's Four   126

The Modern Era: The War on Drugs and Racial Minorities   *128*

The Ultimate Sanction for the Dangerous Classes:
The Death Penalty   *138*

Notes   *143*

4   *Housing the Dangerous Classes: The Emergence*
     and Growth of the Prison System   *145*

Part I: Early Developments of Imprisonment, 1600 to 1900   *145*

The Trafficking of Offenders: Forerunners of the Modern
Prison Industrial Complex   *147*

Early Capitalism and the Emergence of the Workhouse   *150*

Late 18th Century Reforms and the Birth of the Prison
System   *152*

The Development of the American Prison System   *156*
    The Walnut Street Jail   156
    The Pennsylvania and Auburn Systems of Penal Discipline   158
    The Rise of the Reformatory   161
    Convict Labor   163
    Convict Leasing   164

Part II: Twentieth Century Developments in the American Prison
System   *168*

Prison Reform During the Progressive Era   *168*
    Inmate Self-Government   168
    Classification, Diagnosis and Treatment: A New Prison
    Routine   169
    The Decline in Prison Industries   171
    The Big House   172

The Emergence of the Federal Prison System and the System
of Corrections   *173*
    The Federal Prison System   173
    The System of Corrections   175

The Modern Era, 1980 to the Present: Warehousing and the New American Apartheid   177

The American Gulag   183

Some Concluding Thoughts   185

Notes   186

5 *Controlling the Young: The Emergence and Growth of the Juvenile Justice System*   188

Pre-19th Century Developments: The Invention of Childhood   189

A History of Childhood and Adolescence   190

Enter Childhood in the 17th Century   192

Parens Patriae *and Stubborn Children*   197

Defining a Juvenile Delinquent   199

The House of Refuge Movement   200

Conceptions of Delinquency: 1820 to 1860   202

The Fate of the Refuge Movement   203

Ex Parte Crouse: *Court Decisions and Effects*   204

The O'Connell Case   205

Mid-19th Century Reforms   206

The Fate of Mid-19th Century Reforms   211

The Child-Saving Movement and the Juvenile Court   212

Conceptions of Delinquency: 1860 to 1920   214

The Fate of the Child-Saving Movement   216

Twentieth-Century Developments in Juvenile Justice   218

Still Controlling Minorities and the Poor: Current Juvenile Justice Practices   219

Race, the War on Drugs and Referrals to Juvenile Court   220

Racial Composition of Juvenile Institutions   224

High Recidivism Rates and Scandals Persist   225

Notes   230

6 *Perpetuating Patriarchy:*
Keeping Women in their Place   *232*

Women and the Law   *232*

   Patriarchy and Images of Women   232

   Punishing and Controlling Women   234

A History of Women's Prisons   *236*

The Emergence of Women's Reformatories   *239*

   The Role of Racism   240

   Controlling Women's Bodies and Sexuality   242

Girls and the Juvenile Justice System   *244*

   Keeping Girls in their Place: The Development
   of Institutions for Girls   244

   The Child-Saving Movement and the Juvenile Court   244

   The Best Place to Conquer Girls   249

   The Juvenile Court and the Double Standard of Juvenile
   Justice   250

Women and Criminal Justice Today   *254*

   Sentencing Patterns, the War on Drugs and Women   255

   An Outrageous Example: The Pregnancy Police   258

   Women in Today's Prisons   261

   Background Characteristics of Women in Prison   264

Notes   *269*

7 *Crime Control in the New Millennium:*
New Mechanisms for Controlling
the Dangerous Classes   *270*

The Crime Control Industry   *272*

   Taking a Larger View: The Globalization of Crime Control   275

   Millions Under Control of the State   276

The Prison-Industrial Complex: Cashing in on Crime   *278*

   Prisons as a Market for Capitalism   278

   Corporate Interests: The Role of ALEC   282

   Reach Out and Touch Someone   283

   Brother Can You Spare a Bed?   283

   The California Correctional Officer's Union   284

   Rural Prisons: Uplifting Rural Economies?   285

   Some Downsides to Prison Expansion   289

Exploiting Prisoners to Enhance Rural Populations   292

Prison Labor: Auburn Plan Revisited   295

The Privatization of Prisons: More Profits for Private Industry   297

Some Serious Problems with Privatization   299

Private Security: Crime Is Good for Business   301

Other Components of the Crime Control Industry   303

Notes   *304*

8   *Where Do We Go From Here?*   *306*

The Importance of the Economy   *307*

American-Style Capitalism Is the Real Culprit   309

Downsizing and Outsourcing the American Dream and the Growing Surplus Population   313

The Growth and Perpetuation of the Surplus Population (Dangerous Classes)   318

So What Can I Do, You Ask?   *323*

Notes   *325*

References   **327**

Name Index   **350**

Subject Index   **359**

Foreword

Michael Hallett
University of North Florida

Research on punishment is in full-fledged renaissance of late, revealed in part by the release of this second edition of the book you have in your hands—the single best and most comprehensive review of the history of criminal justice from a critical perspective available. As part of a growing body of work bespeaking dissatisfaction with mainstream criminology's myopic focus on hot spots and statistical residues, this book gets to the heart of the matter of social justice versus criminal justice—by exploring the roles of gender, race, and social class in the actual operation of the criminal justice system. Here, a detailed accounting of the fundamental pattern of the history of criminal justice—the exploitation and suppression of the poor and marginal through legal means—is offered to students who are often encouraged to *ignore* questions of social justice entirely. Despite that fact, this book is built on a tradition of scholarship viewing punishment as a social process that evolves, operates, and transforms itself quite independently of crime and criminality—operating instead on the basis of power, wealth, racism, and capitalistic exploitation.

That is, while both crime and imprisonment rates fluctuate over historical periods, the continued pattern of operation in criminal justice over the centuries—as this book thoroughly documents—is a targeted focus on the poor, the politically powerless, and the socially marginal. As Greenberg and West put it: "Sociological analyses of the history of penality have *taken as their premise* that institutionalized punishment practices are not entirely determined by the functional necessity of

---

*Michael Hallett, PhD, is Professor and Chair of the Department of Criminology and Criminal Justice at the University of North Florida. His most recent book, *Private Prisons in America: A Critical Race Perspective* (University of Illinois Press, 2006) won the *Gandhi, King Ikeda Award* from the Martin Luther King Jr. International Chapel at Morehouse College in Atlanta, MLK's alma mater.

preventing crimes" (2001: 638). Many other things are going on in the operation and unfolding of punishment than crime control—such as political posturing by politicians and social entrepreneurs, confinement and demonization of the dangerous classes, artificial management of surplus labor and official unemployment, profit-taking, and not least, the assuaging of middle-class anxieties about crime and vulnerability. From Rothman to Foucault, if the history of criminal justice has taught us anything, it is that punishments always involve dynamics larger than the individual offender. And it is from this perspective that the book begins.

The introductory chapter offers a methodical opening to the tradition of "rabble" management in criminal justice that structures the book, namely through an exposition of the history of jails as holding pens for impoverished debtors. As Shelden notes, "historically the terms crime and poverty (or the old eighteenth-century term *pauperism*) have been used interchangeably" (p. XX). Specifically, readers here find a marked distinction between crime control of offenders versus social control of marginal groups—with a deep-level questioning of the extent to which crime control is the—can be—the actual goal of the criminal justice system as it actually operates. In a capital-based society where the vast majority of citizens managed by the criminal justice system come from the most impoverished class—and the wealthiest two percent of citizens own more than half the available wealth—the groups targeted by criminal justice policy have not been those doing the most damage to society (arguably white collar and business offenders), but those who offended the sensibilities of struggling and middle class white Protestants. Can we control crime without addressing the underlying causes of crime?

The dangerous classes, as it were, are not those objectively harming the social fabric in the most egregious ways—but those, instead, who offend that self-righteous but vague feeling of decency and conformity that has always structured middle-class sensibilities about the necessity for social order and crime control. In Shelden's narrative, the wars on drugs loom large—from Prohibition to the contemporary—criminal justice activities have demonstrably not been about reducing crime or demand for drugs or curtailing addiction—but instead about cracking down on socially reviled groups that have not managed to become part of the mainstream, dominant culture (namely Chinese immigrants in the first instance and poor black males in the second).

In his treatment of the history of policing, Shelden trenchantly documents the birth of the London Metropolitan Police as an outgrowth of bread riots and urbanization, as starving workers unable to find work and displaced by the laws of vagrancy transitioned into the industrial from a feudal economy. In a vitally important passage, Shelden notes:

> The idea that the police would prevent crime by patrolling the streets in search of suspicious activities and/or persons and identifying potential troublemakers was the most important break with the past. The concern over the presence of mobs and radical protests and political parties helps explain the formation of this type of police force. The police could now serve more direct class-control functions (as well as other more routine functions) by patrolling those communities wherein live the poorest and most oppressed people, thereby keeping tabs on them or keeping a lid on potential disorder.

And so it has been ever since.

While the chapters on courts and juvenile justice reveal numerous attempts to overthrow the classist traditions of criminal justice history—through discussions of the political prosecution of Father Daniel Berrigan's protest of the Vietnam War and the child-saving movement of the early 1900s, for example—the book's extensive treatment of the history of the prison system is the most revealing of all, for it is here that the overriding dynamics of the American justice system reveal themselves in their entirety: through a discussion of what Professor Shelden calls the New American Apartheid.

Documenting the evolution of the disparities in punishment for use of crack versus powder cocaine in the United States particularly, Shelden reveals what is arguably the system's over-riding de-facto purpose: controlling all that is not white and male and corporate in society. As Shelden puts it: "As already noted, drug offenses have accounted for most of the increase in prison populations in recent years. However, the prison and jail populations have become increasingly dominated by minorities, especially African Americans, including women." And here you have what in my view is this book's greatest contribution: its discussion of patriarchy as it relates to crime control. Tracing the traditions of patriarchy back to ancient Rome and Greece, Shelden's discussion of the lack of rights for women and slaves sets the context for all that was to come in the social relations of criminal justice: The most powerless (women and minorities) being confined to domestic or unpaid labor—producing more workers and wealth for a system that will invariably exploit them further—the dramatic increase in the incarceration rate of black women in the United States today is the most shocking of all (an increase of over 700 percent).

But perhaps you think this is all just "liberal garbage" or "Marxist trash." In the concluding chapter new to this second edition of *Controlling the Dangerous Classes*, is an expanded discussion of the increasingly global implications of harsh punishment of the poor rooted in the middle-class anxieties of the world's "haves." The book here builds on a tradition that seeks a more fully global and social accounting of the operations of punishment—but takes it a step further: By exploring particularly how populist and expressive fervor for harsh punishment among the world's "haves" relates to broader shifts in the geopolitics and citizenship claims of the world's "have nots," the book offers a glimpse at the increasingly privatized but global expansion of punishment regimes targeted at the poor worldwide. In all our efforts at control of the dangerous classes, Shelden notes, "it is always they who have to change." And that, of course, is where we go wrong entirely—for as this book convincingly documents, the poor and politically powerless of the world are already paying for the greatest crime of all. As Gandhi put it: "The greatest crime of all, is poverty."

Preface

Writing is an art form, a creative act, and an endeavor that is deeply personal. Part of you goes into it. You are making some of your deepest and most cherished feelings public. In doing this, you are exposing yourself and subjecting yourself to the close scrutiny of others. Some may like what you say and some may not. Some may even hate you and level all sorts of accusations your way.

I say these words as a kind of warning to the reader. You may not like what I say. You may not agree with certain premises. I'm not that concerned with this. What I am concerned about is that you take the effort to read what I am saying. What I am saying is deeply disturbing. What I am saying is that our system of justice is deeply flawed. It is deeply flawed mostly because the surrounding culture and social institutions are deeply flawed. The notion of "equal justice" is a kind of oxymoron in American society, since this society is so unequal in so many ways. Unfortunately, such words are not welcomed in our society. We want to hold on to our most cherished beliefs. We don't want to "air our dirty laundry" so to speak. We don't want to admit that the emperor has no clothes nor reveal some dirty truths. We want belief in the myths of Horatio Alger, of democracy, of equality, of unlimited opportunities, of freedom and liberty.

So I must warn the reader at the outset that the book you have in your hands is biased. It presents an alternative view to business as usual when it comes to describing the American system of justice. (The word *biased* is interesting. It comes from a French word that means "slant." Everyone has a slant including writers. There is no such thing as a perfectly unbiased piece of writing—even the Bible is biased!)

My perspective is similar to that presented by Jeffrey Reiman in his book *The Rich Get Richer and the Poor Get Prison*. In the latest edition of this book (the 8th edition), Reiman writes that his book is not a complete survey of the entire criminal justice system and it "is not meant to be a complete recipe for fixing either. Nor is it meant to be a balanced presentation of conservative and progressive views" (Reiman, 2007: xvi). His goal in writing his book is rather to demonstrate that what goes on within the criminal justice system violates people's sense of fairness and that it "does not function the way it says it does" (2007: xvi). The aim in my book is to show that this failure to achieve equal justice for all has been with us from the very beginning—from our early roots in Roman law, through the conquests of William the Conqueror and right up to the writing of the U. S. Constitution.

The first edition of this book was published in 2001, although the writing was completed in the spring of 2000. I will repeat here what I wrote at that time in the Preface, as my views have not changed that much. I will add some closing comments at the end.

This project involves a passion I have had since my graduate school days, namely, the subject of history. I recall that during my graduate school days becoming fascinated by the history of the criminal justice system. While working on my dissertation I would spend literally several hours in the library, not in the sociology or criminology section, but in the history section! I suppose what fascinated me the most was the persistent fact that in so many ways history keeps repeating itself and that we somehow never seem to learn from it. But what I learned most of all is this: Since we often repeat history (as the philosopher Santayana once said something to the effect that those who fail to study history are doomed to repeat it) it occurred to me that *things just don't happen by accident* and that if history does in fact repeat itself then there is a reason for the persistence of some social phenomenon. If we examine something going on today and then go back in history and find that it has occurred not once or twice but repeatedly then the problem is much deeper than we imagined. As sociologists we are suppose to look for patterns of human interaction and social processes. At least that is what some of the leading figures in sociology have suggested (Marx, Durkheim, Weber, and especially C. Wright Mills). If something persists, there must be an important reason. If someone begins to look at the conditions within many juvenile correctional institutions and find that they are often appalling and in some cases violation of human rights, there is the tendency to believe that this is just a product of some current and unusual situation. But if we look deeper, and look at this historically, we quickly learn that this is a pattern that can be traced back at least as far as the houses of refuge in the early 19th century. In so doing we will realize that this current appalling situation is not some aberration, but part of a long tradition. We may realize that this is so because this is how we have always treated those without much power and influence in society. We then know what we are up against if we are going to make changes.

This is what has guided me in the writing of this book. Looking at the past is important only because it takes us to the present and then into the future. Some who read these passages will recognize the influence of one of my favorite historians, Howard Zinn, who has influenced me more than any other historian. It was the first edition of his book, *The Politics of History* (1990) that had a profound influence on me during my graduate school days in the early 1970s. I have never forgotten some of the lessons learned from reading that book, plus his work, *A People's History of the United States* (Zinn, 2005).

I have also learned much from someone who technically is not a true historian (to call someone technically not a true historian seems rather crude as I write these lines, since it suggests that the only people who can possibly be real historians are those with the proper credentials—namely having a degree in the subject—which is obviously not the case), and this someone is Noam Chomsky. Something he wrote in one of his books struck me as being extremely significant and insightful—significant in the sense that he simply asked what should be a rather common-sense question having to do with history. In his book, *Year 501: The Conquest Continues*, Chomsky was writing about the bombing of Pearl Harbor, the "date which will live in infamy" as Franklin D. Roosevelt put it. Chomsky remarked that in all the talk about Japanese aggression, one important question was omitted: "How did we happen to have a military base at Pearl Harbor, or to hold our Hawaiian colony altogether?" In other words, what were we doing there in the first place? The answer is: we "stole Hawaii from its inhabitants, by force and guile, just half a century before the infamous date, in part so as to gain the Pearl Harbor naval base" (Chomsky, 1993: 243). A tough question, to be sure, but the kind that is rarely asked. Such are the kinds of questions I try to raise in this book.

This book is about asking critical questions, like, what is a crime and what is law and whose interests are served by the law and the criminal justice system? And what are the patterns that are constantly repeated? And how does such a system relate to such larger issues as social inequality, social class, race and gender, especially social class?

One final comment is in order, one that needs to be made so that there will be no confusion about my own perspective, which guides the direction and the content of this book. I do not subscribe to some simple, easy to state theory of the law and the criminal justice system. I would not classify myself as an avowed supporter of one theory or another. Obviously, my general orientation (as will soon be obvious) is quite critical, even Marxist in many ways. I am not going to argue that there is some vast conspiracy among the ruling class (and there is in fact a ruling class and they do in fact rule, but their rule is not monolithic; see Domhoff, 1998) to use the law and the legal system in every instance to trample on the rights of ordinary citizens, especially the poor. Nor am I going to argue that every law is a mere reflection of the interest of this class—or any class for that matter. What I will argue is that, when looking at the results of the law in general and the daily operations of the criminal justice system—that is, the outcomes of legal decision—the entire system generally comes down hardest on those with the least amount of power and influence and generally comes down in the most lenient fashion on those with the most power and influence. I am not going to try in this book to advance a new theory of lawmaking. That I leave to others. My purpose here is to show the inherent bias in the American system of law and justice—a bias that is generally based upon social class, but also race, gender, and age—and show how this is grounded in the historical development of the law and the criminal justice system.

This book is not meant to provide an encyclopedic coverage of the history of criminal justice in America. Books by others provide a great deal of detail that is omitted here. This book is rather an introductory overview—a primer if you will—of the subject. There are literally thousands of articles and several recent books that can be consulted if you are interested in probing deeper into this subject. Many of these are found in the bibliography at the end of this book.

Since this book came out it has generated quite a bit of interest. I have talked with many people during the past six years who tell me they have been greatly influenced the book, with one basing a master's thesis on the subject. I especially recall meeting Michael Hallett for the first time (who has graciously agreed to write the Foreword to this new edition). I sat in the back of a room at an American Society of Criminology conference just a few years ago where he was presenting a paper. The subject was convict leasing and he passed around a handout that reproduced some of the information in my book. Upon our meeting after the panel was concluded, he told me that he had been very influenced by my book, for which I was thankful and a bit flattered. I ended up writing the foreword to his book, which expanded upon a few ideas I had brought out in my book (Hallett, 2006). Many others have had similar feelings about the book.

In telling this I am not trying to boast, although it may seem this way. I am simply mentioning this only to illustrate the point I made at the start of this Preface. Our words, as writers, are public and influence people one way or another. This, I believe, is our greatest reward, much more than the royalties we receive (which are rarely very much). To have someone tell you that they have been influenced by what you have said is the greatest reward one can ask for. Therefore, I would like to extend my warmest thanks to all of you who have been influenced by what I have had to say. I sincerely hope that you will be pleased with this second edition.

There are several peple I would like to acknowledge for this second edition. First, a warm thanks to a good friend and colleague, Michael Hallett for writing an excellent foreword. It was nice that you could return a favor. To the people at Allyn and Bacon for giving me a second chance, especially Dave Repetto and Karen Hansen, plus Valerie Heffernan, the project editor with Carlisle Publishing Services. Finally, I extend my love to my wife Virginia for continuing to love me, in spite of my shortcomings and all that has happened in recent years.

R.G.S.

The History of Criminal Justice from a Critical Perspective

One of the 20th century's most eminent historians, Howard Zinn, once wrote, "history is written from records left by the privileged" (Zinn, 1990: 102). By this he merely meant that historical writings tend to be biased and written from the point of view of those in power. Similarly, the history of criminal justice is written largely from the point of view of those in power. In this case we see a history that, among other things, takes the law for granted and too often treats the criminal justice system in a social, political, and economic vacuum. Such standard histories also largely ignore such critical issues as class, race, and gender in the analysis. Moreover, the effect of the development of capitalism is rarely discussed. Issues like racism, inequality, poverty, and class conflict are rarely raised. If they are raised, they are usually done so merely in passing, as if they are aberrations in an otherwise ideal system.

A typical example comes from one of the most popular histories of criminal justice, written by Samuel Walker. At one point he discusses the issue of vigilantism in the 1700s and correctly notes that this was one among many methods of the elite controlling the "dangerous classes." However, he then notes that this phenomenon "formed a violent and ugly scar on the history of criminal justice" (Walker, 1980: 32–33).[1] But was this merely a scar or was it part of a much larger pattern that has repeated itself throughout our history? A more careful look at history reveals that such scars have continued to appear, over and over again, well into the present era (need we look any further than the beating of Rodney King or the systematic incarceration of millions of African-Americans throughout the last part of the 20th and well into the 21st century?).[2]

Howard Zinn also noted that in writing history, the historian cannot be neutral, because "he writes on a moving train." Thus, your history is naturally biased. But so are all the other histories. Zinn notes that "our work is value-laden whether we choose or not" (Zinn, 1990: 35–36). Therefore I would like to state quite categorically that this book is in this sense biased. It takes a critical approach to the subject matter. And what do I mean by a critical approach? The word *critical* comes from two Greek roots: *kriticos* (discerning judgment) and *criterion* (standards). Therefore, the word implies the development of discerning judgment based on standards. Webster's *New World Dictionary* defines *critical* as "characterized by careful analysis and judgment," followed by "critical, in its strictest sense, implies an attempt at objective judgment so as to determine both merits and faults."[3]

A critical approach necessitates the use of our imaginations, and requires us to look at things from perspectives other than our own and to consider the consequences of each perspective. A critical perspective also utilizes what C. Wright Mills called the "sociological imagination." By this Mills meant that the best way to understand the world around us is to "grasp history and biography and the relations between the two within society." More specifically, he wrote that through the use of this method "the individual can understand his own experience and gauge his own fate only by locating himself within his period [of history] . . ." Using the sociological imagination causes us to distinguish between what Mills called "personal troubles of milieu" and "public issues of social structure." By personal troubles Mills referred to those very personal, private matters that "occur within the character of the individual and within the range of his immediate relations with others." A problem becomes a "public issue of social structure" when the issue has to do with "matters that transcend those local environments of the individual" and when "some value cherished by publics is felt to be threatened" (Mills, 1959: 5–8).

Critical thinking includes, among other things, attempting to transcend the current social order and institutional arrangements. Through this process we no longer merely accept "what is." Rather, we attempt to visualize "what could be." Paraphrasing the late Senator Robert Kennedy, some may think about what is and ask "Why?" while others, that is, critical thinkers, think about what could be and ask "Why not?" Michalowski suggests that critical thinking involves exercising "careful judgement or judicious evaluation" and with respect to the critical study of crime such a perspective "demands that we examine not only what the law says is crime but also *why* the law says it is so." To do this we must dig beneath the everyday assumptions and unquestioned truths about crime and examine the social, economic, political, and historical roots of both crime and the ideas about it that are taken for granted (Michalowski, 1985: 14).

A critical historical perspective can help us address the question of "Why not?" because, in looking back, we might be able to see, with greater clarity, what "could have been." Zinn has argued for what he calls "radical history." By this he means a "value-laden historiography" because, as he puts it, you "can't be neutral on a moving train."[4] He suggests five ways history can be useful from this perspective:

(1) "We can intensify, expand, sharpen our perception of how bad things are, for the victims of the world; (2) We can expose the pretensions of government to either neutrality or beneficence; (3) We can expose the ideology that pervades our culture—using "ideology" in Mannheim's sense: rationale for the going order: (4) We can recapture those few moments in the past which show the possibility of a better way of life than that which has dominated the earth thus far; (5) We can show how good social movements can go wrong, how leaders can betray their followers, how rebels can become bureaucrats, how ideals can become frozen and reified (Zinn, 1990: 36–55).

Admittedly, this is quite a task, and in this book I will try to accomplish at least some of what Zinn has suggested. Part of what Zinn is suggesting is that a critical perspective (or in his words, "radical history") seeks to achieve what critical criminologists call *social justice*. By this term, I mean a form of justice that "is appropriate for a society based on cooperative social relations" rather than relations based upon human exploitation and greed (Quinney and Wildeman, 1991: 15). Unfortunately, our modern system of justice takes place within a society that is highly stratified by race, class, and gender. It is my contention that equal justice cannot be achieved in an unequal society. The justice system in American merely reinforces these inequalities. Social justice, in contrast, seeks to eliminate such systemic problems as poverty, racism, sexism, and class inequality, which generate most of the crime we experience.

Social class is of crucial importance in the shape of many patterns of social life, as a multitude of studies have demonstrated (Domhoff, 1998; Gilbert, 1998; Rothman, 1998). However, there are important interconnections between race, gender, and class that always need to be considered.[5] When viewing the history of criminal justice, all three are quite important in that class, race, and gender bias are systemic in American society, which have serious consequences for the criminal justice system, as all other major institutions. It will be shown throughout this book that all three variables have been important in terms of the passage of criminal laws and their enforcement; that is, class, race, and gender bias are operating at every stage. Yet, while not down-playing the importance of race and gender, I will treat class as the most important variable. The reasons should become apparent to the reader; however, some preliminary remarks about the importance of class are in order at this time.

As the title of a recent book suggests, "class counts" (Wright, 1998; see also, Perrucci and Wysong, 2003; Phillips, 2002; Collins et al., 1999; Heintz et al., 2000). As far as the criminal justice system is concerned, social class position determines in large part the following: (1) what behaviors come to be defined as criminal and thus subject to their enforcement; (2) who is defined as a criminal; (3) how far into the criminal justice system a particular case is processed; and (4) the final sentence of a criminal case. Class is also related to whether or not one can make bail, whether or not one has an attorney, and even the quality of the representation (Cole, 1999; Reiman, 2004).

A critical perspective also challenges the conventional wisdom about the nature of our criminal justice system by arguing that the system not only fails in its duty to protect us from crime and make us feel safe, but that it is actually designed to fail. In making this argument we are borrowing the ideas of Jeffrey Reiman who calls this way of looking at criminal justice the "Pyrrhic defeat theory." In military terminology, a *Pyrrhic victory* is where a particular battle is won, but the costs in terms of troops lost amounts to a defeat. Reiman suggests, "the failure of the criminal justice system yields such benefits to those in positions of power that it amounts to success" (Reiman, 2004: 5). Such success comes in the following forms: (1) by focusing primarily on the crimes of the poor and racial minorities, it distorts the crime picture by deflecting the discontents and anger of middle-class Americans toward the poor and racial minorities, rather than toward those in positions of power above them; (2) the American criminal justice system, in its "war on crime," and especially the "war on drugs," makes it look as if the most serious threat comes from the crimes of the poor and racial minorities, when in fact the greatest harms, both in terms of life and property, come from the crimes of the very rich; (3) by focusing on crime control and the punishment of individual offenders the system fails to address some of the major causes of crime. This is what Reiman calls the "ideological" functions of the criminal justice system. By focusing exclusively on the individual offender, writes Reiman, "it diverts our attention away from our institutions, away from consideration of whether our institutions themselves are wrong or unjust or indeed 'criminal'" (Reiman, 2004: 164).

Reiman illustrates this nicely by quoting from Debra Seagal who wrote about a prime-time television "real crime" show that was based upon videotapes of real police arrests. In this article Seagal discusses how focusing on individual criminals diverts our attention away from the social context of crime and, indeed, communicates the idea that these offenders exist in a social vacuum. Seagal writes as follows:

> By the time our 9 million viewers flip on their tubes, we've reduced fifty or sixty hours of mundane and compromising video into short, action-packed segments of tantalizing, crack-filled, dope-dealing, junkie-busting, cop culture. How easily we downplay the pathos of the suspect; how cleverly we breeze past the complexities that cast doubt on the very system that has produced the criminal activity in the first place (Seagal, 1993, quoted in Reiman, 2004: 165).

In a similar vein, one writer has noted that the big hoopla about "family values" by Dan Quayle over both the riots in Los Angeles following the Rodney King verdict and an episode in the TV series *Murphy Brown* (where the main character is a single woman who decides to have her baby out of wedlock and raise it herself) completely ignored the social context of the lives of most women and most inner-city African-Americans. She noted that:

> . . . the erasure of the L.A. uprising in the *Murphy Brown* incident moved the debate away from issues of race, from the condition of inner cities, and from the deteriorating economic base in the United States, to a much safer, symbolic ground. By shifting the debate from the material conditions of inner cities to the discursive field of "family values," both parties occupied a much more comfortable terrain for debate (Stabile, 1993: 289).

This is an example of what is known as symbolic politics (e.g., Gordon, 1994: 4). Similarly, TV crime shows constantly inform the public about the dangerous criminals in our midst without any attempt to try to explain why. The viewer is left with the impression that these criminals come out of nowhere! Reiman concludes by saying that:

> To look only at individual criminality is to close one's eyes to social injustice and to close one's ears to the question of whether our social institutions have exploited or violated the individual. *Justice is a two-way street—but criminal justice is a one-way street.* Individuals owe obligations to their fellow citizens because their fellow citizens owe obligations to them. Criminal justice focuses on the first and looks away from the second.

Thus, by focusing on individual responsibility for crime, the criminal justice system literally acquits the existing social order of any charge of injustice (Reiman, 2004: 166).

The estimated costs of index crimes (based on victimization surveys) are about $105 billion annually. If you factor in intangible costs of pain and suffering (almost impossible to get an accurate estimate of this figure) the total comes to $450 billion. In contrast, the most recent estimate of the costs of corporate and white collar crime is in excess of $1.5 trillion each year (Shelden and Brown, 2004). The list of specific crimes seems endless. The list includes bribery of government officials, defense contract fraud, health care provider fraud, and corporate tax evasion. Moreover, the corporate share of the tax burden has declined from around 25% in the 1950s to less than 10% today (Friedrichs, 2004; Cray, 2005). The list of corporate and white collar crimes also includes price-fixing (costing consumers over $100 million each year), price gouging ("systematic overcharging" with mark-ups as high as a phenomenal 7,000%), false advertising and product misrepresentation, corporate stealing from employees (e.g., cheating workers out of overtime pay, violations of minimum wage laws, and so on), unfair labor practices, surveillance of employees, theft of trade secrets, monopolistic practices, defrauding investors (e.g., the Equity Funding case, which inflated stock prices by claiming $200 million in nonexistent assets), and many more (Mokhiber, 1996: 87; Friedrichs, 2004). And all of this does not even include various forms of what is referred to as occupational crime, such as retail fraud on the part of small businesses, service business fraud (especially prevalent in the car repair industry) and various forms of medical crime, especially Medicaid and Medicare fraud, which is estimated to be as high as $25 billion per year (Friedrichs, 2004).

Reiman notes that what is called a crime has little to do with the objective dangers (Reiman, 2004: 67). Statistically speaking, the gravest threats to us are not from robbers, burglars, rapists and the like. Rather, they are from those who wear a suit and tie to work, or a white medical coat, or who occupy plush offices in corporate headquarters or who occupy powerful positions within the government. Their weapons are ballpoint pins, scalpels, computers, or merely their voices (as when they decide to go to war). Numerous studies have documented the real dangers from corporate and state crime.[6]

The case cannot be overstated that, in general, the criminal justice system focuses primarily on those crimes that have the highest probabilities of being committed by the poorest segments of our society and almost virtually ignores those crimes committed by the richest segments of our society, crimes that actually harm us the most. This is one of the main themes of Reiman's book, aptly titled *The Rich Get Richer and the Poor Get Prison* (Reiman, 2004). In the present book, it will be demonstrated that this tendency has a strong historical basis and has in fact been a constant theme from the very beginning of American history, if not earlier.

Before moving ahead, it is necessary to take a critical view of what is the basic foundation of the criminal justice system, the criminal law. Without the criminal law there is, technically, no crime. But this is more than an academic exercise, for to examine this idea is to begin to expose the law and legal system as an important aspect of social life. But more than this, these perspectives also apply more generally to the entire criminal justice system, not just the criminal law per se. The last perspective to be discussed, the critical perspective, will serve as a general theoretical framework for the entire book.

Perspectives on Criminal Law

Why are some behaviors prohibited by law, while others are not? It doesn't take much analysis to figure out that some very harmful behaviors are perfectly legal—such as the possession and consumption of cigarettes and alcohol, not to mention addictive prescription drugs. However, such drugs as marijuana, heroin, and cocaine are illegal, yet not nearly as harmful as cigarettes and alcohol.

Also, while there is a law that prohibits the killing of another human being (called homicide or just plain murder), in some contexts the taking of a human life can be perfectly legal, such as a police officer killing a citizen who, for instance, threatens his life; the application of the death penalty; killing in the time of war; and the controversial actions of Dr. Jack Kevorkian, the so-called suicide doctor.

Moreover, even if there is clear evidence that one probably took another person's life or committed some other crime, there may be different interpretations of whether or not a law was in fact violated. These interpretations may come from a variety of criminal justice "actors," such as the police (who may look the other way at certain violations) and district attorneys who decide that this was not really a crime (Sudnow, 1965).

Finally, we have behaviors that do tremendous harm to mostly women, namely rape and battering. Theoretically, rape is supposed to be universally condemned, yet numerous studies have documented how in so many instances men accused of rape are not arrested or not prosecuted if arrested or if prosecuted are acquitted, often because certain key actors in the criminal justice system decided that "she deserved it," or "she led him on," and so on. Similar conclusions have been reached with regard to battering.[7]

Thus, we can conclude that the law is more than words on paper. It has a dynamic quality of its own, for it does not exist in a vacuum. Rather, it is a reflection of a particular society at a particular point in time. As Quinney writes, the law "is also a method or *process* of doing something. As a process, law is a dynamic force that is continually being *created and* interpreted. Thus, law in action involves the making of specialized (legal) decisions by various *authorized agents*" (Quinney, 2001: 37). Law is a creation of specific people holding positions of authority; it is not the creation of a divine authority, as was once believed.

The law, because it is a social product, must be viewed sociologically, for the law is first and foremost a social institution complete with a system of roles and status positions (lawyers, judges, legislators, policemen). Also, it contains an ideology, a set of values supportive of the legal system and the existing social order (Quinney, 2002). The law, moreover, is a social process with many different people interpreting and applying the law in various social contexts. How the law is interpreted and applied depends, as we shall see, on many extralegal factors, such as class and race.

A question that has concerned scholars for many years is that of the origins and functions of criminal law. Through the years scholars have offered a variety of different perspectives of the law. These perspectives have been called various names, but for purposes of simplification, there are three main views: (1) the consensus/pluralist, (2) the interest group/conflict, and (3) the critical/Marxist.[8] Each of these three is reviewed in the next section.

Consensus/Pluralist Model

The consensus/pluralist model of law contends that legal norms are a reflection of the values held in common by the majority of the population. In other words, legal norms reflect the will of the people. This is perhaps the oldest and most articulated perspective on criminal law. A variation of this view is that criminal law merely makes official what are common norms or rules of everyday behavior. In other words, what has been custom (e.g., rules followed because everybody has always followed them) eventually becomes the law. From this perspective the criminal law reflects the social consciousness of a society and the kind of behavior a community universally condemns. Thus, the criminal law (and law in general) represents a synthesis of the most deeply held moral values and beliefs of a people or society. The violation of such laws serves, in effect, to establish the "moral boundaries" of a community or society, according to 19th century sociologist Emile Durkheim (1947).

Another variation of this view is that the law functions to achieve social equilibrium or to maintain order. The law is an instrument used to resolve conflicting interests in a society. Roscoe Pound, one of the most famous legal philosophers, believed that the law was a specialized organization of social control as well as a form of social engineering in a civilized society. In Pound's view, without organized social control, man's aggressive self-assertions would prevail over his cooperative social tendency and civilization would come to an end. Hence, criminal law serves as a sort of social "glue." Pound also suggested that the law adjusts social relationships in order to meet prevailing ideas of fair play (Pound, 1922 and 1942; see also Geis, 1964 and Quinney, 2001: 33.)

Another way of expressing the consensus view is the common phrase "there ought to be a law," meaning that people rise up and demand that a certain form of behavior be outlawed. This model is based on the assumption that there is a common consensus by the majority of the people in a society on what is good and proper conduct, an assumption which is highly suspect.

This model, thus, argues three main points. First, law helps to maintain social order and it is the best way to do so—in other words, the only way to maintain order in society is through the law or, as commonly phrased, the "rule of law." Second, law reflects a more or less universal consensus on what is or is not proper behavior. Third, law and the criminal justice system protects public, not private interests. In other words, the law is neutral and helps to resolve conflicts between competing interest groups (and it follows that those who uphold and interpret the law—police, courts, and so on—are neutral as well).

This view also argues that a society needs not only law but also a strong, centralized state to prevent people from becoming barbarians and engaging in what 18th century philosopher Thomas Hobbes (1982) described as a "war of all against all." Such a view assumes that once upon a time humans were simply mean and nasty to one another, thinking only of themselves in a very selfish way, and that there was constant civil strife and war. This, we are told, is just human nature. Yet such a view is contradicted by years of anthropological and historical research, which has proven that prior to our modern era thousands of human societies existed (beginning around 40,000 to 50,000 years ago) in small, economically cooperative groups. This research shows us that state-created law is not the only way to maintain order and peace. But in modern capitalist societies, based as they are on competitive social relations and class (as well as racial and gender) inequalities, the view of human nature as self-centered and in need of control, becomes a rationalization for a capitalist order and leads inevitably to the idea that we need law in order to restrain people's "naturally wicked" ways (Michalowski, 1985: 47–48; see also, Silver, 1967).

Interest Group/Conflict Model

The consensus/pluralist model assumes that law is a reflection of societal needs. This leads us to ask, "Whose needs?" The term *society* is far too general and vague. Such a view assumes that what is good for one group or segment is good for all segments. In a society segmented along class, racial, and gender lines, this is clearly not an appropriate view. The interest group/conflict model of law attempts to answer some of these kinds of questions. This view begins with the basic fact of modern industrialized societies, which are highly stratified and unequal in terms of the distribution of power and life chances. Using this base, conflict theorists contend that the law reflects the interests of some groups at the expense of others. Quinney's *The Social Reality of Crime* perhaps best exemplifies this approach. He states that society is characterized by diversity, coercion, change, and conflict. Law is a result of the operation of interests. More specifically Quinney states, "law incorporates the interests of specific persons and groups . . . Law is made by men, representing special interests, who have the power to translate their interests into public policy" (2001: 35).

In his theory of the social reality of crime, Quinney organized his theory around six interrelated propositions, which are as follows (ibid, 15–25):

1. Crime is a definition of human conduct that is created by authorized agents in a politically organized society.
2. Criminal definitions describe behaviors that conflict with the interests of the segments of society that have the power to shape public policy.
3. Criminal definitions are applied by the segments of society that have the power to shape the enforcement and administration of criminal law.
4. Behavior patterns are structured in segmentally organized society in relation to criminal definitions, and within this context persons engage in actions that have relative probabilities of being defined as criminal.
5. Conceptions of crime are constructed and diffused in the segments of society by various means of communication.
6. The social reality of crime is constructed by the formulation and application of criminal definitions, the development of behavior patterns related to criminal definitions, and the construction of criminal conceptions.

An important component of Quinney's theory is four interrelated concepts, which include: (1) process, (2) conflict, (3) power, and (4) action. By process, Quinney is referring to the fact that "all social phenomena have duration and undergo change." (2001: 8) The conflict view of society and the law is that in any society "conflicts between persons, social units, or cultural elements are inevitable, the normal consequences of social life." Further, society "is held together by force and constraint and is characterized by ubiquitous conflicts that result in continuous change." Power is an elementary force in our society. Power, says Quinney, "is the ability of persons and groups to determine the conduct of other persons and groups. It is utilized not for its own sake, but is the vehicle for the enforcement of scarce values in society, whether the values are material, moral, or otherwise." An excellent definition of power comes from Michael Parenti:

> By "power" I mean the ability to get what one wants, either by having one's interests prevail in conflicts with others or by preventing others from raising their demands. Power presumes the ability to manipulate the social environment to one's advantage. Power belongs to those who possess the resources that enable them to shape the political agenda and control the actions and beliefs of others, resources such as jobs, organization, technology, publicity, media, social legitimacy, expertise, essential goods and services, organized force, and—the ingredient that often determines the availability of these things—money (Parenti, 2002: 4)

Power is important if we are to understand public policy. Public policy, including crime-control policies, is shaped by groups with special interests. In a class society, some groups have more power than others and therefore are able to have their interests represented in policy decisions, often at the expense of less powerful groups. Thus, for instance, white, upper-class males have more power and their interests are more likely to be represented than those of working- or lower-class minorities and women. Finally, by social action, Quinney is referring to the fact that human beings engage in voluntary behavior, which is not completely determined by forces outside of their control. From this perspective, human beings are "able to reason and choose courses of action" and are "changing and becoming, rather than merely being." It is true that humans are in fact shaped by their physical, social, and cultural experiences, but they also have the capacity to change and achieve maximum potential and fulfillment (Quinney, 2001: 8–15).

Quinney's model is based on a conception of society as segmental rather than singular. In a singular society there is a common value system to which all persons conform. The law reflects these common values (this is what the consensus/pluralist model supports). In a segmental society there are numerous segments, each having its own values and interests. Thus, "some values of a segment may be incorporated into some of the criminal laws." Moreover, many segments are in conflict with one another, some segments having values and interests that conflict with other segments. The passage of laws, therefore, is primarily the outgrowth of these conflicting interests. These laws are the product of interest groups who are aware of what their true interests are and organize to promote these interests. The important point here is that the interest structure in modern American society is characterized by an unequal distribution of power and economic resources and those who have the greatest amount are most able to have their interests represented by the law. Indeed, those groups that have little or no power will have little or no opportunity to have their interests represented in the law and in public policies in general. Thus, such powerless groups as women, minorities, youth, and poor people are rarely represented (ibid, 39–41). Quite often laws are passed after vigorous campaigning on the part of various interest groups (or perhaps even one group) or what one writer has called moral entrepreneurs (Becker, 1963). Thus, a group (or groups) lobbies Congress, writes letters to newspapers, and engages in other activities in order to get a piece of legislation written into law. Such groups do not necessarily represent the people; more often than not, they represent themselves or some other small, but powerful group.

A Critical/Marxist Model

The critical/Marxist model of law, which derives largely from the theories of Karl Marx and modern-day Marxist writings, resembles the interest group/conflict model in that it focuses on group conflict and power as important variables, but it differs in many important ways. A critical perspective challenges us to view the law and the legal order in a specific social and historical context. Such a view argues that the law and in fact the entire the legal system is one of many institutions that are part of what Marx called the superstructure of society and therefore operates to help support and perpetuate the substructure or economic base, namely a capitalist economic and social system.

While there are several variations of the critical perspective on law, they can be categorized into two major approaches: (1) the instrumentalist perspective and (2) the structuralist perspective. Each of these variations will be summarized in turn.

The Instrumentalist Perspective.   This is essentially the classical position taken by Marx himself when he asserted that the law and the legal order (and in fact the state itself) serves mostly as an instrument or tool through which the ruling class (that relatively small group that owns and controls most of the wealth in society—or what Marx called the means of production) dominates the society. Marx and Engels summarized this position simply in *The Communist Manifesto* when they wrote "the executive of the modern state is but a committee for managing the common affairs of the whole bourgeoisie" (Marx and Engels, 1955: 11–12).

One of the best illustrations of the instrumentalist position in recent years was postulated by Richard Quinney in *Critique of Legal Order: Crime Control in Capitalist Society*, where he asserted that: "Criminal law is used by the state and the ruling class to secure the survival of the capitalist system, and, as capitalist society is further threatened by its own contradictions, criminal law will be increasingly used in the attempt to maintain domestic order" (2002: 16). The legal order, in short, is used to help keep the ruling class in power. The legal order is also used to keep the subordinate classes "in their place" (i.e., perpetuate a social class system) by defining some of their behaviors as criminal, while ignoring similar or identical behaviors among members of the ruling class or other powerful individuals.

Critics of this position maintain that it is too extreme, that it exaggerates the cohesiveness of the ruling class and its use of the legal order. Not every law is passed to preserve the current social order nor is every law passed solely to represent the interests of the ruling class, as clearly some legislation favors groups other than the dominant class. Often even subordinate classes are represented in legislation, although it can be said that much of this legislation nevertheless does not threaten the basic social order and the class that rules that order. The instrumentalist position also ignores the many occasions when even members within the ruling class have conflicting interests and thus not all of their interests are going to be reflected in law. It may be true that the instrumentalist position is most helpful for analyzing the relationship between social class and law in the earlier eras of American development, but since the relationship between the state and the legal system changes over time, other perspectives need to be considered. In short, say critics, the law does not always support economic interests alone (Lynch and Groves, 2006: 48).

The Structuralist Perspective. This perspective suggests that law is the results of various contradictions inherent within the capitalist system, which in turn create various problems that even the ruling class cannot easily manipulate. Thus, the nature of the capitalist economic system is that law might sometimes operate against the short-term interests of the ruling class but in favor of the long-term interests of the capitalist system as a whole. A classic example was the passage of anti-trust laws in the early 1900s and laws against discrimination in employment, minimum wage laws, consumer protection laws, and laws supporting labor unions (Chambliss and Seidman, 1982; Greenberg, 1991; O'Connor, 1973). In other words, the ruling class does not always get their way.[9]

Those supporting this position also maintain that the state often acts independently from the ruling class, rather than being a mere "instrument" of that class. To be sure, the law can and will be used when the capitalist system appears to be threatened. However, in day-to-day affairs, the various parts of the "superstructure" (e.g., law, ideology, politics, education, media) have a lot of autonomy. Thus, not every political decision, not everything that is taught in school and not every law is a reflection of the narrow interests of capitalists. Chambliss makes the following cogent point on this issue when he notes that every year there are literally thousands of laws passed by various legislators, some local, some national. He then notes that:

> Some laws are clearly passed for the specific interest of an individual; others emerge out of lobbying by groups representing substantial portions of the population; yet others, perhaps the majority, are no more than an expression of the views and interests of legislative committees (Chambliss, 1993: 30).

Having said this, how can we summarize what a critical/Marxist perspective of the law and legal order has to say? The position of the author is that the law is not some mystical force beyond the comprehension and control of human beings. Too often the law is thought of as a cure-all for societal ills. Also, it has been said that society is ruled by law, not by men. On the contrary, it will be argued that society is ruled by men (and not women, it should be noted) and that the law serves to legitimate and sometimes obscure this rule. The Watergate scandal during the Nixon Administration and more recently in the impeachment of President Bill Clinton demonstrated for all that very powerful men run the country, not some abstraction called "the law." Moreover, it has been commonly believed that the law serves as a protective device, which shields the victim and punishes the offender; is capable of righting wrongs; and is impartial, incorruptible, and equitably applied, providing equal justice for all. In the coming chapters, however, examples will be cited in which this has not been the case. In short, it will be shown that this is largely a fiction.

I am not going to make the claim that the law always reflects the wishes or interests of the ruling class—or any other class—at all times. It would be absurd to make such a claim. Quite often, no doubt, members of the ruling class (or the ruling class as a class) could care less about the daily operations of the legal system. Where the law and legal order do reflect the interests of the ruling class is mainly through the dominant definitions and popular conceptions of "crime" and "criminals." As already noted above, these popular conceptions serve the interests of the rich in the sense that they deflect attention away from the crimes committed by their own class. In fact, for all practical purposes the criminal justice system ignores the crimes of the very wealthy and the crimes committed by the state itself.

It also needs to be pointed out that this society is characterized by a tremendous amount of inequality and that a very small proportion of the population does in fact own "means of production." The share of the total wealth going to the top wealth-holders has been on an upward move since the late 1960s, with 1% of the population owning about 47.7% of all financial wealth (stocks, bonds, savings, and so on) in 1998, and the next 19% had 48.2%—up from 43% in 1983 and more than doubling from about 20% in 1976. Roughly the same percentage goes to another 19% of the population, leaving a mere 4% for the remaining 80% (Perrucci and Wysong, 2003; Phillips, 2002; Collins et al., 1999; Heintz et al., 2000). The largest increases in wealth came during the "boom years" of the 1980s and 1990s. Specifically, between 1989 and 1997, the top 1% of the wealth-holders garnered 42.5% of stock market gains, while the next 9% of the wealth-holders took in 43.3% (Collins et al.: 13). During this same period, all other households received proportionately less (ibid; Collins and Yeskel, 2005).

Income inequality, measured by what is known as the Gini Index of Inequality (a scale where 0 means everyone earns the same amount and 1 means one person earns all), has gone up since the late 1960s. Whereas in 1970 the index for the United States was 0.353, in 1996 it was at 0.425, larger than any other industrialized nation (Miringoff and Miringoff, 1999: 105). Indeed, the rich are getting richer, and practically everyone else is getting poorer, and most of the increase has been the result of the "tax reforms" of the Reagan-Bush years in the 1980s, resulting in an estimated $1 trillion going to the very rich (Sklar, 1999; Collins et al., 1999; Phillips, 2002; Bartlett and Steele, 1992).[10] One study found that between 1977 and 1994 the share of after-tax income of the top 1% of all families increased by 72%, compared to a decrease of 16% by the bottom 20% of all families (Shapiro and Greenstein, 1997).

As measured in real dollars (what money will actually buy), the average American worker has not fared well in recent years. While in 1973 the average weekly paycheck was $502 (in 1998 dollars), in 1998 it had shrunk by 12% to $442. Meanwhile, what these workers actually produced (called "productivity") increased by about one-third. In other words, workers produced more for the owners while getting proportionately less. And, as already suggested above, the owners gained quite a bit, to say the least! Between 1977 and 1994, for instance, the top 1% of families saw their after-tax income go up by 72%, while the bottom 20% of families had their incomes decrease by 16% (Collins et al., 1999: 27–32).

As of 2001 (latest figures available), 17.6% of all households had either zero or negative net worth, up from 15.5 percent in 1983 (Collins and Yeskel, 2005: 49). Meanwhile, the savings rate among Americans has dropped tremendously in recent years, going from around 11% in 1984 to 1.4% in 2003; correlated with this has been the rising number of personal bankruptcy filings, almost tripling from 1990 to 2003 (from 661,000 to 1.6 million), while credit card debts more than doubled from 1990 to 2004 (from $243 billion to $735 billion; ibid: 17).

Given this amount of wealth and the power that comes with it, it logically follows that the legal order, in the final analysis, will ultimately be controlled by this small proportion of the population because of the simple fact that they own and control most of the assets of this country (for documentation that there is a ruling class and the extent to which it does in fact rule see Domhoff, 1979 and 1998).

It really doesn't matter that the law does not always side with these rulers, for it does not have to as long as profits can be made and the capitalist system survives. And it is not as if no one else but this small group of capitalists receives the benefits of capitalism, for a lot of other people do as well. Zinn illustrates this in his analysis of the passage of the U.S. Constitution. He notes that the Constitution, and the Bill of Rights, was primarily passed to protect private property, because so many people at that time did in fact own property so it was in their interests to have property protected. But while many people owned property, most owned only a little property, while a small group owned a lot (and they still do today). Zinn notes (Zinn, 1995: 98–99):

> The Constitution, then, illustrates the complexity of the American system: that it serves the interests of a wealthy elite, but also does enough for small property owners, for middle-income mechanics and farmers, to build a broad base of support. The slightly prosperous people who make up this base of support are buffers against the blacks, the Indians, the very poor whites. They enable the elite to keep control with a minimum of coercion, a maximum of law—all made palatable by the fanfare of patriotism and unity.

The Bill of Rights gave just enough liberties to the masses to build support for the ruling class of the period and the government. But, as Zinn notes, what was never made very clear "was the shakiness of anyone's liberty when entrusted to a government of the rich and the powerful." This was shown, for instance, when Congress passed a law that essentially abridged freedom of speech guaranteed by the First Amendment. This was the Sedition Act of 1798 (Zinn, 1995: 99).[11]

Thus, the law and the legal order favor especially the very wealthy, but it favors enough of the rest of the population to appear to be equal. Yet the law clearly has never done a good job supporting the most marginalized sectors of the population: the poor in general, and African-Americans, Native-Americans, and other minorities.

Lawrence Friedman, notable historian of law and criminal justice, had this to say (Friedman, 1993: 101):

> Law is a fabric of norms and practices in a particular society; the norms and practices are social judgements made concrete: the living, breathing embodiment of society's attitudes, prejudices, and values. Inevitable, and invariably, these are slanted in favor of the haves; the top-riders, the comfortable, respectable, well-to-do people. After all, articulate, powerful people *make* the laws; and even with the best will in the world, they do not feel moved to give themselves disadvantage. Rules thus tend to favor people who own property, entrepreneurs, people with good position in society. The lash of criminal justice, conversely, tends to fall on the poor, the badly dressed, the maladroit, the deviant, the misunderstood, the shiftless, the unpopular.

The "Dangerous Classes"

Many of the daily activities of the American criminal justice system have revolved around controlling, regulating, containing, or in some way keeping tabs on those groups deemed dangerous. The term *dangerous classes* was apparently first used by Charles Loring Brace in his book of 1872 called *The Dangerous Classes of New York* (Brace, 1872).

However, there is some indication that the term, as used by Brace, was synonymous with what Marx called the *lumpenproletariat,* first used in his famous work with Engles, *The Communist Manifesto,* originally published in 1848. In the various English translations since then, the term dangerous class has been used instead of lumpenproletariat. In its original usage, Marx and Engels referred to this segment of society as "the social scum, that passively rotting mass thrown off by the lowest layers of old society" (Eastman, 1959: 332). Although this original definition does not include criminal behavior as part of the meaning of the term, nevertheless, Anthony Giddens quotes the following passage from a collection of writings by Marx and Engels (1959: 155) where the authors include, under the heading of lumpenproletariat, "thieves and criminals of all kinds, living on the crumbs of society, people without a definite trade, vagabonds, people without a hearth or home." The key idea that Marx conveyed is that this special segment of society was inevitable under capitalism in that it is "not wholly integrated into the division of labor" (Giddens, 1971: 38). For Marx, this was more of a moral evaluation of a certain segment of society.

A closely related term is what Marx referred to as the relative surplus population or reserve army, which refers to a more or less chronically unemployed segment of the population, primarily because of mechanization, which renders them redundant and hence superfluous as far as producing profits is concerned. This segment helps keep wages down and is absorbed back into the general working population when labor is scarce. This group is also a "lever of capitalistic accumulation" and in fact is "a condition of existence of the capitalist mode of production" (Giddens, 1971: 57). It should be emphasized here that this surplus population should be seen as a much larger category of people than the lumpenproletariat, the latter of which comes closest to what I would refer to as the "dangerous classes."

This population has shown a remarkable growth during the last couple of decades of the 20th century, especially when we consider this on a global scale. Weiss (1999b: 468) suggests that there are three parts to this surplus population as follows: (1) the "officially" unemployed who are actively seeking work; (2) a group of completely discouraged workers at the bottom of the social order; (3) those who are "invisible" because they are not actively seeking work by reporting to state employment offices (those who are counted as unemployed are those who are registered with these state offices).

There is, it should be noted, a dual character to the dangerous classes or surplus population. As Spitzer (1975) has noted, the surplus population has at times been viewed by those in power as a "threat" (viewed as social "junk" or "dynamite"—as was the case with almost the entire working class in the early years of the labor movement during the last half of the 19th century) or as a possible resource (e.g., a form of cheap labor or a group to exploit in order to keep wage levels down). Moreover, the exact nature of this class has changed over the years, ranging from the working class in general in the 19th and early part of the 20th century, to very specific categories in more recent years, such as racial minorities, the underclass and gangs.

The term *dangerous classes* has become quite popular, commonly used in many discussions of the history of crime and criminal justice in this country. It has been recently used by Eric Monkkonen in his historical study of crime and criminal justice in Columbus, Ohio (Monkkonen, 1975) and also by Diana Gordon in her study of drug laws and the "war on drugs" (Gordon, 1994).

Many other writers have echoed the same themes, while using different words. Thus, for example, John Irwin's excellent study on the functions of the modern jail, maintains the view that jails function to manage the "rabble" or "underclass" in society, rather than focus on serious crime per se (Irwin, 1985). Irwin notes that many studies have referred to such terms as *social trash, social refuse, social junk, riffraff, dregs* and the like (ask any police officer and terms such as *asshole, dirt balls*, or *scum bag* will be frequently used). By *rabble* Irwin means the "disorganized" and "disorderly" and the "lowest class of people." They are people who have been regarded as "disreputable" and "detached" from mainstream society. Just like social welfare has been used to regulate the poor, jails have been used for a similar purpose (Irwin, 1985: 2; see also Piven and Cloward, 1972). In this book it will be argued that the entire legal system—from the making of the laws to their enforcement—functions mostly like Irwin's jail: to regulate, manage, and control the "dangerous classes." We could easily substitute rabble or other terms. The meaning is essentially the same. It should be noted at the outset that, historically, the terms *crime* and *poverty* (or the old 18th century term *pauperism*) have been used interchangeably. Even the term *delinquency*, as will be shown in chapter 5, was practically synonymous with the word *pauper* or poor person.

This theme is echoed not only by Irwin, but also by Noam Chomsky in several of his writings (Chomsky, 1994, 1996a, and 1996b) and Jonathan Simon in his historical study of the parole system (1993). In fact, Simon is quite explicit on one of the main functions of the parole system in that it has become part of one of the main functions of the modern criminal justice system, namely, in his words to "secure" the underclass. He argues that in modern times in the middle of "declining public spending on most forms of social support for the poor, criminal justice is one of the few programs left that takes tax dollars from relatively better-off communities and their governments, and spend them on relatively poorer communities and their governments (*even if only to lock them up*)." However, continues Simon, what is happening is that such resources are not used so much to control crime as to contain crime "in the underclass" (Simon, 1993: 258, emphasis in the original). What is even more important to note here is Simon's characterization of what is occurring as what he calls "waste management." He argues that since many of the young males caught up in the criminal justice system may likely become "lifetime clients" of this system, it behooves governments to figure out methods of maintaining this population "at the lowest possible cost." (ibid, 1993) This, says Simon, means that we may have to rethink our reliance upon an increasingly costly penal system. Hence an expansion of parole. It should be noted that Simon was predicting this in a book published in 1993, and since that time the prison system has expanded to reach an all-time high, although to be sure the number of those on probation and parole have also expanded at about the same rate (Glaze and Palla, 2005).

One of the central arguments in this book is that the management of the dangerous classes is not a recent phenomenon. On the contrary, it shall be noted throughout this book that this has always been one of, if not the major, function of the criminal justice system. This argument is based on a Marxian interpretation of one of the negative aspects of capitalism, namely that it produces very distinct social classes with significant differences in the benefits resulting from the huge profits from capitalist enterprises. The very nature of capitalism itself produces periodic economic fluctuations, one result of which is the constant creation of large segments of the population that become superfluous (that is, not needed to produce profits), which in turn often become labeled as dangerous to the more privileged groups. Since we are too civilized to murder or torture this group (as more totalitarian dictatorships do) and we can no longer transport them to another country, they must be in some way managed and controlled. Using the various components of the criminal justice system is one among many methods.[12]

For many years I (and a few others) have been saying this. Most of this discussion has been confined to narrow academic circles. However, someone finally took note of this and, while not writing in the mainstream press, nevertheless reported it in a very good Internet source called "Counterpunch" (Sandronsky, S., 2006). The author makes a very simple point, noting that "in the U.S., market conditions of supply, demand and capital accumulation do in fact help to generate a surplus of labor. In short, there are too many workers for too few jobs. Where do some of these American job seekers end up?" His answer is that many end up in prison.

Many may object to such a broad interpretation of the functions of the criminal justice system, since many of the daily operations of the various components involve dealing with a rather broad cross-section of the public, not just the rabble. Having said that, however, my argument is that the most severe treatment is usually reserved for those at the bottom of the social order, as a cursory look at the inhabitants of the nation's jails and prisons and sitting in the audience within any courtroom will demonstrate. For the more privileged segments of society who run afoul of the law, lighter treatments are made available, as indicated especially when it comes to corporate and white-collar crime (see Friedrichs, 2004).

One result of social inequality is vast differences in the probabilities of having one's behaviors labeled as criminal. Evidence for this is found throughout the social science literature during the last half century or more.[13] Therefore, the legal system responds accordingly and more often than not tends to focus its attention toward those from the less privileged sectors of society—the poor, racial and ethnic minorities and women (especially women of color, who more often than not are also poor, which provides an excellent illustration of the interplay of race, class, and gender) (Messerschmidt, 1997).

I do not intend, in this book, to offer a precise definition of the term *dangerous classes*. I'm not certain it can be done; perhaps it should not be done. I think that, historically, different groups have been so labeled at different points in time. An example, cited many times throughout the course of this book, might better clarify the changing nature of the dangerous classes. I am referring here to various attempts to control the use of drugs. As will be discussed in more detail in chapter 1, among the groups targeted in these drug laws include: (1) the Chinese and opium laws around the late 19th and early 20th centuries; (2) marijuana legislation, which targeted mostly Hispanics and African-Americans during the 1930s; (3) heroin laws, targeting especially African-Americans in the 1950s; (4) various psychoactive drugs (LSD, and so on) used by mostly white "hippies" and antiwar activists, the dangerous classes of the 1960s; (5) crack cocaine used by mostly African-American inner-city youth, along with women (especially minority women) in the 1980s; (6) the continued targeting of racial minorities and the poor in general well into the 21st century. Prohibition laws throughout the 19th and well into the 20th century focused mostly on lower class immigrants, starting with the Irish in the mid-19th century. Most of those in the forefront of the Temperance movement were middle and upper class people who associated most of the problems of urban America with the consumption of alcohol. Corporate leaders argued that drinking (especially in working class saloons) would interfere with productivity and profit. It was no accident that saloons were often the location of much labor organizing and that most of those organizing and most union members were immigrants. So for the dominant classes, "clamping down on drinking and saloons was part of a much broader strategy of social control. . ." In fact, the passage of the 18th Amendment to the Constitution was considered a "blow against Bolshevism and anarchy. . ." (Reinarman and Levine, 1997: 5–6).

Outline for the Book

Throughout this book there will be one overriding theme. This theme can be stated as follows: *The making of laws and the interpretation and application of these laws throughout the criminal justice system has, historically, been class, gender, and racially biased.* More to the point, as Cole has noted, there are really two systems of justice: "one for the privileged and another for the less privileged" (Cole, 1999: 9). Moreover, one of the major functions of the criminal justice system has been largely to control and/or manage those from the most disadvantaged sectors of the population, that is, the dangerous classes. Each of the chapters in this book, from the development of the criminal law, through the development of the police institution and the juvenile justice system and our treatment of women in the system, and the prison system, this theme prevails. Put succinctly, the entire legal system has been and continues to be controlled and dominated by those in power at any given historical period and thus favors those with the most resources at their disposal. Those receiving the brunt of the full enforcement of the law have been predominantly those who make up the dangerous classes.

One way to make this perspective clearer to the reader is to consider the phrase "the golden rule. The golden rule usually refers to the old biblical sentiment of "do under others as you would like them to do unto you." However, there is another meaning attached to this phrase and it is a meaning that most people would probably feel uneasy about, although they might agree. This meaning is: Those who have the gold make the rules.

To admit the truth in this statement is not easy in a country known as a democracy. After all, this is supposed to be a government "of the people, by the people and for the people." Moreover, we are supposed to live under the rule of law not of men.

Most citizens have a sense that a few rich people control things, that money talks and if you have money and power you can get away with almost anything, even murder. Yet the word *class* (and words like *class conflict* and *class oppression*) is a word that is not often used in everyday discourse. (Often when it is brought up by social critics, conservatives will accuse them of fomenting class warfare, a rather ludicrous charge made by those who help perpetuate gross class inequalities.) But it is obvious the average citizen is aware of it—and aware of some of the gross inequalities that exist, even though the media and most politicians avoid referring to it. A poll conducted in the 1990s found that more than 80% of the public feel that the current economic system is "inherently unfair" and more than 70% believe business "has gained too much power over too many aspects of American life" (Chomsky, 1996c: 417).

Classes and class differences are realities in modern American society, and have been since the start of the republic. Perhaps nowhere is this better illustrated on a daily basis—sometimes for all to see—than in our system of justice. Because those who create laws and those who interpret laws are drawn largely from the wealthiest class, it comes as no surprise that those brought into the criminal justice system will be those drawn largely from the lowest social classes. On any given day, in courtrooms all over the country, we have essentially one class passing judgement on another class. Our system is fundamentally a system of class (and racial) justice.

Notes

1. In the second edition of this book, Walker has re-written this section and instead of referring to such incidents as "scars" he suggests that "vigilantism represented the worst aspect of popular justice." Curiously he notes that the "lawlessness" was what he called a "paradox" in that "most organized episodes were led by the wealthy leaders of the community who sought to impose law and order" (Walker, 1998: 37).

2. In a book filled with documented evidence, David Cole (1999) demonstrates the class and racial bias that he argues is built into the modern criminal justice system, a bias that is constantly reinforced daily by criminal justice decision-makers and backed up by Supreme Court decisions. My argument in this book is that what Cole documents for the last half of the 20th century has been a persistent feature of the American criminal justice system from the beginning.

3. I borrowed part of this description of the term from the following website: http://www.criticalthinking.org/about/.

4. Part of this phrase originally came from his book *The Politics of History* (1970: 35), but it is the title of his own personal biography (Zinn, 1994).

5. The subtitle of one popular text (*Class, Race, and Gender*) illustrates this importance (Rossides, 1997).

6. Space does not permit a complete review of these studies. For further documentation refer to studies already cited above, plus the following: Calavita and Pontell (1994); Geis (1996); Poveda (1994); Friedrichs, (2004).

7. The research on this topic is far too numerous to cite here, but for a good summary see Belknap (2001).

8. See the following for extended discussions of these theories: Chambliss and Zatz (1993); Quinney (2001); Michalowski (1985); Lynch and Michalowski (2006).

9. A variation of this view is called the class-dialectical model, which argues that in order to understand the functions of the law one must understand the institutional structure of society and the different social classes that make up a society. True, dominant classes try to preserve those institutions that best add to their hegemony (e.g., economic and political institutions). However, "power is potentially available to the subordinate classes if they become sufficiently class-conscious and politically organized to wrest control or to challenge the control of the means of production. Thus, the power of the dominant class is not absolute" (Whitt, 1993: 266).

10. Bartlett and Steele note that as a result of the 1986 "Tax Reform Act" the average 1989 tax savings for those earning $1 million or more came to $281,033 (a tax cut of 31%), compared to $37 to those earning less than $10,000 (11% tax cut). They also found that during the 1980s the increase in salaries of people earning more than $1 million per year came to 2,184%.

11. One of the founding fathers, James Madison, said that the primary role of the government is "to protect the minority of the opulent against the majority." And his colleague, John Jay, flatly stated that "The people who own the country ought to govern it" (quoted in Chomsky, 1998: 7).

12. Similarly social welfare functions in this way. See, for instance, Piven and Cloward, 1972; see also Chomsky (1994, 1996a) for a similar line of argument.

13. Numerous citations could be listed here, but only the following will be noted: Quinney (2001), Cole (1999), Currie (1998), Walker, Spohn and DeLone (2000), Hawkins (1995). For a good treatment of gender bias see Chesney-Lind and Shelden (2004) and Chesney-Lind and Pasko (2004).

1

Perpetuating the Class System: The Development of Criminal Law

Introduction: Nature and Functions of Criminal Law

The foundation of the modern criminal justice system is the criminal law. After all, technically speaking, there is no crime without criminal law. Criminal law is the body of laws that justify the existence of a criminal justice system. Without criminal law there would be no purpose for a criminal justice system. The U.S. Constitution provides for the creation of laws by state legislatures and Congress. In essence, "Law is the formal statement of authority that is exercised by the state" (Zalman and Siegel, 1994: 13). Executive branch officials, and the courts, are given authority, through provisions in the U.S. Constitution, to enforce these laws. The criminal justice system is the instrument designated by executive branch officials to enforce laws that pertain to criminal behavior. The basis of the American criminal justice system is found within the three branches of our government: legislative, executive, and judicial. The legal authority to establish an official response to crime comes from this structural arrangement. "Legal authority, like other forms of authority, may be enforced by threatening or physically coercing people to comply or by economic rewards" (Terkel, 1996: 200). The legislative branch defines what behaviors are to be prohibited by the criminal law and how the violations are to be punished; the judicial branch (e.g., the courts) interpret these laws and determine whether or not they are constitutionally valid; the executive branch creates the official response in terms of agencies, personnel, and the like.

The legislative branch is the most important of the three branches because these individuals define the behavior the violation of which constitutes crime. Of particular importance are legislatures at the state and local level for the bulk of the criminal acts are violations of state and local laws. In fact, the state and federal legislatures have, in effect, created the two major criminal justice systems: state and federal. Thus, we have state and federal law enforcement systems, state and federal courts, and state and federal prison systems. The reader should be aware of who the individuals are who constitute the legislature, at both the state and local and at the federal level. These groups do not necessarily represent all of the population, since the majority of those who occupy legislative seats (especially at the federal level in the Congress and the Senate) have been predominantly white males from upper class backgrounds (Domhoff, 1998; Bennett, 1994: 439–442; Parenti, 2002).

The most primitive method of settling disputes has been when the powerful overpower the less powerful by force or intimidation. The civilized method, however, is to let a third party handle the matter. The problem, of course, lies in the objective and/or neutral nature of the third party, who may a judge or the court. Is this third party objective or neutral, and is the judge or the court beyond the control of the powerful? If the answer to either question is "no" then the civilized method is simply an impersonation of the primitive method, which is masked to conceal the real identity of the judge or the court agents of the powerful. Through a survey of the history of criminal law it will be demonstrate that the powerful, often at the expense of the powerless, have always maintained control of law. Interestingly, those who have had the most influence in legislating and enforcing law have done so in a way that masks their intentions. Exploring the emergence of modern criminal law is a very long journey far back in time to ancient civilizations. Thus this chapter necessarily begins with a look at how criminal law developed in such early societies as Athens and Rome.

Criminal Law in Ancient Times

The roots of our modern criminal justice system go back to at least ancient times—in Biblical Israel, classical Athens and in Rome—back as far as 1200 B.C. The law and legal system reflected the type of society that existed. In this case we are talking about a highly stratified society, where slaves did most of the work, especially in Athens and Rome. Each of these societies displayed different forms of economic development, which in turn shaped their definitions of and responses to offending behaviors.

Israel was moving from a mostly nomadic existence, based upon the herding of sheep and goats, to an established agricultural society located in the "promised land." Not surprisingly, in Israel the law and criminal justice system reflected the deep religious influences. Wrongful conduct was an offense that threatened the close bonds of society and a wrong committed by any member of "God's chosen people" could bring divine wrath down upon the entire nation (Johnson and Wolfe, 1996: 19–32).

Athens during its classical period (594–404 B.C.) was based upon the commercial activity of the Mediterranean. Rome, a republic, was a constitutional state ruled by aristocrats. Rome was very dependent upon trade and employed a vast army of foreign slaves on its farms, manufactories, and households.

A common theme within these societies was that a harm was essentially a harm against an individual or family, rather than a harm against the state. In fact, the initiation of a criminal case depended upon the initiative of the person wronged or, if he had been killed, by his family or kin folk. Thus, criminal procedure perpetuated the primitive system of revenge. The state did not act as a prosecutor, as we understand the term today, but rather acted as a weigher of evidence and the dispenser of punishment.

Depending upon the offense, the punishment often literally fit the crime, but not always. In the case of homicide, in Israel the law stipulated that one who killed shall be put to death; however, in Athens the punishment was expulsion from Athens and the surrounding countryside. Different punishments were administered depending upon whether or not the killing was intentional. If unintentional, sometimes the families of the victim received some sort of compensation—known as blood money (known as *wergild* in medieval times—to be discussed shortly).

In all three societies, the harshest sanctions were against intentional killers, with lesser penalties for unintentional killers. Sex offenses were dealt with, in general, less severely. Theft was almost always dealt with through some form of compensation. In each system, the victim or victim's family or kin, was responsible for bringing the offender to justice and justice was administered by local officials. Most importantly, in the local courts there was a common practice of relying upon group decisions as being superior to the judgment of any one individual.

Emergence of Criminal Law in Athens

Criminal law, as we understand the term today, developed only when the idea of "private vengeance" was replaced by the notion that the entire community was also victimized. This idea in turn evolved into the notion that the state, which theoretically came to represent the entire community or the people, was also harmed and became authorized to take action. Criminal law, and hence obviously criminal justice, is based upon three key ideas (Quinney, 2001: 44):

1. An offense against an individual is also an offense against the public order and the state.
2. The methods of punishment shall be administered by the state and not solely by the victim.
3. The protection the law provides theoretically should apply to all citizens, not just particular groups.

In Athens the criminal law emerged during the 6th century B.C. At that time Athens was ruled by a small aristocracy that controlled a very large citizenry—the peasant proprietors, the artisans, a lower class of freeman, plus an even lower class of slaves. The discontent this situation produced led the rulers to compromise (they were legitimately afraid of a revolution). The rulers essentially created a system of popular courts and provided for appeals and granted certain rights to every citizen, with the right of all citizens to initiate prosecutions (Quinney, 2001: 46).

Criminal Law in Rome

Until the middle of the 5th century B.C. the law in Rome was devoted mostly to private matters. The Law of the Twelve Tables, the codification of Roman customary law, was essentially a private criminal law in the sense that it was based upon the notion that a victim could seek private vengeance against an offender. This collection of laws was drawn up around 450 B.C. As noted by Tigar and Levy, these Tables "outlined only the simplest of legal principles. . ." and they were characterized "by reliance upon magic and ritual as integral parts of legal procedure and as means for the creation of obligations." This law guaranteed certain rights, but mostly "to the members of the clans that had founded the Roman Republic," that is the ruling class (Tigar and Levy, 1977: 11).

However, as Rome grew from a rural agricultural community to a mighty city-state, the existing law under the Twelve Tables proved to be inadequate. Indeed, this legal system was inadequate to handle the growing conflicts between an urban proletariat and slave population and a powerful, yet small, ruling class. Between the third and second century B.C., the state began to use the criminal law to protect the interests of the ruling class by passing such laws as treason, arson, violence (except violence committed by the state itself) and theft of state property (Tigar and Levy, 47). Indeed, the existing laws did not provide much protection to the growing number of merchants, "whose wealth was increasing at the expense of small peasants and artisans." The emerging society was dominated by traders, bankers, landowners, and the military that protected their interests. The existing labor force of the time was either slave or half-free, mostly conquered and colonized people. The ruling class clearly shaped the law in their favor, yet claimed that this law and legal system was *jus gentium* or a natural law or law that protected all the people. The adoption of the *jus gentium* "reflected the conquest by the new Roman ruling class of its foreign and domestic enemies" (Tigar and Levy, 1977:44).

Acephalous or Non-state Societies and Law

Prior to the Norman invasion of England in 1066, most societies had not been under what we would today call the rule of law. Rather, many societies, as already mentioned above, were under the rule of custom (Diamond, 1974.) As noted by Michalowski, many of these earlier societies were what he termed non-state or *acephalous* societies, a term that means "without a head," that is, with no identifiable ruler. Such a society had no centralized state or government, nor any written law. What is important to note, however, is that most of these societies (and there were literally thousands of them) were "characterized more by order and cooperation than by chaos and competition" (Michalowski, 1985: 45–46). What is significant about these societies is not that they were free from any sort of deviance or what we would call crime, but rather how the people of these societies handled such problems without some sort of centralized authority or state. In these societies deviance was handled informally, since they were essentially disputes between individuals or families.

Acephalous societies are obviously quite different from modern, highly complex capitalist societies. In the former, human relations are more apt to be based upon personal relationships that in turn are based upon mutual obligations and respect. In modern societies, with personal relatedness missing, legal rules are established, which are backed by the threat of punishment, and conformity to such rules too often depends upon the state's ability or even willingness to enforce them or an individual's own commitment to obey them (Michalowski, 1985: 53).

The handling of deviance in these non-state societies was done usually through one of four ways: (1) blood revenge (usually done in cases of homicide where the victim's kin kills the murderer), (2) retribution (typically the victim or the family of the victim returns the harm done with something similar), (3) ritual satisfaction (typically this involves some form of symbolic demonstration of the offender's guilt, such as suffering public ridicule), or (4) restitution (involving some payment to the victim for the harm done). The last type was the most common and it reveals the extent to which the victim is directly involved in the response to the offense; in other words, the focus is more on the victim rather than the offender, unlike our modern court system (Michalowski, 1985: 62–63). Such a response assumed some form of continuing relationship between the victim and the offender, or at least between the two families, something that is obviously missing in today's society (Chambliss and Seidman, 1982; Hoebel, 1973).

Criminal Law in Medieval Times

The fall of the Roman Empire was one of the most important events of early history, a process that took several centuries to unfold. When the final fall came in 426 A.D., criminal law and criminal justice understandably changed. The Dark Ages (so-called because of the confusion and illiteracy that developed) soon began. Christianity became one of the few unifying characteristics of the period, with the Roman Catholic Church being one of the central authority figures and one of the last vestiges of the Roman Empire. Political authority increasingly fell into the hands of local kings and landlords. In the age of feudalism that followed, poor farmers and merchants began to associate themselves with some powerful lord, who provided security to them in return for either services or taxes. The control of crime became based upon kinship groups. Johnson and Wolfe describe the situation at that time as the beginning of the modern nation states and

> a slow accretion of power in the hands of noble families, based upon dynastic alliances and also upon their standing among peoples of similar language, culture and traditions. As territorial magnates consolidated control, their people found new cohesion in their differences from neighboring states and nations; the result was the rapid decline of a pan-European culture that had once been based upon roman culture and the Christian church and its teachings. The other consequence was the rise of a new view of man based upon his individual importance as a member of a kindred group, a clan and a society . . . this new view of man was founded less upon religion or political philosophy and more upon the necessities of a more primitive and violent world. (1996: 36)

A new kind of relationship was formed, one based upon reciprocal rights and duties between the lord and the workers. But there was no unifying legal order, as local customs prevailed throughout Europe, although many were based in part upon Roman law. Tigar and Levy make a similar point that: "The need for survival and military defense, the lack of a Roman governmental presence and of the Roman legions, made possible and necessary a manorial system in which one finds the origin of what later writers were to term feudalism" (1977: 23).

The term *feudalism* can be described as a system whereby land is held by a landlord who grants individuals (peasants) the right to live and work the land as tenants and sometimes perform military service. It is a system based upon the agricultural mode of production with a caste or slave type of social order (Chambliss and Ryther, 1975: 132). Feudalism was legitimated by the institution of serfdom whereby peasants were "legally unfree" and "were deprived of property rights, though they had rights of use" (Bottomore et al., 1983: 166).

The feudal system emerged mostly as a result of the uncertainties of the Dark Ages. Millions of small farmers and artisans were forced into this system because of the need for protection or by direct force. Europe was indeed a dangerous place to live during this period of time as there were invasions from all directions, from Hungarians in the east, the Moors to the south, and Scandinavians from the north. Tigar and Levy further stated that feudalism represented a sort of "retreat into the manor and village of a ruling class deprived of protection by a decayed and dying imperial government" (1977, 24) In other areas it was a shift from a pastoral, nomadic existence to a more stable agricultural life. The ultimate source of the feudal system was "the act of homage" between two men, one the stronger (the lord) and the other the weaker (the vassal). The vassal tilled the land owned by the lord in an "oath-bound relation of dominance and subordination" that lasted the lifetime of the vassal and extended to his heirs. This manoral society predominated throughout Europe until around the 11th century. The manor was self-sufficient, with little trade outside its boundaries, not unlike the slave system in the southern United States (1977: 23–25).[1]

While most people were accustomed to Roman law, each group had its own customary law as well. Eventually most legal principles of Roman law were replaced by local customary laws within the manors. By the end of this period (roughly the 11th to 12th centuries) Western Europe was "under the rule of a patchwork system of local customs, influenced in varying degrees by Roman law" (Tigar and Levy, 1977: 26). Germany, the Low Countries, and what is now the northern part of France, were under their own customary laws. Thus, after the Norman invasion in 1066, English law came under the influence of not Roman law, but Norman law (Tigar and Levy, 1977: 26–27; Johnson and Wolfe, 1996: 36–37).

By the 10th century England was divided into about eight large kingdoms each with some form of centralized authority, namely tribal chiefs. In time they were replaced by kings who became both landlords and military leaders of their kingdoms. In time, compensation for offenses became the responsibility of the king, lord, or bishop, rather than the kinship group (Quinney, 2001: 46). This was the kind of society that existed around the time William the Conqueror became King of England in 1066 following the Norman invasion.

Emergence of Criminal Law in England

American criminal law is largely an outgrowth of the Norman Conquest and the reigns of William the Conqueror (1066–1087) and Henry XI (1157–1189). William the Conqueror, also known as Duke William II of Normandy and King William I of

England, was the bastard son of Robert I, the sixth of Normandy and was born in 1027 or 1028. Thus, he was born into great wealth. His father was a direct descendent of Rolf the Viking (aka Rollo of Normandy) who became the first ruler of Viking, which eventually became Normandy, part of the northern region of France (Douglas, 1964: 15). The Normans originally came from both the Neustria (northern France) and the Vikings from Scandinavia. The Vikings raided the coasts of the British Isles, France, and other parts of Europe between the 8th and 11th centuries. In fact, the period roughly between 796 and 1066 is known as the Viking Age. In other words, William was merely one of a long line of invaders (the Normans eventually ruled not only England and northern France but also part of what is now the southern part of Italy and a small portion of the area near Syria. William became Duke of Normandy in 1035 (at the age of 7 or 8) when his father (Duke Robert) suddenly left for a pilgrimage to Jerusalem, never to return again (Douglas, 1964: 35–37). William ruled Normandy until 1066 when he led his army in the Battle of Hastings against the Anglo-Saxons led by Kind Harold II , who had claimed the throne of England after the death of Edward the Confessor (who was childless), a claim challenged by William.[2]

When William the Conqueror became the king of England (after 14 years of continuous war) the country consisted of many different groups having different life styles and customs. Each group had its own leader and there was no centralized authority or state. The only unifying characteristic was the existence of Christianity. In fact, the major landowner at that time was the Church. One of William's first acts was to unify this diverse land and to declare himself the supreme landlord of the country. Thus, the land that formerly belonged to the several groups or tribes and then different landlords now belonged to the king. During the process, the old English nobility was almost completely wiped out and by the end of William's reign they owned about 8% of all the land in England. Simply put, the old aristocracy was replaced by a new one (Douglas, 1964: 266).

William began his takeover by separating the lay and ecclesiastical (church) courts and began to send his own judges into the different sections of the country in order to enforce the "King's peace." He also replaced existing sheriffs (derived from *shire-reeves*) with his own, very prominent, men (within two generations most of them would become earls). Understandably this move resulted in a great deal of conflict between the church and the state (the church complained about these sheriffs lining their own pockets with some of the money collected in fines or taxes), a conflict that did not subside until the reign of Henry II. In the end, however, the king won (Douglas, 1964: 297). One result was that personal transgressions formerly handled locally and according to the customs of the people became defined as crimes or harms against the state. It became the state's prerogative to punish transgressors and, in many cases, to collect fines, which in addition to the levy of taxes, no doubt added significantly to the king's coffers. Part of the duties of these sheriffs included their relationship with the existing courts, called shire courts. William became involved more directly in local affairs through the "dispatch of members of his own court to conduct local trials of particular importance" (Douglas, 1964: 306).

The new centralized government was stronger and more efficient than ever before. Cheyney describes some of these changes as follows:

> A body of trained, skillful government officials now existed, who were able to carry out the wishes of the king, collect his revenues, administer justice, gather armies, and in other ways make his rule effective to an extent unknown in the preceding period. The sheriffs, who had already existed as royal representatives in the shires in Anglo-Saxon times, now possessed far more extensive powers, and came up to Westminster to report and to present their financial accounts to the royal exchequer twice a year. Royal officials acting as judges not only settled an increasingly large number of cases that were brought before them at the king's court, but traveled through the country, trying suits and punishing criminals in the different shires. The king's income was vastly larger than that of the Anglo-Saxon monarchs had been (1913: 17–18).

This is an important development and should not be passed over lightly. What occurred was that the order of custom (e.g., handling disputes locally and according to the customs of the people) became the rule of law. As Stanley Diamond has observed, "Law arises in the breach of a prior customary order and increases in force with the conflicts that divide political societies internally and among themselves. Law and order is the historical illusion; law *versus* order is the historical reality" (Diamond, 1974: 49). Hence, William the Conqueror enlarged his control of the nation through the coercive power of a state apparatus, an apparatus that stood above the people and represented the interests of the king. By making personal transgressions crimes, the people could be more easily controlled. In short, criminal law served the function of exercising state (i.e., the king's) power.

However, as Max Weber has noted, no political authority can rule through raw force alone (Weber, 1946). Rather, it must rule through a consensus of the governed. Hence, rulers must legitimize their rule. That is, their domination must be seen as legitimate by the people. The ruling class of England began a series of reforms, which solidified its rule and helped legitimate this rule in the eyes of the people. For instance, the state began to use an ostensibly independent and unbiased set of bureaucratic government officials to handle disputes. These officials were known as justices of the peace. The ruling class also separated judicial and legislative functions. Rules of evidence, due process, the use of writs, rights of appeal, and other rules were established. In addition to the above procedures, the use of peers (jurors) to decide guilt or innocence helped legitimize the king's rule. In a sense, it was good logic because, in the minds of the people, if a person was found guilty, it was the fault of his or her peers rather than of the king or his representatives.

The king and other members of the ruling class used additional measures to legitimize their rule. One method was to foster the view of the king as sovereign. The Christian religion lent spiritual support to the king and the state, and hence, the legal system as well. In short, the king could do no wrong. He was answerable only to God. To question the king (or the state or the law) was to question God. The king's law stood as the ultimate morality. The criminal law became, in time, more than mere descriptions of crimes and their punishments. The criminal law, indeed the formal law and legal order itself, became a powerful ideological force that justified the rule by a few. The way this was done in England is shown through a study by Douglas Hay, to be discussed in the next section.

Criminal Law as an Ideological System of Legitimate Control

The thesis that criminal law adds to the hegemony[3] of a ruling class has been given some factual support in an historical account of changes in England's legal order during the eighteenth century. In the opening chapter of *Albion's Fatal Tree: Crime and Society in 18th Century England*, Hay argues that during this period criminal law functioned as an ideological system of control, which served to legitimate and add to the hegemony of the English ruling class. Criminal law, but in particular its enforcement, reinforced the belief that the ruling class was fit to rule and that it served the interests of all the people. There were three aspects of the law as an ideological system: majesty, justice, and mercy (Hay, 1975).[4]

The majesty of the law was emphasized by the excessive formality of the legal system. This formality could be seen in the pomp and ceremony displayed in courtroom activities and when justices visited country villages. It could also be seen when judges used their courts as platforms to address the multitude by making rhetorical statements about "the virtues of authority and obedience, the fitness of the social order," and the inculcation of dominant values supportive of that order, such as respect for the law, the king, and God.

The idea of justice, especially "equal justice for all," was displayed by the hanging of a man of wealth following judgment by a jury of his peers, even though this was indeed a rare occurrence. More importantly, the myriad procedural rules enabled some accused persons, even poor people, to be set free on a technicality. As Hay puts it:

> The punctilious attention to forms, the dispassionate and legalistic exchanges between counsel and judges, argued that those administering and using the laws submitted to its rules. The law thereby became something more than the creature of a ruling class—it became a power with its own claims, higher than those of prosecutor, lawyers, and even the great scarlet-robed assize judge himself. To them, too, of course, the law was The Law. The fact that they deified it, that they shut their eyes to its daily enactment in Parliament by men of their own class, heightened the illusion. When the ruling class acquitted men on technicalities they helped instill a belief in the disembodied justice of the law in the minds of all who watched. In short, its very inefficiency, its absurd formalism, was part of its strength as ideology (1975: 33).

In other words, the law was made to appear as if it had divine origins and that it was above class interests and control. The law's strength an ideological force lay in the belief that the nation was under the rule of law rather than the rule of wealthy men. The myth of the rule of law remains to the present day.[5]

The mercy of the law was shown through the extensive use of pardons of condemned men and the fact that the number of executions remained fairly stable, while offenses punishable by death increased in the eighteenth century. What appeared was a form of what Max Weber called khadi justice in which there was much formalism in the administration of the law, but in which the law "was nevertheless based on ethical or practical judgments rather than on a fixed, 'rational' set of rules" (Hay, 1975: 40). In other words, justice was administered in a very informal, almost ad hoc, manner with few formal procedural rules. Such mercy reinforced the benign paternalism of the ruling class, especially on the numerous occasions when even the poor were granted reprieves. Hay provides the following conclusion:

> Here was the peculiar genius of the law. It allowed the rulers of England to make the courts a selective instrument of class justice, yet simultaneously to proclaim the law's incorruptible impartiality, and absolute determinacy . . . it allowed the class that passed one of the bloodiest penal codes in Europe to congratulate itself on its humanity. It encouraged loyalty to the king and the state (1975: 48–49).

Emergence of the Concept of Crime

The emergence of criminal law (and hence the notion of crime) in England did not occur in a vacuum. Rather, it emerged in the context of larger structural changes in economic and political institutions. As we have already suggested, it reflected a shift from feudalism to nationalism (before this time there was no concept of England, of nation, or of country) and the replacement of blood ties as a basis of social order to ties based on land ownership (i.e., private property). Moreover, the notion of crime carried with it the notion of sin. Furthermore, the concept of *mens rea* (guilty mind) also emerged during this time. Jeffery comments as follows:

> The concept of *mens rea* was derived from the Christian view of sins of the mind. Sins can be punished individually, not collectively, so that the individual and not the clan or family is responsible. Only individuals have souls that can be saved; social groups do not possess souls, and for that reason tribal responsibility gave way to the Christian notion of individual responsibility (1969: 30).

In short, a new legal system emerged along with changes in the social structure. Criminal law and the notion of crime emerged from the transition from tribal law to state law. The differences between these two legal systems can be summarized as follows (Jeffery, 1969: 31):

Tribal Law	*State Law*
Blood tie	Territorial tie
Collective responsibility	Individual responsibility
Family as unit of justice and order	State as unit of justice
Feud or compensation	Punishment

The social structure of tribal society was held together through clans of families, offenses were the responsibility of the collectivity, and it was their duty to settle offenses through either feud or compensation. Under state law (what we have in today's society), the social structure was held together through private property, the individual was solely responsible for his or her actions, and the state stepped in to administer justice through a system of punishment.

There was, however, a much larger change occurring, that of the emergence of capitalism as a dominant economic form and with it the coming of what is known as the "state."[6] This is a society based upon the "centralization of power under some ruler or government with the authority to issue directives and commands binding upon all members of the society" (Michalowski, 1985: 69). As state societies emerge, there also emerges a system whereby the victim of an offense begins to take a back seat in the proceedings, as the state takes over handling disputes. As suggested in the above chart, the individual is gradually substituted for the family or kinship as the offended party. Eventually it is the state itself that is the offended party and is therefore suppose to hereby act as a sort of representative of the victim, rather than the victim's kin.

In time what occurred was the development of a technology capable of producing a surplus of goods and a complex "division of labor," along with a system of stratification and a very "politicized economy." What eventually happened was that a centralized power base arose that began to compel or coerce a surplus from the work force. This eventually led to inequality among different groups, with one group —the group that rises to power and has control over the means of production—having control over most of the surplus and hence wealth. Once this occurs there comes the threat of trouble in the form of "revolutions, peasant and slave uprisings, labor strife, and common crimes as groups or individuals seek to affect either a personal or more general redistribution of wealth and power" (Michalowski, 1985: 74–75). Thus there arises the need for a formal system of "law" to respond to such threats to the prevailing order. Therefore it is not surprising to find the general conclusion among many scholars to the effect that formal law came about only with the rise of "private property." As Jeremy Bentham wrote: "Property and law are born together and die together" (Michalowski, 1985: 75). And this is exactly what occurred, beginning during the period roughly between the 8th and 11th centuries. Several case studies of these changes and how the legal system changed are available. Two of these are discussed in the next section. What these two cases show is that the law and the new legal order placed primary importance in the protection of private property and the social inequalities that the emerging system of capitalism produced (Tigar and Levy, 1977).

Two Case Studies: The Law of Theft and the Law of Vagrancy

Two studies of the origins of two specific criminal laws in early English society provide evidence that the law often reflects the interests of the rich and the powerful and tends to punish mainly the poor and the powerless: studies of the law of theft and the law of vagrancy (Hall, 1969; Chambliss, 1975).[7]

The law of theft dates from the fifteenth century in the famous Carrier case of 1473. The case resulted in a totally new view of the concept of theft. In this case, the defendant, who was hired to carry bales of merchandise to Southampton, opened the bales and absconded with the contents. He was arrested and charged with a felony.

Prior to this case, the necessary element of theft was trespass. The property had to be literally removed from the premises before larceny could legally have occurred. But the accused in this case already had possession of the bales and, hence, technically, could neither have committed trespass nor be charged with theft. The judges broke precedence and ruled that breaking into the bales and removing the contents constituted trespass, because possession of the bales did not mean possession of the contents (today this would probably be considered "embezzlement").

The Carrier case must be understood in the economic and political context within which it occurred. During the time when this case was decided England was in the middle of a commercial revolution. With the onset of industrialism and early forms of capitalist development there came a dependence on foreign trade. King Richard III, a merchant himself, had provided protection to foreign merchants that guaranteed safe passage for their goods. It was in the interests of the commercial class to insure favorable relations with foreign merchants (the complainant in this case just happened to be an Italian merchant) and since the courts were subservient to the crown, they too had to protect the interests of the merchants.

During the 15th century there was a great increase in the number of merchants and Southampton became the leading port of trade. Furthermore, the contents of the bales in this case consisted either of wool or cloth or both, and, coincidentally, they were the leading products of the time. Hence, Hall concludes that "the interests of the most important industry in England were involved in the case" (Hall, 1969: 50). Criminal law—specifically the law of theft—lagged behind the needs of the times (i.e., the needs of the rising merchant class) and was changed to meet these new needs through the Carrier case.

One more important point must be mentioned in this regard. During this period feudalism was disappearing and the Black Death in 1348 (plus various enclosure movements) forced millions of peasants off the land and killed many more. The economic changes brought about by the declining feudal economic system created a new class of "vagabonds" and beggars who were cut adrift from the mainstream of the newly emerging economic system known as capitalism. In short, there were simply not enough jobs to go around and this new class had to develop alternative methods of making a living. One method was stealing. Inciardi make the following summation of this process (1975: 7):

> As trade and commerce developed in seaports and interior cities assuring landowners a ready market for foodstuffs, land became valuable and many peasants were forced from their land. The decreasing yield from the soil, however, led to the initiation of the three-field system, thus forcing additional serfs from the land that had to remain fallow. In England specifically, the economic changes during this period were closely associated with the rise of the rogue and vagabond class. Ownership of land became individual rather than communal. Serfs had attempted to improve their conditions by severing themselves from the soil and accepting wages, but this alternative led to a more intense state of destitution. As sheep farming increased, the enclosure acts, which began in the twelfth century, more drastically affected the peasants, for their lands, as well as waste lands, suddenly became usable as pasture.

Understandably, merchants and landowners wanted to protect themselves from these hordes of peasants who, within a few centuries, would earn the label of "dangerous classes."

Similarly, whereas before the onset of capitalism it was customary for villagers and farmers to be able to freely take wood from the forests (and wild game, fruit, and even the contents of wrecked ships), since it was considered common land, after capitalism emerged these activities were defined by the state as crimes. Thus, criminal law helped in creating private property by defining common rights (e.g., taking of wood) as crimes.[8]

The emergence of the law of vagrancy, and the different uses of this law throughout history, gives evidence that the profit-making classes use the law to control and/or regulate the labor force and groups who are perceived as a threat to their dominance. Chambliss' analysis provides us with this illustration (Chambliss, 1975).

The first vagrancy statute was enacted in 1349 in England. The original law stipulated that it was a crime to give alms to any person of sound mind and body who was unemployed. In actual fact, the law was passed in order to provide a steady supply of cheap labor to landowners and to regulate the labor force. The prime force behind this law was the famous Black Death of 1348 to 1349, the pestilence that reduced the population in England by about one-half. Among the results of this wave of pestilence was the reduction in the size of the labor force and the corresponding reduction in the profits of the lords of the manors and other employers. Cheyney describes it as follows (1913: 104–105):

> After the Black Death the same demesne lands were to be cultivated, and in most cases the larger holdings remained or descended or were regranted to those who would expect to continue their cultivation. Thus the demand for laborers remained approximately as great as it had before. The number of laborers, on the other hand, was vastly diminished. They were therefore eagerly sought for by employers. Naturally they took advantage of their position to demand higher wages, and in many cases combined to work at the old accustomed rates.

This period witnessed a significant change in social class relations and in the composition of the work force. What the new laws indicated was that more and more people were beginning to make their living by working for a wage, whereas before they had not (they worked the land as serfs). Workers were becoming more mobile, searching for the best jobs at the highest wages. In short, it was the beginning of a capitalist economic system (Huberman, 1963). Such a system would become a constant battleground between owners and workers (still going on today). The conflict is at the heart of the capitalist social order: It is the inherent contradiction within a capitalist system whereby the process of producing commodities is essentially a public process involving many different people, while the results of such production (in this case the profits) are privately owned.[9]

In response to this significant change, the landowning class passed a series of laws known as the Statutes of Laborers in 1349. The new laws stipulated that every man "when offered service at these wages must accept it . . . if any laborers, men or women, bond or free, should refuse to accept such an offer of work, they were to be imprisoned. . . ." (Cheyney, 1913: 107).

This was an obvious attempt to respond to the growing poverty and the concomitant threat to social order. It was a period when "bread riots were common and landless farmers poured into English cities" and vagrants were perceived as being a challenge to "social order" (Adler, 1989a: 213). The vagrancy laws passed at this time were consciously designed to control the mobility of the laboring classes and to protect mostly the interests of the landowners. The laws were designed "to curtail the mobility of laborers in such a way that labor would not become a commodity for which the landowners would have to compete" (Chambliss, 1975: 11). The application of such laws was widespread, focusing not only on vagrants but rogues and thieves, along with "gypsies, Irishmen, fortune tellers, university scholars found begging without permission, and peddlers" (Adler, 1989a: 213).

In time the law was altered to adapt to changing social and economic conditions. In 1530 the law was reactivated (after being dormant for several years) as a result of a shift in focal concern from the idle and those refusing to work to such criminal types as rogues and vagabonds, plus others who, as noted earlier, developed criminal careers because of their marginal positions in society and the shortage of employment opportunities. Indeed, the merchants and other capitalist entrepreneurs needed protection from those whose life conditions forced them to steal in order to survive.

It would be a mistake to conclude that it was simply the narrow interests of the capitalist class at work here. Obviously ordinary citizens were concerned with the threats posed by rogues and vagabonds of an earlier era and common criminals throughout 19th and 20th century American society. Vagrancy statutes continued to be used to cover a wide variety of social problems. In fact, as Adler correctly points out, vagrancy codes throughout the 19th century defined *vagrant* in such broad terms that "anyone who threatened social order" could be arrested. On numerous occasions they were used to arrest labor organizers and rebellious workers, tramps and beggars and a whole host of other "undesirables" (Adler, 1989a: 214–215). A study of the use of vagrancy laws in early 19th century St. Louis shows quite clearly that local merchants and capitalists, as well as most ordinary citizens wanted some protection from outsiders such as wanderers and paupers (poor people). After all, their presence was a threat to social order and the creation and maintenance of a stable business climate, the profits of which accrued mostly to the wealthy. However, enough profits trickled down to enough people to mean that many ordinary citizens would naturally perceive threats from rogues, vagabonds, wanderers, and other undesirables. The laws reflected the interests of the capitalist class of St. Louis—and a number of others as well (Adler, 1986). However, the social conditions that created a class of vagabonds, wanderers, petty thieves, paupers, and so on was the result of an expansive capitalist system, which allowed great fortunes to be amassed by a relatively small group of capitalists throughout the 19th century, while creating hordes of poverty-stricken people left completely out of the emerging American Dream.[10] It was left up to the criminal justice system to manage those left out. It has been the case ever since.

From this review we can concur with Adler who appears to be challenging the Marxist interpretation of vagrancy laws, yet his comments seem to support my own interpretation that such laws, like laws in general, do in fact reflect the interests of the dominant classes and seem to concentrate on those deemed undesirable or perhaps even dangerous, while simultaneously being supported by other classes (who are usually the most directly victimized). Thus, the use of the criminal law (in this case vagrancy laws) has in fact been an excellent illustration of controlling the dangerous classes.

The use of criminal law to protect the interests of the dominant classes, its use as an ideological system of control, and its use to secure and protect the foundations of a particular economic system continued as colonists began to settle in America. The development of criminal law in America will be our next topic. The American legal system, with a few modifications was simply an adaptation of English criminal law.

Emergence of Criminal Law in America

In colonial America many of the laws had religious foundations that were based primarily on maxims from the Old Testament (Erickson, 1966; Haskins, 1960; Nelson, 1974; Powers, 1966). The maxim "eye for an eye" was reflected in some of the punishments. There were several capital offenses (i.e., punishable by death), many of which had Biblical foundations. For instance, these offenses included idolatry, witchcraft, blasphemy, bestiality, sodomy, adultery, and cursing or smiting a parent. The Puritan leaders in the Massachusetts Bay Colony developed a conception of a government that was divinely ruled. The "word of God" served as a basis for the newly established order. The governor and his magistrates "were granted power through divine authority. As 'Gods upon earth,' the leaders must be fully obeyed in order that the covenant be kept" (page 61). Governor John Winthrop expressed this view when he stated.

> . . . the determination of law belongs properly to God: He is the only law
> giver, but He hath given power and gifts to man to interpret his laws; and
> this belongs principally to the highest authority in a commonwealth, and
> subordinately to other magistrates and judges according to their several
> places (Quinney, 2001: 61–62).

For Winthrop and other rulers, this was an easy method to secure their own power and legitimacy.

It is clear that the rulers of the Massachusetts Bay Colony used the legal system to secure their conception of order in addition to their hegemony. It is also true that the law was used to persecute those who threatened the traditional religious beliefs. Haskins goes so far as to suggest: "The government of Massachusetts was thus a dictatorship of a small minority who were unhesitantly prepared to coerce the unwilling to serve the purposes of society as they conceived it" (Haskins, 1960: 44–45). The majority of the cases handled in the courts were offenses against morality, such as adultery, cohabitation, fornication, indecent exposure, blasphemy, and the like (Nelson, 1975: 37–38). There were even laws specifically against Quakers, who obviously were a serious threat to the religious rulers of the time. For instance, it was a capital offense for a Quaker to return to the colony after banishment. Three Quakers were hanged in Massachusetts because of the violation of this law (Friedman, 1993: 32). Obviously, crime and sin went hand in hand during this time. However, throughout this period of time instability was constantly at hand and eventually a change that threatened the very foundations of Puritan society came during the 17th century.

Erickson noted several crime waves during the seventeenth century and suggested that these served to help establish the moral boundaries of the Puritan settlement. That is, by enforcing various laws that were violated during these crime waves, the consensus on what was good and proper conduct was reaffirmed (Erickson, 1966). Chambliss offers a different interpretation. He suggests that these crime waves were precipitated "by power struggles between those who ruled and those who were ruled" (1976: 11). The case of Anne Hutchinson is illustrative. This woman began holding meetings in her home, which included religious discussions that gave an interpretation of the Bible that conflicted with the popular beliefs of others in the Commonwealth. She and her followers were accused of being antinomians (a religious sect that opposed the dominant Puritan religion) and subsequently were banished as criminals.

Some 20 years later the emergence of the Quakers created another conflict. They, too, were punished for their "blasphemy." In fact, it was a criminal offense to be a Quaker! Then, in the 1670s, in Salem, the outbreak of "witchcraft" provided the arena for yet another power struggle. This was partly a diversionary tactic used by the rulers at a time when their authority was threatened by England. As Chambliss notes, "the potential diversion of witchcraft served to give at least the appearance of a reaffirmation of authority in the hands of those who ruled" (1976: 14). It is important to note that those who were defiant or hostile to the rulers were the ones put to death. Those who confessed and generally accepted the legitimacy of those in power were spared the death penalty. A total of 19 people were executed, mostly women (Friedman, 1993: 46). (See chapters 3 and 6 for more details on the Salem witch trials.) By labeling others as criminal, heretic, or witch, the rulers were able to reduce conflict and control the rest of the population.[11]

The most noteworthy changes in American criminal law came on the heels of the American Revolution. The rise of the bourgeois class to power (this class consisting primarily of planters, merchants, and lawyers) brought with it attempts to centralize the powers of a new state and, in effect, to control those who threatened the new social order (Takagi, 1975). In other words, criminal law was changed to meet the demands of a changing society. Nelson's study of criminal law in post-Revolution America is instructive. He says that the period immediately following the Revolution was a time of great civil strife and disorder (e.g., Shay's Rebellion). The new rulers "feared organized groups of malcontents bent upon the reconstruction of society . . . they feared such political activity because they expected that it would be economically motivated . . . In short, their fear was that the economically underprivileged would seek material gain by banding together to deprive the more privileged persons of their wealth and standing" (Nelson, 1974: 111). There was a shift in the focal concern of criminal law from enforcing morality toward the protection of private property (owned by a very small minority) and social order. Court cases reflect this shift, for the bulk of the cases after the Revolution concerned property and public order offenses, whereas before the Revolution most cases involved offenses against morality, as noted above.

Laws that explicitly protected the political order of Britain were adopted to serve the same purposes in America. For instance, the Sedition Act was passed in 1798 and provided for the punishment of those who made any statements against the newly formed government. "The law, as well as curtailing loyalty to the British, became an instrument of the Federalists in their attempt to suppress the activities (considered as pro-French) of the opposition Republican Party" (Quinney, 1970: 58) Similarly, the law of treason was used to secure the new order, especially those laws that were antiloyalist, for example, those that disfranchised the loyalists.

The period immediately following the American Revolution was a period of reform of the criminal law. Ideally, the leaders wanted a legal system that was not monarchic and authoritarian, like it was under British rule. In part the new legal codes would follow some of Beccaria's formulations.[12] The Bill of Rights was part of this reform effort and about half of these had to do directly with criminal matters. More than anything else, however, such reforms were an effort by those now in power to create an ideology that the new nation was to be one under the rule of law instead of the rule of men. In fact, of course, it was and continues to be a nation under the rule of men—specifically white, upper class men.[13] The notion of rule of law merely camouflages the nature of power and control in this society. Howard Zinn provides one of the best examples of the concept rule of law as follows (Zinn, 1990: 111):

> The law appears impersonal. It is on paper, and who can trace it back to what men? And because it has the look of neutrality, its injustices are made legitimate. It was not easy to hold onto the "divine right" of kings—everyone could see that kings and queens were human beings. The code of law is more easily deified than a flesh-and-blood ruler. Under the rule of men, the oppressor was identifiable, and so peasant rebels hunted down the lords, slaves killed plantation owners, and revolutionaries assassinated monarchs. In the era of the corporate bureaucracies, representative assemblies, and the rule of law, the enemy is elusive and unidentifiable.[14]

This period also witnessed many other legal reforms, the most important of which was the abandonment of various public punishments (e.g., whippings, the stocks and the pillory), narrowing the number of crimes punishable by death, the creation of a full-time uniformed police (see chapter 2), and the creation of a new prison system (see chapter 4).

More than anything else, however, the reforms merely made it easier for those in power to create a legal system that help reinforced their rule. It is inherently class biased. This can be seen in the writing of the Constitution, written as it was by men of property and wealth (Beard, 1935). Was it any accident that Native Americans, women and slaves were systematically excluded from the creation of the new government? In a sense, the newly emerging criminal justice system became, in Friedman's words, "the strong arm of the stratification system" (Friedman, 1993: 84). Nowhere is this better illustrated than with regards to the matter of race.

Racism and the Law

The development of legal institutions in America corresponded to the development of racist ideologies and the oppression of Native Americans, African-Americans, and other racial and ethnic minorities. The law, especially during the 19th century, was used to regulate and control the labor of minorities. Two groups were especially troublesome (to those in power) by their presence in early American history, and the legal system did its best to keep them in their place. These two groups were Native Americans and black slaves.

When Columbus began his explorations into the new world, it marked the beginning of a "confrontation between the conquerors and the conquered on a global scale" (Chomsky, 1993: 3). The Arawaks, the first Indians that Columbus met, were a peaceful group, and they ran out to greet the visitors, bearing gifts, food, and water. Columbus was to write in his log that, "With fifty men we could subjugate them all and make them do whatever we want" (Zinn, 2005: 1). However, the traits displayed by the Arawaks were not those that stood out among Europeans, "dominated as it was by the religion of popes, the government of kings, the frenzy for money. . ." (Zinn, 2005: 2–3). What Columbus wanted more than anything else was gold in order to finance the conquests of Spain, a society where about 2% of the population owned 95% of the land. He found no gold, but in the process about half of the 250,000 Indians on Haiti were dead within two years; by 1515 there were around 50,000 Indians left and by 1550 there were 500; by 1650 *none* of the original Arawaks were left. It has been estimated that more than 3 million Indians perished in the West Indies between 1492 and 1508, prompting one writer to describe this as "complete genocide" (Zinn, 2005: 1–7).[15]

The law supported the wholesale confiscation of their land throughout the nation and the genocide committed against them. These people were ruled by a foreign law rather than their own customs (in this case, a tribal society ruled by tribal law was overthrown and ruled by a capitalist society and legal system). The peculiar logic of European law maintained that the Indians had only a natural right to the land, but not a civil right. Obviously, from this point of view, the natural right had no legal standing—that is, legal from the point of view of the American conquerors. This entire invasion of North America was based upon an ideology born out of a civilization based upon the relentless drive to amass profits, no matter what the outcome in human terms. And it was a civilization based upon subjugation that confronted a world based more upon egalitarian relations (Zinn, 2005: 13–22).

Many of the broken treaties were supported by the American legal system. Indian land was confiscated through trickery and the white man's law by the use of the legal term *title,* which was foreign to the native language and was an invention of a capitalist money economy (e.g., private property as a new concept). This confiscation, writes Vine Deloria, was supported by the U.S. Supreme Court in the 1903 case, *Lone Wolf v. Hitchcock.*[16] Deloria notes that the court in this case "laid down the principle that the tribes had no title to the land at all. Rather the land was held by the United States and the tribes had mere occupancy rights" (Deloria, 1969: 46). Burns cites another case (*Johnson v. Macintosh,* 1823) where the court ruled that "discovery gave exclusive title to those who made it," thus upholding the claim that whites "discovered" America (Burns, 1974: 264; see also, Brown, 1971). In other words, merely as a result of conquest, native lands became the property of the U.S. government and therefore the Indians were to be considered occupants (de Yoanna and Langeland, 2001).

In the case of African-Americans, the law supported slavery and their kidnapping from Africa. Profits from the slave trade were enormous, as so many have noted—and perfectly legal. Slavery became a form of labor exploitation and a method of controlling the labor market. Numerous laws had to be passed to help perpetuate slavery. Laws were passed in the Carolinas prohibiting free blacks from traveling into Indian country, apparently on the assumption that the two groups might join together. It was common for black and white slaves and servants to run away together, and thus laws were passed to prohibit this. For example, Virginia passed a law in 1661 prohibiting a white English servant from running away with a black slave. In 1691, Virginia passed another law prohibiting interracial marriages. Many slaveholders felt uneasy keeping so many black slaves without many white servants to help keep order on the plantations. So in 1717, Parliament passed laws adding transportation to another country to the list of punishments for crime, resulting in tens of thousands of convicts being sent to various colonies, especially Maryland and Virginia. By the end of the 17th century laws were passed throughout the Southern states that made slavery a perpetual condition for black people. In fact, with the coming of the American Revolution, freedom became a reality for whites only. As Burns notes, the Constitution itself guaranteed the continuation of the slave trade, the return of fugitive slaves, and "the counting of black persons as three-fifths human beings for purposes of taxation and representation" (Burns, 1990: 116).

The various slave codes passed throughout the South became a common method of legalizing slavery. Such codes "legislated and regulated in minute detail every aspect of the life of a slave and of black/white interaction; assured white-over-black dominance; and made black people into virtual nonpersons . . ." (Burns, 1990: 117). It was not merely the plantation owners, but rather the entire community that was involved in the legal regulation of slaves. There were many "slave patrols" and the law authorized these men to pick up runaway and disorderly slaves and slaves who were found without a pass. These are merely a few examples among hundreds (Zinn, 2005: 31, 54–56). What the law did was to codify and express "the basic theorem of slave law" (Friedman). It represented the "massive power of masters and mistresses, and the power of their agents and overseers" (Friedman, 1993: 85). One perfect example of the racist nature of the law in the case of African-Americans can be seen in a law passed in 1855 in the state of Kansas. Here the law stipulated that a white man convicted of rape of a white woman could be sentenced to no more than five years in prison. However, the penalty for a black man for the same offense was castration. Wherever such a law was in force, it was reserved almost exclusively for African-Americans (or in some cases for Native Americans) (Burns, 1990: 115).

Regular courts in the South would deal with the more serious crimes committed by slaves. These cases were, however, mostly property crimes. In some cases slaves convicted of violent crimes were hanged. Not surprisingly, most of these were cases of rape, always involving a white victim. These hangings were well attended and whites made certain that blacks attended, so as to send a clear message that a black person dare not commit a violent crime against a white person. It should be noted that in these cases the white owner would be compensated for slaves put to death. In Louisiana, for instance, the public treasury would provide up to $750 per slave. In South Carolina the value attached was much lower at $122.45 per slave (Friedman, 1993: 88).

After the Civil War the legal system worked to keep African-Americans in their place, with vaguely worded vagrancy laws (reactivated after being dormant), Black Codes, and the famous Jim Crow laws creating segregation in hotels, restaurants, and so on (Woodward, 1955; Shelden, 1980). In short, there was a concerted effort to search for any legal means necessary to maintain the status quo. What many of the legal codes did was to keep so-called free blacks tied to the land (owned by whites) via the system of sharecropping (a throwback to the feudal system and a form of slavery). This became a form of perpetual debt. (The movie *Sounders* dramatically depicts this economic system.) The doctrine of separate but equal was upheld by the Supreme Court in *Plessy v. Ferguson* in 1896. In this famous case, a man named Homer Plessy (who was described as not really black but an "octoroon") purchased a first class train ticket and sat in a "white only" section. He was summarily ejected from the train and tossed in jail in New Orleans. He claimed in his defense that this was in violation of the 13th and 14th Amendment. It went all the way to the U.S. Supreme Court where, by an 8 to 1 vote, the court rejected the appeal. Writing for the majority Chief Justice Henry B. Brown said that the segregation of the races is "natural" and, "If one race be inferior to the other socially, the Constitution cannot put them upon the same plane." (Friedman 1993: 96). In a famous dissent, Justice John Marshall Harlan wrote that the "Constitution is color blind" (Friedman, 1993: 96). Obviously the Constitution was color blind in theory only. In fact, there was really never any intention among the framers of this document to include "lesser" people, like slaves, Native Americans and even women as having "equal rights before the law." In this sense the Constitution has served as an ideological prop for the capitalist system, claiming that this system is "the best of all possible worlds," at least for the minority who reap the most benefits.

Another method of control involved various voting barriers, which were supported by law throughout the South. An example of such legal practices was the "grandfather clause" (a law stipulating that in order for a man to vote his grandfather had to have been eligible to vote, an obvious impossibility for blacks, for no black man had ever been granted the vote in America). In short, the entire legal system, from the wording of specific laws to the penal system (e.g., with convict leasing), helped to maintain white rule in the South after the Civil War (Genovese, 1976; Shelden, 1980; Adamson, 1999; Myers and Massey, 1999). More will be said about this in chapter 4 when the convict lease system—another form of slavery—is discussed.

Other minority groups have fared little better at the hands of the legal system. These groups were often subjugated by means of criminal law in order to provide capitalists a steady supply of cheap labor during the 19th and well into the 20th century. The legal system lent support to and made possible capitalist expansion in the 19th century. For instance, Chinese people were recruited to do the back-breaking work of building the railroads to the West, beginning with the Gold Rush in the 1840s (Dinnerstein and Reimers, 1975: 57). Wu makes the following observation:

> . . . The Chinese were initially brought into the United States to meet the serious labor shortages which then affected economic growth, particularly in California. As a rule, they performed unskilled labor, the kind of strenuous and menial jobs which whites

average person (most could not come up with the required $200) and so rich
speculators bought up most of the land.

- During the Civil War Congress gave 100 million acres to railroads and established a
national bank, resulting in a partnership between big business and the government,
thus guaranteeing huge profits.
- A "Contract Labor Law" passed in 1864 enabled companies to sign "contracts"
with foreign workers if they pledged to give back 12 months worth of wages to help
pay the cost of immigration. (Zinn, 2005: 233–234)

Controlling the Dangerous Classes: Drug Laws as an Example

Perhaps no area of legislation has created more controversy than legislation against
the use of certain drugs. The sordid history of anti-drug legislation is filled with emotions and vested interests. In order to fully understand these laws, we need to examine briefly the history of the use and abuse of drugs.

The use and distribution of opium can be traced at least as far back as the 8th
and 9th centuries when Turkish traders began to seek markets for their homegrown
crop of opium. The trade in opium was rather inconsequential until capitalism began
to replace feudalism around the 16th century (Chambliss, 1977).

Leaders in the opium market at this time were the Portuguese. Since Europe had
little to offer Asia in terms of goods to trade, the Portuguese ships began to raid Asian
vessels in search of marketable goods. What they found was opium, which they could
readily use in trade for tea, silk, spices, and pottery.

As opium dens began to flourish, European powers, through the British East
India Company, gained almost total control. As addiction to opium began to spread
throughout China, the Chinese began to make attempts to stem the flow of the plant.
Britain fought back, defeating the Manchu Dynasty in the Opium War (1839 to 1842)
and gaining possession of Hong Kong, the major port of the opium trade. One result
of the ensuing treaty between China and Britain was that the British were to enforce
laws against smuggling. But while the Chinese law forbade smuggling opium, British
law did not. Thus, Britain was given complete freedom in the control of the opium
trade. After another brief war broke out in 1856, opium was legalized. Hence, the
profit for Britain in opium was increased immeasurably. But a tax was imposed by
China and Chinese farmers were given the right to grow the plant.

During the last half of the 19th century, European countries almost literally took
over as colonies all of Southeast Asia. A famine in China reduced the labor force and
caused thousands of Chinese to immigrate. The Chinese went to major cities in Southeast
Asia and as far away as the United States. They brought with them the British-encouraged
opium habit, which proved to be helpful to colonial governments since those addicted
proved to be a compliant work force. Chambliss comments as follows (1977: 78):

> The opium trade was carefully, albeit corruptly, organized and controlled by an unholy
> alliance between colonial officials, local governments and entrepreneurs who were given
> government franchises to import and sell opium. The profits were substantial. Opium

sales provided 40 to 50 per cent of the income of colonial governments. Opium profits helped finance the railways, canals, roads and government buildings as well as the comfortable living conditions of colonial bureaucrats.

By the 1840s there were over 2,500 opium dens in Indochina, providing for about 45% of all tax revenues.

During the last half of the 19th century the growing of opium in China increased and began to compete with the demand for Indian and Turkish-grown opium. Britain and America (who came upon the scene much later) were soon forced to look elsewhere for profits. The major producing monopoly eventually centered on the Golden Triangle (where Laos, Burma, and Thailand meet). In the meantime, the French began to invest in this trade and eventually took monopolistic control of Indochinese opium. This proved to be a successful weapon against communist insurgence, as the French were able to pay off hill tribes and local leaders who would support the French in this struggle.

Prior to the 20th century, the common attitude toward drug use in both the U.S. and Britain could be characterized as laissez-faire. The use of such highly addictive drugs as opium and cocaine was common and accepted in both Britain and the United States. A survey of 35 Boston drugstores in 1888 discovered that more than three-fourths (78%) of prescriptions refilled three or more times contained opium (Levinthal, 1996: 154).

The use of various forms of cocaine gained acceptance for both its anesthetic and psychopharmacological properties throughout the late 19th century. In fact, by 1883, cocaine was indexed in 50 scientific papers. "Among its uses, cocaine was prevalent as an anesthetic for ophthalmological surgery, and widely prescribed for such respiratory ailments as asthma, whooping cough, and tuberculosis was extensive during this time." Even Sigmund Freud supported its use "as an antidote for morphine addiction and alcoholism, as an aphrodisiac and a cure for asthma" (Trueblood, 1998: 4; see also, Helmer, 1975). Musto notes that many medicines "that could be bought at any store or by mail order contained morphine, cocaine, laudanum, or (after 1898) heroin . . . Hay fever remedies commonly contained cocaine as their active ingredient" (1999, 3). By 1890, cocaine had become the primary ingredient in many elixirs and other restoratives that claimed to relieve a variety of disabilities, such as common colds, asthma, headaches, influenza, and depression. Cocaine was also found in cigars, cigarettes, chewing gum, and various tonics, and most notably, Coca-Cola. Also, until 1903, Coca Cola contained cocaine (Musto, 1999: 3; Trueblood, 1998: 4).

The first influx of opium into the United States came with Chinese workers (commonly known as coolies)[19] starting in the 1850s. Opium was used to combat the psychological pain of their work and as relief from physical illnesses. From the point of view of employers, it was good business (both in a profit sense and in terms of pacifying workers).

Opium came into the United States legally through normal business channels. By the 1880s, however, when mining and railroad building had declined, the United States became concerned with the number of Chinese (and other) immigrants coming into the country. The United States and China agreed to stop Chinese immigration in return for a reduction in opium going to China via American shipbuilders. The first antiopium legislation passed in 1886, making it illegal to trade in opium (Chambliss, 1977: 65).

After the civil war, attitudes began to change and there developed strong opposition toward the smoking of opium; an attitude directed mainly toward Chinese immigrants. Opium smoking—in contrast to opium drinking in the form of laudanum and similar legally prescribed products (used by middle and upper class people)—eventually became associated with criminal activity and demand for the control of opium dens grew. In response, the first recorded drug law in the United States was passed in 1885, an ordinance in San Francisco banning opium dens (Levinthal, 1996: 49, 154–155; United States Sentencing Commission, 1995: 112). To quote a newspaper at that time, such an ordinance was passed for fear that "many women and young girls, as well as young men of respectable family, were being induced to visit the dens, where they were ruined morally and otherwise" (Levinthal, 1996: 155).

Then in 1887, the federal government prohibited the importation of opium by the Chinese, and in 1905 restricted opium smoking in the Philippines. For several years thereafter, "the United States launched a series of international conventions designed to foster narcotics control activity, including the Shanghai Opium Convention of 1909 and the 1911 International Conference on Opium at The Hague" (Trueblood, 1998: 5).

The regulation of opium smoking came to epitomize the widespread fear and hostility of Chinese immigrants. It also "became the catalyst for the ensuing wave of reform sentiment that began to sweep the country respecting the use of any narcotics" (Levinthal, 1996: 50). These fears put extraordinary pressures upon policy makers, the result of which was the passage of the Pure Food and Drug Act of 1906. This Act required manufacturers to disclose the amounts of alcohol or "habit forming" drugs (specifically opiates and cocaine) on product labels, although the law did not restrict the sale or use of these substances (Levinthal, 1996: 50).[20] Moreover, in the South, there was fear from use by blacks whom southerners feared might be likely to attack whites while under the influence (Musto, 1999: 6).

By the turn of the century the opium trade had shifted from India to Turkey and then to Southeast Asia, especially the Golden Triangle. Opium dens were run and organized by the governments of China and other governments in Southeast Asia, and profits supported both local and colonial governments.

In 1898 Bayer (a German pharmaceutical company) began distributing a product that it claimed was nonaddictive and had the same medical value as opium but without the undesirable side effects. It's medical name was diacetylmorphine but was sold under the trade name *heroin*, from the German word *heroisch*, which means heroic and powerful (Inciardi, 2002: 24).

Like the attitude toward opium, as the use of cocaine became increasingly associated with minorities and crime, it was no longer perceived as a benign substance. Myths about the invincibility of "crazed" African-Americans under the influence of cocaine were created and perpetuated through newspaper headlines like one in 1913 that read: "Drug Crazed Negroes Fire at Every One in Sight in Mississippi Town." It was believed that cocaine bestowed such brut strength upon these "animals" that they were impervious to any and all efforts at social control—bullets included (Trueblood, 1998: 5; Goldstein, et al., 1997).

By 1914, almost every state in the nation had passed laws regulating the use and distribution of cocaine, all in the name of "crime control" (Trueblood, 1998: 5). In 1914, the United States passed the Harrison Act, which made it illegal to trade in opium or its derivatives (including heroin) without registering with the federal government and paying taxes. Further interpretations of the act through court rulings (such as the Linder case in 1925) made it illegal to sell or possess these drugs (Lindesmith, 1965). The significance of this legislation was that the law, in effect, shifted attention from one class of drug addicts to another. As Troy Duster notes, prior to the passage of the Harrison Act, the average drug addict was of middle to upper-middle class in origin, with the majority being middle-class housewives, mostly white. "Whereas in 1900 the addict population was spread relatively evenly over the social classes (with the higher classes having slightly more), by 1920, medical journals could speak of the 'overwhelming' majority from the 'unrespectable' parts of society" (Duster, 1970: 11). Thus, antidrug legislation during this era followed previous legislation. In effect, it sought to control the "unrespectable" sector of the population, specifically the dangerous classes (especially racial minorities).

This legislation apparently made little difference as far as the drug business was concerned. After World War I, the heroin and opium business became highly competitive, run by local merchants who made special arrangements with merchant seamen and mercantilists. By 1938, the heroin business had grossed an estimated $1 billion annually (Chambliss, 1977: 67).

As the law and order crackdown on these drugs, Congress became even more punitive. It began enacting a series of laws that place more restrictions on the use and distribution of illegal drugs. Perhaps more significantly, in 1930 Congress created the Federal Bureau of Narcotics to regulate and enforce the new laws. This new agency was charged with enforcing drug laws (excluding alcohol), and the nation's first drug czar, Harry J. Anslinger, was appointed at its first commissioner (Trueblood, 1998: 7; United States Sentencing Commission, 1995: 133). "Anslinger was a staunchly conservative member of the Treasury Department during the prohibition era, who garnered the support of several important conservative U.S. Congressmen during his 32-year tenure—not the least of whom was Senator Joseph R. McCarthy" (Trueblood, 1998: 6; Levinthal, 1996: 51).

Anslinger perhaps best represents the extremes of prohibition in general, as he was a law-and-order evangelist and, in the words of his biographer, "a cross between William Jennings Bryan and Reverend Jerry Falwell" (Gray, 2000: 73–74). He was the perfect fit for the job as the head of the Bureau of Narcotics, as he had formerly been involved in alcohol prohibition in the state of Florida (Gray, 2000: 73–74).

The Depression and the end of Prohibition placed severe constraints on Congress in the allocation of federal spending in general, and spending for the Bureau of Narcotics. Anslinger, desperate for power and money, seized upon several unsubstantiated rumors in the 1930s concerning so-called degenerate Spanish-speaking residents in the Southwest who were going on crime sprees allegedly while smoking marijuana. Anslinger began calling it the assassin of youth and identifying it as the next major public menace (Levinthal, 1996: 51). According to law enforcement, this killer weed, as it began to be referred to, "aroused sexual excitement and led to violent crimes" (Trueblood, 1998: 7; Goldstein et al., 1997). Anslinger used the mass media to spread his gospel about the evils of marijuana. Writing in the popular *American Magazine,* Anslinger used the anecdote to his best advantage to spread hysteria about this drug. A sample of his writings is as follows (quoted in Inciardi, 2002: 35–36):

> The sprawled body of a young girl lay crushed on the sidewalk the other day after a plunge from the fifth story of a Chicago apartment house. Everyone called it suicide, but actually it was murder. The killer was a narcotic known to America as marijuana, and to history as hashish. It is a narcotic used in the form of cigarettes, comparatively new to the United States and as dangerous as a coiled rattlesnake.

Anslinger did not hesitate to use the race angle, as noted in these two stories:

> Colored students at the Univ. of Minn. Partying with female students (white) smoking (marijuana) and getting their sympathy with stories of racial persecution. Result pregnancy (Gray, 2000: 79).
>
> Two Negroes took a girl fourteen years old and kept her for two days under the influence of marijuana. Upon recovery she was found to be suffering from syphilis (Inciardi, 2002: 35–36).

Another illustration appeared in a headline article in the *New York Times* (July 6, 1927) titled "Mexican Family Go Insane." The story read in part: "A widow and her four children have been driven insane by eating the Marijuana plant. . ." In January of 1929 the *Montana Standard*, reporting on that state's passage of a drug law, noted that "Marijuana is Mexican opium, a plant used by Mexicans and cultivated for sale by Indians" (a statement that is patently false, by the way; Inciardi, 2002: 34–35).

The alarmist position of Anslinger found perhaps its best outlet with the movie *Reefer Madness*. This movie has since become somewhat of a classic illustration of the hysteria surrounding certain drugs, showing the "moral decline of innocent young people unwittingly enticed into a deviant subculture of marijuana smoking youth" (Trueblood, 1998: 7). This film was partly responsible for the passage of the Marijuana Tax Act of 1937, which regulated and taxed marijuana at the federal level. A series of state laws followed, criminalizing marijuana possession (Becker, 1963).

However, the Marijuana Tax Act and all the state laws passed in its wake, predictably failed to reduce drug consumption patterns of marijuana. The proposed evils of marijuana failed to materialize and eventually public concern decreased and marijuana was no longer the subject of intense drug legislation.

However, it did not take too long for new drugs to come on to the scene. The 1960s saw a number of amendments to the laws then in effect. In 1961, for example, the United Nations adopted the single convention on narcotic drugs, establishing regulatory schedules of psychotropic substances. In 1962, the Bureau of Narcotics changed its name to the Bureau of Narcotics and Dangerous Drugs. Note the addition of the words *dangerous drugs,* perhaps signifying a shift in policy direction. By this time Anslinger was becoming a liability because of his often uncontrollable tirades. At the urging of President John Kennedy, Harry Anslinger retired (Trueblood, 1998: 7–8; Levinthal, 1996: 51; United States Sentencing Commission, 1995: 114; Musto, 1999: 238).

It is clear that the interests of the people have not been represented in drug control legislation. For the most part, the interests that have been involved have been those of the manufacturers and the federal government, especially the Federal Bureau of Narcotics (now called the Drug Enforcement Administration). Evidence of the latter's influence can be seen in the case of the first antimarijuana legislation, the Marijuana Tax Act. As Becker has noted, the Federal Bureau of Narcotics almost single-handedly (with the help from expert testimony from certain manufacturers) outlawed marijuana with the passage of the Marijuana Tax Act of 1937. However, little concern over the evils of marijuana was evident until the 1960s (it had always been used mainly by lower-class people and minority groups) when middle- and upper-class youths began to use it (Becker, 1963).

In the meantime, two legislative acts (the Boggs Act of 1951 and the Narcotic Drug Control Act of 1956) substantially increased the penalties for possession and sales of drugs tremendously. For instance, in 1956 the penalty for first offense possession was from 2 to 10 years; for second offense possession, the penalty was from 5 to 20 years. Gradually, the use of marijuana spread and so did the number of arrests. The Boggs Act had little impact on marijuana use (Gray, 2000: 85). However, as is typical when it comes to obsessive politics, if getting tough fails, just get even tougher! This is what Congress did when it passed the Narcotics Control Act in 1956. This act doubled the penalties of the Boggs Act and even included the death penalty for certain cases (Gray, 2000: 86).

Then, during the late 1960s, pressures began to build up over the decriminalization of marijuana. One of the prime motivating forces behind the reduction of penalties for possession of marijuana has been the growing number of young people from wealthy and influential families who had been arrested and sentenced to prison. The reform of the marijuana laws in the state of Nebraska is an illustration.

Galliher, McCartney, and Baum evaluated the legislation that resulted in decreased penalties for possession of marijuana in Nebraska in 1969. The bill, which reduced possession to a misdemeanor (a seven-day jail sentence as maximum), was passed without much fanfare. Few notices appeared in the newspapers and there was little debate. In such a conservative state as Nebraska, the authors note, this was quite unusual (Galliher and Baum, 1977).

Further probing found that about six months prior to the bill's introduction a county attorney's son and the son of a college professor were arrested for possession of marijuana. The district attorney prosecuting the case told the authors that he felt that it would be easier to get drug convictions if it was reduced to a misdemeanor. Other district attorneys agreed and said they wanted a law that was enforceable.

The state senator who sponsored the bill promised to make the bill retroactive in order to cover the sons of the college professor and the county attorney. It is apparent that the increasing use of marijuana by middle- and upper-class youth was the prime mover behind this bill. District attorneys, seeking easier convictions (possibly to increase their chances for reelection), were supportive of the bill. The issue of the seriousness of marijuana possession laws only developed with visible and seemingly widespread use among the sons and daughters of the wealthy. "As long as marijuana use appeared only among the poor, the problem of drug convictions didn't emerge for either conservatives or liberals" (Galliher and Baum, 1977: 81).

One of the most notorious examples of vested interests of manufacturers is seen in the passage of the Comprehensive Drug Abuse and Prevention Act of 1970. This act was the outcome of a bill (S-3246) originally called the Controlled Dangerous Substances Act and was introduced in September of 1969 (Graham, 1977).

A few basic facts about the manufacture and distribution of drugs help us understand the significance of this bill. In 1976, drug companies spent around $40 million on magazine advertising and another $97 million on television advertising. Retail sales during 1975 totaled $8,146 million on prescription drugs alone. Obviously, the drug companies had a direct interest in the outcome of this bill.

There were three schedules under the proposed bill, each schedule categorized according to the degree of penalties assessed to violators and the extent of enforcement required. Amphetamines (such as those consumed in the millions by housewives, business executives, truckers, and many other "respectable" people) were placed in Schedule III; hard drugs, such as LSD, heroin, cocaine, and marijuana, were placed in Schedule I.

The U.S. Senate began to hold hearings in September, 1969. Testifying for President Nixon (who was the bill's strongest supporter) was Attorney General John Mitchell. Medical testimony was offered by Dr. Sidney Cohen of the National Institute of Mental Health. He said that "50 percent of the lawfully manufactured pep pills were diverted at some point to illicit channels" (Graham, 1977: 89). Evidence was brought forth that five New York City pharmacies had shortages of from 12% to 50% of their stock in librium and valium (two of the most widely used Schedule III drugs in America). The Bureau of Narcotics and Dangerous Drugs had evidence that these drugs were connected with 36 suicides and 750 attempted suicides. Others testified to the harmful effects of both librium and valium. However, these and many other questions were never fully discussed during the hearings. The bill passed the Senate and went before the House of Representatives on January 23, 1970.

In the House hearings John Ingersoll of the Bureau of Narcotics and Dangerous Drugs testified. Concerning the problem of diversion to illegal sources, he said, "Registration is . . . the most effective and least cumbersome way" (Graham, 1977: 93) to solve this problem. He recommended, among other enforcement efforts, biennial inventories of the stocks of these drugs. Still, there was no guarantee that the drugs would not be diverted into illegal channels.

Dr. Dorothy Dobbs of the Federal Drug Administration testified that amphetamines have limited medical use and that dependency can result and that they cause "extreme personality changes" with "the most severe manifestation" being psychosis (ibid: 1994).

Congressman Claude Pepper of Florida led an investigation team which found a great deal of laxness in drug companies. For instance, an agent of the Bureau of Narcotics and Dangerous Drugs said he was able to pass himself off as a doctor and ordered 25,000 units of amphetamines through two mail order houses in New York.

Several other experts testified to the dangerous effects of amphetamines and other drugs placed in Schedule III. But apparently this testimony was not enough to offset the very favorable testimony given by drug company representatives, such as those from Hoffman-La Roche Labs (a company that earned a profit in excess of $4 billion on librium and valium alone). The bill passed with most of the amphetamines being placed in Schedule III (with very limited restrictions on their manufacture and distribution) (Graham, 1977: 93–97).

Crack versus Powder Cocaine

Among the most controversial developments during the 1980s—and one which reflects one of the themes of this book—is legislation pertaining to cocaine and the obvious differences between the powdered variety and that of crack. Consistent with previous drug "epidemics," the rampant media coverage of crack cocaine during this time created a moral panic of unprecedented proportions. The literature regarding drug scares and the creation of moral panics, suggests that these events are independent phenomena, not necessarily related to actual trends or patterns in drug use or trafficking (Brownstein, 1991: 94). Research on illicit drugs has often emphasized the disparity between the perceived threat of that substance and the actual social harm involved (Jenkins, 1994: 12). And, as Reinarman and Levine have argued, the response of the media and the political establishment appears to have been well out of proportion to the actual dimensions and seriousness of the crack problem (Reinarman and Levine, 1997a; Brownstein, 1991; Zimring and Hawkins, 1991). In fact, examination of the National Institute of Drug Abuse (NIDA) Household Survey in 1991—near the peak of crack's epidemic—finds that less than 1% of the respondents had used crack during the pervious month, and only 1% to 2% of respondents had ever used crack in their lives (Belenko, 1993: 13). The emergence of the crack cocaine epidemic in this country was unprecedented in its media coverage, the public, political, and legislative response. Like no other drug before it, crack became a symbol for America's fear of crime and public order during the 1980s.[21]

Fueled by sensationalized media accounts and political posturing, crack cocaine became the catalyst for the war on drugs (Belenko, 1993; Reinarman and Levine, 1997a). Crack also became the target of a previously unparalleled punitive legislative response, ultimately culminating in the Anti-Drug Abuse Acts of 1986 and 1988. These acts implemented a 100-to-1 quantity crack to powder cocaine ratio for federal sentencing provisions, and criminalized simple possession of as little as five grams of crack cocaine, resulting in a mandatory five years in prison, compared to probation for possession of the same amount of powder cocaine. It should come as no surprise that the former drug has been used mostly by poor African-Americans and other minorities, while the latter has been used by more affluent whites (United States Sentencing Commission, 1995).

The surrounding social and political context of legislation of cocaine was that of the get tough approach to crime that emerged in the late 1970s and early 1980s. During this time period racial and class images dominated the discussion, with the image of the "crack head" being a poor, lower-class African-American male.

As the 1980s began the conservative agenda of the Reagan Administration began to take hold almost immediately. During this time came the reemergence of determinate sentencing (United States Sentencing Commission, 1995: 115). Determinate sentencing came at a time of decreasing public tolerance for crime, a growing skepticism towards rehabilitation, and an increasing acceptance of a more general get tough attitude toward crime (Belenko, 1993: 11). The result was the Sentencing Reform Act of 1984. This act created the United States Sentencing Commission and Determinant Sentencing. Specifically, the act directed the Sentencing Commission to promulgate "a system of detail, mandatory sentencing guidelines to assure more uniform federal court sentencing decisions." In addition, the act abolished parole for defendants sentenced under the sentencing guidelines (United States Sentencing Commission, 1995: 115).

So-called sentencing guidelines became one of the most popular reforms of the 1980s, stemming largely from the perception that judges were too lenient or that criminals were being paroled long before their sentence was due to expire. Many critics lamented the fact that crooks got off too easy and that a 30-year sentence should mean 30 years. A catchy slogan that was eventually used was "truth in sentencing" (Gest, 2001: 54). Part of the move toward sentencing guidelines stems from a tendency within any capitalist society to make things efficient, streamlined, systematized, or just plain bureaucratized so as to make outcomes more predictable. This was clearly seen around the turn of the 20th century with the rise of what came to be called scientific management. This was a system devised by Frederick Taylor in an attempt to increase factory production by getting the most work out of each worker and to do so with some scientific rationale. The more general aim was not to increase production but rather to figure out a method of making a profit in the most systematic way. In time this need for efficiency and predictability had a spillover effect, as it impacted many other areas of social life, including the criminal justice system.[22]

It was at this time that crack cocaine suddenly appeared on the streets of America. Crack, or "rock" cocaine as it was originally referred to, first began to be reported around November 1984. The first published report about rock cocaine described it as the "drug of choice" in the ghettos of Los Angeles. This report appeared in the *Los Angeles Times* with the ominous title of: "South Central Sales Explode into $25 'Rocks'" (*Los Angeles Times*, 1984; Klein, Maxson and Cunningham, 1991).

Within six months there was "a barrage of almost daily media coverage focused on crack use flooded into American Households, catapulting concerns regarding illicit drug use to the forefront of the public agenda" (Trueblood, 1998: 11). On May 18, 1986, *The New York Times* published a front page article entitled "Opium Dens for the Crack Era," which described the "pernicious and addictive qualities" of crack cocaine (Brownstein, 1991: 85).

The media coverage peaked in June and July 1986 following the death of Len Bias in June 1986 from an apparent overdose of crack cocaine—at least this was the official version (see the following discussion). That same year Don Rogers of the Cleveland Browns professional football team died from a cocaine overdose. However, the death of Len Bias became the catalyst for subsequent Congressional legislation to enact the strict 100-to-1 ratio for sentencing of crack cocaine. During the

Congressional Hearing that was to follow on July 15, 1986, "Bias's death was cited 11 times in connection with crack cocaine" (United States Sentencing Commission, 1995: 123).

Bias died of cocaine intoxication the day after he was the second player drafted in the National Basketball Association's College draft in 1986 by the Boston Celtics (the death of "ordinary" African-Americans from similar causes would never cause such publicity—after all, they were not worth millions in profits to the Boston Celtics). Although the method of cocaine ingestion that killed Bias was not known at the time of his death, Bias' death was surrounded by newspaper articles running head-lines and stories containing a quote from Dr. Dennis Smyth, Maryland's Assistant Medical Examiner, "Bias probably died of free-basing cocaine" (United States Sentencing Commission, 1995: 122). Yet, despite the fact that two other medical ex-aminers in the same office found that Bias' death probably had nothing to do with crack cocaine, Dr. Smyth's assertions received the bulk of the coverage (United States Sentencing Commission, 1995: 122).

During July 1986 alone, there were 74 evening news segments regarding crack cocaine, many of which were reinforced by the erroneous belief that Bias death was due to a crack cocaine overdose. About a year later, during the trial of Brian Tribble (accused of supplying Bias with cocaine), Terry Long, a University of Maryland bas-ketball player who participated in the cocaine party that led to Bias's death, testified that he, Bias, Tribble, and another player snorted powder cocaine over a four-hour pe-riod. Tribble's testimony, however, received limited media coverage (United States. Sentencing Commission, 1995: 123).

The U.S. Congress, with support from then President Reagan, used the Bias in-cident to push through Congress legislation that increased sentences for drug offend-ers. Millions of African Americans were living in poverty, and all of a sudden Len Bias's death drew attention to the African-American community. Of course, nothing was accomplished to alleviate the pains of poverty, but legislators discovered a way to ensure that more African Americans would be sent to prison, and for much longer periods of time, through the Anti-Drug Abuse Act of 1986. In 1980, African Americans made up 23% of all those arrested for drugs. Now, the majority of all drug convictions involve African Americans (Cole, 1999; Parenti, 1999; Miller, 1996; Human Rights Watch, 2000, 2003).

In the months leading up to the 1986 elections, more than 1,000 stories ap-peared on crack cocaine in the National Press, including five cover stories each in *Time* and *Newsweek*. NBC News ran 400 separate reports on crack cocaine, 15 hours of air time. *Time* called crack cocaine the "issue of the year" in its September 22, 1986 issue; *Newsweek* called it the "biggest news story since Vietnam and Watergate" (June 16, 1986). The CBS news program *48 Hours* ran a documentary entitled "48 Hours on Crack Street," which became the most watched documentary in televi-sion history (Johnson, Golub, and Fagan, 1995: 275). ABC News termed crack as a "plague that was eating away at the fabric of America" (Belenko, 1993: 23; Reinarman and Levine, 1997b: 20–22).

Similar to other moral panics, the creation of the crack epidemic was a product of the media in its relentless drive to make news and thus make profits. These types of panics have been described as a disconnect between image and reality (Miller, 1996: 155). Although the National Institute of Drug Abuse annual reports suggest that crack cocaine use was limited to an extremely small drug user subculture (1% to 2% of the population), the media's hype regarding the use of this drug became the catalyst for an enormous concern pertaining to its widespread use. This is illustrated by a Gallup Poll showing that respondents described drug abuse as the most important problem facing the country.

Trueblood aptly describes this moral panic in the following manner (1999: 17):

> In the midst of this media frenzy, the election campaign of 1986 became a forum for politicians to try to out-platform one another in their efforts to demonstrate their concerns and the need for swift draconian measures of social control with respect to drug abuse. Interestingly, the creation of this particular drug panic allowed the development of a conservative agenda, even during a predominantly liberal Congress. With conservatives and liberals alike quickly acknowledging the newest drug "menace," silence regarding this issue would too readily be interpreted as being "soft" on drugs.
>
> The ensuing reactionary agenda toward drug users and traffickers resulted from social, political, and ideological forces. Emerging during an era of increasing momentum toward strict punishment of drug users and dealers, and with a presidential administration that had a strong ideological focus toward individual accountability and an aversion for sociological and economic explanations of social problems, the spread of crack cocaine into the inner city provided a convenient scapegoat for diverting attention from pressing social and economic problems and blaming a specific powerless group for social disorder.

As the election year progressed, the media, police officials and politicians provided a continuous barrage of heated rhetoric concerning the alleged widespread use and abuse of crack cocaine (Johnson, Golub, and Fagan, 1995: 276). Some of the assertions made in these reports were not supported by scientific data at the time and in most cases turned out to be patently false (United States Sentencing Commission, 1995: 122). Indeed, one of the most interesting aspects of the anticrack crusade was that, unlike previous antidrug efforts, it occurred during a time when there was plenty of research regarding its psychopharmacological and behavioral effects. But the antidrug crusaders ignored the research and used purely anecdotal information derived from media and law enforcement sources to link crack to a wide variety of social problems, including violent crimes, escalation of drug abuse, child abuse, and neglect, and prostitution. One of the most common myths was that crack was instantly addictive and that innocent people were being transformed into compulsive crack smokers. Moreover, crack use was driving people to commit violent crimes and to drop out of the labor force, and that crack gangs were in control (Johnson, Golub, and Fagan, 1995: 276). Most who were in the forefront of developing drug policies knew of some of the research that had been done, which contradicted their views. However, they ignored the research findings. (For more details see Baum, 1997).

The Anti-Drug Abuse Act of 1986 emphasized the use of punishment and social control to fight drug abuse, despite research that overwhelmingly supported the use of treatment and education (Baum, 1997). The 1986 act also established two tiers of mandatory prison terms for first time drug traffickers—a five-year and ten-year minimum sentence. Under the new law, these prison terms are determined solely by the quantity and type of drug involved in the offense (United States Sentencing Commission, 1995: 116). The act further expanded funding for police and corrections, adding to an already growing criminal justice industrial complex, as it authorized $1.7 billion in new money to fight the war on drugs, which was in addition to the already authorized $2.2 billion. A mere 14% of the funds was allocated for treatment and prevention (Johnson, Golub, and Fagan, 1995: 288; Belenko, 1993: 14).

The act distinguished between two forms of cocaine with identical chemical makeup—powder and crack—and isolated crack for more severe punishment. Lesser quantities of crack than powder cocaine would result in the five- and ten-year mandatory minimum penalties applicable to both forms of cocaine, thereby imposing an inconceivable 100-to-1 quantity ratio of powder to crack cocaine (i.e., it takes 100 times as much powder cocaine compared to crack to trigger the mandatory minimum penalties) (United States Sentencing Commission, 1995: iii).

In reviewing the legislative history of this act, Congress's conclusions respecting the dangerousness of crack cocaine relative to powder cocaine flowed from four assumptions:

> First, crack cocaine was viewed as extraordinarily addictive: both relative to powder cocaine and in absolute terms. Second, the correlation between crack cocaine use and the commission of other serious crimes was considered greater than that with other drugs. Floor statements focused on psychopharmacological driven, economically driven, as well as systemic crime. Third, the physiological effects of crack cocaine were considered especially perilous, leading to psychosis and death. Fourth, members of Congress felt that young people were particularly prone to using crack cocaine. Finally, there was great concern that crack cocaine's "purity and potency," the cost per dose, the ease with which it is manufactured, transported, disposed of, and administered, were all leading to widespread use of crack cocaine (United States Sentencing Commission, 1995: 118).

Specifically, the Anti-Drug Abuse Act provided the following penalties for first offense cocaine trafficking (Trueblood, 1998: 19):

> *5 grams* or more of crack cocaine
> Or   = Five (5) years mandatory minimum penalty
> *500 grams* or more of powder cocaine
> *50 grams* or more of crack cocaine
> Or   = Ten (10) years mandatory minimum penalty
> *5,000 grams* or more of powder cocaine

The initial set of guidelines became law in November 1987. In January 1989, the Supreme Court upheld the constitutionality of the Sentencing Commission and the guidelines in *Mistretta v. United States*, 488 U.S. 361 (1989).

The 1986 act was expedited through Congress, leaving in its wake a very limited legislative record to which we can refer to explain either the differentiation in the sentencing in crack and powder cocaine or the speed attendant to its enactment. The history of the 100-to-1 quantity ratio that emerged from this act, therefore, can only be understood in the context of the individual members' floor statements pertaining to the act. Senator Hawkins, for example, spoke in support of the 1986 act in terms of the urgency of this legislation. As usual, creating fear among the public is important, especially when citing national security as a reason to be fearful. Hawkins stated that: "Drugs pose a clear and present danger to America's national security."[23] Ironically, this same excuse was used repeatedly during the Cold War, which justified huge expenditures within the Pentagon system (Chomsky, 1992).

As the 1986 elections grew near, the heightened public concern and the media-driven national sense of urgency surrounding the crack problem created a political context in which Congress was pressured to act quickly, so it dispensed with much of the typical deliberative legislative process, including, most importantly, committee hearings. Preliminary versions of this bill proposed various quantity ratios for the sentencing of crack offenders. The original version of the house bill, HR 5484, in fact, contained a quantity ratio of 20-to-1, and was introduced on behalf of the Reagan Administration by Senator Dole. As the 1986 act quickly advanced through the legislative process in late summer and early fall, after consulting with law enforcement professionals, but without holding hearings, the Senate set specific quantity levels for the entire range of illegal drugs, including powder and crack cocaine, that would trigger the five- and ten-year mandatory minimum penalties. The resulting legislation increased the powder cocaine-to-crack ratio from its original form of 20-to-1 to 100-to-1 (United States Sentencing Commission, 1995: 117–120).

Federal circuit courts addressing the constitutionality of crack cocaine penalties have upheld the current federal sentencing scheme, including the 100-to-1 ratio.[24] The courts have held that the penalty distinction was created out of the legitimate congressional objective of "protecting the public against a new and highly potent addictive narcotic that could be distributed easily and sold cheaply" (United States Sentencing Commission, 1995: 118).

It should come as no surprise that the heated media coverage of crack surrounding the elections of 1986 quickly evaporated following the passage of the 1986 act. As media coverage waned, however, so did public concern about drug abuse. A New York Times/CBS poll during 1987 indicated that only 3% to 5% of the public viewed drugs as the most pressing social problem (Belenko, 1993: 25).

During 1988, however, there was a resurgence in media and political attention toward crack. Fueled by the 1988 presidential election, candidates again attempted to gain attention and to demonstrate their toughness against crime and drug use by enacting strict penalties for drug use. Part of this hysteria was caused by George Bush's use of the Willie Horton case (an African-American man on furlough who killed someone; Anderson, 1995; Chambliss, 1999: 13–31). Caught up in the renewed antidrug fervor, Congress again escalated the war against drugs culminating in the enactment of the Anti-Drug Abuse Act of 1988.

Despite a continuing dearth of research regarding the effects of crack, two years after the enactment of the Anti-Drug Abuse Act of 1986, Congress decided that it was time to again get tough on drugs and drafted the Anti-Drug Abuse Act of 1988. Among other features, the act established a new cabinet-level White House Office of

National Drug Control Policy, charging its Director, William Bennett (the "drug czar"), to submit to Congress an annual National Drug Control Strategy (Belenko, 1993: 15; for a good critique of Bennett's views and policies see Baum, 1997).

With respect to crack, Section 6371 of this act established increased Federal penalties for serious crack offenses. It made crack cocaine the only drug under the act with a mandatory minimum penalty for a first offense of simple possession (Zimring and Hawkins, 1991: 105). The act made first time possession of more than five grams of a mixture or substance containing cocaine base punishable by at least five years in prison. Second- or third-time offenders were subject to similar penalties for possessing as little as three or one gram, respectively (United States Sentencing Commission, 1995: 123).

Not surprisingly, there was little debate on the amendments establishing the mandatory minimum crack cocaine possession penalties. Senators argued, without factual evidence, that the supply of cocaine was greater than ever before. It was also argued that crack cocaine causes greater physical, emotional, psychological damage than any other commonly abused drug (United States Sentencing Commission, 1995: 125). The 1988 act passed the Senate by an almost unanimous vote (87 to 3) on October 14, 1988; shortly thereafter the House followed suit (by a vote of 346 to 11).

On September 5, 1989, President Bush took advantage of the media frenzy in a major televised speech about drug abuse, once again bringing crack to the forefront of public concern. In an attempt to illustrate the rampant proliferation of crack, President Bush waved vials of crack in front of the television cameras, claiming that DEA agents had seized the drugs from a dealer in Lafayette Park, right outside the White House. The shock value was as expected, but it turned out to be a complete fabrication, as it was eventually discovered that the DEA could not find any crack dealers in Lafayette Park. So agents had to lure an uncooperative dealer to the park and make the arrest. Since the speech was written prior to the arrest, the DEA was directed to take whatever steps were necessary to provide the appropriate evidence needed by the President to substantiate these claims (*Washington Post*, 1989). This example illustrates the hype and political hyperbole surrounding the crack epidemic during this time (Jenkins, 1994: 12).

Throughout this period of time, media coverage further intensified fears about crack by focusing on the alleged involvement of gangs (of course, always African American or Hispanic), and the tendency to use random violence; including the claim that crack was spreading into all corners of the nation, including white middle-class suburbs (*Newsweek*, 1988: 65). News articles about gangs and violence invariably quoted local or national law enforcement officials as the only source of information about gang involvement and their role in the spread of crack.[25] For example, a *Washington Post* article on February 22, 1988, described how the Jamaican posses had introduced crack to Washington, DC, and quoted a narcotics task force officer as stating that "crack is just taking over" (Belenko, 1993: 27). Similarly one of the major *Time* magazine stories, relying almost exclusively on reports from police, concluded that the crack war was being lost to gangs (*Time*, 1988: 21).

These accounts however, were soon contradicted by research in the area of gangs, violence, and crack. Indeed, despite accounts of nationally syndicated, highly centralized street gangs dominating crack cocaine distribution, the research supports an alternative view. Specifically, researchers have found that street gangs neither played a predominant role nor appeared to have brought much extra violence of or-ganizational character to crack distribution. Rather, it was concluded that crack distribution could be attributed to drug dealers, not street gangs (Klein, Maxson, and Cunningham, 1991: 626).[26]

The media continued to develop this theme, focusing its attention, as always, to the potential vulnerability of the white middle-class (a classic use of fear tactics). For example, the *New York Times* published a full-length editorial called "Crack—A Disaster of Historic Dimensions," in which the author portrays crack as "uniquely de-structive," and a threat that has "spread to middle America" (*New York Times*, 1989a). Also, in its Sunday edition, the *New York Times* began a two-part series with a front page article entitled "The Spreading Web of Crack," stating that "Crack, which has been devastating entire inner-city neighborhoods, has begun to claim significant num-bers of middle- and upper-class addicts, experts have found" (*New York Times*, 1989b). The image of not only crack but the specter of a growing underclass of mostly African-American crack dealers invading middle America is evident in these stories.

The research completely contradicts the above claims, however. The evidence is quite clear that most drug-related violence is confined to people who live in or near drug communities and neighborhoods. Also, few people are likely to be the stereo-typic innocent bystander of drug-related violence. In fact, data from New York City Police Department during the first half of 1990 reveal that only 1.4% of all homicide victims were innocent bystanders (Brownstein, 1991: 95–96).

Finally, although it appears from the research that drugs and violent crime are clearly related, the extent to which that relationship may be causally related is the sub-ject of much discussion. The research by Paul J. Goldstein suggests three models of that relationship. Psychopharmacological (crime resulting from behavioral effects of the drug), economically compulsive (crime committed by persons who are financially driven to support their drug habits) and systemic (crime related to the market and dis-tribution of a drug). What Goldstein's research found was that, contrary to media ac-counts, violent crime surrounding crack use is primarily confined the inner cities and is a result of the violence attendant to the marketing and distribution of crack cocaine (Goldstein et al., 1997; Baumer, 1994).

The Impact of the Drug Laws Passed in the 1980s

A reasonable question a reader might pose at this time is: What has been the result of the legislation passed during the 1980s? Consider some of the following statistics:[27]

- Convictions for drug law violations (mostly possession) accounted for more than *one-half* of the increase in state prison inmates during the 1980s and early 1990s. Between 1985 and 1995 the number of prisoners in state institutions who had been convicted of drug offenses went up by 478%, while the number in federal prisons went up by 446% (more than 80% of the increase in the federal prison population during this time was because of drug convictions).

- Between 1990 and 2000 the percentage of federal prisoners convicted of violent crimes went from 17% to 10%. Meanwhile, number incarcerated for drugs accounted for the largest percentage of the total growth (59%), followed by public-order offenders (32%). As of 2001, 55% of those in federal prisons were in for drug offenses.
- In 2005 more than 1.8 million were arrested for drugs (about 43% for marijuana alone, mostly possession).
- In the federal system, the average sentence for a drug offense is now about 75 months, compared to 65 months for a violent felony.
- Between 1980 and 1997 drug arrests tripled. During this same period, the number of people going to state prison for a violent crime went up by 82%; for a non-violent crime, up 207%; for a drug offense, up 1,040%.
- A drug offense is the most serious offense for 72% of women in federal prisons and 30.4% of women in state prisons; also, between 1986 (the year mandatory sentencing was enacted) and 1996, the number of women sentenced to state prison for drug crimes went up tenfold (from around 2,370 to 23,700), and this has been the main cause of the increase in the imprisonment of women.
- In the federal system, during about the same period of time, the sentences of those convicted on drug charges increased from an average of 55 months to 80 months; by contrast, the average sentences for murder during this time period actually decreased from 162 months to 117 months, while for all violent offenses the average sentence declined from 133 months to 88 months.
- Recent figures show that in the federal system 55% of all drug defendants are what we call low-level offenders, such as street dealers, while only 11% are classified as high-level dealers.

These figures are just a sampling of the human wreckage resulting from the punitive policies used by this country during the three decades. The war on drugs has targeted mostly the poor and racial minorities, and in turn has helped to create a prison-industrial complex. (More will be said about this subject in subsequent chapters.)

Part of the problem is that the manufacture and distribution of illegal drugs is a huge business enterprise. The UN report entitled *World Drug Report 2005* reported that the illegal drug market for 2003 was an estimated $13 billion at the production level and $94 billion at the wholesale level, while in the United States alone it was an estimated $322 billion (based on retail prices and taking seizures and other loses into account. The report noted that the value of these drugs "increase substantially as they move from producer to consumer." This same report estimated that the profits in this business are enormous. For example, in 2001, one kilogram of heroin in Pakistan sold for an average of $610; in the United States its value was an average of $25,000 per kilogram (United Nations Office on Drugs and Crime, 2005: 127). A report by the U.S. Office of Drug Control Policy found that the cost of heroin at the retail level declined from about $1,974.49 per gram in 1981 to $361.95 per gram in 2003. At the wholesale level, the cost went from $1,007.60 per gram in 1981 to $139.22 per gram in 2003. The report also noted that the average purity of heroin on the U.S. market at the retail level went from about of 11% in 1981 to about 32% in 2003; at the wholesale level the value increase from 12% to 46% (Office of National Drug Control Policy, 2004: 62–63).

A report by the U.S. Office of Drug Control Policy found that the cost of heroin at the retail level declined from about $1,974.49 per gram in 1981 to $361.95 per gram in 2003. At the wholesale level, the cost went from $1,007.60 per gram in 1981 to $139.22 per gram in 2003. The report also noted that the average purity of heroin on the U.S. market at the retail level went from about of 11% in 1981 to about 32% in 2003; at the wholesale level the value increase from 12% to 46% (Office of National Drug Control Policy, 2004: 62–63). A study by Abt Associates estimated that between 1989 and 1998, Americans' personal expenditures alone went from $39 billion to $77 billion yearly on cocaine and $10 billion to $22 billion on heroin (Abt Associates, 2000: 5).

In comparison, the estimated economic costs of alcohol abuse is around $148 billion, compared to drug abuse costs of around $97 billion, of which 60% are related to law enforcement and imprisonment—only 3% were from the victims of drug-related crime. A recent survey found that more than 48 million Americans use alcohol an average of one or more days each week, which is more than the sum total of those who have ever tried cocaine, crack, and/or heroin (an estimated 30 million), and two and a half times the number who have used marijuana once in the last year alone (referring to 1998, an estimated 18.7 million) (Substance Abuse and Mental Health Services Administration, 1999).

It has long been recognized that alcohol plays a huge role in criminal behavior. Fagan summarizes the literature as follows: "Alcohol use has been associated with assauitive and sex-related crimes, serious youth crime, family violence toward both spouses and children, being both a homicide victim and a perpetrator, and persistent aggression as an adult. Alcohol 'problems' occur disproportionately among both juveniles and adults who report violent behaviors" (quoted by Dilulio, 1996: 15; See also: U.S. Department of Justice, 1998). One survey found that about 40% of offenders under some sort of supervision within the criminal justice system (probation, parole, jail, prison) were using alcohol at the time of the offense for which they were convicted. This same survey found that about 60% of jail inmates said they drank alcohol on a regular basis during the year prior to their current conviction; about two-thirds of these had been in some kind of alcohol treatment program at some point in time (Greenfield, 1998).

Whose Interest Does the Law Serve?

Given what has been said in the preceding pages, one question might be raised: Do *all* criminal laws operate in the interest of powerful groups? More specifically, does the *passage* of every criminal law serve only these interests? The reader may wonder about such laws as those prohibiting homicide and assault. It would be absurd to suggest that every criminal law on the books was passed solely to preserve the interests of the rich and the powerful. It is a lot more complicated than that.

This issue gets to the heart of the three models of the law noted in the introduction to this book. From a consensus standpoint, law reflects values held by everyone in a society and does not represent the narrow interests of a ruling class. From the interest-groups/conflict perspective, law reflects certain interests as opposed to other interests of various competing "interest groups" in a society. From a critical/Marxist point of view, law mainly reflects the needs and values of a ruling class.

There is no easy answer to this question, but some attempt at an answer should be provided. To begin with, upon reviewing the history of criminal law, one has to conclude that law has often in fact reflected the interests of the ruling class. More than that, however, the law has been used to a large extent to enhance the power of a ruling class and/or to control groups in a society perceived as dangerous—whether these groups be black slaves, Native Americans, vagrants, union organizers, lower class immigrants, or simply the poor.

This is not the same thing as saying that each and every criminal law represents ruling class interests only—or the interests of any other group for that matter. There is also the distinction to be made between the intent of a specific law and the result in terms of a law's interpretation and enforcement. Returning to Quinney's Social Reality of Crime theory, recall one of his propositions stated that: "Criminal definitions are applied by the segments of society that have the power to shape the enforcement and administration of criminal law" (2001:18) And that, "Behavior patterns are structured in segmentally organized society in relation to criminal definitions, and within this context persons engage in actions that have relative probabilities of being defined as criminal" (Quinney 2001:20). Thus, it may very well be that the intent of a specific law has not been to reflect the sole interests of a ruling class, the result has been unmistakable: those who have been arrested and processed through the criminal justice system have consistently been those drawn from the bottom of the social class structure.

Let's take a specific example, a law that should theoretically reflect the interests of all the people and should show the least amount of bias: laws concerning the crime of homicide. Once upon a time homicide was defined by custom as a tort, but when it became a concern for the state, restitution was replaced by a debt to society. The current law against homicide is not as clearly defined as one might expect. Typically, such laws refer to acts such as the willful taking of another person's life (premeditated murder), the accidental yet negligent taking of another life (as in a fight), or killing someone while committing another crime (as in robbery). Yet, what is missing from the law of homicide are such cases as (1) the production of goods that can cause harm or even death to consumers (as in the case of the Ford Pinto and numerous other cases), (2) various working conditions that can result in death for many (e.g., black lung disease among miners, the manufacture of the chemical kepone), and (3) the perpetuation of poverty conditions that cause infant mortality and other forms of sickness and death suffered by the poor (Hepburn, 1977; Chambliss, 1993; Breggin and Breggin, 1998). The real-life circumstances of an offense rarely correspond to abstract statements codified into law. The interpretation of homicide varies tremendously. On the one hand, police can shoot fleeing felons and executioners can carry out the death penalty, while soldiers kill in war under direct orders. States may engage in mass murder and genocide (including the United States).[28] And, of course, the killing of millions of Jews by Germany was sanctified by German law (and was turned into a crime mostly because Germany lost the war; Chambliss, 1993: 37). An appropriate commentary, although written in 1936, further illustrates this point. Gustavus Myers, in his book *History of the Great American Fortunes*, in commenting on the fortune of the Astor family, wrote:

> Is it not murder when, compelled by want, people are forced to fester in squalid, germ-filled tenements, where the sunlight never enters and where disease finds a prolific breeding-place? Untold thousands went to their deaths in these unspeakable places. Yet, so far as the Law was concerned, the rents collected by the Astors, as well as by other landlords, were honestly made. The whole institution of Law saw nothing out of the way in these conditions, and very significantly so, because to repeat over and over again, Law did not represent the ethics or ideals of advanced humanity; it exactly reflected, as a pool reflects the sky, the demands and self-interest of the growing propertied classes . . . (quoted in Zinn, 2005: 233–234).

It would be an exaggeration to suggest that all laws serve the interests of a ruling class or any other particular group. Some laws do serve such interests, as we have seen, and many acts committed by powerful people are not considered criminal. We need only a passing reference to the costs to our society of corporate crime each year. According to FBI figures about two people will be murdered within the next hour (most often by a gun or knife). However, according to one recent study about 56,000 Americans die on the job every year or from such occupational diseases as black lung, brown lung, asbestosis, and various other cancers related to various occupations (about six per hour) (Mokhiber, 1996: 62). Another estimate puts the number of annual deaths from work-related death at between 65,000 and 100,000, with deaths from job-related diseases ranging from a low of 136,800 to a high of 390,000. Work-related accidents kill an estimated 10,700 and cause an estimated 1.8 million disabling injuries each year (Friedrichs, 2004: 71; Cullen, 2002). One author estimates that the overall work-related death rate is around 115 per 100,000, compared to a homicide rate of around 8 per 100,000 (Michalowski, 1985: 325–338).

As noted in the introduction to this book, corporate and white collar crime cost the American people an estimated $1.5 trillion each year. These white collar crimes violate numerous laws on a persistent basis. Laws that were enacted ostensibly to serve the interests of the general public; yet the enforcement of these laws is practically nonexistent. Perhaps it is because these offenders came from the highest echelons of society, were pillars of the community and in the minds of most people they were not really criminals or at least they were not perceived as dangerous, which is in part due to a massive system of propaganda put forth by this same class (Chomsky, 1989). Yet collectively these particular offenses cost more than 100,000 lives and trillions of dollars each year! For the most part, these are indeed *white* collar crimes, for they are committed overwhelmingly by wealthy white males. In fact, there is no way anyone can argue that the worst crimes are committed by racial minorities. Yet within our criminal justice racial minorities (and the poor in general) are overwhelmingly subjected to the actions of the criminal justice system and fill our jails and prisons.

It is a rare occurrence when a perpetrator of a corporate or state crime goes to prison (as in some of the Enron cases).[29]

Thus, the most important point is that most laws that are enforced the most vigorously happen to be those most likely to be violated by relatively powerless groups, especially the poor and racial minorities. It can also be the case, as illustrated in this chapter, that the legal system can be used to oppress or otherwise control certain groups. The law can indeed be a selective instrument of class justice, as the critical/Marxist view of the law contends. Friedman makes an appropriate and astute observation about our laws and legal institutions: "Laws and legal institutions are part of the system that keeps the structure in place, or allows it to change only in approved and patterned ways. The criminal justice system maintains the status quo" (Friedman, 1993: 830). Friedman goes on to note that most people want the status quo, or at least the parts they have (even if it may be little). They obviously don't want others to harm them or take their property. However, some have a lot more than others and have a lot more power. Hence the law "protects power and property" and keeps the distribution of wealth intact, while keeping those at the bottom in their place (1993: 830).

Friedman also observes that in the beginning, the American republic was supposed to be based upon "justice, equality, and opportunity." But looking back we see something quite different, as Friedman notes:

> We see a republic created, on the whole, by and for white Protestant men; behind the flag-waving and the Fourth of July parades, we see the hideous grinning faces of inequality, oppression, biases overt and covert, cruelty, lack of understanding, intolerance. This was no pure or ideal democracy; far from it . . . It was a half democracy, an adolescent democracy, a smug democracy . . . criminal justice followed, as it always did, the pattern of social norms. It fell, as it always has fallen, more heavily on the underclass, on the deviants, on the "outs". . . Criminal justice was the strong arm of the stratification system. It was part of the process that made subordination real. And subordination was real, most notably, for American blacks; also for members of other minority races; and for the poor, the deviant, the unpopular (1993: 84).

Finally, Zinn's comments on the notion of the rule of law are appropriate here. He observes that in modern capitalist democracies abstract rules and a legal order has replaced feudal lords and kings (as we noted earlier in this chapter). Thus the law gives the appearance of being impersonal. He notes that the law

> . . . is on paper, and who can trace it back to what men? And because it has the look of neutrality, its injustices are made legitimate. It was not easy to hold on to the "divine right" of kings—everyone could see that kings and queens were human beings. A code of law is more easily deified than a flesh-and-blood ruler (Zinn, 2005: 373).

When we had the rule of men those who were oppressive could be readily identified. But in our own era we have impersonal bureaucracies, large corporations and laws contained within not easily understood state penal codes (e.g., California Penal Code, Nevada Revised Statutes). The law hides unequal wealth and power and theoretically treats everyone the same. Paraphrasing the French philosopher Anatole

France, the law prohibits both the rich and the poor from sleeping on park benches and traffic laws treat every driver alike (both the driver of a 20-year-old car and the driver of a limousine are both equally subjected to the speed laws). This is the great equality of the law in societies beset by huge disparities of wealth (Milovanovic, 1994: 18).

The legal order punishes—very severely in some cases—those who rise up to protest inhumane social conditions, whether we are talking about abolitionists and union organizers in the 19th century or civil rights protesters in the 1960s or antinuclear protesters in the 1990s. Those who challenge the status quo will often come face to face with the raw power of the state. I would like to close this chapter with another quote from Howard Zinn, who wrote: "What life is best worth living—the life of the proper, obedient, dutiful follower of law and order or the life of the independent thinker, the rebel?" (1997: 402).

Notes

1. A variation of this form of society still existed in the United States during and immediately after slavery, known as the *sharecropping* system. A derivative of this was the "plantation prison" that emerged in the South after the end of the Civil War, lasting well into the 20th century. This will be discussed in chapter 4.

2. Some of this information is taken from Wikipedia, the free encyclopedia. Here are some specific websites: http://en.wikipedia.org/wiki/Rolio%2C_Count_%28or_Duke%29_of_Normandy; http://en.wikipedia.org/wiki/Normandy; http://en.wikipedia.org/wiki/Normans; http://en.wikipedia.org/wiki/Battle_of_Hastings. There are many details of the Norman Conquest that are beyond the scope of this chapter. The reader is encouraged to examine some of these websites for more detail and to consult the Douglas book cited here.

3. The term *hegemony* refers to the dominance of one group or nation over another, especially its influence or authority. If, for instance, a king has hegemony over the masses of people within his domain, his values, opinions, etc. are generally accepted and are thought to be proper or "the way things should be," even though there may be other, more valid opinions and values. Thus, the king (or some other powerful ruler) rules through the consent of the governed, so that force only needs to be used sparingly. Most ruling classes throughout history, especially in capitalist societies, have had this sort of hegemonic control over the society. In short, rulers maintain their dominance because the majority of the people have been convinced (often through the use of sophisticated forms of propaganda) that such rulers are acting in the best interests of the people, even though they are not always doing so. For further elaboration on the use of propaganda as a means of control in capitalist democracies see, for instance, Chomsky (1989).

4. For a critique of this book see Langbein, 1983; see also a rebuttal by Linebaugh, 1985.

5. Howard Zinn makes a crucial point about the rule of law when he observes that whereas in previous eras (such as early English society) the rule was by "flesh and blood" humans that people could actually see, that is, "the oppressor was identifiable, and so peasant rebels hunted down the lords, slaves killed plantation owners, and revolutionaries assassinated monarchs. In the era of the corporate bureaucracies, representative assemblies, and the rule of law, the enemy is elusive and unidentifiable" (Zinn, 1991: 111). In other words, in the modern era we are under the authority of a neutral and impersonal law, rather than a king.

6. The concept of *state* has been almost impossible to define precisely. One of the best definitions comes from Miliband who writes that "the state" is not a thing as such, but rather it "stands for a number of particular institutions which, together, constitute its reality. . ." (Miliband, 1969: 49–54). He goes on to note a *state system* consists of what we normally regard as the "government," including the Congress, the Senate, and other similar institutions (e.g., Parliament in England) along with various administrative units (e.g., regulatory commissions), the military, the police

and judicial system. One of the keys to understanding the state is that it is related to the business of rule as Poggi notes. Poggi defines the state as a "complex set of institutional arrangements for rule operating through the continuous and regulated activities of individuals acting as occupants of offices. The state, as the sum total of such offices, reserves to itself the business of rule over a territorially bounded society. . ." (Poggi, 1978: 1) This definition gets to the heart of the matter since the state is involved in ruling the society, that is, in some form of domination over others. The key question is, "For whose benefit?".

7. A very serious critique on Chambliss' interpretation of vagrancy laws was done by Adler (1989a), followed in the same issue of this journal by a rebuttal by Chambliss (Chambliss, 1989), which in turn was followed by Adler's rebuttal to Chambliss (Adler, 1989b; see also Adler, 1986). Reading the dialogue between these two scholars might best be described as an academic version of a "cat fight," which left me concluding that nobody won the contest. It was more of a draw than anything else. Where appropriate I will reference these authors in this section of the chapter.

8. See the following for discussion of this subject: Ditton (1977), Marx (1975), Linebaugh (1976). The articles by Linebaugh and Ditton are reproduced in Weiss (1999).

9. This relationship forms an important component—perhaps the most important component—of Marx's analysis of capitalism. This is spelled out in some detail in Marx's own work, especially the classic *Capital*. The interested reader may find a far more readable summary of these issues in Marx, K. *The Economic and Philosophic Manuscripts of 1844*. Buffalo, NY: Prometheus Books, 1988; an insightful analysis of some of these issues can be found in Heilbroner (1985). For a contemporary account of some of the negative aspects of this conflict, see Chomsky (1999).

10. For a fascinating analysis of the accumulation of wealth by a relatively small group of robber barons, see Josephson (1962). See also Zinn (1995, especially Chapter 11).

11. The phenomenon of "witch hunts" was not a new phenomenon and it certainly did not end with the Salem case. Throughout history there have been instances where those in power engaged in activities aimed at ferreting out those who threatened the status quo. To engage in witch hunting essentially means to look for excuses to control or even get rid of those who threaten the social order, often based upon vague definitions

of the threatening behavior. This often includes guilt by association or guilt by accusation. The Inquisition was a classic example. It was also a good example of the process of scapegoating, which is part of the witch-hunting phenomenon. Thus, those in power can claim that instead of themselves and their rule there are others, in this case, witches, that are the source of major social problems. And it is no accident that the majority of those accused of witchcraft (and later of being communists) have been the poor. The phenomenon of "moral panics" is similar. In every case, the witch hunt or the moral panic takes place during times of great social conflict, change and upheaval. In the 20th century we have witnessed such witch hunts as the Red Scare during the late 1910s and early 1920s, the McCarthy communist witch hunt in the early 1950s, the targeting of African-American, antiwar and other activists groups in the 1960s and early 1970s, and the more recent attempts to control minorities via the war on drugs and war on gangs. For further study of this fascinating phenomenon (including moral panics) see the following: Harris (1978), Pfohl, (1994), Erikson (1966), Cohen (1972), Goode and Ben-Yehuda (1994).

12. This is in reference to the famous book written by an Italian Cesare Beccaria, originally published in 1774, which set out to establish some consistency in the criminal code. See Beccaria (1963).

13. Throughout American history, often during times of upheaval and social change, those in power will take a few otherwise isolated cases, and reassert the importance of the rule of law, especially during those times when it would appear to any sane observer that the nation is in fact under the rule of men and not of law. A case in point was the investigation of President Bill Clinton concerning his sexual relationship with a White House intern. On numerous occasions members of Congress and various political pundits referred to this case as about the rule of law. Speaker of the House Newt Gingrich flatly denied (despite overwhelming evidence to the contrary) that the "Starr Report" (a report by the Office of Independent Counsel) was not about sex, but about the rule of law (as reported on CNN, September 22, 1998). Similar comments were repeatedly heard during the Watergate hearings in the early 1970s.

14. On the same page this quote taken from Zinn gives an example from John Steinbeck's famous novel *Grapes of Wrath* where a farmer, whose land is about to be taken away from him,

takes his gun out and threatens the tractor driver who is about to bulldoze his house. The driver says he is taking orders from a bank in Oklahoma City, who in turn was taking orders from a banker in New York. The frustrated farmer then asks "Then who can I shoot?"

15. Zinn notes that out of an estimated Indian population of around 10 million when Columbus landed, less than a million would eventually be left after the various wars and diseases introduced by Europeans. He cites one tragic example: On Martha's Vineyard in 1642 there were about 3,000 Wampanoags; by 1764 there were only 313. On nearby Block Island, they numbered between 1,200 and 1,500, but by 1774 there were only 51 (Zinn, 1995: 16).

16. 187 U.S. 553, 23 S.Ct. 216, 47 L.Ed. 299 (1903). For details about this case see the following website: http://www.utulsa.edu/law/classes/rice/ussct_cases/Lone_Wolf_v_Hitchcock_187_553.htm. The court stated that: "But the right which the Indians held was only that of occupancy. The fee was in the United States, subject to that right, and could be transferred by them whenever they chose."

17. Examples of these laws included a San Francisco ordinance that made it against the law to operate a laundry except if the building was made of brick or stone. Since no buildings were made of such materials at this time, this meant that Chinese owners were in violation of the law. If a white person owned the building, the law was waived (Friedman, 1993: 99).

18. The following is a statement from a Congressional Senate Report, dated 1876 (ironically on the first anniversary of the Declaration of Independence, which declared that "all men are created equal"): "The burden of our accusation against them [the Chinese] is that they come in conflict with our labor interests; that they can never assimilate with us; that they are a perpetual, unchanging, and unchangeable alien element that can never become homogeneous; that their civilization is demoralizing and degrading to our people. . ." Quoted in Leong (1998).

19. The word "coolie" comes from a Dutch word to describe a "dock laborer" and also a Chinese word meaning "bitterly hard use of strength." It became a racial slur in America and was even a legal term. California passed the "Anti-Coolie Act" in 1862 to tax Chinese workers and also as a method of discouraging them from coming to America. Source: http://en.wikipedia.org/wiki/Coolies.

20. When the United States became involved in the Vietnam War, they too took advantage of the opium trade. The CIA became a major trafficker in this huge industry. The profits from the opium trade resulted in huge financial savings on the part of the Southeast Asian leaders. American planes helped ship the opium to Saigon where it was processed into heroin and either sold to American GIs or shipped to the United States, often in the coffins of American soldiers (McCoy, 1973). For a similar account, focusing on the connection between the CIA and the Contras, see Webb (1998) and especially Cockburn and St. Clair (1999).

21. One method whereby the dominant classes can more easily control the masses is through scare tactics whereby you create large-scale fear (even if the fear is totally unjustified, as in this case) and create demand for "law and order." The fear almost always creates simultaneously the need for scapegoats for various social ills, so that close scrutiny of the real sources of the problems—the activities of the dominant classes—is not done. For further discussion of this phenomenon see Chomsky (1989, 1994). For a good discussion of the use of fear, see Glassner (1999).

22. One example is in the field of education. See Spring (1972: 95–96).

23. 132 Cong Rec. 24, 436 September 26, 1986.

24. Some examples are: *United States v. D'Anjou*, 16 F.3d 604 (4th Cir.), *cert denied*, 114 S. Ct. 2754 (1994) (equal protection); *United States v. Angulo-Lopez*, 7 F.3d 1506 (10th Cir. 1993), *cert denied*, 114 S. Ct. 1563 (1994) (equal protection, cruel and unusual punishment); *United States v. Thurmond*, 7 F.3d 947 (10th Cir.,1993), *cert denied*, 114 S. Ct. 1311 (1994) (equal protection, due process); *United States v. Jackson*, 968 F.2d 158 (2d Cir.), *cert denied*, 113 S. Ct. 664 (1992) (vagueness); *United States v. Simmons*, 964 F.2d 763 (8th Cir.), *cert denied*, 113 S. Ct. 632 (1992) (due process, equal protection, cruel and unusual punishment); *United States v. Levy*, 904 F.2d 1026 (6th Cir. 1990), cert denied, 498 U.S. 1091 (1991) (vagueness); *United States v. Cyrus*, 890 F.2d 1245 (D.C. Cir. 1989) (equal protection, cruel and unusual punishment). But see *United States v. Davis*, No. 93–0234 (N.D. Ga. Aug. 26, 1994) (invalidating heightened statutory penalties for cocaine base as impermissibly vague based on lack of scientific distinction between "cocaine" and "cocaine base.").

25. The use of experts is one of the five main filters Herman and Chomsky cite in their propaganda

model of the news media. Such filters are used to frame issues in a way that distorts reality and serves the interests of the rulers (Herman and Chomsky, 2002).

26. Similar media accounts associating crack and random violence were also a central theme to media stories in 1988 and 1989 (Brownstein, p. 85). The CBS network, in an effort to capitalize on the revived crack hysteria, inaugurated its 1989–90 season on *48 Hours* with a three-hour special, "Return to Crack Street," which constructed a compelling picture of the realities of drug-related violence that was spreading and becoming random in its selection of victims. This documentary, and other media reports of its time, typified the media's attempt to present crack as being out of control, extending its reach into white Middle America (Belenko, 1993: 27; Reinarman and Levine, 1997b).

27. The following statistics are taken from the following sources: Mauer (2006); Ziedenberg and Schiraldi (2000); Maguire and Pastore (1996); Drug War Facts http://www.drugwarfacts.org.; http://www.drugwarfacts.org/prison.htm; FBI, *Uniform Crime Reports*, 2005 http://www.fbi.gov/ucr/05cius/arrests/index.html.

28. There is quite a bit of literature documenting the complicity of the U.S. government in killings and torture on a grand scale. These instances are well documented in the following works: Chomsky (1988, 1993); Chomsky and Herman (1979); Parenti (1995); Blum (1996, 2000), Kinzer (2006).

29. For a compilation of news reports on this case see the following Internet sites: http://www. chron.com/news/specials/enron/; http://news.findlaw.com/legalnews/lit/enron/#documents; http://topics.nytimes.com/top/reference/timestopics/people/s/jeffrey_k_skilling/index.html?excamp=GGBUenroncase; http://www.nytimes.com/2006/09/19/business/19enron.html?ex=1163998800&en=f1e6c2f9ec8736d9&ei=5070.

2

The Development of the Police Institution: Controlling the Dangerous Classes

In the fall of 2006, in a suburb of New Orleans, the local sheriff has made some waves with his approach to fighting crime in his district by suggesting that his deputies would stop, search and run background checks on young black males congregating in high-crime areas. A few years earlier he had stated that "If we see two young blacks driving a rinky-dink car in a predominantly white neighborhood, they'll be stopped" (Foster, 2006).

The police of today are the most visible representatives of the state. Of all the criminal justice agencies, the police receive the largest share of government funding, which came to about $72 billion in 2001.[1] The police are usually viewed as being in the forefront in the war on crime or as representing the thin blue line between civilization and anarchy. Yet the police, as an institution of social control and as an occupational subculture, are probably the least understood. To develop an understanding of the police, we need to trace the historical development of this unique institution. This is the aim in the present chapter. As we will see, policing as an activity of a governmental unit is not new; however, the police as an institution and distinct bureaucracy, as we know it today, is a rather recent invention, unique to modern capitalist societies.

Early Police Systems

Police systems have differed over the years depending on the prevailing economic and political systems. Not every type of society has had an organized police system. As a general rule, the more stratified a society, the greater will be the reliance on formal methods of social control, in this case, organized police forces (Chambliss and Seidman, 1982: 34). As a corollary to this general principle, we might add that police forces in stratified societies have always functioned to help maintain class and racial control and in effect help perpetuate the existing stratification system. (The news item that opens this chapter is one among thousands of examples of this general principle.) In so doing, the police, as an institution, have functioned to serve the interests of dominant groups (Bacon, 1939). Quite often, as we will see, a police system has developed as a response to organized threats against the dominance of a small ruling class, especially in 19th century American society.

One of the earliest known police systems existed in Babylonia during the years when Hammurabi issued his famous code (2181–2123 B.C.). It appears that the police during this period were under the direct control of monarchs, the ruling class of the period. One police historian has stated that: "The Babylonian monarchs possessed vast landed estates, the feoffee being bound to come up when summoned and serve as soldier or slave-driver or policeman" (Reith, 1975: 179). Later, in the years before Christ, several societies, ruled mostly by kings and monarchs, had strong, efficient central governments, with order maintained by a *gendannerie* (totalitarian police force) as well as standing armies.

In early Greece there existed a law enforcement system known as the kin-police in which, in a sense, all citizens were policemen. In other words, it was a self-sufficient and self-policing community. In time, however, prosperity created greater wealth concentrated in the hands of a few and "created social classes and political and other parties in the state, and the need of these to put individual and class interests before the interests of the community as a whole" (Reith, 1975: 191).

During the years of the Roman Empire policing again took the above-noted forms. Rome had many of the characteristics of stratified societies elsewhere. The inequalities that existed created wars, internal strife, and riotous behavior among the masses. Reith states that:

> Successful wars and the loot and wealth with which they provided some Romans in the capital altered and enhanced the status and divisions and power of classes and factions in the Roman community. Abundance and cheapness of slaves enabled the rich to exploit the land, dispossess the older class of peasant farmers, and, in consequence, Rome became crowded with an increasingly large population of aimless, workless, discontented and often hungry malcontents, for the control of whose power of insurrection there was only the weak machinery of oratory . . . Against the activities of swarms of discontented slaves, only repressive measures were possible . . . (1975: 214)

After many years of civil strife, Augustus (63 B.C.–14 A.D..) took control and maintained law and order with an Imperial police force known as the Vigiles, a combination of police and firemen. Among the expressed goals of this force was that of "arresting thieves and returning fugitive slaves" (Kelly, 1975: 9). Augustus had a police force of 10,000 in a city with a population of about three-quarters of a million, or one policeman for every 75 citizens (Reith, 1975: 226). Today, by comparison, we have one police officer for every 300 or 400 citizens.

As noted in chapter 1, as Rome shifted from a mostly rural agricultural society to a rather large city-state, the previous informal social norms (e.g., Twelve Tables) could no longer function effectively, as there were growing conflicts between the rulers and a growing proletariat and slave population.

One interpretation of the rise of the Roman police is that it resulted from the need to control crime in the streets, which allegedly was rising quite rapidly (although there is no hard data to confirm this). This view also suggests that among the causes of this crime wave included the absence of adequate street lighting, inefficient law enforcement, minority problems (this was not specified in the source consulted here), and the existence of swamps outside the city, which made "a perfect hideaway for the marauders and fugitives who victimized Rome" (Kelly, 1975: 6). This interpretation apparently takes the perspective of those in power since crime in the streets often consisted of riots and rebellions on the part of slaves and other oppressed people. Considering the degree of inequality that existed in Rome during that time, one of the major functions of the police was to protect the property and powerful positions of the rulers.

To use a comparative analogy, we might look briefly at the police system in the Southern states of America, especially during the days of slavery. Here police forces were established to control the slaves, especially to prevent any protests they might wage (and there were many and the potential was always present). Indeed, as one noted historian has written, these patrols were established to "curb runaways, hold down interplantation theft, and prevent the formation of insurrectionary plots" (Genovese, 1976: 22). In many instances, these patrols "whipped and terrorized slaves caught without passes after curfew" (1976: 617). After the Civil War, police forces were increased, but their major function remained the same: control the black population. As in Rome, Southern police were enforcing the law, the law of those in power.

Not much is known about the police after the fall of the Roman Empire, except that with the coming of feudalism social control came to be a function of individual kings and nobles with their own private armies. Organized police forces as we understand the term did not exist during this period of time. This was to change following the Norman invasion in the 11th century.

The Emergence of the Police Institution in England

Prior to the development of capitalism, English society was organized around a feudal system of production, with kings, barons, and various landlords constituting the ruling class. As we saw in the previous chapter, William the Conqueror created his own unique legal system, complete with justices of the peace and various kinds of police forces.

Prior to the Norman invasion, policing was a community responsibility (as it was in all feudal societies). Each village in England was divided into units of 10 families, called tythings. In each tything a person known as a tythingman was responsible for keeping order in his section of the village (his section being similar to what are called beats in modern policing). A system known as the mutual pledge system was used whereby small sums of money were awarded to citizens who reported crimes to the tythingman or who responded to the tything-man's "hue and cry" (an announcement that a crime had occurred). In addition to catching thieves, the tythingman also reimbursed those who lost property (Reith, 1975: 26). The mutual pledge system and other forms of citizen participation in crime control were forerunners of the vigilante, the bounty hunter, and similar forms of citizen arrest.

As villages grew, tythings were combined to form hundreds (each with 10 tythings) that were policed by constables. These hundreds were eventually combined to form shires (what we would today call counties). As noted in chapter 1, these shires were policed by individuals known as shire-reeves or sheriffs. Eventually, the Normans established the vicecomes to take the place of the sheriffs. "The shire court of the vicecomes became, often, merely an instrument for collecting unjust and oppressive fines and taxes" (Reith, 1975: 28). The tythingman later became known as the chief pledge. This officer came under the authority of the Knights of the Shire (under direct authority of kings) who also became known as justices of the peace. By the fourteenth century the chief pledge came to be known as the petty constable and later on the parish constable.

The constabulary system became the dominant form of policing in England until early in the 19th century, and was even copied in America. "The constable did not use his power to discover and punish deviation from the established laws. Rather, he assisted complaining citizens if and when they sought his help" (Parks, 1977: 196). The constable served during the day while at night citizen volunteers took turns as night watchers. Policing, in other words, became a community responsibility and was under the control of the community. The constable, more-over, was not concerned with preventing crime in the sense that we know it today. That is, he did not spend his time ferreting out potential criminals. This was to change in the 19th century.

This form of policing could not survive the growth of population, the rise of the cities and, especially, the emergence of a capitalist economy with the parallel emergence of class divisions. In this new type of society the voluntary observance of the law no longer held the social order together. According to Reith, such a system of social control seems to never survive

> . . . ineffective from the advent of community prosperity, as this brings into being, inevitably, differences in wealth and social status, and creates, on this basis, classes and parties and factions with or without wealth and power and privileges. In the presence of these divisions, community unanimity in voluntary law observance disappears, and some other means of securing law observance and the maintenance of authority and order must be found (1975: 210).

What should be added to the above statement is that authority and order is defined by those in power and that typically means keeping the masses under control. The gradual transition to capitalism in the 18th century brought with it increased class divisions and a growth of a large propertyless and powerless surplus population. The presence of this mass of humanity posed a definite threat to the prevailing social order and the ruling class. And this brought forth demands for a highly organized and centralized police force, primarily to control the dangerous classes.

The Metropolitan Police of London

Feudal society in England was coming to a close by the 15th and 16th centuries as capitalism began to take over as the dominant economic form. By the end of the 17th century the enclosure movements and other repressive actions by the emerging bourgeoisie had forced many landless peasants to the cities in search of jobs, a process vividly described by Karl Marx (Marx, 1977: 27–31). As one might expect, the masses of propertyless peasants began to engage in various forms of revolt and criminal activity in response to their plight. The propertied classes attempted to contain this revolt and discontent and to generally maintain order. One of the first attempts to maintain order was the organization of the famous Bow Street Runners by Henry Fielding, a famous police reformer of the time. This was accomplished during the 1740s, at about the time that new criminal careers were emerging, such as pirating, highway robbery, begging, and many others (Reith, 1975: 135; Lyman, 1975: 13).

After the formation of the Bow Street Runners economic conditions began to worsen in England and by 1770 prices were rising faster than wages. One result was the famous Gordon Riots, a revolt by members of the working class against rising prices. Parliament and property owners (often indistinguishable) became alarmed and fearful of the presence of mobs. The police, as usual, were criticized for their general inefficiency and inability to control the riots and the military had to be called to the scene. The police, it should be noted, often agreed with the protesters (and often lived in the same neighborhoods) and hence were not neutral enough for those in power, whereas the military were (Lyman, 1975; Critchley, 1975). Whenever riots threatened the estates of the ruling class, local magistrates called out various associations of the gentry to put down the riots. Sometimes the army or militia were called out, but local magistrates distrusted their loyalty. Even though the local gentry resisted the formation of a full-time police force, the rulers' tendency to call out the army risked further problems. More importantly, from the perspective of the merchants, riots disrupted the marketplace and hurt business (Humphries and Greenberg, 1993).

A contemporary observer echoed the sentiments of many when he noted that there was "A large mass of unproductive population . . . without occupation or ostensible means of subsistence . . . hundreds of thousands go forth from day to day trusting alone to charity or rapine; and differing little from the barbarous hordes which traverse an uncivilized land" (Miller, 1999: 5).[2] In London the more well-to-do classes "fled from the poor, and as the gulf between the classes grew the poor seemed more threatening and unreachable" (1999: 5).

As the geographical extent of trade expanded, it became more and more difficult to prevent theft based upon the previous methods of informal, almost ad hoc and individualistic methods. In 1798 Patrick Colquhoun, a successful Glasgow businessman (known as the Father of Glasgow), wrote a very influential book called *A Treatise on the Police of London* in which he stated: "The sole intention of the author . . . is to secure the inhabitants of the Metropolis against the alarming consequences to be dreaded from the existence of such an atrocious and criminal confederation . . ." (Lyman, 1975: 18). Colquhoun estimated that this confederation numbered around 115,000 out of a total population of 999,000 (11.5%).

He was apparently most concerned about rioters and other people who made up the dangerous classes. Colquhoun also commented that "The evil propensities incident to human nature appear no longer restrained by the force of religion, or the influence of moral principle" (Miller, 1999: 6). Another contemporary estimate said there were 150,000 "roughs and ruffians" in London (Miller, 1999: 121). One model of policing that was present at that time was the Thames River Police, which was originally established as a sort of private police force financed by the West India Company merchants doing business in the port of London (they financed about 80% of the force) in order to reduce losses to property due to theft and other threats to maritime commerce. Although it was a short-lived enterprise (it was abolished two years later and replaced by the Marine Police Establishment), it served as a forerunner of things to come (Critchley, 1975: 51–54; Spitzer, 1993: 586).

Up until around 1820 there continued to be strong resistance to the formation of an organized, 24-hour police force. For many people in London "the cop on the beat was an ominous intrusion upon civil liberty. Englishmen feared an importation of despotic France's secret political police. . ." (Miller, 1999: 4). There was also a strong tradition in England of handling offenses as private matters. As suggested above, for a number of years, police officers were hired by private individuals to recover their stolen property or to solve whatever crime had been committed. A magistrate in 1821 said that "officers in abundance are loitering about the police offices, in waiting for hire. Protection is reserved for individuals who will individually pay for it" (Richardson, 1974: 7). The police had to engage in some clever propaganda by sending different messages to different social classes, since support of the idea of a police force was viewed more favorably among the higher social classes (Miller, 1999: 4).

In the meantime, economic conditions continued to worsen in England. In 1807, for instance, England blockaded French ports, resulting in severe unemployment and a rise in hunger and poverty among workers. A severe winter in 1810 and a harvest failure in 1812 added more problems. The use of machinery by factory owners began to displace workers, who soon became mere appendages to the machines. As expected, the workers began to protest. One of the most famous revolts was the Luddite Riots in late 1811 and early 1812. The workers destroyed machines and generally disrupted the entire factory system, a system that was quite oppressive (men, women, and children working up to 16 or 18 hours per day under grueling conditions).

The government's response was to make the destruction of machines punishable by death! The War of 1812 resulted in increased profits and temporarily calmed things down as employment rose. But a depression between 1815 an 1822 resulted in widespread unemployment and more unrest. The Corn Laws of 1815 increased the price of bread, which was a mainstay of the poor, thus resulting in increased poverty and rioting. Once again the government responded with repressive measures by passing the famous Six Acts (known also as the Riot Acts) which prohibited unauthorized drilling and authorized the seizure of seditious and blasphemous literature. (Ironically, the British passed similar laws against American colonists prior to the Revolution.) Events during the 1820s convinced Parliament and other powerful leaders that armed intervention of the military was doing more harm than good (e.g., resulting in a decline of legitimacy toward Parliament and the existing police). The death of 11 and wounding of 500 to 600 citizens who were peacefully attending a lecture (labeled as a mob by local magistrates) convinced the majority that some alternative was needed.

The depression temporarily ended around 1822, but a panic in 1825 resulted in the closing of many banks, the lowering of wages, and a rise in unemployment, all of which brought about a new wave of riots and protests by workers. There was a growing sense that the old methods of informal social controls were not working as the population was growing rapidly (London's population doubled between 1750 and 1820) and the "rich segregated themselves from the poor" (Miller, 1999: 5).

Sir Robert Peel

During the 1820s there were several protests and doubts were being raised by the elites about the effectiveness of the military to control the situation. For example, in 1823 the Duke of Wellington called for a full-time police force "to preserve the lives and properties of His Majesty's subjects against domestic insurrection and disturbance" (Miller, 1999: 7).

At this time Sir Robert Peel (known as Bobby, after whom the London bobbies were named) became Home Secretary and for several years worked with other supporters, and, finally, after many years of debate, the Metropolitan Police Act was passed, in 1829 (Lyman, 1975: 21–28). It was modeled in part after the Thames River Police. The formation of the Metropolitan Police of London was supported primarily because of a growing concern by those of wealth and power about the presence of mobs and the rabble. Such a concern is not unique in history, and many a police force has been established for this reason.

Several reports have noted that there was ostensibly a rise in crime immediately preceding the formation of the new police force. However, most of the crime (as reflected in arrest and court data) was of a rather petty nature and grew out of the class conflicts of the period. Two different sources support this contention. Michael Ignatieff reports that the rate of males going to trial went from 170 per 100,000 population in 1824 to 240 in 1828 and 250 in 1830. The proportion committed for vagrancy increased by 34% between 1826 and 1829, and it rose by 65% between 1829 and 1832. Over half of the prison population during this period consisted of those convicted of vagrancy, poaching, petty theft, disorderly conduct, and public drunkenness. Only 25% of those awaiting trial in local jails or serving actual sentences were there for indictable crimes; deserters and debtors constituted the rest. The new police increased the already growing crackdown on minor offenses. Thus, during the 1830s about 85% of all arrests were for drunkenness, disorderly conduct, and similar minor crimes (Ignatieff, 1978: 179–185).

Wilbur Miller noted that from 1831 to 1941 total arrests increased by 41%, with less than half ever convicted and no more than about 6% ever going to trial. What is interesting to note is that the figures do not include drunks who were discharged at the police station, a policy abandoned in 1833. Miller reports that in 1831 there were a total of 59,037 arrests, of which 23,787 (40%) were drunks discharged at the station (Miller, 1999: 88). The heavy emphasis on minor offenses, which were committed mainly by the poor and the working class, reflected the trend toward the regulation and control of the dangerous classes.

Peel was of critical importance in the creation of the first police bureaucracy. He was not only a large landowner, a shrewd politician (a Tory) and the son of a wealthy manufacturer and was able "to weld the alliance of landowners, manufacturers, and fractions of the petty bourgeoisie that finally succeeded in establishing a bureaucratic police force in England." (Humphries and Greenberg, 1993: 481). The establishment of a full-time, salaried bureaucratic police system was seen as a more efficient method of social control that represented two new developments in the history of policing: (1) rule through an essentially impersonal bureaucracy that seemingly represented the more general interests of society as a whole, rather than the ruling class; (2) "A deeper, more finely tuned penetration of formal control into everyday life" (Humphries and Greenberg, 1993: 481).

The Metropolitan Police Act was passed in 1829 without serious opposition. The passage of this act and the creation of the London police represented the centralization of the state—a definite sign of the times as the capitalist system began to grow rapidly (Lynch and Michalowski, 2006: 145).

Peel sought to legitimate his police force in the eyes of the people by arguing that the police would serve the interests of all the people. He stressed that the new role of the police would be the prevention of crime through increased patrols, on the assumption that more police automatically resulted in less crime (a claim that has never been empirically demonstrated). The police would have a civilian character, since they would be recruited from the ranks of the working class. The police, moreover, would be service oriented (Lyman, 1975: 33–36). Alan Silver has offered another explanation behind the passage of the Metropolitan Police Act, namely, that it would shield the rulers from the masses. He writes:

> If the power structure armed itself and fought a riot or a rebellious people, this created more trouble and tension than the original problem. But, if one can have an independent police which fights the mob, then antagonism is directed toward the police, not the power structure. A paid professional police force seems to separate "constitutional" authority from social and economical dominance (Sliver, 1967: 11–12).

Hence, there was a shift from control of policing on the community level (as it was with the constable form of policing) to control by the state (which in turn was under the direct control of the rulers).

The idea that the police would prevent crime by patrolling the streets in search of suspicious activities and/or persons and identifying potential troublemakers was the most important break with the past. The concern over the presence of mobs and radical protests and political parties helps explain the formation of this type of police force. The police could now serve more direct class control functions (as well as other, more routine functions) by patrolling those communities wherein live the poorest and most oppressed people, thereby being able to keep tabs on them or to keep a lid on potential disorder. Moreover, because their role shifted to that of the prevention of crime, the police eventually became the scapegoats for increasing crime rates. Also, the focus of the police on individual offenders or potential offenders shifted the causes of crime away from social conditions to the individual.

There is a great deal of evidence that the wealthy classes and the working classes and the poor shared different views of the police. Richardson notes that a "parliamentary committee of 1834 noted the possibility of abuses of power; still it found the Metropolitan Police 'well calculated to maintain peace and order . . .' and further found that the police were 'one of the most valuable of modern institutions' " (Richardson, 1974: 14). Yet, Richardson continues, the poor and the working classes "considered the police more as an element of control than as a group of protectors. In a sense the police monitored the behavior of the dangerous classes so that the comfortable and satisfied could sleep more soundly at night or not be annoyed by the sight of public drunkenness" (1974: 14).

The Development of the Police Institution in the United States

Early forms of policing in America were similar to those existing in England prior to the early 19th century. We have already referred to the Southern police system, where police forces consisted primarily of slave patrols before the Civil War. In the North, especially in such large cities as New York, Boston, and Philadelphia, the rulers hired out their own police to serve as night watchers, some specifically to guard warehouses and homes. At times the militia was called upon to suppress disorders, which were common during the late 18th century. For the most part, however, policing in Colonial America was at the community level, with some form of constabulary system dominant (Parks, 1977; Center for Research on Criminal Justice, 1977: 21–22). Throughout Colonial America the local sheriff and constables were the backbone of law enforcement. The night watchman patrolled the streets in larger communities. Constables and night watchmen, incidentally, were ordinary citizens. Eventually the Dutch introduced a paid watch system in New York (1648) and in Boston a similar system was adopted (1663); both were soon abandoned because they were too expensive. The sheriff was generally appointed by the governor and he became the chief law enforcement agent in the county, with numerous duties (jury selection, in charge of local jails, and so on). Just like night watchmen and constables, however, the sheriff was often neglectful of his duties and incidences of corruption were common (Friedman, 1993: 28–29).

In New York City, as late as 1845, there were 100 marshals in addition to a part-time watch of around 1,000 men known as constables. These police officers were not salaried but were paid fees for recovering stolen property or providing other police services. At night, a group of volunteers served as watches (Richardson, 1975: 22).

Most historians agree that the growth of population, increased immigration, the emergence of class divisions, and resulting urban disorders were the major factors associated with the rise of an organized police force (Bacon, 1939; Lane, 1967; Richardson, 1970; Silver, 1967). Richardson, writing of the New York Police, argues that between 1830 and 1845 there was "a marked upsurge in crime, vice, and disorder . . ." in addition to ". . . rapid population growth with sharp increases in immigration, heightened distinctions between class, ethnic, and religious groups with consequent social strain, and a dizzying economic cycle of boom and bust" (Richardson, 1975: 16). He also contends that the city was no longer "a homogeneous community with a common culture and shared system of values and moral standards" (1975: 16). In a similar vein, Lane notes that Boston was plagued with some of the same changes. He notes especially: "Riot, one of the first problems recognized as beyond control, dramatized the need for force. The leaders of government were firmly set against popular violence as a means of political and social protest" (Lane, 1967: 24–25). Ironically, the leaders of the American Revolution supported popular violence as a means of political and social protest. Apparently, these same leaders (and the next generation) did not apply the same logic to the protests of other oppressed groups. This is a point that both Lane and Richardson fail to point out.

Most police historians (such as Lane and Richardson) claim that the above changes inevitably resulted in a breakdown in normal mechanisms of social control and the development of a full-time organized police force. The following statement by Kalmanoff epitomizes this conventional view of the rise of the police in the United States:

> While the need for social control diminishes in the presence of increasing stability, rapid or extensive change will necessitate the development of new or improved mechanisms of maintaining social order. As in England, the Industrial Revolution in the United States was accompanied by profound and rapid social change. Traditional social patterns were disrupted by the migration from rural to urban areas, the inevitable competition for employment, and the pressures of urbanization. The problems of transition were aggravated by the extremely heterogeneous nature of American society and by the constant influx of new immigrants from Europe and other areas. Social dislocation, economic development, and a growing class structure in the United States demonstrated the inadequacy of the prevailing methods of social control, particularly in rapidly developing urban areas (Kalmanoff, 1976: 36).

This point of view generally takes the form of the popular consensus argument by suggesting that the people were supportive of the newly created police forces in the mid-19th century. The organization of a full-time organized police force was the result of actions taken by business and political leaders in large cities in the North. In fact, there was a great deal of opposition on the part of the working class. According to one view:

> Workers did not accept such exploitative conditions (i.e., union busting, depressing wages and other practices on the part of employers) without resistance. This took its most organized form in labor strikes which directly threatened the high profit levels that employers maintained through the exploitation of workers (Center for Research on Criminal Justice, 1977: 23–24).

In Lynn, Massachusetts, for instance, workers on three occasions organized to defeat shoe-manufacturer mayors; here the largest issue was the strikebreaking activities of the police.

Two recent studies, one by Harring and McMullin on the rise of the Buffalo police and one by Harring on the Milwaukee police challenge some of the conventional interpretations of the rise of the police. It is true, as Harring and McMullin argue, that the rise in disorders required new methods of social control. However, these new methods were those perceived as necessary by those in power. Indeed, the business leaders in the major cities of the North felt threatened by the specter of urban disorder, the presence of mobs, and the dangerous classes. The attitude toward these groups (and the working class in general) was similar to white attitudes toward blacks in the South: these powerless groups would seize power. The studies by Harring and McMullin and by Harring present evidence that (1) the size of the police force increased more rapidly than both the rise in population and the increase in crime; (2) crime was primarily of the public order variety, such as disorderly conduct, vagrancy and the like; and (3) the police were created and under strict control by business and political leaders. Let us pursue this matter further with a closer look at the rise of the police in Buffalo, New York (Harring, 1976, 1978; Harring and McMullen, 1975).

An Illustrative Case: Buffalo, New York

Both Lane and Richardson argue that in New York and Boston the rise of a full-time police force in the 1840s and 1850s followed a rapid increase in crime and disorder. But there is no evidence that these periods contained more crime and disorder than earlier periods. The period just before the American Revolution and for decades to follow witnessed a great deal of crime and disorder (e.g., Shay's Rebellion). Moreover, the population of eastern cities was not as homogeneous prior to the 1840s as both Lane and Richardson suggest. Rather, these cities were quite heterogeneous with a well-defined class structure, numerous ethnic groups, and the existence of slums (Harring, 1976: 55).

Additional evidence indicates that the rise in police personnel did not correspond to a rise in crime. This is evident in Boston as well as in Buffalo (Ferdinand, 1967). Harring and McMullin show the figures on arrests, population growth, and the changes in police personnel in Buffalo. Harring and McMullin note that, in Buffalo, between 1873 and 1880 the police force actually declined, as did total arrests, but population increased by about 32%. Between 1880 and 1890 the police force increased by over 100%, while population increased by about 67%. Then, between 1890 and 1900, the size of the police force increased by about 80%, twice the percentage increase of the population. Hence, the theory that an increase in population causes an increase in the size of the police force fails to explain why the growth of the police was far greater than the increase in population.

At first glance, one might conclude that there is a close relationship between the increase in the size of the Buffalo police force and crime. But crime, as measured by arrests (as it is here), is open for interpretation. Between 1873 and 1900 total arrests rose by about 125%, population increased by about 200%, and the police force increased by 259%. However, notice that the percentage of arrests that were of the public order variety, which included at that time such offenses as drunkenness (public), disorderly conduct, vagrancy, plus the charge of being a tramp. It is well known that such charges are usually rather vague and depend solely on police discretion. In Buffalo, for each year, these offenses constituted the majority of all arrests (ranging from 59% to 74% of the total), but between 1885 and 1900 they averaged 70% or more of all arrests.

What is also interesting from this study of Buffalo is the fact that the overall rate of the police force increased by only 20% during the entire period, but actually decreased by 28% between 1873 and 1880, whereupon it began to increase quite rapidly, going up by two-thirds (67.7%) between 1880 and 1900. Similarly, the overall arrest rate decreased by about 50% between 1873 and 1885, only to be almost exactly reversed between 1885 and 1900 as it went up by almost exactly 50%. Similarly, the arrest rate for public order offenses decreased by around one-third from 1873 and 1880, only to increase by a phenomenal 469% between 1880 and 1900! Meanwhile the arrest rate for crimes of violence did not show any apparent pattern, going down by 55% between 1873 and 1885, then up by 72% between 1885 and 1890, then down by 7% from 1890 to 1895, and then back up again by 21% between 1895 and 1900.

It just so happens that this period witnessed the greatest amount of political unrest in Buffalo, as elsewhere in the nation.[3] Moreover, Harring and McMullin found that most of those arrested during periods of political unrest were laborers who were charged with these offenses in the context of social and political struggles (Harring and McMullin, 1975: 12).

It is also interesting to note that the percentage of arrests that were crimes of violence remained fairly constant throughout this period: ranging from a low of 0.6% in 1873 to a high of 1.1% in 1880, but averaging less than 1% of the total. Hence, crime in the streets did not consist of direct personal harm to individuals, but rather it consisted of primarily harm (or political threats) to industrialists as thousands of workers struggled to gain union recognition and a decent standard of living, behavior that was labeled by the industrialists of Buffalo as criminal. Clearly the rabble were getting out of line and needed to be contained.[4]

The conventional analyses of the rise of the police also cite the importance of urban disorders, especially what is commonly referred to as rioting. It is true that this was of major concern during these times, just as riots were a major concern during the time of slavery in the South and during the American Revolution. But it was of major concern to those who held positions of economic and political power: in the South, the white plantation owners; in the North, manufacturers; during the Revolution, the British. Indeed, throughout the nineteenth century there were widespread political turmoil and resistance as workers, in response to gross exploitation by capitalist owners, sought to gain some form of democratic control of their lives, especially the workplace. The owners used various techniques to keep workers in line, such as hiring scabs to work while workers were on strike, token advancement of leaders, and, more commonly, the use of both private and public police forces. The police became the tools of the owners in many cases, for they were ordered to break up strikes and arrest workers on vague charges, such as disorderly conduct. Not surprisingly, Harring and McMullin found that arrests for these offenses increased during periods of rioting and declined sharply after the turmoil came to a close.

Not coincidentally, the greatest economic crisis in U.S. history up to that period occurred in 1893, with 642 banks failing and 16,000 businesses closed. Unemployment stood at around 20%. Labor unions, starting to get a foothold in the country, organized mass protests. In 1892 alone strikes occurred all over the country, including Buffalo, and they continued for many years thereafter. Only a few years earlier the infamous Haymarket bombing occurred in Chicago in 1886, when about 3,000 workers assembled at Haymarket Square. About 180 policemen were ordered to be present. A bomb exploded, killing seven policemen. Eight so-called anarchists were arrested, tried, convicted and sentenced to death, despite little evidence that they did it; four were hanged, one committed suicide in jail and three were eventually pardoned by Illinois Governor John Altgeld and sent to prison. To the present date, no one knows who threw the bomb and serious questions have consistently been raised about the guilt of those arrested. This case drew international attention and would continue to draw protests well into the 20th century. Subsequent to this event, police continued to be hired by industrialists to quell labor protests, which often led to indiscriminate violence against protestors and arrests and imprisonment on disputed or minor charges (Zinn, 1995: 265–276).

Finally, most historians cite the inevitable problems of overcrowding, slums, and so on, as causing problems in social control and giving rise to increases in police manpower. But this view overlooks the fact that it was primarily the low wages paid to immigrant workers that created slums, not to mention forced segregation and other forms of discrimination. There's nothing inevitable about this, since human beings, not the laws of nature, are doing this. Harring has written:

> Industrialization occurred in the context of cut-throat competition among capitalists in which low wage levels were a major source of profits. Skill levels were reduced to facilitate the control of workers and to reduce wages. Frequent depressions further reduced wages and made workers' income highly unstable. (1976: 57)

The police throughout this time were under direct control of upper class business and political leaders, thus lending support to the notion that they were the tool of the ruling class. For instance, in Buffalo between 1872 and 1900 there were 17 police commissioners, of which 14 were businessmen. There were also 9 police superintendents, of which 4 were businessmen. These businessmen were concerned, first and foremost, with protecting business interests which, usually, were contrary to the interests of the workers. In Buffalo, labor problems were cited more often than crime as a justification for additional police personnel, according to annual police reports. One police report in 1893 reveals that in response to a strike the entire police force was ordered on duty; many other reports reveal identical responses. Police were also ordered to break up the meetings of workers who were attempting to organize unions. In addition, since Polish immigrants in Buffalo were especially troublesome, the police department set up special Polish precincts to help control them and to aid in their (i.e., Polish) socialization (Harring and McMullin, 1975: 10–13).

In Buffalo, New York, Boston, and most other industrial cities the police were actively recruited from working-class communities. At first, many officers were reluctant to exert the kind of control their superiors (i.e., the upper class) wanted. But the owners often bribed them, such as offering them more pay than given other workers, hiring police from one immigrant group to control another immigrant group (e.g., Irish police controlling Italians and Poles), and other measures (Harring and McMullin, 1975: Center for Research on Criminal Justice, 1977: 26–27).

The Rise and Growth of Private Policing

A discussion of 19th century developments would be incomplete without some reference to the phenomenon of private policing. Private policing emerged during the same period that public police forces emerged. Thus, private policing arose with the growth of industrial capitalism and working-class protests. Like the early fee-for-service constables, private policing has enabled the rich to purchase their own protection from crime. Hence it is a class-based institution (Lynch and Groves, 1989: 90–91). While the public police concentrated their efforts on maintaining social order, the private police concentrated on the protection of the private property of the capitalist class (Lynch and Groves, 2006; Weiss, 1978).

What is important to emphasize here is the distinction between private and public order. On the one hand, the origin of the police—in this case a public police—was related to the need for some form of public peace. As noted by Shearing and Stenning, there has also been the notion of a private peace, which relates to the idea that while "the state is the public authority and all other authorities operating within its territory are subordinate to it," the state can, at its discretion, "define separate private peaces so long as they are not in conflict with the public peace." Shearing and Stenning also note that corporations have been legally defined as analogous with "persons" and hence "have a right to a sphere of private authority over which they have undisturbed jurisdiction" (Shearing and Stenning, 1987: 11–15).

What is especially significant in this context is the emergence of the idea of the corporation as a person with all the rights accorded to people in general, as noted in the 14th amendment guaranteeing that all persons have the right to due process. This was a carefully calculated move on the part of corporate owners and their lawyers during the so-called Gilded Age (roughly the last 25 years or so of the 19th century when huge fortunes were amassed by the robber barons; see Josephson, 1962). This change formally came about in 1886 with the Santa Clara case in California during which the U.S. Supreme Court ruled that a corporation should be treated like a person and that ordinary people were conceived as having their own liberties intertwined with the corporation and therefore "taking away corporate rights was equivalent to challenging their own constitutionally guaranteed rights." (Derber, 1998: 126–131). In other words, an artificial person (which was what the corporation was in fact), had the same rights as real people. Thus the old idea that a corporation was under public control (which it was at first) was transformed into completely new entity unto itself with all the rights and privileges of citizens. It gave unprecedented freedom to corporations to do basically whatever they wanted (1998: 126–131).

What this development also revealed was the close connection between corporations and the state, since it was a branch of the state (the courts) that helped create the corporation as a private entity. But more than this, this relationship eventually expanded to include many other state entities, including the U.S. Secret Service and the Department of Justice. As union protests escalated during the late 19th century, the courts began to side with corporations, charging that the corporation's due process rights were being violated by strikers. The courts began to issue injunctions against strikers, while calling out the National Guard and the U.S. Army to quell disturbances, as the federal government looked the other way. It was a clear example of "usurpation of state power by private interests" (Weiss, 1987b: 111).

The first private security agency (and the most popular, even today) was Pinkertons, established in Chicago during the 1850s. The main purpose for the establishment of this agency was to provide additional protection to private corporations and secondly to provide supplemental services to the Chicago police department.

After the Civil War the Pinkertons shifted from routine detective work to industrial spying, first for railroad companies and later for other private corporations. For the next several decades, Pinkertons worked for private corporations in their battles against working-class union activities. Their activities were generally confined to four important strike services: (1) labor espionage (providing spies at the workplace), (2) strikebreakers (hired especially as scabs to replace striking workers), (3) strike guards (those who protected private property during strikes), and (4) strike missionaries or those who "mingled with striking employees or townspeople, either to urge strikers to violence or to act as propagandists against the strike" (Weiss, 1978: 39) During the period 1869 to 1892 this force participated in 77 strikes. Among the most famous included the Homestead (Pennsylvania) strike against the Carnegie Steel Company, which left 12 dead (10 of them strikers) (Weiss, 1978: 39).

A Senate hearing (which followed the Homestead strike) culminated in several criticisms of Pinkertons, which in turn was followed by several pieces of legislation (known as anti-Pinkerton laws). Most of this legislation was ineffective because several states began to establish their own private security forces to help break strikes, with Pennsylvania establishing a state police force specifically to deal with strikes.

Violence against strikers and other working-class activities reached a peak during the late 1910s and early 1920s, such as the violence against the International Workers of the World, the Palmer Raids, and the violence against striking workers in Ludlow, Colorado, in 1914.[5] As Weiss reports: "These agencies and corporations stockpiled huge arsenals of weapons, including millions of dollars worth of machine and hand guns, sickening gas, tear gas and deadly chloropicrin" (Weiss, 1978: 42). Finally, during the Great Depression when strike activity reached a new high, part of Roosevelt's New Deal reforms focused on private policing. As collective bargaining became institutionalized, violence on the part of private security forces became unnecessary, although they continued most of their antilabor activities (especially industrial spying).

Pinkerton's and other security forces have continued to serve the need of private industry, with their primary emphasis being on protecting firms from employee theft and shoplifting, in addition to other guard duties. Private security forces have expanded their role to include guarding buildings at night and serving as watchmen, for apartment complexes and even enclosed housing districts.

The Growth of the Police Institution in the 20th Century

By the end of the 19th century almost every major city had a full-time police force. While the police (including private police, such as the Pinkertons) were often used to suppress strikes, many of the daily duties of police officers were of the service variety. At times police officers helped provide overnight lodging services for the homeless, they supplied coal for poor families, they served soup in special kitchens for the hungry, and so on (Radelet, 1977: 35). Such functions were an apparent contradiction since the police were often called on to oppress these same people. In time, most of these services were to be handled by charity organizations, so that the police could do real police work.

Another function of the police, one which created a great deal of animosity among the people, was to control liquor. Public drunkenness became a popular form of human activity as saloons and taverns replaced the home as a favorite place to drink during the late 19th century. These places also became favorite hangouts of workers, often becoming places where political meetings were held. Then came the Temperance Movement. According to Parks, the Temperance Movement started with the mission that the consumption of alcoholic beverages should be moderate, rather than excessive. In time, the major concern shifted to that of abstinence. Total abstinence became a symbol of power and respectability, and those who did not abstain were to be punished. Thus came the passage of laws regulating the drinking habits of millions of Americans. More importantly, however, the Prohibition Movement that followed (resulting in a Constitutional Amendment) was an effort on the part of powerful groups to control the dangerous classes, specifically the immigrant working classes. The police were called on to enforce these laws. Since the public was sharply divided on the issue, the police were often caught in the middle. And, since many police officers engaged in drinking behavior of the type that was outlawed, many were reluctant to enforce the law. The police often solved the problem by doing no more than the minimum. Eventually this led to a great deal of corruption (Parks, 1977).

The fact that the police were often unable (or, in some cases, unwilling) to maintain order and suppress dissent led to many criticisms. These criticisms came from all segments of society. Working class organizations, such as unions and radical political parties, complained of harassment and brutality, while business and political leaders complained of laxness and corruption. One study concluded that:

> By the beginning of the 20th century, many Progressives in business, government, and the universities were becoming strongly critical of the police. They regarded most

police departments as corrupt and ineffective, subservient to local politics and totally incapable of providing the level of protection they felt a highly interdependent business society required. A main stimulus for their dissatisfaction with the performance of the police was the apparently rising rate of crimes against property . . . The traditional police forces, according to the Progressives, were not only failing to put a stop to rampant crime and political agitation, but were actually aggravating them through the use of misguided and outmoded strategies (Center for Research on Criminal Justice, 1977: 32).

The period known as the Progressive Era (1890–1920) saw numerous reforms throughout society, including the criminal justice system. Since this period of history is so important, especially with regard to the criminal justice system, some brief comments are in order. This review should be kept in mind as it also relates to the other chapters in this book, since so many criminal justice system changes occurred during this era.

The Progressive Era

The literature covering the period known as the Progressive Era is voluminous. There have been many different interpretations of this movement, specifically concerning (1) the origins of this movement, the nature of its leadership, and the general social objectives; and (2) the amount of success and social value to society. Arthur Link suggests that there was not a progressive movement as such. Rather, there were several different progressive movements. There was "the effort of social workers and students of the labor question to bring the state and national governments to the side of women, children, and other unprotected groups" (Link, 1967: 68). There was a movement aimed to rid the nation of widespread corruption in the cities and to restore representative government to the cities. There was also a movement to make state governments more responsive to the people and as instruments of social welfare, rather that subservient to corporations. Finally, "there was a progressive movement on the national level, the main thrusts of which were attempts to subject railroads, industrial corporations, and banks to effective public control" (1967: 68).

Few scholars disagree, however, as to the total effect of this period on American history. "The foundations of the society we live in today were created between 1880 and 1920 by industrialization, urbanization, and immigration. Those forty years were America's 'take off' point into modernity. . ." (Mann, 1963: 1).

Indeed, the last half of the 19th century and first two decades of the 20th century witnessed such widespread social problems as poverty, unemployment, economic crises, labor unrest, crime, and delinquency. Many people were aroused to action by the works of the muckrakers, a group of writers (e.g., Upton Sinclair, Ida Tarbell, Lincoln Steffins) who published books and articles that exposed many urban problems. Large numbers of professionals, educators and businessmen, who came to be known as Progressives, responded by agitating for a wide variety of reforms.

Many of the problems, as perceived by the Progressives, stemmed from overcrowded slums and the high concentration of immigrants within these areas. The

Progressive's solution was to educate and assimilate the foreigners (immigrants were often called worse), while improving the more pressing problems of the cities through local (mostly volunteer) action.

There has been some debate concerning the social backgrounds of the Progressives. Some historians, such as Russell Nye (1951), have argued that they were Midwestern, small-town people. Others, such as Hofstadter, have focused on their urban origins, arguing that the leaders were among the educated middle class. Hofstadter maintains that these reformers were most concerned about their own future positions, specifically referring to their status anxiety as driving forces of reform activities, rather than the plight of the poor, for instance (Hofstadter, 1955).

One of the most convincing arguments is that reformers were strongly influenced (and dominated by) the business sector. Both Hays, and particularly Wiebe, show how business leaders strongly supported such reforms as the regulation of the railroad and communications industry, the conservation movement, antitrust reforms, and the Federal Reserve Act (Hays, 1959; Wiebe, 1967). Wiebe has shown that business, professional and educational groups organized on a national basis to spread their desire for nationalization, integration, and regulation, in short, the efficiency of economic and political institutions.

In recent years a group known as the New Left Historians has provided a radical/Marxist interpretation to this period. Gabriel Kolko, for instance, has described the period as a "triumph of conservatism" because "there was an effort to preserve the basic social and economic relations essential to a capitalist society . . ." (Kolko, 1963: 2). Progressivism, says Kolko, was "the political rationalization of business and industrial conditions, a movement that operated on the assumption that the general welfare of the community could be best served by satisfying the concrete needs of business" (Kolko, 1963: 2–3). William A. Williams (1988) suggests that this period brought about the triumph of a new corporate order (in his words, the Age of Corporate Capitalism). One result was the adaptation of the major institutions of society, indeed the life of most citizens, to this new order. This new economic order was "designed to accumulate large amounts of capital, resources, and labor and apply them to the rational, planned conduct of economic activity through a division of labor and bureaucratic routine" (Williams, 1988: 2).

It has also been argued that many reforms (especially those concerned with education, juvenile justice, and criminal justice) resulted in extending bureaucratic controls to many areas of social life in order to regulate and control those on the bottom of the social order. Piven and Cloward, for instance, have argued that public relief (and other ameliorative) programs emerge during "occasional outbreaks of civil disorder . . . and are then abolished or contracted when political stability is restored" (Piven and Cloward, 1971: xiii). One of the most popular aims of reformers was that of increasing and extending the functions of the government in order to solve social problems. Many reforms concerned with improving the efficiency of the legal system ended up by adding several new bureaucracies, especially on the national level (with the emergence of such organizations as the FBI) (Walker, 1998).

Most of the New Left historians have argued that business leaders supported most reforms (many of which were passed as compromises, following lengthy debates in the House and Senate) because they feared social revolution. This interpretation is understandable since labor unrest and the growth of the Socialist party during this period obviously threatened the interests of capitalists. Kolko argues that most of the legislation of the period, in effect, if not intentionally, sought to regulate the economy in the interests of private profit and property (Kolko, 1963; see also Weinstein, 1968, and Tipple, 1970).

Link's conclusion, however, is just the opposite. He calls the progressive movement "one of the most significant and fruitful reform movements in American history" (Link, 1967: 70). He particularly praises what he calls the social justice movement, which involved the attempt to improve the lot of the underprivileged. He writes that the accomplishments of social justice reformers "constituted perhaps the greatest single triumph of the social justice movement before the First World War" (Link, 1967: 71–72). However, even judging by Link's own account the results of these reforms were quite mixed.[6]

Howard Zinn observes that while "ordinary people benefited to some extent from these changes," the most fundamental conditions changed very little "for the vast majority of tenant farmers, factory workers, slum dwellers, miners, farm laborers, working men and women, black and white" (Zinn, 1995: 341–342). It was clear, says Zinn, that a lot of the reforms were instigated to "head off socialism." Zinn quotes a privately circulated memo from the National Civic Federation which stated that: "In view of the rapid spread in the United States of socialistic doctrines," there was a need for "a carefully planned and wisely directed effort to instruct public opinion as to the real meaning of socialism" (1995: 346).

Indeed, there was a concerted effort by big business to preserve the capitalist system, since it was being criticized so harshly. One method was the emergence of a public relations industry to sell the capitalist story to the masses. Thus began, around the time of World War I, an intense propaganda effort, let by such experts as Walter Lippman, the dean of U.S. journalists, who urged the manufacture of consent since "the common interests very largely elude public opinion entirely, and can be managed only by a specialized class. . ." Harold Lasswell would later note that we should not succumb to "democratic dogmatisms about men being the best judges of their own interests." Instead, the elites are the best judges and what was needed was "a whole new technique of control, largely through propaganda" mostly because of the "ignorance and superstition" of the masses of people. After all, "rationality belongs to the cool observers," noted Reinhold Niebuhr who eventually became "the official establishment theologian" of the government and who suggested that what was needed was for elites, via the media and the advertising industry, to provide the necessary illusions so that the right course of action can be followed, all for the common good (all quotes from Chomsky, 1989: 16–17). Such necessary illusions included intense propaganda about the emerging juvenile justice system and that such a system would act in the best interest of the child, especially the children of the poor.[7] The illusion was that those in authority would know what is best for children, better in fact that the parents (see chapter 5.)

Whether or not these reforms were successful probably depends upon one's own ideological views and the time period within which one is writing. From a conservative standpoint (represented by Link) they were, in fact, progressive, while from a radical standpoint (represented by Kolko and Zinn and others) they were failures or, at best, uplifted only a handful of the underprivileged. The latter interpretation better fits the available evidence since so many people (as Zinn notes), especially blacks and immigrants, benefited little and experienced a wave of repression throughout the period (e.g., the rise of the Klu Klux Klan, the Red Scare, the Palmer Raids on immigrants, and the passage of anti-immigration laws). The benefits of reforms aimed at children and youth can also be questioned, as we shall see in chapter 5 (Walker, 1998: 151–152).

There is no questioning the fact that American society underwent some radical transformations during this period. What did in fact occur was the bureaucratization of many areas of social life, resulting in the control, regulation, and efficient functioning of the major institutions of society and the establishment of many regulatory agencies of social control (Weber, 1946; Haber, 1964).

Police Reforms During the Progressive Era

Concerning the police, some of the major goals of reformers included the following:

1. *Centralization*. This was necessary because, said reformers, the existing police were too close to local communities and under the control of local politics. Apparently the police institution had not as yet become completely separated from influences of local communities, although, to be sure, such a process was by this time well under way. Reformers aimed to tighten the control of the police, leaving it in the hands of high-level administrators, such as police commissioners.

2. *Professionalism*. Reformers sought to professionalize the police by filtering out incompetent or unskilled police and replacing them with educated and highly skilled officers. This tactic also included the abolition of community residence requirements, which no doubt contributed to many officers' inability to control working-class strikers. This reform should sound familiar since professionalism has been strongly recommended by many special crime commissions, including the Wickersham Commission in the 1930s and the President's Commission in 1967, as well as the National Advisory Commission in 1973.

3. *Technology*. A third method of improving the police was to increase the reliance on the use of technology. This strategy was supposed "to replace the traditional police reliance on fear and brute force" (Kalmanoff, 1976: 42), especially in dealing with riots and other forms of protests. One of the most notable changes was the introduction of the call box system in the 1880s and the two-way radio in 1929.

4. *Crime Prevention*. A fourth tactic was to beef up efforts toward preventing crime. Two specific methods were to be developed: (1) cooperation with schools, welfare agencies, and the like in order to identify potential delinquents and other troublemakers (e.g., in the schools); (2) increasing contacts with troublesome groups directly, especially youth. One example of these efforts was the crime prevention division of the Berkeley police that worked closely with the child guidance clinic. (Center for Research on Criminal Justice, 1977: 35–39).

Police departments all over the country were plagued with problems of graft and inefficiency during the late 19th century. One of the most common solutions to this and other internal problems was the introduction of the civil service system. At times civil service (and other reforms) was aimed at throwing the rascals out. Indeed, police and political corruption (e.g., Tammany Hall in New York City) were believed to go hand in hand. But civil service reform involved more than this. As Richardson states: "The civil service program became intertwined with a larger program to eliminate 'politics' from the government of cities, to make urban government a matter of administrative efficiency rather than political conflict" (Richardson, 1974: 64). In effect, such a form of government was to take away influence from poor and working-class (especially immigrant) neighborhoods. As far as the police system was concerned, promotions began to be made through competitive examinations (before promotions were largely made based on who you knew). Yet the reality was much different from what the new laws stipulated, for "political influence remained strong in promotions . . . Police commanders exercised too much power in too many sensitive areas . . . and politicians and others constantly sought to get 'their' policemen promotions and the right assignments" (1974: 64).

New Developments in Private Policing

Labor struggles continued well into the 20th century and the police—both public and private (including state police, the National Guard, and the army)—continued to be used to control labor unrest. However, during the Depression era of the 1930s, the rights of labor were finally recognized with the passage of the Wagner Act (National Labor Relations Act) in 1935, which backed up workers' right to organize. But corporate America immediately began to resist and fight back with the beginnings of intensive corporate propaganda (Fones-Wolf, 1994: 5–25; Carey, 1995). This involved large public relations industry to sell the capitalist story. This included "convincing workers to identify their social, economic and political well-being with that of their specific employer and more broadly with the free enterprise system" (Fones-Wolf, 1994: 6). This was perhaps best summarized with the famous phrase, "What's good for General Motors is good for the country." Certainly corporations had a lot to worry about: between 1936 and 1944 membership in unions went from about 4 million to around 14 million, as strikes continued throughout the 1930s—4,000 strikes in 1937 alone (Weiss, 1987b: 112).

Henry Ford, while considered by some a great innovator, among workers he was known as a tyrant "who demanded from his workers absolute obedience and machinelike behavior to complement his technocratic vision of the ideal factory" (Weiss, 1987b: 113). An illustration of this can be seen at his River Rouge plant where 80,000 workers were employed in what can be called, for all practical purposes, a prison-like environment. Weiss quotes the following description, which summarizes what this factor was like:

They do not whistle while they work; they do not even whisper. Only the tools they use make any sound as they demonstrate the efficiency of mass production. Their silence is a tribute to the Machine-Age Pavlovs who determine from week to week just how much men can stand before running amok (1987b: 114).

To enforce this prison-like atmosphere corporations like Ford (and Bethlehem Steel) hired thousands of spies and sluggers (private detectives) who were working with hundreds of private detective agencies. At one point Henry Ford had his own in-house police department, with as many as 3,500 men employed (Ford called this the Ford Service Department). At times this was augmented by various community groups, including the Knights of Dearborn and the legionnaires. In response to this, the ACLU pressed for a Congressional investigation. Finally, in the face of incredible opposition from a strengthened union movement and the Roosevelt administration, there began a turnaround in both the philosophy and strategy of corporate management. What occurred was a shift toward what became known as public relations (actually a nicer sounding word than *propaganda*) from the usual robber barons approach known as slugging (Weiss, 1987b).

As World War II ended, there were expectations of the lowering of wages and the inevitable strikes by workers as a response. Management was understandably concerned with the new power of labor. Instead of relying on old methods of social control (noted above), the new head of Ford (Henry Ford II, who took over in September, 1945) created a new industrial relations position within Ford. This method entailed recognizing unions, but putting union leadership on the defensive where they would be "held accountable to the *company's* demands" (Weiss, 1987b: 122).

Despite this effort, more strikes occurred in 1946. One result was Congressional action culminating in the passage of the Taft-Hartley Act in 1947, which included sanctions against unions for such activities as mass picketing, wildcat strikes, walkouts, and so on. The act increased union power over their own members, which transformed them into not only "agents of labor peace, *but agents of the state as well*" (Weiss, 1987b: 124, quoting Lipsitz, 1982). In short, labor officials became, in effect, policemen, so that reliance upon private police, state police, and so on would no longer be required. As Weiss notes, "the slugging-detective style of labor discipline became inappropriate and dangerous. Under the new system, as long as union bosses limited contract demands to wage and hour considerations, negotiations could be 'reasonable' " (1987b: 125). Various strike-breaking efforts of union leaders (i.e., their policing activities) was supported by federal law under the Taft-Hartley Act. This style of policing represents a continuum of policing from public forms of policing with public accountability at one end, to those forms with "special powers and accountable only to private interests" at the other end (Weiss, 1987b: 127).

One of the most important changes in the police institution during this century has been its increasing bureaucratization. There are more and more specialized areas and more and more tasks to be performed. The emergence of special detective bureaus is an example of this. We have, in most police departments, such detective divisions as burglary, robbery, homicide, vice, and juvenile, to mention just a few. The average police officer now spends most of his or her time performing rather routine clerical tasks, such as interviewing victims of crimes (in which long and detailed crime reports often have to be filled out), writing traffic tickets, and many others.

One result of these changes is the growing alienation of the beat police officer. The automobile, along with the geographical mobility of citizens and the emergence of suburbs, has contributed to this alienation. In particular, the uniformed police officer is alienated from real police work (e.g., conducting investigations, making important arrests, and so on and from the people he or she is supposed to serve). Gone are the days of the walking beat cop who knew everybody (such as Bumper Morgan in Joseph Wambaugh's *The Blue Knight*, 1974). Now the beat is an impersonal one and the city is seen through the glass windows of a squad car. Yet the functions remain basically the same.

This does not mean, however, that uses of certain police forces to control those defined as dangerous ceased to exist, because in the era following World War II various efforts were made to control a new dangerous class that had emerged in the 1960s, namely urban, lower-class African Americans.

Policing the Ghetto in the 1960s

In the 1960s many began to conceive of the ghettos within the inner cities of America as analogous to imperialized colonies (Blauner, 1972; Tabb, 1970). Not unlike today, such ghettoes are almost totally separated from the rest of society (both literally and figuratively speaking). Part of this separation can be seen in some of the most common problems that plague these areas. These problems include poverty, unemployment and underemployment, substandard housing, inadequate social services, high crime rates, and high rates of alcohol and drug abuse.

Blauner described the colonization of African Americans in terms of five major components. First, there is a forced, involuntary entry. Second, the colonizers carry out policies that constrain, transform, or destroy the culture of the colonized. Third, government bureaucracies and the legal system itself administer control over the lives of the colonized. "The colonized have the experience of being managed and manipulated by outsiders who look down upon them" (Blauner; 1972: 84). Fourth is the element of racism. "Racism is a principle of social domination by which a group seen as inferior or different in alleged biological characteristics is exploited, controlled, and oppressed socially and psychically by a superordinate group" (1972: 84). Finally, there is a separation according to labor status, with the colonized assigned the menial and unskilled tasks and often relegated to the "surplus labor force" (1972: 84).

The colonial model was extended to explain the role of the police in the ghetto as an army of occupation in that they began to be viewed as an alien force of soldier in enemy territory. Several studies during the late 1960s demonstrated that the police were not only perceived by ghetto residents as outsiders, but they actually were outsiders in many respects (e.g., not from the same neighborhood). This was true even when applied to African-American officers (Kelly, 1976).

Another element of a colonial police force noted by Blauner was expressed as the goals of containment, regulation, and control. Blauner noted that: "They constrict

Afro-Americans to black neighborhoods by harassing and questioning them when they are found outside the ghetto . . ." (1972: 97–98). In the survey by Kelly noted above it was found that ghetto residents believe that the police virtually ignored serious crime (especially crimes against residents by absentee merchants, land-lords, and other representatives of the business community as well as government) and spend too much time on relatively minor offenses. Many also believed that most police ignored serious personal crimes, as long as it was black against black.

The goal of containment was most apparent with regard to collective disorders, such as the riots of the 1960s in such locations as Watts, Detroit and Newark. Blauner noted at the time that: "In the final analysis they [the police] do the dirty work of the larger system by restricting the striking back of black rebels to skirmishes inside the ghetto, thus deflecting energies and attacks from the communities and institutions of the larger power structure" (Blauner, 1972: 99; see also Balbus, 1973).

Police Corruption: A Continuing Problem

Corruption has been a constant within the police institution. During the early years of the American police, there were constant problems associated with various kinds of corruption among not only individual police officers, but entire departments as well. As Walker notes, one could easily conclude that corruption was the main business of the police in the 19th century. Police routinely received payoffs to look the other way at various illegal activities. This was, of course, during the era where almost entire local governments were in one way or another corrupt. It was the era of Tammany Hall and other political machines that made corruption seem almost normal (Walker, 1998).

Various reforms during the Progressive Era and after did little to stem the tide of police corruption. Evidence of this comes from the first of many blue ribbon government commissions investigating corruption and other aspects of the criminal justice system throughout the 20th century. The first was the Wickersham Commission in 1931 (National Commission on Law Observance and Enforcement, 1931), which found corruption within police departments to be common. President's Johnson's Crime Commission in the 1960s (such as the Task Force Report on the Police) came up with findings almost identical with the Wickersham Commission (President's Commission, 1967b).

Greater detail of corruption has often come with investigations that have focused on one city. One of the most popular was the Knapp Commission on Police Corruption in New York City in the early 1970s. This investigation stemmed from allegations brought forth by plainclothes patrolman Frank Serpico who became quite a celebrity (his story became a best-selling book, a movie starring Al Pacino, and even a TV series). In the words of the Commission's final report: "We found corruption to be widespread" (Knapp Commission, 1975: 235).

Specifically, they found that plainclothesmen were involved in a pad or collections of payments (up to $3,000 per month) from several gambling estab-lishments. The share per month per officer ranged from $300 to $400 in midtown

Manhattan to $1,500 in Harlem. Serpico charged that 19 Bronx plainclothesmen received an average share (called a nut by the police) of $800. The Commission also found that Brooklyn plainclothesmen brought in an average nut of $1,200 (see also Maas, 1975).

Payoffs in narcotics enforcement (known as scores) were common. The commission found a pattern "whereby corrupt officers customarily collected scores in substantial amounts from narcotics violators. These scores were either kept by individual officers or shared with a partner and, perhaps, a superior officer. They ranged from minor shakedowns to payments of many thousands of dollars . . ." (Knapp Commission, 1975: 235). The largest payoff discovered was $80 000.

In Reading, Pennsylvania, back in the 1950s, the entire city was controlled by organized crime. In the 1960s, in New York City, a close advisor of Mayor Lindsay, James Marcus, was deeply meshed in corrupt political activities with organized crime figures. In Newark, New Jersey, in 1969, a scandal broke out involving the mayor, other city officials, and the police department (Quinney, 1979: 211–212).

In a study conducted for the President's Commission, Gardiner (1969) reported on one medium-sized city (he used the pseudonym of Wincanton) where it was found that corruption had been common for many decades. Specifically, it was found that "Mayors, police chiefs, and many lesser officials were on the payroll of the gambling syndicate . . ." (Gardiner, 1969: 104). According to this report, the head of these illegal operations was controlled the police department. A police chief was quoted as saying, "Hollywood should have given us an Oscar for some of our performances when we had to pull a phony raid to keep the papers happy" (1969: 111). The leader, Irv Stern, was able to "secure freedom from State and local action" (1969: 112) One investigation found "that Stern had given mortgage loans to a police lieutenant and the police chief's son" (1969: 112). Finally it was found that "Most policemen . . . began to ignore prostitution and gambling completely after their reports of offenses were ignored or superior officers told them to mind their own business. State policemen, well informed about city vice and gambling conditions, did nothing unless called upon to act by local officials" (1969: 114).

As the Knapp Commission suggested, officers tend to be socialized into a police subculture that supports various forms of deviant activities. The Commission distinguished between the bad apple theory and the group support theory of police corruption. Stoddard, in another study (of a police department in the southwestern part of the country) found widespread support for certain forms of deviance among officers. Specifically, Stoddard found the existence of an informal code that supported deviancy. Rookies were pressured to go along with this code and failure to do so resulted in group ostracism. "Lack of acceptance not only bars the neophyte from the inner secrets of the profession but may isolate him socially and professionally from his colleagues and even his superiors" (Stoddard, 1975: 262). Thus, while the bad apple theory suggests that police corruption stems only from a few bad apples in an otherwise clean barrel, the group support theory suggests that the barrel is not so clean after all and that deviancy, while not indulged in by all police officers within a department, is nevertheless condoned by most officers.

The study by Stoddard, as well as the Knapp Commission's findings, suggests that it is the honest policeman who is the exception. Stoddard quotes one policeman who, in reference to a fellow officer, said: "You've got to watch him, because *he's honest!*" (1975: 268). The Knapp Commission found an intense amount of group support within the police department in New York City and "a stubborn refusal at all levels of the department to acknowledge that a serious problem exists" (1975: 238).

However, both the bad apple and group support theories fail to adequately explain police corruption as a persistent phenomenon throughout our history. Both perspectives imply that a new kind of police officer is all that we need (perhaps of the Serpico variety). But the historical consistency of corruption and the social, political, economic, and legal context of it suggests that this type of reform will not solve the problem. One reason is the fact that so much money is involved and that there are very powerful interests (usually on the part of respectable people) enmeshed in police corruption. In other words, there is evidence to suggest that police corruption is not the problem; the problem appears to be that the economic and political structure of our society breeds corruption. A study by Chambliss lends support to this view (1975b).

Chambliss found corruption to be widespread in Seattle, Washington, as he studied the problem through personal observation over a period of several years. This corruption did not involve police officers only. It also involved members of organized crime, key political and business figures, as well as high-ranking police officials. In particular, Chambliss discovered that all of these individuals participated in such illegal activities as gambling, prostitution, loan sharking, and many more, while individual police officers took bribes of substantial amounts. Most of these activities were restricted to the fringes of slum communities, where respectable citizens could participate but not be seen by their fellow citizens. The police made a few token arrests and even some well publicized raids, but of course, they avoided involving influential citizens.

Chambliss suggests that there existed a symbiotic relationship between the law enforcement bureaucracy and the major suppliers of vice in Seattle. He concludes:

> The gambling, prostitution, drug distribution, pornography, and usury which flourish in the lower-class center of the city do so with the compliance, encouragement, and cooperation of the major political and law enforcement officials in the city. There is in fact a symbiotic relationship between the law enforcement-political organizations of the city and group of *local,* as distinct from national, men who control the distribution of vices (Chambliss, 1975b: 150).

The implications of Chambliss' findings are far-reaching. He further concludes that in the study of organized crime there has been an overemphasis on the criminal and

> . . . a corresponding de-emphasis on corruption as an institutional component of America's legal-political system. Concomitantly, it has obscured perception of the degree to which the structure of America's law and politics creates and perpetuates syndicates that supply the vices in our major cities (1975b: 144).

Continuing, Chambliss concludes:

> Organized crime becomes not something that exists outside law and government but is instead a creation of them, or perhaps more accurately a hidden but nonetheless integral part of the governmental structure. The people most likely to be exposed by public inquiries (whether conducted by the FBI, a grand jury, or the Internal Revenue Service) may officially be outside of government, but the cabal of which they are a part is organized around, run by, and created in the interests of economic, legal, and political elites (1975b: 144).

Another implication of this study is that it becomes evident that law enforcement is a form of class domination, especially in the case of vice laws. As Chambliss found out (and as most observers have noted), those who were arrested were mainly small-time, lower-class people. The well-to-do who actively participated in these vices were rarely, if ever arrested. From this perspective, the police serve to perpetuate profit-seeking ventures of the private enterprise system (i.e., privately run by a small minority).

The average police officer is, of course, caught in a bind between demands by the powerless for a more equal share of the wealth and power and the powerful and property holders who want to keep what they have. The most common solution is to practice crime control when dealing with the poor but to observe due process when dealing with the privileged (Chambliss and Seidman, 1971: 365). In his study Chambliss found (Chambliss, 1975b: 146–147):

> . . . the law enforcers do what any well-managed bureaucracy would under similar circumstances—they follow the line of least resistance. Using the discretion inherent in their positions, they resolve the problem by establishing procedures which minimize organizational strains and which provide the greatest promise of rewards for the organizations and the individuals involved. Typically, this means that law enforcers adopt a tolerance policy toward the vices, selectively enforcing these laws only when it is to their advantage to do so. Since the persons demanding enforcement are generally middle-class persons who rarely venture into the less prosperous sections of the city, the enforcers can control the visibility and minimize complaints by merely regulating the ecological location of the vices.

In case you might think that this problem has disappeared, still another police corruption scandal in (you guessed it) New York City (actually the Bronx) prompted yet another commission in 1994, known as the Mollen Commission. Once again, widespread corruption was discovered. Not only this, police brutality was apparently normal. One officer was known as the Mechanic, because "I used to tune people up" (police jargon for a beating). As usual, most of the recipients of this tune up were African Americans or Hispanics (Cole, 1999: 23). In the same city of New York still another scandal has occurred; in fact, two big scandals that began to make the headlines in 1999. One involved the arrest and gang rape of a Haitian man, while another involved the killing of another man, who was riddled with no less than 41 bullets! As of this writing (February, 2000), both cases are still pending.

Lest you think that police corruption is a problem of the past, consider a recent scandal in Los Angeles, centering on a special antigang unit called CRASH (Community Resources Against Street Hoodlums). The unit was originally called TRASH (the "T" stood for Total); the name was changed for obvious reasons. Under this program the police engaged in surveillance and harassment. Their explicit purpose was, to use one officer's words, to jam suspected gang members—to harass and then move on, making no arrest in most cases. Officers were rotated out of the unit after two or three years and thus never had a real opportunity to develop detailed knowledge about the communities (Klein, 1995: 164–165).

During one five-week period in 1995, gang-squad officers were accused of brutalizing and violating the rights of two families in their homes. These cases cost taxpayers about $1 million to settle the family claims. In one case, a 15-year-old was hit in the mouth with a shotgun butt, and his father was suffocated until he passed out and was later taken to the hospital. According to police records, there was not even an internal investigation conducted of these incidents. The department appears to have ignored the claims. It has been reported that at least twelve officers were relieved of duty for illegally shooting suspects, planting evidence, beating one man, falsifying evidence, and many other crimes. All twelve belonged to the LAPD's elite CRASH antigang unit. But that was the least of their troubles, as it turned out.

There are those who suggest that American law enforcement has overstepped its boundaries. Those boundaries are defined by the U.S. Constitution and the Bill of Rights. In some cases, those boundaries are defined through criminal statutes (Miller, 1996; Parenti, 1999; Cole, 1999). Time and time again, law enforcement has been confronted with acts of brutality and abuse of authority. Rodney King (Los Angeles, 1992), Malice Green (Detroit, 1992), Waco, Texas (1993), and the Rampart scandal (Los Angeles, 1999). Time and time again, the explanation has been directed to the bad-apple theory. The problem may not be the apples at all. The problem may be the barrel.

By late October 1999, the Los Angeles Police Department (LAPD) recognized the dilemma they were in. A LAPD lieutenant revealed that the Rampart investigation had revealed that a sergeant in the antigang unit had given officers instructions to plant guns on suspects, and that evidence of stealing drugs and using prostitutes to sell drugs was part of the routine by some LAPD police officers. The investigation into the LAPD Rampart station became significantly larger than police officials had early revealed publicly. In fact, as the investigation continued, it was revealed that the sergeant had done more than simply give orders to plant weapons on suspects. He also helped to create fictitious crime scenes such as the one where one 19 year old, Francisco Ovando, was shot in 1996, framed, and falsely imprisoned. There was hard evidence that members of the CRASH unit stole drugs from dealers and then employed street prostitutes to sell the drugs for their own profit. One officer indicated that the CRASH unit officers behaved like the gangs they were supposed to police (*Los Angeles Times*, 1999a).

In mid-November it was revealed that Rampart police officers conducted random stops and confrontations involving minor offenses that resulted in beatings and detention of citizens. Although 40% of the Rampart officers were Latinos, residents indicate that those officers were among the worst. Some people indicated that even the Latino officers would refer to them as wetbacks and often asked them why they did not go back to Mexico. Some people indicated that Rampart officers set them up so they could not acquire legal residency status. One area resident, Al Pina, 36, who moved to the area to take a job as vice president of the local community development corporation, stated that he was surprised to see the number of random stops conducted by Rampart police. In fact, Pina was also stopped by three officers, restrained, and searched, as another officer held a gun on him. When the officers released him, he asked why he had been singled out for such treatment. Officer David Solis told him he fit the profile of a drug dealer. Pina, a clean-cut former Air Force sergeant, said he had never felt so humiliated in his life. In another case, Juan Jimenez, 20, a United Parcel Service stock clerk, indicated he had been detained and handcuffed by police at least twelve times in 1999. He was en route to night school or to his volunteer job where he tutored children. On one occasion, Jimenez had been mugged, and he called the police. When the police responded, they handcuffed and searched him. In poor neighborhoods, everyone becomes a target for police abuse of power (*Los Angeles Times*, 1999b).

In 1998, Walter Rivas was arrested and framed by Officer Michael Buchanan. Buchanan asked Rivas, "Who do you think they are going to believe, are they going to believe you or me?" (*Los Angeles Times*, 1999c). The focus on Buchanan placed the arrest and conviction of hundreds into question. Buchanan was relieved of duty in October 1999 in connection with another case, in which he and Officer Perez had framed a suspect (1999c). By mid-December, it was projected that as many as 3,000 criminal cases may have been affected by questionable police tactics including perjury and planting evidence on suspects (*Los Angeles Times*, 1999d).

By February, 2000, investigators found evidence that at least 99 people had been framed, with a total of 32 convictions having been overturned. A Los Angeles City Councilman called for an independent investigation (*Los Angeles Times*, 2000; *Washington Post*, 2000). It has also been suggested by the Mayor of Los Angeles that, in order to settle the law suits that have already begun (with more predicted to follow), money from the national tobacco industry settlement (up to $300 million) be used to help cover these lawsuits. What is important to note here is that this money was supposed to be used for health, education, and other social programs (Jablon, 2000). It should also be noted that the victims of this corruption have been overwhelmingly the poor and racial minorities.

That corruption has become almost synonymous with government and big business has been documented by the Watergate and other scandals during the past several decades. For instance, several reports have concluded that the men involved in Watergate had several things in common. First, many of the Watergate defendants were employed or had been employed by either the CIA or the FBI or by both. Second, many of these men had been involved (at least indirectly) with such incidents as the Bay of Pigs, a plot to assassinate Fidel Castro and overthrow his regime, and the assassinations of John and Robert Kennedy. Third, many of these men had close ties to organized crime figures. In fact, several reports have indicated that there is strong evidence linking the Office of Strategic Service (OSS)—which eventually became the CIA—with Lucky Luciano and Meyer Lansky (two famous Mafia members); Thomas Dewey (former governor of New York and presidential candidate against Truman in 1948); John and Allen Dulles; and Richard Nixon. According to one report (Leslie, 1977; see also Nohn, 1976), Lucky Luciano, with help from the CIA, "began an international smuggling ring for the syndicate's narcotics industry" (Leslie, 1977: 9). Further, "the CIA called on Luciano in 1947 when communist strikers shut down the port of Marseilles to American shipping. He supplied hit men while the CIA supplied money and weapons" (1977: 9). Frank Sturgis, one of the Watergate burglars, had been a gun smuggler for Castro and later became a CIA undercover agent. He and Robert Maheu (FBI agent, Howard Hughes' assistant, involved in Watergate); John Roselli, Sam Giancanna, and Santo Trafficante (all connected with organized crime); Richard Helms (former CIA director); and E. Howard Hunt (CIA agent, consultant to White House counsel Charles Colson, Watergate burglar) were involved in the Bay of Pigs incident.[8]

The CIA was also involved in the overthrow of the Allende government in Chile in 1971, with the full support of the State Department and the Nixon administration, mostly at the insistence of some of the leading American corporations doing business there. The CIA has also been involved in the Iran-Contra Scandal in Nicaragua in the 1980s and Guatemala in the 1950s. In each of these cases, corporate interests were being threatened by insurgent movements and democratic elections of leaders who wanted to nationalize various industries (Kinzer, 2006; Blum, 1995, 2000; Chomsky, 1988, 1993).

Another example was the FBI's counterintelligence efforts to subvert the Black Panthers and other radical groups in the 1960s, an effort known by the code word COINTELPRO (Blackstock, 1975; Cockburn and St. Claire, 1999). This program's name was an acronym for counterintelligence program. It was started in 1956. Under the close scrutiny and direction of J. Edgar Hoover, the FBI waged a war against almost all organizations that could be considered subversive—ranging from antiwar organizations to civil rights groups. According to a memo from FBI director J. Edgar Hoover, the purpose of this program was to expose, disrupt, misdirect, discredit or otherwise neutralize subversive organizations. In fact, if any black leader emerged, Hoover wanted the Bureau to "pinpoint potential troublemakers and neutralize them before they exercised their potential for violence" (Cockburn and St. Claire, 1999: 69).[9]

High on Hoover's list was Dr. Martin Luther King Jr., who became a principal target. The FBI tapped his telephone conversations, threatened his life, committed blackmail to discredit him, and even sent him a letter suggesting that he commit suicide. All of this was eventually confirmed in a Senate hearing headed by Frank Church in 1976, it was discovered that the FBI conducted more than 200 black bag jobs, where FBI agents broke into offices and homes of mostly black radical groups in order to destroy equipment, steal and copy files, take money, plant drugs, and even in one case start a fire that destroyed the Watts Writers Workshop in Los Angeles. Blackmail, illegal surveillance tactics, arson, perjury, smear campaigns, and allegations of assassination were a few of the methods used by the FBI and local law enforcement against civil rights and antiwar movement members.

The word *neutralize*, in this discussion, should be taken to mean within intelligence organization's assassination (commonly used historically by the CIA). The FBI launched a major offensive against the Black Panther Party (BPP). By the mid-1960s, peace marches and peaceful demonstrations for civil rights clashed with the less patient, more confrontational strategies of organizations like the Black Panther Party (BPP). According to various sources, at least six and maybe seven Black Panther leaders were killed with the help of the FBI. The most famous killings were the assassinations of Fred Hampton and Mark Clark in Chicago. These two were shot in their sleep by Chicago police, who had been provided with a detailed floor plan of the house by an FBI informant (who had, incidentally, drugged Hampton and Clark).

As such BPP leaders as Huey P. Newton, Bobby Seals, and Eldridge Cleaver began to embrace the words of Malcolm X to resist the white power structure, they began to promote the notion of self defense as means to attain civil rights. To a power structure that was well enmeshed in the practice of economic and racial exploitation and oppression, talk about self-defense by the lower classes, and particularly blacks, was frightening. In fact, when members of the BPP began arming themselves, within the parameters of California law, the power structure was more than frightened—they were terrified. Ronald Reagan, then governor of California, urged the state legislature to quickly change the law and disarm the BPP.

FBI files made available to the public through the Freedom of Information Act reveal that the file on the BPP in Winston-Salem, North Carolina, had accumulated nearly 2,900 pages. There were Black Panther Party affiliates in most cities across the United States during the 1960s and early 1970s. This suggests that tens of thousands of pages on the Black Panther Party, as a whole, may have been collected.

Antiwar organizations, such as Students for a Democratic Party (SDS), were also targeted by law enforcement under COINTELPRO. Abbie Hoffman, a leader in the antiwar movement, had more than 13,000 pages in his FBI file. COINTELPRO barely made a ripple in the national press at the time it was revealed. This was because at about the same time, Watergate made the headlines and dominated the news for several years. Apparently crimes by or against elite groups matter more than crimes against or by the powerless.

Another example came in 1971 when there were several burglaries of members of the Michigan Socialist Workers Party (in Detroit), which involved the theft of membership lists, rather than valuables ordinarily taken in burglaries. Several years later a U.S. District Court Judge ruled in favor of the Socialist Workers Party in their suit against the Attorney General of the United States. The judge stated that the FBI's activities constituted a violation of the constitutional rights of the party. The judge identified many crimes committed by the FBI, including at least 208 surreptitious entries (this did not include the Michigan case). The Detroit case (and many others like it) barely made a ripple in the national press. At about the same time that these cases (including the breakup of the Black Panther Party) were occurring all over the country, Watergate made the headlines and dominated the news for several years (Chomsky, 1999b).

It should be obvious why Watergate received so much attention: those subjected to the FBI's terrorist tactics (see Chomsky, 1999b; Blackstock, 1975 for details) were among the dangerous classes (at this time the radicals trying to form an alternative political party and African Americans seeking justice), whereas the victims of Watergate (and most of the perpetrators) were men of power. And this crime was rather petty in comparison to the crimes committed by the state during the same time period.

Space does not permit a complete discussion of COINTELPRO (see previously cited references for detail), but it should be mentioned at least in passing that the FBI has had a history of involvement in these kinds of activities. The Bureau of Investigation was founded in 1908 ostensibly to enforce the Sherman Anti-Trust Act and the Alien and Sedition Acts and was immediately involved in controversy and various illegal and quasi-legal behaviors. They spent most of the time serving as an instrument for the protection of big business. The Bureau was also involved in many antiunion activities. For example, the first time that the Sherman Act was enforced was against a labor union, charging them with restraint of trade (Michalowski, 1985: 178). This agency was involved in gross violations of civil liberties during the infamous Red Scare of 1919 to 1920, largely under the leadership of one of its staff members, a man named John Edgar Hoover. COINTELPRO is merely one of the FBI's largest undertakings.

Quinney summarizes the connection between big business, organized crime, politics, and law enforcement as follows: "The connection among crime, business, and the state continues to be covered up by the federal government's law enforcement agencies. . . . To disclose a nationwide criminal conspiracy would require the FBI to investigate and expose gangster friends and supporters deeply involved in business and politics" (1979: 215).

The above examples are known as state crimes, a topic rarely discussed. Yet the death toll and economic devastation of crimes committed by the U.S. government is beyond description. Crimes of the state include several different kinds of harmful behaviors and they all have at least one thing in common: they are generally committed against powerless people and they are rarely, if ever, called crimes. Although there are several definitions, the one offered by Michalowski and Kramer will do. They call this state-corporate crime and define it as "illegal or socially injurious actions that result from a mutually reinforcing interaction between (1) policies and/or practices in pursuit of the goal of one or more institutions of political governance and (2) policies and/or practices in pursuit of the goals of one or more institutions of economic production and distribution" (Michalowski and Kramer, 2006: 20).

Examples of these harms include the following: the violation of environmental, safety, and health standards at federal nuclear weapons production facilities by private contractors; the famous Iran-Contra Affair (cooperation between the CIA and private arms dealers); and the intervention by our government into the affairs of Third World countries in support of dictatorships and the overthrow of democratically elected governments, all in support of private corporate interests. The last category is particularly interesting, since our government is supposed to be "making the world safe for democracy." Among some specific examples of these interventions include: Guatemala (1950s), Zaire (1960s), Dominican Republic (1961–1962), Indonesia (including East Timor, 1960s–1970s), Greece (1967), Chile (1973), Angola (1975),

Libya (1980), Grenada (1980s), El Salvador (1980s), Nicaragua (1980s), Haiti (late 1980s, early 1990s), to name just a few in a long list of mostly CIA-backed atrocities, all in the name of private profit and political domination.[10]

One particularly gruesome example—and one almost completely ignored by the mainstream press (however, it has finally received world-wide attention in light of elections for independence in August, 1999)—was what amounted to genocide in a little country known as East Timor. East Timor, a portion of Indonesia, just north of Australia, was a country of around 600,000. This country, rich in oil and other resources, became a pawn of the Indonesian dictator Suharto (who had overthrown the democratically elected President Sukarto, with CIA backing by the way) who, along with abundant arms from the United States, killed around 200,000 innocent citizens in what has been described as the worst example of genocide (on a per-capita basis) since the Holocaust.[11]

Still Controlling the Dangerous Classes: The "War on Drugs"

Let's begin this section by considering some of the following statistics:[12]

- In 2005 the police arrested 1,846,351 people for drug law violations, compared to 1,476,100 in 1995 (a 25% increase); in 1975 a total of 601,400 were arrested for drugs, while in 1985 a total of 811,400 were; thus between 1985 and 2005 the percentage increase was 127%.
- During the year 2005, almost half (47%) of the total arrests for drug law violations were for pot (786,545). Of those, about 90% were arrested for possession alone. The total number arrested represented an increase over 1999, when 704,812 were arrested for pot.
- So far in 2006 (as of November 13) more than 1.3 million have been arrested for drugs (just under 684,000 for pot alone, mostly possession).
- Between 1980 and 1997 drug arrests tripled. During this same period, the number of people going to state prison for a violent crime went up by only 82%; for a nonviolent crime, up 207%; for a drug offense, up 1,040%.
- Recent figures show that in the federal system 55% of all drug defendants are what we call low-level offenders, such as street dealers, while only 11% are classified as high-level dealers.

The war on drugs has similarly targeted minority groups, but especially African Americans. Indeed, there is abundant evidence that this war has been in reality a war on African Americans, on a scale that is unprecedented in American history. Research by Jerome Miller found that during the 1980s and early 1990s in Baltimore African Americans were being arrested at a rate six times that of whites, and more than 90% were for possession (Miller, 1996: 8; see also Currie, 1993; Tonry, 1995; Mann, 1995; Chambliss, 1995; Lockwood, Pottieger, and Inciardi, 1995). More specifically, Miller found that in Baltimore in 1981 only 86 black youths were arrested for drugs, compared to only 15 whites; by 1991 the of black youths arrested had increased to 1,304 (an increase of 1,416%), compared to a mere 13 for white youths (a drop of 13%).

However, the rate of illegal drug use among minorities is actually lower than for whites. One survey found that that whites constituted 72% of all illegal drug users, while blacks constituted only 15% and Latinos another 10%.[13] And yet, blacks constitute 36.8% of those arrested for drug violations, over 42% of those in federal prisons for drug violations. African Americans comprise almost 58% of those in state prisons for drug felonies; Hispanics account for 20.7%. Among persons convicted of drug felonies in state courts, 33% of the white defendants went to prison, compared to 51% of the black defendants received prison sentences (these figures are a bit misleading and underestimated the proportion of minorities since Latinos are included in both racial groups) (Durose and Langan, 2001).

A study of Maryland by the Justice Policy Institute (2003) showed the following differences in 2003. While blacks constitute only 28% of the population of that state, they are two-thirds of all drug arrests and an astounding 90% of those incarcerated on drug convictions.

One study noted that almost all (99%) drug trafficking defendants in federal courts between 1985 and 1987 were African Americans (Baum, 1997: 249). In some cities, the proportion of felony defendants who were African American was quite high. For example, African Americans constituted 93% of all felony defendants in Wayne County (Detroit), 90% in Baltimore and 85% in Cook County (Chicago) and Kings County (Seattle), but only 14% in Maricopa County (Phoenix) and 9% in Honolulu (Reaves, 1998: 43).

A Justice Department study found that the growth in the state prison population between 1990 and 2000 accounted for by drug convictions was 27% of the total growth among black inmates, 7% of the total growth among Hispanic inmates, and 15% of the growth among white inmates (Harrison and Beck, 2002: 13). One study found that in the year 1986, before mandatory minimums for crack cocaine offenses became effective, the sentence for drug offenses for blacks was only 11% higher than for whites. However, a mere four years later that percentage had soared to 49% higher for blacks (Meierhoefer, 1992: 20).

A 1980s study found evidence of substantial increases in minority youths being referred to juvenile court, thus increasing the likelihood of being detained. But, cases of the detention, petition and placement of minorities nevertheless exceeded what would have been expected given the increases in referrals. There has been an increase in the formal handling of drug cases, which has become a disadvantage to minorities. "Given the proactive nature of drug enforcement, these findings raise fundamental questions about the targets of investigation and apprehension under the recent war on drugs" (McGarrell, 1993, quoted in Miller, 1996: 258). A study of Georgia's crack-down on drugs found that the higher arrest rate for African Americans was attributed to one single factor, as reflected in the following quote from a police official: "it is easier to make drug arrests in low-income neighborhoods . . . Most drug arrests in Georgia are of lower-level dealers and buyers and occur in low-income minority areas. Retail drug sales in these neighborhoods frequently occur on the streets and between sellers and buyers who do not know each other. Most of these sellers are black. In contrast, white drug sellers tend to sell indoors, in bars and clubs and within private homes, and to more affluent purchasers, also primarily white" (Fellner, 1996: 11).

A more recent report by Human Rights Watch concluded that the war on drugs results in an increase in arrest rates for drug offenders as well as an increase in racial discrimination among arrestees. Blacks are more likely to be arrested for drug offenses than whites (Human Rights Watch, 2000). The Human Rights Watch continued by stating "Throughout the 1970s, for example, blacks were approximately twice as likely as whites to be arrested for drug-related offenses. By 1988, the national anti-drug efforts was in full force and blacks were arrested on drug charges at five times the rate of whites" (Human Rights Watch, 2000). Hence, blacks represented 37% of all drug arrestees nationwide and blacks represented 53% of all drug arrestees in urban areas (Human Rights Watch, 2000).

In most instances, racial disproportions in drug arrests indicate demographic factors. Drug enforcement is highly concentrated in vast urban and metropolitan areas, where illicit drug use is considered to be high (Human Rights Watch, 2000). It is also said that "Since more blacks, proportionately, live in these areas than whites, black drug offenders are at greater risk of arrest than white offenders. But within metropolitan areas, politics and law enforcement priorities have determined how drug arrests would be distributed" (Human Rights Watch, 2000).

The main area of concentration during the drug war has been in low income minority neighborhoods. When the popularity of crack began in the early 1980s, these neighborhoods suffered from "disorder, nuisance, and assault on the quality of life that accompanied increased drug dealing on the streets as well as the crime and violence that accompanied the development of crack distribution systems" (Human Rights Watch, 2000). Distressed neighbors in these concentrated areas forced the police and political officials to do something about the drug issue. As a result, the crack cocaine dilemma fed the media frenzy with sensationalized stories which ultimately led politicians to seek electoral votes by "getting tough on crime" (Human Rights Watch, 2000).

Although crack is the least consumed illicit drug in the United States, the war on drugs has managed to target the possession and sale of crack cocaine among blacks. Human Rights Watch notes that crack cocaine in black neighborhoods became a primary concern for "complicated and deep-rooted set of racial, class, political, social, and moral dynamics" (2000). Not surprisingly, the general public identifies both crime and drugs with those whom are collectively poor, urban, and black. Human Rights Watch concluded their report as follows:

> The war on drugs precipitated soaring arrests of drug offenders and increasing racial disproportions among the arrestees. Blacks had long been arrested for drug offenses at higher rates than whites. Throughout the 1970s, for example, blacks were approximately twice as likely as whites to be arrested for drug-related offenses. By 1988, however, with national anti-drug efforts in full force, blacks were arrested on drug charges at five times the rate of whites. Nationwide, blacks constituted 37 percent of all drug arrestees; in large urban areas, blacks constituted 53 percent of all drug arrestees.

Even greater disparities in drug offender arrest rates have been documented in individual states. For example, Human Rights Watch's analysis of drug arrests by race in the state of Georgia for the years 1990–1995 revealed that, relative to their share of the population, blacks were arrested for cocaine offenses at seventeen times the rate of whites. In Minnesota, drug arrests of blacks grew 500 percent during the 1980s, compared with 22 percent for whites. In North Carolina, between 1984 and 1989, minority arrests for drugs increased 183 percent compared to a 36 percent increase in white drug arrests (Human Rights Watch, 2000; see original report for sources of the data reported here).

Clearly, the police are continuing to carry out their historical mandate to control the dangerous classes, which today means African Americans and other minorities, in addition to the poor in general.

Notes

1. This information comes from the Sourcebook on Criminal Justice Statistics, one of the best all around resources available http://www.albany.edu/sourcebook/pdf/t14.pdf.

2. This statement came in an 1821 by a writer named George Mainwaring (*Observations on the Present State of the Police of the Metropolis.*) London; quoted in Miller, 1999: 120.

3. For a good description and summary of this period of labor unrest see Zinn (2003), especially chapter 11.

4. For a modern variation on this theme, see Chomsky, 1994.

5. For a more complete discussion of the Ludlow Massacre see Zinn, 1990: 79–101.

6. For opposing views on the outcome of progressivism see Mann (1963); for a good critique of progressivism see Zinn (1970, 2005).

7. Corporate propaganda is rarely discussed and in fact the first serious academic studies of this phenomenon did not appear until recently (Carey, 1995; Fones-Wolf, 1994), although it had been used at least since around the time of World War I. As Carey has noted, corporations and political leaders have actually feared true democracy and thus corporate propaganda has been used to, as the title to Carey's book suggests, take the risk out of democracy. See also Herman and Chomsky (2002).

8. The connection between the participants in Watergate and other scandals has been amply documented. See the following for examples: Borosage and Marks (1976), Agee (1974), Marchetti and Marks (1974), Smith (1972), and Nohn (1976).

9. Most of this information is taken from the following sources: Cockburn and St. Claire (1999); Chomsky (1999b); Donner (1980); Garrow (1981); Churchill and Vander Wall (1988, 1990).

10. A complete listing and detailed discussion of these and other state crimes can fill an entire book—in fact they fill several books. See references noted previously.

11. Extensively documented in Chomsky (1996a, chapter 7), Parenti (1995:26–27), and Zepezauer (1994: 30–31).

12. The following statistics are taken from the following sources: FBI, *Uniform Crime Reports* (various years); Mauer (2006); Ziedenberg and Schiraldi (2000). Maguire and Pastore (1996); Drug War Facts, 2000. http://www.drugwarfacts.org; Drug War Facts, 2004 http://www.drugwarfacts.org/prison.htm.

13. Among the surveys that can be cited include the following: Substance Abuse and Mental Health Services Administration (1998); Maguire and Pastore (1999: p. 343, Table 4.10; p. 435, Table 5.48; and p. 505, Table 6.52); Beck and Mumola (1999, p. 10, Table 16).

3

Processing the Dangerous Classes: The American Court System

Introduction

In the winter of 1999, in a Michigan court, a young African-American male was sentenced to prison. An observer of this sentencing wrote the following words:

> In February 1999, a young African-American male was sentenced to prison for the crime of burglary in a Michigan court. Sitting behind the young man was an older woman who wept and an older man who simply placed his head in his hands and just sat there. The couple appeared to be the young man's parents. After informing the young man of his sentence, the judge made a profound, concluding statement that "justice had been served." After the judge left the courtroom, two officers of the court walked over to the young man—one on each side—and instructed him to "come with us." The defense attorney patted the young man's shoulder, turned, and walked away. There was no exchange of words between this young man and his white attorney. The older couple stood up. The woman reached out to her son, but the officers would not allow the young man to take her hand. He was quickly ushered out of the courtroom. The older man put his arm around the woman and they walked out of the courtroom. The woman was crying profusely. He tried to comfort her. Following them out of the courtroom, they got into a very old vehicle and drove off. Exhaust fumes could be seen for nearly a block before they turned at an intersection and disappeared. This observation is not an isolated event in the annals of American jurisprudence. It is jurisprudence history, and it is repeatedly enacted in criminal courtrooms across America. Some form of "justice" may have been served in the courtroom episode noted above, but it was not *social* justice.[1]

The American criminal courts are a major link within the criminal justice system; they stand between the police and the correctional system. This system is a major institution in American society.

One does not have to travel very far in America without a reminder of the central role of the courts. Pass through any town of any size in this country and the local courthouse will often stand out among all of the buildings one will see. In fact, in many towns the courthouse lies literally in the center of town, often with many other important government offices found within (or in close proximity to) this building (local police or sheriff's department, jail, city hall, post office, and so on). In many small towns you will find the courthouse surrounded, in a circular fashion, by several small businesses. The courthouse grounds are often neatly landscaped, with park benches and picnic tables. And invariably you will find, in huge letters, the phrase "Justice for All" or similar words, along with perhaps the symbol of the blind lady of justice nearby plus the American and the state flags.

The courts are certainly one of the busiest of all government institutions and they differ from most other institutions in at least two important ways. First, the courts are places where citizens most directly interact on an individual basis, rather than in groups (with some exceptions, to be sure). Second, it is the courts where people go to "get what is their due" or "have their day in court," whether this be a small claims case or a traffic case or even as victims in a criminal case. Yet at the same time the courts are perhaps one of the least understood institutions—at least as far as the general public is concerned. Public opinion polls consistently find that the public is more ignorant of the court system than any other institution. Also, surveys consistently show that the public often feel that they have been mistreated by the courts and dealt with in a disrespectful way. The public comes to the court system wanting some resolution, either protection or punishment; too often they get neither and their claims are often treated as trivial or frivolous. This is especially the case among ordinary, working-class citizens (Merry, 1990).[2]

In the United States today there are federal and state courts, and each with its own hierarchy with jurisdictional distinctions. The Supreme Court is at the top of the federal court hierarchy, followed in succession by the U.S. Courts of Appeal (with 13 circuits), an assortment of district courts (some having both general and local jurisdictions, while others have only federal jurisdiction), and administrative quasi-jurisdictional agencies (e.g., Federal Trade Commission, National Labor Relations Board, and so on.). The U.S. Supreme Court is composed of eight associate justices and one chief justice. Cases are advanced to the U.S. Supreme Court through a writ of certiorari from the U.S. Courts of Appeals, and from state supreme courts (Vago, 1997; Neubauer, 2005). At the very bottom of the federal court hierarchy are U.S. magistrates who adjudicate minor criminal cases, conduct preliminary stages of felony cases, and oversee numerous civil cases. State supreme courts head the state court hierarchy. Some states also have intermediate appellate courts. State supreme courts are courts of last resort for appeals requiring interpretation of state law.

Below these higher courts are, in order of succession, trial courts of original and general jurisdictions, and at the bottom are courts of limited jurisdiction. The trial courts typically deal with serious felony and major civil cases, but in some instances they also adjudicate misdemeanor cases. A simpler way to view the institution of courts is to recognize that in both the federal and state court systems there are trial courts (with varying degrees of jurisdiction) and there are appellate courts. Trial courts serve as a trier-of-fact body of this institution (take witness testimony, examine evidence, apply procedural rules, and so on), whereas the appellate courts base their decisions on the trial court's record and the constitutionality of lower court decisions made within that record (Vago, 1997; Neubauer, 2005).

The court has been defined as "an agency or unit of the judicial branch of government . . . which has the authority to decide upon cases, controversies in law, and disputed matters of fact brought before it" (Rush, 1994: 78). Such a definition is frequently associated with concepts like justice, fairness, impartiality, objectivity, and other similar superlatives. Actually, the court is not an agency, nor a component of any agency, but "more like an independent branch of government stipulated in both the Constitution of the United States and in state constitutions" (Turkel, 1996: 139). On the surface, this statement suggests that the court is autonomous to other branches of government and other institutions but, as we will see, the court is simply another political government institution often with an agenda far removed from any notions of justice and impartiality.

Criminal courts have been described as "marketplaces in which the only commodity traded seriously is time" (Jackson, 1984: 77). Civil courts can be viewed in a similar vein, with the exception that the commodities traded are power and privilege. This commodity of power and privilege allow corporations to do pretty much as they will: (1) it removes people from their homes (relocation of Native Americans), (2) it decides which parent receives custody of children in divorce cases, (3) it controls women's bodies (e.g., abortion issues), (4) it decides who can work and who cannot (labor issues), and (5) keeps people living in poverty (welfare issues). This commodity controls and impacts many other social issues that face contemporary society. Obviously this view implies, at the very least, that the court is not justice-oriented, objective, or impartial. In fact, this view suggests that the court operates in a stock-market atmosphere with justice reduced to the eyes of the beholder, and where fairness is replaced by whims of power. Such a definition also considers the ideology of the court to be interest-serving. And the function of the court is limited to efficiency. This is not any different than many other institutions within capitalist society.

Most people do not think of the court as a self-serving institution that conceals its true identity behind a cloak of justice, fairness, impartiality, and so on. Rather, most people choose to view the court as simply an guardian of justice. Of course, justice is whatever we want it to be at a given point in time. It is typically said that justice is served if the court's decision favors us or our ideas about the disposition of a case in which we are familiar. We tend to turn on that definition when the court's decision is against us, or against what we think the court ought to have done, resulting in the charge of "injustice." Thus, when a defendant stands before the sentencing judge, after being found guilty of a crime, and is informed that he or she is sentenced to a term in prison, many applaud the decision and say that justice has been served. Few consider another form of justice that is relevant to most criminal cases, that of social justice, which necessitates the consideration of concepts such as race/ethnicity, sex/gender, and social class. And when the topic of social justice is brought up, it is generally rejected with contempt or, at the very least, dismissed as simply another example of liberal thought that fails to recognize that all poor or disadvantaged people do not commit crimes.

A review of the history of the courts demonstrates that while justice has often been served, social justice has not generally been served. This problem can be traced back to the very beginning of the American court system during colonial times.

The Development of the Modern Court System: The Colonial System

Following the American Revolution, although there were significant changes within the entire governmental structure, including the criminal justice system, our modern courts have their roots within colonial society. Early American courts, and their administration of justice process, were microcosms of the British judicial system. As in England, which regarded the Parliament as the highest court, colonial legislatures were the highest courts and one of their legal functions was to serve as courts of appeal. Throughout the 17th century, colonial courts emerged into a three-tiered court system (very much like state courts are arranged today). Below the legislature high courts were Superior courts where governors or their designates presided over criminal trials, as well as civil trials that were previously heard in lower courts. The lower courts handled most of the trials, and levied and collected taxes. These lower courts also provided residents with socializing opportunities, and a place to conduct business and engage in lively political discussions (Knappman, 1994). "Ordinary people *used* the courts to get justice for themselves, vindication, restitution; and in criminal as well as civil matters" (Friedman, 1993: 31). The courts were also used as places to vent frustrations and anger, thus assisting in the stability of colonial society (Chapin, 1983, 1996). These in turn were copied, with a few modifications, from England's court system.

The original charter of the Massachusetts Bay Colony created two types of courts: a general court and a court of assistants. The former acted as both a legislative body and the highest court, while the latter (which consisted of the governor, deputy governor, and magistrates) was in charge of appeals from the lower courts, which came to be known as county courts. These county courts were the heart of the local system of criminal justice—the same kinds of courts found in most cities and towns today (described above). What is perhaps most interesting about these courts was the fact that they performed so many different functions: probate, spending money on road and bridge repairs, various forms of licensing, providing the maintenance of the local ministry, regulation of wages, and of course all matter of criminal cases (Friedman, 1973: 35).

Within these county courts the person who performed most of the day-to-day duties was the justice of the peace. These individuals were appointed by the governor (who was himself an appointment of the English king) and were controlled, for all practical purposes, by the local elites. Actually this office took the place of the local magistrate in the 1860s (Friedman, 1973: 35). More will be said about this in the following paragraphs.

For all practical purposes, judicial authority within the colonies was in the hands of the governor, who in turn was under the control of England. Not surprisingly, as British rule became increasingly unpopular, the courts (and the entire legal system itself, but especially judges and most lawyers) were viewed as mere extensions of the King of England. In fact, lawyers were not exactly welcomed within the colonies, although as time passed their knowledge and skills became more appreciated and in demand (Glick, 1983: 36; Friedman, 1973: 84).

Elite Dominance of the Legal Profession in Colonial America

As the legal profession grew during colonial times, it became more and more specialized as increasing numbers of lawyers participated in formal training. At first, of course, few attended college, since there were no law schools in the early years of the colonies, so that lawyers either had no training at all, save for informal reading, or they went to England for their training, attending what was known as the Inns of Court in London. These were not law schools as we know them today; in fact, they were "little more than living and eating clubs" where in theory "a man could become a counselor-at-law in England without reading a single page of any law book." However, they did "read law and observed English practice" (Friedman, 1973: 84).

Most other lawyers learned the trade through apprenticeships with older lawyers. In fact, some of the most famous lawyers of the 18th century, many of whom directly participated in the writing of the Constitution, received their training this way. Among the notables included Thomas Jefferson and James Wilson (both signed the Declaration of Independence). Some lawyers were actually imported directly from England to assist in the governance of the colony, such as Nicholas Trott, who came to South Carolina in 1699 as their attorney general. It should be noted that most lawyers did the work on a part-time basis, as they usually were men of considerable means and thus had to spend a lot of their time managing their property. In Maryland, for instance, most of these part-time lawyers listed their regular occupations as planters. This is not to say that some lawyers were not poor and struggled with their finances, as so many did. Yet, the legal profession, then as now, soon began to be dominated by an upper crust of wealthy and powerful individuals, such as those classified as founding fathers. Of the 35 men listed as founding fathers, 20 were lawyers (Friedman, 1973: 85; Wilson, 1974).

An excellent illustration of the domination of the legal profession by the upper class comes from two studies of Massachusetts lawyers during the latter part of the 18th century (McKirdy, 1984; Flaherty, 1984). The author of one study (Flaherty, 1984) focuses on some of the first lawyers to practice criminal law in the state. He notes that there were only 15 practicing lawyers in 1740, which increased to 25 by 1762 (this group achieving the newly created rank of barrister), and 71 by 1775. During the first years of the Superior Court (1692–1710) there were very few lawyers that did any criminal cases. There were only a few lawyers considered to be the leading practitioners during the first half of the 18th century. These included Thomas Newton, John Valentine, John Read, Robert Auchmuty, and John Overing. Each of these individuals either came from prosperous families or became prosperous on their own, many achieving prestigious positions in Massachusetts politics and the legal profession (e.g., Attorney General, Advocate General, Judge of the Admiralty Court).

The other study (McKirdy, 1984) provides a detailed profile of every lawyer (including judges) during the 10 years immediately prior to the American Revolution. The results are revealing—yet not too surprising. There were 33 judges in the sample and 81 lawyers. As for the judges, 22 went to Harvard College (in itself indicative of a wealthy background). As for their occupational background, of those with a listed occupation other than being a lawyer, all but one was a physician, merchant or other businessman, or a gentleman. One was a minister, one was a soldier and one was a tutor at Harvard.

As for the lawyers, most read like a "who's who" in Massachusetts society. Almost all (89%) attended college, either Harvard (72%) or Yale (17%). Practically all of them either came from wealthy families (e.g., owners of much land, proprietors, well known ministers) or rose to positions of power and influence (e.g., judges, attorneys general, senators). Included are some rather famous names, such as John Adams (one of the founding fathers), David Noble (famous as a judge and merchant), James Otis (Speaker of the House, Attorney General, member First Revolutionary Council) and James Otis, Jr. (famous patriot, Representative to the General Court, elected Speaker of the House, Robert Paine (son of Thomas Paine), Timothy Pickering (Adjunct General of the Continental Army, U.S. Senator and U.S. Congressman, U.S. Postmaster General, Secretary of War), Josiah Quincy, Jr. and Samuel Quincy (of the famous Quincy family), William Read (son of John Read, one of the leading lawyers in the state, Deputy Judge of the Vice Admiralty Court, Judge of the Suffolk Inferior Court of Common Pleas), Timothy Ruggles (Brigadier General of the state militia, Speaker of the House), and Theodore Sedgwick (Representative to the General Court, state senator, member of the Continental Congress, U.S. Congress, U.S. Senate, Massachusetts Supreme Judicial Court) (McKirdy, 1984: 339–358).

Processing Criminal Cases: The Justice of the Peace in Colonial America

A particularly fascinating case study was done on one specific justice of the peace by the name of John Clark (Osgood, 1984). This study is based upon some rare records left by Mr. Clark himself in a 269-page book, which contain 1,379 entries. The entries cover the period between 1700 and 1726. What is most revealing from the data contained in these entries are the kinds of cases handled in Clark's court. Although it does not provide much detail about the backgrounds of criminal defendants, the occupations of some are presented (more detail is provided for civil cases, including the occupations of those who won the case and those who lost).

As far as criminal cases are concerned, out of 264 cases, 127 (48%) involved the crime of breach of peace. Typical of the religious influence of the times, three offenses taken together constituted almost one-third of the cases (31.8%)—profane swearing, profane cursing (it is not clear what the difference was in these first two), and profaning the Sabbath. Theft cases were 11% of the total.

Other cases that were handled included various civil (mostly violation of contracts) and administrative matters (the most common of which was a category called violating a municipal ordinance). Grand jury presentments amounted to a total of

35 cases, with the most common being selling liquor without a license. However, it is interesting to note that there were two cases presented by the grand jury that involved the charge of uncleanness, and one each of the following charges: bawdy house, neglect of worship, and a man and wife fornicating (where they fornicated was not specified!) (Osgood, 1984: 148–149).

The occupations of those involved in criminal matters are given on only 13 cases, the most common of which was the category unknown (5 cases). The occupations of those involved in civil cases were more often listed. They included such varied occupations as innholders, cordwainer, mariner, victualler (tavern keeper), joiner (a carpenter who specializes in doors and windows), and shipwright (Osgood, 1984: 150–151).

Upholding Morality

It is obvious that during the colonial era cases involving various morals charges tend to dominate the courts, as noted in some of the cases in the previous section. Religion and sex influenced early American courts and processes. Religion was woven into codes throughout the colonies, but was most evident in the northern colonies as reflected in the Massachusetts Bay Colony. "In one part of the *Laws and Liberties of Massachusetts . . .* The code contained a list of 'capital laws.' Each one came equipped with citations from the Bible" (Friedman, 1973: 34). This is not surprising given the fact that the Bible had such a profound impact on the earliest settlers, especially among New England Puritans. The Massachusetts Code of 1648 made the following offenses punishable by death: "Idolatry, witchcraft, blasphemy, bestiality, sodomy, adultery, rape, man stealing, treason, false witness with intent to take a life, cursing or smiting of a parent, stubbornness or rebelliousness on the part of a son against his parents . . . " (Haskins, 1969: 37). Most of the codes were more or less reproductions straight out of the Bible.

However, when it came to enforcing these laws during actual court cases, the bark of the rulers was louder than their bite, as juries usually refused to convict on these charges or simply refused to convict at all. Apparently these laws were established to instill fear more than anything else (Haskins, 1969: 44). Those that were convicted were usually sentenced to pay restitution (in cases of theft) and/or to receive such punishments as whipping, the stocks, the pillory, and other forms of public punishment. It was probably also the case where many citizens refused to go along with the repressive laws laid down by the rulers. Many jurors showed disrespect toward authorities, such as judges, while many a citizen simply chose to ignore the immorality of their fellow citizens, perhaps because they engaged in similar behavior. Indeed, as several studies have noted, the sexual behavior of colonial citizens was often quite loose. Also, there was much drinking and carrying on among citizens. In Essex County, Massachusetts, many women were pregnant on their wedding day and about 60% of these brides were prosecuted, but apparently without much success! (Walker, p. 30; see also, Chapin, 1983 and Flaherty, 1972).

In most other cases, justice was quite individualized, with numerous being dismissed outright. One study found that about one-third of the cases examined virtually disappeared from the records, presumably having been dismissed (Walker, 1998: 30; see also, Greenberg, 1974). This was perhaps most clearly in evidence in capital cases, as most were reduced to a lesser offense (e.g., reducing murder to manslaughter) and most of those who were actually sentenced to death were eventually pardoned. Evidence of such leniency can be seen in the fact that between 1624 and 1664 in New York, there was only one execution (Walker, 1998: 35; see also, Greenberg, 1974; Hindus, 1980; Mackey, 1982).

If there was one area where there was evidence of the occasional repressive features of colonial, especially Puritan, law, it was in the case of the famous witch trials in Salem, Massachusetts. This will be covered in the next section.

Hunting for Witches and Religious Dissidents

In early Massachusetts society several typical religious-based offenses were heresy (which was often the foundation for the offense of witchcraft), blasphemy, Quakerism, and violation of the Sabbath (Friedman, 1973; Knappman, 1994; Dailey, 1991; Evans, 1989; Chapin, 1989; Morgan, 1958; Semmes, 1970). Women were often singled out for the prosecution of these offenses. This is not too surprising, since women were considered property, and lived an existence of servitude and compliance. When they failed to comply with these rigors, they were brought before the court.

In 1637 and 1638, Ann Hutchison was charged with traducing the ministers and their ministry and heresy. Tried twice, the civil trial took place in November 1637 and the religious trial was held on March 22, 1638. She was placed on trial for her religious views and because she crossed the boundary established for women—she had held religious meetings. Mrs. Hutchison was found guilty and the sentence was banishment (Evans, 1989; Dailey, 1991). Because it was winter, her sentence was modified and she remain confined in the colony until spring. Throughout her confinement Mrs. Hutchison continued to express her views, and this demonstration of defiance resulted in the second trial, where after being found guilty on the basis of her spiritual views, was excommunicated and ordered banished. In 1643, Mrs. Hutchison was killed by Indians in what eventually became New York. The historical significance of these trials exhibit the interest in curtailing religious dissent and the control of women in the Massachusetts Bay Colony (Knappman, 1991; Dailey, 1989).

Judith Catchpole was an indentured servant. She arrived in Maryland in January 1656. Eight months after her arrival, she stood trial for infanticide and witchcraft. Her accuser, William Bramhall, himself an indentured servant, had arrived in Maryland with Ms. Catchpole. He had made allegations that she had given birth and subsequently murdered the child. He also accused her of several acts of witchcraft. Before the trial began, Mr. Bramhall died. Interestingly, an all-woman jury was selected. After hearing the testimony of this case, the female jurors took it upon themselves to examine Ms. Catchpole, after which they testified, under oath, that Ms. Catchpole had never been pregnant. The jurors discarded the witchcraft charges outright, and found her not guilty of infanticide. This case presents an interesting paradox. On one hand, we see women subjected to judicial process without any substantiated evidence. Second, the pragmatic response of the court to use women jurors for expert evaluation (Knappman, 1991; Semmes, 1970).

During the summer of 1659, upon visiting two imprisoned Quakers in Boston, Mary Dyer found herself imprisoned and charged with the offense of Quakerism. She was found guilty, and sentenced to banishment. Several months later, Mary Dyer returned to Boston. Perhaps Mary Dyer's fate had been sealed nearly 22 years previous when she stepped forward and clutched Ann Hutchison's hand after the latter had been excommunicated and banished. Nevertheless, for her act of defiance against judicial authority, Mary Dyer was sentenced to death, and was hanged on June 1, 1659. In 1959, the Massachusetts General Court authorized the construction of a seven-foot statue of Mary Dyer. The inscription reads, "Witness for Religious Freedom." Today this monument rests on the lawn of the Boston State House (McHenry, 1983; Tolles, 1971). The Puritans, who left England to avoid religious persecution, became religious persecutors, and the judicial process gave that persecution legitimacy.

In 1692, 200 people were brought to trial in Salem, Massachusetts. Their charge was witchcraft. Charges of witchcraft were not alien to the colonies; witchcraft was a crime in England and was an offense in the colonies. This case is significant in the history of American jurisprudence for several reasons. First, it demonstrates the courts willingness to support religious persecution and to wage war against women. Second, it demonstrate that Massachusetts Bay Colony was willing to engage in witch-hunts very much like Europeans had done for centuries, but with less frequency. But most of all it reflected the court's willingness to respond to times of anxiety and social unrest—the same causes of witch persecutions in Europe—through violence. In 1684, the Massachusetts Bay Colony had lost its charter, and became a component of the New England Dominion. Political autonomy and the titles to land were threatened.

During the 1691 to 1692 winter, Betty, the daughter of Reverend Samuel Parris, and her 11-year-old cousin were being entertained by a Caribbean slave girl named Tituba. Other girls were invited, and their ages ranged from 12 to 20. The girls began exhibiting strange behavior. Tituba, falling to the floor and experiencing convulsions, began barking like a dog. Thereafter, the other girls began acting strangely. The entire community was horror stricken. After a thorough investigation, the girls named the slave girl, Sarah Good who was a near derelict, and Sarah Osburn. On February 29, 1692 the three were arrested. Several months later, May, the jails of Salem were packed with people accused of witchcraft. The trials were conducted from June through September, 1692. Some of the evidence allowed in the trials included visions seen by the townspeople. Twenty-nine people were convicted. Nineteen people were hanged, and the remaining convicted persons were released over a period of years. The significance of these trials champions the notion that women were obviously persecuted, and that in times of social peril, looking for scapegoats proved an adequate distraction. It was the court, in its entire legal splendor, that legitimated the persecution and scapegoating (Knappman, 1991; Friedman, 1993; Starkey, 1949). And the persecutions and scapegoating did not cease as the colonies entered the 18th century.

After the Revolution: The Federal System and the Supreme Court

After the American Revolution a federal court system emerged, complete with various appellate courts and of course the United States Supreme Court. This was an important development in the history of criminal justice. Following the American Revolution there was quite a debate between those who believed that there should be a federal court system and those who did not. This debate was actually part of the much larger debate concerning whether or not there should be a strong central government to begin with. Thus, the anti-Federalists versus the Federalists. In time the Federalists won out, although with some compromises, such as establishing district courts (via the Judiciary Act of 1789 and the Reorganization Act of 1801) that were empowered to enforce federal laws, but structured along state lines where judges had to be residents of that state. Various state courts were soon established by state legislative bodies (Neubauer, 2005: 41–42).

Of major importance was the creation of the highest court of the country, the Supreme Court, established in 1789 with the passage of the Judiciary Act. If there was ever an instance where evidence of the upper-class bias of the legal system was the clearest, the composition of the United States Supreme Court is just such an instance. It was created by a special Senate committee, headed by Oliver Ellsworth (who wrote the bill), who later became the third Chief Justice (Schwartz, 1993: 14). Throughout the history of the Supreme Court, its members have been drawn overwhelmingly from the upper crust of society. This was especially the case in the 19th century, as almost all came from the landed gentry and were schooled in the most prestigious, mostly Ivy League universities (Schmidhauser, 1960). The very first court, 1790 to1801, reflects this class bias, as did the second court, the Marshall Court, 1801 to 1836 (one of the most influential in the early years). Those selected for the first Supreme Court were: William Cushing (a Harvard graduate, ranked third in his class, Chief Justice of the Massachusetts highest court), John Jay (one of the founding fathers, member of the Continental Congress, the first Secretary of State; he was appointed by George Washington as the first Chief Justice), John Rutledge of South Carolina (a large slaveholder, a founding father who was one of the signers of the U.S. Constitution), James Wilson of Pennsylvania (another founding father, born in Scotland and attended the University of Edinburg, taught the classics at the College of Philadelphia, member of the Continental Congress), James Iredell of North Carolina (served as state judge and the attorney general), and John Blair of Virginia (a judge on the Virginia Supreme Court of Appeals). Subsequent appointments to this first court (because of resignations of Jay and Rutledge) included Samuel Chase (a founding father who served in the Continental Congress and was Chief Judge of the Maryland General Court, and was one of the signers of the Declaration of Independence) (Schwartz, 1993: 17; Wilson, 1974).

The 1801 to 1836 court was headed by none other than John Marshall. Marshall, of Virginia, was one of the founding fathers, and was a member of the

Virginia Ratification Committee, who eventually served as the U.S. Commissioner to France, the U.S. Congress, and Secretary of State. Marshall's biggest case was, of course, the famous *Marbury v. Madison* in 1803, which established the Supreme Court's power to review the constitutionality of cases (Schwartz, 1993: 39–41).

The Supreme Court has been a consistent supporter of the concept of private property. And it is not unusual that the very first case it heard involved property. In the case of *Chisholm v. Georgia*, argued in 1793, the Court considered a suit concerning the claim for the delivery of goods. The issue was whether or not a state could be sued in federal court by a citizen of another state (the Court ruled that a state could in fact be sued) (Schwartz, 1993: 20–21). While a complete review of Supreme Court decisions is beyond the scope of the present chapter, suffice it to say that in time, in the words of Howard Zinn, the Court "was doing its bit for the ruling elite" (Zinn, 1995: 254). Continuing, Zinn argues,

> How could it be independent, with its members chosen by the President and ratified by the Senate? How could it be neutral between rich and poor when its members were often former wealthy lawyers, and almost always came from the upper class? Early in the nineteenth century the Court laid the legal basis for a nationally regulated economy by establishing federal control over interstate commerce, and the legal basis for corporate capitalism by making the contract sacred (1995: 254).

A simple review of some key Supreme Court decisions in the 19th century will demonstrate Zinn's point. Two cases typify the court's bias. One is the now infamous separate but equal cases of *Plessy v. Ferguson*, was noted already in chapter 1. The obvious racist nature of this decision needs no elaboration. The other is the court's handling of cases falling under the *Sherman Anti-Trust Act* passed by the Senate in 1890, following years of agitation and protests. It came about during the infamous Gilded Age, described by Friedman as "the factory age, the age of money, the age of the robber barons, of capitol and labor at war" (Friedman, 1973: 296). It began soon after the close of the Civil War. It marked, in a sense, the triumph of capitalism. What followed was an era that witnessed the amassing of great wealth, mostly off the backs of immigrant workers, many very young. The result was the concentration of wealth in the hands of a small, very ruthless minority of capitalists, appropriately called the robber barons.[3] There was such a public outcry at the ruthlessness of these capitalists that the U.S. Senate had to do something. That something was the Sherman Act, which was theoretically supposed to make illegal the crux of the problem: monopolistic practices (often referred to as the trusts) and restraint of trade.

Unfortunately—and typically—this act did little to alleviate the problem. The wording was so vague as to be almost meaningless—it never defined *monopoly* or *restraint of trade*, which was what it was supposed to regulate! Further, the act failed to set up an enforcement mechanism—no separate administrative agency was established. Mostly it was smoke and mirrors, mere public relations. What is really important to realize here is that this law was ultimately most often used against labor unions and especially as a strike-breaking tool (Friedman, 1993: 118). The result is nicely summarized by Zinn as follows:

> In 1895 the [Supreme] Court interpreted the Sherman Act so as to make it harmless. It said a monopoly of sugar refining was a monopoly in manufacturing, not commerce, and so could not be regulated by Congress through the Sherman Act (*U.S. v. E. C. Knight Co.*). The Court also said the Sherman Act could be used against interstate strikes (the railway strike of 1894) because they were in restraint of trade. It also declared unconstitutional a small attempt by Congress to tax high incomes at a higher rate (*Pollock v. Farmers' Loan & Trust Company*). In later years it would refuse to break up the Standard Oil and American Tobacco monopolies, saying that the Sherman Act barred only "unreasonable" combinations in restraint of trade (1995: 260).

Zinn goes on to quote a New York banker who gave a toast to the Supreme Court for ruling in the interests of those in power and who were the important people, saying that the Court was the "guardian of the dollar, defender of private property, enemy of spoliation, sheet anchor of the Republic" (1995: 260). Yes, indeed, private property was indeed defended against the unreasonable restraints placed against the rulers by those merely trying to earn a decent wage. But, after all, it was what judges wanted, what big business wanted, and it was (and still is) their views and interests that are important!

The Supreme Court continued to make these kinds of interpretations of the law so as to favor, more often than not, those with power. Take the Fourteenth Amendment, which declared that no person shall be deprived of property, "nor shall any State deprive any person of life, liberty, or property without due process of law." Eventually the Court began to interpret this amendment not as a protection for blacks, but as a protection for corporations, ruling on many occasions that a corporation was a person. This they did in convincing fashion in the case of *Wabash Railway v. Illinois* (1886) in which the Court ruled that states could not regulate commerce, only the federal government could (Friedman, 1993: 394; Zinn, 1995: 255). Between 1890 and 1910, of all the Fourteenth Amendment cases brought before the Supreme Court, 288 dealt with corporations and a mere 19 dealt with black citizens (Zinn, 1995: 255). One critic has noted that: "This alteration to the business world was designed to do two things, encourage involvement of the working and middle class and relieve some of the financial strain from the business owner. With the humans removed from the corporation a transformation occurred, corporations shifted from being public servants to seeking profits for imaginary stockholders" (Emerson, 2006).[4] During the first four decades of the 20th century the Supreme Court invalidated more than 200 economic regulations (Emerson, 2006, citing Kelly, 2001: 53). One Supreme Court Justice, Samuel Miller, said in 1875 that it was useless to "contend with judges who have been at the bar the advocates for forty years of railroad companies . . . " A statement by Supreme Court Justice David J. Brewer in 1893 summarizes the dominant view of how the law reflects the will of the rich and powerful. He stated quite matter-of-factly that:

> It is the unvarying law that the wealth of the community will be in the hands of the few . . . The great majority of men are unwilling to endure that long self-denial and saving which makes accumulation possible . . . and hence it always has been, and until human

nature is remodeled always will be true, that the wealth of a nation is in the hands of a few, while the many subsist upon the proceeds of their daily toll (Zinn, 1995: 255).

How can one in any way conclude that the courts could ever be dispensers of equal justice, given these attitudes and the distribution of wealth and power?

Post-Civil War Changes in the Court System

The biggest changes in the American court system came after the Civil War, largely because of the huge growth in population, especially the emergence of large cities. The old agrarian court system of small-town American could no longer handle the changes. New courts emerged, including small claims courts, so-called lower courts (often called municipal courts or justice of the peace courts, which handle misdemeanors, including traffic citations) and felony courts (often called superior courts, district courts and the like) and juvenile courts (begun in 1899). Just to give the reader an idea of this growth, in Chicago alone by the early 1930s there were over 500 separate courts (Neubauer, 2005).

Along with the general growth in the court system came the emergence of the grand jury. The grand jury originated in the 12th century as a result of a struggle between Henry II and the church. Henry wanted to remove the jurisdiction of the church in cases in which members were charged with a crime (and received the benefit of clergy). The church was generally more lenient and gained money through the collection of fines. The grand jury consisted of a panel of 16 men created by the king to investigate and bring charges against people who were suspected of law violations. The king created a citizens police force to gain control over the prosecution of criminal cases. In time, an accusation by a grand jury became equivalent to a guilty verdict, since the king had so much control over it (Clark, 1975: 9).

By the 17th century two changes in criminal justice had altered the role of the grand jury. First, petit juries (trial juries) began to replace trial by ordeal (e.g., placing an accused's hand in boiling water). Second Parliament emerged and its taxing power replaced the grand jury's function of levying fines. However, during the 17th century the grand jury continued to be used as a means of political control and repression, such as when Charles II used it to attempt a Catholic control of the Protestants by seeking indictments against the Duke of York (Clark, 1975: 9–10).

The first grand jury in America was instituted in Massachusetts in 1635. By 1683 all the colonies had them. During the colonial period grand juries initiated investigations frequently since there were no police forces and no office of public prosecutor as we know them today. Grand juries, moreover, were quite independent at this time.

After the American Revolution the grand jury was included in many state constitutions and was included in the Fifth Amendment ("No person shall be held to answer for a capital or otherwise infamous crime, unless on a presentment or indictment of a Grand Jury . . . "). The purpose of a grand jury was to have a body that would shield the citizen against abuse by the state. In reality, however, it tended to be more protective of the privileged and powerful than the average citizen. For instance, when the Federalists were in power (e.g., John Adams) the grand jury was used to indict the Republicans (or anti-Federalists), especially for charges of treason under the sedition laws. However, even the Republicans, when they came to power, used the grand jury against their political enemies (e.g., Thomas Jefferson's indicting Aaron Burr) (Clark, 1975: 20–21).

The prosecutor has had a unique role within the court system, often viewed as the gatekeeper of the system in that he or she is in charge of screening cases and deciding whether or not to prosecute. Historically, the domain of the prosecutor (i.e., the functions, roles, duties, jurisdiction of the prosecutor) has changed drastically. In colonial times the victim had a much larger role. Usually, the victim hired a private prosecutor (usually a privately retained lawyer) for the case, judges and juries played a more influential role. Trials were the order of the day, and these were of a very swift duration, after which the convicted offender was "hanged, banished, lashed, or given in servitude to the victim until he made good his debt" (McDonald, 1979: 22). At this time, of course, there were no prisons as such, no hilly authorized police force (as we saw in an earlier chapter), and no public prosecutor. In other words, the *state* had not as yet stepped in to dominate the criminal justice process. In a small, relatively homogeneous and agriculturally based society, there was little need for a centralized state apparatus. All of this was to change during the 19th century with the coming of the Industrial Revolution.

In the 19th century the entire criminal justice system underwent some noteworthy changes. By the end of the 18th century, shortly after the American Revolution, the states began to enact legislation creating public prosecutors and state prisons. The result was that the "domain of the victim of crime in the criminal justice system was greatly reduced. He no longer played a correctional role; and his role in the investigation and apprehension of criminals was minimized" (McDonald, 1979: 24).

We have already seen how the police emerged as a distinct occupation in the 19th century. The use of the grand jury began to diminish as the states, in their constitutions, "either did not provide for a grand jury system or provided for one but also allowed for the option of proceeding by way of information filed by the prosecutor" (McDonald, 1979: 24). The prosecutor's domain expanded considerably. The victim of a crime was beginning to be largely ignored, while the criminal justice process was placed into the hands of experts, a group of trained professionals who ostensibly would have the knowledge and motivation to serve the public. Also in the 19th century there was an increase in the police's authority in the charging decision. In fact, until the present century, the police had almost total control of this crucial decision. Today, however, the functions of the police, the prosecutor, judges, and juries, as well as the penal system, are fairly distinct.

An overview of the history of the courts would not be complete without some reference to an important component of the criminal justice system, which is critically related to the courts. This component is the jail. The jail is important—and should be discussed in connection to the courts—for at least two reasons. First, it is usually the second stage of the criminal justice process following an arrest. Throughout history, the jail has been used primarily as a place of temporary detention prior to a defendant's first appearance in court. Second, the length of time a defendant spends in jail is strongly related to the final disposition by the court. Indeed, in the majority of cases the real reason people are held in jail awaiting trial is that they simply cannot afford to post the bond, not because they are dangerous or are likely to commit further crimes. Numerous studies, covering more than 40 years, have consistently demonstrated two major points: (1) whether or not one is released from jail pending the final disposition of the case is strongly dependent upon both the class and race of the defendant—minorities and the poor are far more likely to remain in jail and (2) comparisons of those who remain in jail and those released show that those released fare much better in terms of the likelihood of being convicted and if convicted the likelihood of being sentenced to a term of imprisonment. These studies are too numerous to summarize in their entirety here.[5]

The Jail: Managing the Rabble

In his study of the modern jail, John Irwin argues that one of the main functions of this institution has been to manage the rabble or the underclass—two terms that can be used synonymously with dangerous classes (Irwin, 1985). A common procedure for releasing a defendant pending his or her court appearance is that of bail, which is a form of security that a defendant puts forth, which guarantees that he or she will appear in court whenever requested. In most jurisdictions a defendant can, in effect, buy his or her freedom. In most jurisdictions bail is set on misdemeanor charges by a police official, usually a desk sergeant at the station house where the defendant was booked. For felonies, bail is typically set by a judge in a courthouse during the initial appearance (Neubauer, 2005: 177).

According to the Fifth Amendment to the U.S. Constitution, no person can be held, "nor deprived of life, liberty or property, without due process of law." Also, according to legal principles, one is presumed innocent until proven guilty beyond a reasonable doubt, and there can be no punishment without conviction, nor can one be detained for the purposes of punishment. The reality of criminal justice is often just the opposite. On any given day, thousands of people are held in jail awaiting court appearances (sometimes for several months). They have not been proven guilty; they are there simply because they cannot afford bail.

This is nothing new, as any cursory review of the history of jails, both in America and elsewhere, will show. The modern jail actually originated in England with the Norman Conquest in the 11th century. Under Henry II the jail (or to be more precise, the English term *goal*) began to take on characteristics and functions known today. Henry II sought to establish at least one jail in each county, under the control of a local sheriff. By the 13th century all but five counties had a jail. It should be noted that the county sheriff was a royal appointment, "a functionary who upheld his master's interests against local powers" (McConville, 1998: 268).

It is obvious that from the very beginning jails were almost exclusively used to house the poor. In fact, a term often used interchangeable with jail was that of debtor's prison. McConville notes that it was ironic that, on the one hand the financing of local jails depended upon user fees paid to jailers, yet on the other hand, the majority of jail inmates "were drawn chiefly from the poor and powerless classes" (McConville, 1998: 269). One 18th-century reformer noted that such fees were extracted "from misery" (1998: 269). Not surprisingly, corruption was rampant during this entire period, yet little was done to correct the problem. This was probably because, then as now, much profit was to be made from the existence of crime. The jails of London functioned as "brothels, taps, criminal clubs, and asylums for thieves, robbers, and fraudsmen, and when their raw material—prisoners—threatened to run out, minions would bring false charges to replenish the supply" (McConville, 1998: 270). Also not surprisingly, the well being of the prisoners was virtually ignored. As a result of their poverty, many either starved to death or died from some disease.

By the middle of the fourteenth century London jails became used as a method to extract payment from those in debt—hence the term *debtor's prison*. Even though most who ended up in jail because of this could not pay their debts—since the means to do so were taken away by the mere fact of being in jail—the actual function of the jail in this case was more as a threat than anything else. Some debtors selected to remain in jail until their death, since this would thereby cancel their debt and save their families from being charged (McConville, 1998: 271–272).

Even though technically the jail of people because of their debts ceased to exist by the nineteenth century, nevertheless many still went to jail on the charge of contempt of court, which essentially served the same purpose as before and still does today—usually for failure to pay a fine.

Jails in the American colonies served similar functions, but in time became temporary holding facilities for those awaiting court appearances or those serving short sentences. The use of bail dates back to early English society (at least as early as 1000 A.D.) and was originally established to insure that an accused appeared for trial (Goldfarb, 1965, 1975). This practice goes back to the practice of mutual responsibilities of the collective; more specifically, groups of ten families (under the control of the tithingman (see chapter 2) to insure obedience to the law. The families in effect pledged to ensure the defendant appear in court. Crime prevention in those early years was a collective responsibility, which was very practical in small, agrarian communities. Such a concept no longer applies in modern societies, characterized by much mobility and anonymity. Bail has thus come to stand for a different sort of pledge—a monetary or property form of pledge, often through the defendant's family, relatives or friends. The problem today is, of course, the fact that most accused people come from the poorest sectors of society (McConville, 1998: 279).[6]

Jails historically served still another function. For years, starting at least as far back as the mid-14th century, jails were almost synonymous with what were then called workhouses or poorhouses (see chapter 4 for a more detailed discussion of these institutions). More specifically, this function of the jail can be traced directly to the Ordinance of Labourers (or Statutes of Labourers) passed in England in 1349, brought about in part because of the Black Death (see chapter 2 and the discussion of the Law of Vagrancy) which forced the vagabond and other undesireables to accept work at the prevailing wage or go to the workhouse. The Elizabethan Poor Law of 1572 further contributed to this development. This law distinguished between the common criminal and the unworthy poor. Hard labor (which evolved into the infamous rock pile, the chain gang and similar punishments of our modern era) became a standard form of punishment for those not even convicted of a crime, but only because of their poverty. In time it became difficult to distinguish between the pauper (the common term for a person living in poverty) and the vagabond (those who wandered about the country without working). Eventually, in the United States, these two terms were replaced by *welfare dependent* and *petty persistent offender* and in time even the mentally ill (McConville, 1998: 282–284).

A recent case reported in the *New York Times* illustrates the charge that the modern jail functions like a poorhouse and that bail is a form of ransom. The case involves a Hispanic man charged with "sexually assaulting a quadriplegic man for whom he worked as a home health aid." (Finder, 1999: 33–34). He was unable to raise the $5,000 for his bail. Consequently he spent 19 months in jail awaiting his trial, since he refused to plead guilty. He was finally found not guilty. Ironically he spent more time in jail awaiting this decision than he would have spent had he pled guilty to a lesser charge. After some careful investigation (by a member of the public defender's office who was finally able to find time to conduct an investigation because his case load was so high) it was discovered that the alleged victim had made similar complaints to the home care agency that hires helpers to take care of people, like the victim, who need constant care (Finder, 1999: 33–34).

This brief history of the jail illustrates very clearly the theme of this book. Jails have been used mostly to, in Irwin's term, manage the *rabble*—another term for the dangerous classes. And, by logical extension, the criminal courts (especially the so-called lower courts) have served the same purpose.

The 1960s: The Warren Court and the Reaffirmation of the Right to Counsel

A history of the American court system would not be complete without a review of the significant events of the 1960s, during what became known as the Warren Court, named after the Chief Supreme Court Justice, Earl Warren. This was a period marked by tremendous upheavals and social movements: civil rights, women's liberation, antiwar, and others. Many began to take a close look at issues that had long been smoldering under the surface, issues related to the core of American democracy. The criminal justice system, not surprisingly, stood squarely in the center of the debate. Several significant Supreme Court decisions were made during this time. The first had to do with the Sixth Amendment guarantee of the right to counsel, among other rights.

In a 1932 decision the U.S. Supreme Court ruled that defendants had a right to counsel in cases in which the death penalty might be imposed (*Powell v. Alabama*, 1932). This case left unanswered the problem of providing counsel in cases in which the defendant was too poor to afford a lawyer in noncapital cases. This was partially answered in *Betts v. Brady* (1942) where the Supreme Court ruled that there was no such guarantee in state courts unless the defendant could show that to be deprived of counsel would result in a denial of due process. This decision was overturned in a landmark decision in *Gideon v. Wainwright* (1963) where the

Court ruled that a defendant accused of a felony even in a noncapital ease should be provided counsel.

In *Gideon* the Supreme Court was faced with an ideological challenge to the myth of equal justice for all. It was shown that Clarence Earl Gideon, who had asked for counsel but was denied, had to act as his own lawyer and that he was no match against an experienced prosecutor. It was found that any lawyer would have been able to prove that Gideon was innocent (as a subsequent trial was to show). It was a clear case of the fact that being poor (which Gideon was) led to a denial of due process. (For a fuller treatment of this case, see Lewis, 1964.) The Supreme Court stated the obvious:

> Reason and reflection require us to recognize that in our adversary system of criminal justice, any person hauled into court who is too poor to hire a lawyer, cannot be assured a fair trial unless counsel is provided for him. This seems to us an obvious truth, Governments, both state and federal, quite properly spend vast sums of money to try defendants accused of crime. Lawyers to prosecute are everywhere deemed essential to protect the public's interest in an orderly society. Similarly, there are a few defendants charged with a crime, few indeed who fail to hire the best lawyer they can get to prepare and present their defense. That government hires lawyers to prosecute and defendants who have the money hire lawyers to defend are the strongest indications of a widespread belief that lawyers in criminal courts are necessities, not luxuries. . . . From the very beginning, our state and national constitutions and laws have laid great emphasis on procedural and substantive safeguards designed to assure fair trials before impartial tribunals in which every defendant stands equal before the law. This noble ideal cannot be realized if the poor man charged with crime has to face his accusers without a lawyer to assist him.

Several years later (1972) the Supreme Court ruled that indigents accused of misdemeanors must also be provided with counsel in cases that can lead to imprisonment (*Argersinger v. Hamlin*, 1972). The right to counsel was eventually extended to various critical stages of the criminal justice process, starting with custodial interrogation (*Miranda v. Arizona*, 1963) continuing through subsequent hearings, such as the preliminary hearing (*Coleman v. Alabama*, 1970) and police lineups (*United States v. Wade*, 1972).

In theory, all defendants, rich and poor alike, have a guarantee of counsel. But the real issue is the quality of counsel and the question of whether or not justice is being served. Can the average defendant receive the best counsel, given the bureaucratic nature of the court system? Can every defendant get the kind of counsel that O.J. Simpson had? Obviously not, given the degree of inequality existing in our society. Do public defenders and other lawyers for the poor provide the same kind of defense that a rich man would receive from a retained lawyer, as was the case for Simpson? Given the fact that the majority of those in prison come from poor backgrounds, had public defenders, and had to await their trial in jail, the answer to these questions has to be "no."

Soon after the Gideon decision both state and federal courts began making some policy changes concerning the effectiveness of counsel issue, one of which included the adoption of what became known as the mockery of justice standard. This standard means that "only circumstances so shocking that they reduce the trial to a farce satisfied defendants' claim of ineffective counsel" (Samaha, 1999: 541–542). However, critics immediately charged that this was too vague, subjective and narrow to be of any practical use. Under this guideline even defense lawyers "who appeared in court drunk did not violate this standard" (Samaha, 1999: 541–542). The courts have even failed to fine ineffectiveness when the defense counsel used heroin and cocaine during the trial, even when the counsel stated that he was not prepared, when an attorney on a capital punishment case could not name a single Supreme Court decision concerning the death penalty, and even when the attorney was suffering from Alzheimer's disease! (Cole, 1999: 78–79).

Most jurisdictions eventually abandoned this guideline and adopted the reasonably competent attorney standard. This was not much of an improvement, as it states that a lawyers' performance would be measured against the "customary skills and diligence that a reasonably competent attorney would perform under similar circumstances" (Samaha, 1999: 542). The Supreme Court attempted further clarification in *Strictland v. Washington* (1984), but without much success at operationalizing effective counsel.

There are still serious gaps in the right to counsel. The Supreme Court has ruled that this right applies to all critical stages in the criminal justice process. But critical stages only include those that occur after formal charges have been filed. Critical stages do not include the investigative stop, the actual arrest, a search following an arrest, and even custodial interrogation. This is because the Sixth Amendment guarantees the right to counsel in all criminal prosecutions—in other words after the defendant has been formally charged by the prosecutor (Samaha, 1999: 354–355). The trumpet of Gideon (to use the title of Anthony Lewis' book) has been muted considerably over the years (Cole, 1999: Chapter 2).

Even though defense counsel is a right at each of these critical stages of the criminal justice process, most defendants do not have attorneys to call upon immediately following arrest (probably the case for the majority of defendants). What happens in the majority of cases is that counsel is assigned by the court (or the case assigned to the public defender's office) during the initial court appearance (Benner, Neary, and Gutman, 1973: 24; Neubauer, 2005). It is important to note that the average defendant is allowed just one lawyer rather than an entire team as is the case during celebrity cases like O.J. Simpson (not to mention the dozens of investigators, expert witnesses, and so on).

Under the assigned counsel system a court appoints a specific attorney to handle a case. This is common throughout America, especially in large urban courts where about three out of every four defendants are indigent and therefore too poor to hire their own attorney (Wice, 1985); in some areas the percentage is even higher, such as in Seattle where the proportion of felony defendants who were indigent in a recent year was 88% and in Monterey, California 92% of felony defendants were indigent (Hanson and Chapper, 1991).

The judge usually has a list of lawyers in private practice in a particular county or a list of those who have volunteered to serve as counsel for indigents. Unfortunately, these lawyers are typically young and inexperienced and take the cases because they need the money or the experience or both. And the money won't make them rich, as their hourly fees generally range from $25 to $40. This system is similar to managed care in the health system, where in cases of psychotherapy, therapists are hired by insurance companies to see eight to ten clients each day for a much lower rate. Not surprisingly, the care received by clients in each case suffers. Here is another instance of money talks. Thus, justice is itself a commodity and fits in nicely within the overall capitalist framework of commodity production (Lynch and Michalowski, 2006).

A more recent system that has emerged is the contract system, used in a few, but growing number of counties. As implied by the term *contract*, local governments sign contracts with local attorneys to handle indigent cases. This represents a sort of privatization of due process, as one study concluded (Worden, 1991, 1993). It is a process where a system of competitive bidding is often done, with the result being that the lowest bidder, and not necessarily the best bidder, often wins the contract. Typical capitalist mentality operating here! It should come as no surprise that several states have filed suits and in one case the practice was ruled unconstitutional (*Smith v. State*, 1984).

It is apparent that providing attorneys for indigent defendants is not a high priority. To begin with, among the three major components of the criminal justice system, the least amount of annual expenditures goes to the general category of judicial and legal. In 1993, this segment received around $21 billion, compared to $44 billion for police, and just under $32 billion for corrections (Maguire and Pastore, 1997: 3). Expenditures on counsel for the indigent represent a very small percentage of this total. According to most recent data (1986) only about $1 billion went toward public defenders offices. This represented an increase from only $200 million in 1976, ironically prompting some critics to complain about the rising costs (Neubauer, 2005:113). A study in Virginia found that, after accounting for overhead costs, the hourly rate for court-appointed attorneys came to $13; in Kentucky this rate comes to around $8.50 per hour; in Alabama there is a statutory limit of $1,000 for all felonies and only $2,000 for capital crimes, while in Kentucky and Tennessee there is a $1,000 minimum for all noncapital felony cases; in Mississippi it is $1,000 per case, which amounts to just over $2 per hour (Cole, 1999: 83–84). In short, poor people get attorneys working for poverty wages.

The retained counsel system is generally far superior, especially if a defendant can afford the fees. The main reason for this is that with enough money, private attorneys can hire investigators and spend more time collecting evidence, finding witnesses, and taking other measures to insure an adequate defense. This is particularly true if the attorney works for a law firm and the defendant is out on bail to assist in his or her own defense.

The American court system was put to some rather severe tests during the late 1960s and early 1970s during what have been called radical-criminal trials. This marked an important segment of the history of criminal justice. The following section briefly explores this topic.

Traditional vs. Radical-Criminal Trials

The Traditional Criminal Trial

In the more traditional trial of a criminal case there are a number of roles, each with its own behavior expectations. We can conceive of the trial as analogous to a theater production. The major roles are those of judge, prosecutor, defense attorney, bailiff, marshal, defendant, member of the jury, spectator, and member of the press.

The judge's role is that of a neutral arbitrator, the defense attorney's role is that of one speaking out on behalf of the client, the prosecutor represents the people or the state (which is supposed to be synonymous), and the defendant is supposed to be passive and is not expected to want (or have the ability) to defend himself or herself. The spectator is supposed to be passive, sit quietly, and observe (as do all others) proper courtroom demeanor.

The judge is perhaps the most interesting actor and the most symbolic. He or she sits high above all the action, with the American flag on one side and the state flag on the other side. The judge dresses in a black robe and is addressed as "your honor." All are supposed to rise when the judge walks in. The traditional symbol of justice, a woman with blindfolds, is prominently displayed either inside the courtroom or near the main entrance outside the building.

Adherence to these symbols and the formalities and power relations within the courtroom processes themselves serve to legitimize (if not to mystify) the existing judicial system and the law. The judge, the court, and the law often become synonymous with or symbolic of god and country. Failure to adhere to these symbols can result in a contempt of court citation and/or removal from the courtroom.

Until the late 1960s and early 1970s the social, political, and/or economic context within which justice was meted out rarely entered into the courts (notable exceptions include the trials of the International Workers of the World and Sacco and Vanzetti during the early part of this century; Zinn, 1995: 367). Usually the issues focused on the narrow concerns of individual criminal acts and the guilt or innocence of individuals. This, of course, has corresponded with the traditional legal notions of mens rea (individual guilt) begun around the 11th century in England (see chapter 1). During the late 1960s and early 1970s several radical-criminal trials questioned the legitimacy of the judicial system.

Challenging the System: Radical-Criminal Trials

During the late 1960s and early 1970s several trials sent shock waves through the legal establishment. The defendants in these radical-criminal trials, or political trials, already held in contempt society's traditional economic and political institutions and desired to create very fundamental changes. Eventually, as Sternberg notes, "It dawned upon these defendants that far from being 'agents' of the other institutions of power, the courts themselves were another creator and center of the very status quo they were determined to change" (Sternberg, 1974: 279). These defendants viewed the criminal courts as agents of powerful interests or, more specifically, as representatives of a ruling class and constituting an oppressive institution. Many defendants sought to raise what they believed to be important moral and political issues "in an effort to generate jury sympathy for the defendants and the cause they represented" (Barkan, 1977: 324).

Indeed, many did not attempt to deny that they had committed the alleged criminal act. What they often did was deny that the act was, or should be, in itself criminal. Thus, to them real guilt or innocence was not the issue. A defendant in the 1969 Milwaukee Twelve draft-card burning case said: "I'm not saying the jury should find us innocent. I'm simply hoping that the court will allow us to demonstrate the reasonableness of our belief and to (let the jurors) decide for themselves whether, in fact, it was reasonable" (Barkan, 1977: 324).

Phillip Berrigan, one of the Baltimore Four accused of draft-card burning and sentenced in April 1968, tried, in his remarks to the court, to place this conviction in a larger perspective. He wrote:

> But whatever work is useful to describe our nation's plight, we ask today in this court: What is lawful about a foreign policy which allows economic control of whole continents, which tells the Third World, as it tells our black people, "You'll make it sometime, but only under our system, at the pace we decide, by dole, by handout, by seamy charity, by delayed justice. Don't try it any other way!" What is lawful about peace under a nuclear blanket, the possible penetration of which impels our leaders to warn us of one hundred million American casualties? . . . What is lawful about the rich becoming richer, and the poor poorer, in this country or abroad?. . . . [T]hese are not times for building justice; these are times for confronting injustice. This, we feel, is the number-one item of national business—to confront the entrenched, massive, and complex injustice of our country. And to confront it justly, nonviolently, and with maximum exposure of oneself and one's future (Berrigan, 1970: 11–12).

For Berrigan, then, the burning of draft cards was an act of civil disobedience, and the fact that it was unlawful was irrelevant. What was relevant was the war in Vietnam, racism abroad and at home, the discrepancy between the rich and the poor. However, the court, ostensibly being above politics, could decide only the issue of guilt or innocence and as a result sentenced the Baltimore Four to prison.

In some cases the defendants sought to show the jury that the federal government itself was involved, in the sense that FBI agents (agent provocateurs) were responsible for the alleged crimes or in some cases even set up the defendants. This was especially true in the Gainesville Eight trial against the Vietnam Veterans against the War. The government charged them with conspiring to disrupt the Republican National Convention in 1972. However, the government itself ended up on trial. In this case, as Fred Cook states, "The government, in effect, was found guilty" (Cook, 1974: 75).

In some radical-criminal trials the tactics used by the defendants challenged the authority of the court and court officials, to the utter disbelief of the latter. The large number of contempt citations, the gagging and shackling of Black Panther Bobby Seale during the Chicago Seven trial, and other forms of punishment demonstrate "the depth and breadth of a culture shock experienced by officers of the criminal court" (Sternberg, 1974: 280). The Chicago Seven trial perhaps best illustrates these points and exposes the often farcical nature of court proceedings. The defendants used several tactics to challenge the legitimacy of the court:

- Direct and verbal attacks on judges and other officials or on the judicial process itself. The defendants often insisted that they be allowed to speak for themselves.
- Ignoring the proceedings, such as by refusing to stand when the judge entered the courtroom or reading books or magazines during the proceedings.
- Mocking legal procedures, such as when Jerry Rubin appeared in a black robe, or unresponsive answers were given to what court officials thought were straightforward questions, such as when Abbie Hoffman gave "Woodstock Nation" as his address.
- Refusing to limit interactions to traditional actors inside the courtroom. The defendants in the Chicago Seven trial often argued with prosecution staff in the hallways, and many gave speeches attacking the proceedings and gave them to large audiences, often in front of the courthouse.
- Attempts to restructure and even reverse traditional roles, as when Bobby Seale charged the judge with "contempt of the American people."
- Defendants planning and standing together in solidarity in their challenges to the court (with shouts of "Right On!").

Defendants in radical-criminal trials often helped their lawyers with defense strategy and discussed moral and political issues while on the witness stand (often bringing charges of immaterial and irrelevant from prosecutors and judges, who would warn them to stick to the issues). Many defendants chose to represent themselves because of certain restrictions placed on lawyers. A lawyer, having been socialized into courtroom procedures, typically seeks a purely legal remedy (e.g., acquittal, shortened sentences), which often involves compromises and accommodations. A lawyer who behaves otherwise is likely to be disbarred. Defendants in the White House Seven trial (1973), charged with praying for peace on the White House lawn, stated:

> We could not bring ourselves to be represented by counsel, feeling that to do so would be participating in a kind of cat-and-mouse game with the government. We felt that rather than seeking to support our legal innocence in court, it was our simple duty to speak the truth of how we were led to that place (Barkan, 1977: 328).

Defendants who act as their own lawyers are often given some latitude by judges because such defendants are considered ignorant of "traditional rules of evidence and proper courtroom procedure" (Barkan, 1977: 329). However, defendants' ignorance of proper courtroom procedures can be turned to their own advantage, enabling them "to inject political or moral issues into the proceedings" (1977: 329–330).

The role of spectator underwent rather drastic changes and, in fact, changed from one of mere spectator to one of active participant in de-legitimating the court.

Audience participation was almost a daily event at most trials. Attempts to control spectators were largely unsuccessful. Most of them had ideologies very similar, if not identical, to those of the defendants. Defendants, then, viewed audiences as their people and their interventions as the will of the people. Sternberg comments as follows:

> It follows that the intervening audience in the radical trial was invariably on the side of the defendants and hostile to the institutionalized judiciary. In the progressive and interactive dialogue among and between defendants and members of the audience . . . an increasingly strengthened structure of "resonating sentiments" emerged. At the same time, the dissonance of sentiments between the court on the one hand and the defendants and the audience on the other became magnified. Examples were the massive support the audience gave to Bobby Seale in the courtroom, time after time answering his defiant raised and clenched fist with cries of "Right On"; the solidarity the New York Panther defendants displayed with a spectator whom Judge Murtaugh ordered removed for interrupting the proceedings, one defendant saying, "If she goes out, we go out!"; the concerted outrage of the entire audience when Judge Hoffman bound and gagged Seale; the continuous open as well as sub rosa exchange between defendants and audiences in New York and Chicago, as if the official court personnel were either absent or simply did not count. In all these instances, audience and defendants constructed a mutually supportive and subversive social reality under the very gavel and noses of the judge, prosecutors and marshals (Sternberg, 1974: 285–286).

From the perspective of judges and other court officials, nothing like this had ever happened. So entrenched were they in the formal rules and regulations that they utterly failed to comprehend the radical position. Moreover, the trials themselves raised some important constitutional issues, such as the Sixth Amendment guarantee of the right to confront witnesses directly, and both the Sixth and Fourteenth Amendments, which guarantee a public trial. In 1970, the Supreme Court ruled that defendants waived the right to confront their accusers by disorderly behavior and that they could be bound and gagged or even expelled. The Court did not rule on the issue of guaranteeing a public trial. From the defendants' perspective in these cases, a public trial meant just that—a truly *public* hearing with active participation by members of the audience.[7]

These trials did, however, reveal the court system for what it is: a system in which dissent is stifled, in which the rule of law and corresponding ideologies are legitimated, and in which larger issues of social, economic, and political justice are ignored. In short, the court system merely processes defendants and does nothing about the causes of crime. It is a court system resembling a microcosm of a capitalist society in which exchange and bargaining between unequals goes on, all in the name of justice.

This is quite typical in a capitalist society, where commodities are produced socially but owned privately. In other words, commodities are produced mainly for private profit rather than for social good. Within the justice system, "justice will be pursued socially, but the benefits of justice will accrue to particular individuals," (Lynch and Michalowski, 2006: 99), especially those with power. The courts are agencies that attempt to rectify problems caused by the capitalist system itself, such as gross social inequalities. As such, the courts are attempting to solve a social problem by merely punishing individuals. By focusing almost exclusive attention on individual offenders, the courts merely reinforce the myth that individuals, rather than the surrounding social system, need correcting. This ideology is further reinforced by the mystique of the law displayed every day in every court—the extreme formalism of the court process, with the swearing on the bible, the robes of the judges, the ubiquitous scales of justice signified by the blind lady—which masks what is really occurring in the outside world (Lynch and Michalowski, 2006: 99). The various radical-criminal trials of the 1960s and 1970s, along with the system's response to mass civil disobedience during the riots of the 1960s and more recently the riots following the Rodney King decision, demonstrated clearly how the courts are unable to deal with these outside issues (Feagin and Vera, 1995: 103–108: Balbus, 1973).

If the reader thinks that such trials are part of a bygone era, think again. A recent case called the St. Patrick's Four has raised similar issues. One of the main differences in this case is that it has not made any headlines, thanks to a mostly timid press that caters to the powers that be.

The St. Patrick's Four

The radical-criminal trials of the 1960s and early 1970s were not an isolated event in American history. Indeed throughout the 20th century there have been numerous cases where otherwise ordinary citizens ended up in court on various charges stemming from antiwar protests.[8] It should come as no surprise, therefore, that another American involvement in war would elicit the same protests. On March 17, 2003, four peace activists in Ithaca, New York, poured their own blood inside a military recruiting center on the eve of the U.S. invasion of Iraq. They did not try to flee, but rather knelt down in prayer and waited to be arrested. This was the first indictment against antiwar protestors since the Vietnam War era (Komp, 2005).

The people involved were hardly among the criminal class. They were Daniel Burns, 43; Clare Grady, 45; Teresa Grady 38; and Peter DeMott, 57—all members of the Magnificat Catholic Worker community in Ithaca. All admitted their guilt, but testified they committed their act in order to protect American soldiers in the military and their fellow human beings in Iraq.

The four argued that their actions were legal because the invasion of Iraq was illegal under international law. Also, since the United Nations had not approved the invasion of Iraq, such acts that constituted war crimes. Under the Nuremberg Principles of international law, "individuals have international rights and duties to prevent crimes against humanity which transcend the national obligations of obedience imposed by the individual state. They further argued that if their actions were indeed illegal, they were authorized under the defense of necessity because the harm they caused was far smaller than the harm they were trying to prevent" (Quigley, 2005).

Like the radical-criminal trials of the 1960s, one of the St. Patrick's Four defendants, Daniel Burns, asked the jurors to look at the context of their actions, stating that:

> The immediate context for the justice of our action is the Pre-emptive Invasion of the War of Iraq. An invasion opposed by the United Nations, opposed by most nations in

this world, and founded on lies about weapons of mass destruction, and an invasion that has cost a billion dollars a day, hundreds of American sons and daughters, and thousands of our Iraqi sisters and brothers. Also we ask you to look at the justice of our action in light of the context of international law. Why was the invasion opposed by the UN and many of our allies? Because international law only allows an attack on another country in self defense or with approval of the UN security council—and we had neither. And the Nuremberg principles provide a legal defense for people seeking to prevent war crimes. No jury would convict 4 people of breaking and entering if they broke into a burning house to try to save a child. Here, the building was on fire—as Iraq is now, and we broke in to try to save our troops and the innocent Iraqis. We did not save them, but justice says we should not be punished for trying. So, we end where we started. We ask for justice. We ask for justice for the people of Iraq and our troops. We ask for justice for world peace. We ask for justice to say no to pre-emptive illegal war (Quigley, 2005).

Like the earlier radical-criminal trials, the trial drew hundreds of protesters (but not most of the national media).

After deliberating for 20 hours, the jury was deadlocked, with 9 to 3 favoring acquittal. But soon thereafter, the federal government stepped in an attempt to make this a federal conspiracy case charging that "by force, intimidation, and threat" (Zawerucha, 2005): the four impeded an officer of the United States, plus damage to property and two counts of trespass, which could lead to as much as six years in prison. This was unprecedented in American history and is contrary to the double-jeopardy provision of the Fifth Amendment to the Constitution. In the new case, the defendants were not allowed to use many of their key defenses, such as citing the Nuremberg Principles and violations of international law. Federal Judge Thomas J. McAvoy ruled that such a defense is outside the scope of the federal court and that "an illegal war does not provide a justification for violating criminal laws of the United States" (Zawerucha, 2005).

Many experts familiar with the case have argued that this a blatant attempt to silence dissent. The American Civil Liberties Union said that starting a separate federal prosecution for a "clearly nonviolent protest suggests that the government may be more motivated by the message than by the conduct of the defendants" (Zawerucha, 2005). Law Professor Scott Horton (who was once a member of the Council on Foreign Relations and worked at the Department of Defense) stated that "There should have been no action brought against them. What they are doing is punishing citizens expressing displeasure to what their government has done" (Zawerucha, 2005).

On October 26, 2005 the defendants were found not guilty of the most serious charge of conspiracy and guilty of two lesser misdemeanor counts. They face up to six years in prison. Public interest lawyer Bill Quigley of Loyola University, who acted as a legal advisor for the defendants, stated that "The decision to acquit on the conspiracy charge, a felony, is a huge victory, given the narrow parameters within which the four could present their defense and given the restrictions on deliberations. This is a major setback in the government's efforts to criminalize dissent" (Mager, 2005). In a page out of the trials of the late 1960s, one of the defendants, Claire Grady, made the following opening statement in their trial:

> We are here today, the four of us parents, facing very serious charges. In a case that I believe is about love, truth, and the power of peaceful non-violent symbolic action. We are moved out of love—the love God shows us, the love we share as family and community, the love we grow into, that reaches out to all people, especially those most in need. Especially those who suffer at the work of our hands and policies. We seek the truth! The WHOLE truth. The truth about our part in the bigger picture. We are open to dispelling the lies that lead to bloodshed and the killing of the innocent. We are not able to turn a blind eye to our part, not able to remain silent, not able to stand idly by. We put our lives on the line. Peacefully, prayerfully, we undertook this non-violent symbolic action to show the awful truth about war. To show our non-cooperation with it, and to sound the alarm, to warn others, especially our beloved youth who are also victims of war, who have been lied to, and whose honorable intentions and bravery have been exploited (Mager, 2005).

They were all sentenced to four months in federal prison on January 27, 2006. Theresa Grady gave the following statement upon her sentence. Part of this statement brings back the memory of Martin Luther King's famous "Letter from a Birmingham Jail"[9]:

> This court and the jury were intended to be a check and balance to tyrannical government. You instead have sentenced our nation, its young in particular, to continue trammeling international laws which our own nation has fought for, helped to create, and upholds in the woefully neglected constitution! Leaving us a nation fearful to do anything about the great crimes of our government, from which our souls both collectively and individually are sorely aching. Not to mention the victims of its violations. I will always act believing in the goodness of all people and the gravitation of people's conscience towards rightness, justice and truth. This courtroom has been no exception in this application. Please go forward with your good conscience and employ the dusty laws, which sit unused in the books. They are crying to be used in the name of justice! The victims of war will applaud you. They are the victims of torture, the victims who are our service people and their families.[10]

Moving into the first years of the 21st century we find that little has changed. However, one significant change has been that the people who are increasingly appearing in the nation's courts—and hence jails—are racial minorities (especially African Americans) charged with drug law violations, the results of a war on drugs that has been rather successful, since it appears obvious that the intent was to control the minority population, especially those included among the growing underclass—the modern equivalent of the dangerous classes of a century or more ago (Human Rights Watch, 2000). The next section will cover this topic.

The Modern Era: The War on Drugs and Racial Minorities

As the two previous chapters point out, the war on drugs has had a huge impact on the criminal justice system. With the emphasis placed almost totally on a legalistic

TABLE 3.1 *Sentences in Federal Courts for Drug Law Violations,*
1950–2005 (Percent incarcerated and average sentence in months)

Year	Percent Incarcerated	Average Sentence
1950	77	22
1960	82	73
1970	52	65
1980	78	55
1990	86	79
2005	96	86
% increase (1950–2005)	25	291

Source: Sourcebook on Criminal Justice Statistics, 2005 (http://www.albany.edu/sourcebook/pdf/t5382005.pdf).

response to the drug problem the police have responded with literally millions of arrests for drug possession and sales during the past two decades. Not surprisingly there has been a predictable impact on the criminal courts and the rest of the criminal justice system.

To give the reader an idea of the impact the drug war has had on the court system, one of the chapters in a fascinating book by journalist Mike Gray is illuminating. Through a series of interviews with both defense attorneys and prosecutors in a Chicago court, Gray describes courtroom deals made and the manner in which the drug dealers are taken care of. He notes that one of the consequences of the huge influx of drug cases is the establishment of a totally separate courtroom reserved for drug cases only. Further, officials had to create two separate shifts: one during the day and the other at night. What is perhaps most interesting is that during the day the majority of defendants are white, while during the nightshift most are racial minorities (Gray, 2000).

Sentencing in the federal system for drug offenses shows some startling changes during the past half-century. As shown in Table 3.1, between 1950 and 2005 the proportion of those going to prison for drug offenses rose from 77% to 96%, while the average sentence has risen by 291%.

A common view holds that the drug war has aimed its efforts to rid the nation of dangerous drugs or what former President George Bush called the "scourge of the nation" (Baum, 1997). Aside from the obvious fact that the most dangerous drugs are tobacco and alcohol (as demonstrated by the large number of deaths resulting from their use), one would assume that enforcement efforts would equally target all of those who use the outlawed drugs (marijuana, cocaine, and so on). However, this is not the case. In May of 2000, The Drug Policy Litigation Project reported that African Americans comprised of 35% of those arrested for drug possession, 55% of those convicted, and 74% of those incarcerated (Gunja, 2003). The next several pages display sample tables and graphs that illustrate these discrepancies based on race. The evidence is overwhelming that the drug war disproportionately targets African Americans.

TABLE 3.2   *Results of the National Household Survey on Drug Abuse in 1994 and the National Survey on Drug Use and Health in 2004*

Population	1994	2004
Current Drug Users	12.6 Million	19.1 Million
Percent of the Population	5.8%	16.1%
Gender		
Men	7.9%	9.9%
Women	4.3%	6.1%
Race or Ethnicity		
White	6.0%	8.1%
Black	7.3%	8.7%
Hispanic	5.4%	7.2%
American Indian/Alaskan Native	N/A	12.3%
Asian	N/A	3.1%
2 or More Race	N/A	13.3%
Type of Drugs		
Marijuana	81.0%	76.4%
Cocaine	0.7%	0.5%
Heroin	1.7%	0.1%
Methamphetamine	N/A	0.2%

Source: The 1994 National Household Survey on Drug Abuse Report and the 2004 National Survey on Drug Use and Health Report.

To begin with, it is clear from numerous studies that there are few racial differences in actual illegal drug use. The Substance Abuse and Mental Health Services (SAMHSA) sponsored an annual survey called the National Household Survey on Drug Abuse (NHSDA). By year 2002, this same survey was then changed to the National Survey on Drug Use and Health (NSDUH) (Substance Abuse and Mental Health Services Administration, 2004).

As noted in Table 3.2, there are few racial differences in illegal drug use among adults. Surveys also show few racial differences among high school students (Grunbaum, 2003). In 2003, the National Survey on Drug Use and Health (NSDUH) reported an estimate of "5.9% of women aged 18 or older met the criteria for the abuse of or dependence on alcohol or an illicit drug in the past year" (Substance Abuse and Mental Health Services Administration, 2005). NSDUH further states that "rates of abuse of or dependence on alcohol or illicit drugs among women aged 18 or older were highest among American Indians or Alaska Natives (19.9%), followed by whites (6.3%), blacks (4.5%), Hispanics (4.4%), and Asians (3.4%)" (Substance Abuse and Mental Health Services Administration, 2005).

TABLE 3.3　*Court Commitments to State Prison, by Crime Type, 1980–2000*

Offense	1980	1992	2000	% Increase, 1980–1992	% Increase 1992–2000
Total	131,215	334,301	924,700	155	177
Violent	63,200	95,300	173,200	51	82
Property	53,900	104,300	262,000	94	151
Drugs	8,900	192,000	319,700	1,046	67

Sources: Mauer, M. *Americans behind Bars: The International Use of Incarceration, 1992–1993.* Washington, DC: Sentencing Project, 1994; Gilliard, D. K., and A. J. Beck. *Prisoners in 1993.* Washington, DC: Bureau of Justice Statistics, 1994; Durose, M. R. and P. A. Langan, "Felony Sentences in State Courts, 2000." Washington, DC: Bureau of Justice Statistics, 2003.

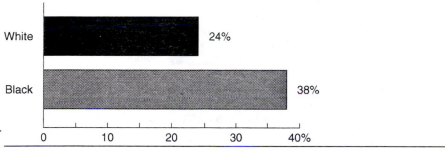

FIGURE 3.1　*Drug Offenders as a Percent of State Admissions by Race.*

Source: Incarcerated America, Human Rights Watch Backgrounder, April 2003 (http://www.hrw.org/backgrounder/usa/incarceration/).

Numerous studies have illustrated the differential conviction and sentencing rates for drug cases. Data on court commitments to state prisons during the 1980s and early 1990s clearly show the dramatic changes for drug offenses. Between 1980 and 1992, sentences on drug charges increased by more than 1,000%. In contrast, there was a more modest increase of 51% for violent offenses. Since 1992, the percentage increases for drugs have slowed down compared to other offenses, but still constitute a huge chunk of the state prison population, illustrated in Table 3.3. Race played a key role in these increases, especially during the late 1980s and early 1990s. The number of African Americans sentenced to prison for drug charges increased by over 90%, almost three times greater than white offenders (Maguire and Pastore, 1996: 550). Between 1985, when the drug war really took off, and 1995, the number of African American inmates sentenced for drug crimes increased by 700% (Currie, 1998: 12–13).

Looking at those in custody based on various censuses of state and federal prisons show that drug convictions constitute 24% of the admissions to state prisons for whites, but 38% for blacks, as shown in Figure 3.1. Figure 3.2 shows the racial discrepancy for all the states in the country.

TABLE 3.5 *New Prison Admissions per 100,000 by Race and County of Sentencing, for Dane and Milwaukee Counties, 1996*

Offense	White* (Milwaukee)	White* (Dane)	Black (Milwaukee)	Black (Dane)	B/W (Milwaukee)	B/W (Dane)
Total	58	41	943	2059	16.4	49.7
Homicide	2	1	36	14	15.1	26.2
Assault	6	6	88	373	14.0	67.3
Robbery	7	3	144	256	19.9	96.8
Sex Assault	9	5	67	166	7.8	34.9
Theft, burglary, etc.	15	12	215	332	14.1	28.6
Drugs	10	3	300	560	30.7	193.0*

*White is white non-Hispanic.
Source: Oliver, P. (2002). *Racial Disparities in Criminal Justice.* Madison: University of Wisconsin. Rates per 100,000 population within race, and black/white ratios.

TABLE 3.6 *Average Sentence Length for Offenders Convicted of Various Crimes in U.S. District Courts, by Race, 1992 and 2003 (sentences in months)*

	1992	2003
White		
Violent	92.4	91.2
Drugs	73.6	67.6
Black		
Violent	103.9	109.7
Drugs	106.9	110.5

Source: Sourcebook on Criminal Justice Statistics, 1996. Washington, D.C.: Department of Justice, Bureau of Justice Statistics, 1996, p. 474; *Sourcebook on Criminal Justice Statistics, 2003,* Table 5.21 (http://www.albany.edu/sourcebook/pdf/t5212003.pdf).

justice system" (Human Rights Watch, 2000). Though drug statutes may appear to be impartial, organizations such as the Drug Policy Litigation Projects and the Human Rights Watch have expressed their concern on on how these laws are actually enforced.

Not only were more African Americans sentenced for drug crimes, but also the severity of their sentences increased compared to whites. In 1992, in the federal system, the average sentence length for African-American drug offenders was about 107 months, compared to 74 months for white drug offenders; in 2003 the gap was even greater, with the average sentence for whites for drug offenses decreasing to 67.6 months, compared to an increase for blacks from 106.9 to 110.5 months (see Table 3.6). There has been a huge discrepancy when comparing powder and crack

TABLE 3.7   *Drug Offenders Sentenced Under the U.S. Sentencing Commission Guidelines, by Race, Powder Cocaine, and Crack, 2003*

Race	Powder Cocaine		Crack Cocaine	
	N	%	N	%
White	1,037	17.7	363	7.0
Black	1,815	30.9	4,203	81.4
Hispanic	2,938	50.1	542	10.5
Other	77	1.3	58	1.1

Source: Sourcebook on Criminal Justice Statistics, 2003, Table 5.39, (http://www.albany.edu/sourcebook/pdf/t539.pdf).

TABLE 3.8   *Drug Felony Convictions in State Court by Gender and Race in 2002*

Gender	
Male	83.0%
Female	17.0%
RaceWhite	27%
Black	47%
Other	27%

Source: Rainville, Gerard and Brian A. Reaves. *Felony Defendants in Large Urban Counties, 2000.* Washington, DC: Bureau of Justice Statistics, December 2003. (http://www.ojp.usdoj.gov/bjs/pub/pdf/fdluc00.pdf).

cocaine sentences in the federal system. In 2003, for instance, African Americans constituted a phenomenal 81% of those sentenced for crack cocaine, compared to around 30% of those sentenced for powder cocaine; Hispanics fared even worse for powder cocaine, constituting half of all of those sentenced (Table 3.7). The reader should keep in mind data on actual drug use, noted in Table 3.2.

Drug offenses accounted for 37% of all felony convictions in state courts in 2000. Males constituted 81% of those convicted of drug charges and females 19%. Race figures prominently in these data. As shown in Table 3.8, of all the drug defendants, blacks were 47%, compared to 27% for whites and 27% for Hispanics.

An earlier and more detailed study came from a U.S. Department of Justice report that examined felony defendants in the largest 75 counties in 1994 (Reaves, 1998). Here we can see the effects of the war on drugs and its impact on the nation's court system during this period of time; we also can clearly see the effects of race. African Americans constituted over half (56%) of all defendants and 62% of those charged with drug offenses.[11] In some cities, the proportion of felony defendants who were African American was quite high. For example, African Americans constituted 93% of all felony defendants in Wayne County (Detroit), 90% in Baltimore, and 85% in Cook County (Chicago) and Kings County (Seattle), but only 14% in Maricopa County (Phoenix) and 9% in Honolulu (Reaves, 1998: 43).

Many of these defendants had prior experiences with the justice system. For example, about one-fourth (24%) were on probation or on parole, and another 12% were on pretrial release status at the time of their most recent arrest. These figures varied by offense, with 39% of the drug defendants having an active status within the criminal justice system at the time of their arrest, while 45% of those were charged with public-order offenses. Also, about two-thirds (68%) had at least one prior arrest, with 23% having had 10 or more prior arrests. The most likely persons to have had prior arrests were drug offenders and public-order offenders (72%). Just over half (56%) had at least one prior felony arrest, with about one-fifth (22%) having had five or more prior felony arrests. Moreover, over half (55%) had had at least one prior conviction, with 38% having prior felony convictions (mostly of a nonviolent nature). Clearly these defendants were no strangers to the criminal justice system.

The majority of these defendants (62%) were released pending the final disposition of their cases. Of these, the most common form of release was on their own recognizance and through some form of financial release (surety bond, and so on). The median bail amount for those released was $5,000; the median for those detained was $15,000. Most of the defendants who were released were set free within 24 hours (51%), with more than three-fourths (79%) being released within one week. Most (76%) of those released made all of their court appearances. Those charged with violent crimes were the most likely to make all of their court appearances (85%); drug defendants were the least likely (71%). Of those who were rearrested while on release status, only 15% were rearrested for a new offense (Reaves, 1998: 19).

A total of 72% of these defendants were ultimately convicted—61% on a felony charge and 11% on a misdemeanor charge. Not surprisingly, few of those convicted ever went to trial (4% of those convicted of a felony and none of those convicted of a misdemeanor). Of those not convicted, most had their cases dismissed. It is interesting to note that those charged with violent offenses were the most likely to have their cases dismissed (36%). Also not surprisingly, more than three-fourths (79%) of those who were detained were convicted, compared to only 67% of those released; 84% of the drug defendants who were detained were convicted, compared to 69% of the violent offenders (Reaves, 1998: 8–14, 24).

The largest percentage of convictions were for drug offenses (31%), property crimes ranked second (accounting for 29% of the total), and violent crimes ranked third (16%). In terms of sentencing (more on sentencing follows), those convicted of violent crime were the most likely to be sent to prison (76%), with public-order offenders a close second (71%), and drug offenders third (68%, with 75% of those convicted of trafficking sent to prison). All together, two-thirds (67%) of those convicted were sentenced to prison. Not surprisingly, violent offenders received the harshest sentences (median of 72 months); the median sentence for drug offenders was 36 months (48 months for traffickers). Unfortunately, no cross-tabulations are provided for race and sentencing in this study, but given data presented in other tables in this chapter, we know that race is crucial (Reaves, 1998: 8–14, 24).

One of the explanations for these trends can be found in recently enacted get tough sentencing legislation. One example has been called mandatory sentencing. These types of sentences result from mandates by state legislatures (almost always resulting from local or even national political moods, frequently during election years) that certain kinds of offenders who commit certain types of crimes be sentenced to a term in prison for a set minimum amount of time. In some states there are laws such as "use a gun, go to prison," which gives neither judges nor prosecutors any discretion.

A popular variation of this is known as habitual offender laws. These sentencing laws stipulate that after an offender is convicted of so many serious crimes (usually two or three major felony convictions), the individual is sentenced to a very lengthy term in prison, often for life (sometimes without the possibility of parole). Perhaps the most infamous of these laws is Three-Strikes and You're Out, which began in California in the early 1990s. A product of political posturing and the cynical desire among politicians to get votes by playing on public fears of crime, legislation in California and elsewhere used the popular baseball phrase to obtain the needed support. Almost instantly, the catchy phrase became part of American popular culture. This would be the ultimate get tough stance on crime, showing little regard for the consequences. Originally passed in 1993 in California, the legislation was suppose to impose extremely harsh sentences after a conviction for a third felony (specifically, in California the third strike would result in a sentence of 25 years to life). Theoretically, it was suppose to get tough on the toughest criminals—mostly repeat, serious, especially violent offenders. It was, unfortunately, based upon the erroneous assumption that the criminal justice system was too lenient on criminals (when in fact just the opposite was occurring); it was also based upon a few celebrated cases, especially the kidnapping and murder of Polly Klass (Walker, 2006).[12] It has also been described as "politicized crime control policy" (Benekos and Merlo, 1995: 4).

The consequences of Three Strikes and You're Out have been as follows: (1) it has had virtually no impact on crime; (2) instead of locking up serious offenders, the bulk of those sentenced have not fit the stereotype of the superpredator and many have been relatively minor offenders (in California, by March of 1999, more had been sentenced for marijuana possession than the combined total for those sentenced for murder, rape, and kidnapping); (3) a very uneven application of the legislation across different jurisdictions; (4) it has resulted in both jail and prison overcrowding, especially in California (not to mention the increase in court costs because of a decline in plea bargaining caused by an increase in cases going to trial); (5) not surprisingly, a huge discrepancy when it came to race and class, with the impact being felt on those who are poor and/or racial minorities (in California, while African Americans accounted for only 7% of the total population, they accounted for 20% of all felony arrests, 31% of the state's prisoners, and 43% of those sentenced for the third strike; Campaign for an Effective Crime Policy, 1998).[13]

Whether we are talking about early English society or the modern criminal courts, the court system in the United States tends to focus its attention primarily on those from the less privileged sectors of society. The courts have been dominated by persons drawn primarily from the more privileged sectors of society, especially the highest court, the United States Supreme Court. The recent war on drugs has been in effect a war on minorities, especially African Americans. This will become especially apparent when the history of the next component of the criminal justice system is examined, the prison system.

Before turning our attention to the prison system, some attention should be paid to the ultimate penalty, capital punishment. Not surprisingly, the most likely recipients of this penalty have been the dangerous classes, especially African Americans. The next section examines this topic.

The Ultimate Sanction for the Dangerous Classes: The Death Penalty

Capital punishment is one of the oldest forms of punishment, dating back several thousands of years. It has had a long and turbulent history in America. It has gone through periods in which most states either abolished it altogether or never used it and periods in which it was commonly used (Sellin, 1967; Bedau, 1964). The first American execution was in 1608. Since then, there have been 15,536 recorded executions. Early colonists brought the English tradition of execution to America. Since the laws tended to have their roots in religious practice, a variety of offenses were punishable by death. For example, some of the earliest executions were for bestiality, sodomy, piracy, concealing a birth, and witchcraft (Espy and Smykla, 2004). Executions became more frequent in the late 1800s and peaked in the 1930s when the United States averaged 167 executions per year. State sanctioned executions began to decline in the 1940s until reaching an all-time low between 1960 and 1976. Since the mid 1990s, however, the execution rate has been increasing.

Two landmark Supreme Court decisions in the 1970s rekindled the controversy surrounding the death penalty: *Furman v. Georgia* (1972) and *Gregg v. Georgia* (1976). After these two decisions were handed down, the use of the death penalty sentences increased dramatically. Between 1977 and 1995, there were 4,857 sentenced to death, with 313 of these actually executed. (Between 1930 and 1967 there were 3,860 prisoners executed in the United States, more than in any other democratic nation.)

In *Furman v. Georgia* there were nine separate opinions, one from each of the justices. In 1969, William Furman accidentally shot and killed an occupant of a home he was burglarizing. He was tried and convicted. The jury took only an hour and a half to sentence him to death. According to Justice Brennan's opinion, "the jury knew only that he was black and that, according to his statement at trial, he was 26 years old and worked at Superior Upholstery."[14] The primary issue in the Furman ruling was a lack of consistency in capital sentencing due to a lack of guidelines for jurors. Essentially, the ruling found that then existing statutes were unconstitutional due to their arbitrary and capricious application and their great potential for racial discrimination. Importantly, the Court did not rule that the death penalty in and of itself constituted cruel and unusual punishment in violation of the Eighth and Fourteenth Amendments of the Constitution.

Following the Furman ruling, 37 states reformulated their death penalty statutes in an attempt reduce arbitrariness by providing guidelines for judges and jurors. These new laws were upheld in a series of Supreme Court decisions in 1976.[15] The most widely cited is the case of *Gregg v. Georgia*. In the case of *Gregg v. Georgia* the Court upheld the Georgia statute calling for the death penalty for murder. The primary issue in the Gregg decision was not whether capital punishment was cruel and unusual, but whether or not the process of death sentencing was rational and objectively reviewable. The Court outlined two principles to guide legislatures in crafting their statutes. First, the statutes were required to provide objective criteria designed to limit sentencing discretion, and second, the Court required that judges or juries consider the character of the defendant. The Court ruled: "A punishment must not be excessive, but this does not mean that the states must seek the minimal standards available. The imposition of the death penalty for the crime of murder does not violate the Constitution." In two other decisions the Court ruled similarly (*Proffit v. Florida,* 1976 and *Jurek v. Texas,* 1976). However, in *Coker v. Georgia* (1977) the Court ruled that the death penalty for rape constituted cruel and unusual punishment.

Before *Furman v. Georgia*, appeals were not mandatory and many death row inmates did not pursue them. In fact, one-quarter of the prisoners executed in the 1960s had no appeals at all, and two-thirds never had their cases reviewed by a federal court (Bohm, 2003). The Supreme Court, in an attempt to achieve fairness in the process, ordered a mandatory review. Presently, most retentionist states automatically review both the conviction and sentence. The appeals process has been streamlined in recent years (Dieter, 1997). One important change in the appeals process since the *Gregg v. Georgia* ruling is that the Supreme Court will no longer consider issues raised for the first time pursuant to last-minute pleas for stays of execution, particularly when the claims could have been raised in prior petitions.

Since the Furman ruling, 38 states have revised their death penalty statutes in an attempt to reduce arbitrariness. Typically, these statutes require a bifurcated trial. Phase one includes the presentation of evidence and aggravating factors for the purpose of a finding of guilt or nonguilt. When the jury convicts, the penalty phase begins. During this phase the prosecution urges the jury to return a death verdict and the defense presents mitigation evidence. The primary difference between the new and old statutes is the required presentation of aggravating and mitigating evidence. To be death eligible, a homicide must be accompanied by one or more aggravating factors. These are statutory and are different in each state. For example, some statutes list armed robbery and rape as aggravating factors. Mitigators are also statutory and vary by state. For example, some statutes list diminished capacity due to drugs or alcohol as mitigation.

After a de facto abolition of the death penalty, it was reactivated in 1977 with the execution of Gary Gilmore by a firing squad in Utah (this state is the only one that allows the prisoner a choice between a firing squad or hanging). Since 1976 more than 5,000 people have been sentenced to death (although the number has declined in recent years (from 317 in 1996 to 125 in 2004) and 1,045 of them have been executed. During this period, the racial breakdown of those executed was 57% white, 34% black, and the remainder other races. As of September 1, 2006, 38 states plus the federal government had the death penalty; four of these states have had no executions since 1976 (Kansas, New Hampshire, New Jersey, and New York). As of April 1, 2006, there were 3,370 inmates on death row. California leads the way as far as the total number of death row inmates (652); Texas is second (404), and Florida is third

(392). Texas leads the country in executions since 1976 with 393, Virginia a distant second with 97. The South accounts for more than 80% of all executions since 1976; it also has consistently had the highest murder rate in the country.[16]

Race figures prominently in the imposition of the death penalty. For instance, of the 4,172 prisoners executed between 1930 and 1995, over half (52%) were African Americans. Between 1930 and 1972, a total of 455 were executed for rape and 89% were African Americans. When considering the race of the victims, race once again enters into the picture. For instance, 82% of the victims of those executed were white, whereas about 50% of the victims of all homicides were African American. Several studies have noted that there are vast discrepancies in the application of the death penalty according to the race of the victim and the race of the offender. Where the victim is white and the offender is African American, the death penalty will be given about 35% of the time, compared to only 14% when the relationship is reversed (i.e., African-American victim and white offender); the death penalty will be given in 22% of the cases where whites kill whites and only 6% of the cases where African Americans kill African Americans (Baldus et al., 1990). The study by Baldus et al. also found that the race of the victim played a key role in the prosecutor's decision to seek the death penalty and a jury's decision to impose it. Even after controlling for an astounding 200 variables, Baldus et al. still found race to be the most significant variable! Other recent studies have arrived at identical results. These studies, by the way, examined data from several different states (Gross and Mauro, 1989; Radelet, 1981; and Amsterdam, 1988).

It is not as if these findings are new. Almost 40 years ago Wolfgang, Kelly, and Nolde (1962) studied 439 cases of men sentenced to death in Pennsylvania for murder between 1914 and 1958. They found that 20% of the whites had their sentences commuted to life imprisonment, whereas only 11% of the blacks did, a statistically significant relationship. In an even earlier study, Johnson (1941) examined homicide cases in Richmond, Virginia, and in five counties in North Carolina during the 1930s. He found that the death penalty was most often applied when the victim was white and the offender was black, and the least likely when both the offender and the victim were black (see also Garfinkel, 1949).

Studies of rape have also found a strong relationship between the race of the victim and the imposition of the death penalty. Elmer Johnson, in a study of rape cases resulting in the imposition of the death penalty in North Carolina between 1909 and 1954, found that blacks were more likely than whites to be executed. A study of Florida cases found that blacks who raped whites were much more likely to receive than if the situation were reversed (cited in Wolfgang and Reidel, 1975: 369). Wolfgang and Reidel also studied 3,000 rape convictions in 11 southern states between 1945 and 1965. They found: "Among 1,265 cases in which the race of the defendant and the sentence are known, nearly seven times as many Blacks were sentenced to death as whites" (1975: 371–372). They also found that 36% of the blacks who raped whites were sentenced to death, while all other racial combinations resulted in only 2% being sentenced to death. These relationships held true even when they held constant such other factors as prior record and contemporaneous offenses (e.g., murder while committing robbery) (see also Bowers, 1974).

Many of these studies gained some prominence in one of the most significant Supreme Court cases concerning the death penalty, that of *McCleskey v. Kemp* in 1987. It was here that research concerning the race of the victim was cited. Not surprisingly the case originated in Georgia, just as did Furman and Gregg. The defendant, Warren McCleskey, an African American, was convicted of killing a white police officer. Part of the defense strategy was to use the study by Balbus. Despite the overwhelming evidence in support of the importance of the race of the victim, the Supreme Court rejected the appeal. While accepting the validity of the Balbus study, the Court nevertheless ruled that, regardless of statistical correlations, in the case of McCleskey, there was no evidence that *"any of the decisionmakers in McCleskey's case acted with discriminatory purpose"* (quoted in Walker et al., 2007: 248, emphasis added). The Court also suggested that at best, all that could be shown was a "discrepancy that appears to correlate with race" (2007: 548).

What is perhaps most interesting about this ruling is that the Court appeared to be afraid of what the logical conclusions of such evidence might be. Justice Powell, writing for the majority, noted that such evidence "throws into serious question the principles that underlie our entire criminal justice system . . . if we accepted McCleskey's claim that racial bias impermissibly tainted the capital sentencing decision, we would soon be faced with similar claims as to other types of penalty" (Kennedy, 1997: 336). Not surprisingly, the ruling came in for immediate attacks, including four dissenting justices (Blackmun, Marshall, Brennan, and Stevens). Heaven forbid, they suggested, that others may challenge such obvious biases, "even women" (wrote one justice). One scholar noted sarcastically that concluding that "at most" there appears to be a "discrepancy" is like saying that "at most" the many studies on lung cancer "indicate a discrepancy that appears to correlate with smoking" (Kennedy, 1997: 336). Most of the critics voiced the opinion that this ruling sent a message that racial bias is perfectly constitutional. McCleskey was eventually executed in the electric chair on September 26, 1991. The famous Justice Thurgood Marshall, who joined two other justices in a dissent for a stay of execution, stated that it appears that "the court values expediency over human life . . . " (Walker et al., 2007: 252).

David Cole has argued that it would be nearly impossible to prove that a prosecutor and a jury have imposed the death penalty in a particular case because of the defendant's race. He notes that there are long-standing rules that prohibit defendants from obtaining discovery from the prosecution and therefore "unless the prosecutor admits to acting for racially biased reasons, it will be difficult to pin discrimination on the prosecutor" (Cole, 1999: 135). In short, says Cole, "defendants are precluded from discovering evidence of intent from the two actors whose discriminatory intent the *McCleskey* Court required them to establish" (Cole, 1999: 135).

Subsequent cases on this issue had almost identical results. In one such case, that of *Dobbs v. Zant* (a 1989 case in, naturally, Georgia!), the Court rejected the appeal even though several jurors referred to African Americans as "coloreds" and two admitted using "nigger" in their conversations. Even the defense attorney (a court-appointed attorney) admitted using nigger and believed that African-Americans make good basketball players, but not teachers (Cole, 1999: 135).

In other words, the Supreme Court has concluded that "discrimination is inevitable," a "natural by-product of discretion" and hence "constitutionally acceptable" (Cole, 1999: 137). So there you have it, the highest court in the country that espouses equal justice for all is telling us, in effect, that racial bias is supported by the United States Constitution! Some members of Congress responded to the *McCleskey* decision by adding a Racial Justice Act to the Omnibus Crime Bill of 1994. By a slim majority, the House voted for this provision, which would have allowed those on death row to challenge their sentence based upon statistical evidence of race discrimination in capital cases, as had McCleskey. But it was defeated in the Senate and dropped from the 1994 bill. Senator Orin Hatch (R-Utah) remarked, quite candidly, that this "so-called Racial Justice Act has nothing to do with racial justice and everything to do with abolishing the death penalty . . . It would convert every death penalty case into a massive sideshow of statistical squabbles and quota quarrels" (quoted in Kennedy, 1997: 346). What more can be said, given this kind of worse-case scenario logic?

Since the Court reinstated capital punishment in 1976 new issues emerged that have caused courts and legislatures to continue the reconstruction and reformulation of death penalty law. Two more recent evolutions involved the execution of mentally retarded defendants and juvenile defendants. *Mental retardation* is described as substantial limitations in functioning that is characterized by significantly subaverage intelligence and limitations in skills related to self-care, communication, social skills, and work. The Court first addressed the issue of mental retardation and execution in 1989 in the case of *Penry v. Lynaugh* when it cited a "lack of national consensus" on executing the mentally ill and upheld the constitutionality of the practice. In 2002, however, the Court changed its position.

By 2002, most death penalty states banned the practice of executing mentally retarded defendants, public opinion polls revealed that a majority of Americans were opposed to the practice, and the American Bar Association established a policy opposing executions of those deemed to have an IQ of 70 or below. Clearly, a national consensus had formed. In turn, the Supreme Court declared in *Atkins v. Virginia* that executing an individual who meets all of the three criterion outlined by the American Association on mental retardation.[18]

In a similar fashion, the Supreme Court changed its position on executing juvenile offenders. When polls indicated that the public opposed the execution of juvenile offenders, the Supreme Court banned the practice in *Roper v. Simmons*. The Court's 2005 ruling came despite a history of allowing juvenile executions in its *Stanford v. Kentucky* and *Thompson v. Oklahoma* rulings. In short, the courts and legislators respond to public outcries of cruel and unusual punishment. In listening and responding to these concerns they are legitimizing capital punishment, which allows the practice to endure.

One issue that is often overlooked (but fortunately not forgotten by critics of the death penalty) is that of those wrongly convicted. One detailed study found evidence of some 400 defendants sentenced to death who turned out to be innocent, with an estimated two dozen who were actually executed—and many more spent years in prison. Not surprisingly, a disproportionate number have been African Americans (Radelet, Bedau, and Putnam, 1992).

During the past two decades more attention has been focused on the possibility that people could be sentenced to death when there may be some question about their guilt. A Columbia University study of 4,578 cases between 1973 and 1995 found that there were serious reversible errors in almost 70% of capital cases that were reviewed. Death sentences were overturned in two-thirds of the appeals, with 95 death row prisoners having been completely exonerated. The use of DNA testing has resulted in 107 persons being released between 1989 and 2002, 12 of whom were on death row. Total error rates have reached as high as 70% in some courts (Liebman et al., 2002; Weinstein, 2002a). The most recent data (2006) reveal that since 1973 a total of 123 people have been summarily released from death row, acquitted at retrials, had charges dropped, or were pardoned in light of evidence of their innocence declared innocent after being on death row, some for many years.[19]

Meanwhile, the use of the death penalty has increased, as appeals have declined and the process from conviction to execution has been stepped up. More are being executed every day. A few states, such as Texas, have turned this into a sideshow (to use Hatch's terminology) with crowds of people outside applauding as soon as the defendant is executed. African Americans and other minorities continue to receive the death penalty in numbers far greater than their proportion in the general population. Almost without exception, the executed are drawn from the ranks of the dangerous classes. Indeed, the death penalty is the ultimate penalty for this class.

Notes

1. The observations of a Detroit courtroom were made in February, 1999 by William B. Brown, Professor of Sociology at the Western Oregon. Portions of the first several pages of this chapter are adapted from Shelden and Brown (2003).

2. In recent years there has been a great deal of publicity concerning an alleged growth in frivolous lawsuits. Such a claim is not supported by the fact, as several studies have shown a decrease in the total number of lawsuits. For evidence see Association of Trial Lawyers of America (2005) and Bureau of Justice Statistics (2005).

3. See the classic study by Josephson called *The Robber Barons* (1962). Here he lays bare the greed and corruption, and often criminal behavior, of the richest men in America: Rockefeller, Vanderbilt, Carnegie, Mellon, Harriman, Gould, Frick, Morgan, and a host of others. Ironically, only one other period of American history has seen such concentration of wealth in such a small number of hands, and that period is the last two decades of the 20th century and the beginning of the 21st century, the period we are in as these words are written!

4. In the case of *Dartmouth College* (1819), the Supreme Court validated the corporation as a "private entity" immune from government intervention (Kelly, 2001: 130).

5. The connection between time spent in jail (and whether or not a defendant is detained in the first place) and final disposition has been documented by numerous studies. Among the most important of these studies include: Bynum (1982), Clarke and Koch (1976), Foote (1954), Ares, Rankin, and Sturz (1963), Farrell and Swigert (1978), and Patterson and Lynch (1991).

6. A 1992 study found that nationwide about 80% of felony defendants in the 70 largest counties were indigent (Cole, 1999: 66).

7. *Illinois v. Allen,* 397 U.S. 337 (1970).

8. For examples during both World War I and II; see Zinn, 2005.

9. This letter has become one of the most famous documents ever written and has been reproduced on many occasions. To read this letter go to the following website: http://almaz.com/nobel/peace/MLK-jail.html.

10. "Human Rights Award Recipient, Teresa Grady, Sentenced in Federal Court." Posted January 27, 2006 by Katie Quinn-Jacobs (online: http://stpatricksfour.org/?q=tgradysentence&PHPSESSID=01b0322fefa1a1f02213702a92d63504).

11. Baum (1997: 249) cites a study that found that almost *all* (99%) drug-trafficking defendants between 1985 and 1987 were African Americans.

12. Ironically, the father of Polly Klass, Marc Klass, has publicly criticized this type of legislation. He has formed the nonprofit KlassKids Foundation which, among other goals, seeks means of prevention rather than merely harsh reaction. He wrote the foreword to Peter Elikann's critique of the current demonization of children as superpredators (Elikann, 1999).

13. Space does not permit a detailed coverage of the "three strikes" law, but the reader is encouraged to read the report by the Campaign for an Effective Crime Policy (cited in the text) plus the text by Shichor and Sechrest (1996).

14. *Furman v. Georgia,* 408 U.S. 238 (1972).

15. See *Proffit v. Florida,* 428 U.S. 242 (1976); *Jurek v. Texas,* 428 U.S. 262 (1976); and *Gregg v. Georgia,* 96 Sup. Ct. 2902 (1976).

16. This discussion and all statistics cited are drawn from the following sources: Sellin (1967); Bedau (1996); Haas and Inciardi (1988); Radlett, (1989); "Capital Punishment USA—An Overview" (online: www.geocities.com/trctlll/overview); "Death Row Inmates by State" (online: www.deathpenalty info.org/DRowInfo); "Execution Update" and "Death Row Statistics" (online: www.deathpenalty info.org); see also http://www.deathpenaltyinfo.org/FactSheet.pdf.

17. *Penry v. Lynaugh,* 492 U.S. 302 (1989).

18. The criteria include: (1) substantial intellectual impairment; (2) impact of that impairment on everyday life of the individual; (3) appearance of the disability at birth or during the person's childhood.

19. This information comes from the Death Penalty Information Center. (2006). *Innocence and the Death Penalty* (online: http://www.deathpenaltyinfo.org/article.php?did=412&scid=6#inn-st). For a fascinating story of a man who spent 17 years on death row before being exonerated see the following: Democracy Now! "The Story of Harold Wilson: Convicted of Triple Murder, Sentenced to Die, Exonerated after 17 Years in Prison," Tuesday, December 20th, 2005 on the Internet: http://www.democracynow.org/article.pl?sid=05/12/20/1434244.

Housing the Dangerous Classes: The Emergence and Growth of the Prison System

Despite popular beliefs, imprisonment has little to do with actual levels of crime. Rather, imprisonment is one among many forms that have developed over the years to contain and house those individuals who are part of the dangerous classes. The basic argument in this chapter is that the development of the prison as a place of punishment corresponds not to crime but to much larger structural changes in the surrounding society and the specific social and historical context. In this case, the emergence and growth of the prison system corresponded to the emergence and growth of capitalism as a dominant economic form. Given that, as Marx predicted, capitalism continually produces a relative surplus population or reserve army of unemployed, certain mechanisms have been needed to somehow contain or manage this group, especially the lowest stratum, which Marx called the lumpenpropetariat. Recall in the Introduction this relative surplus population refers to a more or less chronically unemployed segment of the population that has become redundant or superfluous as far as producing profits is concerned. Prisons and other forms of total institutions have been among the major mechanisms for such containment.[1]

Part I: Early Developments of Imprisonment, 1600 to 1900

In their book *Punishment and Social Structure*, Rusche and Kirchheimer state their basic thesis on the relationship between the economic base of a society (or the mode of production) and the dominant form of punishment:

> . . . the mere statement that specific forms of punishment correspond to a given stage of economic development is a truism. It is self-evident that enslavement as a form of

punishment is impossible without a slave economy, that prison labor is impossible without manufacture or industry, that monetary fines for all classes of society are impossible without a money economy. On the other hand, the disappearance of a given system of production makes its corresponding punishment inapplicable. Only a specific development of the productive forces permits the introduction or rejection of corresponding penalties. But before these potential methods can be introduced, society must be in position to incorporate them as integrated parts of the whole social and economic system.

They note that in the history of punishment several epochs can be distinguished during which different penal systems and modes of punishment were predominant. Thus, during the early Middle Ages penance and fines were dominant; during the later Middle Ages a harsh system of corporal and capital punishment prevailed; during the late 18th and early 19th centuries imprisonment became the dominant form (Rusche and Kirchheimer, 1968: 6–8).

It should be noted that for centuries there have been forms of imprisonment, but almost always for short periods of time while an offender waits for the final decision on the case. Even in ancient Roman times there were places called prisons, but in reality they were like the modern equivalent of jails. In Venice, for instance, a popular tourist attraction is the Palazzo Ducale, which includes a courthouse and a prison (called the *I piombi* or "the Leads"). (One famous prisoner was Casanova, who managed to escape.[2]) The prison was reached via the Bridge of Sighs (the prisoners were heard sighing on their way to their cells). Public hangings were right next to the big canal next to St. Peter's Square. The Palazzo Ducale (also known as the Doge's Palace) was the seat of the government of Venice for centuries. In addition to being the home of the *Doge* (the elected ruler of Venice) it also contained the courts and—until its relocation across the Bridge of Sighs—the city jail.[3] Virtually every major city and town in the Roman Empire—and for that matter most of Europe—had some form of jail (often spelled *gaol* in old British English fashion). The *Catholic Encyclopedia* reports that in ancient Rome there were jails and the supervision of them was part of the regular duties of the local government (*triumviri capitalse*) until the middle of the 3rd century.[4]

The major concern in this chapter is to examine the reasons why imprisonment became a dominant mode of punishment during the late 18th and early 19th centuries. Specifically, this chapter is concerned with explaining why the prison emerged as a dominant place for punishment. Prior to this period of time punishment was harsh and public, often taking the form of a spectacle, with public whippings, hangings, hard labor in city streets, and so on (Foucault, 1979: 9).

Along with the prison system there emerged a new form of penal discipline. Rather than merely physical punishment imposed upon the body, we find a form of discipline aimed at the mind. This took such forms as daily rituals and routines, the inculcation of various attitudes and values (e.g., habits of industry and the Protestant ethic), hard labor, and the use of solitary confinement. This form of discipline arose simultaneously with the emergence of almost identical forms of discipline in the newly emerging factory system; and both arose along with the emergence of a capitalist mode of production. The evidence to be brought forth here suggests that the prison system and the new forms of discipline imposed upon prisoners served the major function of providing a pliant and stable work force, in addition to controlling in some way those segments of the population that do not or cannot fit into the prevailing social order (Melossi, 1978).

Through such an overview we can see how closely connected to the development of American capitalism the prison system has been. In fact, the 18th century philosopher Jeremy Bentham's invention of the panopticon penitentiary was used almost simultaneously as a design for the early factory system. (There will be more about this shortly.)

It should also be noted that the design of public schools was influenced by the design of the prison. This should not be too surprising since there was a need for social control of children and a need to prepare them for factory work. In fact, the connection between compulsory schooling, the new factory system, and various forms of punishment in penal institutions is apparent. The late Neal Postman noted that "with the growth of large industrial cities and the need for factory and mine workers, the special nature of children was subordinated to their utility as a source of cheap labor" (Postman, 1994: 53). Although writing about England, historian Lawrence Stone's comments are relevant for America, as he notes that one of the effects of industrial capitalism was "to add support for the penal and disciplinary aspects of school, which were seen by some largely as a system to break the will and to condition the child to routinized labour in the factory" (Quoted in Postman, 1994: 53).

Before turning to a discussion of the earliest forms of imprisonment, it is necessary to take a brief look at one of the earliest forms of punishment; one that has direct ties to the drive for profit within the capitalist mode of production. The subject is the trafficking of offenders.

The Trafficking of Offenders: Forerunners of the Modern Prison Industrial Complex

Scott Christianson, in his historical work *With Liberty for Some: 500 Years of Imprisonment in America* suggests that there is a connection not often seen when examining imprisonment, namely that between prison and slavery. He observes that slavery has often been viewed as a form of punishment and also that prison systems have often resembled a form of slavery (Christianson, 1998: xii). Michael Hallett has arrived at a similar conclusion when discussing the connection between slavery, convict leasing, and the modern growth of private prisons. He notes that the shipping of both convicts and debtors to America to work on colonial tobacco or cotton plantations "had already proven cost-effective for the Crown" (Hallett, 2006: 41).

Christianson observes that early descriptions of Spanish and French slave trades often used the terms *slave* and *prisoner* interchangeably. There is another obvious connection: one between prisoners, slaves, and private profit. Indeed, as we shall see shortly, penal slavery is a more apt description of American prisons, especially in the early years where so many criminals ended up being shipped from England to Southern plantations as source of cheap labor, often serving several years as apprentices. "Eventually plantation owners found that they could save even more money by using black slaves, since they could keep them for life" (Christianson, 1998: 6, 10).

The point raised here is that the growth and development of capitalism itself required cheap labor wherever it could be found, starting with children who were seized (often called napping) for shipment to American colonies to be servants. This practice became so common that the term *kidnapping* was often used (Christianson, 1998: 12). Here we find the beginnings of a prison industrial complex by providing cheap labor to help the newly emerging businesses. A trade in prisoners thus began, starting in the early 17th century when thousands of prisoners (slaves) were transported from England to America. It is true that American history is a history of immigration, but then American colonial history is mostly a "story of the immigration of prisoners" (Christianson, 1998: 13). Indeed, these prisoners "manned the ships" and they "were carried to the colonies to work in the mines and fields" and were "brought in chains from African and Europe to the Caribbean and the Americas as slaves" (1998: 13).

The early fortunes in America were not normally made through hard work by risk-taking entrepreneurs as American folklore would have us believe. Rather, most of these fortunes were the result of the "seizure, imprisonment, shipment, and sale of human beings to America," without which "immense fortunes would not have been made from tobacco, sugar, and rum" (Christianson, 1998: 15). In fact, some of the earliest trading companies from Great Britain had their own private lockups or prisons, which they used to temporarily house those on their way to the colonies. Operating these private prisons became quite profitable, a "lucrative clandestine trade in many ports," (1998:18) which also led to even more profit-making businesses, such as those manufacturing leg irons and similar hardware. Transportation expanded the social control function of the state with little or no cost, since "it relied on private entrepreneurs" (Hallett, 2006: 42). It was in fact driven by British colonial imperialism.

This trafficking of prisoners was for many years one of the most common forms of sentencing, especially after England made so many crimes punishable by death, which resulted in the increasing use of pardons. These pardons were not done for purely humanitarian reasons; as such a system provided a steady stream of cheap labor for colonial merchants. In fact, Parliament passed an act to assist these new businesses in the colonies, an act that allowed the courts to sentence offenders to transportation to the colonies instead of to the gallows, resulting in literally thousands of offenders shipped to America to be servants for a period of usually seven years. Christianson gives one example, a man named Jonathan Forward, a merchant in London who had contacts in Maryland. He was able to obtain a nice little subsidy from the crown: "three pounds for each Newgate prisoner and five pounds for every convict taken from the provinces. In exchange, he agreed to ship any and all criminals sentenced to transportation, and to pay all costs, including gaol [i.e., jail] fees, for their conveyance" (Christianson, 1998: 23–24). Forward was already experienced in the slave trade, so this was nothing new to him. Forward began collaborating with Jonathan Wild who provided many felons for transportation to the colonies. On one occasion, in August of 1718, a total of 106 prisoners were put on board the ship *Eagle*, a ship well-known for transporting slaves. Forward maintained a virtual monopoly on this business for more than 20 years. Transporting criminals remained a lucrative business throughout the 18th century. This business was described as one carried out by the "most corruptible class" of traders. In an ironic twist to this story, Forward's business was eventually taken over in 1771 by a young Glasgow trader by the name of Patrick Colquhoun, who eventually became a famous police reformer (Christianson, 1998: 23–24).

In time, transportation became the most common form of punishment in Great Britain. Between 1720 and 1765 Parliament passed 16 laws making transportation the required form of punishment for a wide variety of mostly minor crimes, such as poaching and perjury; at one point around 16,000 debtors were released from prisons and sent to the new colony of Georgia, a project led by one James Edward Oglethorpe, who was the deputy governor of the Royal African Company and a leading figure in early American history. It has been estimated that more that 20,000 prisoners came from England to Virginia and Maryland, plus at least another 10,000 from Ireland. Additional estimates, from various sources, puts the total number of prisoners transported to America at more than 50,000, representing at least one quarter of all British emigrants to America during the 18th century. Some say this estimate is too low. And it does not even include those sent from France, Spain, and Denmark (Christianson, 1998: 24–25; see also Blomberg and Lucken, 2000: 19–20). It can even be said that transportation marked the end of public punishments (e.g., public whippings, stocks, and pillory), the kind of punishments more appropriate for a colonial society based upon agriculture and the notion of crime as sin (Blomberg and Lucken, 2000).

One more point needs to be made and that is the fact that even back in colonial days there was a dual system of justice, one for the well-to-do and one for the poor. Public punishments and eventually transportation was reserved for the poor, while fines were leveled against the well-to-do. Not much has changed in 400 years.

The growing capitalist system certainly benefited from a steady supply of prisoners! So much for traditional notions of hard work and individual initiative as reasons for amassing huge fortunes! It should be noted that on their return voyage these convict vessels often brought with them colonial exports like tobacco, wheat, and pig iron. Profits often exceeded 30%! One convict trader wrote to his partner that their business "if properly managed will in a few years make us very genteel fortunes" (Christianson, 1998: 25).

Like African slaves, prisoners were often viewed as human cargoes and mere commodities. Advertisements were posted throughout the colonies noting the planned arrival of a particular convict vessel, in a manner almost identical to the arrival of African slaves. As we will note in a later chapter, for African Americans, the American prison system became little more than a substitute for chattel slavery.

If you think that such trafficking is a thing of the past, relegated to the dustbin of history, think again. Transporting prisoners is not only common today, but it is a big business. A recent survey by the Associated Press shows that 11 states export an estimated 8,700 prisoners to other states because of space shortages. This figure does not include the District of Columbia, which has no prisons, that has about 5,800 inmates spread out all over the country in both federal and private prisons (Crary, 2004). It is ostensibly saving the states money, which they would have had to pend on either new prisons or expansions of existing prisons. Examples include the state of Connecticut sending prisoners 500 miles to Jarratt, Virginia.[5] Other examples include Hawaii, which sends 1,439 prisoners to prisons run by Corrections

Corporation of America in Oklahoma and Arizona; Vermont is sending about 700 prisoners to Kentucky and Tennessee; Alaska sends more than 700 to Texas and within the next three years may send as many as 1,000; ironically, Arizona, which houses some prisoners from Hawaii (noted above) nevertheless sends more than 600 to Texas!

However, they may be cutting off their nose to spite their faces, since transporting prisoners to far away places makes it almost impossible for prisoners to maintain contacts with family members. It has long been recognized that a key to parole success is maintaining close ties with family members while incarcerated. A case in point is the family of Barbara Fair (a social worker in New Haven, Connecticut) who has three sons sent to prison on drug charges, who says the pain of this separation "is felt most keenly by Keijam Tucker, her son in Virginia, because he rarely sees his three young daughters. Even though most of the Connecticut inmates find the visitation and smoking policies more lenient in Jarratt than at Connecticut prisons, Tucker, 28, has formally requested a transfer to his home state—to no avail. Mrs. Fair says 'He'd take the deplorable conditions here in Connecticut just to see his daughters. They're growing up without him' " (LA Times Online, Crary, 2004).

The corrections commissioner of Vermont, Steven Gold, said the state would like to get back the prisoners they are sending to Virginia (at the prison in Jarratt) back home soon. Their plan is to create more space in their prisons by placing more offenders in community-based programs. Gold said that: "We recognize that when offenders are separated from their families and support systems, it has an impact on their current lives and their eventual re-entry" (LA Times Online, Crary, 2004). Corrections Corporation of America (CCA), the largest private prison company in the world, holds 55,000 inmates in 60 facilities in 20 states; CCA has more than 6,000 out-of-state prisoners in their various facilities around the country (LA Times Online, Crary, 2004).

Early Capitalism and the Emergence of the Workhouse

In order to understand the rise of the modern prison system we need to consider some of the earlier forms of imprisonment, namely workhouses or houses of correction. These institutions emerged in the late 15th and throughout the 16th century during which time we find the beginnings of what Marx called the "expropriation of the agricultural population from the land." It was the beginning of the transformation of a feudal society to a capitalist society. It was also a part of history written in blood and fire "for it was literally the case that small farmers and peasants were often killed and had their homes or huts burned" (Marx, 1977: 375). It was also the beginning of the famous "enclosure movements" (in 1489), a form of robbery against the poor by landlords, which lasted well into the 19th century in England and Scotland as formerly common land was transformed into private property (Chambliss and Ryther, 1975: 186–187).

This process turned a mass of propertyless and powerless peasants into a mass of wage-laborers (or proletarians) who were forced to emigrate to the cities and towns in search of work. However, there were more people than there were occupations and jobs available (a condition that has remained throughout the history of capitalism).

This created a problem in "social control" in terms of how to control the newly created surplus population. Marx stated the problem as follows:

> The proletariat created by the breaking-up of the bands of feudal retainers and by the forcible expropriation of the people from the soil, this free and rightless proletariat could not possibly be absorbed by the nascent manufactures as fast as it was thrown upon the world. On the other hand, these men, suddenly dragged from their accustomed mode of life, could not immediately adapt themselves to the discipline of their new condition. They were turned in massive quantities into beggars, robbers and vagabonds, partly from inclination, in most cases under the force of circumstances. Hence at the end of the fifteenth and during the whole of the sixteenth centuries, a bloody legislation against vagabondage was enforced throughout Western Europe. The fathers of the present working class were chastised for their enforced transformation into vagabonds and paupers. Legislation treated them as "voluntary" criminals, and assumed that it was entirely within their powers to go on working under the old conditions which in fact no longer existed (Marx, 1977: 896).

In other words, the new class of paupers, vagabonds, beggars and vagrants was created by and in turn "criminalized" by the state and sentenced to a term of confinement at hard labor in the houses of correction. These houses of correction were among the first in a long line of institutions (including modern forms of welfare) established for the control and regulation of this "surplus population" created by capitalism (Quinney, 1980: 131–140).

The first house of correction was known as the Rasphaus, which opened in 1596 in Amsterdam (Sellin, 1944, 1976; Shank, 1978). In this and similar institutions that sprang up throughout Europe and later in America we find the beginnings of the shift toward punishment of the mind in the form of the inculcation of habits of industry. The intention of the Rasphaus "was to discipline the inmates into accepting a regimen analogous to an 'ideal factory,' in which the norms required for capitalist accumulation were ingrained in the code of discipline" (Shank, 1978: 40). Furthermore, the organization of these workhouses "anticipated the compulsive regimens of isolation and hard labor to be pursued far more thoroughly in the penitentiary" (Ignatieff, 1978: 13–14). These workhouses, which were often appropriately called poorhouses,[6] were more fully developed in the late 18th and early 19th centuries in the shape of a gigantic "workhouse for the industrial worker himself" known as the "factory" (Marx, 1977: 388–389); as will be noted later, many have suggested that the factory was at least partly modeled after the penitentiary). When released from these workhouses, the inmates would theoretically willingly adapt to the regimentation of the factory and other forms of labor under the new capitalist system (Rusche and Kirchheimer, 1968: 42).

Most forms of punishment during the 17th and 18th centuries were harsh and public, as suggested earlier. Corporal and capital punishments were the norm, even for minor offenses. During the 18th century, however, the harshness of the punishments began to produce inconsistent results. Instead of acting as a deterrent and promoting respect for the law and for the ruling class, public punishments often turned into public demonstrations. For instance, the English judicial system even went so far as to engage in processionals as condemned men were transported through the streets toward the gallows at Tyburn outside of London. The ritual of such hangings "was taken over by the crowd and converted into a thieves' holiday and poor people's carnival" (Ignatieff, 1978: 88). These hangings were constantly "attended with disruptions, threatened rescues, disorders, brawls and riot" (1978: 89). Such disturbances became almost weekly occurrences and by the end of the 18th century were reminding the rich of the Gordon Riots, which was "an alarming sign of a new cleavage between elite and the poor" (Linebaugh, 1975: 67). It wasn't too long before hangings were conducted within prison walls, out of sight of the public (Linebaugh, 1975: 67).

In other words, the existing methods of justice were often irrational and inconsistent, and often producing results quite the opposite of those intended. This gave rise to a series of reforms (ostensibly humanitarian) toward the end of the 18th century, which culminated in the birth of a new system of punishment, the modern prison.

Late 18th Century Reforms and the Birth of the Prison System

Crime and punishment during the 18th century in England was characterized by corruption, inefficiency, discretion, and local control (especially by local justices of the peace). As capitalism grew, so did the power of the capitalists and at the same time so did the conflicts with those groups trying to resist the new forms of production and the newly emerging ruling power, the bourgeoisie.

A constant complaint of reformers centered on the inefficiency and corruption of local jails and workhouses. The management of these institutions was solely in the hand of local jailers and justices of the peace. There was wide variation in the kind of discipline used, there was unequal treatment of the rich and the poor, and many criminal justice workers were paid fees and thus open to bribery on a constant basis. Moreover, there was an inmate subculture, which exerted a great deal of control over what took place within these institutions. Those in control, however, looked the other way and, as long as they reaped profits (e.g., payments for preferential treatment) these abuses were ignored. Another problem was overcrowding, which became so bad that there was much rebuilding and enlargement of facilities between 1766 and 1776 (Ignatieff, 1978: 35–43).

One attempt to relieve the overcrowding was the introduction of convict hulks whereby convicted offenders were sentenced to serve a period of time aboard ships, a form of galley slavery. Many convicted offenders had their sentences commuted and were placed aboard ships and even transported to newly conquered colonies, where there was a need for abundant cheap labor (Rusche and Kirchheimer, 1968: 57; Barnes and Teeters, 1959: 295–305; Barnes, 1972: 61–92; Ives, 1914; Shaw, 1966; Ekirch, 1987).

Several notable reformers, such as Cesare Beccaria, Jeremy Bentham, and John Howard became famous for their critique of the arbitrariness, excesses, and inefficiency of the criminal justice system. These and other reformers represented two major currents of thinking within the penal reform movement. One current advocated reform of the law along rational lines; that is, they wanted the laws to be explicit and the punishments proportionate of the offense and applicable to all, regardless of the circumstances. This was the essential argument of the classical school of criminology, especially Beccaria who argued that the punishment should fit the crime. Similarly, Bentham argued that punishment should be consistent and physical punishment should not differ according to the emotions of the punisher. For the punishment of whipping, for instance, he recommended a whipping machine whereby each whip would be like all the others. In other words, punishment should become a science (Ignatieff, 1978: 75).

Another strand of thought advocated the implementation of new modes of penal discipline that would more efficiently inculcate habits of industry and help maintain social order. This corresponded to new thinking about crime and criminals. Bentham, for instance, said criminals were like children and persons of unsound mind, who lacked self-discipline. They had "infantile desires," which "drove them to ignore the long-term cost of short-term gratifications" (Ignatieff, 1978: 66–67). As already noted, it was Bentham who designed the famous panopticon style of prison, which also became useful to those who would later design the factory, since it involved a central administration area that allowed complete surveillance of inmates at all times. This style of prison construction was designed to be a cost-effective means to control large numbers of prisoners. Bentham can be view as a kind of entrepreneur who hoped to become wealthy from this design. In fact, he developed this model not just for prisons but also for houses of industry, poorhouses, hospitals, factories, mental institutions, and even schools (Hallett, 2006: 41).

Social control was complete within such a system, like similar social control systems in the factory. Also, the regimentation within these early prisons predated almost identical regimentation in many factories. As Rothman notes, both the early prisons and the factories "emphasized regularity and punctuality" and by "instilling order in its inmates, the prison was, in effect, helping to guarantee discipline and regularity in those who arrived each morning at the factory gate" (Rothman, 1998: 111; this also applied to the routine in the reformatory, to be discussed later in this chapter).

Along similar lines we have the views of John Howard, who was perhaps the most well-known and well-traveled prison reformer. Howard was heavily influenced by Quaker asceticism which stressed silent prayers, suffering and self-discipline. This led him to advocate a strong disciplinary regime within the prison system. He also believed that criminals were sinful and lost souls estranged from God. Much of his thinking was derived from a branch of knowledge known as materialist psychology. According to this view, what was needed was a strict regime of routinization and repetition, which would result in the internalization of moral duties. The best place for this kind of reformation was within a total institution (Goffman, 1961). Some have even called Howard the father of solitary confinement who even advocated this form of punishment for his own son (Ignatieff, 1978: 49–67; McGowen, 1999). Howard's ideal of a prison was that of a "structurally secure, spacious and sanitary" institution which would "embody a reformatory regime of diet, work and religious exercises" and "subject to a formal code of rules and systematic inspection" (Hogg, 1979: 10).[7]

Reformers wanted a system of punishment that would be perceived as legitimate (for there was a crisis in legitimacy at this time) and to do so the reformers

154 Chapter 4 • Housing the Dangerous Classes

needed to reconcile the apparent opposites of deterrence and rehabilitation, punishment and reform, just as factory owners had to reconcile the apparent conflict between profit and benevolence. The answer lay in the establishment of strict rules that would remove discretion of those in authority. Thus, both guards and inmates were to be routinized by an explicit system of rules. To do away with the inmate subculture they would institute the famous silent system. Constant surveillance of the inmates by guards and of guards by special inspectors, and of the entire operation by the general public was also advocated (Ignatieff, 1978: 76–78).

Some prison reformers, including Howard, were influenced by hospital reformers of the period. The hospital reformers wanted to habituate the poor to cleanliness, since the sicknesses of this class of people "were interpreted as the outward sign of their inward want of discipline, morality, and honor" (Ignatieff, 1978: 60–61). Physical diseases were correlated with moral problems and it was believed that the poor needed to be taught to be clean and godly, tractable, and self-disciplined. And "once the bodies of the poor were subjected to regulation, their minds would acquire a taste for order" (60–61).

It is hardly a coincidence that similar behavior was required of factory workers. Among the men who actively supported Howard's reforms were leading scientists, academics and manufacturers. Ignatieff further stated that the manufacturers were:

> . . . best known as the fathers of the factory system and scientific management. Besides introducing mechanization, extended division of labor, and systematic routing of the work process, they also devised the new disciplines of industrial labor: punch clocks, bells, rules, and fines. In order to reduce turnover and stabilize the labor force in their early factories, they provided schools, chapels, and homes for their workers in model villages. Regimentation along these lines would uplift the morals of the workers and eliminate their vices, according to the reformers. If this type of regimentation did not produce the desired results, there was always the workhouse and the prison (1978: 62).

Howard and other reformers believed that crime was a product of unregulated, undisciplined, and immoral lives and the required corrective was a strict regime of routinization and regulation, including the repentance of one's sins (hence the name *penitentiary*). Michel Foucault describes the new form of punishment, which he called a gentle form of punishment, as follows:

> As for the instruments, these are no longer complexes of representation, reinforced and circulated, but forms of coercion, schemata of constraint, applied and repeated. Exercises, not signs: sign-tables, compulsory movements, regular activities, solitary meditation, work in common, silence, application, respect, good habits. And, ultimately, what one is trying to restore in this technique of correction is . . . the obedient subject, the individual subjected to habits, rules, orders, an authority that is exercised continually around him and upon him, and which he must allow to function automatically in him (1979: 128–129).

The prison became one among many controlling institutions "designed to shape an emerging industrial proletariat" (Weiss, 1987a: 338). It was obvious that neither the control of crime nor humanitarianism was the major factors in prison developments; rather, "discipline and surveillance were the objectives of the new institutional web" (1987a: 339).

One of the most important guiding principles of prison reform was the principle of less eligibility. Simply put, less eligibility means that the conditions (or the standard of living) within the prison (or those dependent on welfare on the outside) should never be better than that of the lowest stratum of the working population. This would, theoretically, act as a deterrent to crime (or poverty) since people would choose to work under the prevailing conditions of free labor rather than commit crime and go to prison. In other words, people would freely choose to sell their labor power on the open market rather than seek alternative methods of subsistence and face a possible prison sentence. This principle still operates today, even though the theory behind it has never been proven to be correct (Rusche and Kirchheimer, 1968: 94; Melossi, 1978: 75; Hogg, 1979: 11).

The result of reform efforts during the last half of the 18th century was the passage of the Penitentiary Act of 1779 in England. This act created bard labor houses that would avoid the inefficiency and corruption of the old houses of correction, but the ideal work force free from corruption and willing to accept a regime as regulated as those of the inmates could not be found. Prisoners usually refused to work as diligently as superintendents wanted them to, and guards would slack off and even accept bribes. Overcrowding, a problem common today, was also a problem then (Ignatieff, 1978: 106).

The Penitentiary Act failed to deter crime and eliminate corruption. English society continued to experience crises, which grew worse during the 1790s and the first two decades of the 19th century. It was during this time that the first national penitentiary was opened at Millbank in 1813. But even the opening of this prison did not solve the problem. The regimes of hard labor, solitary confinement, and meager diets (all recommended by Howard and other humanitarian reformers) resulted in prisoner revolts, many of which were widely supported by those in the free society. One result was the return of whipping and other forms of physical oppression. One of the most interesting innovations in punishment during the 1820s was the treadwheel. The prisoners, holding onto bars, moved their feet in a walking motion in order to make the treadwheel go. The famous silent system in which prisoners were prohibited from talking to one another was also introduced at this time. Meanwhile crime and prisoner rebellions increased.

As more and more formal systems of control replaced informal systems of control (especially with the formation of the London Metropolitan Police in 1829) sentences to prisons and jails increased dramatically. For instance, when a new prison was opened at Pentonville in 1842 the rate of imprisonment was 326 per 100,090 population, an almost twofold increase from the rate of 170 in 1824. Among the new methods of control introduced in Pentonville were the removal of such privileges as communication with friends and family, an increase in the number of guards, and transportation to Australia following release, which almost amounted to a life sentence, even for minor crimes (Ignatieff, 1978: 179, 200).

The imposition of a new regime of penal discipline in England was part of a much larger movement to increase the hegemony of the new bourgeois society. Such

dominant middle-class values as hard work, respect for law and property, thrift, obedience, and so on, were held up as analogous to a religion (in a sense it was a religion,
influenced as it was by the Quakers and other religious groups). The image of the
prison served to confirm the dominant values implicit in their hegemony and the de-
votion of respectable, law-abiding citizens to such values. Perhaps more importantly,
the newly emerging penal system should be viewed as part of a much larger network
of institutions (e.g., family, education, religion) that would act to reproduce capitalist
social order. Neither the control of crime nor altruism was the motivating force.
Rather the motivation was discipline and surveillance (Staples, 1997). While some
reformers were motivated by genuine concern over the poor and the downtrodden
(as have so many over the years), the net result has always been the same: social
(especially class) control.[8]

Crime was viewed as a moral problem and, like poverty, was a simple choice.
Hogg sums up the goal of the prison system and penal discipline in early English society as follows:

> The sanctity of property and middle class standards of propriety had little relevance to
> communities whose very economic survival and conditions of life involved their trans-
> gressions in a myriad of everyday, and mostly petty, ways. The desire to moralize, disci-
> pline and reform the habits of these classes was the prime motivation for penal and other
> reforms in the second half of the century, as it had been in the period before (1979: 14–15).

Developments in America followed more or less along the same lines. The emphasis was on discipline of the laboring and dangerous classes and the inculcation of
those habits that were to be the very essence of "capitalist work management" (Melossi,
1978: 75). The next section will be devoted to a discussion of these developments.

The Development of the American Prison System

The Walnut Street Jail

The use of imprisonment as a mode of punishment did not occur until the late 18th
century in America. A penal reform movement actually can be traced back as far as
the efforts of William Penn in 1682. Penn was in the forefront of a movement to abolish the death penalty for many crimes and to introduce a new method of punishment
modeled after the Dutch workhouse, which seemed to correspond closely to the
Quaker thinking of the time (Melossi and Lettiere, 1998: 21).

Throughout Colonial America the most common form of punishment was a combination of banishment and various forms of public punishments, such as the stocks, the
pillory, and branding (e.g., branding the letter "T" on a thief's forehead). The use of
workhouses as a place of confinement was usually a last resort (Rothman, 1971,
Chapter 2; Powers, 1966). The primary method of social control in such a society was
rather informal, with local families, the community and the church providing most
forms of punishment. Toward the middle of the 18th century imprisonment in jails and

workhouses came to be reserved more and more for the poor. Many workhouses came to be called poorhouses. In Pennsylvania in 1766 the government established a house of employment reserved for those classified as "rogues, vagabonds and other idle and dissolute persons" (Takagi, 1975: 20).

Shortly after the end of the American Revolution a group of prominent citizens, such as Benjamin Franklin, Benjamin Rush, William Bradford, and Caleb Lownes, came together to update the criminal code of 1718. The new law, passed in 1786, authorized a penalty of "hard labor, publicly and disgracefully imposed" (Takagi, 1975: 20; see also Barnes, 1972: 81). Prisoners were to be sentenced to perform hard labor in the city streets. However, as in England during the processionals of condemned men, convicts began to draw crowds of sympathetic people. Shortly thereafter, a group calling themselves the Philadelphia Society for Alleviating the Miseries of Public Prisons amended the law and in 1788 suggested that sentences be more private and even called for solitary confinement within the confines of the Walnut Street Jail. The reason that this was done is that the new bourgeois class, having just gained power as the dominant class, wanted to promote stability and social order, in addition to respect for the law and for the new government. Placing prisoners on city streets did not result in such respect; placing them indoors would "export out of public view the sufferings and degradations heaped upon the poor" (Takagi, 1975: 23).

The Walnut Street Jail became the first state prison in America, and it was part of a much larger effort to create a powerful and centralized state apparatus. This state apparatus not only helped secure the new order, but it also helped perpetuate the existing class divisions. Takagi states that: "The success of the Revolution at home was brought about by the creation of a class divided society based upon private property and the ratification of the new Constitution was to guarantee the privileges and power of the bourgeoisie" (Takagi, 1975: 22–23). In fact, James Madison made it quite clear when he wrote in *The Federalist Papers* that: "The diversity in the faculties of men, from which the rights of property flow, is not less an insuperable obstacle to a uniformity of interests. The protection of these faculties is the first object of government" (Madison, 1961: 78). Continuing, Madison argues that one of the duties of a government or state is to regulate various interests, including "a landed interest, a manufacturing interest, a mercantile interest, a moneyed interest, with many lesser interests . . ." 1961: 79).

There were, indeed, class divisions at the end of the 18th century. And there was a great deal of disorder, stemming mainly from economic crises and general uncertainty over the future of American society. Shay's Rebellion was just one among several popular revolts of the time against the existing form of government and economy (Zinn, 1995: 90–96). It was also the early beginnings of the newly emerging ruling class of business people who would eventually become the tools and tyrants of the government, "overwhelming it with their force and benefiting from its gifts" (Chomsky, 1996b: 124) It was a system characterized by the replacement of the old feudalistic monarchy of England (which the American Revolution fought against) by the rule of a small business elite. It was becoming obvious at that time that some of the original supporters of the American Revolution (such as Thomas Jefferson) became alarmed at what was occurring. It was, in short, becoming less like a democracy (which the ruling class feared) and more like a ruling oligarchy with the "new spirit of the age: gain wealth, forgetting all but self" (Hill, 2001).

Prominent Americans, including those belonging to *the Philadelphia Society for Alleviating the Miseries of Public Prisons,* were concerned about maintaining social order. As Rothman writes: "What in their day was to prevent society from bursting apart? From where would the elements of cohesion come?" (Rothman, 1971: 58). The major worry, as Rothman suggests, was whether the poor would "corrupt society" and criminals would "roam out of control" (1971: 59). Thus, continues Rothman, comprehension and control of deviance "promised to be the first step in establishing a new system for stabilizing the community, for binding citizens together . . . And here one also finds the crucial elements that led to the discovery of the asylum" (1971: 59). In the end, the prison system became one among several methods of reforming and controlling the dangerous classes.[9]

While imprisonment slowly became a dominant method of punishing offenders, there also began to be some changes in the methods of penal discipline. Specifically, there was for a time two contrasting methods, which came to be known as the Pennsylvania and Auburn systems.

The Pennsylvania and Auburn Systems of Penal Discipline

Many reformers of the period believed that criminals lacked respect for authority and proper work habits, which could only be accomplished through a system of penal discipline emphasizing hard labor. Other reformers believed that the criminal was a sinner and needed to repent for his crimes. The idea of penance is said to have originated in the medieval monasteries of Europe for monks who had sinned or committed crimes (Melossi and Lettiere, 1998: 22). This could only be accomplished through the use of solitary confinement and no contact with other prisoners or with the outside world. These two views (although having more similarities than differences) came to be known respectively as the Pennsylvania and Auburn systems of penal discipline and prison construction.

The Pennsylvania system was modeled after some of the beliefs of John Howard. Two prisons were constructed during the early 19th century in the state of Pennsylvania. The first was opened in 1826 in Pittsburgh (known as the Western Penitentiary); the other was opened in 1829 in Cherry Hill, near Philadelphia (known as the Eastern Penitentiary). The architecture of these prisons (especially the one at Cherry Hill) reflected the basic plan for solitary confinement. The cells were arranged like spokes on a wheel, all radiating from a common central area. Each cell had an outside exercise yard. Each prisoner was allowed short periods in this yard for daily exercise, but most of the time was spent inside the cell working at some menial task. Each prisoner was blindfolded as he entered the prison to begin his sentence and was prohibited from contact with other prisoners. Only approved visitors from the outside were allowed to visit the prisoner (Barnes and Teeters, 1959: 338–339).

The Auburn system, which emphasized work in association with other prisoners, began in New York and was supported by some of the most prominent citizens of the state, including Thomas Eddy (noted financier and philanthropist), political leader and one-time governor De Witt Clinton, and governor and jurist John Jay. The first prison modeled after this plan was called the Newgate Prison, which opened in New York in 1797. (This prison was named after one by the same name in England.)[10] It closed in 1828 when a new prison called Sing Sing was opened and the Newgate prisoners were transferred to the new facility. In 1821 the second prison was opened in Auburn (Barnes, 1972: 132).

The Pennsylvania model soon came into disfavor because so many prisoners died or became insane, and there was a significant rise in the number of suicides as well. In the Auburn system prison administrators developed what has become known as the congregate system and the silent system. Prisoners worked together during the day but were not allowed to speak to one another and they were kept in solitary confinement at night. This system became the most dominant one and was followed by hundreds of prisons throughout the nation during the 19th century.

While ostensibly calling themselves and their new system at Auburn humanitarian, supporters of the system were as cruel as those who had come before them and the system they created was almost as repressive as those that existed in previous years. Elan Lynds, the first warden at Auburn, introduced the famous lock-step (prisoners would march single file, while shuffling their feet and keeping their eyes right) and was a strong advocate of the use of whipping, including the use of the cat-o-nine-tails. Lewis Wright, head of the Prison Discipline Society of Boston, was a firm believer in the Auburn system and published several tracts in support of it. In one he wrote as follows about the Auburn prison:

> The whole establishment, from the gate to the sewer, is a specimen of neatness. The unremitted industry, the entire subordination and subdued feeling of the convicts, has probably no parallel among an equal number of criminals. In their solitary cells they spend the night with no other book but the Bible, and at sunrise they proceed, in military order, under the eye of the turnkeys, in solid columns, with the lock march, to their workshops: thence, in the same order, at the hour of breakfast, to the common hall, where they partake of their wholesome and frugal meal in silence . . . When they have done eating, at the ringing of a little bell, of the softest sound, they rise from the table . . . From one end of the shops to the other, it is the testimony of many witnesses that they have passed more than three hundred convicts, without seeing one leave his work, or turn his head to gaze at them. There is the most perfect attention to business from morning till night, interrupted only by the time necessary to dine, and never by the fact that the whole body of prisoners have done their tasks, and the time is now their own, and they can do as they please . . . (Barnes, 1972: 136–137).

The famous Frenchmen Gustave de Beaumont and Alexis de Tocqueville, who toured American prisons during the first half of the 19th century, noted that while the Pennsylvania system produces more honest men the New York system (i.e., Auburn) produces more obedient citizens (DeBeaumont and de Tocqueville, 1964). They also could have added that the Auburn system attempted to produce an ideal worker for the factory system, a worker who was obedient, passive, silent and who would not complain about the grueling working conditions.

In time the Auburn system became the most dominant not simply because it was more profitable, but that it fit nicely within the larger structure of capitalism, characterized as it was by the need for cheap labor. Early prison factories resembled factories on the outside and for a time prisoners produced goods that were sold in the free market on the outside. While this may have been an important factor, it was certainly not the only factor. Perhaps even more important was the fact that as a mode of penal discipline the Auburn system was ideally suited for an emerging capitalist society in that it attempted to inculcate habits of hard work, punctuality, and other routines that would fit nicely into the regime of the factory system.

The penitentiary also fit into the overall pattern of republicanism, the view that society can only be held together through a free market, promoted by an active state. Consistent with this belief system was the need for individuals to become self-governing. Benjamin Rush had suggested the penitentiary might become a sort of gateway to the new republic by producing Republican machines, that is, human beings who were uncivilized or had lost their civilization and who would be transformed into good workers and citizens. In order to accomplish this task, the very souls of these men had to be conquered so that they could enter into a conversation with the other members of the American covenant.

One consequence of such a plan was "the extermination of those whose souls (if they indeed had been endowed with one) could not be reached, such as the native inhabitants of North America" (Melossi and Lettiere, 1998: 25–26; see also de Tocqueville, 1961). In other words, those who were unable or unwilling to accept the new order. It is interesting to note that de Tocqueville, in his classic work, *Democracy in America*, had noted that while the Native American was much too different to become part of this new order, the other race (the colored) would, once freed, be exposed to the new penitentiary regime. This, as we will see later in the chapter, is exactly what happened. As to the Native Americans, genocide was the preferred method (Melossi and Lettiere, 1998: 25–26; see also de Tocqueville, 1961).[11]

While the penitentiary was objected to by many Christian ministers, it was widely supported by state governments and the wealthy as an important mechanism to protect private property. Moreover, the apparent love for punishment was closely related to the love for democracy on the part of Americans. Furthermore,

> Democracy is the expression of the will of the people. Who counters that will, which expresses itself into the law, has to be punished . . . Right or wrong, black or white: who is (or is perceived to be) on the wrong side of the law, shall be punished. But alas, as with everything else in society, who breaks the law and is powerful (economically, politically, ethnically, racially, culturally and in regard to gender, and so on and so forth), can afford a full use of the safeguards that a developed legal system provides them with. For others, tough luck (Melossi and Lettiere, 1998: 28).

Finally, a capitalist system, based as it is on competition, cannot survive without various rewards and punishments. And those at the bottom of that order are viewed as being more tempted to violate the law in order to get ahead, based upon the notion that they have less to lose and more to gain. Thus, those individuals need to be more carefully watched and controlled. This was noted by many observers, including de Beaumont and de Tocqueville (Melossi and Lettiere, 1998: 28; de Beaumont and de Tocqueville, 1964).

The Rise of the Reformatory

During the first half of the 19th century several reformers and students of the prison system noted with dismay the brutality that existed within these institutions. The Frenchmen de Beaumont and de Tocqueville commented that while American society provided the most extended liberty, the prisons offered the spectacle of the most complete despotism (de Beaumont and de Tocqueville, 1964). As crime and disorder continued to rise in America, reformers searched for some alternative to the existing regimes of custody that prevailed. Some began to believe that prisoners should be rehabilitated and re-educated and should be allowed to earn their freedom while learning a specific trade. These beliefs led to the introduction of such well-known practices as the indeterminate sentence, parole, and vocational and educational training. All of these programs emerged with the rise of a new type of prison, known as the reformatory (Barnes and Teeters, 1959: 417; Barnes, 1972: 144).

The reformatory idea received its impetus from Captain Alexander Maconochie, who headed the penal colony on Norfolk Island in Australia. Maconochie introduced the mark system whereby a prisoner's sentence would be reduced if he obeyed prison rules (the modern version is known as good time). This worked as follows:

> Every convict, according to the seriousness of his offense, instead of being sentenced to a given term of years, had a certain number of marks set against him which he had to redeem before he was liberated. These marks were to be earned by deportment, labor and study, and the more rapidly they are acquired the more speedy the release (Barnes, 1972: 145).

About the same time, in England, Sir Walter Crofton introduced the so-called Irish system, which included the indeterminate sentence and parole. In the reformatory system here in America the ideas of Crofton and Maconochie were combined with such innovations as classification of inmates according to offense, personality, and other characteristics. If the prisoner proved he was *reformed* (a term which has never been precisely defined), he was given a pardon or what was known as a ticket-of-leave. The prisoner was still under some sort of supervision by the state until the expiration of his sentence. This practice was copied in America and came to be known as parole (Simon, 1993).

The reformatories were designed ostensibly to transform the dangerous criminal classes into "Christian gentlemen and prepare them to assume their 'proper place' into . . . hard-working, law-abiding lower class citizens" (Pisciotta, 1994: 4). These institutions would also inculcate into them good old fashion American values such as "habits of order, discipline, self-control, cheerful submission to authority, as well as respect for God, law, country, and the principles of capitalism and democracy" (1994: 4).

All of these programs were put into practice in a new prison at Elmira, New York, called the Elmira Reformatory, which was opened in 1877 (an institution which still stands today). Under the administration of Zebulon Brockway (a popular prison reformer and administrator and also an author of several books), a wide variety of programs were introduced. Among these were included industrial and academic education, religious services, library facilities, an institutional newspaper, and a gymnasium. The development of the reformatory came at a time of new hope among penologists of the period, exemplified by the first annual meeting of the National Congress of Penitentiary and Reformatory Discipline, in Cincinnati in 1870 (this organization is today known as the American Correctional Association). It was here that Brockway electrified the audience with his presentation on "The Ideal of a True Prison for a State" (Walker, 1998: 95), which came to be called the new penology.

Brockway's proposal was influenced by a study done by two penologists of the period, Enoch Cobb Wines and Theodore Dwight, who published *Report on the Prisons and Reformatories of the United States and Canada* in 1867 (Wines and Dwight, 1973). Wines and Dwight urged the development of a new type of institution in order to separate veteran and younger criminals, which they called an adult reformatory. Such an institution, they said, would "teach and train the prisoner in such a manner that, on his discharge, he may be able to resist temptation and inclined to lead an upright, worthy life" (Pisciotta, 1994: 11).

The recommendation was taken up by New York with an 1870 act that created the Elmira Reformatory, with the aim of housing "male first-time offenders between the ages of sixteen and thirty" and providing "agricultural labor" and "mechanical industry" (Pisciotta, 1994: 12). Following the Declaration of Principles put forth at the 1870 Congress, this institution would specifically provide treatment based upon the new medical model (see discussion of this term later in the chapter) using the indeterminate sentence, along with a very carefully calculated system of classification, "intensive academic and vocational instruction, constructive labor, and humane disciplinary methods" (Pisciotta, 1994: 13). An intensive period of parole would follow, thereby theoretically extending treatment into the community.

Brockway became its first and most popular administrator and he called his new institution a reformatory hospital and college on the hill. However, the Elmira Reformatory under Brockway became a military-like fortress, which emphasized coercion and restraint and ushered in a new era of treatment. Brockway defined reformation as the "socialization of the anti-social by scientific training while under completest governmental control" (Platt, 1977: 67–68). However, the Elmira reformatory "became like a garrison of a thousand prisoner soldiers . . . By means mainly of the military organization . . . The general tone had gradually changed from that of a convict prison to the tone of a conscript fortress" (1977: 67–68). In reality, it became benevolent repression under a strict military form of discipline, rather than reform (Pisciotta, 1994: 22).

The Elmira Reformatory (and other reformatories) failed to live up to its promise of reforming criminals and it ". . . failed signally to provide the right sort of psychological surroundings to expedite this process [of reformation]. The whole system of discipline was repressive, and varied from benevolent despotism, in the best instances, to tyrannical cruelty in the worst" (Barnes, 1972: 147). Elmira was originally built to house 500 inmates, but by 1899 it housed around 1,500. This prompted one writer of the period to state: "What had begun as a bold experiment lost the inspiring impulse of its first promoters, and became routine work and mass treatment" (Platt, 1977: 68). Beatings were routine, often done in the bathroom (called the slaughterhouse by inmates). Brockway himself administered some of the punishment. He was described by inmates as a different man at these times, as if he enjoyed the beatings.

Brockway rationalized this by calling it part of his scientific criminology and renaming corporal punishment as positive extraneous assistance, and solitary confinement was dubbed "rest cure cells" (Walker, 1998: 97–98). This was the new penology of the period!

However, Elmira (and so many other asylums) was never specifically designed for any other purpose than custody and control. More than this, it was a system of class control, for the prisons (then and now) were populated by the poor, the powerless, and (especially during the 19th century) immigrants. Commenting on the insane asylums and houses of refuge (for juveniles), Rothman states that these institutions "were two more bricks in the wall that Americans built to confine and reform the dangerous classes" (Rothman, 1971: 210).

Convict Labor

Throughout the history of prisons the concept of work in its various forms has been of utmost importance. This has been part of the more general belief that idleness is the devil's workshop and that criminals lack the work ethic" (Morash and Anderson, 1978). Thus, most prison regimens have utilized some form of work as a form of punishment (Miller, 1974). It can also be said that the use of inmates as a form of cheap labor has been part of the capitalist system from the beginning, as owners seek to maximize profits however they can include using the cheapest form of labor, whether it be slaves, immigrant labor, or inmates. Such exploitation persists to the present.

In the 19th century three different forms of convict labor emerged: the contract system, the state-use system, and the convict lease system. The prisons in the North tended to emphasize the contract system whereby prisoners produced goods to be sold (at a profit) to private companies, which in turn sold the goods in the free market. This was part of the Auburn system, since the congregate style of work was more applicable for the emerging industrial system of labor. This was especially the case during the Civil War, which created a need for various products, such as cloth, hosiery, shoes, and so on (Weiss, 1987a: 336). The exploitation of convict labor was part of a much larger process of capitalist exploitation. Barnes and Teeters note:

> But it was the rise of the merchant-capitalist in America, in the period following 1825, that breathed life into prison industry. Here was an intermediary who was glad to furnish the raw material and take the finished product at an agreed-upon rate. The system of contract labor was only one incident in the rise of the merchant-capitalist, of which home labor and the sweat-shop were other phases in his attempt to obtain cheap labor. Through this system prisons became profit-making enterprises, which was one reason why the Auburn system name to its dominant position (Barnes and Teeters, 1959: 528).

A variation of the contract system was the lease system. Under this system, prisoners were hired out to private businesses and worked away from the prison during the day. Through this method thousands of prisoners in several states helped build railroads, bridges, roads, and other projects. This system soon gave rise to the notorious chain gang, which still exists in many forms, mainly in the South (more about this follows). The contract system was abandoned soon after the end of the Civil War, particularly in the Northeast and Midwest, as organized labor mounted a serious campaign against the use of prison labor. What happened next was that the state took over under the so-called state-use system. Under this system, prisoners produced goods that would be used within the state system (e.g., other prisons, schools, hospitals, and so on). Today this is the most common form of prison labor, although variations of the old contract system have begun to emerge with many private companies using inmate labor. More will be said about this subject in the final chapter.

The systems of convict exploitation discussed in the preceding paragraphs soon disappeared in the North, but another system, convict leasing, had become popular in the South shortly after the Civil War. This is discussed in the next section.

Convict Leasing

Following the Civil War there emerged a method of punishment that demonstrates the fact that penal changes reflect much deeper changes in the political economy of a society. In the Southern states prisons were not used extensively prior to the end of the Civil War. After the war, however, the South was faced with some rather serious economic, political, and social problems. Political and economic recovery were among the first priorities because the economy of the South, based as it was on a slave mode of production, was being replaced by a capitalist mode of production. Another crucial problem was what to do with the newly freed slaves. What the white ruling class commenced to do was to begin the systematic oppression of blacks and maintain a system of caste rule that would replace a system of slavery (Shelden, 1979, 1993b). What happened was that the sharecropping system replaced slavery as a legal method of controlling the labor of African Americans. A system of agricultural (and eventually industrial) peonage emerged and was supported by such informal methods as vigilantism, intimidation, Jim Crow laws, and the like (Weiss, 1987a: 345).

Convict leasing was introduced throughout the South for one main reason: free blacks represented such a threat to white supremacy, convict leasing would be just another form of chattel slavery that would function to keep the black race in a subordinate position. Some might argue that this was one way to provide an abundant source of cheap labor to help rebuild the war-torn South (Shelden, 1979, 1993b). While this is no doubt partly true and an abundant supply of cheap labor was in fact readily available, this form of labor was not much of a help in the enormous task of rebuilding that faced the South (Sellin, 1976: 145; Weiss, 1987a: 345–347).

The emergence of convict leasing just happened to coincide with the demise of transportation of criminals, since the supply of white indentured labor had practically come to a halt. This "exacerbated the importance of slavery in colonial America" (Hallett, 2006: 43) and the doctrine of white supremacy "conveniently began to thrive during this period, with the exploitation-derived benefits of the African slave trade quickly surpassing those of white indentured servants" (2006: 43).

It was no accident that convict leasing developed only in the South and not the North. According to Hallett and several other scholars (Lichtenstein, 1996; Ayers, 1984; Colvin, 1997) convict leasing not only helped resolve the major economic crises facing the South, but also it kept white supremacy alive. It was, as Lichtenstein noted, New South slavery as it facilitated a form of industrial slavery by taking advantage of the existence of farms and plantations and the general exploitation of black labor (Hallett, 2006: 48, referencing Lichtenstein, 1996: 1–16).

The subjugation of African Americans became common throughout the South after the war. Several laws were passed (or old ones were reinstituted) that helped keep the African-American population in its place, such as vagrancy, loitering, disturbing the peace, and Jim Crow laws, to name just a few. When these methods failed, the use of force was used, especially lynching (and lynching increased after the war). Indeed, as several writers have documented, the use of force to keep African Americans in a subordinate position increased dramatically after the war, one example being the rise of the Ku Klux Klan (Cable, 1962; Johnson, 1930; Friedman, 1970; Meier and Rudwick, 1970; Woodward, 1955, 1969). There occurred a black crime problem during this time as former slaves tried to adjust to their freedom while being in an economically destitute position. Southern courts sentenced many to long sentences for minor crime, resulting in what one historian called a flood of criminals (mostly black) into the Southern prisons (Oshinsky, 1996; Ayers, 1984).

One result of this practice was the shift in prison populations to predominately African American following the war. Data for Tennessee prisons demonstrated this change. As indicated in Table 4.1, African Americans represented only 33% of the population at the main prison in Nashville as of October 1, 1865, but by November 29, 1867, the percentage had increased to 58.3%. By 1869 it had increased to 64% and it reached an all-time high of 67% between 1877 and 1879; a slight decrease in the number of inmates (especially African American) between 1880 and 1898 can be explained in part by the opening of two branches of the main prison—Brushy Mountain and Inman—in the 1890s. As indicated in Table 4.2, the population of

TABLE 4.1   *Racial Composition at the State Prison at Nashville, Tennessee, 1865–1914*

Date	Total	White	Black	Percent Black
Oct. 1, 1855	200	134	66	33.0
Nov. 29, 1867	485	202	283	58.3
Oct. 1. 1869	551	198	353	64.0
Dec. 1, 1874	963	380	583	60.5
Jan. 1, 1877	997	326	671	67.3
Jan. 6, 1879	1,183	372	781	67.7
Dec. 1, 1880	1,241	420	621	66.1
Dec. 1, 1898	899	324	575	63.9
Dec. 1, 1900	1,110	418	692	62.3
Dec. 1, 1902	923	408	525	55.7
Jan. 1, 1910	1,060	395	671	62.9
Dec. 1, 1912	1,206	474	732	60.7
Dec. 1, 1914	1,243	520	723	58.2

Sources: Taylor, 1941: 42; Tennessee Board of Prison Commissioners, 1896–1914; U.S. Census Bureau, 1918: 288–290.

TABLE 4.2   *Racial Composition at Brushy Mountain State Prison, Tennessee, 1898–1914*

Date	Total	White	Black	Percent Black
Dec. 1, 1898	525	64	441	84.0
Dec. 1, 1900	634	127	507	79.9
Dec. 1, 1902	762	145	617	80.9
Jan. 1, 1910	747	131	616	82.5
Dec. 1, 1912	704	139	565	80.3
Dec. 1, 1914	616	131	485	78.7

Sources: Tennessee Board of Prison Commissioners, 1896–1914; U.S. Census Bureau, 1918: 288–290.

Brushy Mountain Prison was predominantly African American, much more so than at the main prison. The only data available for the Inman branch are for prisoners on hand as of December 1, 1898. At that time there were only 58 prisoners, all of whom were African American (Shelden, 1979: 465–466).

Data from other states also illustrate the predominance of African Americans in the Southern prison system after the war. In 1888 the prison at Baton Rouge, Louisiana, held 85 whites and 212 African Americans; in 1875 in North Carolina 569 African Americans and 78 whites were sentenced to prison (Sellin, 1976: 149–159).

The actual increase in the populations within Southern prisons is staggering, as Tables 4.1 and 4.2 indicate. In Georgia there was a tenfold increase in prison populations during a four-decade period (1868–1908); in North Carolina the prison population increased from 121 in 1870 to 1,302 in 1890; in Florida the population went from 125 in 1881 to 1,071 in 1904; in Mississippi the population quadrupled between 1871 and 1879; in Alabama it went from 374 in 1869 to 1,878 in 1903 and to 2,453 in 1919 (Mancini, 1978: 343).

Convict leasing involved leasing out prisoners to private companies that paid the state a certain fee. The convicts worked for the companies during the day (convicts were usually not paid) outside the prison and returned to their cells at night. The sole aim of convict leasing "was financial profit to the lessees who exploited the labor of the prisoners to the fullest, and to the government which sold the convicts to the lessees" (Sellin, 1976: 146–147). One example was a lease system in Alabama. As Sellin explains it: "In 1866, the governor of Alabama leased the penitentiary to a contractor who was charged the sum of five dollars and given a sizable loan. The legislature granted him permission to work the prisoners outside the walls; they were soon found in the Ironton and New Castle mines" (1976: 150). In Tennessee by 1870 convicts were being leased from the main prison at Nashville to three separate railroad companies in Tennessee. During the 1880s the legislature appropriated about $14 million to relieve the railroad companies that had suffered great losses during the war. It is no exaggeration that convicts rebuilt Tennessee's railroads. In 1871, coal mining companies began to use convict labor and by 1882, more than half of the convicts at the Nashville prison were leased out. In 1884, the Tennessee Coal, Iron and Railway Company took complete control and leased the entire prison population (Shelden, 1979: 467).

Convicts were eventually classified "according to their ability to meet productivity quotas," along with "endorsing the use of violent methods such as whipping to exact higher productivity" (Hallett, 2006: 51). The state, having rented prisoners to private contractors, essentially washed its hands when it came to oversights. At least under the slave system the owners had some kind of obligation to take care of them. Under convict leasing, there was no such obligation. Little wonder historian David Oshinsky titled his book *Worse than Slavery* (1996), a book about the infamous Parchman Prison in Mississippi.

Mancini describes how one company, especially the owner Joseph E. Brown, made huge profits from convict leasing in Georgia:

> In 1880 Brown, whose fortune could be estimated conservatively at one million dollars, netted $98,000 from the Dade Coal Company. By 1886, Dade Coal was a parent company, owning Walker Iron and Coal, Rising Fawn Iron, Chattanooga Iron, and Rogers Railroad and Ore Banks and leasing Castle Rock Coal Company. An 1889 reorganization resulted in the formation of the Georgia Mining, Manufacturing and Investment Company. This rested largely on a foundation of convict labor (Mancini, 1978: 342).

The convict lease system was cruel and inhumane, to say the least. Deaths were common and the treatment caused much sickness and suffering. In a coal mine in Georgia convicts were routinely whipped if they did not produce the daily quota of coal (Mancini, 1978: 347). In Alabama inmates were punished by being placed in a sweatbox during the day in the hot sun. A Louisiana newspaper reported that "it would be more humane to impose the death sentence upon anyone sentenced to a term with the lessee in excess of six years, because the average convict lived no longer than that." Indeed, the death rate in 1896 was 20% (Sellin, 1976: 153). The mortality rate for inmates in the South was 41.3% per thousand convicts, compared to a rate of 14.9% in the North (McKelvey, 1968: 183). A common method of punishment was water torture—this was "where one is strapped down, face up, nostrils held shut, with barrels of sometimes boiling water poured down the throat" (Hallett, 2006: 50). Also, because these were leased prisoners and now owned (as in slavery) whether or not they lived was not important. If one died, they simply could get another one to replace him (Mancini, 1996).

The convict lease system, as such, disappeared, yet other forms of convict labor continued (and still exist today) in various forms. McKelvey notes: "But the lease system was doomed by its decreasing usefulness to the state, and it was not abandoned until profitable substitutes were perfected" (McKelvey, 1968: 185). These other systems included plantations, industrial prisons, and the famous "chain gang," which still exists today. The chain gang actually developed alongside the convict lease system as one of the two major forms of convict labor. Weiss provides us with the following graphic description of this system: "Chained together in fetid bunkhouses, suffering malnutrition and exposed to rampant disease, these hapless charges suffered one of history's most degrading punishments" (Weiss, 1987a: 345). It should be noted that the vast majority of those on these chain gangs were African Americans, often convicted for merely being black.

Part II: Twentieth Century Developments in the American Prison System

Prison Reform During the Progressive Era

As noted in the previous chapter, the Progressive Era brought about widespread changes in how American society responded to crime and other social problems. Reformers focused on practically all emerging problems of a growing capitalist society. As with all aspects of the criminal and juvenile justice system, the prison system became the focus of the many efforts by reformers to make changes. Some of the most popular prison reforms will now be discussed.

Inmate Self-Government

Progressive prison reformers sought to achieve the aims of rehabilitation inside the prison walls. These reformers reversed some of the principles of earlier reformers in that the prison should be as similar to the outside society as possible. The major principle that organized their efforts was the view of the prison as a community. Thus, they set about to humanize, individualize, and democratize the prison. For instance, they wanted to abolish the lock step and striped uniforms, liberalize visitation rules and correspondence, abolish the silent system, and introduce a number of amusements, such as movies, sports, exercise, bands, and so on (Rothman, 1980: 118–119).

One illustration of Progressive prison reforms was the Mutual Welfare League, an attempt to introduce the idea of inmate self-government into a prison. The chief organizer of this bold attempt was Thomas Mott Osborne, the head of the New York Prison Reform Commission. Osborne was probably the first to spend time inside a prison anonymously, which he did at the Auburn Prison in 1913. His experiences led him to conclude that the regime in this prison was too repressive, particularly the silent system and total isolation (solitary confinement). He came away with the conclusion that inmates must learn to be responsible for their own conduct. When he became warden of Sing Sing Prison in 1914 he established a Mutual Welfare League. Under this plan prisoners would elect a Board of Delegates, who would in turn elect an Executive Board. The Executive Board would be the rule-making and enforcement body of the prison. The League would also present inmate grievances. The aim of such a program was to make inmates "not good *prisoners*, but good *citizens* . . ." (Rothman, 1980: 121).

At first the experiment seemed to work, as sales of products produced by prisoners increased by almost $40,000 between 1913 and 1914. Also, discipline seemed to have improved. One indication of this was that in 1914 only 155 prisoners were treated for wounds, compared to 363 the year before. In time, however, the experiment failed, mainly because disciplinary problems seemed to have increased after the first year (a charge that might be debatable) and newspapers and the prison superintendent accused Osborne of coddling prisoners. Charges of mismanagement were brought against Osborne, but he was exonerated. He eventually resigned in disgust. One outcome of this experiment was the discovery of the importance of an inmate subculture, a subject that has been extensively studied since then (Walker, 1998: 152–153; Barnes and Teeters, 1959: 499–501).[12]

Classification, Diagnosis and Treatment:
A New Prison Routine

Perhaps the most enduring of all prison reforms during this era was the emergence of individualized treatment, based upon what has become popularly known as the medical model, which argues that the offender is sick or suffering from some form of disease and, like a physical illness, must be diagnosed and cured. The reasons for this development are many and varied. One source has to be the development of the positive school of criminology—a major shift in the thinking about the nature and causes of crime. Coming from a variety of both European and American writers, this school of thought stressed the importance of social, psychological, and biological facts in crime causation. However, it was mainly the psychological perspective (with the parallel development of the practice of social work) that led to the development of the medical model and individualized treatment. Individualized treatment stressed the importance of viewing each offender as a separate case to be individually diagnosed and treated (just as you would be if you visited a doctor's office with a physical ailment).

A related source was the emergence of the academic and professional fields of social work, sociology and psychology. In the early years of these disciplines, there was a constant effort to attain respectability and to map out areas of domain. The prison eventually became a convenient laboratory for the scientific study of human behavior and social organization. In each of these disciplines the so-called case study method prevailed. This method emphasizes the study of the individual (although it can be applied to specific groups and institutions). In the case of the problem of crime, the emphasis shifted to the study and treatment of the individual offender (largely ignoring the law itself and the surrounding social context).

Both psychologists and psychiatrists were in the forefront of prison reform during the Progressive Era. Their first goal was the establishment of diagnostic centers where each new prisoner would be individually diagnosed and classified. "They would interview, examine, and test the inmate, determine his aptitudes and his potential for rehabilitation, then assign him to the appropriate place [i.e., institution]" (Rothman, 1980: 122). To accomplish this would require the establishment of a variety of institutions. According to Ernest Hoag and Edward Williams, two California psychiatrists, criminals could be classified according to five categories: "those capable of learning a trade, those best suited for agriculture, the insane, the defective, and the psychopathic" (1980: 123). On the whole, then, psychologists and psychiatrists viewed the prison as analogous to a hospital (as did John Howard over 100 years earlier). These reformers came to view the prison as an institution that could be transformed "into treatment centers which would diagnose the ailment and deliver the appropriate antidote" (1980: 123).

In order for offenders to receive this treatment, reformers insisted upon a sentence that would give prison personnel enough time to perform such as task. The answer was to be the indeterminate sentence. This sentence entailed no fixed amount of time on a particular sentence. Reformers believed that under such a sentence prisoners became more responsible for their own rehabilitation (Rothman, 1980: 69). Between 1890 and 1915 a total of 26 states had passed some type of indeterminate sentence law (Miller, 1974).

Classification became a permanent part of the 20th century penal institution. Some form of classification had always been used in prisons. The first known type was a simple one of segregating offenders by sex and age, which was done at the Walnut Street Jail. In the 1840s the insane were separated and placed in separate institutions, while African Americans were always been segregated from whites, if not in totally separate institutions, at least within each institution. During the last half of the 19th century classification came in the form of separations according to recidivists—first offenders, sex deviates from the rest of the population, and the like. Eventually there were grades of offenders based upon good behavior or progress (often with different uniforms or some type of insignia to distinguish them). Also, in many prisons the trusty system was developed whereby a select group of prisoners are given some responsibility, the most common (and notorious) of which has been to act as a guard (Barnes and Teeters, 1959: 466–467, 496–498). This system survived until at least the 1960s, when it came under attack as a result of a series of scandals within the Arkansas prison system (Murton and Hyams, 1969).

In reality, classification was and still is based upon concerns for custody. The various classification schemes discussed above appealed to prison wardens because they would simplify custody. In particular, they would segregate the troublemakers from the general population, in addition to child molesters and other sex offenders, potential suicides and escapees (Rothman, 1980: 124).

Psychiatrists and psychologists, in all their theories about criminal behavior, never could come up with specific cures that were workable. "For all their allegiance to a medical model," says Rothman, in reality "they had no medicines to prescribe" (Rothman, 1980: 125). One result was that, instead of in-depth psychotherapy and individualized attention, inmates were subjected to a highly regimented prison routine that would include work and education, with the emphasis on work. A special prison committee in New York concluded that: "Work is to be the foundation around which every activity revolves in every prison" (1980: 126). The routine within these prisons would ideally keep prisoners busy and a system of rewards would, hopefully, help prisoners learn to function according to rules and regulations, therefore making better prisoners rather than better citizens on the outside.

Yet even the above, rather modest, reforms were not adopted uniformly in every prison in the country. "Change was piecemeal, not consistent, and procedures were almost nowhere implemented to the degree that reformers wished. One should think not of a Progressive prison, but of prisons with more or less Progressive features" (Rothman, 1980: 128). Probably the most consistent change was the abandonment of striped uniforms (only four southern states still had them by the mid-1930s), the lockstep and the silent system. Most prisons began to allow inmates freedom of the yard (i.e., to mingle, talk, exercise, and so on for an hour or two each day outside of their cells in an open area), more recreation (especially baseball), and movies. However, treatment never became a reality, since most states were reluctant to spend the necessary money

and custody considerations always came first. In fact, despite all the rhetoric of individualized treatment, by 1926 there were only a small handful of full-time psychiatrists and psychologists.

The failure to implement treatment programs can also be attributed to the fact
that the medical model rarely went beyond diagnosis, for there was no specific cure
available for criminal behavior. Even educational and vocational training was limited.
Austin MacCormick, noted prison reformer and eventual director of the Bureau of
Prisons, concluded in 1929 that: "Save for a few exceptions, we are tolerating a tragic
failure. There is not a single complete and well-rounded educational program in all
the prisons and reformatories for adults in America" (Rothman, 1980: 136). In short,
the bottom line was (and still is) custody, since whenever the goals of treatment and
custody conflicted, custody won (and still usually wins).

The reality of American prisons became one of idleness and boredom. Vocational
training was at best extremely limited. The amount of work available was quite limited,
which is ironic since so many had believed that work was highly reformative. An attorney general's report in the mid-1930s found that 60% of the nation's prisoners were idle.
One reason was the fact that most forms of inmate labor common in the 19th century
had largely disappeared. This change deserves more detailed attention.

The Decline in Prison Industries

By the end of the Progressive Era the lease and contract methods of inmate labor had
begun to disappear from the scene. Three other systems became the most common:
state account, state use, and public works. Table 4.3 illustrates these changes.

The state account and the state use systems are very similar, the major difference being that in the former the goods are sold on the open market and in the latter
the products are used by other state agencies. The latter is the most often used today.
Public works uses prisoners in the building and/or repair of highways, streets, bridges,

TABLE 4.3 *Percent of Prisoners Employed Under Different Systems of Labor, Selected Years*

System	Year						
	1885	1895	1905	1914	1923	1932	1940
Lease	28%	19%	9%	4%	0%	0%	0%
Contract	40	34	36	26	12	5	0
Piece-Price	8	14	8	6	7	11	0
State Account	0	0	21	31	26	19	12
State Use	26	33	18	22	36	42	59
Public Works	0	0	8	11	19	23	29
Total	100	100	100	100	100	100	100

Source: Barnes and Teeters, 1959: 535.

and similar projects. Between 1914 and 1915 there was a so-called good roads system, which involved using prisoners to build and improve public highways. This movement may have been related to the arrival of the automobile on a large scale during this period. Colorado and Washington, among other states, took advantage of this brief experiment (Walker, 1980: 154).

A variation of public works was the infamous chain gang, which emerged in the South after the Civil War in the form of prison camps. This system emerged out of the lease system when, because the convicts often refused to work and many escaped, they were placed in chains while they worked. One notorious chain gang was called by one writer the American Siberia (Powell, 1891). This particular chain gang was a camp in Florida, where turpentine was extracted in a semitropical jungle atmosphere where the only labor that could be obtained was that of convicts. "Prisoners worked in gangs, chained together in filthy bunkhouses, exposed to dysentery and scurvy" (Barnes and Teeters, 1959: 378). After several exposés, covering most of the southern states, plus government investigations, the chain gang has all but disappeared, although some form of this system still exists in the South.

The final phase of the decline of prison industries came during the 1930s. Because of the economic decline of the Great Depression, a total of 33 states passed various laws that prohibited the sale of prison-made goods on the open market. Two federal laws, the Hawes-Cooper Act of 1929 and the Ashurst-Summers Act of 1935, prohibited the interstate shipment of prison-made goods. As a result, the traditional forms of prison industries, for all intents and purposes, ceased to exist (Allen and Simonsen, 1998: 44–45).

Instead of a treatment-oriented prison, what really became dominant during the Progressive Era was a type of prison popularly known as "The Big House." An analysis of prison developments during this period of time would not be complete without a discussion of this type of prison.

The Big House

We can trace the overall growth of the American prison system in terms of six major eras: (1) 1790–1830: early American prisons; (2) 1830–1870: the Pennsylvania and Auburn systems; (3) 1870–1900: reformatories; (4) 1900–1946: The Big House; (5) 1946–1980: the correctional institution; (6) 1980 to the present: warehousing.[13] The last two eras have seen the greatest growth in the prison system. Thus, while in 1900 the prison population stood at around 50,000, by 1935 it was over 120,000. In 1900 there were 81 state prisons and reformatories, while at the end of the 1930s there were over 100. In 1990 there were a total of 1,287 prisons (80 federal and 1,207 state prisons); by 1995 there were a total of 1,500 prisons (125 federal and 1,375 stateprisons), representing an increase of about 17%. The federal system experienced the largest increase, going up by 56%. In some cases, the capacity within the prison has increased—some megaprisons can hold from 5,000 to 10,000 inmates (Austin and Irwin, 1997: 66). As of 2005, there were about 1.5 million prison inmates and 750,000 jail inmates, bringing the total to about 2.2 million prisoners (Harrison and Beck, 2006).

The Big House became the dominant type of prison until the late 1940s and early 1950s. This prison was typically a huge, granite structure, capable of housing 2,000 or more prisoners, with some housing more than 4,000. These institutions were theoretically supposed to eliminate the most abusive forms of punitiveness and prison labor within existing prisons (Rotman, 1998:165). Most had large cell blocks with three or more floors or tiers of cells, usually housing one or two men in each cell. Many were built in the late 19th century, such as Jackson (Michigan), San Quentin (California), Joliet (Illinois), and Sing Sing (New York), while most were built in the 20th century, such as Stateville (Illinois) and Attica (New York) (Irwin, 1980: 3; Killinger and Cromwell, 1973: 47). Irwin provides perhaps the most graphic description of the Big House:

> This granite, steel, cement, and asphalt monstrosity stood as the state's most extreme form of punishment, short of the death penalty. It was San Quentin in California, Sing Sing in New York, Stateville in Illinois, Jackson in Michigan, Jefferson City in Missouri, Canon City in Colorado, and so on. It was the place of banishment and punishment to which convicts were "sent up." Its major characteristics were isolation, routine, and monotony. Its mood was mean and grim, perforated here and there by ragged-edged vitality and humor (Irwin, 1980: 5).

Although it was, in a sense, an industrial prison, with factories producing various goods, most prisoners spent their time in relative idleness toward the end of the 1930s. When they did work, one of the major products was license plates.

Thus ends another chapter in prison reform. The reform agenda during the Progressive Era ran up against the hard realities of the prison. The 20th century prison, mostly in the form of the Big House, was this reality. Rothman concludes his analysis of prison reforms during this period with the observation that the reality of the prison "is not one of the inmates exercising in the yard or attending classes or taking psychometric tests, but of the physical presence of the walls" (Rothman, 1980: 157–158). It was these high walls (some as high as 30 feet above the ground) that helped wardens and guards keep their jobs, for legislatures and the general public seemed to be content with one thing: maintaining a quiet joint (i.e., no riots, no escapes, and a smooth running institution).

We now turn to the final phase in the history of prisons with the development of the Federal Bureau of Prisons and the so-called correctional institution.

The Emergence of the Federal Prison System and the System of Corrections

The Federal Prison System

Until 1895 prisoners convicted of federal crimes were housed in state prisons. The number of prisoners housed in state prisons more than doubled from 1,027 in 1885 to 2,516 in 1895. During this period of time federal prisoners were used as contract labor. But in 1897 Congress outlawed this practice and eventually it was decided that these prisoners should be transferred to a separate institution (Rotman, 1998:166). Thus, federal prisoners began to be housed at Fort Leavenworth, an old military prison in the eastern part of Kansas. In time a new prison was built nearby, which opened in 1928. In the meantime two additional federal prisons were being built by the federal government, one in Atlanta and the other on McNeil Island, Washington. Atlanta was opened in 1899 and McNeil Island was opened in 1907 (Allen and Simonsen, 1998: 538–539).

The passage of several federal laws (e.g., Mann Act in 1910, Harrison Narcotic Act in 1914, Volstead Act in 1918, Dyer Act in 1919) resulted in an increase in federal prisoners. Subsequently, in 1925 Congress authorized the construction of a federal reformatory at Chillicothe, Ohio and the construction of the first federal prison for women, which was opened in 1927 at Alderson, West Virginia (Allen and Simonsen, 1998: 538–539; Rotman, 1998: 167).

A more significant development was the overall increase in the role of the federal government in the fight against crime. This was due in part to an alleged crime wave during the 1920s and 1930s. Most of this crime wave was created by the news media as they sensationalized various gangsters and such famous criminals as Bonnie and Clyde, John Dillinger, Ma Barker, and Alvin Karpis, not to mention such organized crime figures as Al Capone. As noted in chapter 2, a major role was played by the Federal Bureau of Investigation. In 1929 the Federal Bureau of Prisons was officially established, thus completing the federal law enforcement bureaucracy (Allen and Simonsen, 1998: 539–540; Walker, 1998: 159–163; Rotman, 1998: 167–168).

With the creation of the federal prison system and the passage of new federal laws, new federal prisons were constructed. The most famous of these new prisons was Alcatraz (opened in 1934), located on an island in the San Francisco Bay area, directly across from the famous Fisherman's Wharf. Alcatraz, probably more than any other federal prison, typified the new crackdown on crime and on hardened criminals, especially organized crime figures and famous criminals like John Dillinger and Al Capone. An escape-proof prison located on a small island in the San Francisco Bay, it became one of the most notorious failures on the new penology as it hardly put a dent in the increasing crime rate of the next two decades. It was finally closed in the early 1960s and is now merely a tourist attraction. It was replaced, however, by a "super-max" prison at Marion, Illinois (Rotman, 1998: 168).[14]

The Federal Bureau of Prisons helped develop a new system of classification, new prison industries, a federal system of probation and parole, and new educational and vocational training programs. Perhaps the most important was the new system of classification. First, there was a classification system according to types of prisons. Five different types of facilities were developed: penitentiaries, reformatories, prison camps, hospitals, and drug treatment facilities. Second, within each facility classification was done according to age, offense, sex and other criteria. In the 1970s the federal system established a classification system based upon security level. Five levels were established: minimum (mostly federal prison camps—many are next to military bases where many inmates provide additional labor for the military base), low (double-fenced perimeters and mostly dormitory-style living arrangements), medium (cell-type living arrangements and double-fenced perimeters with electronic detection systems), high (most commonly known as U.S. penitentiaries, with high security perimeter double fences or walls, along with very close supervision of inmates in cell-type housing), administrative (special needs institutions—pretrial defendants, noncitizen detainees and, more importantly, the housing of the "extremely dangerous, violent, or escape-prone inmates") (Allen and Simonsen, 1998: 540–546).

The System of Corrections

With the federal government leading the way, a new era of penology began to emerge, especially after World War II. This new penology ushered in a new type of prison system complete with a new terminology. Thus began the age of the correctional system and a host of new prison workers, whom Irwin has called correctionalists. These individuals were a "growing body of college-educated employees and administrators of prisons, parole, and probation and a few academic penologists. . . ." (Direct quote from Irwin.) These individuals "were convinced and were able to convince many state governments and interested segments of the general population that they could reduce crime by curing criminals of their criminality" (Irwin, 1980: 38–39). Instead of a prison there was to be a correctional system; in place of prisoners or convicts, we would have inmates; and guards were magically transformed into correctional officers (Barnes and Teeters, 1959: 440). The prison system remained a system to house the "dangerous classes," but the new terminology seemed to be an attempt to mask its true functions and create the false impression that something positive was being accomplished within the walls.

Many of the "Big Houses" were replaced by shiny new correctional centers. In line with a "new" era of "treatment," there also emerged a new classification for these new prisons, according to the degree of security that was apparently needed. Thus, we find *maximum, medium*, and *minimum* security correctional institutions. Examples of minimum security prisons (most without walls) included the California Institution for Men at Chino (a state institution); a federal institution at Seagoville, Texas; and another at Wallkill, New York.

Part of the new penology[15] included the emergence of what many have called the rehabilitative ideal or the emphasis (originally called for in 1870) on *treatment* (a term that was changed to *rehabilitation*). It appears that, after floundering for several decades, the proposals of the 1870 prison meetings were to be finally implemented. During the decades of the 1940s and 1950s correctionalists would implement this new penology according to three essential procedures: the indeterminate sentence, classification, and specific treatment programs (Irwin, 1980: 40; Rotman, 1998: 169–170). Classification was to be done by a special team of psychologists, social workers, counselors and other professionals who would form a special classification committee to determine the proper course of treatment for the prisoner. The new penology even went so far as to create a name change for the American Prison Association (formerly the Congress of Penitentiary and Reformatory Discipline), calling it the American Correctional Association in 1954—a name that exists to the present day. New names were invented to replace old, punitive practices; thus, the hole (solitary confinement) was renamed the adjustment center. Even Soledad Prison in California was renamed the California Treatment Facility (see discussion that follows). And in place of the old granite walls, they built tall fences (today reinforced with razor wire, with some wired with electricity) and guard towers (Rotman, 1998: 170). But for all practical purposes, they remained essentially prisons or what Goffman called total institutions (Goffman, 1961).

The indeterminate sentence was implemented in most states. While some reformers (such as psychologist Karl Meninger) advocated a sentence of zero to life for all offenders (in other words, literally a sentence of indeterminate length), most state legislatures implemented a modified version, such as 1 to 10 years for larceny, passed in California. More power was granted to parole boards as a result of indeterminate sentencing laws. Ideally, parole boards would release an offender only when they felt he or she was rehabilitated. But this assumed that those in charge of the prisons "had procedures for identifying and changing criminal characteristics, which they did not, and that parole boards had procedures for determining when these changes had occurred, which they did not" (Irwin, 1980: 41–42).

While classification was supposed to be improved so that criminal behavior could be cured, the procedures adopted never attained this ideal. On the one hand, theories of criminal behavior never have been developed sufficiently to affect an adequate cure for criminality and treatment programs have never been fully implemented in most prisons. On the other hand, classification (and most other prison procedures) continued to be determined by concerns over custody and security. Thus, the classification procedures tended to ignore a prisoner's treatment needs, however ill defined.

The most common treatment program to be implemented during these years (mainly the 1950s) was group counseling. However, even this was not too successful, since the pay was insufficient and the location of most prisons was far from ideal (many were located in rural areas, many miles away from urban areas). As a result, group counseling sessions were led by those not fully qualified to do so. Further, these sessions became a sort of game played by prisoners since they were led to believe that by attending even their chances for parole would be greater, and perhaps even their sentence shortened. In other words, most who did attend (and not all did) did so not to change their behavior and attitudes, but to get an early release.

Academic and vocational training programs were more easily implemented, yet these too were far from effective. Most of the vocational training programs did not begin to equip prisoners with marketable skills on the outside. In fact, most of these programs were tied into the daily maintenance of the prison (e.g., cooking and baking). Also, most prisons lacked modern equipment and techniques (Irwin, 1980: 46).

For the most part, the prisons of the post–World War II era continued pretty much the way they had before. Rotman's assessment captures the basic problems of rehabilitation within these prisons when he writes that:

> . . . despite the rhetoric of rehabilitation, this new wave of treatment euphoria shared with previous efforts the same paucity of practical realizations. Because of the limited professional possibilities offered by the penitentiary setting, the treatment staff was still generally composed of less qualified individuals. In addition, there was a permanent conflict, ideological and professional, between the custody and the treatment staffs regarding issues of discipline and security (Rotman, 1998: 169).

Irwin's comments echo those of Rotman, as he writes that:

> The public and most government policy makers continued to demand that prisons first accomplish their other assigned tasks: punishment, control, and restraint of prisoners. In addition, the new correctional institutions were not created in a vacuum but planned in ongoing prison systems which had long traditions, administrative hierarchies, divisions, informal social worlds, and special subcultures among the old staff. The new correctionalists were never able to rid the prison systems of the old regime, though often they tried; and the old timers, many of whom were highly antagonistic to the new routine, resisted change, struggled to maintain as much control as possible, and were always successful in forcing an accommodation between old and new patterns. So correctional institutions were never totally, or even mainly, organized to rehabilitate prisoners (Irwin, 1980: 46–47).

Irwin discusses at length the history of Soledad Prison in California as an example of the failure of post–World War II developments. (Irwin himself was an inmate at this prison during the 1950s.) It was originally established as a medium security, treatment-oriented prison for younger and more trainable prisoners. Its original name implies it goals: California Training Facility. The prison had no granite walls (like Big Houses) but instead a high fence (although with gun towers at several locations, indicating that the new penology was still concerned over custody and security). There was a library, a hospital, an education building, gym, and other accoutrements of the new penology. They offered several vocational training programs, elementary and high school programs and a counseling program. The overall environment was not as harsh as in most of the older prisons.

It did not take too long for this new treatment-oriented prison to succumb to the realities of prison life and became just another prison. Prisoners became aware of the fact that the new treatment was in reality, simply a new method of control and, moreover, that rehabilitation was ineffective (as evidenced by the high rate of return of prisoners who had participated in Soledad's treatment programs). Further, an influx of African Americans and Chicanos created racial divisions, which was further acerbated by a growing militancy of African-American prisoners during the late 1960s. Prison administrators took advantage of these divisions (as most still do today) in order to better control the prison and maintain a quiet joint (a common divide and rule technique). Thus, by the 1960's Soledad was like most other prisons in America, with a heavy emphasis on custody and control. It eventually fell victim to the many disturbances within the entire prison system, highlighted by the killing of the celebrated George Jackson in January, 1970 (Irwin, 1980: 47–90).

The Modern Era, 1980 to the Present: Warehousing and the New American Apartheid

It should come as no surprise to find that most prisoners today are still drawn from the bottom of the class structure, have few marketable skills, little formal education, and poor work records, and are disproportionately nonwhite. Prisons still house the dangerous classes. More ominously, however, the modern American prison system is becoming to look more like a gulag than ever before (Christie, 2000; Richards, 1990). Also, it is clear that the prison system is becoming a form of apartheid as for the first time in our history African Americans constitute a numerical majority of prison, as well as jail inmates. Before we examine these and other characteristics in more detail, let us look at the population of today's prisons as a whole.

The most recent data show that as of June 30, 2005 there were 2,186,230 people behind bars. The overall incarceration rate was 738 per 100,000 population (up from 601 in 1995), placing the United States first in the world for overall incarceration rates per 100,000 population.[16] We are way ahead of other industrial democracies, whose incarceration rates tend to cluster in a range from around 55 to 120 per 100,000 population, with some well below that figure, like Japan's rate of 58. England is slightly above this range at 142.[17] The average incarceration rate for all countries of the world is around 80 per 100,000. Thus, America's incarceration rate is almost nine times greater than the world average (Currie, 1998: 15; Kuhn, 2001). The Norwegian criminologist, Nils Christie, in the third edition of his groundbreaking book on the crime control industry, noted that there is a huge difference between the United States and our northern neighbor Canada. Canada's incarceration rate is about 129, about one-fifth our rate. He notes, by the way, that these two countries are essentially the same (in terms of the economic and political systems) except for one important difference: Canada has more of a social safety-net (various welfare benefits) than does the United States (Christie, 2000: 31).

While these increases were noteworthy during the later 1980s, they were most pronounced during the first half of the 1990s, as you can see from Tables 4.4 and 4.5. What Table 4.4 clearly shows is how the rates in recent years compare over time.

TABLE 4.4   *The Growing Prison Population, 1925–2005*
(rates per 100,000 in state and federal prison)

Year	Number	Rate
1925	91,669	79
1935	144,180	113
1945	133,649	98
1955	185,780	112
1965	210,895	108
1975	240,593	111
1985	480,568	202
1995	1,085,363	411
2005	1,461,132	491
% increase (1975–2005)	507	342

Source: Maguire, K. and A. L. Pastore (eds.) (1997). *Sourcebook on Criminal Justice statistics—1996;* Washington, DC: Department of Justice, Bureau of Justice Statistics, p. 518; Harrison, P. M. and A. Beck. (2006). "Prisoners in 2005." Washington, DC: Bureau of Justice Statistics, November (http://www.ojp. usdoj.gov/bjs/pub/pdf/p05.pdf).

For comparative purposes Table 4.6 illustrates population changes in other parts of the criminal justice system. Here we find data on the number on probation and parole, in addition to those in prison and jail for the period 1980 to 2005. Note that while the prison and jail populations were growing rapidly, so too were the two other parts of the system.

How do we explain this phenomenal growth? In a word, *drugs!* Indeed, the war on drugs, which really took off during the mid-1980s, began to have its effects on jail and prison populations by the early 1990s (Baum, 1997; Miller, 1998; Currie, 1993). As noted in Table 4.7, between 1982 and 2002 the number of state prison inmates who had been convicted of drug offenses went up by 948%! By comparison, only modest increases were seen for violent and property offenders.

TABLE 4.5   *Inmates Held in State or Federal Prisons or in Local Jails, 1985–2005*

Year	Total	Federal or State Prisons	Local Jails	Rate/100,000
1985	742,580	487,594	254,986	313
1995	1,585,586	1,078,542	507,044	601
2005 (6/30)	2,186,230	1,431,468	747,529	738
% Increase				
1985–1995	114	121	99	92
1995–2005	38	33	47	23
1985–2005	194	194	193	136

Source: Proband, S. C. 1997. "Jail and Prison Populations Continue to Grow in 1996." *Overcrowded Times* 8, 4 and "Corrections Populations Near 6 Million." *Overcrowded Times* 9 (June); Harrison, P. M. and A. Beck. 2006. "Prisoners in 2005." Washington, DC: Bureau of Justice Statistics, July (http://www.ojp.usdoj.gov/bjs/pub/pdf/p05.pdf).

TABLE 4.6   *Adults on Probation, in Jail or Prison, and on Parole, 1980–2005*

Year	Total	Probation	Jail	Prison	Parole
1980	1,832,350	1,118,097	163,994	329,821	220,438
1985	3,011,500	1,968,712	254,986	487,593	300,203
1990	4,348,000	2,670,234	403,019	743,382	531,407
1995	5,335,100	3,077,861	499,300	1,078,545	679,421
2005	7,058,000	4,162,536	747,529	1,446,269	784,408
% Increase					
1980–2005	285	272	356	339	256

Source: Glaze, L. E. and S. Palla (2005). "Probation and Parole in the United States, 2004." Washington, DC: Bureau of Justice Statistics, November 2005 (http://www.ojp.usdoj.gov/bjs/pub/pdf/ppus03.pdf).

TABLE 4.7   *State Prison Inmates, by Offense, 1988–1994*

Offense	1982	1992	2002	% Increase (1982–2002)
Violent*	215,300	369,100	624,900	190
Property	114,400	181,600	253,000	121
Drugs	25,300	168,100	265,100	948
Public Order	17,800	56,300	87,500	392

*Violent offenses include murder, negligent and non-negligent manslaughter, rape, sexual assault, robbery, assault, extortion, intimidation, criminal endangerment, and other violent offenses.

Source: Bureau of Justice Statistics (http://www.ojp.usdoj.gov/bjs/glance/tables/corrtyptab.htm).

The decade of the 1980s witnessed the most dramatic changes. For instance, data on court sentencing shows that between 1980 and 1992, court commitments to state prisons on drug charges alone increased by more than 1,000 Figures from U.S. District Courts (federal system) show that whereas in 1982 about 20% of all convictions were for drugs, by 1994 this percentage had increased to about 36%. During this same period of time the proportion of those convicted on drug charges who were sentenced to prison increased from 74% in 1982 to 84% in 1994, and their actual sentences increased from an average of 55 months in 1982 to 80 months in 1994; the average sentences for murder during this time period actually decreased from 162 months to 117 months, while for all violent offenses the average sentence declined from 133 months to 88 months (Maguire and Pastore, 1997: 468, 472). Put somewhat differently, while in 1980, 19 out of every 1,000 arrested for drugs were sent to prison, in 1992 an incredible 104 for every 1,000 were sent to prison! (Melossi and Lettiere, 1998: 42, quoting Holmes, 1994). Incidentally, on any given day, almost 60% (58.6%) of all federal prisoners are serving time for drug offenses; of these 40% are African American (Maguire and Pastore, 1997: 576).

Numbers and rates tell only half the story. To see what is happening to our prison system we need to take a careful look at who is incarcerated. In general, we can conclude that modern prisoners occupy the lowest rungs on the social class ladder, and they always have. The modern prisons system (along with local jails) is a sort of ghetto or poorhouse reserved primarily for the unskilled, the uneducated, the powerless and, in increasing numbers it is being reserved for racial minorities, especially African Americans. This is why this system is being called the new American apartheid.[18]

One of the most dramatic changes in the demographics of American penal institutions in recent years has been the phenomenal increase in the proportion of African Americans and other minority groups who are locked up. Not surprisingly, this change can be attributable largely to the war on drugs.

As already noted, drug offenses have accounted for most of the increase in prison populations in recent years. However, the prison and jail populations have become increasingly dominated by minorities, especially African Americans,

TABLE 4.8   *Adults in Local Jails, by Race, 1985–1994 (rate per 100,000)*

Year	White	Black
1985	73	368
1990	106	568
1995	122	700
2005	166	800
	% Change	
1985–2005	127	117

Source: Bureau of Justice Statistics. "Correctional Populations in the US, 1998" (http://www.ojp.usdoj.gov/bjs/pub/pdf/cpus9802.pdf); Harrison, P. M. and A. Beck. 2006. "Prisoners in 2005." Washington, DC: Bureau of Justice Statistics, July (http://www.ojp.usdoj.gov/bjs/pub/pdf/p05.pdf).

TABLE 4.9   *State Prison Inmates by Offense and Race, 1986–2002*

Offense	1986	1991	2002	% Increase	
				1986–1991	*1986–2002*
Violent					
White	88,591	121,865	213,800	37.6	141
Black	119,694	150,972	257,300	26.1	115
Property					
White	63,785	74,612	114,900	17.0	80
Black	58,833	70,668	88,400	20.1	50
Drugs					
White	14,174	29,845	64,500	110.6	355
Black	14,201	80,304	126,000	465.5	787

Sources: Bureau of Justice Statistics, *Sourcebook on Criminal Justice Statistics—1995*. Washington, D.C.: Department of Justice: Bureau of Justice Statistics, p. 550 *Sourcebook on Criminal Justice Statistics—2003* (http://www.albany.edu/sourcebook/pdf/t600012002.pdf).

including women. Table 4.8 shows recent trends for jail populations. The numbers should be self-explanatory; likewise for Table 4.9, showing especially the drug connection, with a 784% increase for black prisoners for drugs, double the increase for whites. The most recent figures available (2005) are shown in Table 4.10. Here again, we see the incredible racial discrepancies at every age group. This table also shows the rate for the Hispanic population, a group that was once lumped together with whites as far as prison populations go. The differences remind me of the old 1960s

TABLE 4.10   *Inmates in State or Federal Prisons and Local Jails, June 30, 2005 (rate per 100,000)*

	Male				Female			
Age	**Total**	**White**	**Black**	**Hispanic**	**Total**	**White**	**Black**	**Hispanic**
Total	1,371	709	4,682	1,856	129	88	347	144
18–19	1,739	905	5,306	2,072	116	76	257	168
20–24	3,291	1,627	10,486	3,878	27	206	611	317
25–29	3,462	1,682	11,955	3,884	299	220	720	287
30–34	3,122	1,693	10,472	3,640	342	255	855	312
35–39	2,765	1,562	9,425	3,111	364	260	957	322
40–44	2,240	1,299	7,575	2,649	264	177	751	264
45–54	1,214	658	4,401	1,873	110	70	323	138
55+	260	167	879	562	12	9	26	26

Source: Harrison, P. M. and A. J. Beck (2006), "Prison and Jail Inmates in Mid-Year 2005." Washington, DC: Bureau of Justice Statistics, May 2005 (http://www.ojp.usdoj.gov/bjs/pub/pdf/pjim05.pdf).

TABLE 4.11   *Lifetime Chances of Going to State or Federal Prison for the First Time*

Race	**1974**	**1991**	**2001**
White male	2.2%	4.4%	5.9%
White female	0.2%	0.5%	0.9%
Black male	13.4%	29.4%	32.3%
Black female	1.1%	3.6%	5.6%
Hispanic male	4.0%	11.1%	17.2%
Hispanic female	0.4%	1.5%	2.2%

Source: Bonczar, T. P. (2003). "Prevalence of Imprisonment in the U.S. Population, 1974–2001." Washington, DC: Bureau of Justice Statistics, August, 2003.

phrase: "If you're white, you're alright; if you're brown, stick around; if you're black, stay back."

The most dramatic representation of the racist nature of the criminal justice system can be seen in Table 4.11. A black male born in 1974 had about a 13% chance of ending up in prison; the percentage more than doubled by 1991 (thanks largely to the drug war). The most recent figures show that a black male child born in 2001 has almost a one-third chance of ending up in prison. Also see the noteworthy increases for Hispanic males.

Many African Americans have been unjustly subjected to some of the more repressive types of legislation passed in recent years, such as "Three Strikes and You're Out" and various habitual offender laws. A study by the National Council on Crime and Delinquency found evidence of systematic racial bias in Florida's habitual criminal law. Specifically, they discovered that African-American offenders were about twice as likely to receive this type of sentence, even when controlling for the current offense and prior record (Irwin and Austin, 1997: 52).

Finally, we should note the well-publicized statistic that in 1995 around one-third of all African American males in their 20s are either in jail, in prison, on probation or on parole, a figure that stood at one-fourth around 1990 (Mauer, 1995).

The American Gulag

As noted above, the present American prison system is beginning to resemble in many ways the gulags of Russia. One of the first, and most popular, exposures of gulags came with the publication of Russian author Alexander Solzhenitsyn's *The Gulag Archipelago* (1970). This book exposed literally thousands of prison camps spread throughout the Soviet Union, mostly in isolated areas like Siberia. These concentration camps originally emerged in the 1920s under Lenin and then expanded even further under Stalin. The number of prisoners grew from around 350,000 in 1929 to more than 1.5 million by 1931. These were forced labor camps set up ostensibly to help the growth of industrialization following the Russian Revolution (Conquest, 1995; Harris, 1997).

Gulags persist to the present day, not only in Russia, but also in such countries as China, North Korea, and the Sudan. A recent report noted the existence of Gulags in Canada during the 1930s, known as Project 51 in Lac Seul, Northern Ontario (Collins, et al., 1996; Lilly, 1993; Pasqualini, 1993; Wu, 1996).

One might conclude from the above that the gulag phenomenon is typically seen as either an aberration (such as Canada's Project 51) or something restricted to Third World or totalitarian societies. However, a close look at the modern American prison system might suggest otherwise. Indeed, at least two recent authors have suggested as much. In the early 1990s, Norwegian criminologist Nils Christie suggested that the crime control industry was beginning to look like the equivalent of the Russian gulag (Christie, 1993). A paper by Richards also used the term *gulag* to describe the modern prison system (Richards, 1990). We don't have to look very far back in history to find almost the exact equivalent to gulags in this country, especially in the West, with the emergence of so-called relocation centers to house Japanese-Americans during World War II.

Today the American prison system has many of the same characteristics of gulags. Prisons are literally found in just about every part of the country, with the bulk of them (especially those built during the past 20 years) in rural areas. There is also a great deal of human rights abuses in American prisons (and also jails and juvenile correctional facilities) such as cruel and unusual punishment (e.g., long periods in solitary confinement) and extreme brutality and violence. Moreover, there is much forced (and cheap) labor, much of which produces great profits for corporations.

To give the reader an idea of the "gulag-look" of the American prison system, we compare the states of Texas, Michigan, and California—three states that have obviously found building prisons a lucrative business. One of the most interesting things about the American prison system is that since the beginning most of these institutions have been located in rural areas.

Texas is a classic example, which now boasts of over 100 prisons (most have been built since 1980 and 80 have been built in the 1990s). An example of the rural nature of most of these facilities can be seen by sampling some of the towns where they are located (population according to the 1990 census): Iowa Park (6,072), Teague (3,268), Dilley (2,632), Brazoria (2,717), Kennedy (3,763), Dalhart (6,246), Marlin (6,386), Rusk (4,366), Richmond (9,801), Woodville (2,636), Woodville (2,636), Navasota (6,296), Fort Stockton (8,524), Childress (5,055), and Cuero (6,700). A check of the 1998 *Rand McNally Road Atlas* reveals that several Texas prisons and other facilities are located in towns not even found on the map! Places like Lovelady, Midway, Tennessee Colony (with three separate prisons each housing over 3,000 inmates!), Rosharon (with no less than four prisons housing over 6,000 inmates), and a privately run prison in a town called Venus (with 1,000 inmates). These institutions are found literally in every part of the state.

The Texas prison system has more than 42,000 employees, operates its own health services system (with more than 8,000 personnel, including 200 doctors) and has 35 lawyers working for them. Farming is big business for the prison system, with control over more than 134,000 acres (about 200 square miles), operating the largest horse and cattle herds in the entire state (more than 10,000 head of cattle and around 1,500 horses). The system also operates 42 factories within 32 prisons under its own Texas Correctional Industries. The most recent figures (December 31, 2005) show that there are just over 169,000 inmates in the state prison system and an incarceration rate of 691 (ranked second in the nation), according to the Bureau of Justice Statistics (Harrison and Beck, 2006: 1).

As of 1996, Michigan had 39 prisons and 15 prison camps, the majority of which were built in the 1980s. The rural nature of the prisons in this state is just like Texas. Some examples include: Munising (2,783), Baraga (1,231), Carson City (1,158), Grass Lake (903), Coldwater (9,607), Ionia (5,935), New Haven (2,331), St. Louis (3,828), Newberry (1,873), Eastlake (473), Freeland (1,421), Plymouth (9,560), Standish (1,377), and Lapeer (7,759). Kinchebe (not on map, nearest town is Rudyard, pop. 900).[19] Typical of recent trends, there are a total of four facilities in Kinchebe alone, one of which is located on an abandoned Air Force base, purchased by the state in 1978. The facility at Newbury was opened in 1995 on the site of a former state mental institution.[20] As of December 31, 1997, there were 44,771 inmates and an incarceration rate of 457 (ranked ninth in the nation, excluding the District of Columbia) (Proband, 1998b).

Not to be outdone, California also fits well into the gulag mentality. As of spring, 1996, there were 32 state prisons (in 1980 it had just 12 prisons!) plus 38 forestry camps and a multitude of community facilities. Largely as a result of the recent Three Strikes and You're Out laws, it is anticipated that by 2001 the state will have around 250,000 inmates (it had 157,547 as of December 31, 1997 and an incarceration rate of 475, tenth in the nation, excluding the District of Columbia) and around 50 prisons). Some examples of the rural nature of California's prisons include: Avenal (9,770), Susanville (7,279), Techachapi (5,791), Calipatria (2,690), Baker (650), Imperial (4,113), Chowchilla (5,930), Blythe (8,428), Soledad (7,146), Ione (6,516), Crescent City (4,380), Coalinga (8,212), Jamestown (2,178), and Adelanto (8,517).

Some Concluding Thoughts

We live in times of great uncertainty and rapid social change as millions just barely eke out a living while a very small minority become richer and richer. As the title of Jeffery Reiman's book says, "the rich get richer and the poor get prison" (Reiman, 1998). However, it is more than what Reiman has suggested. As we move into the new century we find more and more of our citizens relegated to the ranks of what Marx once described as the surplus population, a population rendered unneeded or superfluous as far as creating profits are concerned. With more and more corporate downsizing has come the disappearance of semiskilled and unskilled jobs once filled by urban minorities, especially African-American males. But this group is still very much with us and, from the point of view of those in power, they need to be managed in some way. The prison system seems to be the mechanism of this form of management.

It is especially ironic that we are experiencing what politicians are calling the end of welfare as we know it. The irony is that we are experiencing a new form of welfare and it's called the prison system. And since there has not been a significant rise in the kinds of crimes that have historically resulted in prison sentences (burglaries, larcenies, robberies, murder, and so on) and we cannot use the crude techniques of control common in totalitarian societies (e.g., torture, genocide), we have invented new crimes and new criminals to justify prison expansion, namely drugs. But of course only certain kinds of drugs, used by certain classes of people are targeted.

It should also be emphasized that following the social unrest of the 1960s the problem of discipline became greater than ever before, exemplified by the problem of crime. For conservatives it was also a crisis in values—especially the value of hard work and responsibility. (Out of this concern came the hot political agenda of family values during the late 1980s.) As Melossi and Lettiere perceptively note, the current era has been one marked by what the famous French sociologist Emile Durkheim called anomie, a breakdown in social norms and the disjuncture between the culture (traditional goals, such as success) and the social structure (legitimate institutions that help meet these goals). Two common outcomes of this includes an increase in various forms of crime and deviance and a strong effort by those in power to restore and defend the old order through the use of various forms of social control, typically the most coercive forms (the legal system). Continuing, Melossi and Lettiere observe that during recent years crime:

> . . . became a master-metaphor to designate what was wrong with American society, with the criminals certainly, but also with work absenteeism, students taking over campuses, pot-smokers, free-sex lovers, rebellious minorities, "liberated" women and so on and so forth. At the same time, "punishment," and the connected concept of "individual responsibility" increasingly became a master-metaphor of what "the cure" ought to be (Melossi and Lettiere, 1998: 37–38).

This conservative reaction reached its zenith during the Reagan years in the 1980s, when the rate of imprisonment went zooming upward, and the targets were mostly minorities, especially African Americans who may face the following possible scenario within the first two decades of the 21st century: a majority of all African-American males between 18 and 40 will be in prison or jail! (Estimates provided by Mauer, 1994; Miller, 1996; Tonry, 1995).

Are we not engaging in our own form of slow genocide, a sort of disenfranchisement of urban minorities? Have we not created a new, more modern form of apartheid? And in order for us to do this it is necessary to use certain scientific-sounding labels, like sociopath or criminal personality. Of course the traditional, gut-level terms are also used, like dangerous classes, predators, thugs, gangs, and the like. It is not "our kind" that are being sent to prison, it is "them," "those people," and so on. This way we can wash our hands of any responsibility.

We have come a long way from the workhouses of the 16th and 17th centuries. But the functions of the modern prison system—ironically in the richest country in world history—remain the same: providing housing for those groups deemed dangerous, a label being used more and more disproportionately to define people with dark skin.

Notes

1. The classic discussion of total institutions is found in Goffman (1961). For one of the most recent treatments of the tendency to contain the dangerous classes, see Irwin (2005).

2. This is discussed on the Wikpedia encyclopedia: http://en.wikipedia.org/wiki/ Giacomo_ Casanova#_ref-Casanova-prisons_0. Here a reference is given to the following book, written in French: Giacomo Casanova (1787). *Histoire de ma fuite des prisons de la République de Venise qu'on appelle les Plombs*. Leipzig. Shonfeld.

3. The author personally saw this on a trip to Italy during the winter of 2006–2007.

4. See the following website: http://www. newadvent.org/cathen/12430a.htm.

5. Jarratt, Virginia has a population of 589, typical of the locations where a majority of prisons that have opened in the past decade or so. It is located in the southern part of the state, about 70 miles south of Richmond, just off Interstate 95. The name of the prison is Greensville Correctional Center, opened in 1990, which now has a population of 3,007. (http://www.vadoc.state.va.us/ facilities/ institutions/ greensville. htm).

6. For an excellent treatment of the subject of poorhouses, see Wagner, 2005.

7. The reader may note a connection between religion, conservative thought, and punishment in this discussion. It is beyond the scope of this chapter to explore this subject in any detail. For a good analysis of this, see Shelden, 2004.

8. Weiss refers to a study of the emergence of the prison system in Massachusetts and South Carolina by Hindus, who argued, "The profit,

production, and discipline goals of the prison [in Massachusetts] were the same as those of the factory" (1987: 339). What is perhaps most interesting here is the fact that factory owners were often active in prison reform. Weiss reproduces an interesting quote from this source as follows: "The largest single category of arrests in Massachusetts was liquor-related offenses. Arrests for vagrancy and the entire area of sex-related crimes also show that a particular value system was being upheld through law, rather than simply that limited list of crimes against persons and property, prosecution for which few would object to." See Hindus (1980: 227 and 251). Virtually every major historical study has noted that the vast majority of arrests throughout the 18th and 19th centuries were for mostly public order and similar crimes. See, for instance, Ignatieff (1978).

9. It should be noted that Rothman (using a consensus argument) continually suggests that Americans wanted social order, and so on, never mentioning the fact that it was a relatively small ruling elite that wanted a certain kind of order, one that would primarily benefit their own class. See Chomsky (1996a) for further elaboration on this theme.

10. For an interesting account of the original Newgate prison in England visit the following website: http://www.oldbaileyonline.org/ schools/ journey.html.

11. For a discussion of the treatment of Native Americans and evidence of genocide, see Chomsky (1993) and Zinn (1995). It should be noted that while the incarceration of African

Americans was almost nonexistent in the South prior to Emancipation (with a rate of only 8.34 per 100,000), in the North the free African Americans were incarcerated at a rate of 289.91, compared to a rate of only 26.23 for whites; ironically a difference higher than it is today (late 1990s). After 1870, of course, the South began to catch up with the North in the incarceration rate of African Americans, jumping up to a rate of 120.35 versus only 42.56 for whites. Melossi and Lettiere (1998: 27, citing Sellin, 1976: 133–144 and Sabol, 1989). In the South the role of the penitentiary was seen as an acceptable and more humanitarian method of punishing white offenders, since most white southerners believed capital and corporal punishments were appropriate methods of punishing black offenders (see Weiss, 1987a: 343).

12. For a more detailed story of Osborne, see Tannenbaum (1933). It is probably no accident that this experiment did not last. While the official goal of prisons has been to prepare inmates to be responsible and productive citizens, in fact prisons have operated as if they wanted to produce just the opposite. There is a tendency to reinforce dependency and irresponsibility, which, in effect, reproduces the class structure.

13. The first five were suggested by Irwin (1980) while the last period (covering the years since Irwin's book), was suggested by Robert Weiss (personal communication).

14. This prison is located in the southern part of Illinois, within a short distance from Southern Illinois University. While a graduate student at this university in the early 1970s, the author visited this prison on several occasions as part of a special education program organized by a group of inmates (joined by fellow graduate student and now noted authority on prisons, Robert Weiss). I recall very vividly the experience of going inside this prison. It looked and felt and sounded like a prison, much more so than any other prison I have visited. The experience was at first frightening, not because the inmates were dangerous (some were, of course, but those I met were not), but because of the look and feel of the prison, with the steel locks, block walls, the sound of cell doors closing behind me (an unmistakable echo that gave me the message loud and clear that this was in fact a prison). What was particularly eerie was on the occasions when I went about the time the sun was setting and around the spacious grounds (covered with trees and freshly mowed lawns) I could see several deer roaming around. The contrast between the freedom displayed by these deer and the deprivation of freedom displayed by this very imposing prison was incredible. I have never forgotten that sight—and I wish I had a camera at the time! In time Marion became infamous for the behavior modification programs within its walls and the large number of political prisoners it held.

15. The reader no doubt notices that the phrase new penology has already been used to describe the rhetoric of the 1870 Prison Congress meetings and the reforms during the Progressive Era. This is testimony of how history so often repeats itself. The latest new penology was mainly "old wine in new bottles."

16. Bureau of Justice Statistics, online: http://www.ojp.usdoj.gov/bjs/pub/pdf/pjim05.pdf.

17. "U.S. Prison Population Continues Rising." CNN News, April 24, 2005. http://www.cnn.com/2005/US/04/24/prison.population.reut/index.html?section=cnn_us.

18. This is similar to the argument provided by Massey and Denton (1993), who were describing the old American apartheid.

19. It should be noted that there are at least eight prisons in the Northern Peninsula alone (Munising, Baraga, Newberry, Kinchebe, and Marquette (pop. 21,900)), housing more than 5,000 inmates.

20. It is ironic that many state mental institutions were closed in the 1960s and 1970s as part of a deinstitutionalization movement, only to have many of the same buildings now housing prison inmates. It has been estimated that as many as 70% of prison inmates suffer severe mental problems (Schlosser, 1998; interviewed by Terri Gross, "Fresh Air," *National Public Radio,* December 3, 1998).

5

Controlling the Young:
The Emergence and Growth
of the Juvenile Justice System

This chapter traces the development of the juvenile justice system from colonial times to the present. It will begin with a brief discussion of how the misbehavior of children and youth was dealt with in colonial society and turn to the build-up of institutions dealing with juvenile delinquents in the early 19th century. The chapter will close with a discussion of the reforms that took place in the last half of the 19th century, culminating in the modern juvenile court and juvenile training schools.

From our current historical vantage point, this is not a story with a happy ending. Indeed, we have continued to succumb to what we will refer to here as the edifice complex. By this we mean that we have continued to view the solution to many human problems as requiring some form of *edifice*—a courthouse, an institution, a detention center, and so on. Yet at the same time, we have succumbed to the *Field of Dreams* syndrome—"If you build them, they will come." In other words, as soon as you construct these edifices they will be filled almost immediately. This is one of the themes advanced in this chapter.

Another major theme that will be advanced here is that diversion for juveniles, in its various forms, has been used throughout history. Each new institution (e.g., reform schools, training schools, and group homes) has been established on the heels of the failure of old institutions, which have become overcrowded, inhumane, and costly. Each new institution has supposedly been more humane and would alleviate some of the problems created by existing institutions. However, in time these institutions have become as harsh and overcrowded as those they have replaced. The edifices have continued to be built and, lo and behold, they (inmates, guards, administrators, and so on) keep coming.

The third, and major, theme of this chapter is that the juvenile justice system has been used mostly to control the behavior of the children of the urban poor, especially racial and ethnic (Irish) minority groups. More informal—and less

188

repressive—mechanisms have been reserved mostly for the children of the more privileged classes.

Pre-19th Century Developments: The Invention of Childhood

Once upon a time there were no children and no concept of adolescence. This is not to say that there were not persons under the age of 18 or under the age of 10 for that matter. In his excellent book, *The Disappearance of Childhood*, Neil Postman charges that "it is quite possible for a culture to exist without a social idea of children. Unlike infancy, childhood is a social artifact, not a biological category. Our genes contain no clear instructions about who is and who is not a child, and the laws of survival do not require that a distinction be made between the world of an adult and the world of a child" (Postman, 1994: xi). He further notes that the word *children* is no more than about 150 years old and the custom of celebrating a child's birthday did not exist until around 1800. It should also be noted that until the late 19th century the term *adolescence* or even *teenager* was not part of the language.

Another way of putting this is to say that puberty is a biological fact, while childhood and adolescence is merely a social fact. There is no biological reason why, for several years after the onset of puberty young people cannot assume most adult roles. In fact, back before our own industrial revolution, where farming was the dominant way of life, a boy was considered a man as soon as he could fire a weapon or plow the fields or do countless other things men did. Similarly, a girl became a woman soon after puberty, when she was able to get pregnant. A close examination of anyone's family history will show women giving birth starting as young as 13 or 14. Ironically, despite our own cultural prescriptions for children under 18 (legally speaking, in most states a child is anyone under 18), we think nothing of certifying a 14- or 15-year-old as an adult for committing a serious crime. (Another irony is that if after being certified as an adult this person is sentenced to probation and is still under 18, then he still does not have the privileges that adults have, such as voting, drinking, and so on.)

In recent years we have seen what can be described as an extension of childhood and adolescence well beyond what was considered normal 150 years ago. A 20- to 22-year-old college male may be seen on any college campus acting rather childish, doing all sorts of idiotic things that would have been unthinkable a century ago. But a century ago, there was no social need for him to behave this way, because his 19th century counterpart would have been married with two or more children and either working on the farm or, increasingly as the 20th century appeared, working in the mines and factories. In fact, the high-school middle school youths of today were working 14 hours a day 150 years ago! This was before child labor laws were passed, as more and more immigrants flooded the shores of this country to fill the jobs previously held by 10- to 15-year-olds. It was no accident that compulsory schooling came about during the same period of time, for something had to be done about those youths displaced by the new immigrant labor force. Ironically, some 150 years later, several million adult workers have been displaced by a new wave of cheap labor, either in the form of so-called illegal aliens from Mexico or Third World workers willing to work for peanuts to make the clothes you are wearing as I speak (check the labels in your closet or inside your baseball cap).

The reason this subject is being brought up here is that the main subject of this chapter is juvenile delinquency, which is nothing more than various forms of deviance committed by persons under a certain biological age, one which has been rather arbitrarily set by adult legislators in the various states. Much of the behavior that is brought to the attention of juvenile courts around the country would not be crimes if it were not for the fact that we have set this arbitrary age for dividing childhood from adulthood. Just to give you an idea of the arbitrary nature of this age, while most states set the age at 18, many set it at 17 and even a few use 16, prompting the logical question of Why the difference? Is there something that the states that use 16 or 17 know that the other states do not know?

Shortly we will introduce the concept of status offenses as those crimes that are specific to those under the age of adulthood. Status offenses include running away from home, truancy, being unmanageable or incorrigible, curfew violations, liquor law violations, and smoking cigarettes. The absurdity of these laws is demonstrated that in one state you can drink at 16 and in another you get arrested; in one state you can run away from home, but in another state you get arrested (even if you had a very good reason for running away, such as fleeing from an abusive parent).

But we are getting away from our story here. Let's look briefly at the history of childhood and adolescence.

A History of Childhood and Adolescence

In a long view of history, even the concept of childhood is of relatively recent vintage. According to Aries, art in the Middle Ages (500 to 1400 A.D.) did not even attempt to portray childhood, instead depicting children as little men and women (Aries, 1962). Adolescence as a separate social category did not appear until the 19th century; during earlier periods (when life expectancies often went little beyond the age of 40), young adults constituted the backbone of society. Prior to this time, infancy ended around age seven and adulthood began immediately. There was no intervening stage for the simple reason that it was totally unnecessary. In fact, it was not until around the 16th century when there were books on the subject of child rearing. In the medieval world childhood was invisible (Postman, 1994: 18).

In fact, the family as we know it today did not really exist in the Middle Ages. Until about the 14th century one's family meant mostly a person's legal heredity line with an emphasis on the blood ancestry rather than merely the conjugal unit. Aries shows this through paintings of the period, showing either a solitary figure or large groupings of people, usually in public, with few scenes inside a dwelling. "The family," writes Firestone, "was composed of large numbers of people in a constant state of flux and, on the estates of noblemen, whole crowds of servants, vassals, musicians, people of every class as well as a good many animals, in the ancient patriarchal household tradition" (Firestone, 1970: 75).

More importantly for our purposes here, during the Middle Ages there was no such thing as childhood as we know it today. It was literally the case that the people of this time were not conscious of children as a distinct social category. Paintings reflect this, as they usually depict children as sort of "miniature adults." In most families these children were wet-nursed and then sent to another family for a period of apprenticeship to a master, usually some sort of domestic service. This usually lasted from about age 7 to 14 or 18. (Keep in mind that during this time, there were no special words to describe these "little adults.") The child never developed a heavy dependence upon his or her parents, since the typical household included all sorts of adults, not just the immediate family—there were visitors, friends, distant relatives, servants, and so on. Therefore, the typical child had very limited contact with a biological parent, which is totally unlike today. This is what today we would call a true "extended family" (Firestone, 1970: 76–77).

More crucially, children were never totally segregated into special quarters, schools, or even activities. There were no children's toys, special games, nor children's clothing (paintings show children dressed up as adults). All activities were shared with adults within the community. The aim was to get them ready as soon as possible for adult life. After all, children were valuable sources of labor for communities and families (Firestone, 1970: 78).

A key reason for the lack of distinction between adults and children was the lack of reading and the fact that throughout the Middle Ages communications were oral. During this time, childhood ended at around the age of seven. Why seven? Because that is generally the age when children have command over speech and are able to understand what adults are talking about. They are able to know all the secrets of the adult world, including sexual secrets. In fact, throughout this period of time children became exposed to all sorts of adult behavior. They were, in short, not *innocent* as we understand the term today. They no doubt were very much aware of all sorts of sexual behavior on the part of adults, perhaps even witnessing it on many occasions. Of course, what this means is that adults did not worry about protecting them from sexual and other adult behavior. Moreover, there was no concept of shame since this rests upon the notion that there are secrets that adults must keep from children and hence it would be shameful to disclose them. Not to worry during the Middle Ages because such shame is based upon a clear distinction between the adult and the child's world, which did not exist at that time and hence there were no institutions to help express such a distinction (Postman, 1994: 15).

It should also be noted that during the Middle Ages the Catholic Church determined that the age of seven was when a person knew right from wrong and could reason. Further, the "oralism of the Middle Ages helps us to explain why there were no primary schools. For where biology determines communication competence, there is no need for schools. Postman notes that the "seven-year-old male was a man in every respect except for his capacity to make love and war" (Postman, 1994: 14). In short, "there was no separate world of childhood. Children shared the same games with adult, the same toys, the same fairy stories. They lived their lives together, never apart" (1994: 14–15). Paintings by various artists of the time showed how the culture of the period did not hide anything from children. There was no evidence for toilet training in the early years and not surprisingly no hesitancy to discuss sexual matters in front of the children. In fact, there was no such phrase as "not in front of the children!" (Postman, 1994: 16–17).

Another interesting thing about the Middle Ages is that there was a very high mortality rate among children. "In part because of children's inability to survive, adults did not, and could not, have the emotional commitment to them that we accept as normal. The prevailing view was to have many children in the hope that two or three might survive. On these grounds, people obviously could not allow themselves to become too attached to the young." It is interesting to note that it was not until around the late 14th century that children were included in wills (Postman, 1994: 17). Prior to around the 16th century there were no books on child-rearing and few about mothers in their role as mothers. Simply put, childhood ended at seven and adulthood began at once, with no intervening stages, no adolescence and no teenager. There was also no special children's jargon. One writer noted: "Of all the characteristics in which the medieval age differs from the modern, none is so striking as the comparative absence of interest in children" (Postman, 1994: 18–19).

Enter Childhood in the 17th Century

This slowly began to change with the development of capitalism starting after the 14th century when we saw the beginnings of the modern family. Along with this change came a new vocabulary to describe children and childhood. By the 17th century special children's toys began to emerge along with special games for children.

Paintings reveal the change, for most begin to show scenes of children with their mothers (e.g., the infant in the arms of Mary) and scenes inside homes with children and their parents. Some writers, such as the philosopher Rousseau, began to develop an ideology of childhood and even worried about the purity and innocence of children and about their exposure to vice. Whereas in previous ages there was almost total independence for children, there gradually became almost total dependence. (The child savers at the end of the 19th century were almost obsessed about children's exposure to vice and eventually passed laws prohibiting children from loitering near saloons and other places where adults engaged in various kinds of sexual acts. There will be more about this later in the chapter.)

One of the key institutions for segregating children from adults and perpetuating the differences was the school. More importantly, however, was that the school emerged along with the printing press, books, and reading. All of this came about simultaneously with the emergence of capitalism and a market society where a new generation of workers needed to be socialized to take their place in the coming industrial order (Spring, 1972). A small family became the ideal place for such socialization.

With the coming of books came a sharp distinction between those who could read and those who could not. Also, books became a way of achieving fame and fortune and having one's words and their work last forever, which in turn created a new sense of self, a unique individual identity. It follows logically that as personal identity developed, it would apply to different age groups, especially children. Soon the idea of childhood became part of the human vocabulary. Adults learned to read first and eventually it became the custom that the young would have to become adults by learning to read. Prior to this time they automatically became adults, since no one could read. And in order to learn to read children would have to attend school and thus

European society invented schools and in so doing invented childhood (Postman, 1994: 36).

We must also remember that all of this occurred during the period known as the Renaissance (1300–1600). This was a vast social movement that swept away old feudal customs and institutions, made for gains in intellectual development, and paralleled the emergence of capitalism throughout the Western world. The old feudal order was gradually disappearing, an order that did not include the concept of childhood. It became a period of learning, the growth of commerce and exploration, which in turn created a need for binding contracts, deeds to property and maps, all of which required printing and eventually an educated public. Within about 100 years after the invention of the printing press the foundations of modern science were laid, with the year 1543 standing out. This was the year that Copernicus and Vesalius published their famous books on astronomy and anatomy respectively (Postman, 1994: 35).

Eventually, the idea of childhood emerged mostly because this group of individuals had become separated from the adult world. They had been separated "because it became essential in their culture that they learn how to read and write, and how to be the sort of people a print culture required" (Postman, 1994: 37). Part of the reason for this was that merchants, the emerging capitalist class or *bourgeoisie* needed their children to be able to read and write in order to handle the paperwork of their business enterprises (1994: 38).

To give you an idea of the impact of these developments, consider the growth of schools in England. During the 16th century villages all over England requested schools be built in order to provide instruction for their children. One survey found that whereas in 1480 there were 34 schools in England, by 1660 there were 444, a growth of more than 1200% in less than 200 years. Because schools were designed "for the preparation of a literate adult, the young came to be perceived not as miniature adults but as something quite different altogether—unformed adults. School learning became identified with the special nature of childhood" (Postman, 1994: 39). The word *schoolboy* became popular and was synonymous with the word *child* (1994: 40–42).

One result of this development was that infancy came to be seen as ending when the command of speech was achieved, while childhood began "with the task of learning how to read." In fact, the word *child* came to be defined back then as an adult who could not read or an adult who was "intellectually childish" (Postman, 1994: 42).

More importantly, however, what happened was that as soon as you had a separate category of people based upon one characteristic—in this case the inability to read—other characteristics would eventually be noticed and perhaps amplified. One student of the history of schooling and childhood observed that as childhood became a distinct social and intellectual category, different "stages of childhood became visible" because they were "segregated at schools, receiving special printed materials geared to distinct stages of learning . . ." Even more importantly, what also emerged were separate "peer groups" and a distinctive "youth culture" (Postman, 1994: 43, quoting Eisenstein, 1979: 133–134).

Eventually even the clothing for children became different for the first time in history, as reflected in paintings from the period. Not surprisingly, a special children's jargon emerged and, of course, the inevitable books on pediatrics. Also, in the Middle Ages it was common for the same name to be given to different children, followed by a number to indicate birth order. By the 17th century, however, children started receiving different names. Finally, and predictably, children's literature began to appear in the mid-18th century with the publication in 1744 of a book called *Jack the Giant Killer*. By the end of the century there were several books known as juvenile literature (Postman, 1994: 43).

Social class has a bearing here, for childhood began as a "middle-class idea, in part because the middle class could afford it" (Postman, 1994: 43). It was not for another century or so when this idea filtered down to the lower classes, which is why so many children of the lower classes worked in the mines and factories well into the end of the 19th century.

What must also be remembered is that learning in a school setting required the development of incredible self-control, which runs counter to the natural inclinations of children. Children's natural exuberance had to be slowed down and controlled. This is why, starting around the 16th century both schoolmasters and parents began to "impose a rather stringent discipline on children. The natural inclinations of children began to be perceived not only as an impediment to book learning but as an expression of an evil character" (Postman, 1994: 46). Children soon came to be seen as "inclined to evil" (1994: 46) and hence needing to be controlled. This development should not be passed over lightly, for here we may find one of the earliest developments of social control mechanisms for a group based upon age and the earliest forerunners to the modern juvenile justice system. Remember that this is based upon a cultural change in the surrounding society, which in turn was influenced by important economic and political changes as well. Children's natural inclinations can be translated to something like independence—as an adult has. Thus, at one point in human history there was no need to control this age group simply because it did not exist, whereas at the point where it was created by adult society, there followed a need for new forms of social control. This new system was to be public schools.

It would not be too much of an exaggeration to say that the most significant development during the past 500 years or so was the coming of industrial capitalism and the factory system. What the early capitalists needed more than anything else was a steady supply of cheap and compliant labor. As many scholars have noted, the public school system, especially in England and the United States, was mostly a system used to "break the will and to condition the child to routinized labor in the factory" (Postman, 1994: 53). This may be somewhat of an exaggeration, since most children did not yet attend these schools, especially the children of the poor who were used to keep the new factories operating. The cruelty of these new factories toward children is illustrated in the following passage written by an 8-year-old girl in the mid-19th century:

> I'm a trapper in the Gauber Pit, I have to trap without a light, and I'm scared. I go at four and sometimes half-past three in the morning and come out at five and a half past. I never go to sleep. Sometimes I sing when I've light, but not in the dark: I dare not sing then (Postman, 1994: 53).

Revelations such as these eventually led to legislation that prohibited the employment of children in the mines, that is, "children under the age of ten!" (Postman, 1994: 53).

For now it is important to note that prior to the 19th century any sort of deviance (however defined) on the part of children was dealt with on a relatively informal basis. Although there were often strict laws governing the behavior of youth (especially in New England), they were rarely enforced, and the severe punishment corresponding to many laws concerning children and youth were rarely administered. For example, regarding the typical response by the Quakers, Hawes reports: "When a child misbehaved, either his family took care of his discipline or the Quaker meeting dispensed a mild and paternalistic correction" (Hawes, 1971: 18). The use of almshouses or other forms of incarceration was rarely made against members of one's own community.

This is not to say that children were never punished, for indeed they were, and often brutally. Punishments of children who committed crimes were often severe and were similar to those meted out to adults. In England, for instance, as late as 1780, children could be convicted and hanged for more than 200 crimes! Postman recounts the hanging of a 7-year-old girl for stealing a petticoat! What is important to note, however, is that committing crimes against one's own children was hardly noticed, but to do so against other children would be severely punished, for the simple fact that this type of crime was considered "damaging the property of others" (Postman, 1994: 53). There was also a "reign of terror" against many children of the poor throughout England during the 18th and well into the 19th century, with them being relegated to the notorious workhouses (about which Dickens often wrote), the textile mills, the mines, and prisons (Postman, 1994: 54).

The legal responsibility of children in the United States was formulated according to Common Law principals. Blackstone's commentary on children's criminal incapacitation, written in 1796, was incorporated in American law. Blackstone noted that:

> . . . the capacity of doing ill, or contracting guilt, is not so much measured by years and days, as by the strength of the delinquent's understanding and judgement . . . at eight years old he may be guilty of a felony. Also under fourteen . . ., and could discern between good and evil, he may be convicted and sentenced to death. Thus a girl of 13 has burnt for killing her mistress, one boy of 10, and another of 9 years old, who had killed their companions have been sentenced to death, and he of 10 years actually hanged. . . Thus also in very modern times, a boy of ten years old was convicted on his own confession of murdering his bedfellow; there appearing in his whole behavior plain tokens of mischievous discretion; and as the sparing this boy merely on account of his tender years might be of dangerous consequence to the public, by propagating a notion that children might commit such atrocious crimes with impunity, it was unanimously agreed by all the judges that he was a proper subject of capital punishment (Blackstone, 1796: 23–24).

Thus, children were judged to be incapable of criminal offenses before the age of 7. Between the ages of 7 and 14, they were presumed innocent unless evidence of a criminal state of mind could be presented. Youth at the age of 14 who participated in criminal or delinquent behavior were considered adults and treated as such.

Two illustrations of Blackstone's opinion can be found in *State v. Aaron* (4. N.J.L. 263, 1818) and Stage's case (5 City-Hall Recorder, New York City, 1820). In *State v. Aaron*, a young male slave of 11 years was accused of murdering another young child. Before and during the trial he denied the crime, but was convicted and sentenced to death. The second case involves a group of children between the ages of 7 and 14 who were indicted for grand larceny. George Stage, who was 8-years-old at the time he was arrested, was caught while trying to escape from a private house with a stolen bear skin. He was convicted and sentenced to three years in the state prison.

Platt (1977) documents 14 cases (between 1806 and 1882) on the criminal responsibility of children in the United States. Of these 14 cases, 7 children were indicted for homicide, 1 for manslaughter, 5 for various degrees of larceny, and 1 for malicious trespass. In 10 instances, the jury returned a verdict of not guilty, one child was found of guilty of trespass but the sentence was not reported, 2 children aged 11 and 12 were executed, and the remaining child was sentenced to three years in a state prison. Granted that these cases were unusual and involved appellate court decisions, they nevertheless suggest that the criminal law recognized at that time that some children under 14, particularly children of color, were held as responsible for their actions as adults.

Prior to around the mid-1700s there was not much serious crime to speak of, neither among adults nor children. For the most part, the behavior and the control of children was largely a responsibility of parents and perhaps other adults in the community. Eventually various laws were passed calling for the punishment of parents who failed to perform their duty to control their children. In cases in which children's misbehavior was especially troublesome, apprenticeship of some form was often the punishment meted out. Also, various forms of corporal, and in rare cases, capital punishments were carried out (Bremner, 1970; Bernard, 1992: 44–45; Rendieman, 1979).

One of the major reasons for this type of response was the fact that the labor of children and youth was so much in demand (although in the South, slaves were more readily available). More importantly, however, children and youth were usually viewed as small adults and treated as such. As several historians have noted, there was actually no concept of adolescent or teenager prior to the onset of industrialism and the emergence of capitalism during the late 18th and early 19th centuries. Young people had relatively close ties to their families and communities until about the age of puberty. Kett has noted that in agricultural communities "physical size, and hence capacity for work, was more important than chronological age . . ." (Kett, 1977: 13). Autobiographies and biographies are replete with instances of young people beginning to work at ages as young as 6 or 7 during the colonial period and even well into the 19th century. Typically a boy between 7 and 14 would engage in minor jobs, such as running errands, chopping wood, and so on, while after that age apprenticeship into some trade was taken up (1977: 13–18).

The importance of children and youth to the family income should be stressed. As Kett notes:

> Children provided parents in preindustrial society with a form of social security, unemployment insurance, and yearly support. As soon as children were able to work in or out

of the home, they were expected to contribute to the support of their parents; when parents were no longer able to work, children would look after them (1977: 23).

There were, of course, class distinctions during this period. Many poor children were sentenced (because they were poor rather than their misbehavior per se) to several years of hard labor as apprentices, either to wealthy landowners or to ship captains (Bremner, 1970). Kett further notes that:

> Poor farm children were forced out of the home early, children of prosperous, landowning farmers left home at a somewhat later age and returned home more frequently; children of wealthy manufacturers and merchants left early, but because of parental preference rather than necessity. The degree of freedom also depended on social class. To the extent that poor households were more frequently disrupted than wealthy ones, poor children often had more de facto freedom (unless bound as paupers), although, it must be added, there was little that they could do with their freedom (Kett, 1977: 29).

Before the 19th century, then, the deviant behavior of young people was handled largely on an informal basis. This does not imply that all was well with the treatment of youths in previous centuries. Children were, for example, subjected to some extreme forms of physical and sexual abuse (de Mause, 1974; Empey, 1979). Strict laws governed the behavior of children; however, in the United States, these laws were used only infrequently (Hawes, 1971; Rothman, 1971; Sutton, 1988). Almshouses (a word used synonymously for workhouses and jails up until the 19th century) and other forms of incarceration were rarely used to handle the misbehavior of members of one's own community, and incarceration for long periods of time was almost nonexistent. In cases where children's misbehavior was especially troublesome, apprenticeship (this usually involved sending a youth away from home to live with someone who could teach him a trade) was often used as a form of punishment (Rendleman, 1979). For the most part, the control and discipline of children was left up to the family unit (Krisberg and Austin, 1993: 9).

Parens Patriae *and Stubborn Children*

The appearance of adolescence as a social category coincided with an increasing concern for the regulation of the moral behavior of young people (Platt, 1977; Empey, 1979; Postman, 1994). Although entirely separate systems to monitor and control the behavior of young people began to appear during the early part of the 19th century, differential treatment based upon age did not come about overnight. The roots of the juvenile justice system can be traced to much earlier legal and social perspectives on childhood and youth. One of the most important of these was a legal doctrine known as *parens patriae*.

Parens patriae has its origins in medieval England's chancery courts. At that point it had more to do with property law than children; it was, essentially, a means for the crown to administer landed orphans' estates (Sutton, 1988). *Parens patriae* established that the king, in his presumed role as the father of his country, had the legal authority to take care of his people, especially those who were unable, for various reasons (including age), to take care of themselves. For children, the king or his authorized agents could assume the role of guardian to be able to administer their property. By the 19th century this legal doctrine had evolved into the practice of the state's assuming wardship over a minor child and, in effect, playing the role of parent if the child had no parents or if the existing parents were declared unfit.

In the American colonies, for example, officials could "bind out" as apprentices "children of parents who were poor, not providing good breeding, neglecting their formal education, not teaching a trade, or were idle, dissolute, unchristian or incapable" (Rendleman, 1979: 63). Later, during the 19th century, *parens patriae* supplied (as it still does to some extent), the legal basis for court intervention into the relationship between children and their families (Teitelbaum and Harris, 1977).

Another legal legacy of the colonial era that relates to the state's involvement in the lives of youth is the Stubborn Child Law. Passed in Massachusetts in 1646, it established a clear legal relationship between children and parents and, among other things, made it a capital offense for a child to disobey his or her parents. This statute stated in part:

> If a man have a stubborn or rebellious son, of sufficient years and understanding (viz) sixteen years of age, which will not obey the voice of his Father, or the voice of his Mother, and that when they have chastened him will not harken unto them: then shall his Father and Mother being his natural parents, lay hold on him, and bring him to the Magistrates assembled in court and testify unto them, that their son is stubborn and rebellious and will not obey their voice and chastisement, but lives in sundry notorious crimes, such a son shall be put to death (Sutton, 1988: 11).

This law was grounded in the distinctly Puritan belief in the innate wickedness of humankind, wickedness that required, for one thing, that children be subjected to strong discipline. This law was unique in several other respects: It specified a particular legal obligation of children; it defined parents as the focus of that obligation; and it established rules for governmental intervention should parental control over children break down.

It is important to consider the full implications of the notion of the state as parent, and more especially, father—a concept that is implied in both the *parens patriae* doctrine and, to some extent, in the Stubborn Child Law. The objects of a patriarch's authority have traditionally included women in addition to children (see chapter 6 for further discussion of patriarchy). The idea of patriarchy has also reinforced the sanctity and privacy of the home, and the power (in early years, almost absolute) of the patriarch to discipline wife and children (Dobash and Dobash, 1979: Chapter 1). Further, the notion of *parens patriae* assumes that the father (or, in this case, the state or king) can legally act as a parent with many of the implicit parental powers possessed by fathers. Therefore, as we shall see, governmental leaders would eventually utilize *parens patriae*, once a rather narrowly construed legal doctrine, to justify extreme governmental intervention in the lives of young people. Arguing that such intervention was "for their own good," the state during the 19th century became increasingly involved in the regulation of adolescent behavior.

In the United States, interest in the state regulation of youth was directly tied to explosive immigration and population growth. Between 1750 and 1850 the population of the United States went from 1.25 million to 23 million. The population of some states, like Massachusetts, doubled in numbers, and New York's population increased fivefold between 1790 and 1830 (Empey, 1979: 59). Many of those coming into the United States during the middle of the 19th century were of Irish or German background; the fourfold increase in immigrants between 1830 and 1840 was in large part a product of the economic hardships faced by the Irish during the potato famine (Brenzel, 1983: 11). The social controls in small communities were simply overwhelmed by the influx of newcomers, many of whom were either foreign born or of foreign parentage.

This was to change, slowly at first, with the transition to capitalism (specifically the factory system in the New England area) during the late 18th and early 19th centuries. With the breakup of colonial society, in addition to the beginning of immigration, came an influx of poor, homeless young people, many of whom flocked to the cities of the Northeast, particularly New York. With this increase came a growing concern among prominent citizens about the perishing and dangerous classes, as they would be called throughout the 19th century. With the shift from agriculture to industrialism came the age of adolescence and with this age came the problem of juvenile delinquency and attempts to control it.

Defining a Juvenile Delinquent

The term *juvenile delinquent* originated around early 1800s and had two different meanings that correspond to the two words being used: (1) *delinquent*, which means "failure to do something that is required" (as in a person being delinquent in paying taxes) and, (2) *juvenile*, meaning someone who is "malleable, and not yet 'fixed in their ways,' " and subject to change and being molded (i.e., redeemable). By the 1700s, with colleges and private boarding schools developing, various informal methods of social control of more privileged youth emerged (this paralleled the emergence of capitalism and the need to reproduce the next generation of capitalist rulers). Eventually, more formal systems of control emerged to control working and lower class delinquents around the early 1800s, including the juvenile justice system and uniformed police.[1] In other words, the attitude that even working and lower class offenders could be redeemed developed (Bernard, 1992: 49–55).

It should be noted that informal systems of control have always been reserved for the more privileged youths, while the less privileged have been subjected to formal systems of control. However, if we examine history closely, with few exceptions it has almost always been the case that minority youth have been much more likely to be viewed not as juvenile delinquents (i.e., malleable and thus redeemable) but as hardened criminal and not redeemable (since by definition adults are more fixed in their ways and less redeemable). Little wonder that such a great proportion of those certified or waived to adult court in recent years (i.e., viewed as unredeemable adult criminals) have been minorities. This also demonstrates that what kinds of behaviors and what kinds of people end up being labeled as delinquent has always been quite subjective. Like beauty, delinquency is in the eye of the beholder.

The House of Refuge Movement

During the early 19th century prominent citizens in the cities of the East began to notice the poor, especially the children of the poor. The parents were declared unfit because their children wandered about the streets unsupervised and committing various assortments of crime just in order to survive. Many believed that here was the major source of problems in social control and forerunners of even greater problems in the future. Poor and immigrant (in this era the Irish) children, their lifestyles, and social position would soon be associated with crime and juvenile delinquency.

Rothman suggests that there was an assumption that the causes of criminality were to be found not only in the above social conditions of the cities, but also in family upbringing. He notes that one belief was foremost, namely, that "parents who sent their children into the society without rigorous training in discipline and obedience would find them someday in prison" (Rothman, 1971: 70). Reformers, upon examining the life histories of adult convicts, found that early childhood transgressions were the prelude to worse things to come. Here we find the beginnings of the use of the concept of pre-delinquency, a notion that has continued in its popularity to the present day.[2]

As attention began to focus on the children of the poor, another problem was noticed. Many observers found that young children, some as young as six or seven, were locked up with adult criminals in jails and prisons and were also appearing with increasing regularity in criminal courts. Child reformers believe that such practices were not only inhumane, but would also inevitably lead to the corruption of the young and the perpetuation of youthful deviance or perhaps a full-time career in more serious criminality.

A number of philanthropic associations emerged in eastern cities to deal with these problems. One of the most notable was the Society for the Reformation of Juvenile Delinquents (SRJD), founded in the 1820s.[3] A member of this group, lawyer James W. Gerard, expressed a view that was typical of other members of this society when he commented that most of the children appearing in the criminal courts of New York were "of poor and abandoned parents" whose "debased character and vicious habits" resulted in their being "brought up in perfect ignorance and idleness, and what is worse in street begging and pilfering" (Hawes, 1971: 28).

The solution that was offered became one of the most common solutions to the problem of delinquency in years to come: remove the children from the corrupting environments of prisons, jails, unfit homes, slums, and other unhealthy environments and place them in more humane and healthier environments.

The SRJD, composed primarily of wealthy businessmen and professional people, convinced the New York legislature to pass a bill in 1824 that established the New York House of Refuge, the first correctional institution for young offenders in the United States. The bill created the first statutory definition of juvenile delinquency and authorized the managers of the refuge "to receive and take into the House of

Refuge '. . . all children as shall be convicted of criminal offenses . . . or committed as vagrants' if the court deems that they are 'proper' objects" (Hawes, 1971: 33).

The general aims of the House of Refuge, including the conceptions of delinquents, are reflected in the following extract from the SRJD (Abbott):

> The design of the proposed institution is, to furnish, in the first place, an asylum, in which boys under a certain age, who become subject to the notice of our police, either as vagrants, or homeless, or charged with petty crimes, may be received, judiciously classed according to their degree of depravity or innocence, put to work at such employments as will tend to encourage industry and ingenuity, taught reading, writing, and arithmetic, and most carefully instructed in the nature of their moral and religious obligations, while at the same time, they are subjected to a course of treatment, that will afford a prompt and energetic corrective of their vicious propensities, and hold out every possible inducement to reformation and good conduct (Abbott, 1938: 348).

It should also he noted that according to the SRJD a *juvenile delinquent* was defined as a child who broke a law, or who "wandered about the streets, neither in school nor at work and who obviously lacked a 'good' home and family" (Hawes, 1971: 33).

The statutes contained vague descriptions of behaviors and lifestyles that were synonymous with the characteristics of the urban poor (especially Irish immigrants). Being homeless, begging, vagrancy, and coming from an unfit home (as defined from a middle-class view point) are examples. The legislation that was passed also established specific procedures for identifying the proper subjects for intervention and the means for the legal handling of cases. According to law, the state, or a representative agency or individual, could intervene in the life of a child if it was determined that he or she needed *care and treatment*, the definition of which was left entirely in the hands of the agency or individual who intervened.

Immigrants received the brunt of enforcement of these laws, especially children of Irish parents. Pickett notes that a house of refuge superintendent accounted for a boy's delinquency because "the lad's parents are Irish and intemperate and that tells the whole story. . ." (Pickett, 1969: 6, 15). The results of such beliefs are reflected in the fact that between 1825 and 1855 the percentage of commitments to the refuge that were Irish went as high as 63 (1969: 15).

That the delinquency statutes more often described a way of life or social status (e.g., poverty) is attested to by the fact that of the 73 children received at the New York Refuge during the first year of operation, only 1 had been convicted of a serious offense (grand larceny), 9 were committed for petty larceny, and 63 (88%) were committed for what Abbott describes as "stealing, vagrancy and absconding" (Abbott, 1938: 362) from the almshouse. From such descriptions it appears that their major crime was simply being poor.

The majority of those committed to the New York House of Refuge were children whose parents came from working-class backgrounds, many of whom could be classified as working poor or just plain poor. A check of occupations of those whose parents held jobs (and most did not hold jobs) shows that the most common was listed as common laborer; washerwoman ranked second; and masons, plasterers and bricklayers ranked third. The occupation of washerwoman is indicative of the common phenomenon of the period among many urban dwellers that men were forced to leave their families in order to find work elsewhere, leaving children and their mothers to fend for themselves. It should also be noted that women and children were the primary work force in many factories in the Northeast (Pickett, 1969: Appendix).

It seems that the reformers and institutional officials believed that they had the qualifications not only to judge those on the bottom of the social order but also to govern or otherwise intervene in the latter's best interest. Mennel makes the following astute observation:

> Early 19th century philanthropists also undertook charitable work for their own protection. They feared imminent social upheaval resulting from the explosive mixture of crime, disease, and intemperance which they believed characterized the lives of poorer urban residents. Without relieving the poor of responsibility for their conditions, these philanthropists saw in their benevolences, ways of avoiding class warfare and the disintegration of the social order. The French Revolution reminded them, however, that the costs of class struggle were highest to advantaged citizens like themselves (Mennel, 1973: 6).

Conceptions of Delinquency: 1820 to 1860

The conceptions about delinquency and theories attempting to explain the phenomenon of delinquency played an important role in child-saving activities and their accomplishments during the first half of the 19th century.

Mennel notes that "during the 18th century juvenile delinquency slowly ceased to mean a form of misbehavior common to all children and instead became an euphemism for the crimes and conditions of poor children" (Mennel, 1973: 6). By the 19th century such a view became quite dominant in popular thinking. According to Pickett, the managers of the New York House of Refuge believed that the major causes of delinquency were, in order of importance: ignorance, parental depravity and neglect, intemperance, theatrical amusements, bad associations, pawnbrokers, immigration, and "city life in general" (Pickett, 1969: 191). A crude environmental view prevailed throughout this period as poverty, family rearing practices (of the poor), and other social and psychological factors were typically associated with delinquency (Pickett, 1969: 191). A report by a Unitarian minister in 1830 stated that three-fourths of the young picked up by the police were from families that looked to their children to help support them. Instead of citing the inequalities that existed at the time and the exploitation on the part of factory owners (who employed large numbers of children), the report said that this condition was due to the "idleness and intemperance of the parents" (Bremner, 1970: 613). The report further noted that these children "are every day at once surrounded by temptation to dishonesty" (1970: 613).

Rothman notes that the family was generally considered a major source of the problem. He writes that such phrases as "poor upbringing," "bad habits," "drinking," and "immorality" (indicative of an anti-Catholic bias so common at that time) were commonly heard. Other factors commonly associated with crime and delinquency included the lack of respect for authority and failure to abide by the work ethic (even though the vast majority of the Irish worked hard, struggling to achieve the American Dream). All of these were characteristically associated with the behavior, lifestyles, and living conditions of the urban poor (especially Irish-Catholics) (Rothman, 1971: 58).

It is generally true that reformers often blamed social conditions as the primary cause, and therefore beyond the control of individual youths. At the same time, however, they blamed the youngsters themselves (and their parents as well), at least indirectly. Time and again reformers stressed that it was up to the individual to avoid the temptations that such social conditions produced. A report by the SRJD noted that the youths in the refuge were "in a situation where there is no temptation to vice . . . and where, instead of being left to prey on the public, they will be *fitted* to become valuable members of society" (Hawes, 1971: 44). It was as if the evil conditions of the inner cities were like bacteria that were in the air and that some were immune while others were not. Therefore, the goal of reformation was to immunize individuals who had come down with the disease of delinquency or predelinquency. The physical analogy has been with us ever since.[4]

The Fate of the Refuge Movement

Social reformers, such as the SRJD and the "child savers" of the late 19th century (to be discussed later in this chapter), have often been described as humanitarians with love in their hearts for the unfortunate children of the poor. According to the SRJD: "The young should, if possible, be subdued with kindness. His heart should first be addressed, and the language of confidence, although undeserved, be used toward him" (Hawes, 1971: 45). The SRJD also said that he should be taught that "his keepers were his best friends and that the object of his confinement was his reform and ultimate good" (1971: 46).

The results of the actions by these reformers suggest that the best interests of the child were usually not served. Children confined in the houses of refuge were subjected to strict discipline and control. A former army colonel working in the New York House of Refuge said: "He (the delinquent) is taught that prompt unquestioning obedience is a fundamental military principle" (Mennel, 1973: 103). It was strongly believed that this latter practice would add to a youth's training in self control (evidently to avoid the temptations of evil surroundings) and respect for authority (which was a basic requirement of a disciplined labor force). Corporal punishments (including hanging children from their thumbs, the use of the "ducking stool" (a practice of tying someone to a chair and ducking them in and out of a pool of water, often a lake or pond) for girls, and severe beatings, solitary confinement, handcuffs, the ball and chain, uniform dress, the silent system, and other practices were commonly used in houses of refuge (Pisciotta, 1982).

Following the lead of New York, other cities constructed houses of refuge in rapid succession. Within a few years there were refuges in Boston, Philadelphia, and Baltimore. It soon became evident, however, that the original plans of the founders were not being fulfilled, for crime and delinquency remained a problem. Also, many of the children apparently did not go along with the benevolence of the managers of the refuges. Inmates often staged various protests, riots, escape attempts, and other disturbances, which were almost daily occurrences (Pisciotta, 1982; Hawes, 1971: 47–48; Bremner, 1970: 689–691). While at first limiting itself to housing first offenders, youthful offenders, and predelinquents, the refuges in time came to be the confines of more hardened offenders (most of whom were hardened by the experiences of confinement) and soon succumbed to the problem of overcrowding. Such a fate would return time and time again to plague institutions built throughout the 19th and 20th centuries, even to the present day.

While the early 19th century reforms did not have much of an impact on crime and delinquency, they did succeed in establishing methods of controlling children of the poor (and their parents as well). Rothman concludes: "The asylum and the refuge were two more bricks in the wall that Americans built to confine and reform the dangerous classes" (Rothman, 1971: 210). While the poor and the working classes were usually viewed as lazy, shiftless, and dangerous, the trait that tended to strike the most fear into the hearts and minds of the privileged was idleness. Indeed, an idle mass of underprivileged and deprived people was an obvious threat to the security of the upper class. Little wonder, then, that the major assumptions about the causes of crime and delinquency continuously stressed idleness, lack of the work ethic and respect for authority. It is important to emphasize lack of respect for authority because *authority* usually means those in power, who do the hiring and firing, the ruling class and its representatives. To achieve respect for authority is to legitimize a particular social order and set of rules. When one lacks respect for authority one has, among other things, not granted legitimacy to the existing order and ruling class. Because of this, it becomes important to instill such values in the minds of citizens, especially those who violate the law or otherwise behave contrary to role expectations. The SRJD asked citizens to visit the House of Refuge in New York "and see that idleness has become changed to industry, filth and rags to cleanliness and comfortable appearance, boisterous impudence to quiet submission" (Hawes, 1971: 44). Ideally, the result of orderly asylums such as these would be the production of passive, happy, contented workers who would gladly, upon release, submit to authority and accept their assigned place at the bottom of the social order and cause no further trouble. In the following quote Rothman is describing the function of the prison, but his description could very easily apply to houses of refuge: "The functioning of the penitentiary . . . was designed to carry a message to the community. The prison would train the most notable victims of social disorder to discipline, teaching them to resist corruption" (Rothman, 1971: 107–108).

The rhetoric of the founders and managers of houses of refuge obviously fell far short of the reality experienced by the youth held in these facilities. A look at one of the most significant court challenges to the refuge movement provides additional insight into the origins of the juvenile justice system.

Ex Parte Crouse: *Court Decisions and Effects*

Argued in 1838, *Ex Parte Crouse* arose from a petition of habeas corpus filed by the father of Mary Ann Crouse. Without her father's knowledge, Crouse had been committed to the Philadelphia House of Refuge by her mother on the grounds that she was incorrigible. Her father argued that the incarceration was illegal because she had not been given a jury trial. The court noted that Mary had been committed on a complaint that said "that the said infant by reason of vicious conduct, has rendered her control beyond the power of the said complainant [her mother], and made it manifestly requisite that from regard to the moral and future welfare of the said infant she should be placed under the guardianship of the managers of the House of Refuge."[5] The Court rejected the appeal, saying that the Bill of Rights did not apply to juveniles. Based upon the *parens patriae* doctrine, the court asked, "May not the natural parents, when unequal to the task of education, or unworthy of it, be superseded by the *parens patriae* or common guardian of the community?" Further, the Court observed that: "The infant has been snatched from a course which must have ended in confirmed depravity . . ."[6] Note here that the logic was accepted, even though one of Crouse's parents (her father) felt able to care for her. Also note that they were making predictions of future behavior based upon rather vague criteria, which was becoming quite common at the time and would continue to be a common practice for years to come.

The ruling assumed that the Philadelphia House of Refuge (and presumably all other houses of refuge) had a beneficial effect on its residents. It "is not a prison, but a school," the Court said, and because of this, not subject to procedural constraints. Further, the aims of such an institution were to reform the youngsters within them "by training . . . [them] to industry; by imbuing their minds with the principles of morality and religion; by furnishing them with means to earn a living; and above all, by separating them from the corrupting influences of improper associates."[7]

What evidence did the justices consult to support their conclusion that the House of Refuge was not a prison but a school? Not surprisingly, only testimony by those who managed the institution had been solicited. This was probably because the justices of the Supreme Court came from the same general class background as those who supported the houses of refuge and believed the rhetoric of these supporters. In short, they believe the promises rather than the reality of the reformers. A more objective review of the treatment of youths housed in these places, however, might have led the justices to a very different conclusion. For instance, subsequent investigations found that there was an enormous amount of abuse within these institutions. They were run according to a strict military regimen during which corporal punishment (girls in one institution were ducked under water and boys were hung by their thumbs), solitary confinement, and a silent system were part of the routine.[8] Work training was practically nonexistent, and outside companies contracted for cheap inmate labor. Religious instruction was often little more than Protestant indoctrination (many of the youngsters were Catholic). Education, in the conventional meaning of the word, was almost nonexistent.

The O'Connell Case

A most intriguing addendum to the history of the houses of refuge—and to the *Crouse* case—came in 1870 with a Chicago case concerning a boy named Daniel O'Connell in the case of *People v. Turner* (1870). This young boy was incarcerated in the Chicago House of Refuge, not because of a criminal offense, but because he was "in danger of growing up to become a pauper" (People v. Turner, 1974). His parents, like Mary Crouse's father, filed a writ of *habeas corpus*, charging that his incarceration was illegal. What is most intriguing about this case is that although the facts were almost identical to the *Crouse* case, the outcome was the exact opposite.

The case went to the Illinois Supreme Court and this court concluded that, first, Daniel was being punished not treated or helped by being in this institution. (Recall that the court had concluded that Mary Crouse was being helped.) Second, the Illinois court based its ruling on the realities or actual practices of the institution, rather than merely on good intentions as in the Crouse case. Third, the Illinois court rejected the *parens patriae* doctrine because they concluded that Daniel was being imprisoned and thus they based their reasoning on traditional legal doctrines of the criminal law. They therefore emphasized the importance of due process safeguards. In short, while the court in the Crouse case viewed the houses of refuge in a very rosy light, praising it uncritically, the court in the O'Connell case viewed the refuge in a much more negative light, addressing its cruelty and harshness of treatment (Bernard, 1992: 70–72; *People v. Turner,* 1974). Because of the O'Connell case, only children who had committed felonies could be sent to reform schools.

One reason for the different rulings in these two cases may stem from gender. Mary Ann Crouse was committed to a House of Refuge and the court deemed this appropriate for her moral and future welfare. On the other hand, the similar O'Connell case, the court overturned the institutional commitment based on due process (for more detail, see Chesney-Lind and Shelden, 2004).

The O'Connell decision was to have far-reaching effects in the development of the movement to establish the juvenile court in Chicago in 1899. While this will be covered in more detail shortly, it needs to be mentioned in passing at this time that the founders of the juvenile court established this institution in part as a method of getting around the argument in the O'Connell case. In the 1905 case of Frank Fisher (ironically another Pennsylvania case), the court returned to the logic used in the Crouse case. In this case, the Pennsylvania Supreme Court ruled as follows:

> To save a child from becoming a criminal, or continuing in a career of crime, to end in maturer [sic] years in public punishment and disgrace, the legislatures surely may provide for the salvation of such a child, if its parents or guardians be unwilling or unable to do so, by bringing it into one of the courts of the state without any process at all, for the purpose of subjecting it to the state's guardianship and protection.[9]

In time, this case would be overturned in 1967 in the Gault case.

Mid-19th Century Reforms

America in the mid-19th century was a nation constantly moving west. The settlements in newly conquered territories were in need of labor. Farm laborers, helpers in retail stores, washerwomen, and kitchen girls were among the kinds of work needed as capitalism spread its tentacles across the land.

Simultaneously the eastern cities like New York, Boston, and Philadelphia were overpopulated with immigrants from all over Europe. Fleeing economic ruin, political repression, starvation, and religious persecution, they came by the millions. The capitalist class promised jobs for everyone, along with freedom and the good life. But for most, the reality was quite different. The immigrants that were found in overcrowded tenements and slums soon became the dangerous classes, a term applied to them by those in power.

Especially troublesome for those in power were the very young, those labeled as street urchins, the abandoned waifs, and the children of the urban poor. They, along with their adult counterparts, needed to be controlled in some way, the newly emerging justice system—both the adult and juvenile—would provide this function, along with schools and other institutions and programs. One such program was the placing out system introduced by the New York Children's Aid Society (see following discussion).

About the same time, many began to complain about the conditions of the houses of refuge. Not satisfied that these institutions were doing an adequate job of reformation, new methods were recommended. In Massachusetts, for instance, the first compulsory school law was passed in 1836, thereby creating a new category of delinquent, the truant, and a new method of controlling youths. New York passed a similar law in 1853. The objective of these laws was that of controlling rather than educating the children of the poor. As Bremner states (speaking of the New York law): "This legislation was an instrument for placing abandoned and neglected children [of the poor] in institutions" (Bremner, 1970: 456). In New York the Association for Improving the Conditions of the Poor established the *New York Juvenile Asylum* in 1853. The primary aim of this association was to create a "suitable House of Detention" for "beggars, truants, waifs," and other "morally exposed children and youth" 1970: 739. It would remove them from "dangerous and corrupting associates and place them in such circumstances as will be favorable to reform, and tend to make them industrious, virtuous, and useful members of society" (1970: 820). Such promises should now sound familiar.

The connection between compulsory schooling, the new factory system and various forms of punishment in penal institutions is apparent. As Postman notes, "with the growth of large industrial cities and the need for factory and mine workers, the special nature of children was subordinated to their utility as a source of cheap labor" (Postman, 1994: 53). Although writing about England, historian Lawrence Stone's comments are relevant for America, as he notes that one of the effects of industrial capitalism was "to add support for the penal and disciplinary aspects of school, which were seen by some largely as a system to break the will and to condition the child to routinized labour in the factory" (Stone, 1969: 92, quoted in Postman, 1994: 53).

Public school reforms would continue to have a close connection to juvenile justice reforms. In his book, *Education and the Rise of the Corporate State*, Joel Spring writes that:

The more general concern of industrialists was that schools produce an individual who was cooperative, knew how to work well with others, and was physically and mentally equipped to do his job efficiently. A cooperative and unselfish individual not only worked well with his fellows in the organization *but was more easily managed* (Spring, 1972: 43, emphasis added).

William H. Tolman, cofounder of the American Institute of Social Service, commented in 1900 on the importance of the kindergarten program, saying that: "The lessons of order and neatness, the discipline of regulated play . . . are acquisitions, making the child of greater value to himself, and, if he can follow up the good start which has been made for him, tending to make him of greater wage earning capacity . . ." (Spring, 1972: 36). Tolman further stated that children would be coming into the shops of the employers "in a few years; how much better for you [the employers] that their bodies have been somewhat strengthened by exercise, and their minds disciplined by regulated play" (1972: 37).

Such innovations in public schooling as kindergarten, extracurricular activities, home room, and organized playgrounds combined to teach children the benefits of cooperative work, discipline and respect for authority, not to mention submission to the needs of the group. (Individual initiative was apparently not encouraged.) It was not by accident that many of these programs were also established to prevent and control delinquency.

Representatives of the business world began an all-out campaign to support new forms of education, which would train the future workers of America (Bowles, 1975). At first they began with their own educational programs along the lines of improving employee morale and relations between management and the worker. For instance, corporations brought about such programs as the social secretary (to "maintain constant personal contact with the workers" (Spring, 1972: 36)), employee associations and clubs, periodic employee benefit gatherings, Sunday School programs, company magazines, and even their own public schools (including day-nurseries and kindergartens). The establishment of nurseries and kindergartens functioned to free "both parents for work either in the factory or home" (Spring, 1972: 36). The Plymouth Cordage Company used such a system because: "The company believed that by removing the children from the house for part of the day the mother could give her undivided attention to housework" (Spring, 1972: 36). The rationale given by this company was that the husband would function better at work coming from a clean home with hot meals. Another function of kindergartens was to promote the role of women as the natural caretakers of children, as they enabled teachers to get into the homes of workers and thus interest mothers in children's work (Spring, 1972: 36).

Eventually corporations began to put pressure on local communities to have the public school system perform some of these functions. Obviously to do so would save business a great deal of money. As Spring concludes:

These industrial programs for the management of workers became models for the type of activities adopted by the public school. . . In some cases actual programs, like home economics, were transferred from factory education activities to the public schools to produce workers with the correct social attitudes and skills (Spring, 1972: 22).

In short, the school system evolved "to meet the needs of capitalist employers for a disciplined labor force, and to provide a mechanism for social control . . ." (Bowles, 1975: 219).

Rather than eliminate inequality and increase upward social mobility, the school system had the function of maintaining class differences. One method adopted was what is now known as the tracking system. There was pressure placed upon schools to change the curriculum to one of a multiplicity of course offerings, which would correspond to the major strata of the occupational world. A report by the National Education Association in 1910 stated that: "The differences among children as to aptitudes, interests, economic resources, and prospective careers furnish the basis for a rational as opposed to merely a formal distinction between elementary, secondary, and high education" (Cohen and Lazeron, 1975: 186). Ellwood Cubberly, an educational reformer, wrote in 1909 that:

> Our city schools will soon be forced to give up the exceedingly democratic idea that all are equal, and our society devoid of classes . . . and to begin specialization of educational effort along many lines in an attempt to adapt the school to the needs of these many classes . . . (Cohen and Lazeron, 1975: 187).

Reforms in public schooling were closely related to the problem of juvenile delinquency, as stated earlier.[10] For example, in 1916 the Alfred Binet Intelligence Test was established. Henry Goddard, one of the leaders in the development of this test, believed that intelligence testing was the key to reducing delinquency and claimed that the public schools could be used as clearing houses to pick out potential delinquents, especially the category he called the low intelligence "defective delinquent" (Mennel, 1973: 96–99). Thus, the public schools became agencies of social control and a crucial element in the prevention and control of delinquency. Teachers, guidance counselors, truant officers, school social workers, and school psychologists became part of this vast network of social control within the school system. Actually the desire to use the schools for this purpose was recognized long before, as Charles Loring Brace stated in 1880 that ". . . in the interests of public order, of liberty, of property, for the sake of our own safety and the endurance of free institutions . . ." what is needed is a ". . . strict and careful law, which shall compel every minor to learn to read and write, under severe penalties in the case of disobedience" (quoted in Platt, 1974: 370).

While it can certainly be argued that the school system ultimately meant upward mobility for some (usually those already from privileged classes), for the majority, however, it meant remaining in their original class position. For African Americans and other minorities the situation was worse. This was especially the case in the public schools of the South, which were patterned after a social order based upon caste and class and the concept of separate but equal (Shelden, 1980).

Some reformers, such as Charles Loring Brace, believed that a family-type setting, preferably in the country, would offset the often brutalizing and impersonal setting of houses of refuge. Actually, such a move had begun as early as the 1830s in Boston when prominent citizens felt the need to establish a reform school for boys who had not yet been convicted of a crime but nevertheless still roamed the streets and were in need of discipline. What was needed, they said, was an institution that stood somewhere between the houses of refuge and the public school system. The result was the Massachusetts State Reform School for Boys, opened in 1849. A similar school was opened for girls in Lancaster in 1855, the first of many such institutions based on the "family system" (Brenzel, 1983). The first family system for boys was the Ohio State Reform Farm, opened in 1857 (Bremner, 1970: 705).

In the meantime, a placing out system had emerged in the New York area, the most famous of which was the one operated by the New York Children's Aid Society. What this group did was place children "out west" (to use their phrase, referring to anywhere west of the Allegheny Mountains) in family-type institutions (such as the Ohio Reform School), in actual residences (similar to what today we know as foster homes) or on farms. Millions of children came west in what were commonly referred to as orphan trains (Holt, 1992). The following comment by Charles Loring Brace, founder of the Children's Aid Society, indicates that economic factors played an important role and that many of these children provided landowners a cheap source of labor:

> The United States have the enormous advantage over all other countries, in the treatment of difficult questions of pauperism and reform, in that they possess a practically unlimited area of arable land. The demand for labor on this land is beyond any present supply . . . It is of the utmost importance to them [the farmers] to train up children who shall aid in their work [referring to children whom the Children's Aid Society placed] (Abbott, 1938: 138).

It is interesting to note one of the methods used by the Children's Aid Society. The Society divided New York City into sections and assigned to each section a visitor (part of the Friendly Visitor Program, one that was popular throughout the nation; such a role would eventually evolve into that of social worker). Hawes describes what these visitors did:

> The visitors would go from house to house, trying to persuade the families to send their children to the public schools or to the industrial schools of the Children's Aid Society. When a visitor found a homeless or neglected child, he took him to the central office of the society, where, after securing the parent's consent—if they could be found—it prepared to send him to a farmer's home in the West (Hawes, 1971: 101).

Usually the parents could not be found because they were away during the day (when the visitors called) either working or seeking work. One might understandably wonder what happened if the parents refused to cooperate with such a practice. While the records of what those on the bottom of the social order thought of things are typically incomplete, if known at all, a few notable cases suggest that these parents, and their children as well, did not always passively succumb to the benevolences of the reformers.[11]

For example, the Baltimore House of Refuge had a case in which a mother attempted to get her daughter from a home where she had been placed by the Refuge. The officials reported:

> After we had found a home for the little girl, the mother made an application for her, which we refused. She succeeded in finding where the child was, and demanded it. The man with whom we had placed her was quite firm, and refused to surrender her, but told the mother that if she conducted herself well, the mother might visit her. She threatened legal proceedings, but our power over the child was superior to hers and thus the injudicious interference of the parents was prevented (Bremner, 1970: 693–694).

Other incidents of parents trying to maintain their rights over the power of the state are reported by Rendleman. He notes that during the last half of the 19th century the number of court cases challenging the state's power over children increased. In reviewing these cases he concludes that most commitments were for either poverty or "poyerty plus" (e.g., begging, poverty, destitution, neglect, and dependency) and in some cases, says Rendleman, it is difficult to tell why children were being taken away from their parents in the first place. Court decisions give evidence that children were not committed to institutions because of any violation of the law or because of failings by parents, "but simply because the parents were poor and behaved as poor people always have." There was "an unspoken assumption that the state had an equal if not superior interest in the children and the burden was on the parents to show to the contrary" (Rendleman, 1979: 104–106).

The Fate of Mid-19th Century Reforms

Toward the end of the 19th century it was clear to many that earlier reforms and the existing institutions were doing little toward the reformation of delinquents and the reduction of crime. However, as Rothman has noted, the asylums constructed during the early and middle 19th century failed yet persisted because the original intention to reform gave way to custody. The primary reason for this was a pragmatic one: Once perceived as a threat to all, the dangerous classes could no longer be banished or merely whipped as they were during the colonial period. They had to be controlled physically, for to banish them might result in their being a danger to another community (Rothman, 1971: 240).

While it is certainly true that custody became the order of the day, some reformers never gave up and soon began to agitate for more effective reformation. Upset with the ruling in the O'Connell case, they sought ways of getting around it. They began to argue for an extension of the current system to include a special court for hearing children's cases. But in believing that reformation was not working, reformers were saying, in effect, that control was ineffective. Hence, additional reforms were merely new measures to control and regulate the deviants, potential deviants, and the poor in general (Piven and Cloward, 1972).

Part of the new upswing in reform activities was a result of the changes occurring in American society during the last half of the 19th century: greater industrialization and urbanization, a new wave of immigrants, general unrest and revolt by workers, periodic economic crises in the capitalist system, and other problems. Chicago, the main site of the child-saving movement, had grown from a small town of around 5,000 in 1840 to a huge city of a million and a half by the end of the 19th century, mostly accounted for by immigrants (Bernard, 1992: 84).

There was also a noteworthy change in the labor market structure, especially as it affected youth. In the 1880s, with the growth of factories came the movement of both journeymen and apprentices into the ranks of the industrial proletariat and where teenage helpers posed a constant threat to the wage-earning abilities of young adult journeymen. Skilled crafts began to exclude teenage youth and hence these youths were forced to take factory jobs, most of which were dead-end jobs. Thus, between 1865 and 1900 "the ranks of unemployed veterans who flooded into New York, Philadelphia, Chicago, and other great cities after Appomattox were swelled in hordes of young tramp laborers who drifted from place to place and job to job" (Kett, 1972: 147). Many of these youths became what the Schwendingers have called redundant workers or what Marx referred to as the relative surplus population (Schwendinger and Schwendinger, 1976: 13). Little wonder they behaved in delinquent ways.

New theories of crime and delinquency had emerged by this time, heavily influenced by the positivist school of criminology. This school of thought popularized the so-called medical model of deviance. The Progressive Era ushered in a new series of reforms commonly known as the child saving movement and resulted in the establishment of new institutions to "care for, control, and protect" errant and wayward youth. One such institution was the juvenile court.

The Child-Saving Movement and the Juvenile Court

Like their earlier 19th century counterparts, the child savers were a group of upper-middle and upper-class whites with business and professional backgrounds. Also, they were threatened by the deleterious social conditions in the slums of Chicago and other cities. Surveys by noted reformers Z. R. Brockway and Enoch Wines found that children were still being kept in jails and prisons with adult offenders. The child savers dedicated themselves to saving these children and diverting them from the adult criminal justice system.

The result of their efforts was the establishment of the juvenile court. The new legislation of the period (first in Chicago and Denver in 1899, then elsewhere) created new categories of offenses and extended the state's power over the lives of children and youth. Because of the O'Connell case, only children who had committed felonies could be sent to reform schools. A method of "nipping the problem in the bud" was needed. The logic the reformers used was to define the new juvenile court as a sort of chancery court, upon which the doctrine of *parens patriae* was based. Only in such a court, argued the child savers, could "the best interests of the child" be served. The 1899 Illinois Juvenile Court Act simply removed from the jurisdiction of the criminal courts all cases involving juveniles (at first the upper age was 16, later it was raised to 17) and then to formally establish the juvenile court. Thus, the problem arising out of the O'Connell case was immediately solved (Bernard, 1992: 88–89).

The new laws that defined delinquency and predelinquent behavior were broad in scope and quite vague: (1) the laws covered the usual violations of laws also applicable to adults; (2) the laws covered violations of local ordinances; (3) the laws included such catchalls as vicious or immoral behavior, incorrigibility, truancy, profane or indecent behavior, growing up in idleness, living with any vicious or disreputable person, and many more. These would eventually be known as status offenses (Platt, 1977: 138).

It should be noted that prior to the passage of the Juvenile Court Act in Chicago in 1899 several states already had laws defining these status offenses. For instance, in 1895 Tennessee passed an act to provide county reformatories. Under this act a county could commit "infants under the age of 16" if

> . . . by reason of incorrigible or vicious conduct, such infant has rendered his control beyond the power of such parent guardian or next friend, and made it manifestly requisite that from regard to the future welfare of such infant, and for the protection of society he should be placed under the guardianship of the trustees of such reformatory institution (Shannon, 1896: 1087–1088).

Children could also be committed as vagrants or if they were "without a suitable home and adequate means of obtaining an honest living, and who are in danger of being brought up to lead an idle or immoral life" (Shannon, 1896: 1087–1088). Even the Tennessee code reproduced, almost word-for-word, the original act that created the Philadelphia House of Refuge in 1826 (see the case of *Ex Parte Crouse*, discussed previously).

Influenced by the dominant eclecticism prevailing in the field of criminology, reformers believed that delinquency was the result of a wide variety of social, psychological, and biological factors. They believed that one must look into the life of the child offender in intimate detail in order to know the whole truth about the child. The judge of the juvenile court was to be like a benevolent, yet stern father. The proceedings were to be informal without the traditional judicial trappings. There was neither a need for lawyers nor constitutional safeguards because first of all the cases were not criminal in nature and second the court would always act in the best interests of the child. The court was to be operated like a clinic and the child was to be diagnosed in order to determine the extent of his condition and to prescribe the correct treatment plan, preferably as early in life as possible.

Even the terminology of the juvenile justice system was, and to some extent still is, different. Children in many parts of the United States are "referred" to the court rather than being arrested; instead of being held in jail pending court action, they are "detained" in a "detention center" or "adjustment center"; rather than being indicted, children are "petitioned" to court; in place of a determination of guilt, there is an "adjudication"; and those found guilty (i.e., adjudicated) are often "committed" to a "training school" or "reform school" rather than being sentenced to a prison.

Envisioned as a benevolent institution that would emphasize treatment rather than punishment, the juvenile court turned out to be a mixture of the two orientations. The confusion can be traced to the mixed legacy of the court that combined a puritanical approach to stubborn children and parental authority with the Progressive

Era's belief that children's essential goodness can be corrupted by undesirable elements in their environments. Finckenauer (1984: 116; see also Feld, 1999) termed the mixture "ambivalent" or "even schizophrenic."

The attention of the juvenile court and its supporters was mainly against the children of the poor, especially immigrants. One critic has suggested that the juvenile court served "as a literal dumping ground" (Schlossman, 1977: 92). The court provided an arena "where the dependent status of children was verified and reinforced, and where the incapacities of lower-class immigrant parents were, in a sense, certified" (1977: 92).

The juvenile court system extended the role of probation officer, a role originally introduced in the mid-19th century in Boston.[12] This new role was one of the primary innovations in the 20th-century juvenile justice system and the role became one of the most crucial in the entire system. Schlossman writes that "nothing in a child's home, school, occupation, or peer-group relations was, at least in theory, beyond" (Schlossman, 1977: 99) the purview of the probation officer. The probation officer "was expected to instruct children and parents in reciprocal obligations, preach moral and religious verities, teach techniques of child care and household management" (1977: 99).

Part of the probation officer's role was likened to that of an exorcist, for he was required to, in a sense, ward off or "exorcize" the evil temptations of the city. One reformer, Frederic Almy, wrote in 1902: "Loving, patient, personal service" would provide the "*antiseptic* which will make the *contagion* of daily life harmless" (Schlossman, 1977: 99, emphasis added).

Conceptions of Delinquency: 1860 to 1920

Social reformers in America accepted a form of "soft determinism" and the "notion that behavior is determined by forces outside the individual actor's control" while operating on the assumption that "if criminal behavior was determined by knowable biological or psychological or social conditions, those conditions could be identified and changed, *at least at the individual level*" (Faust and Brantingham, 1974: 3, emphasis added). However, as implied in the preceding quote, while causal factors were external to the individual (such as poverty, bad housing, inequality), the emphasis was and would continue to be on the individual offender.

Most of the reformers tended to accept the version of Social Darwinism known as Reform Darwinism, the view that man was not completely helpless and that man's progress enabled him, through positive science, to step in and improve his lot. With the help of such writers as Charles H. Cooley and Charles Henderson, reformers tended to accept the nature versus nurture view, with heavy emphasis on the nurture side of this dichotomy (Cooley, 1974; Henderson, 1974). However, taken as a whole, the environmental view that combined bad homes and evil surroundings dominated the thinking throughout the 19th and early 20th centuries. There is little evidence that the prevailing views have changed very much.

There was also a belief that intervention should be stressed and that potential criminals and delinquents could and should be identified and treated at the earliest age possible. Such a belief had been quite dominant throughout the 19th century.

The juvenile court was supposed to be one of the chief means through which intervention would be made. The court also enlisted the help of other programs and institutions to carry out such a program. Thus, it is not too surprising to find that public schools, recreation programs, public playgrounds, boys' clubs, YMCAs, and other organizations all helped in dealing with the problem of delinquency, especially in their role of identifying and containing so-called predelinquents (Shelden, 1976; Shelden and Osborne, 1989).

The general images or stereotypes of delinquents and criminals had not changed much since the early 19th century. For example, Charles Loring Brace, in commenting on the dangerous classes, said that those who participated in the New York Draft riots of 1863 (protesting being drafted to fight in the Civil War) were "street children grown up" (Bremner, 1970: 757). He further commented that this class:

> . . . has not begun to show itself, as it will in eight or ten years, when these boys and girls are mature. Those who were too neglected or too selfish to notice them as children, will be fully aware of them as men. They will vote. They will have the same rights as ourselves, though they have grown up ignorant of moral principle, as any savage or Indian. They will poison society. They will perhaps be embittered at the wealth, and the luxuries, they never share. Then let society beware, when the outcast, vicious, reckless multitudes of New York boys, swarming now in every foul alley and low street, come to know their power and use it (Bremner, 1970: 757).

As this quote suggests, the images of delinquents were often contradictory. On the one hand they were often viewed in a sympathetic light, suggesting they needed help; on the other hand, they were feared and described in some of the most racist and vicious ways.

Many of the child savers, like their earlier 19th-century counterparts, suggested a number of social factors as causal forces of delinquency. But few carried their arguments to the logical conclusion, that changing environmental factors was necessary, at least those social conditions that benefited the privileged. The solution continued to focus on the control, rehabilitation, or treatment of individual offenders or groups of offenders from a particular segment of the population (including those identified as predelinquents). The existing social structure was accepted as good and necessary, but there was a need to lead those who went astray back so that they could fit into the existing social order and class system. Unfortunately, the only place they were permitted to fit was at or near the bottom of that order.

Most of the programs advocated during this period placed primary emphasis on the individual and his or her moral and other personal shortcomings and received justification from psychological, psychiatric, and psychoanalytic theories of delinquency just beginning to emerge during the late 19th century. Such as approach was exemplified in the works of G. Stanley Hall and William Healy, both of whom worked closely with the juvenile courts in various cities. These writers advocated a clinical approach (using the medical model), one that stressed the need for a scientific laboratory to study delinquents. One such laboratory was the juvenile court.

The Fate of the Child-Saving Movement

The child savers claimed that they had ushered in new innovations in penology, especially with the establishment of industrial and training schools. Actually, the methods used were variations of earlier methods used in houses of refuge and other institutions. Most of the new institutions of the 20th century were placed in rural areas, a practice that was in part a reflection of the belief in rural purity, a product of the popular anti-urban bias among so many child savers. It was assumed that the "temptations" of city life would be offset by placement in such a setting. The juvenile court was to be the primary placing agency, thus serving a function similar to that of the Children's Aid Society when it placed children "out west."

The emphasis within these institutions remained relatively unchanged from previous methods. Restraint, control, the teaching of good work habits (e.g., cleaning floors, waiting on tables, milking cows, cooking, and so on), respect for authority, and a quasi-military model continued to be the hallmark of these institutions.

An example of the kinds of institutions opened during this period was the Shelby County Industrial and Training School, located near Memphis, Tennessee. Opened in 1904 in a farming community, it emphasized farm labor and the development of habits of industry through various forms of work and education. One of its founders stated that the *school* (a term often substituted for prison) would be:

> a place where we could educate the youths confined there in the practice, as well as the science, of agriculture; a place where they could be taught to get the best results from the cow in the way of milk, butter and beef; a place where they could not only raise cotton, but could learn to make it into cloth; a place where they could acquire a knowledge of carpentry, blacksmithing, shoemaking, broommaking, designing, horticulture, floriculture, etc.; in fact a place where from whence they could go with a technical knowledge which would enable them to take a position in the world as useful citizens.[13]

In a report in 1912 the Board of Directors stated, in glowing terms, how successful this institution had become:

> The boys in the several departments of work and in the school room have shown commendable interest in work and study. All are in school half of every weekday, under the instruction of a thoroughly competent lady school teacher. In the several departments of work, habits of industry have been cultivated which must prove a helpful training for future usefulness. The half-day work and half-day school, which has been in practice in these institutions for years, is now appealing to our public school authorities as a necessary advance in youthful development
>
> There has been no attempt in the past to indulge in expensive and often impracticable methods. Our work in all departments is necessary, practical and productive. On the firm and in the garden the actual use of the implement in the hand of the boy, under intelligent supervision, must produce results—and does—which means an abundance of fresh vegetables in their season for our tables and feed for our dairy cows and other stock.

> In the bakery and kitchen . . . the boys, under the supervision of a lady teacher of domestic science, are kept exceedingly busy . . . The laundry force and the boys who do the endless scrubbing, sweeping and dusting lie all being taught the necessity of work . . .[14]

Thus, even the most menial work was made respectable, so that these youths would fit into their appropriate labor force position upon release.

This institution was closed in 1935 amid a great deal of controversy, with two grand jury reports criticizing its methods and lack of results (in terms of a high recidivism rate and overcrowding) (Shelden, 1992).

The new penology (as it was called at the time; see chapter 4), perhaps best represented by state and county reformatories, industrial and training schools, and the like, emphasized menial labor that helped produce profits for both the state and private industry. For instance, the Illinois State Reform School (opened in 1871 at Pontiac) signed contracts with a Chicago shoe company, a company that manufactured brushes and a company manufacturing cane-seating chairs. And this was called the educational program at this institution (Platt, 1977: 105). The training in such institutions was suppose to, in the words of the famous penal reformer Frederick Wines, "correspond to the mode of life of working people," and should "be characterized by the greatest simplicity in diet, dress and surroundings, and *above all by labor*" (Platt, 1977: 50, emphasis added).

In many of these institutions (such as the one in Memphis) a lot of emphasis was placed on agricultural training, despite the fact that America was fast moving toward an industrial society. The reformatory regime aimed to teach middle class values but lower class skills. Bookishness was expressed as something undesirable while menial labor was described as an educational experience. Waiting on tables, cleaning, cooking and the like were to be taught to the "colored boys" in these institutions, according to the National Conference of Charities and Correction. Reformers aimed to "get the idea out of the heads of city boys that farm life is menial and low . . ." (Platt, 1977: 59–60).

It should be said at least in passing that the above characterization of the child savers and the juvenile court is essentially correct omits one important ingredient, one that even Platt now recognizes. Platt has recently noted that "there is a tendency to overstate the power of the state, reify the child savers' victims, and minimize issues of agency, resistance, and engagement. For example, historian Eileen Boris suggests that many immigrant families turned to the child savers for help in controlling their wayward children. The early juvenile justice system, says Boris, 'was more interactive than the concept of social control suggests' " (quoted in Platt, 2006: 3). David Tanenhaus gives a fresh look at a sample of 3,000 cases in the Chicago Juvenile Court right after it first opened. From his analysis, we get a picture of great hope that children will be treated by the law in a much more humane manner. Although not always successful, in comparison with the most recent trends of treating juveniles more (e.g., via zero tolerance policies, certification as an adult), the original juvenile courts seem mild by comparison (Tanenhaus, 2004).

The juvenile court system rapidly spread throughout the country following the lead of Chicago and Denver (both opened in 1899). Juvenile institutions, such as industrial and training schools and reform schools, continued to develop and expand.

Twentieth-Century Developments in Juvenile Justice

During the period roughly between 1920 and the 1960s there were relatively few structural changes within the juvenile justice system. In Illinois, beginning around 1909, the juvenile court began experimenting with the intensive psychological study and treatment of youthful deviance. The Juvenile Protective League, under the leadership of such notables as Julia Lathrop (head of the U.S. Children's Bureau), Jane Addams (famous reformer and founder of Hull House; Addams, 1910), Julian Mack (judge of the Boston juvenile court), and William Healy (famous psychologist), established a child guidance clinic. In this clinic the medical model of delinquency was epitomized. Thus, under the direction of Healy, child guidance clinics focused their attention and energies on the individual delinquent, one who was generally viewed as maladjusted to his or her social environment. By 1931 there were over 200 such clinics around the country (Krisberg and Austin, 1993: 32–35).

During the 1920s and 1930s the profession of social work grew to prominence (Lubove, 1965; Kunzel, 1993). This field began to dominate the treatment of individual delinquents and interpreted delinquency as stemming from conflicts within the family. Even today, social work methodology has a strong influence within the juvenile justice system.

Another development, the Chicago Area Project, which had its theoretical thrust from the famous Chicago School of Sociology and the works of Clifford Shaw, focused on community organization to prevent delinquency. From this perspective, delinquency stemmed from the social disorganization of slum communities rather than from the exploitation inherent in the capitalist system. Hence, the solution would be found in "fostering local community organizations to attack problems related to delinquency," (Krisberg and Austin, 1993: 35–42) such as poverty, inadequate housing, and unemployment.

Much of the effort focused on reducing gang delinquency, which was so prevalent in Chicago and other large cities (Liazos, 1974: Thrasher, 1927). However, such programs did little to alter the social reality of economic deprivation and other structural sources of delinquency. Krisberg and Austin comment that:

> . . . Chicago at that time was caught in the most serious economic depression in the nation's history. Tens of thousands of people were unemployed, especially immigrants and blacks. During this period, a growing radicalization among impoverished groups resulted in urban riots. The primary response by those in positions of power was an expansion and centralization of charity and welfare systems. In addition, there was considerable experimentation with new methods of delivering relief services to the needy [e.g., Hull House]. No doubt, Chicago's wealthy looked favorably upon programs like the Area Project, which promised to alleviate some of the problems of the poor without requiring a redistribution of wealth and power (Krisberg and Austin, 1993: 33).

The decade of the 1960s brought about some hope for significant changes, but such hope lasted barely into the 1970s. At least two developments stand out during this period of time. One development was the intrusion into the business of juvenile justice by the United States Supreme Court. Such famous court cases as *In re Gault* (1967),[15] *Kent v. United States* (383 U.S. 541, 1966), *In re Winship* (397 U.S. 358, 1970), among others, promised significant reforms. Sadly, most of the promise was never realized, especially with regard to institutionalizing youth.

The second development, which had some major impact, came on the heels of the efforts of Jerome Miller in the state of Massachusetts, who managed to close most of the reform schools opened in the 19th century (Miller, 1998). Despite the success of the closure of most of their institutions and the development of workable alternatives throughout the country, the recent "get tough" policies do not signal hopeful signs. Krisberg and Austin have observed that: "Most jurisdictions still rely on placement in institutions, with conditions reminiscent of reform schools 100 years ago. Children continue to be warehoused in large correctional facilities, receiving little care or attention" (Krisberg and Austin, 1993: 49).

The get tough movement has especially targeted minorities, as more and more institutions have become dominated especially by urban African Americans (Pope and Feyerherm, 1990; Miller, 1996; Shelden, 2006). Moreover, young women continue to be subject to a double-standard as minor offenses too often result in some form of incarceration (Chesney-Lind and Shelden, 2004). Also, many institutional systems have become huge bureaucracies with a vested interest in keeping a certain percentage of youth incarcerated.

Let's take a closer look at the current situation, where we find that the juvenile justice system is still focusing almost exclusively on controlling minorities and the poor. Sadly, this is even truer today than it was almost 200 years ago.

Still Controlling Minorities and the Poor: Current Juvenile Justice Practices

In 2005, the police made about 1.6 million arrests of those under 18 years of age.[16] Just under one-fourth (24%) of these arrests were for index crimes, with property offenses accounting for the vast majority of all arrests in this category (82% and the bulk of these were larceny-theft, mostly shoplifting). However, these figures represent a rather small percentage of all youths under the age of 18 who committed acts that could be considered delinquent. It should be noted that the majority of all youth commit some offense that could theoretically result in a referral to the juvenile court, yet few end up with an arrest.

As shown in Table 5.1, race figures prominently in juvenile arrest statistics. As noted here, while African-American youths make up about 12% of the juvenile population, in 2003 their rate of arrests for all crimes was almost double what it was for white youths. More dramatic differences are seen for violent crimes, where the arrest rate for African-American youth was around four times greater than white youths, which was actually not as great as what it was in 1980 and in 1990. For drug offenses, however, the differences are even more dramatic. Thus, whereas in 1980 white youths had a higher rate than African Americans, by the early 1990s the difference was reversed, with black youth's arrested at a rate more than four times greater than whites.

TABLE 5.1   *Juvenile Arrest Rates (per 100,000 age 5–17),*
for Selected Offenses, by Race, 1980–2003

	1980		1990		2003	
	White	*Black*	*White*	*Black*	*White*	*Black*
Index Crimes:						
Violent	105	632	105	656	93	359
Property	1290	2679	1070	2169	615	1126
Total	1395	3311	1175	2825	708	1485
Drugs	219	196	125	632	269	446
Total (all arrests)	3980	6300	3339	7088	2988	5111

Percent Change:	*1980–1990*	*1990–2003*	*1980–2003*
Total Index:			
White	−16	−40	−49
Black	13	−47	−55
Violent:			
White	0	−11	−11
Black	4	−45	−43
Property:			
White	−17	−43	−52
Black	−19	−48	−58
Drugs:			
White	−43	+115	+23
Black	+222	−29	+128
All Offenses:			
White	−16	−11	−25
Black	13	−28	−19

Source: FBI, *Uniform Crime Reports, 1980,* p. 205, *Uniform Crime Reports, 1989,* p. 191, *Uniform Crime Reports, 1998,* p. 229; *Crime in the United States, 2003,* p. 274. Washington, DC: U.S. Department of Justice.

By 2003, the gap narrowed considerably. Elsewhere in Table 5.1 we see the percentage changes over these years. What is noteworthy is the fluctuations during this period, with black arrest rates jumping by more than 200 percent during the 1980s, while white arrest rates increased the most in the 1990s, as the black arrest rate decreased. Overall, however, black arrest rates increased the most between 1980 and 2003.

Race, the War on Drugs and Referrals to Juvenile Court

It is impossible to talk about juvenile court processing without reference to race and, in recent years especially, drug offenses. Race often plays an indirect role in that race relates to offense which in turn affects the police decision to arrest. Race may also relate to the visibility of the offense. This is especially the case with regard to drugs.

There is abundant evidence that the war on drugs has, in effect, resulted in a targeting of African Americans on a scale that is unprecedented in American history. As the research by Jerome Miller has shown, young African-American males have received the brunt of law enforcement efforts to "crack down on drugs." He notes that in Baltimore, for example, African Americans were being arrested at a rate six times that of whites and more than 90% were for possession (Miller, 1996: 8; Currie, 1993; Tonry, 1995; Lockwood, Pottieger and Inciardi, 1995).

While the arrest rate in Baltimore for both races among juveniles for heroin and cocaine possession was virtually the same in 1965, by the 1970s the gap began to widen and by 1990 the arrest rate for African Americans stood at 766, compared to only 68 for whites in the year 1990. Overall, in 1980 the national rate of all drug arrests was about the same for black and white juveniles; during the early 1980s the arrest rate for whites dropped by one-third, while the rate for blacks remained about the same. But as the war on drugs expanded, the arrest rate for black youths went from 683 in 1985 to 1,200 in 1989, which was five times the rate for whites; by 1991 it went to 1,415. An even more alarming study in Baltimore found that total arrests for black youths was around 86 in 1981 (versus 15 for whites); by 1991 that number had increased to 1,304 for blacks, compared to a mere 13 for white youths (Miller, 1996: 86).

Nationally, between 1987 and 1988 the number of whites brought into the juvenile court remained virtually the same (up 1%), but the number of minorities referred to the court increased by 42% (Miller, 1996: 84–86). In Miller's study of Baltimore, he found that during 1981 only 15 white juveniles were arrested on drug charges, compared to 86 African American juveniles; in 1991, however, the number of whites arrested dropped to a mere 13, while the number of African-American youths arrested skyrocketed to a phenomenal 1,304, or an increase of 1,416%. The ratio of African-American to whites youths arrested went from about 6:1 to 100:1 (Miller, 1996: 86). A close look at juvenile court cases illustrates the role of race in drug cases. According to 1999 national data the drug referral rate for blacks was 11.3 per 1,000 juveniles, nearly twice the rate for whites (5.8) and 4 times the rate for youth of other races (2.7) (Office of Juvenile Justice and Delinquency Prevention, 2003).

A study by McGarrell found evidence of substantial increases in minority youths being referred to juvenile court, thus increasing the likelihood of being detained. But, cases of the detention, petition, and placement of minorities nevertheless exceeded what would have been expected given the increases in referrals. There has been an increase in the formal handling of drug cases, which has become a disadvantage to minorities. "Given the proactive nature of drug enforcement, these findings raise fundamental questions about the targets of investigation and apprehension under the recent war on drugs" (McGarrell, 1993: 46). As noted in a study of Georgia's crack-down on drugs, the higher arrest rate for African Americans was attributed to one single factor: " . . . it is easier to make drug arrests in low-income neighborhoods. . . . Most drug arrests in Georgia are of lower-level dealers and buyers and occur in low-income minority areas. Retail drug sales in these neighborhoods frequently occur on the streets and between sellers and buyers who do not know each other. Most of these sellers are black. In contrast, white drug sellers tend to sell indoors, in bars and clubs and within private homes, and to more affluent purchasers, also primarily white" (Fellner, 1996: 11).

Regardless of whether race, class or demeanor is statistically more relevant, one fact remains: growing numbers of African-American youths are finding themselves within the juvenile justice system. They are more likely to be detained, more likely to have their cases petitioned to go before a judge, more likely to be waived to the adult system, and more likely to be institutionalized than their white counterparts (Walker, Spohn and DeLone, 2007). While some of this relates to the nature of the offense, as we have shown, the likelihood of one race being associated with a particular offense, especially drugs, cannot be denied.

This point is underscored in an analysis of national figures on race and the juvenile justice system (Building Blocks for Youth, 2000). Jeffrey Butts, a researcher at the Urban Institute, commented that: "*At each stage of the process, there's a slight empirical bias. And the problem is that the slight empirical bias at every-stage of the decision-making accumulates. By the time you reach the end, you have all minorities in the deep end of the system*" (Center on Juvenile and Criminal Justice, 2004, emphasis in the original). The statistics clearly support this contention as shown in Figure 5.1. Whereas African-American youth constitute only 15% of the total population, they are 26% of those arrested, 44% of those detained, 46% of those sent to adult court and 58% of those who end up in state prison.

Quite often the discrepancies are even starker when we look at individual cities. A recent study in Columbia, South Carolina illustrates this point (Moore, 2004). In Columbia, while African Americans make up less than 20% of the total juvenile population, they constitute 60% of all juvenile arrests. In fact, between 1995 and 2003 the number of black youths arrested has increased, while the number of whites arrested has decreased. In fact, in 1996 the arrest figures were almost split evenly between whites and blacks (50% black, 49% white), but in 2003 it was 60% black and

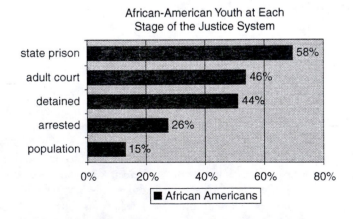

FIGURE 5.1   *Percent African-American Youth at Each Stage of the Juvenile Justice Process.*

Source: Building Blocks for Youth, "And Justice for Some." April, 2000 (http://cjcj.org/jjic/race_jj.php).

TABLE 5.2 *Offense Profile of Detained Residents by Sex and Race/Ethnicity for United States, 2001 (Rate per 100,000 Juveniles)*

Most Serious Offense	Total	Sex		Race/Ethnicity				
		Male	Female	White	Black	Hispanic	American Indian	Asian
Total	88	141	34	52	225	111	134	37
Delinquency	85	137	30	50	218	106	117	36
Person	27	44	9	14	74	34	29	15
Violent Crime Index*	17	30	4	7	51	24	16	11
Other Person	10	14	5	7	23	9	13	4
Property	21	35	6	13	52	25	32	8
Property Crime Index**	18	29	5	11	45	20	27	7
Other Property	4	6	1	2	8	5	5	1
Drug	7	12	2	3	22	8	8	1
Public order	9	14	3	5	22	12	15	4
Technical violation	21	32	10	14	47	28	34	8
Status offense	4	4	3	3	7	4	16	1

* Includes criminal homicide, violent sexual assault, robbery, and aggravated assault.
** Includes burglary, theft, auto theft, and arson.

Source: Sickmund, M., Sladky, T. J., and Kang, W. (2004) "Census of Juveniles in Residential Placement Databook" (http://www.ojjdp.ncjrs.org/ojstatbb/cjrp/asp/Offense_Detained.asp?state=0&topic=Offense_Detained&year=2001&percent=rate).

only 39% white. The police have concentrated their patrols in increasing numbers in the city's near Westside, a 12-square-block of mostly black residents. Not surprisingly, the detention rate of black youth is far greater than for whites.

The most current national figures reveal similar patterns. The same data presented in Table 5.2 are translated into rates per 100,000 juveniles. Here we clearly see the racial discrepancies. Regardless of offense, African-American youths are far more likely to be detained than their white counterparts. Indeed, reading downward within this table we see the fact that for all delinquent offenses black youths are about 4 times more likely to be detained (a rate of 225 versus 52), while for personal crimes the ratio is just over 5:1; the differences are most pronounced for drug offenses, with black youth more than 7 times more likely to be detained.

Racial bias is cumulative, starting long before a youth is ever contacted by the police. More will said about racial differences in the rates of detention and institutionalization later in the chapter, but suffice it to say at this point that black youths are found in detention centers and juvenile correctional facilities at a rate that is four times that of whites. Such differences remain regardless of offense charged. They are seven times more likely to be detained if charged with a drug offense and six times more likely to be committed on a drug charge.

While some may believe that the overrepresentation of minority youth is a result of their committing more crimes than whites, such is not the case, as indicated by self-report surveys and surveys on drug use (actually showing that whites are more likely than minorities to use illegal drugs.[17] It may be the result of differential police policies (e.g., targeting low-income, mostly minority neighborhoods) or the location of some offenses in more visible places (especially drug use). Regardless of the reasons, studies have shown race to be a very important factor (Shelden, 2006: Chapter 11; Walker, Spohn and DeLone, 2007).

Jerome Miller, reflecting on his own 30 plus years of working with youthful offenders, notes that one of the problems within the modern juvenile justice system is the method of diagnosing youth and recommending appropriate dispositions. He notes that the treatment options that the diagnostician has in mine helps to determine the actual diagnosis of the youth, rather than the other way around, as we generally assume. In reality, he notes, "the theory-diagnosis-treatment flow runs backward. The diagnostician looks first to the means available for handling the client, then labels the client, and finally justifies the label with psychiatric or sociological theory. Diagnosis virtually never determines treatment; treatment dictates diagnosis" (Miller, 1998: 232).

Increasingly, the juvenile courts, perhaps giving in to the law and order rhetoric of the past two decades, have begun to rely upon one of the most extreme disposition within the juvenile justice system, namely certifying a youth as an adult. It is as if they have said: "We give up! We have done everything we can think of to help you." They are, in effect, disposable children.[18]

Racial Composition of Juvenile Institutions

As suggested above, incarceration is a fate that awaits many minority youths. The percentage of incarcerated youth who are racial minorities has risen steadily over the years. National figures show that in 1950 only 23% of those in training schools were minorities; in 1960 this figure was 32%; in 1970 it was up to 40%; in 1989 minorities constituted 60% of those in public training schools; in 1997 the percentage stood at 66%. It is interesting to note that the majority of youths confined in private facilities are white. This is no doubt because most of the costs are paid for by family members, usually through their insurance (Walker, Spohn and DeLone, 2007: 223–224; U.S. Department of Commerce, 1975: 419).

Not surprisingly, the overall rate of incarceration was considerably higher for minorities. The latest (2001) census of committed juveniles (see Table 5.3) reveals such stark contrasts as: (1) the overall rate for black was 634, compared to a rate of 253 for Hispanics and only 155 for whites; (2) even considering the most serious offense charged, commitment rates for minorities far exceeded those of whites, such as: personal crimes, the black rate was 231 compared to only 50 for whites and 89 for Hispanics; drug offenses, the black rate stood at 70, the Hispanic rate was 25, compared to merely 11 for whites (in other words, for drug offenders, the black incarceration rate

TABLE 5.3   *Offense Profile of Committed Residents by Sex and Race/Ethnicity for United States, 2001 (Rate per 100,000 Juveniles)*

	Committed							
		Sex			Race/Ethnicity			
Most Serious Offense	Total	Male	Female	White	Black	Hispanic	American Indian	Asian
Total	246	417	65	155	634	253	468	83
Delinquency	233	403	55	145	608	247	432	79
Person	85	147	20	50	231	89	174	29
Violent Crime Index*	59	106	9	32	166	66	129	20
Other Person	26	41	11	18	65	23	44	9
Property	73	128	16	49	176	74	137	27
Property Crime Index**	61	107	13	41	146	63	115	23
Other Property	12	21	3	8	30	12	22	4
Drug	22	39	4	11	70	25	23	5
Public order	25	44	4	16	61	28	42	8
Technical violation	28	45	11	18	69	30	55	10
Status offense	12	14	10	10	26	7	36	4

* Includes criminal homicide, violent sexual assault, robbery, and aggravated assault.
** Includes burglary, theft, auto theft, and arson.

Source: Sickmund, M., Sladky, T. J., and Kang, W. (2004) "Census of Juveniles in Residential Placement Databook" (http://www.ojjdp.ncjrs.org/ojstatbb/cjrp/asp/Offense_Committed.asp?state=O&topic=Offense_Committed&year=2001&percent=rate).

was more than six times greater than for whites; (3) in every other offense category, whites had the lowest rate and blacks had the highest, with Hispanics in the middle. The distribution of these rates, with blacks first, Hispanics second and whites third, remind me of a phrase heard repeatedly during the civil rights movement of the 1960s: "If you're white, you're alright, if you're brown, stick around, if you're black, stay back."

High Recidivism Rates and Scandals Persist

It has been almost 200 years since the New York House of Refuge was founded. Institutions for juvenile offenders have repeatedly suffered from scandals, violence, corruption and high recidivism rates. It is almost as if there is a giant umbilical cord stretching from those houses of refuge to current correctional institutions. Little has changed, except that modern institutions are more expensive to operate and the architecture fits in with the modern era. I have seen them up close.

In 1999 a new super-max youth prison was opened in North Las Vegas in order to house those offenders classified as Level IV—the highest classification in the state based upon their alleged degree of "dangerousness." This was a new category, created according to a youth's prior record, was based upon a point system—the more points, the more dangerous the youth was. Careful investigation by the author discovered that there was literally no scientific rationale for the point system and no research was cited that would warrant such a point system. Not surprisingly, the higher the level of classification, the greater the percentage of minorities. This institution, called Summit View Correctional Center, was built and operated by a private company called Correctional Services Corporation. Within one year of opening the prison was beset by a number of problems, not the least of which was the fact that there were too many empty beds (a certain number were needed in order to make a profit). This was mostly because the state could not find enough dangerous youth to qualify for Level IV (in fact, for a time the prison borrowed a few Level III youths from the detention center at the juvenile court in Las Vegas). But they did find a large number of minority youths to house in this prison, for a recent census revealed that about 80% of the youths were minorities. I was once given a tour of this institution. It reminded me of the "supermax" prison in Marion, Illinois (which I personally visited on several occasions when I was a graduate student at Southern Illinois University in 1976). Summit View looked like a prison, smelled like a prison, and sounded like a prison.[19]

One of the most famous (or infamous, depending upon your view) of the modern institutions is the California Youth Authority (CYA). An entire chapter could be devoted to describing this monumental failure. Suffice it to say that during the past 25 years or so it has demonstrated that there has been little improvement upon the old houses of refuge. A series of three reports surfaced back in the 1980s condemning practices within the CYA (Lerner, 1982, 1986; Lerner, DeMuro, and DeMuro, 1988). All three reports documented extreme brutality and the lack of meaningful treatment within these institutions. The third and final report noted that the CYA institutions "are seriously overcrowded, offer minimal treatment value despite their high expense, and are ineffective in long-term protection of public safety" (Lerner, DeMuro, and DeMuro, 1988: 11). At the time the CYA was over 150% capacity with 9,000 wards packed into institutions designed for 5,840. The report further noted that the Youthful Offender Parole Board played a key role in the overcrowding, resulting in the legislature cutting its budget by one-third because of the board's failure to follow its own guidelines. The report called the board a "structural anomaly" and recommended it be abolished (1988: 11).

CYA scandals have persisted to the present day. In the fall of 2004 the CYA was once again rocked by revelations of extreme brutality, suicides, horrible physical conditions and almost total failure to live up to its mission statement. A special report in *U.S. News and World Report* noted: "At the Heman G. Stark Youth Correctional Facility here, the K&L disciplinary lockdown is known as 'the Rock.' Here dim corridors are lined with the steel doors of a dozen concrete cells. The air is dank, and the drip-drip of water echoes quietly, thanks to the perpetually leaking showers. On the mental health unit, shouts and curses bounce off the walls. In a cell, a young man with his head down paces silently, back and forth, back and forth." The writer of this report said it was "just another day at Stark" and quoted one expert who called the CYA system "a very dangerous place" with "an intense climate of fear." Last year at Stark there were almost 300 attacks—"more than double the previous year's total" (Cannon, 2004).

A report in May, 2004 found revealed that a CYA officer was caught on video letting his German shepherd bite a 20-year-old prisoner on the leg, even though the inmate was following orders and lying on the floor. This was the second such episode in four months caught on tape at a CYA institution in Stockton (Warren, 2004a).

Still another report on the news of two more deaths within a CYA institution revealed "excessive rates of violence; inadequate mental health care and educational services; overuse of isolation cells; and deplorable conditions, including feces spread all over some of the cells. Some boys were being forced to sit or stand in cages while attending classes, a 'normal' situation in the state's Kafkaesque system." Going even further the report noted that:

> Just as shocking as the litany of CYA abuses is the fact that institutions such as Preston Training School simply don't work. A growing body of research shows that young people incarcerated in large institutions get rearrested more frequently, and for more serious crimes than their counterparts with similar delinquency histories who are not incarcerated. For example, a study that compared matched samples of offenders in Arkansas found that the incarceration experience was the single greatest predictor of future criminal conduct, dwarfing the effects of gang membership or family dysfunction. It's not surprising then, that more than nine out of 10 CYA "graduates" are back in trouble with the law within three years of their release. On top of that, the CYA system costs taxpayers a whopping $85,000 a year per youth. It seems likely that if the majority of CYA youths came from white, middle-class neighborhoods, the public would never stand for its failures and abuses (Bell and Stauring, 2004: XX).

Numerous additional reports appeared in the *Los Angeles Times* during 2004 that echoed this report.[20] One of these reported on a special senate hearing where state Senator Gloria Romero (D- Los Angeles) said, after reviewing a report that was part of a class action suit filed by a group of CYA wards that called the conditions chilling where some inmates were kept in "steel-mesh cages not much bigger than phone booths" (Warren, 2004c). Romero said the CYA was "totally failing in its mission to rehabilitate youths." She called it a system "that is in chaos, ruled by fear and neglect," despite an expenditure of more than $80,000 annually on each young offender (Warren, 2004c).

A class action law suit was filed in 2002 alleging unconstitutional treatment of inmates. A report in the *Los Angeles Times* summarizes this case:

> Last year, the lawsuit was refiled in state court as a taxpayer action, alleging, in essence, that the CYA was improperly spending state funds on unlawful practices. The plaintiff is Margaret Farrell of Reseda, whose nephew, mentally ill inmate Edward Jermaine Brown, was locked in a filthy isolation cell for 23 hours a day for seven months, the lawsuit said.

The toilet in the cell often did not function and Brown was fed "blender meals," a whipped mix of food groups, through a straw pushed through his cell door (Warren, 2004c).

Since the lawsuit was filed, the CYA has closed the housing unit where Brown was locked up and stopped the blender meals (Warren, 2004d).

Then there is the following report of a judge ordering that no more youth be sent to the CYA:

San Mateo County abruptly halted sending children and teenagers to the California Youth Authority this week, responding to newspaper accounts of brutal and inhumane conditions inside the statewide juvenile prison system. Initiated by presiding juvenile court Judge Marta Diaz, the action makes San Mateo the second Bay Area county planning to keep youths in their home counties, rather than subjecting them to conditions of confinement inside the state's 10 lock-up facilities. Tuesday, San Francisco Supervisor Tom Ammiano introduced a moratorium on all non-mandatory commitments to CYA. Supervisors will vote on the moratorium at a meeting next week. Probation officials are also taking action, responding to recently released state-commissioned reports that detail a climate of ward-on-ward brutality and harsh institutional treatment, including confining youths in cells 23 hours per day. The CYA reviews found that substance-abuse treatment was below national standards, and the reports concluded that mental-health services were failing the majority of inmates, ages 12 to 25, who suffer from psychiatric disorders (de Sá, 2004).

This was reported in the *San Jose Mercury News* and was followed up by a series of reports in the fall further documenting the travails of the CYA.[21]

The settlement of the lawsuit stipulated that the CYA had better get their act together. The CYA "agreed to a set of short-term fixes, including the development of a system to separate vulnerable inmates from dangerous ones, reducing the time prisoners spend in isolation cells, and improvements in the handling of inmates on suicide watch" (Warren, 2004d: XX). Part of the settlement requires independent experts who have been hired to study the CYA. In their first report, released in February, 2004, they portrayed a system in which violence was, in their words, "off the charts" and in which "medical care, psychiatric treatment, education services, gang management, and suicide prevention were inadequate."

It is unlikely that this will result in significant changes. Note that in the above statement that they will only reduce time spent in isolation cells and make improvements in the way they handle kids who are on suicide watch. Thus, isolation will still be used. Note the words of one critic who said that "This agreement does not transform the CYA, it merely brings it up to a tolerable level. The danger is that the governor will tie a ribbon around this and call it a day, when there's a lot more that needs to be done to re-engineer the system." Critics have pointed out "that what's missing is any requirement that the state house inmates in smaller living units, as opposed to the massive prison-like facilities that typify the CYA. Most researchers believe—and several states have proved—that small groups more effectively foster the human connections troubled youths need to turn around their lives" (Warren, 2004d).

An audit by the Office of the Inspector General was released in January, 2005, accusing the CYA of "failing to give offenders the education and training that could save them from a life of crime" (Rieterman, 2005). A story in the *Los Angeles Times* noted that the CYA youth prisons "are still confining too many wards for 23 hours a day," and the audit called such a practice "ineffective and dehumanizing." The report "found that 27 youths at a Chino detention facility were locked up around the clock, except for five-minute daily showers. And 39 youths at a Stockton facility were locked down for more than 30 days, with three kept in their cells for more than 200 days. Numerous other wards, the audit found, were receiving little in the way of required teaching and counseling designed to help prepare them for their eventual release." The Inspector General, Matthew Cate, stated that the "most troubling" finding of the report "is that many of the deficiencies that have not been corrected are central to the Youth Authority's core mission of rehabilitating the young people entrusted to its care" (Reiterman, 2005).

On January 31, 2005 the State of California signed an agreement with juvenile justice advocates (who had brought the law suit noted above) and filed it in Alameda County Superior Court. The agreement puts "therapy and positive reinforcement at the heart of California's youth prison system, rejecting today's more punitive approaches in favor of models that have been successful in other states" (Warren, 2005). The court order resulting from the lawsuit says that the CYA must (Warren, 2005).

- Shift to an "open programming" model, as opposed to one that confines inmates in their cells for long stretches at a time, at all prisons by May 2. Under the change, inmates must be released for education, meals, treatment and recreation on a daily basis, and dangerous youths would be separated from those considered vulnerable.
- House youths in the facility closest to their homes. This addresses a chief complaint of families, who often live hundreds of miles from their incarcerated children, making visits difficult.
- Involve families in the therapy provided to youths, unless it would be considered detrimental to the inmate.
- Emphasize "positive reinforcement rather than punitive disciplinary methods" to encourage good behavior.
- Require all staff who work with youths to be trained in rehabilitative and treatment services.

What is occurring here may be a political solution to pacify a public that is largely uninformed about the realities of youth prisons. By *political solution,* I merely mean that a band-aid may be used to fix a totally ruptured system that may need to be abandoned. It remains to be seen whether or not the court order will be effective. Given the history of reforms the changes are most likely to be cosmetic in nature. The promise that treatment will be provided rings very hollow, since they have promised that from the day the CYA was opened more than 60 years ago. There are simply too many with a vested interest in keeping the system the way it is. It is *déjà vu* all over again.

Notes

1. Thus, informal systems of control have always been reserved for the more privileged youths, while the less privileged have been subjected to formal systems of control. However, if we examine history closely, with few exceptions it has almost always been the case that minority youth have been much more likely to be viewed not as juvenile delinquents (i.e., malleable and thus redeemable) but as hardened criminals: not redeemable (since by definition adults are more fixed in their ways and less redeemable). Little wonder that such a great proportion of those certified or waived to adult court in recent years (i.e., viewed as unredeemable adult criminals) have been minorities.

2. One of the persistent problems in our response to crime and delinquency is that when trying to make predictions based upon certain risk factors, as is done with various health problems (e.g., cancer), is that there are too many false positives where you predict that someone will become a delinquent and the prediction turns out to be false. Most kids, even those at high risk, will never become adult criminals.

3. This group was formerly called the Society for the Prevention of *Pauperism* (another word for poverty). For a discussion of this group and a detailed description of its upper-class backgrounds, see Pickett (1969: 21–49).

4. Although Platt was writing about the later 19th century child savers (to be discussed later in this chapter) his comments summarize the prevailing view throughout this century: "If, as the child savers believed, criminals are conditioned by biological heritage and brutish living conditions, then *prophylactic* measures must be taken early in life." Famous prison reformer Enoch Wines commented that "They are born to it, brought up for it. They must be saved" (Platt, 1977: 45, emphasis added; see also Platt's comments on the term *predelinquent* and how such youth needed to be "immunized" against the "disease of delinquency" on p. 107).

5. The wording used here is taken verbatim from the law, passed in Pennsylvania in 1826, which authorized the House of Refuge, "at their discretion, to receive into their care and guardianship, infants, *males under the age of twenty-one years,* and *females under the age of eighteen years*, committed to their custody . . ." (emphasis added). Note the obvious distinction based upon gender. This exact same statute was reproduced in numerous state laws throughout the 19th century. I found an example in my own study of Memphis,

Tennessee (Shelden, 1976; Shelden and Osborne, 1989).

6. *Ex Parte Crouse,* 4 Wharton (Pa.) 9 (1938); for the significance for girls see Shelden, 1998).

7. *Ex Parte Crouse.*

8. All of these charges are well documented in the following works: Mennel, 1973; Hawes, 1971; Bremner, 1970; Pisciotta, 1982. Abuses within the juvenile justice system have continued to the present, with one scandal after another throughout the 20th century. There has been a big scandal concerning the California Youth Authority, as will be noted later in this chapter (see Cannon, 2004).

9. *Commonwealth v. Fisher,* 213 Pa. 48 (1905).

10. For a fuller discussion of this topic from the perspective of an active reformer of the period see Addams, 1909.

11. In my own study of the origins of the juvenile justice system in Memphis, Shelden found several instances where commitments to the county training school were challenged in court, some successfully. See Shelden (1976, 1992).

12. The origins of probation can be traced to the efforts of a man named John Augustus, a Boston shoemaker who, during the 1840s volunteered to take on the responsibility of supervising offenders in the community as a substitute to sending them to prison or jail. Since then this rather unique idea has become highly bureaucratized with the average probation officer supervising between 50 and 100 offenders. The spirit of volunteerism and the offering of a helping hand in the name of true benevolence toward one's human being has turned into a job as a career bureaucrat. Many who engage in this line of work are overwhelmed by the responsibilities and often care little about the persons they supervise. In fact, the supervision is often little more than surveillance, which usually consists of a few phone calls. In many instances probation officers follow the motto found on the wall of a California probation officer which read: "Trail 'em, Surveil 'em, Nail 'em, and Jail 'em" (Miller, 1996: 131).

13. *Memphis Commercial Appeal,* July 21, 1903.

14. *Memphis Commercial Appeal,* July 16, 1912.

15. The case of *In Re Gault* involved a 15-year-old Arizona boy named Gerald Gault who was adjudicated as a delinquent in juvenile court and committed to the Arizona Industrial School for the

period of his majority (21-years-old) because he and some friends made an obscene phone call to a neighbor. The U.S. Supreme Court ruled that Gault had been denied certain fundamental rights (like the Illinois court did in Danny O'Connell's case), such as the right to counsel. Writing for the majority, Justice Abe Fortus stated that "Under our Constitution, the condition of being a boy does not justify a kangaroo court." For the full text of this case (and many others, including the O'Connell case) see Faust and Brantingham, 1974; see also Platt, 1977: 161–163.

16. FBI, Uniform Crime Report. http://www.fbi.gov/ucr/05cius/data/table_38.html.

17. A good review is found on my website: Esona, D. and R. G. Shelden. 2006. "Racial Disparities and the Drug War." http://www.sheldensays.com/Res-fourteen.htm.

18. See Golden's (1997) insightful account of the more general problem of how children are treated within the modern welfare system, a system designed, along with the justice system, to control the dangerous classes. It is interesting to note that ironically as the government has, in the last years of the 20th century, been "ending welfare as we know it" (to use a popular political sound bite) we are in the process of increasing the use of the prison system (on both the juvenile and adult level) to serve basically the same general purpose.

19. Shelden, R. G. "If it looks like a prison . . ." *Las Vegas City Life,* August 13, 1999. An update is found on my website: http://www.sheldensays.com/i_told_you_so.htm.

20. Examples include the following: Warren, Leovy, and Zamichow (2004); Warren (2004b); Warren (2004c).

21. Bailey and de Sá (2004). These and subsequent reports can be found on the website for the Center on Juvenile and Criminal Justice (http://cjcj.org/press/index.php).

6

Perpetuating Patriarchy: Keeping Women in their Place

Women and the Law

Patriarchy and Images of Women

Several stereotypical images of women have helped shape not only the law, but also the definitions of what behaviors and what kinds of persons are considered criminal. Among some of the most popular of these images include the following: (1) woman as the pawn of biology (i.e., controlled by biological forces, such as the menstrual cycle, beyond her control); (2) woman as passive and weak; (3) woman as impulsive and nonanalytic (i.e., they act illogically and therefore need the guidance from the more analytical man); (4) woman as impressionable and in need of protection (i.e., she is childlike and gullible and therefore need more protection from men); (5) the active woman as masculine (i.e., whenever she breaks away from the traditional roles, it is deemed unnatural or even masculine); (6) the criminal woman as purely evil (i.e., when a woman falls from grace she must really be evil, since she is so inherently pure to begin with); (7) the Madonna-whore duality (a woman is either a virtuous person or the paragon of evil or the seductress) (Rafter and Stanko 1982: 2–4; Pollock, 1996: 4).

Given these images, it is not surprising to find that there has been a tradition in law, going back as far as ancient Rome and Greece, which holds that women are perpetual children and the only adults are men. In ancient Greece, for instance, only men could be citizens in the political arena and most of the slaves were women (and women in general were treated as slaves). In Rome both the status of women and slaves was improved somewhat as they were incorporated into the family under the rule of *Patria protestas* (power of the father). This term implied not so much a family relationship, but rather a property relationship. The woman had to turn over any income she received to the head of the household and had no rights to her own children, no rights to divorce, or for that matter, no rights to life outside of the family. According to Roman law, unlike slaves, women could not be emancipated. A woman's relationship to her husband was designated by the concept of *manus* or hand. From this is derived the modern practice to ask a woman's father for "her hand in marriage" (Eisenstein, 1988: 58–59; Terkel, 1996: 6–7).

The attitudes that shaped these practices are revealed in several different sources, from the Bible to statements by Aristotle. Aristotle said that it is only natural that the man is superior and the woman inferior and equally naturally it follows that one governs and the other is governed. In the Bible there are numerous references to this natural state of affairs. In Corinthians (I, 11:3, 9) it is written that: "The head of every man is Christ; and the head of the woman is the man . . . Neither was the man created for the woman; but the woman for the man." In Timothy (2:11–12): "Let women learn in silence with all subjection. But I suffer not a woman to teach, nor to usurp authority over the man" (quoted in Parenti, 1994: 143).

Such control of women is consistent with the system known as patriarchy. In her excellent treatment of this subject, Gerda Lerner defines *patriarchy* as "the manifestation and institutionalization of male dominance over women and children in the family and the extension of male dominance over women in society in general. It implies that men hold power in all the important institutions of society and that women are deprived of access to such power" (Lerner, 1986: 239). The legal institution is one among these various institutions mentioned by Lerner that are ultimately controlled by men and by extension is used to control women. Lerner describes it best by an analogy with a stage in a theater:

> Men and women live on a stage, on which they act out their assigned roles, equal in importance. The play cannot go on without both kinds of performers. Neither of them "contributes" more or less to the whole; neither is marginal or dispensable. But the stage set is conceived, painted, defined by men. Men have written the play, have directed the show, interpreted the meanings of the action. They have assigned themselves the most interesting, most heroic parts, giving women the supporting roles.

Continuing the analogy, Lerner notes that as women become more aware of this inequality, they begin to protest, asking for more roles, and more equality in determining what is assigned. At times they may upstage the men and at other times they may pinch-hit for a male performer. Yet even when they win equal access to desired roles, they must first qualify according to terms set by the men, who are the judges of whether or not women measure up. Preference is given to women who are docile and those who act differently are punished—by ridicule, ostracism, and exclusion. In time women realize that getting equal parts does not translate into equality, as long as the script, stage setting, the props, and so on are controlled by men (Lerner, 1986: 12–13).

While women's subordinate status existed before capitalism emerged as a dominant mode of production, contrary to the strictly Marxist interpretation,[1] it is nevertheless true that capitalism has made things worse. This is because "capitalism rewards the impulses of exploitation, accumulation, competitiveness, ruthless self-interest, individualized aggrandizement, scarcity psychology, and indifference to the sufferings of the disadvantaged" (Parenti, 1994: 149). Capitalism also "relies on sexism as a diversionary force" by focusing on issues other than class inequality, such as abortion, sexual morality, etc. rather than a "critical examination of who gets what, when, and how." Further, under capitalism "wealth is accumulated by expropriating the labor power of the worker," (1994: 150) and both sexism and racism makes this that much easier. Women, moreover, are often blamed by conservatives for what ails the society; they are convenient scapegoats (e.g., charges that too many are in the workforce demanding equal pay, or too many are welfare queens, and so on).[2]

Perhaps more importantly, women are viewed as commodities. Parenti describes the process of *commodification* as "the process of objectifying and transforming the female appearance and body to fit marketable (that is, marriageable) standards." Women have gone through hundreds of different procedures over the years (e.g., stretching lips and necks, flattened breasts during certain times and again expanded them at other times, painted nails and lips, and so on) mainly in order to "gain the attention and approval of men, to persuade men to 'buy' them either as wives or workers" (Parenti, 1994: 150).

Punishing and Controlling Women

What has happened when women have not conformed to these images or in someway acted "out of place" or did not fit the image of a commodified female? Throughout world history women offenders have been subjected to differential forms of punishment that reflects their subservient position. In the Middle Ages a pregnant woman might receive lenient punishment if she were to "plead her belly," yet could be burned at the stake for the crime of adultery or for murdering her spouse (the latter of which still receives harsher punishment than men murdering their wives). Prior to the rise of imprisonment in the 19th century, daughters and wives who were unwanted were often forced into convents and similar institutions, along with political prisoners, the mentally defective and other outcast persons (Dobash, Dobash, and Gutteridge, 1986; Lorde, 1988).

Much of Roman law was eventually incorporated into the English common law, which in turn was copied (with few significant changes) in America. For several years the only law book used was Blackstone's famous *Commentaries on the Laws in England*, originally published in 1765. American family law incorporated Blackstone's famous dictum that the husband and wife are as one and that one is the husband (Eisenstein, 1998: 58–59).

Not surprisingly, in early American law the wife could not sue, execute a deed and engage in any other similar practices, without consent of her husband. Women were denied the vote until 1921 and in general laws that were "designed to protect the interests of 'persons' simply did not apply to women" (Chambliss and Courtless, 1992: 31). In fact, the Supreme Court ruled in 1867 that a woman who had completed law school and had passed the bar in Illinois, nevertheless had no right to practice law! Using the prevailing logic of the time, the court stated in their ruling that the "natural and proper timidity and delicacy which belongs to the female sex evidently unfits it for many of the occupations in civil life. . ." and that the "destiny and mission of women are to fulfill the noble and benign offices of wife and mother" (1992: 31).

Throughout Colonial America women had no identity, other than their relation with their father or later with their husband. The husband had rights over his wife that

FIGURE 6.1 *Punishments for Women in Colonial America.*

Source: From *Curious Punishments of Bygone Days*, by Alice Morse Earle, 1896 (http://www.getchwood. com/punishments/curious/index.html).

resembled in many ways the rights of masters over their slaves. Even if a man killed his wife, he would be treated under the law with far more leniency than if his wife had killed him. In fact, a man killing his wife was treated almost the same as if he had killed an animal or a servant. Colonial law was often very specific about women and some crimes were, in effect, women's crimes and were severely punished. For instance, the crime of being a common scold was applied "to a woman who berated her husband or was too vocal in public settings." The most appropriate punishment for scolding was the ducking stool, the branks and branding (see Figure 6.1). The former was placing the female offender in a chair and ducking her in a pool of water several times, for the purpose of drowning her. The latter was a type of metal headgear placed over the head of a woman who was accused of scolding. If the woman tried to move her tongue to speak, sharp spikes would dig into her.

In colonial America several women were singled out for committing various crimes that were religiously based. As discussed in chapter 1, Anne Hutchinson was persecuted for expressing alternative religious views and eventually banished from Massachusetts in the 1630s. Perhaps the most famous case was that of Mary Dyer. As noted in chapter 3, she sympathized with the Quakers, was subsequently convicted and hanged in Boston in June, 1659 (McHenry, 1983; Tolles, 1971; Knappman, 1991; Semmes, 1970). Two centuries later the state of Massachusetts constructed a statue of her, which presently stands in front of the state capitol of Boston, ironically across the street from the famous Commons where about 100 years after her death American patriots "gathered for drill to fit for freedom." The inscription on her statue reads "Witness for Religions Freedom."

Then there were the infamous witch hunts, both in Europe and in the American colonies. These witch hunts stand as classic examples of the use of the legal system to punish women who dared challenge the male power structure. In New England during the 1600s at least 36 women were executed for the crime of being a witch. The crime of witchcraft was one among many religious-based laws on the books during colonial times. This was clearly an effort to exert almost complete control by Puritan leaders. Women who were unattached—as wives, sisters, and daughters of men—received the most severe treatment. Most of the so-called witches were merely women who were outspoken in their views or had a great deal of informal power either as healers or as community leaders (Pollock, 1996: 7–90). Such odd behavior was labeled by those in power as a form of mental illness or just plain crazy behavior. One study noted that much of the witchcraft craze stemmed from anxiety over inheritance, a system that would keep property—and hence power—in the hands of men. Not surprisingly many accused as witches stood to inherit property as there were no male heirs. Many, incidentally, were beyond their childbearing years and hence unneeded by the male hierarchy (Karlsen, 1987).

While woman played an active role in efforts to pass three key Civil War amendments to the Constitution (Thirteenth, Fourteenth, and Fifteenth Amendments), ironically these amendments that extended equal protection to all persons ignored women. In other words, these "equal rights amendments to the Constitution simply did not apply to women" (Terkel, 1996: 177–178). It was not until 1971, in the case of *Reed v. Reed* (1971) that the court said that under the U.S. Constitution women were persons.

The feminist movement of the 19th century led to several significant changes in the legal status of women. The Married Women's Property Acts gave women certain property rights that had heretofore been denied and the issue of domestic violence led to the passage of laws in some parts of the county, as it was for the first time considered a crime. In the first part of the 20th century, women made some gains in the workplace. Yet despite these new laws, women's gains were often only illusory. The law and legal system remained male dominated and women continued to be treated as second class citizens (Terkel, 1996: 177–178; see also Faludi, 1991; C. MacKinnon, 1989; Sokoloff and Price, 1995: 23–25).

The unequal treatment of women by the law is perhaps nowhere better demonstrated than their treatment by the criminal justice system and the use of imprisonment as a method of control. In the next section the historical development of women's prisons will be reviewed. This rather sordid history not only illustrates the brutal treatment of women as a group, but the class and racial dimensions of such treatment.

A History of Women's Prisons

Prior the 19th century women offenders were generally housed within the same quarters as the men, although kept separate. Reports of early jails and workhouses note the often deplorable conditions in which men, women, and children were all thrown in together, along with the mentally ill and both petty and serious offenders. In colonial America few women offenders were incarcerated, which is not surprising since few were incarcerated in general. Of those who were arrested, most were charged with violations of rather minor religious-type laws (e.g., violation of the Sabbath, adultery), and these were white women only. When they were arrested, they were held in local jails for trial and the normal punishment was often some sort of public reprimand, such as whipping or the stocks and the pillory (Collins, 1997: 5).

For African-American women the situation was obviously quite different, as the majority were legally slaves and those who were not were indentured servants (Sellin, 1976). Most violations of laws were handled informally within the plantation, but occasionally the slave owners had to rely on the local criminal justice system. In such cases they often used what were called Negro Courts. These were set up specifically for slaves who violated laws that were applicable to slaves but not whites. Among the crimes (often considered felonies) they were charged with included striking the master three times (punishable by death). Incidentally, death and even incarceration was rarely taken against slaves since such action was not profitable for the owners (unlike today as prisons are quite profitable). It was not until after the Civil War when African Americans began to appear in penal institutions in large numbers, largely as a result of various Jim Crow laws and the infamous Black Codes (Shelden, 1979). Many were subjected to the infamous convict lease system (see chapter 4).

As already noted in this book, the early American jails were often mere extensions of the earlier workhouses and almshouses. The Newgate prison (New York), opened in 1797, was the first institution for felons only, and women offenders were housed in an area separate from men (Collins, 1997; Rafter, 1990: 4–5). By 1835 there appeared several institutions with separate quarters for women offenders, notably in Maryland and New York (Collins, 1997).

Treatment of prisoners, both male and female, changed dramatically around the 1820s with the founding of the Auburn State prison, originally housing both men and women, although in separate quarters. Overcrowding soon set in (and condition that would plague prisons up to the present date) and there was little interest in the women offenders, who at that time were viewed with particular distaste. In fact, conditions were so bad that the prison chaplain once remarked that it was bad enough for male prisoners, "but to be a female convict, for any protracted period, would be worse than death" (Freedman, 1981: 16). When Newgate Prison was closed in the 1820s, the men were all eventually transferred to Auburn prison, but the women were sent to Bellevue Penitentiary in New York City. However, conditions were so horrible at Bellevue, that a women's annex was built at Mount Pleasant, New York, on the grounds of Sing Sing Prison, and opened in 1839 (Watterson, 1996: 196; Rafter, 1990: 6). Around the same time a women's annex was built on the grounds of the Ohio Penitentiary and opened in 1837. During this period of time it was widely believed that women offenders should be treated more harshly than their male counterparts. This belief was justified by the argument that the female offender was more depraved than her male counterpart since, having been born pure, they had fallen further from grace than had their male counterparts and, in fact, she was often blamed for the crimes of men (Freedman, 1981: 17–18).

Most of the activities female prisoners performed in these early prisons (activities still performed today) were designed to fit them for the duties of domestic life. At first there was little or no separation of male and female prisoners. Several noted reformers, such as Elizabeth Fry, a famous Quaker reformer (1780–1845), along with such notables as Dorothea Dix (1802–1887), Clara Barton (1821–1912), and Josephine Shaw Lowell (1843–1905) began to advocate separate facilities and other reforms. One of the first results of reform activities was the hiring of female matrons, beginning in Maryland after the Civil War. It is interesting to note that the majority of 19th and early 20th century prison reformers were not only women, but members of the upper class. As Freedman's study of these 19th century reformers shows, the roster reads like a who's who of the American elite, not an uncommon occurrence, as most reforms were carried out by members of the elite (Platt, 1977).

Only a small number of women were imprisoned in the early 19th century, and when they were they were confined in separate quarters or wings of male prisons. Not surprisingly, the conditions of their confinement were horrible—filth, overcrowding, and a great deal of sexual abuse by the all-male guards. Typical of such conditions were those found at the Auburn Penitentiary in upstate New York where at one time there were 70 women inmates housed together in a one-room attic. In 1826 a woman named Rachel Welch became pregnant while in solitary confinement and died shortly after childbirth from the flogging received from a prison guard (Rafter, 1990). Sexual abuse was so accepted that in the Indiana State Prison, a prostitution service was set up for the male inmates using female prisoners as prostitutes (Freedman, 1981: 15).

It was after the Civil War when the imprisonment of women began to increase, as it did for men. This is not too surprising since the end of this war signaled, in a sense, the triumph of Northern capitalism over the agricultural South (Genovese, 1965). As noted in chapter 4, the increase in imprisonment rates was particularly noteworthy for African Americans, especially in the South. And this was the case for women as well as men. The rate of convictions for women increased enough to justify the building of more prisons.

Separate facilities for women gradually began to emerge following the 1870 meeting of the National Congress on Penitentiary and Reformatory Discipline in Cincinnati. At this time women and children were often housed in the same prisons as men. One of the resolutions of this conference was that the goal of prisons should be rehabilitation rather than punishment. In 1873, the first prison for women was opened, the Indiana Women's Prison. Watterson notes that:

> It embraced the revolutionary notion that women criminals should be *rehabilitated* rather than punished. Young girls from the age of sixteen who "habitually associate with dissolute persons" and other uneducated and indigent women were ushered into the model prison apart from men and isolated from the "corruption and chaos" of the outside world. The essential ingredient of their rehabilitative treatment would be to bring discipline and regularity into their lives. Obedience and systematic religious education would, it was felt, help the women form orderly habits and moral values (Watterson, 1996: 198).

Several other women's prisons were opened over the next 40 years, including the Massachusetts Prison at Framington (1877), the New York Reformatory for Women at Westfield Farm (1901), the District of Columbia Reformatory for Women (1910), and the New Jersey Reformatory for Women at Clinton (1913). These institutions would be separate, home-like institutions where women would have an opportunity to mend their criminal ways and learn to be good housewives, helpmates, and mothers (Watterson, 1996: 198).

There was a flurry of women's prison reform activities between 1870 and 1900. Freedman suggests that four major factors contributed to the rise of the women's prison movement during this time: (1) an apparent increase in female crime after the war and an increase in women prisoners; (2) the women's Civil War social service movement; (3) the emergence of charity and prison reform movements in general, many of them emphasizing the problem of crime and the notion of rehabilitation; and (4) the beginnings of a feminist movement that emphasized a separatist approach and a reinterpretation of the notion of the fallen woman (Freedman, 1981: 14).

The alleged crime wave among women following the war primarily involved the wives and daughters of men who had died in the war. The large number of deaths during the war created a class of poor women who began to be arrested on mostly public order offenses and offenses against morality (Freedman, 1981: 14).

Several reformers placed the blame of the rise of female criminality on the attitudes and sexist practices of men. One noted reformer, Josephine Shaw Lowell, complained that many women "from early girlhood have been tossed from poorhouse to jail, and from jail to poorhouse, until the last trace of womanhood in them has been destroyed" (Freedman, 1981: 59). She condemned law officer's who regarded women "as objects of derision and sport" and who "wantonly assaulted and degraded numerous young women prisoners" (Friedman, 1981: 60). Many specifically blamed the double standard whereby men condemned female sexual activity while condoning their own and, moreover, arrested and imprisoned prostitutes but not the men who enjoyed their services. Finally, reformers complained of male guards in prisons where women were confined. Investigations found that women "may be forced to minister to the lust of the officials or if they refused, submit to the inflection of the lash until they do" (Freedman, 1981: 60).

Reformers argued that women prisoners would be treated more fairly and would stand a better chance of being reformed if they were confined in separate institutions controlled by women. Reformers countered male resistance by arguing that "the shield of a pure woman's presence" would enable them "to govern the depraved and desperate of her own sex" (Freedman, 1981: 61). The reformatory would be the institution that would provide the needed reform.

The Emergence of Women's Reformatories

Rafter's historical account of the rise of women's prisons noted that two major types of prisons emerged during the 19th century. One type was the custodial prison. As its name implies, these institutions emphasized custody and security as the main goals.

The custodial prison resembled the classic penitentiary, originally designed for male prisoners and their purpose was as the name suggests, to warehouse (or in modern vernacular, to *incapacitate*). There were three main types of custodial prisons for women: (1) those that were either within or attached to male prisons; (2) prison farms in the South; (3) totally independent prisons. The first type was the most common (Rafter, 1990: 83). The second type was the reformatory (discussed in chapter 4). The reformatories, in contrast, were supposed to be more treatment oriented.

The first reformatories relied on domestic routines and, upon release, women were placed in suitable private homes as housekeepers. These institutions, and most to follow, were all designed according to the cottage plan whereby separate housing facilities would be as nearly as possible like an average family home that would teach these women to become good homemakers. While the women reformers often claimed to be staunch feminists, the organization of prison life they created was perfectly suited to keep women in their traditional place. In fact, the design won the approval of many skeptical men, one of whom commented that: "Girls and women should be trained to adorn homes with the virtues which make their lives noble and ennobling. *It is only in this province, that they may most fittingly fill their mission*" (Freedman, 1981: 62, emphasis added by Freedman). The end result, of course, would perpetuate women's traditional roles of dependency as housewives and maids. Even a cursory look at women's prisons today reveals that little has changed, especially the treatment of women as children and training them to continue their domestic roles.

Freedman suggests that although reformers "claimed that their goal for each inmate, as for each prison, was female self-sufficiency, they trained women inmates for dependency in domestic employment and in other ways treated them as juveniles, referring even to elderly prisoners as 'girls' and setting up cottage households with the inmates in the role of children" (Freedman, 1981: 61). Even a cursory look at women's prisons today reveals that little has changed, especially the treatment of women as children and training them to continue their domestic roles.

The Role of Racism

Not too surprisingly, most of the women in custodial institutions were African American, whereas most in reformatories were white. Thus, the energies of prison reformers like Elizabeth Fry and Dorothea Dix were, in effect, directed toward white women prisoners. For African-American women prisoners, the custodial prisons where most of them were housed represented merely a continuation of their slave status prior to the Emancipation Proclamation (Rafter, 1990).

This was especially the case in the South, where a form of penal servitude served as a replacement for the old slave plantations. African-American women prisoners were often, like their male counterparts, leased out to local businesses such as farms, mines, and railroads to work on various kinds of chain gangs. According to the 1880 census, in Alabama, Louisiana, Mississippi, North Carolina, Tennessee and Texas, more than one-third of the 220 African-American female prisoners were leased out, compared to only one white woman prisoner out of a total population of 40 (Rafter, 1990).

TABLE 6.1   *Racial Composition in State Prisons, by Sex and Region (1880, 1904, and 1923)*

	Total State Prisoners	*Males*	*Females*	
	%Black	*%Black*	*%Black*	*%Black, General Population*
1880				
Northeast	8.1	8.2	7.0	1.6
Midwest	12.2	11.8	29.0	2.2
South	73.0	72.4	85.8	36.0
West	18.0	18.0	20.0	0.7
1904				
Northeast	12.6	12.2	18.2	1.8
Midwest	22.5	22.0	48.4	1.9
South	72.7	73.0	90.2	32.3
West	9.1	8.9	26.1	0.7
1923				
Northeast	15.2	15.1	15.4	2.3
Midwest	19.7	19.6	22.0	2.3
South	60.3	59.6	79.6	26.9
West	7.1	7.0	10.0	0.9

Source: Rafter (1990: 142).

The proportion of African-American women prisoners was even higher than their male counterparts in some states. In New York, for instance, 44% of the women inmates were African American, compared to a percentage of only 20% for African-American men. In Tennessee, in 1868, *every female inmate was African American*, compared to around 60% of the male prisoners (Rafter, 1990).

The overrepresentation of African Americans varied widely by region. As noted in Table 6.1, in 1880, the percentage of women prisoners who were African American ranged from 7% in the Northeast to 85.8% in the South. By 1904, the proportion of African-American women in northern prisons had increased to around 18%, while in the South the percentage increased to 90%. By 1923, both percentages had decreased somewhat to 15.4% and 79.6% respectively. This latter decrease may be attributed to the rise of reformatories during the interim period, which were much more likely to house white inmates. Indeed, in 1923 almost two-thirds (64.5%) of the women in-mates in custodial prisons were African American, compared to only 11.9% in refor-matory institutions. Ranges by specific institutions were marked. Between 1860 and 1934, fully four-fifths (80%) of the inmates at the Tennessee Penitentiary for Women were African American, in contrast to only 3% at the Albion State Prison in New York (Rafter, 1990: 142–146). Not surprisingly, the early prison system reflected the seg-regation in the general society, as African American women were housed in prisons where there was little or no hope of any sort of rehabilitation (i.e., custodial prisons), while white women were most likely to be sentenced to reformatories where there was at least a formal commitment to rehabilitation (Rafter, 1990; Collins, 1997).

The federal prison system for women developed much later than the state prison system. Women convicted of federal crimes were generally sentenced to state prisons, but as the number of female inmates grew after the Civil War, efforts were made to open the federal system to women. The first of the federal prisons for women only was in Alderson, West Virginia, which opened in 1927, when it housed 50 women in a total of 14 cottages. By 1929, there were more than 250 inmates, most of whom had violated various drug laws (the Harrison Act of 1914 outlawed several kinds of drugs) and the Volstead Act of 1919 (Prohibition). Largely in response to the rise of organized crime (which was a direct result of Prohibition), legislation passed in 1930 that created the Federal Bureau of Prisons, which authorized the construction of several new prisons (Collins, 1997: 21).

The proportion of women in prison who are African American has continued to increase over the years. Historically, African-American women have been most likely to be incarcerated in southern prisons. For instance, in 1880 African-American women constituted 86% of the female inmates in the South, compared to only 7% in the Northeast, 29% in the Midwest and 20% in the West. In 1904, these percentages had increased in every region, with the South leading the way at 90%, with the Midwest catching up with 48%. By 1978, African-American women constituted half of the total female prison population (Rafter, 1990: 142). As will be noted later in the chapter, in all sections of the country African Americans were imprisoned in numbers vastly disproportionate to the percentage in the general population. Their percentages declined somewhat by the end of the 1980s and early 1990s, largely as a result of an increase in Hispanics, but also as a result of more white women being sentenced on drug charges.

Controlling Women's Bodies and Sexuality

Although the number of prisons and prisoners increased significantly after the Civil War, the number of prisons for women and the rate of imprisonment soared after the turn of the century. Part of this increase was no doubt a reflection of the class conflicts of the period as more and more immigrants came to America and labor continued to challenge capitalist rule. Nativism and racism was rampant. As Rafter has noted, there was a social purity movement during this period of time as the behaviors of many immigrants shocked the moral sensibilities of the upper classes. In response, those in power attempted to control these classes through the use of formal methods of social control, especially the selective enforcement of various morals offenses (Rafter, 1988). The Women's Prison Association of New York issued the following statement in 1906:

> If promiscuous immigration is to continue, it devolves upon the enlightened, industrious, and moral citizens, from selfish as well as from philanthropic motives, to instruct the morally defective to conform to our ways and exact from them our own high standard of morality and legitimate industry.

Continuing, the writer of the above statement asked rhetorically, "Do you want immoral women to walk our streets, pollute society, endanger your households, menace the morals of your sons and daughters? Do you think the women here described are fit to become mothers of American citizens? Shall foreign powers generate criminals and dump them on our shores?" (Rafter, 1990: 93–94).

Throughout the late 19th and early 20th century reformers constantly focused on women's sexuality because there was a widespread belief that promiscuity and venereal disease was the latest scourge in society. By housing these wicked and immoral women in newly constructed reformatories, it was believed that they could be treated and cleansed of their diseases and thus rendered capable of serving men upon their release. Most of this effort was directed toward promiscuous girls, as we will see later in this chapter.

Clearly, to those in power, there was an obvious threat here and serious steps needed to be taken. This was part of a much larger campaign to stamp out the growing labor movement that had begun during the last half of the 19th century. These were not just ordinary criminals but were social scum threatening the very foundation of the social order!

Proof that the criminal justice system focused on morals offenses, rather than the usual violent and property crimes, can be seen in the commitment offenses of many women offenders that ended up in the reformatories. Women sent to reformatories were convicted mostly of public order offenses. In the Albion Reformatory (New York), for instance, 81.4% were convicted of public order offenses, the most common of which was disorderly conduct, followed by sex-related offenses. Similarly, in the Ohio Reformatory, just over half (53%) were convicted of public order offenses. More specific examples of public order offenses included a variety of what can be called morals offenses, such as lewd and lascivious carriage, stubbornness, idle and disorderly conduct, fornication, serial premarital pregnancies, keeping bad company, adultery, and even venereal disease. One woman was sent to Albion Reformatory for five years on the charge of having had "unlawful sexual intercourse with young men and remaining at hotels with young men all night" (Rafter, 1990: 107). Another woman had quit school, had a brief affair with a soldier, contracted a venereal disease and was hospitalized, and subsequently sent to the reformatory. Another women was raped by her father (who made her pregnant) and was subsequently sentenced for running around with men while she was seven months pregnant (1990: 107–119, 161).

The reformatory was clearly an attempt to control not just women offenders, but a particular class of women, in this case, lower- and working-class immigrant women. Part of this was a backlash against the thousands of immigrant women who entered the labor force and began to lead relatively independent lives. This was what disturbed the ruling classes: young women on their own and doing what they please. Indeed, young women were by the thousands were leaving home and instead of getting married right away (as was their innate duty), they enjoyed the life of the single, independent woman. They began to smoke, drink, going to dance halls (precursors of modern night clubs) and, heaven forbid, engaging in premarital sexual relationships! The reformatory would certainly do its best to try and cure this problem. In so doing, the reformatory was one among many attempts to extend the power of the state over the lives of the lower and working classes, especially immigrants.

Custodial institutions, such as Tennessee State Prison, the state prison at Auburn, New York and the Ohio Penitentiary contained women convicted primarily of property offenses (mostly larceny). There was also a clear racial difference in the two types of institutions: in custodial prisons the majority were African American, while reformatory institutions housed mostly whites (Rafter, 1990: 146). While many were convicted of violent offenses, the context within which these violent crimes occurred paralleled most of those of today among women offenders: the killing of a spouse or lover, after years of abuse. Cases cited by Rafter are illustrative of this context. In one case, heard by the Tennessee Supreme Court, the defendant was only 18 or 19 and her husband was 50 and he had abused her severely. In one instance she "was seriously injured by a blow to the ovaries" and on another occasion "he had hit her on the head with a poker" and in general "treated his wife cruelly and inhumanly, frequently whipped, cursed and abused her" (Rafter, 1990: 110).

The control of women by the criminal justice system has not been confined to adults. Indeed, the developments noted above paralleled similar, if not identical, efforts to control young women and girls. This will be the subject of the next section of this chapter.

Girls and the Juvenile Justice System[3]

Keeping Girls in their Place:
The Development of Institutions for Girls

As noted in the previous chapter, the *parens patriae* doctrine was first challenged in the case of *Ex Parte Crouse* (1938). It is noteworthy that the case involved a young girl, Mary Ann Crouse, for it raises the question of how the juvenile justice system responded to girls and young women. As also noted in the previous chapter, the Crouse case raises questions about the role of the state as a parent. Judges in the 19th century, when asked to review the care of juveniles, were reluctant to examine too closely state intervention into minors' lives if it was justified in familial terms. Ironically, such reviews were not undertaken even if a parent so requested (as in the Crouse case). The remainder of the 19th century witnessed intensification of the notion of the state as parent, which posed a significant threat to the everyday lives and rights of girls.

The Child-Saving Movement and the Juvenile Court

The Progressive Era (1890–1920) ushered in another shift and codification of attitudes toward youths in American society. While social activists of the era used some of the language of the Stubborn Child Law, their initiatives ushered in unprecedented government involvement in family life and more specifically into the lives of adolescents (Teitelbaum and Harris, 1977). The shift culminated in the creation of an entirely separate system of justice: the juvenile court. The child-saving movement (for more detail see the previous chapter) had a special meaning for girls.

The child-saving movement made much rhetorical use of the value of such traditional institutions as the family and education: "The child savers elevated the nuclear family, especially women as stalwarts of the family, and defended the family's right to supervise the socialization of youth" (Platt, 1977: 98). But while the child savers were exalting the family, they were crafting a governmental system that would have authority to intervene in familial areas and, more specifically, in the lives of young people in ways that were unprecedented.

Based on an assumption of the natural dependence of youth, the juvenile court was charged with determining the guilt or innocence of accused underage persons and with acting for or in place of defendants' parents. The concern of the child savers went far beyond removing the adolescent criminal from the adult justice system. Many of their reforms were actually aimed at "imposing sanctions on conduct unbecoming youth and disqualifying youth from the benefit of adult privileges" (Platt, 1977: 199). Other students of the court's history have expanded on this point. They assert that the pervasive state intervention into the life of the family was grounded in colonial laws regarding stubborn and neglected children. Those laws incorporated the thinking of their time, that "parents were godly and children wicked," (Teitelbaum and Harris, 1977: 34) yet most child savers actually held an opposite opinion, that children were innocent and either the parents or the environment was morally suspect. Although the two views are incompatible, they have nevertheless coexisted in the juvenile court system since its inception. At various times one view or the other has predominated, but both bode ill for young women.

One of the unique features of the new juvenile, or family, courts was that they focused to a great extent on monitoring and responding to youthful behaviors that were indicative of future problems in addition to being violations of the law. For instance, part of the Tennessee juvenile code included the phrase "who are in danger of being brought up to lead an idle or immoral life" (Shelden, 1981: 432). Thus girls and their moral behavior were of specific concern to the child savers. Scientific and popular literature on female delinquency expanded enormously during this period, as did institutions specifically devoted to the reformation of girls (Schlossman and Wallach, 1978; Odem, 1995; Messerschmidt, 1987).

The child savers were keenly concerned about prostitution and such other social evils as white slavery (Schlossman and Wallach, 1978; Odem, 1995; Rafter, 1988: 54). Ironically, while child saving was a celebration of women's domesticity, the movement was not without female leaders. In a sense, privileged women found in the moral purity crusades and the establishment of family courts a safe outlet for their energies. As the legitimate guardians of the moral sphere, upper-middle-class women were seen as uniquely suited to patrol the normative boundaries of the social order. Embracing rather than challenging these stereotypes, women managed to carve out for themselves a role in the policing of women and girls. Many early activities of the child savers revolved around monitoring the behavior of young girls, particularly immigrant girls, in order to prevent their straying from the path of correct and lady-like behavior (Feinman, 1980; Freedman, 1981; Messerschmidt, 1987; Gordon, 1988; Odem, 1995).

Just exactly how women, many of them highly educated, became involved in patrolling the boundaries of working-class girls' sexuality is a depressing but important story. Initially, upper-middle-class women reformers were focused on regulating and controlling male, not female sexuality. Involved in the social purity movement, these reformers had a Victorian view of women's sexuality and saw girls as inherently chaste and sexually passive. If a girl lost "the most precious jewel in the crown of her womanhood," (Odem, 1995: 25) to their way of thinking, it was men who had forced them into sexual activity.

The protection and saving of girls, then, led these women to wage an aggressive social movement aimed at raising the age of consent (which in many parts of the country hovered at 10 or 12 years of age) to age 16 or above. The pursuit of claims of statutory rape against men was another component of this effort, and such charges were brought in a number of cases despite evidence that in about three-quarters of the cases Odem reviewed in Los Angeles, the girls entered into sexual relationships with young men willingly. Led largely by upper- and upper-middle-class women volunteers, many of whom were prominent in the temperance movement (like Frances Willard), this campaign, not unlike the Mothers Against Drunk Driving (MADD) campaign of later decades, drew an impressive and enthusiastic following, particularly among white citizens (Odem, 1995).

African-American women participated in other aspects of progressive reform, but they were less than aggressive on the pursuit of statutory rape complaints. They suspected that any aggressive enforcement of these statutes was likely to fall most heavily upon young African-American men (while doing little to protect girls of color), and this is precisely what occurred. Of the very small number of cases where stiff penalties were imposed, African-American men were frequently sent to prison to reform their supposedly lax and immoral habits while white men were either not prosecuted or given probation (Odem, 1995).

Efforts to vigorously pursue statutory rape complaints ran headlong into the predictable staunch judicial resistance, particularly when many (but not all) cases involved young, working-class women who had chosen to be sexually active. Eventually, as Odem's work documents, reformers (many of them now professional social workers) began to shift the focus of their activities. Now it was the delinquent girl who was the focus of reform and "moral campaigns to control teenage female sexuality" (Odem, 1995: 4) began to appear. Reformers during this later period (1910–1925) assumed that they had the authority to define what appropriate conduct was for young working-class women and girls, which of course was based upon middle-class ideals of female sexual propriety. Girls who did not conform to these ideals were labeled as wayward and thus "in need of control" by the state in the form of juvenile courts and reformatories and training schools (Odem, 1995: 5).

Perhaps the clearest example of the ironies of this sort of child saving is Alice Stebbins Wells, a social worker who became the first policewoman in the United States. In 1910, she was hired by Los Angeles Police Department because she argued that she could not serve her clients (young women) without police powers. Her work, and the work of five other female police officers hired during the next five years, was chiefly "to monitor 'dance halls, cafes, picture shows and other public amusement places' and to escort girls who were 'in danger of becoming delinquent to their homes and to make reports to their parents with a proper warning'" (Odem and Schlossman, 1991: 90).

Women reformers played a key role in the founding of the first juvenile court in Los Angeles in 1903 and vigorously advocated the appointment of women court workers to deal with the special problems of girls. This court was the first in the country to appoint women referees, who were invested with nearly all the powers of judges in girls' cases. Women were also hired to run the juvenile detention facility in 1911. The logic for this was quite clear: "in view of the number of girls and the type of girls detained there . . . it is utterly unfeasible to have a man at the head of the institution," (Odem and Schlossman, 1991: 190) declared Cora Lewis, chairman of the Probation Committee, which established the Juvenile Hall. The civic leaders and newly hired female court workers "advocated special measures to contain sexual behavior among working class girls, to bring them to safety by placing them in custody, and to attend to their distinctive needs as young, vulnerable females" (1991: 190).

The evolution of what might be called the girl-saving effort was a direct consequence of a disturbing coalition between some feminists and other Progressive Era movements. Concerned about female victimization and distrustful of male (and to some degree female) sexuality, prominent women leaders, including Susan B. Anthony, found common cause with the more conservative social purity movement around such issues as the regulation of prostitution and raising the age of consent. Eventually, in the face of stiff judicial and political resistance, the concern about male sexuality more or less disappeared from sight, and the delinquent girl herself becomes the problem. The solution: a harsh maternal justice meted out by professional women (Odem, 1995: 128).

Girls were the losers in this reform effort. Studies of early family court activity reveal that almost all of the girls who appeared in these courts were charged with immorality or waywardness (Chesney-Lind, 1973; Schlossman and Wallach, 1978; Shelden, 1981). The sanctions for such misbehavior were extremely severe. For example, the Chicago family court sent half the girl delinquents but only a fifth of the boy delinquents to reformatories between 1899 and 1909. In Milwaukee, twice as many girls as boys were committed to training schools (Schlossman and Wallach, 1978: 72). In Memphis, females were twice as likely as males to be committed to training schools (Shelden, 1981: 70).

In Honolulu during 1929 and 1930, over half the girls referred to juvenile court were charged with immorality, which meant there was evidence of sexual intercourse; almost a third (30%) were charged with waywardness. Evidence of immorality was vigorously pursued by both arresting officers and social workers through lengthy questioning of the girls and, if possible, males with whom they were suspected of having sex. Other evidence of exposure was provided by gynecological examinations that were routinely ordered in most girls' cases. Doctors, who understood the purpose of such examinations, would routinely note the condition of the hymen. Girls were twice as likely as males to be detained for their offenses, and spent five times as long in detention on average as their male counterparts. They were also nearly three times more likely to be sentenced to the training school. Indeed, half of those committed to training schools in Honolulu well into the 1950s were girls (Chesney-Lind, 1973).

Not surprisingly, large numbers of girls' reformatories and training schools were established during the Progressive Era, in addition to places of rescue and reform. For example, Schlossman and Wallach note that 23 facilities for girls were opened during the 1910 to 1920 decade (in contrast to the 1850 to 1910 period, when the average was five reformatories a decade), and they did much to set the tone of official response to female delinquency. These institutions were obsessed with precocious female sexuality and were determined to instruct girls in their proper place (Schlossman and Wallach, 1978: 70).

According to Pisciotta, there was a slight modification of the *parens patriae* doctrine during this period. The training of girls was shaped by the image of the ideal woman that had evolved during the early part of the 19th century. According to this ideal, which was informed by what some have called the separate-spheres notion, a woman belonged in the private sphere, performing such tasks as rearing children, keeping house, caring for a husband, and serving as the moral guardian of the home. In this capacity, she was to exhibit qualities like obedience, modesty, and dependence. Her husband's domain was the public sphere, that is, the workplace, politics, and the law. He was also, by virtue of his public power, the final arbiter of public morality and culture (Pisciotta, 1983: 264–268; see also Daly and Chesney-Lind, 1988). This white middle-class cult of domesticity was, of course, very distant from the lives of many working- and lower-class women who by necessity were in the labor force. Borrowing from Sheila Rothman (1978), Pisciotta notes that the ideal woman was like a Protestant nun. A statement by the Ladies Committee of the New York House of Refuge summed up the attributes early court advocates sought to instill:

> The Ladies wish to call attention to the great change which takes place in every girl who has spent one year in the Refuge; she enters a rude, careless, untrained child, caring nothing for cleanliness and order; when she leaves the House, she can sew, mend, darn, wash, iron, arrange a table neatly and cook a healthy meal (Pisciotta, 1983: 265).

The institutions established for girls set about to isolate them from all contact with males while training them in feminine skills and housing them in bucolic settings. The intention was to hold the girls until marriageable age, and to occupy them in domestic pursuits during their sometimes lengthy incarceration. The child savers had little hesitation about such extreme intervention in the lives of girls. They believed delinquency to be the result of a variety of social, psychological, and biological factors, and they were optimistic about the juvenile court's ability to remove girls from influences that were producing delinquent behavior. As noted in chapter 5, the juvenile court was established to function in a way totally unlike other courts (e.g., the juvenile court judge as a benevolent yet stern father, informal procedures, and so on).

Nowhere has the confusion and irony of the juvenile court been more clearly demonstrated than in its treatment of girls labeled as delinquent. Many of these girls were incarcerated for noncriminal behavior during the early years of the court.

The Best Place to Conquer Girls

Brenzel's history of the first reform school for girls, the State Industrial School for Girls in Lancaster, Massachusetts, established in 1856, and other studies of early training schools are vivid accounts of the girls and the institutions. The Lancaster school was intended "to be a school for girls—for the gentler sex . . . with all the details relating to employment, instruction, and amusement, and, indeed, to every branch of domestic economy" (Brenzel, 1975: 41). Such rhetoric would eventually find its way into the other training schools for girls. In Memphis, the Home of the Good Shepherd, established in 1875, was designed for the "reformation of fallen . . . women and a home or house of refuge for abandoned and vicious girls" (Shelden, 1981: 58). Moreover, because the girls had fallen from grace, they needed to be saved for the "preservation of the State's young manhood. . ." (1981: 58). Lancaster's first superintendent, Bradford K. Pierce, echoed this sentiment: "It is sublime to work to save a woman, for in her bosom generations are embodied, and in her hands, if perverted, the fate of innumerable men is held" (Brenzel, 1983: 4).

Lancaster, a model for all juvenile training schools, was to save children from perversion through conversion. Loving care and confinement in an atmosphere free from the sins and temptations of city life, would redirect girls' lives. What sorts of crimes had the girls committed? Over two-thirds had been accused of moral rather than criminal offenses: vagrancy, beggary, stubbornness, deceitfulness, idle and vicious behavior, wanton and lewd conduct, and running away (Brenzel, 1983: 81). Of the first 99 inmates at Lancaster, only slightly over half (53%) were American-born. Significantly, at least half of the girls had been brought to Lancaster because of the actions of parents and relatives. Similarly, many girls in the Home of the Good Shepherd in Memphis had been brought into the juvenile court because of running away, incorrigibility, or various charges labeled by the court as immorality, including sexual relations that ranged from sexual intercourse to kissing and holding hands in the park (Shelden, 1981: 63). In a study of juvenile court records in four cities around the turn of the century, Schlossman and Wallach, arrived at the same conclusion: immorality seems to have been the most common charge against females. Included under the rubric were coming home late at night, masturbating, using obscene language, riding at night in automobiles without a chaperone, and strutting about in a lascivious manner (Schlossman and Wallach, 1978: 72).

Clearly, early training schools were deeply concerned with female respectability and hence worked to control the sexuality of lower- and working-class adolescent girls. As Rafter noted, such control within the institutional regime was supposed to train so-called loose, young women "to accept a standard of propriety that dictated chastity until marriage and fidelity thereafter" (Rafter, 1990: 159).

These institutions for girls strove for a family-like atmosphere, from which, after having been taught domestic skills, girls would be released to the care of other families as domestic workers. Gradually, however, vocational training in appropriate manual skills (sewing and the cutting of garments), age-group classification, and punishment characterized the institutional regime. By the late 1880s, Lancaster had devolved into a "middle place between the care of that Board [Health, Lunacy and

Charity] and a Reformatory Prison." Lancaster's original goal of establishing a "loving family circle" had been supplanted by "harsh judgement, rudimentary job training and punitive custody" (Brenzel, 1983: 153, 160).

The Juvenile Court and the Double Standard of Juvenile Justice

The offenses that bring girls into the juvenile justice system reflect the system's dual concerns: adolescent criminality and moral conduct. Historically, they have also reflected a unique and intense preoccupation with girls' sexuality and their obedience to parental authority. What happened to the girls once they arrived in the system?

Relatively early in the juvenile justice system's history, a few astute observers became concerned about the abandonment of minors' rights in the name of treatment, saving, and protection. One of the most insightful of these critical works is Paul Tappan's *Delinquent Girls in Court* (1947). Tappan evaluated several hundred cases in the Wayward Minor Court in New York City during the late 1930s and early 1940s, and concluded that there were serious problems with a statute that brought young women into court simply for disobedience of parental commands or because they were in "danger of becoming morally depraved" (Tappan, 1947: 33) He was particularly concerned that "the need to interpret the 'danger of becoming morally depraved' imposes upon the court a legislative function of a moralizing character" (1947: 33). Noting that many young women were being charged simply with sexual activity, he asked, "What is sexual misbehavior—in a legal sense—of the nonprostitute of 16, or 18, or of 20 when fornication is no offense under criminal law?" (1947: 33).

Tappan believed that the structure of the Wayward Minor Court "entrusted unlimited discretion to the judge, reformer or clinician and his personal views of expedience," and cautioned that, consequently, "the fate of the defendant, the interest of society, the social objectives themselves, must hang by the tenuous thread of the wisdom and personality of the particular administrator" (Tappan, 1947: 33). The arrangement was deeply disturbing to Tappan: "The implications of judicial totalitarianism are written in history" (1947: 33).

A more recent study, of the Los Angeles Juvenile Court during the first half of the 20th century, supplies additional evidence of the juvenile justice system's historical preoccupation with girls' sexual morality, a preoccupation that clearly colored the Los Angeles court's activity into the 1950s. As Brenzel and others found, the majority of these girls were from immigrant families and/or from the lower and working classes.

Odem and Schlossman reviewed the characteristics of the girls who entered the court in 1920 and in 1950. In 1920, 93% of the girls accused of delinquency were charged with status offenses; of these, 65% were charged with immoral sexual activity though the majority (56%) had engaged in sex with only one partner, usually a boyfriend. The researchers found that 51% of the referrals had come from the girls' parents, a situation they explained as working-class parents' fears about their daughters' exposure to the "omnipresent temptations to which working class daughters in particular were exposed to in the modern ecology of urban work and leisure" (Odem and Schlossman, 1991: 196). The working-class girls had been encouraged by their families to work (in fact 52% were working or had been working within the past year), but their parents were extremely ambivalent about changing community morals and some were not hesitant about involving the court in their arguments with problem daughters.

Odem and Schlossman also found that the Los Angeles Juvenile Court did not shirk from its perceived duty. Seventy-seven percent of the girls were detained before their hearings. Both pre- and post-hearing detention were common and clearly linked to the presence of venereal disease. Over a third (35%) of all delinquent girls and over half being held for sex offenses had gonorrhea, syphilis, or other venereal infections. The researchers noted that the presence of venereal disease, and the desire to impose treatment (which in those times was lengthy and painful) accounted for the large numbers of girls in detention centers. Analysis of court actions revealed that although probation was the most common court response (61% were accorded probation) only 27% were released on probation immediately following the hearing. Many girls, it appears, were held for weeks or months after initial hearings. Girls not given probation were often placed in private homes as domestics or they were placed in a wide range of private institutions, such as the Convent of the Good Shepherd or homes for unmarried mothers. Ultimately, according to Odem and Schlossman, about 33% of the problem girls during this period were sentenced to institutional confinement (Odem and Schlossman, 1991: 198–199).

In a more detailed analysis, Odem (1995) has demonstrated that in the Los Angeles Juvenile Court women court officials acted as a sort of maternal guardians as they attempted to instill in these working-class girls a middle-class standard of respectability by "dispensing the maternal guidance and discipline supposedly lacking in the girls' own homes. Referees and probation officers scolded their charges for wearing too much makeup and dressing in a provocative manner" (Odem, 1995: 142). Odem quotes one juvenile court referee who commented that: "Any girl who will go before the public with her hair and eyelashes beaded and paint on her face is going to attract attention . . . [and] is surely inviting trouble" (1995: 142). Girls were also chastised for visiting amusement resorts that the court thought "inappropriate and dangerous for adolescents" (1995: 142) and that sex before marriage was simply wrong.

It is obvious these court officials were quite obsessed with the sexuality of these young women. Odem notes that after a girl was arrested, "probation officers questioned her relatives, neighbors, employers, and school officials to gather details about her sexual misconduct and, in the process, alerted them that she was a delinquent in trouble with the law" (Odem, 1995: 143). Following this they were usually detained in juvenile hall and further questioned about their sexual behavior, asking her to give a complete sexual history, starting with their first act of intercourse, while pressuring them to reveal the names of all their partners, the exact times and locations of sexual activities, as well as the number of times they had sex. Further court discipline was leveled to those who did not give complete information (1995: 143–144). Not surprisingly, no such obsessive concern was evident when it came to the sexual behavior of boys.

Between 1920 and 1950 the make-up of the court's female clientele changed very little: the group was still predominantly white, working class (69% in 1920 and

73.5% in 1950 though the number of African-American girls rose from 5% to 9% during this same time), and from disrupted families. However, girls were more likely to be in school and less likely to be working in 1950.

Girls referred to the Los Angeles court in 1950 were overwhelmingly referred for status offenses (78%) though the charges had changed slightly from 1920 charges. Thirty-one percent of the girls were charged with running away from home, truancy, curfew, or general unruliness at home. Nearly half of the status offenders were charged with sexual misconduct, though again this was "usually with a single partner; few had engaged in prostitution" (Odem and Schlossman, 1991: 200). The rate of venereal disease had plummeted; only 4.5% of all girls tested positive. Despite this, the concern for female sexual conduct "remained determinative in shaping social policy" (1991: 200) in the 1950s.

Referral sources changed within the intervening decades, as did sanctions. Parents referred 26% of the girls at mid-century; school officials, about the same percentage in 1950 as 1920 (21% and 27%), and police officers, a greater number (54% compared with 29% in 1920). Sanctions shifted somewhat, with fewer girls detained before their hearings in 1950 (56% compared with 77% in 1920), but the Los Angeles court placed about the same proportion of girls in custodial institutions (26% in 1950, 33% in 1920).

Studies continue to pick up on problems with the vagueness of contemporary status offense categories, which are essentially buffer charges for suspected sexuality. Consider Vedder and Somerville's observation in the 1960s that although girls in their study were incarcerated in training schools for the "big five" (running away from home, incorrigibility, sexual offenses, probation violation, and truancy) "the underlying vein in many of these cases is sexual misconduct by the girl delinquent" (Vedder and Sommerville, 1970: 147). Such attitudes were also present in other parts of the world. Naffine wrote that in Australia official reports noted that "most of those charged [with status offenses] were girls who had acquired habits of immorality and freely admitted sexual intercourse with a number of boys" (Naffine, 1987: 13).

Another study, conducted in the early 1970s in a New Jersey training school, revealed large numbers of girls incarcerated "for their own protection." When asked about this pattern, one judge explained, "Why most of the girls I commit are for status offenses. I figure if a girl is about to get pregnant, we'll keep her until she's sixteen and then ADC (Aid to Dependent Children) will pick her up" (Rogers, 1972: 223–246).

Andrews and Cohn reviewed the handling of cases of ungovernability in New York in 1972 and concluded that judges were acting "upon personal feelings and predilections in making decisions" (Andrews and Cohn, 1974:1401). Included among their evidence were statements made by judges. For example: "She thinks she's a pretty hot number; I'd be worried about leaving my kid with her in a room alone. She needs to get her mind off boys" (1974: 1401).

Similar concern about premature female sexuality and the proper parental response is evident throughout the comments. One judge remarked that at the age of 14 some girls "get some crazy ideas. They want to fool around with men, and that's sure as hell trouble." Another admonished a girl, "I want you to promise me to obey your mother, to have perfect school attendance and not miss a day of school, to give up these people who are trying to lead you to do wrong, not to hang out in candy stores or tobacco shops or street corners where these people are, and to be in when your mother says" (Andrews and Cohn, 1974: 1404).

Empirical studies of the processing of girls' and boys' cases between 1950 and the early 1970s documented the impact of these sorts of judicial attitudes. That is, girls charged with status offenses were often more harshly treated than their male or female counterparts charged with crimes. Gibbons and Griswold for example, found in a study of court dispositions in Washington State between 1953 and 1955 that girls were far less likely than boys to be charged with criminal offenses, but more than twice as likely to be committed to institutions (Gibbons and Griswold, 1957: 109). Some years later a study of a juvenile court in Delaware discovered that first-time, female status offenders were more harshly sanctioned (as measured by institutionalization) than males charged with felonies. For repeat status offenders, the pattern was even starker: female status offenders were six times more likely than male status offenders to be institutionalized (Datesman and Scarpitti, 1977: 70).

The double standard of juvenile justice also appeared in countries other than the United States. Linda Hancock found in Australia that females (most of whom were appearing in court for uncontrollability and other status offenses) were more likely than males to receive probation or institutional supervision. In addition, females charged with criminal offenses received lesser penalties than males and females brought to court under protection applications (Hancock, 1981: 8). Another study found that females in England were less often fined and more often placed on supervision or sent to an institution than males (May, 1977). In another English study, Smart reported that 64% of females and 5% of males were institutionalized for noncriminal offenses (Smart, 1976: 134). In Portugal in 1984, 41% of the girls were charged with status offenses but only 16.8% of the boys were placed in institutions. Likewise, a study of a juvenile court in Madrid revealed that of youths found guilty of status offenses, 22.2% of the girls but only 6.4% of the boys were incarcerated (Cain, 1989: 222–225).

In short, numerous studies of the juvenile courts during the past few decades suggest that court personnel participated directly in the judicial enforcement of the sexual double standard. Such activity was most pronounced in the system's early years, but there is evidence that the pattern continues, in part because status offenses can still serve as buffer charges for sexual misconduct. Some of the problem with status offenses, although they are discriminatory, is understandable. They are not like criminal cases, regarding which judges have relatively clear guidelines. Standards of evidence are delineated, elements of the crime are laid out in the statutes, and civil rights are, at least to some extent, protected by law.

In status offense cases judges have few legal guidelines. Many judges apparently fall back on one of the orientations built into the juvenile justice system: the puritan stance supportive of parental demands, more or less without question; or the progressive stance, whereby they take on the parental roles. These orientations were severely tested during the 1970s, when critics mounted a major drive to deinstitutionalize status offenders and divert them from formal court jurisdiction (for more detailed information about the deinstitutionalization movement see Chesney-Lind and Shelden, 1998: 187–190).

Women and Criminal Justice Today

One thing that cannot be overlooked in any analysis of women, crime, and criminal justice is the interrelationship between class and race. Indeed, the vast majority of female offenders, especially those who end up in prison, are drawn from the lower class and are racial minorities (Daly, 1992; Miller, 1986; Chesney-Lind and Pasko, 2004; Pollock, 2002).

Women's crime cannot be separate from the overall social context within which it occurs. In recent years the plight of women has not improved a great deal. While women have entered into the labor force in increased numbers in recent years (to around 60% versus less than 40% in the 1950s), their employment is found largely in traditional, female occupations, especially in retail trade and service occupations. Women still constitute over 90% of all nurses, 75% of all teachers (except colleges and universities), almost 80% of all secretarial and administrative support positions (e.g., clerical work, cashiers, and so on), and about 80% of all the hairdressers and other personal service occupations. Furthermore, while gains have been made, women still earn less than men—and their gains have come largely because so many men have been eliminated from the labor force. In fact, while in 1960, 89% of all married men and 32% of married women were in the labor force, in 2002 the male percentage had decreased to 70%, while the female percentage had increased to 61%. Also, a far greater proportion of women are working part-time: in 2002, just over one-fourth (27.1%) of women workers worked part-time, compared to about 12% of the men (statistics here are from the U.S. Department of Labor, 2004).

More importantly, increasing numbers of households are being maintained by women with children. While in 1960 only 6% of all families with one or more children were headed by a woman, by 2003 this figure had doubled to 12%. Not surprisingly, race plays a role here, for 53% of all black families were headed by a woman in 2003, compared to only 18% of white families.[4] In 1999, more than two-thirds (68%) of all American children lived with two parents, down from 77% in 1980. However, 74% of white children and 63% of Hispanic children lived with two parents, compared to only 35% of all black children.[5] The vast majority of children living with one parent live with their mother, who is far more likely to be living in poverty.

A recent report[6] noted that "women who head households have a median net worth of $27,850 compared with $86,100 for all American households. Their incomes are lower, too." Moreover, they had a median income of $20,000, compared to $39,000 for all U.S. households. Also, "a far higher percentage of women-headed households (41 percent) are likely to rank in the bottom fifth of income earners than are all American households, of which only 19 percent rank as low in terms of income." The report suggests that such a discrepancy "can be attributed to less education overall, less likelihood of being employed, lower income, and having only one paycheck instead of two to rely on."

Single-parent women are far more likely to be living in poverty. In 1959, only 20% of all poor families were headed by women; in 2003 more than three-fourths (78%) of all families living in poverty were headed by a woman.[7] In 2003, the poverty rate for blacks was 24%, compared to only 8% for whites. In 2001, single-parent families made up 90% of all of those living in poverty. This latter fact is what is sometimes known as the feminization of poverty, which may be somewhat misleading, suggesting that this problem is racially neutral. In fact, however, poverty hits racial minorities (especially minority women) far more than whites: in 2002 the poverty rate for black single mothers was 38%, while for Hispanic single mothers it was 36%; in contrast, the rate was 24% for whites.[8]

One specific example of the role of class and race is demonstrated in a very detailed and sophisticated study by Daly of a sample of women offenders in a court system in New Haven, Connecticut. From a larger sample of 397 cases, this study focused in depth on a smaller sample of 40 men and 40 women who were sentenced to prison (that is, they went through all of the stages of the criminal justice process). Of the 40 women, 24 (60%) were African American, 5 (12%) were Puerto Rican, and the remainder (28%) were white. Half of the women were raised in single-parent families, and only 2 of the women were described as growing up in middle-class households. Most of these women were described by Daly as having grown up in families "whose economic circumstances were precarious," (Daly, 1992: 23) while in about two-thirds of the cases their biological fathers were "out of the picture" while they were growing up. Only one-third completed high school or the equivalent GED (General Education Diploma). Two-thirds "had either a sporadic or no paid employment record" (1992: 24) and over 80% were unemployed at the time of their most recent arrest.

Not surprisingly, the same kind of profile has been given by a nationwide survey conducted by the American Correctional Association (1990), a detailed study by Miller on a group of women offenders in Milwaukee (1986) and studies of women prisoners by Rafter (1990), Freedman (1981), and Pollock (2002), along with studies of female juvenile offenders (Chesney-Lind and Shelden, 2004).

Sentencing Patterns, the War on Drugs and Women

As noted in previous chapters, there is no way we can separate the phenomenal growth in prison populations from the war on drugs, a war that has targeted huge numbers of African Americans. While there is little relationship between race and illicit drug use, African Americans are far more likely to be arrested and sent to prison. For women, the poor in general and African Americans in particular have been singled out. According to one report, during the 1990s "drug offenders accounted for the largest source of the total growth among female inmates (36 percent) compared to male inmates (18 percent)" (Austin et al., 2000: 8). As of 2004, almost one-third (31.5%) of all women prisoners were convicted of drug offenses; in federal prisons, this figure was 65% (Harrison and Beck, 2005; Bureau of Justice Statistics, 2005). In contrast in 1979 only 10% of women in state prison were drug offenders (Donziger, 1996; US Department of Justice, 1994).

A study by the Sentencing Project found that between 1986 and 1995, drug offenses account for about one-third of the rise in male prison population but half of the increase in the female prison population. During this period, the number of women incarcerated for drug offenses soared by 888%, while those incarcerated for other crimes went up by a more modest 129%. Data from states where the drug law penalties are especially high reveal an even more dramatic change. In New York, for instance, under the infamous Rockefeller drug laws, drugs accounted for an incredible 91% of the increase in women's prison population; in California, drug offenses accounted for 55%; but in direct contrast, in Minnesota, a state less committed to sentencing drug offenders to prison, drug law violations accounted for just 26% of the increase (Mauer et al., 1999).[9] Speaking of California, one report revealed that whereas in 1980, only 12% of women admitted to prison were drug offenders, by 1990 this figure was 47% and by 1999 stood at half (50.1%). This report further noted that during the past 40 years there has been a 210% increase for women drug offenders, compared to only an 187% increase for men. Nationwide, between 1974 and 2001 the number of people sent to prison for the first time, largely because of drug offenses.[10]

It should be noted that this is not just the case for women offenders, but for all offenders in recent years. A report by the Bureau of Justice Statistics noted that about two-thirds of the growth in the prison population between 1974 and 2001 was because of an increase in the rate of first-time incarceration, that is, people being sentenced to prison for the first time ever. The report further noted that the percentage of all women ever incarcerated more than doubled from 0.2% to 0.5% (Bonczar, 2003).

Much of the increase in women prisoners comes from the impact of mandatory sentencing laws, passed during the 1980s crackdown on crime. Under many of these laws, mitigating circumstances (e.g., having children, few or no prior offenses, non-violent offenses) are rarely allowed. One survey found that in the early 1990s just over half (51%) of women in state prisons had one or only one prior offense, compared to 39% of the male prisoners. A survey of California prisons found that during the fiscal year 1998, almost two-thirds (64%) of the women were first-time nonviolent offenders (Donziger, 1996: 152). Another report noted that between 1986 (when mandatory sentencing was enacted) and 1996, the number of women sentenced to state prison for drug offenses soared tenfold (from about 2,370 to 23,700) (Amnesty International, 1999: 26).

What needs to be underscored is the fact that arrests on drug charges for women reflect their secondary status in the big world of illegal drug dealing. Figures from the Department of Justice show that women are "overrepresented among low level drug offenders" and are "not principal figures in criminal organizations or activities." Regardless, they nevertheless receive sentences that are similar to high-level drug offenders (Amnesty International, 1999). A detailed study of New York State found that in 1998 a total of 63% of those sent to prison were convicted of the lowest-level drug offenses, what are called felony classes C-E (Human Rights Watch, 1999). A report by Women in Prison Project of New York noted that in that state when the harsh Rockefeller Drug Laws were passed in 1974, only 400 women were in prison and only 100 were in for drugs. By 2004, however, around 2,900 women were in prison, with 40% in for drugs; almost 87% of the women in for drugs were either black or Latina. Between 1986 and 1995, an incredible 91% of the increase in women sent to prison was because of drug law enforcement (Women in Prison Project, 2005).

Another study notes that women most often serve as mules (those who carry drugs for the drug cartels and other high-level dealers) for boyfriends or lovers, often doing so because of threats to their lives. One report viewed this situation in the following terms:

> Women of color who act as couriers in the underground, "informal" drug economies, are economically discriminated against, as in the mainstream, formal economies. Just as male counterparts, female couriers are small time players in economy controlled by narco dictators, drug lords and barons, military and intelligence agencies, the police, organized crime, and so on. In a male dominated industry, male couriers are able to realize a greater share of profits, unlike females who are paid a flat rate, tricked or simply coerced into trafficking in drugs. Some drug-dealers have suggested that these women are used as decoys for smugglers on their flight who pass easily through customs with large quantities of cocaine or heroine (*Saxakali Magazine,* 1997).[11]

Another report, this one from England, supports the above view, as it reads in part:

> The huge number of Jamaican women coming into Britain with their stomachs full of cocaine is pushing the already overcrowded female prison system to breaking point. More than 10% of the women currently in jail are Jamaican drug mules who swallowed rubber wraps of cocaine and boarded flights to this country.
>
> A Guardian investigation has established that the long sentences being served by the 450 Jamaican couriers are stretching resources to the limit while failing to act as a deterrent to the desperate women prepared to smuggle drugs.
>
> The crisis has deepened since July, when a glut of women prisoners were sentenced before the courts went into summer recess. Women are regularly being bused around as prisons try to find them cells and overcrowding is blamed for the unprecedented number of suicides within female jails: 17 women have taken their own lives since August last year.
>
> Jamaican drug couriers have been identified as a key factor in the overcrowding problem. At a time when cells are in short supply, the prison service has been forced to dedicate four of the 17 women's jails to housing foreign women (Gillan, 2003).

A recent report by the American Civil Liberties Union (ACLU) notes that women are indeed very small cogs in the illegal drug market, with many getting involved as "a means of supplementing income in the face of unemployment, low-wage and unstable jobs, lack of affordable housing, and cuts to social programs such as child care, social assistance, and health care" (ACLU, 2005). In many cases their role is "limited to answering telephones or living in a home used for drug related activities" (ACLU, 2005). The case of Chrissy Taylor is typical, as this ACLU report explains:

> Chrissy Taylor was incarcerated at the age of 19 based on her marginal involvement in her boyfriend's scheme to manufacture methamphetamine. Her boyfriend asked her to go to a store in Mobile, Alabama to pick up a shipment of chemicals. Based on his assurance that the mere purchase and possession of the chemicals was legal, she went to the store and bought them. As it happened, agents from the Drug Enforcement Administration (DEA) were working with the chemical store in a reverse-sting operation. The agents sold Chrissy the chemicals and then arrested both her and her boyfriend, not for possession or purchase of the chemicals—neither of which is in and of itself illegal— but for possession with intent to manufacture methamphetamines (2005: 11).

The ACLU report cites a case study of more than 60,000 federal drug cases by the *Minneapolis Star Tribune*, which found that "men were more likely than women to offer evidence to prosecutors in exchange for shorter sentences, even if the information placed others, including the women in their lives, in jeopardy" (ibid; the study referred to is Rigert, 1997). The study found that because women are such minor players in the drug business, they rarely had any useful information for prosecutors. Whatever information they do have, they are reluctant to divulge it, since doing so might endanger loved ones. Thus, they have "less currency with which to bargain their way out of harsh sentences" (ibid).

Thus, the recent efforts to get tough on crime has had a most negative impact on female offenders, as more and more are finding their way into the nation's prison system. As a matter of fact, largely because of the war on drugs, the number of new women's prisons has dramatically increased in recent years. Whereas between 1940 and the end of the 1960s only 12 new women's prisons were built, in the 1970s a total of 17 were built and 34 new prisons were built in the 1980s (Donziger, 1996: 148).

An Outrageous Example: The Pregnancy Police

Perhaps the most outrageous form of judicial sexism comes from the attempt to criminalize pregnant women addicted to drugs, especially crack cocaine. A study by Siegel, appropriately called "The Pregnancy Police Fight the War on Drugs," reveals one of the most repressive sides to the war on drugs. It was during the height of the war on drugs, in the late 1980s that "crack babies" began to make the headlines. Over 200 prosecutions were directed toward women as overzealous prosecutors misused the law (stretching the limits of legal reasoning) against women. Siegel cites the racial bias in such a crackdown by observing that in Florida in 1989 more than 700 pregnant women in public and private clinics were tested for drugs. There was virtually no difference by race in the percentage who tested positive (15.4% of the white women tested positive versus 14.1% of the African-American women), yet African-American women were almost 10 times more likely to be reported to the authorities for drug abuse (Siegel, 1997: 251).

One woman in North Carolina was charged with assault with a deadly weapon (that weapon being crack cocaine) with the intent to kill her fetus. She was sentenced to 20 years in prison. In another case a woman was charged with felony child neglect when her child tested positive for cocaine. Fortunately, most women charged were spared the maximum punishments by sympathetic judges, although some were not.

One woman who did not escape punishment was a Florida woman who was convicted (her first conviction ever) of drug trafficking for "delivering drugs to her infant through the umbilical cord." This woman had sought treatment for her cocaine addiction, but could find no program that would accept her. After giving birth, with no complications, those attending nurses and doctors said the baby looked and acted perfectly normal. Routine tests revealed cocaine in her system and the hospital notified authorities, whereupon she was arrested and eventually convicted, sentenced to 1 year in jail and 14 years of probation. In South Carolina a total of 18 women were charged with criminal neglect of their fetuses (Siegel, 1997).

According to Siegel, hundreds more women were subjected to civil proceedings seeking to deny them custody of their children. Not surprisingly, black and poor women have been the most likely targets of such actions. Studies have shown that in most hospitals poor women are summarily denied drug treatment if they are pregnant. This is part of the blame the user mentality of the drug czar William Bennett who took over the war on drugs during the 1980s.

The media, as usual, hopped on the bandwagon after discovering the crack baby phenomenon. "News footage of emaciated preemies—sustained by tubes and electronics at staggering cost—sickened viewers all over the country. Here were the fruits of indulgence, the horrifying issue of women whose moral compasses were so screwed up they had essentially abandoned their babies in the womb." So-called experts said that these babies were "beyond salvation." The media erroneously interpreted a statistic from a study by Chicago pediatrician Ira Chasnoff who, it was reported, said that 10% of the women in the hospitals surveyed were on cocaine. In reality, Chasnoff was simply misquoted, for what he said was that 10% of the pregnant women surveyed had "*at some time* in their lives, used *some kind* of drug, which included casual use of marijuana" (Gray, 1998: 108–109).

As usual, it became easier to avoid looking at such relevant problems as poverty and racism. During the entire drug scare propaganda during the 1980s, the so-called crack baby became a very convenient symbol. In time careful research showed that this was more hype than fact. For instance, one research study found that less than 2% of all newborns were exposed to cocaine and that such exposure rarely had any effect on the baby's health. So-called crack babies are really poverty babies. Siegel concluded that: "Mothers who use crack were convenient scapegoats for conservative administrations to blame in order to divert the public's attention away from the declining social and economic conditions affecting increasing numbers of Americans" (Siegel, 1997: 257).

A more recent case illustrates the extent of the repressiveness of the drug war. This is a story about a South Carolina black woman who is serving 12 years in prison for murder. Her crime was giving birth to a stillborn child because she took cocaine while pregnant. While there is no research evidence that links cocaine use and stillbirth, prosecutors didn't care. This woman became the first in the nation to be convicted of murder for using cocaine while pregnant (Talvi, 2003).

As of December, 2003 South Carolina was the only state with a child abuse law that could be applied to viable fetuses. This particular case was appealed to the U.S. Supreme Court, which decided not to review it. The attorney who took the appeal to the Supreme Court was joined by 27 medical and drug policy groups (e.g., American Public Health Association, American Nurses Association, and the American Society of Addictions) who wrote that the prosecution of this case "contradicts the clear weight of available medical evidence, violates fundamental notions of public health, and undermines the physician–patient relationship" (Talvi, 2003).

This case (*Ferguson v. City of Charleston*) was also supported by the ACLU, which noted in their brief that: "In the past several years, the state has increasingly intruded into the lives of pregnant women, policing their conduct in the name of protecting fetuses. Pregnant women have been forced to undergo unwanted cesareans;

they've been ordered to have their cervixes sewn up to prevent miscarriage; they've been incarcerated for consuming alcohol; and they've been detained, as in the case of one young woman, simply because she 'lack[ed] motivation or [the] ability to seek medical care'" (ACLU, 2000, citing Kolder et al., 1987). The ACLU further noted that in 1989 the City of Charleston adopted a policy called the Interagency Policy on Cocaine Abuse in Pregnancy (IPCAP) was created and under this policy pregnant women were subject to warrantless searches "if they met any one of several criteria, including no or minimal prenatal care; unexplained preterm labor; birth defects or poor fetal growth; separation of the placenta from the uterine wall; a history of drug or alcohol abuse; or intrauterine fetal death . . ." (2000). Among the horrendous examples of overzealousness, the ACLU notes that during the first few months of the program "women were immediately arrested after they or their newborns tested positive for cocaine. One woman spent the last three weeks of her pregnancy in jail. During this time she received prenatal care in handcuffs and shackles. Authorities arrested another woman soon after she gave birth; still bleeding and dressed in only a hospital gown, she was handcuffed and taken to the city jail" (2000).

In 1994, the Civil Rights Division of the U.S. Department of Health and Human Services began investigating whether the civil rights of African American patients were violated, whereupon the IPCAP was dropped completely. Incidentally, a total of 30 women were arrested under the policy and 29 were African American (ACLU, 2000).

Following the *Ferguson v. City of Charleston* decision, South Carolina began to go after other women in a similar situation. The next case they took to court was another black woman, who used cocaine during her pregnancy. Shortly thereafter, prosecutors in Honolulu went after a native Hawaiian for the death of her two-day-old son. She was charged with using crystal methamphetamine during her pregnancy. It should be noted that the South Carolina law could be applied to pregnant women who smoke, drink alcohol, work around certain chemicals, and even change cat litter, all of which would constitute activity that might cause potential harm to a fetus (Talvi, 2003). Completely ignored by the drug warriors is the fact that children are more likely to be at risk of harm from prenatal exposure to cigarettes and alcohol (Fetal Alcohol Syndrome). One study created the label of Fetal Tobacco Syndrome to "draw attention to the extraordinarily high miscarriage and morbidity rates associated with prenatal exposure to cigarette smoke."[12]

Child abuse charges are still being made against pregnant women in such states as New Mexico, Arizona, Alabama, Colorado, Georgia, Missouri, North Dakota, and New Hampshire. In some cases women are being jailed "for endangering the fetus by not getting to the hospital quickly enough on the day of delivery and by not following doctor's advice to get bed rest" (Paltrow and Ehrlich, 2006). There have been numerous cases where pregnant women gave birth while in jail.

Recently a number of organizations, such as the Drug Policy Alliance, have come out against the criminalization of pregnancy. Recent research has challenged the connection between drug use and pregnancy problems, noting that various other social factors are more important. One survey of the literature found that less than 5% of birth defects are because of drug use and problems such as low birth weight and other fetal development problems stem mostly from the lack of prenatal care

(Lindesmith Center, 1999). One fact, often overlooked, is that many poor women are discouraged from seeking help for their pregnancy for the simple fact that they may be reported to the police for drug use.

The lawyer who took the above-referenced case to the Supreme Court has commented that race enters into the picture, which is not surprising. She notes that:

> Because the problem of cocaine use in pregnancy was presented predominantly as a problem of the African-American community it is deeply intertwined with issues of race, race discrimination, and the legacy of slavery: while illicit substance abuse crosses all race and class lines, this particular debate has focused on low-income African-American women, many of whom rely on welfare. Because it involves women and pregnancy, the issue of drugs and pregnancy is inseparable from issues concerning the status of all women as well as with sex and sexuality (Paltrow, 1999; see also Roberts, 1997).

Women in Today's Prisons

Women are the fastest rising group in American prisons. Driven largely by the drug war, the total number of women offenders somewhere within the criminal justice system (jail, prison, probation, and parole) grew by 81% between 1990 and 2000, compared to a more modest 45% growth for men. Among those on probation, women offenders jumped by 76% compared to only 37% for males during this time. Women in jail rose by 89% versus a 48% increase for men. The most gains were seen for women prisoners and women on parole. These increases were 108% and 105% respectively, compared with increases of 77% and 31% for men (Bloom, 2003). The sharp numerical gains are illustrated in Figure 6.2.

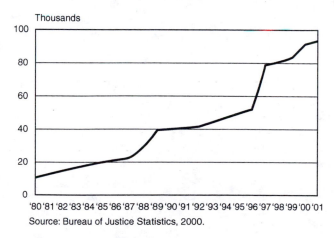

Annual Prison Admissions for Women

Source: Bureau of Justice Statistics, 2000.

FIGURE 6.2   *Annual Prison Admissions for Women.*

Source: Women Coping in Prison Study, Clinical and School Psychology University of Virginia, Charlottesville, VA. 22904. Data from Bureau of Justice, 2000 (http://curry.edschool.virginia.edu/prisonstudy/home.html).

TABLE 6.2   *Incarceration Rates of Men and Women,*
State and Federal Institutions, 1925–2003

Year	Total	Male	Female	Ratio
1925	79	149	6	24.8:1
1935	113	217	8	27.1:1
1945	98	193	9	21.4:1
1955	112	217	8	27.1:1
1965	108	213	8	26.6:1
1975	111	220	8	27.5:1
1985	202	397	17	23.4:1
1994	389	753	45	16.7:1
2003	482	915	62	14.8:1
% increase				
(1975–1985)	82	81	113	
(1985–2003)	139	130	265	
(1975–2003)	334	316	675	

Source: Maguire, K. and A. L. Pastore (1995). *Sourcebook on Criminal Justice Statistics—1995.* Washington, DC: Department of Justice, Bureau of Justice Statistics, p. 556; Harrison, P. M. and A. J. Beck (2004); "Prisoners in 2003." Washington, DC: Bureau of Justice Statistics, p. 4.

About one-half of the women in prison are black and they are eight times more likely than white women to be incarcerated. In contrast, around two-thirds of the women on probation are white. Looking at women's incarceration as a whole, fully two-thirds are either African American or Hispanics. About 11 of every 1,000 women will be in prison at some point in their lives. For minorities this ratio is even greater: 15 out of every 1,000 Hispanic women and 36 of every 1,000 African-American women will end up in prison at some point in their lives, compared with only 5 of every 1,000 white women (Bloom, 2003).

The incarceration rate for women remained fairly stable for most of the 20th century, ranging from 6 per 100,000 population in 1925 to 8 in 1975. After 1975, these rates changed dramatically, doubling to 17 in 1985 and then almost tripling to 45 by 1994, followed by an increase to 62 in 2003. As of December 31, 2003 there were a total of 101,179 women in federal and state prisons (compared to only 8,850 in 1976), constituting 7.2% (versus 3.6% in 1976) of all prisoners.[13] These latest figures represent an incredible numerical increase of 1,043% and an increase of 100% in their proportion of all prisoners during the past 30 years. Moreover, as indicated in Table 6.2, the incarceration rate of women increased by 675%, compared to an increase of 316% for men.

Once again, race enters the picture here, because African-American females have an incarceration rate that is almost eight times higher than their white counterparts (Beck, 2000; Harrison and Karberg, 2003). Much of the increase in women's incarceration rate comes from the impact of mandatory sentencing laws, passed during

TABLE 6.3   *Rate of Sentenced Prisoners in State and Federal Prisons, by Race and Gender, 1980–2002*

Gender and Race	Incarceration Rate			% Increase, 1980–2002
	1980	1990	2002	
Males:				
White	168	339	450	168
Black	1,111	2,376	3,437	209
Females:				
White	6	19	35	483
Black	45	125	191	324
Black/White ratio:				
Males	6.6:1	7.0:1	7.6:1	
Female	7.5:1	6.6:1	5.5:1	

Source: Beck, A. J. and D. K. Gillard (1995). "Prisoners in 1994." Washington, DC: Bureau of Justice Statistics, August;. Harrison, P. M. and A. Beck. (2003). "Prisoners in 2002." Washington, DC: Bureau of Justice Statistics, July.

the 1980s crackdown on crime. Under many of these laws, mitigating circumstances (e.g., having children, few or no prior offenses, nonviolent offenses) are rarely allowed. One survey found that just over half (51%) of women in state prisons had none or only one prior offense, compared to 39% of the male prisoners (Donziger, 1996: 152). It should also be noted that drug convictions account for the bulk of these increases, as has been the case for all prisoners, as I will note following. What is of critical importance for women offenders is the fact that more than 80% of them have children and in most of these cases the women have sole responsibility to take care of them.[14] Table 6.3 illustrates the racial and gender difference in incarceration rates.

One very poignant story illustrates a serious flaw within the legal system and how it can have a negative impact on children. The story, as reported in the *San Francisco Chronicle*, concerns a 10-year-old girl whose mother is in prison and is dying. The girl wrote to the sentencing judge "I don't want my mommy to die in that place by herself. I want her to come home first so we can hug her and take lots of pictures together. Will you please let her come home before God takes her to His home? Please?" The case involved a 51-year-old woman imprisoned at the Valley State Prison for Women in Chowchilla and who, in late 2003, was given six months to live, as she is suffering from liver cancer and cirrhosis of the liver caused by hepatitis C. At this time she had 20 months left on a 6-year sentence for—you guessed it—possession of 6.3 grams of cocaine. Her only hope of survival was a liver transplant, but she had been denied treatment at the University of California at Davis. According to the report, no woman had ever been granted permission to obtain an organ transplant.

The director of the California Department of Corrections broke precedence and granted her an early release under the compassionate release law. But this requires approval from the judge. According to this report, the prospects of getting released were not good. In the previous two months, two terminally ill women had died in custody despite having become eligible for compassionate release. "They died hospitalized and bed ridden, shackled to their beds and guarded 24 hours a day by security officers earning overtime pay" (Edmondson, 2003).

One of the problems is the fact that the majority of women are in prisons more than 100 miles from their children, which helps account for infrequent visits. One survey found that the distance from the prison "accounted for over 43% of the reasons cited by mothers for infrequent or absent visitation with their children" (Bloom and Steinhart, 1993).

These increases do not match the increases in women's crime as measured by arrests, except if we consider the impact of the war on drugs along with greater attention to domestic violence. During this period of time there has been a very dramatic change in the criminal justice system's response to female drug use, as it has for all illegal drug use, as well as domestic violence. In the latter case, such increased attention to domestic violence has led to an increase in arrests of women for both aggravated assault and other assaults (Chesney-Lind and Pasko, 2004). More specifically, between 1994 and 2003, drug arrests for women increased by 35%, compared to a 20% increase for men. In 1994, drug violations constituted just under 8% of the total arrests for women (7.9%); in 2003 they were almost 10% of the total (9.5%). Arrests for other assaults went up by 32%; these offenses were 8% of the total arrests for women in 1994 and 9.5% of the total in 2003. Total arrests for all offenses went up by 12.3% during this time.[15] Of all female offenders sentenced in federal court in 2002, 39% were charged with drug offenses. Among black women, 46% were charged with a drug offense; for Hispanic women the percentage was 44%; for white women the percentage was 36%.[16]

Background Characteristics of Women in Prison

This war on crime and war on drugs has really been, in effect, a war on women and minorities. As are male prisoners, most women in prison are poor and uneducated, but more women prisoners are minorities than is the case with men.

One of the most recent surveys on women in prison found that (Greenfeld and Snell, 1999):

- Incarcerated women are twice as likely as women in the general population to have grown up in a single parent household.
- 47% of female inmates (compared to 37% of male inmates) had at least one immediate family member who had been incarcerated.
- One third of female inmates and one quarter of male inmates report a parent/guardian abused alcohol or drugs.
- 57% of women in state prisons reported that they were physically and/or sexually assaulted at some point in their lives.
- Female inmates who had been abuse victims were more likely to be imprisoned for a violent offense.
- Most women in prison are unmarried.

As indicated here, there are significant racial differences. While a majority on probation (62% are white), the majority of those in prison are minorities, with blacks leading the way. Most are between the ages of 25 and 44; a much higher percentage in prison are between these ages; those on probation or in local jails are considerably younger (about one in five are under 25). Married women are in the minority, with almost half of those in local jails or state prisons have never been married. As for education, a greater proportion of federal prisoners have a minimum of a high school diploma or GED, with more than one-fourth (29%) having been to college; 40% or more on probation, in local jails or in state prisons never finished high school (Greenfeld and Snell, 1999).

One important finding from this survey is the high number of children of the women in the system. Just over 70% of these women have children under the age of 18, with a total of 1.3 million children all together. The report also notes that male prisoners in state prisons have fathered more than 1.3 million children, which is about 11 times more than the number of children attributable to women prisoners.

The report also notes that the economic circumstances of most of the women were more difficult than their male counterparts. Only about 40% had been employed full time prior to their most recent arrest (compared to 60% of male prisoners). About 37% of these women had incomes of less than $600 per month (compared to 28% of the men)—well below the poverty level. Almost 30% of these women had been receiving public assistance.

Alcohol and substance abuse were common among these women. About half of the women in state prisons had been using alcohol and/or drugs at the time of their most recent arrest; about 40% having been under the influence of drugs when their most recent crime occurred. Another 29% of women in state prisons were under the influence of alcohol at the time their latest crime was committed. About one-fourth of the women were daily drinkers, while 60% had been using drugs regularly the month prior to their latest offense. Around one-third of the women said the offense they committed was for the purpose of getting money to buy drugs.

In contrast to men, women in state prisons were much less likely to have no prior convictions (35% versus 23% of the males); an additional 17% of the women had only one prior conviction. As for their most recent offense, only 17% of the women (versus 31% of the men) were convicted of a violent crime; 39% of the women (29% of the men) were convicted of drugs; 36% of the women were convicted of a property crime (compared to 28% of the men). Table 6.4 further illustrates some of these statistics.

In California, a survey by the Little Hoover Commission published in December, 2004 reveals stark contrasts between men and women prisoners, especially when it comes to family backgrounds. For instance, the survey found that 57% of the women compared to only 16% of the men had been either physically or sexually abused prior to being sent to prison. Also, 27% of the women and but only 12% of the men were in therapy for mental health concerns. Not surprisingly, 64% of the women had a child under 18 years of age; yet somewhat surprisingly, the survey included the same statistic for men and noted that 57% of them had at least one child under 18. Yet, while 53% of the women were living with their children at the time of

TABLE 6.4   *Characteristics of Women in the Correctional System*

Characteristic	Probation	Local Jails	State Prisons	Federal Prisons
Major Offense				
Violent	9%	12%	28%	7%
Property	44	34	27	12
Drug	19	30	34	72
Public Order	27	24	11	8
Race				
White	62%	36%	33%	29%
Black	27	44	48	35
Hispanic	10	15	15	32
Other	1	5	4	4
Age				
Under 25	20%	21%	12%	9%
25–34	39	46	43	35
35–44	30	27	34	32
45–54	10	5	9	18
55+	1	1	2	6
Marital Status				
Married	26%	15%	17%	29%
Widowed	2	4	6	6
Separated	10	13	10	21
Divorced	20	20	20	10
Never Married	42	48	47	34
Education				
8th or less	5%	12%	7%	8%
Some high school	35	33	37	19
High school grad or GED	39	39	39	44
Some college or more	21	16	17	29
History of Abuse				
Ever	41%	48%	57%	NA
Before 18	16	21	12	
After 18	13	11	20	
Both	13	16	25	

Source: Greenfield, L. A. and T. L. Snell (1999). "Women Offenders." Washington, DC: Bureau of Justice Statistics, December.

their most recent arrest, only 36% of the men were. The report also found that only 40% of the women, compared to 60% of the men, were employed at the time of their arrest (Little Hoover Commission, 2004).

The Little Hoover Commission also found significant gender differences with regard to offenses. Among all those sent to prison in 2003, only 13% of the women but 28% of the men were convicted of violent crimes; almost half (47%) of the women were convicted of a property crime, compared to 31% of the men; 34% of the women were sent up on drug charges, compared to 29% of the men. Fully 42% of the women were classified as low-level offenders, compared to 15% of the men.[17]

Not too much has changed since the last survey of women prisoners was completed back in the late 1980s. In that survey, conducted by the American Correctional Association, most of the women were racial minorities with little education, one-third of whom had less than a high school education. The occupational histories showed that most had worked in low-skill, low-wage jobs in the service and retail trade industries. For almost half (46%) this was the first time they had ever been incarcerated. The most common of the offenses on their current sentence was, not surprisingly, a drug offense (20.7%), with murder second (15%), and larceny-theft third (12%) (American Correctional Association, 1990).

Some of the details provided in this earlier survey were not included in the most recent survey. For instance, in the earlier survey it was revealed that while most had been married at some time, the majority were now either divorced or separated. Indicative of the low social status of many women inmates is the fact that around 30% never had a driver's license or a checking account, while 60% had received welfare assistance at one time or another. Most had at least one child and about 30% had three or more children. More than 40% had their first child when they were under 18, and another 26% had their child when they were 18 or 19 years of age. Research suggests that having children as a teenager puts one at high risk for greater involvement in criminal behavior (Chesney-Lind and Shelden, 2004). Further, such a situation places the children at risk as well. Note that in almost every case, someone other than the child's father has custody of the child, usually grandparents or the mother's siblings.

What is also of interest is the personal background of these women. Almost half had another family member who had been in prison, which is another strong predictor of criminality (Dryfoos, 1991; Shelden, 2006). Indicative of a negative family life is the fact that so many had run away and were abused. In fact, the percent who were abused is a somewhat low number, given what some other researchers have found through other data (Chesney-Lind and Pasko, 2004). And in fact, the American Correctional Association survey upon which these data are based also surveyed a sample of incarcerated juvenile females and these data reveal a far greater pattern of abuse. For instance, among the juveniles an astounding 80% had run away at least once; and 39% reported that they had run away 10 or more times! Also, over half (54%) had attempted suicide at least once. A greater proportion of the juveniles had been physically abused (62%) and sexually abused (54%) than was the case for the adults (American Correctional Association, 1990).

As for substance abuse, the figures show a pattern of rather extensive abuse. Alcohol abuse was common for these women, as 41% used it either daily or once or twice a week. However, for juveniles such abuse was even greater, as 60% had used alcohol either daily or once or twice a week. One-fourth of the adult women used heroin frequently, while around one-third used cocaine and marijuana. Among the juveniles, while the abuse of heroin was minimal and their use of cocaine was roughly the same as the adults, marijuana use was far more prevalent, as almost half (47%) used it daily, while another 17% used it once or twice a week (American Correctional Association, 1990).

It should be stressed that the majority of women in prison have not been career criminals and about half had never been to prison. This is probably indicative of the war on drugs and its effect on women drug users: It has, in effect, criminalized those who in previous years would never have been sent to prison, but would have instead been placed on probation, if they were arrested at all (American Correctional Association, 1990; see also, Owen, 1998).

The most recent study was completed by Barbara Bloom and published by the National Institute of Corrections and the findings from this survey further underscores previous research (Bloom, 2003). Among the key findings is that women's family backgrounds were quite dysfunctional, with the majority having only one parent in the household (normally the mother), while about half had at least one family member who had been incarcerated (compared to 37% of the men in prison). Drugs and alcohol abuse were prevalent within their families and sexual and physical abuse was far more common than women in the general population. Further, most of these women witnessed violence in their families. Some more detailed studies have found that an even greater percentage of women have experienced abuse, such as more than 80% in a California study, and similar high percentages in many other states, such as North Carolina, New York, and Nevada (Owen and Bloom, 1995; Jordan et al. 1996; Browne et al. 1999; Jordan, 2005).

The physical health of these women is much worse than in the general population and more than male prisoners. They are about three times more likely than men to go to sick call every day (20%–35% vs. 7%–10%). About 5% of the women are pregnant when they enter prison. Sexually transmitted diseases are also a much greater problem for women than for men (women are 50% more likely than men to be HIV positive); since 1991 the number of women with HIV went up by 69%, compared to a 22% rise among men (Bloom, 2003).

Mental health issues are more common among women than men. Around one-fourth have been diagnosed with a mental illness; mostly depression, post-traumatic stress disorder (PTSD), and substance abuse. Incidentally, PTSD is strongly related to sexual abuse and other kinds of trauma. Just over one-fifth of women in jail have been diagnosed with PTSD; around one-fourth of women in prison are getting medication for various psychological disorders. Most of these disorders, by the way, are strongly correlated with their experiences of abuse. Many times the failure to examine the backgrounds of these women results in tragedies, such as what recently occurred in a New York jail. In this case a woman who was sent to jail had ". . . a childhood of sexual abuse, a diagnosis of manic depression, a suicide attempt at age 13," (September, 2002) which was noted when she arrived at Riker's Island more than two years ago. She was never seen by a psychiatrist or by the mental health specialist who was caring for her. She was eventually placed by a social worker on suicide watch this past December. The guard on duty did not know she was on suicide watch. She was found hanging from bed sheets (Von Zielbauer, 2005).

As already noted, the majority of these women have children and the most obvious question is: Who is taking care of them? More often than not, it is either grandparents or the state (e.g., foster care). Visits with children while incarcerated are almost impossible, as so many prisons are now in rural areas far away from home, rendering travel extremely difficult. An example is the case of women offenders in Hawaii.

Currently about 80 (roughly 10% of all women in prison in that state) are housed in a prison in tiny Brush, Colorado (population 5,000), a private prison operated by GRW Corp. (Bloom, 2003).

Finally, while a slight majority of women in state prisons (56%) and 73% in federal prisons had a high school diploma, less than half were employed full time at the time of their most recent arrest (compared to almost 60% of the males). Two-thirds of the women never held a job that paid more than $6.50 per hour. Most who did work did so at traditional female occupations, like cosmetology, clerical work, and food service (Bloom, 2003).

Notes

1. For the classic statement on this position see Engels (1972); a good critique of this thesis is provided by Lerner (1986: Chapter 1).

2. For a discussion of how and why capitalism promotes selfishness, greed, the need for power and control, and so on, see Heilbroner (1985, especially Chapters 2 and 3).

3. Portions of the following section are taken from Chesney-Lind and Shelden (2004).

4. *Statistical Abstracts of the United States*, 2004. http://www.census.gov/prod/2004pubs/04-statab/ pop.pdf.

5. Population Resource Center (2001). "Status of Children in America." http://www.prcdc.org/summaries/children/children.html.

6. "Start Your Financial Year Off Right: Free Financial Resources for Women." http://www.womenof.com/Articles/cn_1_26_04.asp.

7. Crouse (2002); see also these reports: U.S. Census Bureau, Current Population Survey, 2002 and 2003 Annual Social and Economic Supplements, Washington, DC; Heintz et al., 2000: 58.

8. See the following articles from the Internet: Institute for Women's Policy Research (2005). "African-American Women Work More, Earn Less." http://www.iwpr.org/pdf/IWPR Release3_29_05.pdf and (2003). "Single Mothers and Their Children Suffered the Most in the Last Year with Persistently High Poverty." September 26. http://www.greaterdiversity. com/employers/emp_articles03/Single_Mothers.html.

9. See also B. Owen, "Women in Prison," Drug Policy Alliance. http://www.drugpolicy.org/communities/women/womeninpriso/.

10. Prisoner Action Coalition (2000). "Women in California Prisons." Berkeley, CA. http://www.boalt.org/PAC/stats/women-prison-fact-sheet.html;

"Study: 1 in 37 U.S. adults have prison experience," CNN.com, August 18, 2003. http://www.cnn.com/2003/US/Northeast/08/17/prison.stats.ap/.

11. This charge has been collaborated by other sources. See Owen (n.d.) and Huling (1995). A report in the *Houston Chronicle* notes that "To arouse less suspicion, the cartels often hire women and children" (July 15, 2000). See "Mules Ferry Drugs across Borders in game of Chance." http://www.chron.com/cs/CDA/ssistory.mpl/special/drugquagmire/603860. Even the State Department verifies this with a brief report called "Things You Should Know Before You Go Abroad." http://travel.state.gov/travel/living/drugs/drugs_1237.html.

12. See also, DiFranza et al. (1995) cited by Paltrow and Ehrlich (2006), who note that "Cigarette smoking has been linked to as many as 141,000 miscarriages and 4,800 deaths resulting from perinatal disorders, as well as 2,200 deaths from Sudden Infant Death Syndrome, nationwide."

13. The 1976 data are found in Shelden (1982: 347); 1999 data are found in Beck (2000).

14. How this has happened is another story; see Owen (1998) and Chesney-Lind and Pasko (2004) for further discussions of this issue.

15. FBI, *Uniform Crime Report*, 2003. http://www.fbi.gov/ucr/cius_03/pdf/03sec4.pdf.

16. Sourcebook on Criminal Justice Statistics, 2003. http://www.albany.edu/sourcebook/pdf/t526.pdf.

17. Surveys in other states reveal the same patterns. See the following: Marcus-Mendoza, S. and R. Briody (nd.) Female Inmates in Oklahoma: An Updated Profile and Programming Assessment. http://www.doc.state.ok.us/DOCS/OCJRC/Ocjrc96/Ocjrc85.htm.

7

Crime Control in the New Millennium: New Mechanisms for Controlling the Dangerous Classes

"While arrests and convictions are steadily on the rise, profits are to be made—profits from crime. Get in on the ground floor of this booming industry now!"[1]

"The opportunities and options in the field are endless."[2]

"If crime doesn't pay, punishment certainly does . . ."[3]

As the above quotes suggest, fighting crime is big business. What many have called the crime control industry is, I would maintain, part of a much larger global network of social control (more about this follows). Crime today, as always, is often front page news. It dominates the local nightly newscasts, complete with film footage of the victims and the perpetrators. Prime time television is often similarly dominated by crime—from full-length movies to so-called live broadcasts of police in action catching criminals. One of my former students wrote a thesis on the subject of the portrayal of the police on prime-time television and among his key findings was that fully one-fourth of all shows were devoted to the subject of crime (Kopp, 2006). Millions flock to the movie theaters every week to see the latest episodes of crime and violence. Crime also becomes a hot item during every election year, with opposing candidates typically trying to see who can be the toughest.[4] Crime also becomes the subject of hundreds of books, both popular fiction and nonfiction as well as academic discourses.

    In words that were written more than 100 years ago, Karl Marx commented sar-
castically about some of the "positive functions" of crime and criminal justice when
he wrote:

> The criminal produces not only crime but also the criminal law; he produces the pro-
> fessor who delivers lectures on this criminal law; and even the inevitable text-book in
> which the professor presents his lectures as a commodity for sale in the market. . . .
> Further, the criminal produces the whole apparatus of the police and criminal justice,
> detectives, judges, executioners, juries, etc. . . . Crime takes off the labour market a por-
> tion of the excess population, diminishes competition among workers, and to a certain
> extent stops wages from falling below the minimum, while the war against crime
> absorbs another part of the same population. The criminal therefore appears as one of
> those natural "equilibrating forces" which establish a just balance and open up a whole
> perspective of "useful" occupations (Marx, 1993: 52–53).

Indeed, fighting crime is a big business, with literally hundreds of companies, large
and small, itching for a slice of a growing pie of profits. Employment in this industry
offers careers for thousands of young men and women, many with college degrees in
criminal justice programs at more than 3,000 colleges and universities.[5] The criminal
justice system alone provides a steady supply of career possibilities, as police officers, prison guards, probation officers, and many more. Most of these jobs offer not
only good starting pay, but excellent benefits and a promise of future wage increases
and job security.[6] Many have formed unions, some of which have become stronger
than any union heretofore. A multitude of businesses, ranging from small mom and
pop security businesses to huge corporations listed on the New York Stock Exchange,
have found it profitable to invest in crime.

    We have witnessed in the 20th century the emergence of a criminal justice in-
dustrial complex (one part of the crime control industry), which has recently taken
over where the military industrial complex left off. The police, the courts, and the
prison system (or what some have called the prison industrial complex) have become
huge, self-serving and self-perpetuating bureaucracies with a vested interest in keeping crime at a certain level. They need victims, they need criminals, even if they have
to invent them, as they have throughout the war on drugs and war on gangs.[7] In short,
it is good that we have crime, otherwise billions of dollars in profits would be lost
and hundreds of thousands of people would be out of work (including the author
of this book). Fighting crime has become, in effect, a Keynesian stimulus to the
economy.[8]

    While elected officials and many others talk about the need to turn the corner
on the crime problem, to make the streets safe for potential victims, what is ignored
is that there is no way crime will be reduced by any significant amount (such as a 50%
reduction) because it would have such a negative impact on our economy. Simply put,
we cannot afford to really put a large dent in the crime problem. Actually, to be more
specific, various special interests (except the average citizen) cannot afford to reduce
crime. In fact, the traditional reasons for putting people in prison—incapacitation,
retribution, rehabilitation—may be giving way to another reason: increasing the profits of big business and providing economic uplift in rural communities. (We might

also note that in effect, taxpayers are subsidizing private industry in that tax dollars pay for prisons and jails, which in turn contract with businesses for various supplies.)

It is also important to note that the overall rate of crime as the new century began was almost the same as it was 30 years earlier. Yet during that same time, expenditures on the criminal justice system soared by 1500% and the incarceration rate went up by 500% (Shelden and Brown, 2002). Regardless, the public's fear of crime has not diminished (Glassner, 1999; Hope and Sparks, 2000). During the 1990s as the crime rate decreased, polls showed a rising fear among the public. For instance, a Time/CNN poll in 1995 found that an overwhelming majority (89%) believed that crime is rising and just over half (55%) were concerned about being a crime victim (Blakely and Snyder, 1997: 151). More recent surveys show continued fear. For example, a recent Gallup poll (2005) found that 67% of the public believes there is more crime than one year ago; in the year 2000 this percentage was 47; in 1992 it was 94%. Another question posed by the poll is "Is there any area near where you live—that is, within a mile—where you would be afraid to walk along at night?" In 1965, 38% answered "yes" to this question rising to 44% in 1992; in 2005 it was again 38%.[9]

We have now entered into a new century and the new millennium offers us many challenges, but at the same time presents some rather pessimistic predictions. What has occurred during the last one-third of the 20th century is that crime and its control has become one of the fastest growing businesses in world history. As the manufacturing base of American has declined, we have seen in its place the rise of a fast growing service industry. Within this industry is found what can be called the crime control industry.

The Crime Control Industry

The crime control industry can be defined as an assortment of public agencies and private companies that profit, to some extent, from the existence of crime. In some cases it is their raison d'etre (e.g., criminal justice agencies, private security firms, and so on). In other cases, benefits come more indirectly. Examples of the latter include the system of higher education, with more than 3,000 criminal justice programs within colleges and universities. Educating people for occupations in criminal justice is a big business, given the large number of those majoring in criminal justice or criminology and planning on a career in this field. Also, one can earn a degree by attending part-time either through the University of Phoenix (with campuses throughout the western United States) or through distance learning companies. An example of the latter is seen in an ad in the July 2005 issue of *Corrections Today* by a company called Distance Learning Systems. Their add reads as follows: "Crime doesn't pay, but a degree in Criminal Justice does!" Through this program, the ad continues, you can "Combine home study, credit by examination and upper level online course work to earn YOUR bachelor's Degree in Criminal Justice!" This issue also contains an ad for Excelsior College, Bellevue University and California University of Pennsylvania, Mountain Empire Community College, all of which offer degrees, certificates, workshops, and other assorted programs.[10] The criminal justice system alone provides a steady supply of career possibilities, as police officers, prison guards, probation officers, and many more. Most of these jobs offer not only good starting pay, but excellent benefits and a promise of future wage increases and job security. Many have formed unions, some of which have become stronger than any other union heretofore (see following discussion).

There are numerous examples of various businesses that may receive profits because of crime, such as hospitals and insurance companies (hospital emergency room visits, doctor's fees, insurance premiums on auto and other insurance covering crime, and so on) and the salaries of those who deal with the victims of crime (e.g., doctors, nurses, paramedics, insurance adjusters). Then, too, there are the profits from the sale of books (e.g., college textbooks, trade books), magazines, journals, and newspapers (and the advertisers who profit from crime stories) as well as profits from television crime shows (and their advertisers) and movies about crime (with the enormous salaries paid to actors and actresses who star in them).

Further examples of the businesses receiving profits from crime include the money collected by courts through various fines (especially traffic tickets), special courses defendants can enroll in as a condition of (or in lieu of) their sentence (e.g., traffic schools, petty larceny programs), plus a totally separate industry involved in the setting of bail (bail bondsmen and the insurance companies involved). Finally, we have to consider the private security industry, with profits almost impossible to estimate (ranging from companies that provide security guards to the makers of all sorts of security devices like locks and barbed wire, not to mention the security provided to gated communities). As you can clearly see, there are many different entities profiting in some way from the existence of crime.

One of the first to recognize this as an issue was Richard Quinney in his book *Class, State and Crime*, first published in 1977. In this book he wrote that there is what he termed a *social-industrial complex,* of which a criminal justice industrial complex is a part. This much larger complex is "an involvement of industry in the planning, production, and operation of state programs. These state-financed programs (concentrating on education, welfare, and criminal justice), as social expenses necessary for maintaining social order, are furnished by monopolistic industries" (Quinney, 1980: 133). Large corporations, Quinney suggested, have found a new source of profits in this industry, with the criminal justice industry leading the way. Private industry, in short, has found that there is much profit to be made as a result of the existence of crime.

Part of the reason for the growth of the crime control industry is that our society has decided that a technocratic solution to the crime problem is the best course to take. This perspective, which is almost identical to the perspective taken toward the Vietnam War, suggests that the solution to crime requires a combination of science and technology. Such a position was stated well by the President's Crime Commission in 1967. The commission wrote:

> More than 200,000 scientists and engineers have applied themselves to solving military problems and hundreds of thousands more to innovation in other areas of modern life, but only a handful are working to control the crimes that injure or frighten millions of Americans each year. Yet the two communities have much to offer each other: Science and technology is a valuable source of knowledge and techniques for combating crime; the criminal justice system represents a vast area of challenging problems (President's Commission, 1967a: 1).

It is obvious that the government took up the challenge, for since this time the crime control industry has become enormous. It is so huge that it is almost impossible to estimate the amount of money spent and the profits made. Some rough estimates of the size of this industry will be presented in the pages that follow.

One can clearly see the size of this complex by first noting the annual expenditures of the three main components of the criminal justice system: law enforcement, courts, and corrections. In 2001 (latest figures available as of fall, 2006), the total expenditures came to about $167 billion (up from about $11 billion in the early 1970s). The largest amount went to law enforcement ($72 billion), while corrections received just under $57 billion and $37 billion was spent on the courts.[11]

Employment within the crime control industry is growing rapidly, providing many career opportunities for both college students and high school graduates. The most recent data show that in 2001 there were 2.3 million employed within this system, almost doubling the 1.2 million in 1992.[12] The largest component is law enforcement, with just over 1 million employed, followed by corrections with about 747,000, with the courts employing about 500,000.

Chapter 4 presented evidence of the huge increases in the prison population during recent years. What needs to be underscored here is that the mere size of the correctional complex is truly incredible. As noted in chapter 4, the actual number of prisons has increased, along with, in some cases, the capacity within the prison (e.g., megaprisons). According to the Census of State and Federal Correctional Facilities, 2000 published by the Bureau of Justice Statistics, at midyear 2000 there were a total of 1,668 adult correctional facilities, up from 1,464 in 1995 (a 14% increase). The report also notes that there were "264 privately operated facilities under contract with State or Federal authorities to house prisoners—an increase of 140%. The number of inmates held in these facilities rose 459% (from 16,663 inmates in June 1995 to 93,077 in June 2000)." There were 430,033 staff in state and federal prisons, with about two-thirds (270,317) being correctional officers. There were 264 private facilities, up from 110 in 1995.[13] For juveniles, the latest figures are from 1999 and at that time there were a total of about 2,900 facilities (Sickmund, 2002). These add up to more than 4,500 correctional facilities nationwide. It is indeed a huge and constantly expanding industry.

A report by the Urban Institute documents these and other changes in prison construction (Lawrence and Travis, 2004). The authors of the study report that during the past 25 years the number of state prisons went from just under 600 to more than 1,000 in the year 2000, a 70% increase. Put differently, more than 40% of today's prisons did not exist 25 years ago. Just looking at state prisons, the authors note that in 1923 there were only 61 prisons in the country; in 1950 there were 150; in 1974 there were 592; in the year 2000 there were 1,023. The top 10 states in growth increased their prisons by 63% between 1979 and 2000. The top ten were: Texas, Florida, California, New York, Michigan, George, Illinois, Ohio, Colorado, and Missouri. Texas, the authors report, "is in a league of its own, as it added the most prisons (120), currently has the largest number of prisons in operation (137), and experienced the largest percentage increase (706%) (Lawrence and Travis, 2004: 9). (The number for Texas was seven times what they had in 1979).

The authors of the Urban Institute study used a unique method of documenting the growth of prisons by determining what proportion of all counties in the top ten growth states now have a prison, in contrast to 1979. What they found was remarkable. Whereas in 1979 only 13% of the counties had at least one prison, by 2000 almost one-third (31%) did. California topped them all, with 59% of its counties having at least one prison in 2000, compared to only 31% in 1979. In Texas only 3% of its counties had a prison in 1979; in 2000 the proportion soared to 28%. In Florida 45% of the counties had a prison in 1979, but in 2000 more than two-thirds (78%) did. New York State went from 31% to 52% during this time.

Taking a Larger View: The Globalization of Crime Control

In order to better understand the criminal justice industrial complex, I think it is necessary to take a much broader view, one that encompasses the entire world. Thirty years ago Richard Quinney made the following observation: "The legal system at home and the military apparatus abroad are two sides of the same phenomenon: both perpetuate American capitalism and the American way of life" (Quinney, 2002: xxvi). Today these two systems are larger than ever and they spread themselves literally into every corner of the globe.[14] We need to visualize this entire system from a global perspective, as the same technology and world view helps shape both crime control at home and military control abroad, as Quinney suggested.

In many ways the control of crime has taken on many of the characteristics of the military, or what Peter Kraska and others have called the militarization of criminal justice (Kraska, 1999. See also, Arrigo, 1999; Caufield, 1999; Haggerty and Ericson, 1999; Simon, 1993). Echoing Quinney, Kraska makes the point that there is an underlying ideology of militarism that clearly has been borrowed in the war on crime (not to mention the war on drugs), which he defines as "a set of beliefs and values that stress the use of force and domination as appropriate means to solve problems and gain political power, while glorifying the means to accomplish this—military power, hardware, and technology" (Kraska, 1999: 208). This also involves a "blurring of external and internal security functions leading to a more subtle targeting of civilian populations," (1999: 208) plus an ideology that places emphasis on the efficient solving of problems that require the use of state force, the latest and most sophisticated technology, various forms of intelligence gathering, the use of special operations (e.g., SWAT) in both the police and within the prison system, the use of military discourse and metaphors (e.g., collateral damage, under siege) and last, but not least, collaboration with "the highest level of the governmental and corporate worlds, between the defense industry and the crime control industry" (1999: 208).

How big is this network of social control? One way to answer this question is to borrow the popular phrase "follow the money," for the money involved is truly staggering; also to look at employment figures. To begin with, expenditures on the criminal justice system came to $185 billion in 2003, the latest year available.[15] Taking the average annual percentage increase over the past five years, as of 2006 the expenditures would be in just under $260 billion; therefore this figure will be used for the estimates given here. Over two million are employed in the criminal justice system, as of March,

2000 (Beck, Karberg, and Harrison, 2002). Then there is the truly vast private security industry, which includes more than 15,000 firms with annual revenues totally about $40 billion (www.freedoniagroup.com). How many are employed in this industry is not known, but a USA Today report (2003) noted that there are more than 1 million security guards nationwide, also noting that this is a $12 billion industry. Also included is the recently formed Department of Homeland Security, with a budget of $41 billion (Government Security, 2003). Homeland Security includes several different departments, including the Border Patrol, Immigration and Naturalization Services, Coast Guard, Secret Service and many more (www.dhs.gov). According to one estimate about 165,000 are employed within this department.[16] Finally, there's the Pentagon budget, reaching an all-time high of a proposed $401.7 billion in fiscal 2005 (*Government Executive Magazine*, 2004). The total expenditures for all of the above come to about $715 billion. The total number employed in these components is almost impossible to calculate. As for the military, there were about 1.4 million on active duty as of 2003.[17]

The above total leaves out a lot. For instance, we have no idea how many businesses are involved in providing various kinds of products and services to agencies of the criminal justice system, Homeland Security, and the military. Concerning the military, not counted in the Pentagon budget is the cost of the current war in Iraq. The latest count comes to around $362 billion as of January 2007.[18] It is not possible at this time to provide anything more than crude estimates of the number of people employed in private businesses that provide products and services to the various agencies of social control, nor the extent of the revenues obtained from such services. It would be safe to assume, however, that revenues come to several billions of dollars.

If we include the cost of the war in Iraq, then the total amount comes to at least $1 trillion. As for estimating the number employed, if we take the estimated 15,000 firms in the private security industry and assume an average of about 100 employees per firm, we have about 1.5 million in the private security industry (more than the above-referenced 1 million security guards). This would bring the total employed to more than 5 million.[19] Table 7.1 illustrates these estimates.

At a minimum, we have a society that employs over 5 million people (probably more) whose main job is connected in some way with the social control of literally billions of citizens both here and abroad, with expenditures that are more than 1 trillion dollars. Given the money and the number employed, it is safe to say that the control of crime and related security concerns is one of the most important industries in the world.

Millions Under Control of the State

It is probably impossible to estimate the total number of people who, on any given day, are subject to the control functions of the modern American state, whether it is the criminal justice system or the military. We do have, however, some fairly accurate numbers for those under the direct control of the American criminal justice system, especially prisons and jails.

At the end of 2005, there were more than 2.3 million prisoners in the United States, which translates to an incarceration rate of 737 (Harrison and Beck, 2006).[20]

TABLE 7.1   *The Scope of the Social Control Network*
(Crime Control and the Military)

Component	Expenditures (in billions, 2004)
Criminal Justice System	$260
Private Security Guards	12
Department of Homeland Security	41
Pentagon (defense budget, FY 2005)	402
Iraq War	362
Total	$1,077

Component	Employment (in millions, 2004)
Criminal Justice System	2.0
Private Security Guards	1.5
Department of Homeland Security	0.165
Military (active duty)	1.4
Total	5.065

Sources: (see text)

Both of these statistics are all-time highs and highest in the world. Not included in these figures are those detained under the jurisdiction of the Bureau of Immigration and Customs Enforcement (formerly the INS), which totaled 19,562. This number represented a 139% increase over 1995. Additionally, there were 2,322 prisoners held under military jurisdiction, plus 15,735 prisoners held in the custody of correctional authorities in U.S. territories. These numbers together add up to 37,619 (Harrison and Beck, 2006). The total number of prisoners comes to 2,357,978.

It should be noted that our incarceration figures do not include all of those in various community-based facilities (e.g., work-release centers) and incarcerated juveniles. Exact number of those in these various community-based facilities is not available, but as of 2005 there were just under 5 million on probation and parole, up from about 1.3 million in 1980 (Glaze and Bonczar, 2006). The number of juveniles incarcerated was about 102,000 as of 2002 (Sickmund, 2006).

Finally, there is the rather astonishing figure of 47 million American citizens (about one-fourth of the adult population) who have criminal records on file with some state or federal agency! This is a truly amazing statistic (Travis, 2002: 18). (Incidentally, the police made about 14 million arrests in 2005, according to FBI figures.)[21] That brings the total of current and previous criminal justice clients to more than 65 million people, not counting juveniles on probation, parole or under some other form of supervision! It might be said without much exaggeration that the criminal justice system reaches into every nook and cranny of American life.

Looking more carefully at the past 30 years we find that while there have been some fluctuations in the overall crime rate, at this time the official crime rate (index crimes) is about the same as it was in the early 1970s, yet the incarceration rate went up by about 500%. The rate of violent crime actually increased slightly during this period, but the rate of property crime had declined to offset that increase. During this same period of time, expenditures on the criminal justice system increased by 1500% (Shelden and Brown, 2004: Chapter 2). Only one conclusion can be reached: increasing rates of incarceration and expenditures on the criminal justice system has had no impact on the crime rate. The absolute failure of the conservative, hard-line approach to crime is evident.

In the next section a more detailed examination of the fastest-rising component of the entire criminal justice system will be made, the prison industrial complex. As will be shown, it is within this specific industry that the profits from crime appear to be the greatest.

The Prison-Industrial Complex: Cashing in on Crime

The prison industrial complex represents an interconnection among the criminal justice system, the political system and the economic system—just like the military represents a connection with the political and economic system. Politics and economics go hand in hand: How do you think politicians get elected and whose interests do they serve? Think also of the large number of lobbyists in the nation's capital, not to mention the same thing at the local and state level—try to see your senator, congressman, city councilman, or other representative and chances are you will have to wait in line until they see corporate lobbyists (Parenti, 1999). Think for a moment about the building of prisons, jails, courthouses, and police departments and furnishing them with everything they need to keep going (construction costs, electrical, furniture, toilet paper, and so on) and you get an idea of what I am talking about.

A recent illustration of this is revealed in a *Washington Post* report called "7 Federal Prisons to Get Lethal Electrified Fences." According to this story seven high-security federal prisons will get to add "lethal electrified fences" costing around $10 million. A spokesperson for the Federal Bureau of Prisons stated that "This new technology will serve as new security and help us to deter potential escapes, allow us to operate more cost-effectively by reducing the guard towers, the staffing at some of our guard towers."[22] The problem with this is that it is rare to find anyone attempting to escape from a federal prison. Judy Freyermuth, representing the Federal Prison Policy Project, a nonprofit prison reform group, questioned the savings, asking: "How many times have you read of an escape from a federal prison? None." However, the bottom line is that there will be at least one company that builds such fences that will receive the bid.

Prisons as a Market for Capitalism

Within a capitalist society there tends to be an insatiable desire to continue "converting money into commodities and commodities into money" (Heilbroner, 1985: 60). Everything, it seems, is turned into a commodity—from the simplest products (e.g., paper and pencil) to human beings (e.g., women's bodies, slaves). Indeed, within a capitalist society "daily life is scanned for possibilities that can be brought within the circuit of accumulation," (1985: 60) since any aspect of society that can produce a profit will be exploited. Life itself has been commodified.

Part of this drive for profits stems from the ideology of the free market, which is a system of beliefs that under girds the entire capitalist economic system. According to this ideology every individual pursues his or her own personal interests and the result is a collective good for the entire society. It is Adam Smith's invisible hand at work. Corporations are free to do whatever they want.

This free market includes the prison system. The amount of money that flows into the coffers of the prison industrial complex from tax dollars alone is quite substantial. The budget for both state and federal correctional institutions came to $34.1 billion in fiscal year 2000, which represents an increase of almost 80% over 1992. The budgets for probation and parole have also been increasing. While in fiscal year 1992 the average budgets for both systems came to $23 million, in the year 2000 the average was $71 million, an increase of 209%. What is most interesting about the budgets for probation and parole is that the largest increases went to the parole system, with their average budgets going from $25.5 million in 1992 to $43.1 million in 2000, compared to a very modest increase for probation budgets from $55.7 million to $56.3 million. The total budgets for both probation and parole came to just over $1.7 billion in fiscal year 2000. The costs per prisoner per day have been steadily increasing during the past decade, going from about $49 in 1991 to about $58 in 1999. That's about $21,170 per prisoner per year (Camp and Camp, 2000: 84, 88, 186). The most recent figures for the Federal Bureau of Prisons reveal that the budget in fiscal 2002 was $4.6 billion, up from only $330 million in 1980. In 1980 there were only 44 prisons; in 2002 there were 102, with 11 more under construction (Johnson, 2003).

A good illustration of how companies are cashing in on the boom in corrections is found in the amount of advertising done in journals related to this industry. One example comes from two major journals serving the prison industrial complex, *Corrections Today* and *The American Jail*, plus the American Correctional Association's annual directory. (*Corrections Today* is the leading prison trade magazine and the amount of advertising in this magazine tripled in the 1980s.) I have sampled a few issues of these journals and the *ACS Directory* and found advertisements everywhere. Among the companies whose products are advertised here include the following from one issue of *Corrections Today*:

> Prison Health Services, Inc., a company that has, since 1978, "delivered complete, customized healthcare programs to correctional facilities only. The first company in the U.S. to specialize in this area, we can deliver your program the fastest, and back it up with services that are simply the best"; Southwest Microwave, Inc., manufactures fence security, with their latest invention known as "Micronet 750" which is "more than a sensor improvement," it is "a whole new paradigm in fence detection technology"; Acorn Engineering, Inc., with their stainless steel fixtures known as "Penal-Ware" (lavatories, toilets, showers, etc.) and "Master-Trol" electronic valve system; Rotondo Precast, Inc. boasting "over 21,000 cells . . . and growing"; Nicholson's BesTea with "tea for two or . . . two thousand . . . Now mass-feeding takes a giant stride forward . . ."; Northwest Woolen

Mills, manufacturing blanket with the slogan "We've got you covered"; and, "Prison on Wheels" from Motor Coach Industries, with their "Inmate Security Transportation Vehicle." Even insurance companies are getting in on the action, including U.S. Risk Underwriters, "with over 20 years combined experience in liability insurance for the criminal justice system." A company called Control Screening advertises its special Model 6040-M security parcel X-ray scanner with an ad that reads: "Don't allow suspicious packages into your facility." An example of a popular company that has entered the prison market is Western Union offering "an automated solution" for all sorts of payments, from court-ordered payments to commissary needs. Then there is one of the largest food service companies, Aramark, which says it will "trim the fat from your food service." While "your correctional officers are watching the food line, Aramark will be watching your budget." Then there is General Marine Leasing, a company that builds "portable, temporary and modular facilities." Their ad reads: "Overcrowded? Don't let overflow put them back on the street."[23]

This is a small sampling, for there are at least two websites that list company ads aimed at the prison market. One is the Corrections Yellow Pages (http://www.correctionsyellow.com) and another one is simply corrections.com (http://www.corrections.com). Together these contain more than 1,000 different ads. Corrections.com organizes its web page by categories of vendors. For example, under the heading Cleaning/Sanitation there are 20 companies, including Americhem Enterprises (they supply products like industrial degreasers, floor finishers, disinfectants, bowl cleaners, and so on), Champion Industries (specializing in dishwashing machines for prison applications), and Somat Corporation (waste reduction systems for the correctional foodservice industry). This website also claims to be "Home to the Industry's Leading Organizations" and provides a list of 34 different organizations, including both the most popular national groups (e.g., American Correctional Association) and lesser-known regional groups (e.g., Kentucky Department of Juvenile Justice).

The American Correctional Association (ACA) is one of the largest national organizations in the country. Their annual meetings draw hundreds of vendors, usually taking up an entire floor of a hotel or convention center. On the ACA website it mentions the $50 billion or so spent each year on prisons and jails and says to companies, "Don't miss out on this prime revenue-generating opportunity."

The trade journal of the American Correctional Association, *Corrections Today*, has a special issue every July in anticipation of the upcoming annual conference in August. There are more than 200 pages in this special issue. I have a copy of the July, 1999 issue, which includes descriptions from more than 200 different companies, selling everything imaginable. The list includes locks and other security devices, food service, hygiene kits, bedding, blankets, ceiling systems, communications equipment, clothing, weapons, and a wide assortment of architects, engineers and consultants used to build and maintain prisons and jails.

One section of this issue of the journal is devoted to advertising for the famous ACA Exhibit Hall, which they cleverly call the "County Fair Specialty Break." This ad was telling members about the previous winter meetings (these are held every

January at various locations around the country) and reads as follows (bold in the original):

> The excitement of an old-fashioned County Fair was in the air in the Exhibit Hall Tuesday morning for the **1999 Winter Conference Exhibit Hall Specialty Break**. Attendees took a chance for prizes at **Correctional Healthcare Solutions, Inc.'s** Wheel of Fortune and at **Sverdrup Facilities, Inc.'s** Coke bottle ring toss. **Kenall** hosted a dart game for prizes and **HKS** provided a clown juggler who formed balloon animals. **Aramark Correctional Services'** tarot card reader foretold attendees' fortunes as did the palm reader **Norment Detention & Security Group** supplied.

The page shows photos of all sorts of people (including children) having a grand old time, just like an old-fashioned county fair.

Not surprisingly, prison construction itself has become a booming business. During the 1990s a total of 371 new prisons opened. (About 92,000 new beds were added each year.) In 1999 alone, 24 new prisons were opened, at a total cost of just over $1 billion. The average cost of building a new prison came to $105 million (about $57,000 per bed, more than the starting salary of public school teachers and newly hired assistant professors and even some full professors). Also, in 1999 a total of 146 prisons were adding or renovating beds at a cost of $470 million (about $30,000 per bed). As of January, 2000 a total of 29 new institutions were under construction and another 137 institutions were being renovated or adding new beds. Most of the new beds will be in either maximum or medium security institutions, where the costs are the highest. The total estimated costs of these new building projects come to more than $2.2 billion (Camp and Camp, 2000: 76).

The construction of new prisons has become such a big business that there is a special newsletter called Construction Report, just to keep vendors up to date on new prison projects (Dyer, 2000: 13). A Google search on the Internet turns up dozens of companies advertising for prison construction. One example, among many, is Kitchell (http://www.kitchell.com) that, according to their website, "has successfully delivered over 110,000 correctional beds, including over 130 criminal justice projects in 17 states." These projects include 42 state prisons, 29 adult jails, and 30 juvenile facilities. They also build police stations, courts facilities, and camps.

Also found on this search was the website for the North Carolina Department of Corrections (http://www.doc.state.nc.us/DOP/prisons), which includes a chart showing the prisons recently opened or about to open in that state. Between 1989 and January, 2004 a total of 22 correctional facilities (including a youth center and two work farms) were opened. Currently three are under construction, with two due to open in April, 2004 and construction on another prison is set to begin in January, 2005. As of December 31, 2002 North Carolina had 28,772 prisoners and an incarceration rate of 345, a rate considerably below the national average of 476 (Harrison and Beck, 2003). It appears as if this state is hoping to catch up with the rest of the country.

Corporate Interests: The Role of ALEC

A little know fact about the prison industrial complex is an organization known as the American Legislative Exchange Council (ALEC). The mere existence of this organization demonstrates the classic connections between politics, economics, and the criminal justice system. The membership consists of state legislators, private corporation executives and criminal justice officials. More than one-third of state lawmakers in the country (2,400) belong and they are, not surprisingly, mostly Republicans and conservative Democrats. It was started in 1973 by Paul Weyrich (who also cofounded the Heritage Foundation and now is the head of a group called the Free Congress Foundation, a far right conservative group). Their mission is to promote free markets, along with small governments, states' rights, and, of course, privatization. Corporate membership dues range from $5,000 to $50,000 annually. Corrections Corporation of America is a member of this group, which is not surprising. However, members also include a veritable "who's who" of the Fortune 500, such as Ameritech, AT&T, Bayer, Bell Atlantic, Bell South, DuPont, GlaxoSmithKline, Merck & Co., Sprint, Pfizer, to name just a few. Among the companies that have supported ALEC through various grants include Ameritech, Exxon Mobil, Chevron, and several corporate foundations, including the Proctor and Gamble Fund, Exxon Educational Foundation, Bell Atlantic Foundation, Ford Motor Company Fund, among many others.[24]

The website of ALEC is an educational experience in itself. It proudly lists some of the bills it has been involved in getting passed, plus indicates some very important keynote speakers during the past three annual meetings. Among the notables giving speeches include Attorney General John Ashcroft, Secretary of Health and Human Services Tommy Thompson (see following), Secretary of Housing and Urban Development Mel Martinez; President and CEO of American Home Products Robert Essner; Chairman and CEO of Pfizer, Hank McKinnell; Florida Governor Jeb Bush; Secretary of Labor Elane Chao; and ultra conservative syndicated columnist Cal Thomas.[25]

This organization also puts together papers and policy statements on a wide variety of issues reflecting conservative ideas, including one about the myth of global warming. Bill Berkowitz, who carefully follows conservative trends, has noted that ALEC sponsored more than 3,100 pieces of legislation between 1999 and 2000, with more than 400 of these bills passing (Berkowitz, 2002). Within ALEC there is the Criminal Justice Task Force. Among the duties of this group is to write model bills on crime and punishment. Among such model bills they helped draft include mandatory minimum sentences, three strikes laws, truth in sentencing, and the like. One member boasted that in 1995 alone they introduced 199 bills, including truth in sentencing bills, which passed in 25 states. Tommy Thompson, former Wisconsin Governor and current head of Health and Human Services in the Bush Administration, was once a member of ALEC. He was recently quoted as saying that "I always loved going to these meetings because I always found new ideas. Then I'd take them back to Wisconsin, disguise them a little bit, and declare that 'It's mine'." Edwin Bender of the National Institute on Money in State Politics, says that: "Bayer Corporation or

Bell South or GTE or Merck pharmaceutical company sitting at a table with elected representatives, actually hammering out a piece of legislation—behind closed doors, I mean, this isn't open to the public. And that then becomes the basis on which representatives are going to their state legislatures and debating issues."[26] As everyone knows by now, these kinds of laws were a big reason for the swelling of the prison population, which in turn added new markets for capitalist profits.

Reach Out and Touch Someone

The old telephone company ad that advised customers to "reach out and touch someone" has new meaning, since long-distance phone companies have entered into the prison system. Such industry giants as AT&T, Bell South, Sprint, and MCI have found prisons to be an excellent market for long distance business. Indeed, this makes sense because inmates all over the country spend countless hours on the telephone talking with relatives. Of course this requires a collect call, which brings these companies into prison for the huge profits to be made. AT&T has an ad that reads (in upper case letters): "HOW HE GOT IN IS YOUR BUSINESS. HOW HE GETS OUT IS OURS." MCI, not wanting to miss out, went so far as installing, for free, pay phones throughout the California prison system. They levy a $3 surcharge for each phone call made, the cost of which is paid for by the prisoner's relatives. MCI offered the Department of Corrections 32% of the profits (Schlosser, 1998: 63).

This has led to a great deal of controversy in California and elsewhere. In 2002, an investigation by the *Los Angeles Times* found that phone charges benefited the state of California by about $35 million a year as a result of an agreement with long-distance phone companies. Phone charges to relatives of those locked up in the California Youth Authority resulted in about $85 million in revenue for the state in 2001. After several years of pressure, an agreement reached in January, 2001 lowered the charges by 25%. A three-year contract was signed with WorldCom and Verizon that cut rates for adult prisoners by 25% and for juveniles by 78%. As a result of this agreement, the average 11-minute phone call to a family member outside the immediate area will be just over $5 dollars (Warren, 2002).

Brother Can You Spare a Bed?

Finally, there are people known as bed brokers. These individuals act like travel agents, only in this case they help locate jail and prison beds, rather than hotel rooms! An example is a company known as Dominion Management of Edmond, Oklahoma. They will search for a correctional facility with an empty bed for a fee, a sort of rent-a-cell program. Areas suffering from overcrowding are often in desperate need for additional space, the cost of which can run from $25 to $60 per man-day. These bed brokers will earn a commission of around $2.50 to $5.50 per man-day (Schlosser, 1998: 65–66).

In the 1980s, the state of Texas began to use county jails to provide temporary housing to ease overcrowding in the prison system (the District of Columbia began the same thing). They began calling county jails looking for beds. A company known as N-Group Securities in Houston saw a profit. Texas towns were short on jobs and developers began to approach these towns with plans to build more jails. Such Wall Street investment firms like Drexel Burnham Lambert offered to underwrite some junk bonds for the project. However, soon the state of Texas started building prisons—$1.5 billion worth—and the hiring of about 12,000 guards. Thus they now had a surplus of beds and these small towns with new jails were desperate for inmates. So they called other states and began renting their cells, resulting in business from 13 states, from Hawaii to Massachusetts (Burton-Rose and Wright, 1998).

Institutions for young offenders are also a profitable industry. A report by Equitable Securities Research in 1997 is illustrative. The title tells it all: "At-Risk Youth: A Growth Industry." And growing it is with around 10,000 to 15,000 private juvenile-justice service providers. They provide everything from education programs to wilderness camps—a $50 billion per year market (Dyer, 2000: 17). A cursory review of a trade magazine called *Juvenile Offenders* provides many examples of these programs. One of the biggest specific markets relates to the war on gangs.

I could go on and on with numerous examples and give some more reasons why we are in this state of affairs, but we will close with one glaring example of why spending seems to be constantly increasing for the criminal justice system. Two words sum it up: politics and economics. Politics in the sense that elected officials want to be reelected and sounding tough on crime gets votes. Economics in the sense of not only the money to be made by businesses, but also the number of jobs created. Protecting those jobs is often done by strong unions representing criminal justice workers.

The California Correctional Officer's Union

California is a good example of union influence. The California Correctional Peace Officer's Association (the union representing prison guards) has become a potent political force in that state. It was begun in 1957. By the early 1990s it was becoming a powerful political force in California. A recent report noted the following: "The union's impact can be gauged by the rising annual prison guard salary (from $14,440 in 1980 to $54,000 in 2002), the growth in number of state prisons (from 13 in 1985 to 31 in 1995), and large increases in the California Department of Corrections budget (from $923 million in 1985 to $5.7 billion in 2004)" (Institute of Governmental Studies, 2005). In 1992 alone this group was the second largest contributor to political action committees, as they contributed just more than $1 million to various candidates. In 1990, they gave almost $1 million to Pete Wilson's successful campaign for governor. The total contributions given in 1990 were 10 times that given by the California Teachers' Association (Schiraldi, 1994). They contributed $101,000 toward Proposition 184, which created the "Three Strikes and You're Out" law (Burton-Rose and Wright, 1998). Currently they have about 31,000 members who contribute about $22 million dollars a year. They have a staff of 91, including 20 full-time attorneys. They also use the services of five lobbyists and a team of public relations consultants. Their lobbying efforts have resulted in pay raises for correctional officers that bring their salaries to as high as $73,000 (up from $44,000 in

1996), far more than the average teacher and 58% higher than national averages for correctional officers (Center on Juvenile and Criminal Justice, 2006; see also Burton-Rose and Wright, 1998; Cockburn, 1999).

A recent example of the power of this union is their stance toward a program that allows prisoners to earn college credits at Ironwood State Prison in Blythe (Warren, 2003). This program is one among many examples demonstrating that the more education a prisoner receives while in prison, the lower the recidivism rate. But apparently lowering recidivism rates is not on the agenda of this union. In typical exaggerated conservative language, the union complains that it is not right for tax-payers to fund college courses for rapists, murderers and the like. A union memo complained about a similar program at another prison, saying that it is wrong to provide education to prisoners rather than offering tuition assistance "to people in the community who pay taxes and may benefit from these services" (Warren, 2003). A flyer sent to union members working at the Ironwood prison urged them to boycott all management functions and urged them to "Just Say No" to taxpayer-funded college education for inmates, suggesting that "lifers, some of who [sic] are rapist [sic], molesters and murders [sic] receiving a free college education" (Warren, 2003). (Given the poor grammar used in this memo, it might be a good idea that the person who wrote it, the president of the Ironwood State Prison chapter of the union, would enroll in some college-level English courses offered at some prisons.) College officials countered this charge, saying that with this program they were able to expand some of the programs, hire new faculty, and increase opportunities for disadvantaged students not in prison. National figures cited by the *Los Angeles Times* show that such programs are successful and a program in Arizona resulted in a recidivism rate of only 10%, compared to about 60% nationally (Warren, 2003).[27]

The growth in the building of prisons during the past couple of decades has had several unintended consequences, both political and economic. A close look at where most prisons have been built is revealing.

Rural Prisons: Uplifting Rural Economies?

In this country there are more prisoners than there are farmers. It would not be too much of an exaggeration to say that rural America has been pretty much destroyed by factory closings, corporate downsizing, the shift to service occupations and the build-up of chain stores like Wal-Mart. Many rural towns have become "dependent on an industry that itself is dependent on the continuation of crime-producing conditions" (Huling, 2002: 198).

Much of the building of American prisons during the past two decades have been in rural areas, largely because of the promises of economic stimulus to these areas coupled with the cost savings of the states. These figures tell the story: whereas during the 1960s and 1970s an average of four new prisons per year were built in non-metropolitan areas, during the 1980s this average increased fourfold to about 16 per year and during the 1990s went to an average of 24.5 per year. During the 1990s a new prison was opened about every 15 days. During this decade, 57% of all new prisons were in nonmetropolitan counties, which have only 19% of the total population

(Huling, 2002: 198).[28] By the end of the 1990s, there were about 235,000 prisoners and 75,000 workers in the new rural prisons built that decade. Between 1980 and 2000, "more than half of all rural counties added prison work to their available employment mix" (2002: 199). Prisons, along with casinos and animal confinement units for raising or processing hogs and poultry have become the three leading industries in rural areas.

Another example is the North Fork Correctional Facility in Sayre, Oklahoma (pop. 4,144). It is one more in a long list of prisons run by Corrections Corporation of America (CCA). According to the latest count cited on the Oklahoma Department of Corrections web page, there are just over 1,500 prisoners.[29] The prison employs 270 people (most earn between $17,000 and $19,000 per year) and "is responsible for lifting Sayre's spirits and reigniting its economy" according to a report in the *New York Times* (Kilborn, 2001). According to this report, during the 1990s a total of 245 prisons were built in 212 of the country's 2,290 rural counties. Many of these are in the rural Great Plains towns of Colorado, Oklahoma, and Texas "that had been stripped of family farms and upended by the collapse of the 1980's oil boom." About 25 new rural prisons opened each year in the 1990s, in contrast to only 16 in the 1980s and 4 in the 1970s. Population growth naturally followed (especially when prisoners are counted by the census bureau. In these 212 counties, population went up by 12% in the 1990s, compared to a rate of 1.5% in the 1980s. In three Oklahoma cities with new prisons (Hinton, Sayre, and Watonga) the population increased by more than 40% (Kilborn, 2001).

In Sayer, CCA is the largest taxpayer, as the prison pays $411,000 in property taxes, while spending $2.5 million for goods and services in Oklahoma (mostly around Sayre) and also paid about $7 million in wages. "The prisoners are themselves cogs in Sayre's economic engine according to the *New York Times* report, since they "pay the city's 3.5 percent sales tax for the snacks and sodas they buy in the commissary. They also pay a 35 percent to 45 percent tax for the telephone calls, roughly 100 a day, all collect, all long distance" (Killborn, 2001). What is interesting is the fact that all the prisoners have been sent by Wisconsin, "which, because of a space shortage, farms out more than 4,000 prisoners to other states." Moreover, the money received from the long distance phone calls (paid by relatives of the prisons back in Wisconsin), sales taxes, and water and sewer fees, and so on "accounts for nearly all the increase in the city's budget from about $755,000 in 1996, before the prison construction began, to about $1,250,000" in 2001 (Kilborn, 2001).

Typical of the effect of the building of rural prisons, many other businesses have opened to handle the population growth. Near Interstate 40, a Flying J Truck Stop was opened and now employs 117 people and pays around $150,000 year in sales taxes. It is not all positive, as the turnover among prison employees is high (about 70% per year) and there has been a drain on demands for city services. Further, Wisconsin's prison growth has stopped and they will not be sending any more prisoners to other states within 10 years (Kilborn, 2001).

In the small southern Illinois town of Vienna, Illinois (population 1,260) there is a prison and according to the mayor there is no other industry in the town. "They are good jobs at the prisons. People count on retiring from there. They buy cars and they buy houses" (Landis, 2002). This is according to a recent report for *Illinois Issues*. The author of the report notes that "Dozens of small downstate Illinois communities have enjoyed what amounted to a prison construction boom that began in the 1970s and continued well into the 1990s" (Landis, 2002). Between 1990 and 2001, "the state built or planned 21 prisons, work camps and juvenile detention centers at an estimated cost of $818.7 million" (Landis, 2002). In one instance, a maximum security prison in Grayville "offered typical economic incentives to prospective communities: $140 million in state construction spending, 350 construction jobs, 750 corrections jobs and an annual prison budget estimated at $55 million" (Landis, 2002).

There are many states that have several prisons built within a few miles of one another, described by one critic as "penal colonies." In the town of Ionia, Michigan (pop. 10,569) there are six state prisons, which ties it with Huntsville, Texas (pop. 35,078) for the most prisons in any city in the country (Huling, 2002: 206–207). Speaking of Ionia, a story in the *Detroit News* was called "Ionia [Michigan] Finds Stability in Prison: Lockups Provide Fast Growing Community with Jobs" (Street, 2002: 40). Ionia "had recently become one of the state's fastest growing and 'most improved' communities thanks to its five thriving penitentiaries together employing 1,584 workers who collectively made $102 million a year" (2002). Moreover, "penitentiaries, five veritable Great Lakes of cash, provide sustenance to every sector of [Ionia's] once-dry economy: jobs for residents, customers for stores, revenue for the city government," which includes "nearly $1.2 million of the city's $3.8 million budget" (Street, 2005).

There are plenty of other examples. In the Wisconsin town of Stanley (population 1,898) a "spec" prison was completed in the year 2000, built by a company called Dominion Venture Group. The state finally purchased the facility for $75 million in October, 2001. The mayor of Stanley, David Jankoski, stated that "we needed something to bring back vitality to the community . . ." An article in the *Chicago Tribune* (March, 2001) was titled: "Towns Put Dreams in Prisons," referring to many small towns in the southern part of Illinois, areas short on jobs (Clement, 2002).

In the rural heartland of Michigan, Wisconsin, Minnesota, Montana, North Dakota, and South Dakota spending on prisons skyrocketed during the past 20 years. Per capita spending in North Dakota, for instance, went from about $25 to about $75 between 1980 and 2000, while Michigan's per capita spending went from less than $50 to almost $200 during this time. The number of prisoners tripled in Montana and South Dakota and quadrupled in North Dakota and Wisconsin during these two decades. Incarceration rates for these states increased at about the same rate, with Michigan's rate going from about 150 to almost 500 and the rates in both Montana and South Dakota going from under 100 to more than 300 (Clement, 2002).

County and local leaders in these rural areas often engage in a vigorous campaign to get prisons built in their area. In Texas, some town leaders ". . . bombarded the [Texas Department of Prison] with incentives that range from country club memberships for wardens to longhorn cattle for the prison grounds" (Donziger, 1996: 41). In Rush City, Minnesota (pop. 2,102), civic leaders raised $700,000 in donations and another $40,000 from the city to buy the acreage for the site of the new prison. Tiny Shelby, Montana (pop. 3,216) used a $500,000 block grant and another $800,000 in federal grants to pay for the infrastructure so that Corrections Corporation of America (CCA) could build the Crossroads Correctional Facility (Clement, 2002).

Typical of such growth and overall impact can be seen in Michigan's Upper Peninsula where there are nine prisons and four minimum security prison camps; all but two of these were opened during the past two decades. While only 2% of the state's population lives there, about 18% of its prisoners are housed there (Clement, 2002).

In Newberry, in the Upper Peninsula, a prison replaced a mental health center in 1996, which resulted in the county (Luce) having one of the highest ratios of prisoners to total population (13% of the population are in prison). One supporter, a local businessman, said that "the $12 million payroll coming into the community was just a big plus" (Clement, 2002). In Chippewa County (pop. 38,543) there are five state prisons. In Kinross Township, a town of about 6,000, the prisons employ over 1,000 people, making it the second largest employer. Many in Kinross were looking forward to the possibility that McDonald's would open a restaurant, partly because prisoners are allowed to buy food once a month from local restaurants—an obvious captive market (Clement, 2002).

Another example that can be cited is the Pelican Bay State Prison in Crescent City, California (pop. 4,006). Built with a cost of $277 million, it has become the largest employer in the county. Before it was built, Crescent City was a dying town, with most of its population living in poverty or near-poverty (20% unemployment rate). Of the county's 17 sawmills, only 4 were operating, while the fishing industry was dead. During the 1980s, a total of 164 businesses went broke. In typical corporate-welfare fashion, seeing a way out of their predicament local supporters practically gave away land, water, and power to get the prison built. The prison now provides around 1,500 jobs, a payroll of over $50 million and a budget of more than $90 million. The prison also indirectly created more business, such as a $130,000 contract to haul the garbage, a new hospital, a K-Mart, and a new Safeway market. Housing starts doubled since then, as did the value of real estate, while collecting $142 million in real estate taxes, up from $73 million 10 years earlier (Parenti, 1999: 212).

Politicians often seek assistance from private enterprise when it comes to building prisons. Faced with severe overcrowding in the 1980s, New York Governor Mario Cuomo found that real estate prices were far too high near the city of New York, where the majority of inmates are from. So he received help from a Republican state senator from the northern part of New York, who in turn arranged for low prices on land for prisons. What has been the result? While 25 years ago this area had only two prisons, today it has over 20. One prison now occupies land formerly used for the Olympic Village at Lake Placid, while others have opened in abandoned factories and sanatoriums. A total of 36 prisons have been built in this state since 1980 (Duke, 2000). This recent prison boom "has provided a huge infusion of state money to an economically depressed region." These prisons bring in about $425 million in annual payroll and operating expenses—in effect, an annual subsidy of more than $1,000 for each person in the area! The annual salary is around $36,000 for a correctional officer in this area, more than 50% higher than the average annual salary for other workers in the area (Schlosser, 1998: 57–58; Dyer, 2000: 17).

In yet another small town in upstate New York called Malone in the far north-ern end of the state (pop. 6,025), a $180 million supermax prison was recently built. According to one report, prior to its opening, the plan called for holding around 1,500 prisoners in 14- by 8-foot cells for 23 hours per day. (A return to the days of the Pennsylvania System.) The prison ostensibly was to create about 500 badly needed jobs in this part of New York in order to replace the 750 jobs lost at a local shoe fac-tory because of downsizing. And it's not that Malone needed more prisons, for they already had two medium-security institutions! The new prison will bring the prison population in Malone to around 5,000 (of a total population of 6,025). One writer notes that "prisons have become the North Country's largest growth industry . . ." (Wray, 2000: 52). New businesses also tend to follow the building of new prisons—in the case of Malone, four new drugstores and eight new convenience stores (Wray, 2000: 52). A story in the *Washington Post* noted that "If crime doesn't pay, punish-ment certainly does, at least for isolated towns like Malone" (Duke, 2000).

A look at the website for the New York State Department of Corrections (http://www.docs.state.ny.us/faclist.html) shows that there are five prisons in Franklin County (pop. 51,134) where Malone is. According to this website, New York cur-rently has 18 maximum security prisons, 37 medium security prisons, 13 minimum security prisons (4 are designated as shock prisons), three minimum security camps, and one drug treatment campus (in Willard, pop. 600 in western New York on the shores of Seneca Lake) for a total of 72. A recent report notes that less than 40% of the population of New York State lives in what is considered the upstate area; over 70% of the prisoners are from the New York City area, while about 90% of the pris-oners are incarcerated in upstate prisons (Prison Policy Initiative, 2003).

Most of the boom in upstate New York stems from the Rockefeller drug laws passed in the 1970s, which set severe punishments for drug offenders. Prison sen-tences have tripled since the passage of these laws and almost two-thirds (62.5%) were nonviolent drug offenders (Duke, 2000).

One downside to building all these prisons in upstate New York, however, is the fact that hundreds of families of inmates have to make the long bus ride in order to visit their relatives. Ironically, this fact has created yet another business, begun in 1973 by an ex-convict, who founded Operation Prison Gap, which operates a bus service for these families. They now have 35 buses and vans traveling on weekends and holidays (Schlosser, 1998: 58).

Some Downsides to Prison Expansion

Not everyone is happy about locating prisons in small towns and some recent studies have shown little or no economic and social benefits. For instance, in the town of Braham, Minnesota (pop. 1,276), citizens rejected putting a prison there with one local critic saying they would have to change their motto from "Homemade pie cap-ital of Minnesota" to "Prison capital of Minnesota." The prison was located in nearby Rush City, over the objections of a few in that town. In Pembina County, North Dakota, local citizens are protesting the proposed building of a prison there. Opponents are concerned about the negative changes the prison would bring, such as impeding tourism; proponents talk about the jobs that would be created. One supporter hopes that a 500-bed prison will be built, claiming that the impact would be "tremendous," adding that "it's pretty much recession-proof" (Huling, 2002: 204–205). Not all are recession-proof as it turns out. In Bonne Terre, Missouri (pop. 4,039), a new prison was opened in 1995 (the most expensive in the state) and by 2001 the city was in debt with new businesses almost broke because state budget shortfalls delayed the opening of the prison, with an estimated loss of several million dollars (Huling, 2002: 204–205).

As virtually every state is undergoing a budget crisis, cutting back on prison expenses has become one option, including closing some of them. In Illinois, with a budget shortfall of about $1.3 billion for fiscal year 2002, Governor George Ryan closed the old prison at Joliet. He also proposed closing Vienna Correctional Center and the Valley View Youth Center in St. Charles, but later substituted a prison in Sheridan (pop. 2,435) for Vienna (Landis, 2002). Other states are finding that building and maintaining prisons is very expensive and they have already taken steps to alleviate the problem. Examples abound, including the following (Greene and Schiraldi, 2002; Marks, 2003; Butterfield, 2002; Greene and Roche, 2003; Associated Press, 2003):

- Several states have reformed mandatory minimum sentencing laws by returning sentencing discretion to judges, including Alabama, Mississippi, Michigan, Indiana, Connecticut, Louisiana, North Dakota, and Utah.
- Several states (e.g., California and Arizona) have passed special referendums concerning alternative sentencing for drug offenders.
- Some states have instituted parole reforms, including early release.
- Many states are cutting other costs, such as food and health services.
- Some states have closed down entire prisons to save money.[30]
- Some states have put new construction on hold to save money and to find alternatives.

Delays in planned prison construction can have negative effects, however, when surrounding communities are counting on them for economic uplift. One report noted that the "general manager for two hotels in northwest Pennsylvania said a new Microtel Inn a few miles from the vacant Forest County prison is about a third of the way through construction" (Greene and Roche, 2003). The general manager stated that "If it wasn't for prison, there wouldn't be a hotel" (2003). The county has had the highest unemployment rate in Pennsylvania in recent years. A county commissioner stated that "We get people up here for the hunting season and then the trout season and that's about it. As soon as people knew the prison was coming, a lot of that's changed. We've got a lot riding on that prison" (Greene and Roche, 2003).

Another negative point is raised by University of Missouri economist Thomas Johnson, who has said that "prisons generate very few linkages to the economy," (Clement, 2002) by not generating associated industries, like, for instance, an auto plant would—delivery companies, radio assemblers, electronic harness makers, etc. Another critic, a county prosecutor, claims that having a prison nearby has doubled the number of felonies he has had to handle, mostly arising from within the prison (Clement, 2002). An identical experience was reported in Bent County, Colorado (located in the far southeastern part of the state, with a population less than 6,000), as court filings jumped up by 99% after the opening of a private prison in Las Animas (pop. 2,758) (Huling, 2002: 204).

Also, contrary to the expectations of many, most cases the prison jobs do not go to locals, but rather they tend to go to those with seniority and educational backgrounds within the correctional field. Moreover, many prison workers drive long commutes from large urban areas. A study of rural prisons in California revealed that less than one-fifth of the jobs were filled by locals. Despite the fact that the county where Malone, New York is (Franklin) has five prisons in the area, the planned food-processing plant was never built. Also, a $4.5 million sewage-treatment plant that was paid for by the state in order to prepare for one of the prisons increased the amount of nitrate dumped into the Salmon River, described as "a beautiful trout stream treasured by the community" (Huling, 2002: 204). The loans used to build the plant came from the village's bowering capacity, rather than the state, and therefore its taxes have risen, with payments estimated to be more than $1 million per year (2002: 204).

There is some discrepancy in reports of job growth in Malone. One report said that the 750 jobs that opened in their new prison went mostly to people from elsewhere (Huling, 2002: 204). Another report said that the three prisons in Malone brought 1,600 well-paying jobs, noting that one-third of these workers live in the town and the rest from somewhere else in the county. The payroll is around $67 million and one source in the town said that a few small businesses have moved there from Canada, plus there are "new and expanded pharmacies, discount stores and fast-food outlets. Also, there has been an expansion of the hospital and a doubling of the golf course" (Duke, 2000). This rosy picture is not repeated everywhere, however.

In many places where prisons have been built, most of the locally owned businesses have closed, giving way to Wal-Mart, McDonald's, and the like. This is what happened in Tehachapi, California, a small town of just under 11,000 between Mojave and Bakersfield along route 58. Two prisons are located there and 741 local businesses went belly up during the past decade, while being replaced by chain stores.[31]

In one of the most detailed studies, the Urban Institute found little evidence of positive impacts. A study by the Sentencing Project that used 25 years of data from New York State rural counties and looking at employment rates and per capita income "no significant difference or discernible pattern of economic trends" (Lawrence and Travis, 2004: 11, citing King, Mauer, and Huling, 2003) between counties that were home to a prison and counties that were not home to a prison. . . Studies in Iowa and Texas have arrived at similar results (Besser, 2003; Chuang, 1998). This study also noted that the economic benefits from these newly opened prisons "may come from the flow of additional state and federal dollars. In the decennial census, prisoners are counted where they are incarcerated, and many federal and state funding streams are tied to census population counts" (Lawrence and Travis, 2004: 3). Citing a GAO report, they note that "the federal government distributes over $140 billion in grant money to state and local governments through formula-based grants. Formula grant money is in part based on census data and covers programs such as Medicaid, Foster

Care, Adoption Assistance, and Social Services Block Grant. Within a state, funding for community health services, road construction and repair, public housing, local law enforcement, and public libraries are all driven by population counts from the census" (2004: 3).

This study also noted that not all jobs within the prison are filled by local people, largely because of state and union seniority rules, professional certification requirements. One study found that in Missouri 68% of the prison jobs were filled by people living outside the county where the prison was located. The same thing has happened in many other states, such as California and Washington. The Sentencing Project study found that prison construction jobs "impose a variety of requirements that local applicants may not meet." These include the possession of job-specific skills and correctional guard union membership (Lawrence and Travis, 2004: 3; King, Mauer, and Huling, 2003; Street, 2005).

Speaking of the census, we now find that, in effect, prisoners have become valuable commodities—bringing us back in time to the days of the convict lease system in the southern states following the Civil War. It is telling that the impact of such a system has hit African Americans especially hard, as did the convict lease system. Once again, the profit motive takes advantage of cheap, slave labor—only today's slaves are African-American prisoners (Hallett, 2006). This leads me to consider another aspect of the growth in rural prisons, a rather sinister and perhaps even fraudulent development. I am referring here to the use of prisoners to alter census counts in rural areas thereby allowing them to bring in federal dollars.

Exploiting Prisoners to Enhance Rural Populations

It was noted earlier that the increase in the number of prisoners has resulted in the disenfranchisement of large numbers of citizens, especially affected African Americans. Even though prisoners cannot vote in almost every state, they are added to the census counts and these counts are translated into federal dollars pouring into small towns all over the country. This is what one report called the phantom population of rural prisoners (Prison Policy Initiative, 2003). What is happening is that rural communities that have prisons are allowed to pay the U.S Census Bureau money to include prisoners in their census counts, thereby adding substantial numbers to the local population. A *Wall Street Journal* report details how this has happened in the small Arizona town of Florence, which has an official population of 17,054 according to the 2000 census (Kulish, 2001). What this census figure does not reveal is that 11,830 of these residents are prisoners, since Florence, like many other small towns where prisons have been built, is looking to the census count to help them in these financially strapped times.

This began in Florence back in the 1980s and since then has expanded its borders no less than three times. On two occasions the town has paid the Census Bureau for special recounts. This is because for each dollar generated by local taxes and fees, they get $1.76 more because of the prison population. Florence now has "new town offices, a new park and a new senior center . . . The rebuilt little-league facilities boasts a digital score board and dugouts. New police and fire facilities are under construction, and officials are planning a $1 million community center with a pool—all without a local income tax or any substantial increases in sales or property taxes" (Kulish, 2001). In 2001, about $4 million in additional federal funding was expected to be received by the end of the year, according to the *Wall Street Journal* report (Kulish, 2001).

Not surprisingly, Arizona has one of the highest incarceration rates in the country (513 in 2002, ranked 10th in the country), with almost half being either black (14.7%) or Hispanic (33.7%) (Harrison and Karberg, 2003). After Corrections Corporation of America began housing prisoners from Washington, DC in its prison in Florence, the African-American population of the town more than doubled to over 1,500. Florence now has two state prisons, three private prisons, plus the U.S. Immigration and Naturalization Service detention center. This little town can now brag about having "the highest percentage of prison inmates of any U.S. town of more than 10,000" (Kulish, 2001).

Florence is not the only small town to reap such benefits. Calipatria, California has an official population of 7,289, thanks to 4,095 prisoners; Ionia, Michigan has a population of 10,569 that includes 4,401 prisoners—they used some of the federal money to install laptop computers in the town automobiles for officials, including police cars and turned a National Guard armory into a community center (Kulish, 2001). Sussex County, Virginia appears to be the fastest growing county in the country, thanks mostly to the fact that between 1998 and 1999 two new prisons increased its population by 23%. According to the 2000 census, there are 12,504 official residents. Similarly, Coxsackie, New York received an increase in federal funding because its 1990 population was 27.5% prisoners. With a 2000 population of 2,895 it is no doubt set to receive more. Two small Arizona towns, Gila Bend (pop. 1,980) and Buckeye (pop. 6,537) competed to get both adult and juvenile prisons placed in their district. Buckeye won and stands to receive more than $10 million in federal subsidies (Huling, 2002). Malone, New York discussed previously has also benefited. The town may gain more federal dollars because one-third of the total population of 15,000 consists of prisoners (Duke, 2000).

Another benefit of adding prisoners to the U.S. Census count is that it places many of these communities under the official poverty level, thereby qualifying for even more federal funds! Gatesville, Texas (pop. 15,591) qualified for poverty status with its 9,095 prisoners, resulting in the town receiving $4.2 million in state grants, which it used to upgrade water lines and build new roads. Another irony to all of this is the fact that while these prisoners are helping towns qualify for large sums of federal dollars, they are not included in the official unemployment figures. According to one recent study, by including African Americans in the official unemployment figures, the unemployment rate for them increases to almost 40%, while adding about 2% to 3% to the official unemployment figures (Western and Beckett, 1999).

This is a form of "robbing Peter to pay Paul" since these federal dollars are following these prisoners from their original communities. One recent report noted that during the first decade of the 21st century about $2 trillion in federal funds will be distributed based upon the 2000 census count, so that a lot of money will be transferred from poor urban areas to small towns with prisons. Minnesota's state demographer

Tom Gillaspy estimates that the census "directs $2,000–$3,000 per person counted to any given community each decade, *not including additional census-based funding distributed to poor communities*" (Maynard, 2000; emphasis added).

Finally, mention should be made of the impact rural prisons have had on redistricting. One result of the phantom increase in rural populations is in an increase in the voting power of rural districts, many of whom have added additional congressional seats, mostly Republican. The Prison Policy Initiative has argued that by allowing mostly white rural districts "to claim urban black prisoners as residents for purposes of representation resembles the old three-fifths clause of the Constitution that allowed the South extra representation for its slaves . . ." Such a policy also means that legislators in rural areas "can devote more attention to their 'real constituents' " while at the same time those who support building new prisons in their rural areas have additional clout in state legislatures (Prison Policy Initiative, 2003). The state of Florida, already infamous for the 2000 election fraud, will soon have a significant redrawing of political boundaries, thanks to 79,144 (according to the Florida Department of Corrections website (Huling, 2002) prisoners (over half are African American). Gulf County has two prisons that contribute to its population numbers (13,332). The attorney general of Florida issued opinions in 2001 that said county commissions and school boards "*must* include prisoners when redistricting" (Huling, 2002, p. 212). One effect is that voting, in Florida and the other 48 states where prisoners are denied a vote, the voting power of large numbers of mostly minority urban communities are transferred to rural, mostly white areas—also, by the way, heavily Republican. A statement from a former New York State legislator sums up the feelings of many politicians: "When legislators cry 'Lock'em up!' they often mean 'Lock 'em up in my district" (Huling, 2002: 212). I am tempted to conclude that locking up so many urban minorities is one part of a much larger conservative strategy to take over the country!

Todd Clear has noted that the increasing tendency to house prisoners in faraway rural communities amounts to what he calls coercive mobility that has a negative impact on informal methods of social control in poor communities. In many poor neighborhoods, up to 25% of the adult males are behind bars on any given day. This results in the removal of both human capital and social capital from these communities (Clear, 2002). Elsewhere he has estimated that as much as $25,000 per year leaves the community for every man who is incarcerated and this money goes directly to the communities that have the prisons (Clear and Rose, 1999).

Before leaving the subject of rural prisons I'd like to share a recent news item appearing in the *Los Angeles Times* on March 28, 2004. The story was about the small town of Clintwood, Virginia (pop. 1,549), tucked away in a relatively remote area of the far western edge of the state, close to the Kentucky border. The story is familiar: Travelocity (where you can make airline reservations), which was the largest employer in the area (250 jobs) and replaced the dying coal industry, was closing up shop and moving its operations to India by the end of the year.

In the middle of this article, which tells of the potential impact of the job losses that have typified the recent trend of capital flight to foreign countries, there's a passing reference to a prison in the area. The writer of the article notes that there is a joke around the town "that the only secure jobs are at the new state prison, because they are not going to be shipping the convicts to India anytime soon. There are several new lockups around the county, which a lot of people have mixed feelings about" (Streitfeld, 2004). The director of the local Chamber of Commerce stated, with somewhat bitter irony, "It's not quite as bad as being a nuclear waste dump site. But we're the dumpsite for human misery" (Streitfeld, 2004).

A check of the Virginia Department of Corrections website reveals that there is a prison in the small town of Pound (about 10 miles from Clintwood, with a population of 1,089). The name of the prison is Red Onion State Prison, which has an average daily population of 985. This is a maximum security institution opened in August, 1998.[32]

There is still another way that businesses profit from the existence of prisons, one that has a long history, and this is the use of prison labor or what is normally called prison industries. This can be traced back as far as the early 19th century with the emergence of the congregate labor system (Auburn system), noted in chapter 4.

Prison Labor: Auburn Plan Revisited

Currently there are many so-called joint ventures between private companies and the state prison system, which have made millions in profits through prison labor. It is especially tempting for the state of California which, because of "Three Strikes You're Out" legislation, will see prison costs exceed $5.5 billion annually. Convict labor is alive and well throughout the country. Many private companies are taking advantage of cheap inmate labor and the tax breaks provided by California's Joint Venture Program. With the passage of Proposition 139 in 1990, private companies were allowed to use inmates to make products to be sold on the open market. At the time of this report, one company employed 18 inmates at San Quentin to do data entry work for firms such as Chevron, Bank of America and Macy's. Inmates in Ventura were making phone reservations for TWA (now American Airlines) at $5 an hour; on the outside with unionized labor, this would have paid $18 per hour. Low wages are common. In Arizona, 10% of the inmates work for private companies and make less than the minimum wage. Many benefits accrue to private companies, including the fact that they don't have to pay benefits. In Oregon, $4.5 million worth of Prison Blues, a line of jeans, were sold (Parenti, 1999). Other companies using prison labor include Microsoft, Honda, Kaiser Steel, Victoria's Secret, and Lee brand jeans (Wray, 2000).

There are at least 25 states where private businesses have set up shop inside prisons, all under the guise of prison reform—making prisoners pay for their room and board and/or paying restitution to victims and, of course, the old standby rationale: It will give them new skills.

Take the Seattle-based Boeing Corporation, for instance. While making more money than ever before, in 1996 the largest aviation manufacturer in the world (always, of course, taking various subsidies from taxpayers) decided to reduce its workforce of unionized workers and instead take advantage of the growing number in the captive work force in the state of Washington. Micro Jet, a leading manufacturer of aircraft components (with Boeing a major customer) uses the Washington

State Reformatory to make these parts; a nice rent-free factory on prison property (Wright, 1997).

They are not alone in taking advantage of this captive labor force. Other firms doing business there include: Redwood Outdoors (which makes clothes for such famous brands as Eddie Bauer, Kelly Hanson, Planet Hollywood, and Union Bay), Elliot Bay (makes crab pots and fishing industry equipment), A & I Manufacturing (makes blinds), and Washington Marketing Group (a telemarketing company). Paying minimum wages, with no benefits, no unions, no regulations to worry about, and these companies are able to get maximum profits, while the prisoners who work get little in return, after all the various deductions are taken away. One prisoner told Paul Wright (a prisoner who edits the *Prison Legal News*) that he grosses $240 per week, but takes home only $60 after all the deductions. Wright concludes that prison industries in America constitute a "Third World labor model" (Wright, 1997).

In Texas, at the Lockhart Correctional Facility, about 180 prisoners assemble circuit boards for Lockhart Technologies, with a take home pay of about 50 cents an hour. In 1993, this company closed its plant in Austin and simply moved to the prison about 30 miles away. Another company in Washington, Omega Pacific, decided to move its plant from Redmond, Washington, to the Airway Heights Corrections Center near Spokane. The owner of the company, Bert Atwater, was quoted as saying that one of the benefits is that he doesn't "have to deal with employee benefits or workers' compensation," (Wright, 1997) plus worry about workers taking vacation.

As already suggested, the profits from the existence of prisons are dependent upon the continued increase in prison admissions. What if prison admissions begin to decline? We are already seeing some evidence of this. For instance, in New York State there has been a recent downward trend in the number of prisoners, resulting in the reduction of prison staff at many prisons. Specifically, the New York Department of Corrections has frozen hiring at 36 of the state's prisons, with the expectation that they will eliminate just over 600 jobs. One facility in upstate New York is illustrative. A $90 million jail was built in tiny (pop. 2,400) Cape Vincent (near the St. Lawrence River) in 1988. With recent downward trends in prison populations they are worried that what they thought was a recession-proof industry may come to an end. One prison worker said, "Who ever thought crime would go down? Who ever thought we would run out of inmates?" (Rhode, 2001).

And worry they should, as about $2.4 billion per year goes into the state prison system, with millions of dollars going into the upstate economy each year. Salaries for correctional officers start at around $33,000, with raises to $44,000 after 20 years. Not bad in rural areas where the cost of living is so much lower than in the cities.

Still another example comes from the state of Mississippi. According to a report in the *Wall Street Journal*, a prison operated by Wackenhut in Holly Springs ran into trouble finding prisoners to fill about 130 beds. In fact, recently the state found itself with 2,000 more beds than prisoners! The same is happening in South Carolina, with more than 1,000 empty beds. These developments are bad news for corporations like Wackenhut, who depend upon a steady supply of prisoners. In Mississippi, a state representative who was touring one of their prisons, pointed to a prison guard and said "If we don't get [more inmates], she might get laid off." Many who previously support building prisons in Mississippi are now changing their minds. A former police chief who is in charge of the state corrections department, who never had any qualms sending people to jail, now complains that for too many people the only reason to build prisons is to "make money off inmates" and he said that this has "gotten a little too skewed for my liking" (Gurley, 2001). A check of the Mississippi Department of Corrections website revealed that as of the end of February, 2004 there were 20,827 inmates, up from 18,299 as of July, 2005.[33] South Carolina's prison population has increased recently, going from 20,979 in fiscal year 2000 to 24,025 in fiscal year 2004.[34] Apparently these two states are no longer as concerned as they were when this report was written.

Examples of profits being made from designing, building and supplying prisons with various products have now been discussed. However, a key component of the prison industrial complex is the trend of states turning to private companies that specialize in the entire operation of prisons, from the design to the daily operation. The next section explores this topic in more detail.

The Privatization of Prisons:
More Profits for Private Industry

A recent development in the criminal justice field, related specifically to the prison system, is the trend toward what is known as privatization. This is where a private corporation either takes over the operation of a jail or prison or builds one itself and operates it (usually contracting directly with the state). Several years ago researchers warned about the tremendous growth in privatization in general, especially within the private police industry. They quoted one source that called this phenomenon creeping capitalism or the transfer of "services and responsibilities that were once monopolized by the state" to "profit-making agencies and organizations" (Spitzer and Scull, 1977: 20). It should be noted that privatization is a trend that includes more than the criminal justice system. This *contracting out*, as it is often termed, involves a number of services formerly provided by state and local governments, such as public education, health care, waste collection, and many more. Between 1987 and 1995 there were more than 18 types of government services that saw an increase in private-sector involvement (Laursen, 1996).

Privatization has become, in the words of Edward Herman, ". . . one of the mantras of the New World Order. Economic, political and media elites assume that privatization provides undeniable benefits and moves us toward a good society" (Herman, 1997). The movement toward privatization stems from the recent trends toward greater and greater corporate power. This increased power has contributed to the emergence of neoliberal ideology. The core beliefs of this ideology include "the efficiency of the private market, the inefficiency of government, and the dual menaces of inflation and budget deficits" (1997). Herman also notes that: "Part of the design of neoliberal politicians and intellectuals has been to weaken the state as a power center that might serve ordinary citizens and challenge the rule of the market" (1997). Contributing to this trend is the increase in capital flow away from urban centers, leaving them in dire financial straits, as governments ". . . have had to limit business taxes and spending on social benefits in order to provide a 'favorable investment climate,' leaving them under financial stress" (1997).

Through privatization, states can get around voter resistance to prison construction bonds by having private corporations build the prison, who then turn around and send a huge bill to the state and thus taxpayers. This represents a classic case of ". . . socializing the costs and privatizing the benefits" (Dyer, 2000: 245).

As of September, 2001 (latest figures available) there were 142,521 beds in 181 facilities in the United States, the United Kingdom, and Australia. This represents an increase of a mere 3,100 in 1987 (an increase of more than 4500 %!). At that time the largest proportion were under control of two companies, Corrections Corporation of America and Wackenhut (over 90,000 prisoners), with facilities in both the United States and abroad.[35]

The largest, and perhaps the most controversial private prison corporation, is Corrections Corporation of America (CCA). Founded in 1983, the company is headquartered in Nashville, Tennessee and employs more than 15,000 professionals nationwide. I once obtained a copy of their 1995 annual report, at which time they claimed to be the "leading private sector provider of detention and corrections services to federal, state and local governments." There was also a subsidiary, CCA International, which provided similar services in foreign countries. Still another subsidiary was TransCor America, which was touted to be "the nation's largest and most experienced prisoner extradition company." At that time, CCA's stock traded on the New York Stock Exchange. It operated 46 correctional facilities, including one in England, two in Australia, and two in Puerto Rico. This report bragged about its revenues, going from $13 million in 1986 to $207 million in 1995 (an increase of 1492%), while assets increased from $8 million to almost $47 million (an increase of 488%) and stockholders equity had gone from $24 million to $96 million (up 300%).[36]

Since that time, CCA has run into some serious problems. Its stock went as high as $45 in 1998, but bottomed out at merely $0.18 per share, which prompted a Wall Street analyst to comment that the company "has taken a dive that would make a dot-com blush." They eventually merged into Prison Realty Trust—a Real Estate Investment Trust (REIT) that is exempt from corporate taxes providing it meets certain conditions, including distributing 95% of its income to shareholders. However, Prison Realty Trust failed to meet that condition because of cash flow problems and reported a $62 million loss for 1999. In April, 2000 an audit cast doubt about its solvency. All together, CCA and Prison Trust Realty Trust lost $265 million in 1999.[37]

One of CCA's shareholders, Pacific Life Insurance Company, offered a $200 million restructuring plan, while Lehman Brothers refinanced Prison Realty's $1 billion credit line. At the close of business on April 26, 2000 prices closed below $3 per share and on June 7 the stock went back down to $2 per share. However, the very next week the stock rose by $1 per share after news that they had been awarded a $780 million federal contract thanks to the assistance of the former head of the Federal Bureau of Prisons, Michael Quinlan, who became a board member of Prison Realty Trust (typical of private prison companies, which often lure former prison officials to be on their board of directors). A report on the website of The Tennessean noted that two former executives for Prison Realty Trust were to receive severance payments totaling $1.3 million. According to this story, Prison Realty announced plans in December, 1999 to "give up its structure as a real estate investment trust and receive an infusion of up to $350 million from an investor group." (Ward, 2000). This investor group includes The Blackstone Group, Bank of America, and a group with an appropriate name, Fortress Investments (Ward, 2000).[38]

Corrections Corporation of America is still going strong, as seen in the following extract from its website: http://www.correctionscorp.com/aboutcca.html.

> CCA specializes in the design, building and management of prisons, jails and detention facilities and providing inmate residential and prisoner transportation services in partnership with government. The company is the sixth largest corrections system in the nation, behind only the federal government and three states. CCA is the founder of the private corrections industry and is the nation's largest provider of jail, detention and corrections services to governmental agencies. CCA has approximately 66,000 beds in 65 facilities, including 38 owned facilities, under contract for management in 20 states and the District of Columbia. The company manages more than 62,000 inmates including males, females and juveniles at all security levels and does business with all three federal corrections agencies, almost half of all states, and more than a dozen local municipalities. CCA continues its market leadership position in the corrections industry managing over 50% of all beds under contract with private operators in private operators in the United States. CCA joined the NYSE in 1994 and now trades under the symbol CXW.

Apparently the restructuring has paid off—according to CCA's website, the latest price of its stock was $47.22 on November 8, 2006. A facility location map shows that in Texas alone CCA operates 15 facilities and 9 are located within its home state of Tennessee.

Some Serious Problems with Privatization

One of the problems of privatization, especially when it comes to health care, is that profits are placed well above the needs of the people. Nobel Prize winning economist Milton Friedman recently stated that: "Few trends could so thoroughly undermine the very foundation of our free society as the acceptance by corporate officials of a social responsibility other than to make as much money as possible" (quoted in Wolfe, 1999: 12). The article where this comment appears also quotes St. Matthew, who said that "No man can serve two masters . . . you cannot serve God and mammon." In this article it was noted that one of the recent trends in managed care is the phenomenon of "unprofitable patients" who have been "dumped by HMO's because, as a result of their age and attendant medical problems, they were not profitable enough" (Wolfe, 1999: 12). The article then noted the irony that "what is bad news for the dumped patients is obviously good news for Wall Street and the insurance company owners" (1999: 12). The article includes a quote from an editorial in the *New England Journal of Medicine,* which stated:

> The most serious objection to such [investor-owned] care is that it embodies a new value system that severs the communal roots and Samaritan traditions of hospitals,

makes doctors and nurses the instruments of investors, and views patients as commodities. . . . In our society, some aspects of life are off-limits to commerce. We prohibit the selling of children and the buying of wives, juries and kidneys . . . health care is too precious, intimate, and corruptible to entrust to the market (Wolfe, 1999: 11).

The same can be said with the privatization of prisons.

We have seen numerous instances of serious problems with the privatization of prisons and other components of the criminal justice system. Not that the prison system has been all that successful in reducing crime, mind you, but at least prison administrators, and in fact the entire criminal justice system, are at least theoretically accountable to the public, since tax dollars support it. With privatization, there is no accountability. Several scandals demonstrate this, such as escapes, cost over-runs, and so on. Russell Clemens, an economist with the Department of Research for the American Federation of State, County, and Federal Employees, put the problem in perspective when he noted that the various "problems regarding security, staffing, and quality of services have plagued prison privatization from its inception" (Dyer, 2000: 203). He pointed out that in addition to numerous escapes there have been problems pertaining to both health care and food service, which characterize "the low quality of service in privately operated prisons" (2000: 203). The riots at a private prison in New Jersey operated by Esmor Corrections Corporation are illustrative. After this riot there was a lot of media coverage, with the result that Esmor's stock went from $20 per share to $7. Since this riot, numerous private-prison corporations have been caught failing to report problems within their prisons. The reason is simple: such secrecy protects shareholders "from adverse market reactions that would likely occur if a problem were to be reported" (2000: 204).

As already suggested, the profits from the existence of prisons are dependent upon the continued increase in prison admissions. What if prison admissions begin to decline? We are already seeing some evidence of this as discussed earlier.

An analysis of the impact of the privatization of prisons comes from a report by a group known as Good Jobs First. In a detailed study of 60 private prisons (constituting half the total privatized prisons in the country), they found that the promised benefits to state and local governments have failed to materialize. More importantly, however, they found that at least 73% of the prison had received a development subsidy from local, state, or federal government sources, while over one-third (37%) received low-cost construction via tax-free bonds or other government-issued debt securities, 38% received property tax abatements, and another 23% got subsidies for things like water, sewer or utility hook-ups, access roads, and so on. The two largest private companies involved in prison building, Corrections Corporation of America and Wackenhut, were heavily subsidized (78% of CCA prisons and 69% of Wackenhut's prisons were subsidized). The study could find no evidence of whether or not the privatization of prisons had the desired effects on local communities (Mattera and Khan, 2001).

Whether or not privatization of prisons continues (and there are some serious doubts that this trend will continue), prisons and jails will continue to operate, which will still guarantee steady employment for a large workforce, plus continuous profits for those businesses that provide various goods and services (security devices, food, linen, and so on).

Private Security: Crime Is Good for Business

Another part of this complex is the private security business, which is perhaps one of the fastest growing industries in the nation. The total amount of expenditures within this industry came to $52 billion in 1990. In 1990, the private security industry employed over 1.5 million people, outnumbering police officers by a 2:1 margin. In that year more than 2.6% of the workforce was employed in the private security industry, double the percentage it was in 1970 (Farnham, 1992). The latest figures show that this ratio is about 3:1, with more than $100 billion, dwarfing law enforcement expenditures of around $40 billion. This increase has occurred despite an overall drop in reported serious crime during the same period of time. The key, say industry analysts, is that the public still does not feel safe (Buss, 1996).

Owners of businesses are concerned over liability for crimes committed on their premises, which could cost them a great deal even if one preventable incident occurred. Also, overall costs of most security devices have been declining. One company that is benefiting from the public's fear of crime is Security World, a chain of eight stores owned by Winner Corporation of Sharon, Pennsylvania. This is the company that made The Club (auto theft protector) popular. Another big seller is central alarm systems, which accounts for about $3 billion per year in sales (Buss, 1996).

These businesses have a lot to worry about. A study of 197 lawsuits filed against businesses by crime victims found that, of the cases that went to a jury, the awards averaged from $2.2 million for wrongful deaths to $700,000 for robberies. Juries awarded such damages when it was determined that the business lacked adequate security. Insurance companies are encouraging businesses to purchase extra crime insurance, warning businesses "Don't risk a lot for a little" (Buss, 1996).

Private security products for the home is one other example of the cashing in on crime frenzy. According to *Common Cause Magazine*, the American public spent $65 billion on private security products in 1993. It is estimated that this should increase to $104 billion by 2000. Obviously this is fueled by the public's fear of crime, rather the reality of crime. From 1988 to 1992, the sales of home security products increased by 32%. *Common Cause Magazine* estimated that by 1997 one out of every five American homes will be wired with some private security device. This worries law enforcement since about 95% of all home alarm calls received by the police turn out to be false. Thus it is not surprising that the police rarely place such alarm calls on their priority list (*Common Cause Magazine*, 1995).

The residential security market is estimated to be about a $5 billion industry with sales estimated to increase by as much as 30% to 50% during the 1990s. Sales of new home security devices increased by 30% in 1993 alone. Costs range from Radio Shacks simple $9.95 personal alarm to more than $10,000 (Fitzgerald, 1994). Honeywell, ADT Security Systems, and AT&T are leading the pack. Sales in these alarms went from $4 billion in 1986 to $6 billion in 1993, an increase of 50%. Revenues from automobile security devices increased by 15% in 1993, to $540 million. The market for nonlethal weapons, such as mace, is estimated to be around $300 million (Server, 1994). Another company cashing in on crime is Counter Technology, Inc. of Bethesda, Maryland, a company that provides a wide range of security services for its clients (e.g., sensors, fencing, alarms, etc.). The company grew from a mere $88,000 in revenues in 1987 to $14 million in 1994, a jump of more than 1500% (Litvan, 1995).

Private security police, or "rent-a-cop," is another booming industry. During the 1980s, this industry grew at twice the rate of public law enforcement agencies and received 70% more funds. Pinkerton's is among the leaders with revenues exceeding $600 million. There are more than 57,000 private security firms in the country. Presently there are two security guards for every federal, state, and local police officer (Carlson, 1995).

Wackenhut Corporation is the leader in security guard services with contracts with the U.S. Department of Energy, the State Department, and NASA. Revenues in 1990 exceeded $500 million with profits of almost $7 million ($1.80 a share for stockholders). An international firm, it operates prisons and jails in more than 40 countries (Millman, 1991).

Westec Security is a private patrol service, which patrols, for a fee, exclusive neighborhoods. These guards drive around neighborhoods 24 hours a day. The cost per home is $85 per month. Borg-Warner Security has a contract to patrol certain sections of Washington, D.C.'s Georgetown neighborhood with foot patrols. Protection One, based in Culver City, California, earned $22 million in sales last year. The Justice Department estimates that the private protection business does $52 billion worth of business and is growing at about 8% per year. The industry employs about 1.5 million people, about 2.5 times that of public law enforcement (Munk, 1994).

Back in the late 1980s as suburban crime was growing, sales of home alarms went up 80%. Some companies were selling mace, calling it the new stocking stuffer, which one could purchase as a Christmas gift; many were displayed in a candy-cane motif. At one shop, a "fresh display of 36 canisters sold out in three days" (Farnham, 1992: 43).

Paralleling the growth in the private security industry has been the emergence of so-called gated communities. This has been perhaps most apparent in Southern California where, beginning in the late 1960s, literally millions of affluent whites fled to outlying regions, such as Simi Valley to the northwest (site of the first Rodney King trial), and Orange County to the southeast. As the excellent study by Davis shows, what has occurred in this area is the development of "fortress cities" that are divided between the "fortified cells" of the affluent suburbs and "places of terror" in the inner cities (and even the once mostly white, relatively quite San Fernando Valley) "where the police battle the criminalized poor" (Davis, 1992: 224). A recent study of the national growth of these communities found that the number of gated communities went from less than 5,000 in the early 1970s to more than 20,000 as of 1996 and they are growing rapidly. A leading national real estate developer estimates that about 80% of new urban housing projects will be gated. In 1988 alone, one-third of the 140 housing developments in the well-to-do Orange County, California (next to Los Angeles County) were gated—twice the amount than five years earlier. With such developments, little wonder the title of this study is *Fortress America: Gated Communities in the United States* (Blakely and Snyder, 1997: 7).

A recent study of gated communities by Seth Low (2003) brings to mind a perfect illustration of the fort mentality and seeing crime as something inevitable, like natural disasters such as tornadoes and hurricanes. She refers to Oscar Newman's idea of defensible space to segregate the better off from the urban underclass via these gated communities. From this perspective it is useless to address the causes of crime; just fortify your communities.

Low argues that many move into such communities as a way of recapturing their childhood or at least the emotional security they had in their old neighborhoods. In other words, they miss their childhood home. Low quotes one woman who moved into a gated community with a guard house and away from one without this feature, saying that the guard house makes her feel secure. However, all of this fortification comes at a price, both social and psychological. Low asks whether children growing up in such communities become much more fearful than other children. Are such children more vulnerable to drugs, suicide, and other problems? She notes the growing child-protection industry that has capitalized on these fears "as a way to remake the home as citadel and to sell private protective technologies" (Low, 2003: 109). Some have even installed nanny cams to watch children's caretakers. Such actions have shifted the responsibility for protection from the state to private firms. This is the privatization of child care (2003: 110). This is reminiscence of old feudal societies where elites lived behind high walls with a moat around them, separating them from the peasants on the outside.

Other Components of the Crime Control Industry

There are other components of the crime control industry. One important component is the educational system, especially the thousands of criminal justice programs within colleges and universities. There are currently about 3,000 such programs in this country. Nationwide, the average budget of each department or program offering degrees in criminal justice varies considerably, and no firm estimates are available. However, if we take $500,000 (which is about the annual budget for the department where the author works), the total annual expenditures come to around $1.5 billion. Additional expenditures have come in the form of grants from various government agencies (e.g., National Institute of Justice). Total funding for research on the problem of crime in fiscal year 1993 came to $997,023, an increase of almost 700% since 1983 (Maguire and Pastore, 1998).

Other components of this industry that might be included are the following: (1) the profits made by hospitals and insurance companies (from, for instance, hospital emergency room visits, doctor's fees, insurance premiums on auto and other insurance covering crime, and so on) and the salaries of those who deal with victims (e.g., doctors, nurses, paramedics, insurance adjusters); (2) the profits from the sale of books (e.g., college textbooks, trade books), magazine and journal articles, newspaper coverage (and the advertisers who profit from crime stories), television crime shows (and their advertisers), and movies about crime (with the enormous salaries paid to actors and actresses who star in them); (3) the money collected by courts through various fines (especially traffic tickets), special courses defendants can enroll in as a condition of (or in lieu of) their sentence (e.g., traffic schools, petty larceny programs); (4) the money collected by bail bondsmen. One could no doubt think of other categories. The point is that the existence of a crime problem is extremely profitable for millions of people, a few private corporations and the government.

The irony here is that literally thousands of businesses make huge profits off the misery of others. The blood of millions of victims drips from the rafters of Wall Street and all who profit.

Notes

1. An advertising brochure from an investment firm called World Research Group, cited in Silverstein, 1998: 156.

2. Advertising brochure for the University of Phoenix, which claims that you can "earn your degree in 2 to 3 years, in most cases." It offers courses in many different locations, with classes starting almost every month. On the brochure it is noted that "According to the Bureau of Labor Statistics, the field of criminal justice will expand faster than most other occupations through 2008." Courses are taught by "experienced lieutenants, police chiefs, and captains" and "covers the latest theories, techniques, and technologies being used in criminal justice today." A business reply card is included in this brochure.

3. Duke (2000).

4. The 2006 race for the governor of Massachusetts pitted Deval Patrick (a black man and a Democrat) against Kerry Healey (a white Republican). When he was practicing law, Patrick once represented a rapist on appeal, recommending that new DNA evidence be reviewed that might prove his innocence. Healey, who trailed by a wide margin, began to bring up the case in an attempt to show Patrick was "soft on crime" (like George Bush did against Michael Dukakis in the 1998 presidential race when the case of Willie Horton came up). Among her ads was one where she asked "Do you want the next governor to be someone who lets rapists out of prison?" or words to that effect. This time the strategy backfired, as Patrick won by a landslide.

5. These programs typically rank among the top five as far as the number of majors is concerned. At my university, our undergraduate program has 800 majors, putting us second in the entire university.

6. A report in the *San Diego Union* reveals just how financially rewarding such work has become. A review of payroll figures from the California Department of Corrections showed that about 10%

of the prison guards earned in excess of $100,000, chiefly from overtime. The article noted: "Some 2,400 rank-and-file correctional officers' pay exceeded $100,000 in 2005, compared with 557 the year before, a San Diego Union-Tribune analysis of payroll figures shows. One guard grossed $187,000, making him the highest-paid correctional officer in California, according to data provided by the state controller's office. At the historic San Quentin State Prison near San Francisco, one out of five guards was paid more than $100,000 last year" (Schmidt, 2006:). Internet source, no page numbers.

7. For a detailed analysis of the phoniness of the war on drugs see Baum (1997) and Gordon (1994); for a discussion of the war on gangs see Shelden et al. (2004) and Klein (1995).

8. John Maynard Keynes, an early 20th century economist, was most popular for his theory about how government expenditures could stimulate a stagnating economy. In this particular case, expenditures on prisons, jails, courtrooms, police cars, and so on stimulates the economy, creating thousands of jobs in the process.

9. Sourcebook on Criminal Justice Statistics. http://www.albany.edu/sourcebook/pdf/t2332005.pdf and http://www.albany.edu/sourcebook/pdf/t2372005.pdf.

10. These ads are found on pages 27, 90, and 100. This issue of *Corrections Today* includes the annual Buyers Guide containing about 100 pages of ads for about 150 different companies.

11. Sourcebook on Criminal Justice Statistics. http://www.albany.edu/sourcebook/pdf/t14.pdf.

12. Sourcebook on Criminal Justice Statistics. http://www.albany.edu/sourcebook/pdf/t121.pdf and http://www.albany.edu/sourcebook/pdf/t119.pdf.

13. Bureau of Justice Statistics, *Census of State and Federal Correctional Facilities, 2000.* http://www.ojp.usdoj.gov/bjs/abstract/csfcf00.htm.

14. For more detail on the American empire abroad, see Johnson (2004).

15. Sourcebook on Criminal Justice Statistics http://www.albany.edu/sourcebook/pdf/t112003.pdf.

16. Fox_News.com, Jan. 23, 2003.

17. U.S. Census Bureau http://www.census.gov/Press-Release/www/2003/cb03-ff04se.html; see also Johnson (2004: 102).

18. http://costofwar.com/.

19. Also missing from these estimates are the public school security police officers, for which there are no national data available. See Wallace and Pullman (2004).

20. Readers should note that these figures are updated twice each year. To keep up with these trends it may be advisable to bookmark the Bureau of Justice Statistics website: http://www.ojp.usdoj.gov/bjs/.

21. The FBI publishes an annual report called "Crime in the United States, Uniform Crime Reports." http://www.fbi.gov/ucr/05cius/data/table_29.html.

22. "7 Federal Prisons to Get Lethal Electrified Fences." *Washington Post*, July 12, 2005.

23. These ads were selected from several issues of *Corrections Today*, spanning the past 10 years.

24. http://www.capitalresearch.org.

25. http://www.alec.org.

26. www.americanradioworks.org.

27. Ibid. California prison guards have not been without their own share of controversies, including criminal conduct ranging from having sex with prisoners, running drugs into prison, and even manslaughter. One story, appeared the day before the article about complaints against prisoner education programs, cited numerous criminal incidents against some guards, noting that several who are under investigation are collecting their full salary plus benefits while on paid leave. An estimated 109 prison guards were on paid leave for at least 30 days during the past year, mostly while under investigation. The costs to taxpayers are estimated to be "in the millions" (Morain, 2003). Space does not permit a complete discussion of this topic.

28. Ibid; see also Clement (2002).

29. http://www.doc.state.ok.us/Private%20Prisons/privatep.htm.

30. Greene and Roche (2003). These states include Florida, Illinois, Michigan, Ohio, Utah, and Virginia. Other states, like New York, Texas, and Nevada, have downsized unneeded prison space by closing prison housing units.

31. Huling (2002: 202). I have been to Tehachapi on numerous occasions over the years and have been this development first-hand (my parents once lived there).

32. http://www.vadoc.state.va.us/facilities/institutions/redonion.htm.

33. http://www.mdoc.state.ms.us; Camp and Camp, 2000.

34. http://www.state.sc.us/scdc/.

35. The 1987 figures are from Austin and Irwin (2001: 66); the 2001 figures are from Charles Logan's "Private Prisons" (http://www.ucc.uconn.edu/~logan/).

36. www.paulsjusticepage.com/crimepays.story.htm.

37. www.paulsjusticepage.com/crimepays.story.htm.

38. I got onto Fortress Investment's website and found the following statement: "Fortress currently manages over $2.1 billion of private equity capital on behalf of prominent institutional investors and high net worth individuals in two funds:

- Fortress Investment Fund II LLC, a $1.25 billion fund closed in February 2003
- Fortress Investment Fund LLC, an $873 million fund closed in April 2000

The private equity funds primarily make control-oriented investments in asset-based businesses and asset portfolios in the United States and Western Europe. The funds target cash flowing investments that can be acquired at attractive valuations due to structural complexity, distress, or general disfavor within the capital markets. The investment objective of the funds is to generate attractive private equity returns combined with significant downside protection in the form of tangible collateral. Asset-based sectors in which the private equity funds have been active investors include financial services, real estate, energy and power, senior living and the cell tower sector." http://www.fortress-inv.com/site_content.aspx?p=12.

8

Where Do We Go from Here?

Any attempt to reform the criminal justice system, to make it better at achieving justice or reducing crime by any significant amount must confront the existence of the crime control industry and all the profits made off the existence of crime. In short, the criminal justice system—the crime control industry—has, ironically, a vested interested in *not* reducing crime to any great extent. True, we may try to make the current system more efficient at capturing and convicting criminals, but that does not generally result in any significant reduction in the overall rate of crime. Indeed, we have already shown that despite huge increases in expenditures on the criminal justice system over the past 20 years or so, the overall rate of crime has changed little.

The previous chapters on the history of the American criminal justice system should have demonstrated to the reader a systemic class, racial, and gender bias. As the modern crime control industry continues to grow, and as the economy continues to boom for a small segment of the population, while almost completely ignoring the majority, the criminal justice system will continue to target those deemed dangerous, superfluous, and so on. Fighting crime has indeed become a big business with a vested interest in processing more and more citizens through the criminal justice system.

In reviewing the history of criminal justice what we are actually reviewing is the continuous attempt to control crime and in so doing this has been in effect, if not in design, an attempt to engage in the control of the dangerous classes, however this group has been defined over the years. Since crime is still very much with us, perhaps in the new millennium we should be looking elsewhere for our answers.

Although I do not claim to have all the answers, after more than 35 years of studying and teaching about the subject of crime and delinquency, I am convinced that some very fundamental changes need to be made in the way we live and think before we see any significant decrease in these problems. I have previously published these ideas when I was referring to confronting youth crime, but this can also apply to crime in general (Shelden, 1998, 2006). One of the key ideas that I was attempting to convey was this: We are always talking about the problem of delinquency or the problem of youth

306

or that youth in trouble need to change their attitudes, their behaviors, their lifestyles, their methods of thinking, and so on. It seems that it is always they who have to change.

What is invariably included in this line of thinking is the use of labels to describe these youth (and adult offenders too). The labels keep changing, along with changing times. As Jerome Miller has noted (Miller, 1998: 234), we began with possessed youths in the 17th century, moved to the rabble or dangerous classes in the 18th and late 19th centuries, the moral imbeciles and the constitutional psychopathic inferiors of the early 20th centuries. We continued with the psychopath of the 1940s to the sociopath of the 1950s and finally to more recent labels like compulsive delinquent, the learning disabled, the unsocialized aggressive and even the socialized aggressive, and finally the bored delinquent. "With the growth of professionalism, the number of labels has multiplied exponentially" (1998: 234). Miller continues by suggesting that the problem with these labels is that it seems to be a way "whereby we bolster the maintenance of the existing order against threats which might arise from its own internal contradictions" (1998: 234). And it reassures us "that the fault lies in the warped offender and takes everyone else off the hook. Moreover, it enables the professional diagnostician to enter the scene or withdraw at will, wearing success like a halo and placing failure around the neck of the client like a noose" (1998: 234). More importantly, we continue to believe that harsh punishment works, especially the kind of punishment that includes some form of incarceration, so that the offender is placed out of sight and, not coincidentally, out of mind.

But there is a problem here. As noted in this book, throughout the past couple of centuries we have continued to succumb to the edifice complex. We love to build these edifices, no matter what they are called (a new courthouse, a new prison, a new correctional center, a new police station, and so on). Perhaps it is because politicians like to have some kind of permanent structure to leave behind as a legacy so they can tell the people who voted for them to look at this or that building as proof they have done something about crime. Or perhaps it is because they are so profitable and are part of the huge crime control industry. I believe otherwise. I believe that we need to quit looking solely at the troubled youth or criminals as the main source of the problem, or even their troubled families and troubled communities. The problem is much bigger and it goes to the very depth of the nature of American society, to its most basic institutions, especially the economic institution. It is my firm belief that any serious attempt to reduce crime and to achieve social justice will have to first confront the problem of social inequality, which is obviously tied into the economy.

The Importance of the Economy

Today the concentration of wealth and power has narrowed to a point more than any other era in American history. As these words are being written (January, 2007), one of the biggest domestic issues is the economy. The biggest foreign policy issue is the war in Iraq, which continues to drain the treasury of much needed funds (the price tag is at least $350 billion, with some estimates putting to total direct and indirect costs at more than $1 trillion).[1] Certainly it is true that the official unemployment rate is at one of the lowest points in many years. However, it is not so much unemployment that is at issue, for many jobs have been created in recent years. The issue is how well these jobs pay. We have entered into an era where we can be classified as a low wage society. A story in the *Los Angeles Times* back in the fall of 2004 caught my eye and it illustrates this issue very well.

The story centered on Green Bay, Wisconsin, which was the nation's fifth-fastest-growing job market in June, 2004 having tied Laredo, Texas for first place the previous month. While new jobs have been created in Green Bay, the vast majority pay about half of what manufacturing jobs paid. In June, 6,100 jobs were added and 4,800 were in the low-paying service industry, and only 1,300 in manufacturing and construction. The largest gains (2,200) came in the leisure and hospitality fields, which pay an average of $9 an hour, compared to the $18.55 average for all Green Bay employees. Many of Green Bay's displaced workers were with the Paper Converting Machine Company, one of the top-paying companies in the city. According to the story in the *Los Angeles Times*, in recent years the company "has been engaged in a Darwinian competition with overseas rivals that have the advantage of lower costs and undervalued currencies. It has reduced its Green Bay workforce from 1,625 to 918. The company has also wrangled wage concessions from its production workers, lowering the average hourly pay from $22.50 to about $19." The paper industry has been going downhill in recent years and Procter and Gamble shut down one of its plants this year, laying off 135 workers. Georgia-Pacific Corporation, the city's biggest employer, recently announced plans to eliminate 200 mill jobs. Meanwhile, a casino was opened near the airport—a phenomenon common all over the country—with just over 3,000 workers. This is a huge growth industry, but the pay is nothing compared to the old manufacturing jobs. Tourism, one of the largest industries in Green Bay and all over the country, brings in a lot of money to businesses, but creates mostly low-paying jobs (Vieth, 2004). This is the nature of capitalism.

How does this relate to crime? One of the most popular sociological theories of crime is known as strain or anomie theory (Messner and Rosenfeld, 2001). This theory argues that crime stems from the lack of articulation or fit between two of the most basic components of society: culture and social structure.[2] Here we refer to culture as consisting of (1) the main value and goal orientations or ends and (2) the institutionalized or legitimate means for attaining these goals. Social structure, as used here, consists of the basic social institutions of society, especially the economy, but also such institutions as the family, education, and politics, all of which are responsible for distributing access to the legitimate means for obtaining goals.

This lack of fit creates strain within individuals, who respond with various forms of deviance. Thus people who find themselves at a disadvantage relative to legitimate economic activities are motivated to engage in illegitimate activities (perhaps because of unavailability of jobs, lack of job skills, education, and other factors). Within a capitalist society like United States, the main emphasis is on the success goals, while less emphasis is on the legitimate means to achieve these goals. Moreover, these goals have become institutionalized in that they are deeply embedded into the psyches of everyone via a very powerful system of corporate propaganda.[3] At the same time, the legitimate means are not as well defined or as strongly ingrained. In other words, there is a lot of discretion and a lot of tolerance for deviance from the means but not the goals. One result of such a system is high levels of crime.[4]

This view obviously focuses on the importance of the economic institution in generating crime and delinquency. Strong emphasis is therefore placed on the salience of American capitalism in producing certain strains upon its citizens. The economic structure of American capitalism needs to be discussed, especially how it relates to crime and delinquency. Before continuing, a few words need to be said about American capitalism. While a complete and thorough analysis of the capitalist system is beyond the purview of this chapter, some introductory comments seem in order.

American-Style Capitalism Is the Real Culprit

Briefly stated, capitalism is one of several methods whereby societies attempt to meet the basic needs of its citizens in terms of production, and the distribution and consumption of goods and services.[5] Often called the mode of production this economic system consists of two essential parts: (1) the forces (or means) of production (the raw materials, tools, instruments, machines, buildings, and so on, plus the current state of science and technology, and the skills, abilities, and knowledge of the people themselves) and (2) the relations of production, which can be defined as "the specific manner in which the surplus is produced and then appropriated from the direct producers" (Edwards et al., 1986: 7–8).

These relations are essentially class relations, the most common of which are between the owners/managers and the workers (salary and wage earners). The more popular term is that of *social class*, which may be defined as "a group of individuals or families who occupy a similar position in the economic system of production, distribution, and consumption of goods and services in industrial societies" (Rothman, 1999: 5). The most common indicator of one's social class position is that of occupation. Indeed, it can be said that the work people engage in limits their financial status (income and wealth), their social status or prestige, the stability of their employment, the chances for upward social mobility, their general health and longevity, plays a key role in the way they think of themselves, places them within the larger systems of power and authority, and has significant implications for the future of their children. Indeed, in the words of Erik Wright, "class counts" (Wright, 2000). There is probably no other social variable that has a more significant bearing on one's life chances and lifestyles, including the probability of becoming defined as a criminal or delinquent.[6]

Several key questions immediately arise when analyzing capitalism, such as who owns the means of production and who decides how the surplus is to be distributed. The term *surplus* refers to the "difference between the volume of production needed to maintain the work force and the volume of production the work force produces" (Heilbroner, 1985: 33)—meaning, very generally, the margin over and above what is required to meet basic needs and reproduce society (Heilbroner, 1985: 33).

Under most forms of capitalism in today's world, the relations of production are marked by an almost total separation of the workers (i.e., producers) from the means of production. One class—usually referred to as the capitalist class or ruling class— owns most of the means of production (that is to say, a small group, around 1% to 2% of the total population) own most of the factories, land, buildings, wealth, income, and other assets, which in turn translates into an enormous amount of power in society. What is important to note is the fact that wealth itself in its current form is not an end in itself, but rather it is a *"means for gathering more wealth"* which in turn serves "to augment the power of a dominant class" (Heilbroner, 1985: 35).

It is also important to note that inherent in this power relationship is the fact that the typical worker has no choice but to "sell their labor power" (Heilbroner, 1985: 35) to the capitalist. What is especially important here is the fact that possessing capital in all of its forms and owning the means of production leads very directly to the most important ingredient in the relations of production, namely domination. Unlike other forms of domination in history (like the domination of the army, church, and so on) this form involves the power to refuse to sell commodities or buy labor power (Heilbroner, 1985: 39–40). The example of Green Bay, Wisconsin noted previously illustrates the power the large corporations have in simply picking up and moving their factories to low-wage foreign countries.

One crucial difference between the capitalist system and other systems is the drive for profit, which can be almost an obsession. As Heilbroner so aptly puts it, one unique feature of capitalism is "the restless and insatiable drive to accumulate capital" (Heilbroner, 1985: 42). Heilbroner suggests that this can be explained in part by the desire to obtain prestige and distinction among one's fellow human beings, something that was pointed out by Adam Smith. More than any other measure of prestige and distinction, the possession of capital "confers on its owners the ability to direct and mobilize the activities of society..." In short, it is capital that calls the tune and that control over the access to capital "invests their owner with an attribute that goes beyond prestige and preeminence." "This," says Heilbroner "is power." Moreover, wealth itself becomes *"a social category inseparable from power."* And "wealth can only come into existence when the right of access of all members of society to an independent livelihood no longer prevails, so that control over this access becomes of life-giving importance." Quoting Adam Smith, Heilbroner gets to the essence of capitalist society, especially in modern American society, namely that: "Wherever there is great property, there is great inequality. For on rich man, there must be at least five hundred poor, and the affluence of the rich supposes the indigence of the many."[7]

Within our capitalist system, power and control seems to be one of the most distinctive characteristics. The desire to have power and control over others tends to permeate throughout the society, whether we are talking about owners of large multinational corporations or leaders of drug gangs trying to maintain power and control over their local drug markets. It is essentially the same phenomenon, although on much different scales. Within a capitalist society there tends to be an insatiable desire to continue "converting money into commodities and commodities into money." Everything, it seems, is turned into a commodity—from the simplest products (e.g., paper and pencil) to human beings (e.g., women's bodies, slaves). More importantly, the size of one's wealth has no bounds. As suggested earlier, capital rules![8] Indeed, "daily life is scanned for possibilities that can be brought within the circuit of accumulation," since any aspect of society that can produce a profit will be exploited, including the misery and suffering of people who have been victimized by crime (Heilbroner, 1985: 60). Life itself has been commodified.[9]

The accumulation of capital, and hence great wealth and inequality, would not be possible without the assistance of the state. Instead of Smith's "invisible hand of the market" (what is often erroneously called a free market), we have profits that are secured with the assistance of the government, both state and local, in the form of tax loopholes, subsidies and other forms of what is essentially taxpayer assistance. Some call this corporate welfare.[10] In fact, the entire idea of free market capitalism is a myth. As a matter of fact, big business could not exist (and has never existed) without strong support from the government—and hence taxpayers. A recent study by two economists in Holland found that every one of the top 100 transnational corporations in the world (*Fortune* magazine's list) has benefited in some way from their host government; in fact, at least 20 would have folded if they were not given large subsidies from their governments when they faced serious trouble. In fact, true capitalism has never really existed in this country.[11]

The key point that needs to be made here is that capitalism, while bringing about a virtual cornucopia of goods and a standard of living that is the envy of the world, has its negative effects, which is that it produces a tremendous amount of inequality. Within a capitalist system, especially that which exists in American society, such inequality is inevitable and a natural by-product of the system itself. And despite the so-called economic boom in recent years, inequality has become worse.

One of the key concepts originally developed by Karl Marx was the term *reserve army* or *surplus population*. These terms refer to a more or less chronically unemployed or underemployed segment of the population, primarily because of mechanization that renders them redundant and hence superfluous as far as producing profits is concerned. This segment helps keep wages down and is absorbed back into the general working population when labor is scarce. This group is also a "lever of capitalistic accumulation" and in fact is "a condition of existence of the capitalist mode of production" (Giddens, 1971: 57).

What should be made clear is that within a capitalist economic system the development of these class distinctions, especially the existence of a surplus population, is inevitable. Capitalism produces several contradictions, one of which is that between capital and labor or owners and workers. Each group wants to improve their status; specifically, each group wants more of the benefits from the profits derived from production. The owners want more profit, while workers want higher wages and/or more benefits (including better working conditions). This has been a continuous conflict (which is why many call this class conflict inevitable in capitalist societies) throughout the history of capitalism and the battles have usually been won by the owners, although workers have made some very significant gains over the years (but not without constant struggles). Recently, the owners of large corporations have made the most gains. One indication is that while in 1960 the average CEO earned 41 times more than the average worker; by 2003 that ratio had risen to 315 to 1![12]

Whenever there is a discussion of the "underclass" or the poor in general it is really about this "surplus population." This surplus population is an inevitable by-product of *American* capitalism. I emphasize American capitalism for an important reasons: other capitalist democracies (e.g., especially France, Germany, Japan, the Scandinavian countries, and so on) do not have the high degree of inequality and poverty, and hence crime, as exists in the United States, mainly because of the existence of strong institutions like the family and the church that are able to offset the excesses of capitalism. The Norwegian criminologist, Nils Christie, noted that there is a huge difference in incarceration rates between the United States and our northern neighbor Canada. Canada's incarceration rate is about 129, about one-fifth our rate. He also notes that these two countries are essentially the same (in terms of the economic and political systems) except for one important difference: Canada has more of a social safety net (various welfare benefits) than does the United States (Christie, 2000: 31). James Whitman's comparative study of Europe and the United States found huge differences in punishment philosophies and practices, resulting in, among other things, a far greater reliance on imprisonment in the United States—not to mention a higher crime rate. The main reason stems from Europe's social support network, which is lagging far behind in America (Whitman, 2003).

The best-selling book by Barbara Ehrenreich, with the appropriate title *Nickel and Dimed: On (Not) Getting by in America,* presents some of the richest qualitative (and some quantitative) data on current situation under modern American capitalism (Ehrenreich, 2001). It is not a pretty picture. Ehrenreich spent the better part of a year actually working in six different low-wage jobs and trying to make ends meet during this time. The stories she tells of the lives of herself and co-workers reveal the underside of the "American Dream" and the failure of our so-called market economy. The six or eight dollars an hour these workers are making put them all under the official poverty level. Most have to augment their meager wages with either a second job or depend a lot upon other workers in the household (usually a spouse, which in most cases is a husband, since most of the low-wage workers Ehrenreich worked with were women). Even with such additional help, they all struggled daily and their jobs required hard and rather boring labor.

If Ehrenreich's picture is gloomy, think for a moment that these are working poor, which should cause us to ask: what about the nonworking poor? These persons are among what Wilson has called the truly disadvantaged (Wilson, 1987, 1996). A cursory look at the hard data of economic inequality presents still another gloomy picture. If the figures were not bad enough already in the mid-to-late 1990s, here in the early years of the 21st century the situation is even worse. Inequality, in the richest of all nations in the history of the world, is even greater, with a mere 1% of the population possessing almost half of all financial wealth (as noted in the first chapter). Meanwhile, social supports that might reduce poverty and inequality just a bit have been either eliminated altogether or reduced so much that they barely make a difference.

It should be noted that Ehrenreich documented that perhaps the most pressing concern of these working poor was that of finding affordable house and health care. As for house, it almost seems that the nation's housing program consists of recently constructed prisons and jails, which have experienced a boom in the past decade (Shelden and Brown, 2003; Mauer and Chesney-Lind, 2002). As for health care, report after report documents the decline of adequate and affordable health care for a growing number of citizens. The most recent data found that about 75 million Americans lacked health insurance at some point during 2001 or 2002, putting incredible strains on emergency services. As of early 2003, around 16.5% of all citizens lack health insurance, which means around 46 million people (Schmid, 2003). Another source puts the current figure as around 41 million people (Lieberman, 2003: 3–4). Regardless of which figure is accurate, way too many people lack affordable health care.

Moreover, the continuing economic woes facing the country, plus the growing deficits, must necessarily impact millions of families, especially the nation's poor and most marginalized populations. Perhaps more importantly, the spending on the war on terrorism and the conflict in Iraq has already resulted in a budgetary crisis in virtually every state in the nation. The inevitable cutbacks that will certainly follow will naturally have the most negative impact on the lives of ordinary people, but especially the poorest of our citizens. The world inhabited by the poor and the near poor, including Ehrenreich's low-wage workers, must look very bleak at this time.

Downsizing and Outsourcing the American Dream and the Growing Surplus Population

We are presently in the midst of an important era in history, the last stage of the Industrial Revolution (Eitzen and Zinn, 1998: 188–192). Like previous transformations (e.g., from agriculture to manufacturing) several forces are operating to produce this change. These are (1) technological, (2) the globalization of the economy, (3) the movement of capital, and (4) the overall shift of the economy away from manufacturing to information and services.

Among the most important technological changes is the computer chip, which has led to the replacement of many workers by computers and robots. This has, in turn, resulted in a loss of millions of unskilled and semiskilled jobs.

The second force is the globalization of the economy. Presently the U.S. economy is part of a much more competitive world economy. To increase their profits in this competitive world economy, U.S. corporations have had to cut costs, usually by laying off workers or closing plants. The decline in manufacturing has been especially pronounced as will be discussed in the following paragraphs.

The third force involves the movement of capital, or capital flight. This is a process whereby companies have invested overseas, relocated plants within the United States, or engaged in mergers with other corporations. All of these efforts have had the effect of eliminating the jobs of many workers. In fact, multinational corporations that are based in the United States have huge investments in foreign countries, and many pay few if any income taxes.[13] More and more U.S. corporations are finding it very profitable to move most of their manufacturing to Third World countries, where labor is cheap, there are no unions, and there are no restrictions on child labor (and most of this labor is reminiscent of sweatshops in the 19th century) or on worker safety. More than 1,100 American factories (e.g., Ford, General Motors, and RCA) are in northern Mexico (Eitzen and Zinn, 1998: 190).[14]

As already noted, the movement from manufacturing to service has been significant. Whereas in 1960, 31% of the labor force was employed in manufacturing industries, by 2004 this percentage had shrunk by almost two-thirds to a mere 13% (Fisher and Rupert, 2005). In 2004, there were 14 million manufacturing jobs, compared to just under 20 million in 1979 (Congressional Budget Office, 2004). In contrast, the percentage employed in service-producing industries (e.g., transportation, public utilities, retail trade, and services) went from 62% to almost 80%, with the specific category of services accounting for the largest increase (from 13.6% to 28%) (Sklar, 1998). From 1973 to 1989 about 35 million jobs were created, and most of these were in the service sector and about half involved few skills and were low paying. Between 1988 and 1993, 1.7 million high-wage, mostly blue-collar manufacturing jobs were lost, while about a million were created in the lowest-paid service sectors.

As already noted, today the United States could be described as a low-wage society. The average weekly earnings of workers (in 1997 dollars) went from $494 in 1973 to $424 in 1997. As of 1990 an estimated 18% of full-time workers were classified as living under the official poverty line, compared to 12% in 1979 (Bernstein and Gould, 2006). One report recently noted that "More than two-thirds of all poor families with children included one or more individuals who worked in 2003. These individuals typically work a significant amount; in 2002 (data for 2003 are not yet available), family members in working-poor families with children worked a combined total of 46 weeks per year on average" (Center on Budget and Policy Priorities, 2004: 200).[15]

The average wage in constant dollars for full-time workers declined in the late 1970s following a steady increase from the early 1950s. Since the late 1970s wages have leveled off. In short, in terms of what the dollar can purchase, the wages of the typical worker have not changed in 20 years! The effects on the typical male worker have been especially negative. The average male worker has been most affected by these changes. The median earnings of males have decreased, while wages for females have increased, which is partly explained by the rise in low-wage workers from 7.4% of the labor force in the mid-1970s to 13.9% in 1990. In fact, many male workers have in effect disappeared from the labor force. While in the early 1950s almost 90% of the men in America were in the labor force (meaning they were either working or actively seeking work), by the mid-1990s this percentage had shrunk to about 75%.

The average weekly wages, adjusted for inflation, in 2001 were still 13.3% less than their peak value in 1972. Growth in workers' incomes is dropping sharply. In 2001, average annual pay for U.S. workers grew by only 2.5%, down from a 5.9% increase in 2000 (U.S. Department of Labor, 2003).

The data reported in Figure 8.1 tells the story in a nutshell about the changing distribution of wealth and income. In the post–World War II growth period (1947–1979) it was literally the case that a "rising tide lifts all boats." However, since that time it has been more like a "rising tide lifts all yachts."

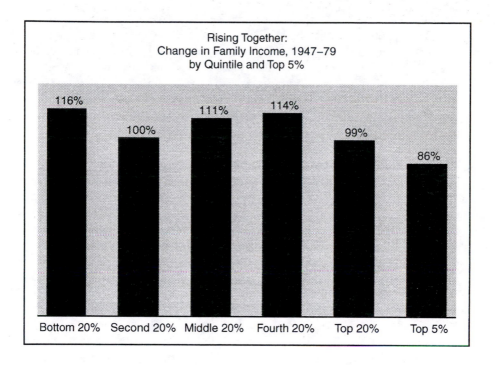

Rising Together:
Change in Family Income, 1947–79
by Quintile and Top 5%

116%   100%   111%   114%   99%   86%

Bottom 20%   Second 20%   Middle 20%   Fourth 20%   Top 20%   Top 5%

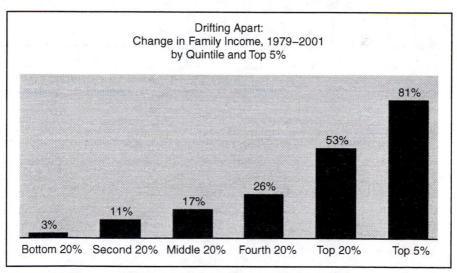

Drifting Apart:
Change in Family Income, 1979–2001
by Quintile and Top 5%

3%   11%   17%   26%   53%   81%

Bottom 20%   Second 20%   Middle 20%   Fourth 20%   Top 20%   Top 5%

FIGURE 8.1   **Income and Wealth Inequality in the United States**.

Source: Analysis of U.S. Census Bureau data in Economic Policy Institute, *The State of Working America 1994–95* (M. E. Sharpe: 1994) p. 37; and U.S. Census Bureau, Historical Income Tables, Table F-3. Cited in: "A Quarter-Century of Growing Inequality," Inequality.org (http://www.inequality.org/facts.html).

During the past four decades the percentage of women in the labor force went from just over 30% to about 60%. A portion of the gains for women may be accounted for by the incredible increase in the proportion of workers employed as temporary workers. In fact, the number of temporary workers increased by 211% between 1970 and 1990. A report from the National Association of Temporary and Staffing Services (the mere existence of this organization is itself most significant) reveals that in the last quarter of 1998 there were 2.94 million temporary workers, up from 1.17 million in 1990. Three-fourths of these workers are employed in two major categories: clerical (40.5%) and industrial (34.5%). Manpower, Inc. and Kelly Temporary Services are among the leading employers in America today, with profits in recent years increasing much faster than most other companies (Folbre, 1995).

Temporary workers are utilized more often in the last two decades and the trend appears to be one which will continue. Labor unions and others decry this use as an exploitation of those who are unskilled and/or uneducated. The temporary workers are, for the most part, using the services of temporary help agencies—thus reducing their net amount of pay (Estevao and Lach, 2001: ii).

Another way of describing this process is what Bluestone and Harrison have called deindustrialization, which is the reduction in our nation's rank in the world economy (Bluestone and Harrison, 1982). A specific example of this occurred in New York City. Between 1970 and 1984 approximately 500,000 jobs, which were in industries that did not require a high school diploma, were lost. These were mostly unskilled and semiskilled jobs typically filled by minorities and young people. During this same period of time the city gained about 240,000 jobs in industries that required more than a high school diploma (Schorr, 1989: 301).

As of 2001, there were about 105 million households (282 million people; in late 2006 we passed the 300 million mark) in America. Of the 105 million households, 25% were single member households while the remaining 75% had two or more members. There were 26% under 18. Most Americans (70%) at that time earned less than $50,000 a year; 31 million of the total households in America earned from $25,000 to $50,000. The typical American household had a net worth of less than $15,000 (U.S. Department of Commerce, 2001). One is certainly tempted to conclude that the American Dream is dead.

While all of this has been going on, the share of the total wealth going to the top wealth holders has been on an upward move since the late 1960s, as noted in the introductory chapter of this book. In short, wealth and power are concentrated more than ever before. All of these recent changes have come during a period of economic prosperity for the country as a whole. A recent series of in-depth articles in the *Los Angeles Times* illustrates the paradox of rising prosperity, but growing insecurity among more and more citizens.[16] This series focused on several families who, by all appearances, are hard workers trying to achieve the American Dream, but through a series of economic shifts, illnesses, or just plain bad luck, had fallen on hard times and experienced unusually high income swings during the course of a single year. The author of this series of reports summarized the apparent paradox of prosperity this way:

> Throughout this series, the *Times* has sought to make sense of an American paradox: why so many people report being less financially secure even as the nation, by many

measures, has grown far more prosperous. The answer, the newspaper has found, *lies in the shifting of economic risks from the broad shoulders of business and government to the backs of working families.*

> Over the last quarter of a century, many safeguards that people once counted on to shield them from financial harm have been weakened or completely lost. These include formal protections such as guaranteed corporate pensions and state and federal unemployment benefits. And they include informal ones, like the loyalty that employers once showed their workers by offering secure jobs with relatively little prospect of long-term layoff. Other cushions that families like the Ryans [one of the families interviewed for this report] have relied on, such as the financial stability that comes with a college education, also have eroded (Gosselin, 2004c; emphasis added).

Several statements in the above quote seem to put the major problem in larger perspective and echoes what many economists (many quoted in this chapter) have been saying in recent years, namely, that in this age of prosperity the wealth trickles up and not down. The safeguards once provided under an informal social contract with corporate America are no longer there. There appears to be a "let them eat cake" attitude.

Likewise, the proportion of Americans living in poverty has increased. As inequality has grown, the social conditions of the most disadvantaged sectors of society have worsened. Massive cutbacks on social spending for programs for the poor have been especially devastating to children. Indeed, one of the most striking facts is that more than one in five children (and over half of all African-American children) now live in poverty. Millions more live under near poverty conditions. The definition of poverty is based upon a certain amount of money needed for a low standard of living—typically a very bare-bones minimum level, for instance, $16,450 for a family of four as of 1998. According to these criteria, 13.3% of all Americans were living in poverty as of 1997; for children (under 18) the rate was 20%. Not surprisingly, racial differences are significant. Thus, for both African Americans and Hispanics the rate was about 27%, more than double the rate for whites (11%). For African-American and Hispanic children the rates were about 37% (Collins and Yeskel, 2005: 29).

This cutoff point has been based upon the same rationale since the 1960s, which was calculated by taking the amount of money needed for a subsistence diet and multiplying it by 3, updated for inflation. However, as many critics point out, food costs now represent a much smaller share of family budgets, while rent and transportation costs have increased and now constitute a larger share of household expenditures. Ehrenreich notes that when the original method for defining the poverty line was devised, 24% of the typical family budget went for food, while housing constituted 29%. By 1999, the food portion had decreased to 16%, while the housing portion rose to 37%.[17] Most critics contend that the official poverty rate should be raised by at least 50%. Using this standard, the official poverty rate would increase to 22.5%, while the percentage of those under 18 would jump up to about 31%. For African Americans and Hispanics, the rates would be 40% and 43% respectively; for African-American children the rates would be 52% and 56% respectively (Heintz et al., 2000: 106–108).

The Economic Policy Institute, after careful review of dozens of studies, arrived at an estimated living wage for a family of one adult and two children of about $30,000 per year, meaning around $14 per hour. As Ehrenreich notes, this budget includes "health insurance, a telephone and child care at a licensed center . . . which are well beyond the reach of millions.... The shocking thing is that the majority of Americans, about 60 percent, earn less than $14 an hour" (Ehrenreich, 2001: 213).

A report by the U.S. Census Bureau found that despite Medicaid, 30% of the poor had no health insurance of any kind during 2000—about twice the share that went without insurance among the general population. The chance of being uninsured varied by race and ethnicity, age, and employment status. About 12% of children under age 18 in the United States—8.5 million young people—lacked coverage for the year. However, the poor were more likely to be uninsured in every category. For white non-Hispanics 10% lacked health insurance coverage in 2000. The rate was 19% for blacks and 18% for Asians and Pacific Islanders. Among people of Hispanic origin, 32% lacked health insurance coverage for all of 2000. Among poor children, 22% were not covered in 2000 (U.S. Department of Commerce, Bureau of the Census, 2000a).

Another Census Bureau report noted that in 1995, 49 million people in America—about one person in five—lived in a household that had at least one difficulty in meeting a basic need during the year before the survey. These included households that did not pay utility bills, did not pay the mortgage or rent, did not get needed medical attention, had a telephone or utility service shut off, were evicted, or did not get enough to eat. The report also noted than 19% of all children lived in households that did not meet basic expenses (Department of Commerce, Bureau of the Census, 2000b).

Not surprisingly, African Americans and Hispanics were more likely than white non-Hispanics to experience difficulties. Greater difficulty was observed among the unemployed and people with a work disability. Renters were more likely than homeowners to encounter problems. People living in a household maintained by a woman were significantly more likely than people living in a household maintained by a man to have problems meeting basic needs (Department of Commerce, Bureau of the Census, 2000b).

This report also noted that in 1995, 1 person in 20 lived in a household where everyone did not get enough to eat. Not getting enough food was strongly associated with income, age, race, and Hispanic origin (Department of Commerce, Bureau of the Census, 2000b).

All of this leads us to the subject of those who fall far below the above-referenced working poor. This is the surplus population, like the invisible poor that Michael Harrington wrote about in the early 1960s (Harrington, 1962). They remain largely invisible today, unless they get "out of line."

The Growth and Perpetuation of the Surplus Population (Dangerous Classes)

One obvious result of these changes has been the development of a category of people commonly referred to as the underclass. It should be emphasized that this term has been the subject of a considerable amount of debate. As one of the leading critics puts it, the term *underclass* has become merely a form of "new wine in old bottles" in that it has replaced some of the old terms like *dangerous classes, undeserving poor, rabble,* and so on. While it is synonymous with persistent and extreme poverty, it is more like a "behavioral term invented by journalists and social scientists to describe poor people who are accused, rightly or wrongly, of failing to behave in the 'mainstream' ways of the numerically or culturally dominant American middle class" (Gans, 1995: 2).

Usually this term is used to, in effect, stigmatize those who fall within the general category of the underclass, the homeless, those who live in the projects, addicts, young poor women with babies, and of course gang members. Needless to say, the term is often used interchangeably with racial minorities.

As noted above, inner cities have been the most negatively affected by these changes. The movement of capital out of the inner cities (capital flight) corresponded to the phenomenon of white flight and the exodus of many middle-class minorities and the decline of the tax base for these areas while the increasing concentration of the poor were left behind. There has also been a corresponding decline in federal funding for social programs, particularly those targeting the urban underclass. This largely occurred during the 1980s with the dawn of a privatization movement, a system aiming to replace federal assistance with private-sector methods of solving urban problems. Among the specific types of programs that suffered included aid to disadvantaged school districts, housing assistance, financial aid to the poor, legal assistance to the poor, and social services in urban areas in general (Cummings and Monti, 1993: 306).

There has been a marked decline in job opportunities, especially for minorities. Many jobs have shifted to the suburbs, as have many basic services and the tax base as well. It used to be common for many minority youth to be able to find unskilled and semiskilled jobs. Today these jobs are disappearing and being replaced by either low-wage service jobs or high-wage jobs requiring advanced skills and education.

A closely related development has been described as the feminization of poverty. This refers to the increase in female-headed households that are most likely to be living in poverty. This has been especially true for African-American women. As a recent census report noted: "In 2004, 28.4 percent of households headed by single women were poor, while 13.5 percent of households headed by single men and 5.5 percent of married-couple households lived in poverty. In 2004, both black and Hispanic female-headed households had poverty rates just under 40 percent" (National Poverty Center, 2006). In 2004, about 33% of African-American children and 29% of Hispanic children lived in poverty, compared to only 10.5% of white children (National Poverty Center, 2006). International comparisons show the United States ranked number one in terms of the overall child poverty rate among industrialized nations, with an overall rate of 25% (Miringoff and Miringoff, 1999: 83–84). The number of children living in poverty declined in the 1990s, only to experience an increase during the past four years (from 2001 to 2003 there was an increase in those living in what is called extreme poverty (families with after-tax income below half the poverty line) (CBS News, 2003).

The welfare reform movement ushered in during the Clinton administration in 1996 significantly reduced the number of citizens on the welfare rolls. Specifically, as of 1999 about 7 million were receiving welfare, compared to just over 12 million in 1996. There has been a negative impact, however, as millions of single mothers who have left welfare are working at poverty wages. One study found that the average wage of these mothers is $6.60 per hour. More than one-fourth of these women are working nights, while two-thirds have jobs without health insurance. Also, more than half of them are having trouble getting decent and affordable child care and paying for such necessities as food and rent.

Still another report noted that whites were leaving welfare at a much faster pace than minorities. One example was in Ohio, where in 1995 just over half of the welfare recipients (54%) were white and 42% were African American, by 1999 these percentages were reversed: 53% African-American and 42% white. In Nevada, between 1994 and 1999 the proportion of whites receiving welfare dropped from 56% to 47%, while the percentage of African Americans increased from 30% to 3% and Hispanics went from 11% to 13%. Research has also shown that it has been much easier to leave welfare for those living away from the inner cities, which obviously helps whites since they are most likely to live in the suburbs (Associated Press, 1999).

Since 1996, the white share of the welfare caseload has declined, while the Hispanic percentage has risen; and the black percentage has been fairly stable. The growing minority share of the welfare caseload seems partly attributable to the increasing number of Hispanics in the low-income population. It is estimated that approximately 41% of current welfare recipients will exhaust their eligibility under the time limits imposed (two years); approximately two-thirds of these families will be racial minorities. Research has found that among those who have left the welfare rolls since 1996, white people earn significantly higher wages during the first three months after exit. From 1997 to 1999, the median hourly wage for whites who left welfare was $7.31; for African Americans it was $6.88, and for Hispanics it was $6.71 (Soss, 2002: 9).

Although the overall poverty rate has declined (that is, the official poverty rate which, as noted previously, is based upon dubious criteria), the African-American poverty rate for 2000 (26.3%) was still more than three times the rate for whites. The percentages for African Americans would no doubt be considerably higher if we included all of those who are currently in prison; as of 2005 over half of all prisoners were African Americans and at least one-third of all African-American males will be either in jail, in prison, on probation or on parole (Harrison and Beck, 2006).

Overall measures of well-being suggest that between 1997 and 1999 conditions improved most for white families. Like the population as a whole, low-income white families experienced gains in family income and less food hardship. Family income also rose among Hispanics. However, as one report noted, *African Americans were the only group to show no statistically significant improvements in well-being during this period of strong economic performance* (Soss, 2002 (p. 9): emphasis in the original).

A Census Bureau report recently underscored what researchers have said for decades, namely that children in two-parent families fare better developmentally than children in single-parent families. More specifically, the report notes that diminished contact with the noncustodial parent can result in a loss of emotion support and supervision from adults. Further, being cared for by someone other than a family member is an increasingly common experience in a child's preschool years (Department of Commerce, Bureau of the Census, 2000c).

The declining social and economic position of African Americans, especially as this relates to young African-American males, whom one author has called an endangered species is significant (Gibbs, 1988). The impact on one particular city, Louisville, Kentucky, is described by Cummings and Monti. They describe the underclass in this city as being "comprised largely of minorities who are increasingly marginal to the city's economy. The neighborhoods populated by the underclass are characterized by high rates of crime, institutional instability, and impoverished households headed by females.... Louisville's new urban poverty is exacerbated by severe dislocations in the manufacturing and industrial sectors of its regional economy" (Cummings and Monti, 1993: 312–313). The unemployment rates among African Americans in Louisville rose from 6.9% in 1970 to more than 20% by the end of the 1980s. Also, in 1970, 45% of births by African-American women were out of wedlock, whereas in 1988 it was 70% (1993: 312–313).

Or consider the city of Rochester, New York, a city that typifies the deindustrialization process. Mike Males, in his book *Framing Youth,* offers the following description:

> I spent two spring days walking Rochester's formerly prosperous neighborhoods, once well fed by its chief employer, Eastman Kodak, and other topside industries. On North St. Paul sits the 10-story Bausch & Lomb plant, abandoned, windows broken. From the bridge, vacant, silent factories flank the roaring Genesee River. To the right is the Kodak Tower, where corporate cutbacks chopped the labor force from 65,000 in past heydays to fewer than 30,000 today.
>
> Rochester's north and westside formerly working-class neighborhoods are shabby. In another decade they will fall into the bombed-out look of Camden, Baltimore, Richmond, and Philadelphia. It is mostly a white city, one-sixth black. Among black youths, poverty has risen from 31 percent in 1970 to 48 percent today. Among white youth, poverty tripled from 8 percent in 1970 to 22 percent now (Males, 1999: 183).

A similar walk or drive through boarded-up, closed-down former factory towns and in cities like Boston, Detroit, Atlanta, Memphis, and Los Angeles reveal identical patterns (as witnessed personally by the authors of this book). Little wonder gangs flourish, as evidenced by the graffiti everywhere, among other indicators.[18]

Jonathan Kozol has written a great deal about the subject of public schools over the past 40 years, focusing specifically on the lack of quality found within poor communities. In one of his latest books, *Savage Inequalities,* there is a chapter devoted to East St. Louis, a city described by the U.S. Department of Housing and Urban Development as "the most distressed small city in America." He quotes a professor at Southern Illinois University who called it "a repository for a non-white population that is now regarded as expendable" (Kozol, 1991: 7–8). The *St. Louis Post-Dispatch* called it "America's Soweto" (Kozol, 1991: 7–8). Not surprisingly, the educational system had been suffering massive cutbacks in funding for many years. Little work was available, what with all the factory closings. Most of the men had largely disappeared, as four-fifths of the births in this city were to single women. The men were either in prison, had died, living in the streets, or "sleeping in small, isolated camps behind the burnt-out buildings" (Kozol, 1991: 15).

Since Kozol wrote not much has changed in East St. Louis. A recent report by the Federal Reserve Bank in St. Louis notes that:

> Between 1960 and 1970, the city lost nearly 70 percent of its businesses. Unemployment soared. Residents moved out of town. The population drain continued for years. Between 1970 and 2000, the city lost 55 percent of its population. . . . As businesses left and the local government struggled, the tax base shrunk. As the tax base shrunk, the local government struggled more. The city eventually had to eliminate all but basic city services, and even those were cut. The city couldn't pay its light bill or pay for its garbage collection. Street lights and stoplights were turned off, and abandoned lots became dumping grounds for trash. Police and fire protection was spotty, at best. Buildings began falling down. Crime and unemployment rose. East St. Louis and devastation became synonymous. Today, for most of the city's residents, things haven't changed much. Poverty is a way of life (Federal Reserve Bank, 2002).

A University of Michigan study noted:

> Once a healthy community of 80,000 residents, East St. Louis quickly deteriorated socioeconomically and scattered a surplus of vacant and poorly maintained lots throughout the city. According to Kenneth Reardon, a professor in the Department of Urban and Regional Planning at the University of Illinois at Urbana-Champaign, "nearly 40 percent of the city's land was either vacant or unattended and 30 percent of its building stock was abandoned" by 1990 (1). Presently, the 38,000 remaining residents suffer from poor educational systems, increased health risks, unemployment, and poverty. The East St. Louis public school district is currently ranked third to last in the state of Illinois (Bell, 1999).

Today in East St. Louis 97% of the population is black, while the median family income is $14,633, about half the state average. Property taxes are about one-fourth of what they were in 1970. In the northern-most part of the city (zip code 62204), half of the residents live in poverty, three-fourths receive welfare, and about a fifth (20%) of all children are born to a teenager (Peterson, 1997). About one-third (33.7%) of the residents aged 25 years or older do not have a high school diploma. In 2002, the overall crime rate stood at 2030 (about 7 times greater than the national average for cities); the murder rate was a whopping 54 (national rate was 5.6), rate of rapes was 225 (versus 33.0 nationally), and the aggravated assault rate stood at 5038 (versus 310 nationally), and the rate of robbery was 853 (versus 146 nationally).[19]

In short, American style capitalism can be seen as the major culprit in producing such high rates of crime and also a huge and expensive criminal justice system. We can continue tinkering with the criminal justice system—expanding programs for offenders, seeking alternative sentencing practices and a host of other remedies.

We have done this throughout American history. Such reforms, unfortunately, fail to reach the majority of those who end up in the criminal justice system and even if they did, there would be more to follow, since we have not addressed some of the underlying causes of crime—especially the growing inequality generated and perpetuated by American capitalism.

So What Can I Do, You Ask?

To begin with, if anyone wants to know where the answers lie and where to begin to look for solutions, I think it prudent that all of us begin by simply looking in the mirror. We should begin by asking ourselves: Is there anything that *I* can do differently? Is there something wrong with *my* attitudes, *my* beliefs, and *my* actions that may contribute to the problem? If we want some answers, begin by searching *within ourselves*. This is the message from many who espouse some of the philosophies of the East. Let me quote from one such source, a book written by a Vietnamese Zen Master and poet Thich Nhat Hanh in his book *Peace Is Every Step*:

> When you plant lettuce, if it does not grow well, you don't blame the lettuce. You look into the reasons it is not doing well. It may need fertilizer, or more water, or less sun. You never blame the lettuce. Yet if we have problems with our friends or our family we blame the other person. But if we know how to take care of them, they will grow well, like lettuce. Blaming has no positive effect at all, nor does trying to persuade using reason and arguments. That is my experience. No blame, no reasoning, no argument, just understanding. If you understand, and you show that you understand, you can love, and the situation will change (1991: 78).

Later in his book, he describes young prostitutes in Manila as follows:

> In the city of Manila there are many young prostitutes; some are only fourteen or fifteen years old. They are very unhappy. They did not want to be prostitutes, but their families are poor and these young girls went to the city to look for some kind of job, like street vendor, to make money to send back to their families. Of course this is true not only in Manila, but in Ho Chi Minh City in Vietnam, in New York City, and in Paris also. After only a few weeks in the city, a vulnerable girl can be persuaded by a clever person to work for him and earn perhaps one hundred times more money than she could as a street vendor. Because she is so young and does not know much about life, she accepts and becomes a prostitute. Since that time, she has carried the feeling of being impure, defiled, and this causes her great suffering. When she looks at other young girls, dressed beautifully, belonging to good families, a wretched feeling walls up in her, a feeling of defilement that becomes her hell.
>
> But if she could look deeply at herself and at the whole situation, she would see that she is the way she is because other people are the way they are ... No one among us has clean hands. No one of us can claim that it is not our responsibility. The girl in Manila is that way because of the way we are. Looking into the life of that young prostitute, we see the lives of all the "non-prostitutes." And looking at the non-prostitutes and

the way we live our lives, we see the prostitute. Each thing helps to create the other . . . the truth is that everything contains everything else. We cannot be, we only inter-be. We are responsible for every thing that happens around us (1991: 97–98).

The thrust of Hanh's book is that before we can achieve peace on Earth, which includes a world without crime and suffering, we have to develop peace within ourselves. How else can we make the world a better place, unless we make our own lives better? How can we tell the criminals in our midst how to live their lives if we do not set good examples? As Richard Quinney has written: "If human actions are not rooted in compassion, these actions will not contribute to a compassionate and peaceful world. If we ourselves cannot know peace, be peaceful, how will our acts disarm hatred and violence" (Quinney, 1995: 10). Without such hatred and violence, there will be no need to even have, much less need to control, the dangerous classes.

We will need much more, I'm afraid. We must join together in a *collective* effort and make the changes that are needed. I place emphasis on *collective* since no one can do it alone. Every major change in world history has come through collective efforts. Usually such efforts have been directed against extreme concentrations of wealth and power—as in the case of the American Revolution, the growth of unions in the late 19th and early 20th centuries, and the civil rights and antiwar movements of the 1960s, to name just a few. It is happening as I write these words, for great numbers of citizens are rising up and demanding the end of the war in Iraq. There is power in great numbers. There are hundreds of progressive organizations working for such changes. A cursory scroll through the Internet will lead to these groups. Join with them and make the world a better place.

I would like to close with a parable I have used before in my writings, which originated with the famous social reformer and agitator of the early 20th century, Saul Alinsky.[20] Imagine a large river with a high waterfall. At the bottom of this waterfall hundreds of people are working frantically trying to save those who have fallen into the river and have fallen down the waterfall, many of them drowning. As the people along the shore are trying to rescue as many as possible one individual looks up and sees a seemingly never-ending stream of people falling down the waterfall and he begins to run upstream. One of his fellow rescuers hollers "Where are you going? There are so many people that need help here." To which the man replied, "I'm going upstream to find out why so many people are falling into the river."

Now imagine the scene at the bottom of the waterfall represents the criminal justice system, responding to crimes that have been committed and dealing with both victims and offenders. If you look more closely, you will begin to notice that there are more people at the bottom of the stream, that they work in relatively new buildings with all sorts of modern technology and that those working here get paid rather well, with excellent benefits. And the money keeps flowing into this area, with all sorts of businesses lined up to provide various services and technical assistance. If you look upstream, you will find something far different. There are not too many people, the buildings are not as modern, nor are the technology that they use. The people working there do not get paid very much and their benefits are not as good as those provided down below, while the turnover is quite high.

Neither do they find businesses coming their way with assistance. They constantly have to beg for money. Moreover, you will often find more women working upstream, since their work in this culture is not as valued as the work men do (men are in charge downstream).

Some people choose to respond to problems related to crime and delinquency by working downstream. This is certainly a noble goal and good people are always needed. As for me, I picture myself as being one who is constantly running upstream, asking "why?" Which way you want to go is up to you. You just have to be able to look yourself in the mirror each day and be able to say "I tried." A lot of work lies ahead.

Notes

1. The following websites show these estimates: http://nationalpriorities.org/index.php?option=com_wrapper&Itemid=182; http://www.milkeninstitute.org/publications/review/2006_12/76_83mr32.pdf; http://www.nytimes.com/2007/01/17/business/17leonhardt.html?em&ex=1169269200&en=0d6743c864e8ea1b&ei=5087%0A).

2. The reader is encouraged to merely browse through any introductory sociology textbook to find numerous references to these two terms. In fact, one definition of *sociology* itself could easily be "the study of culture and social structure."

3. For an excellent discussion of the role of corporate propaganda see the following: Herman and Chomsky (2002); Fones-Wolf (1994); Carey (1995).

4. A more detailed discussion of this theory is found in Shelden (2006).

5. Other modes of production have included mercantilism, feudalism, socialism, and communism. We could even cite some primitive societies and their "hunting and gathering" modes of production.

6. There is a wide body of literature documenting the relationship between social class and crime. Among other works, see Reiman (2007) and Cole (1999).

7. Heilbroner, pp. 42–46). He is quoting from Smith's famous work *The Wealth of Nations* (1976: 709–710).

8. For a more complete discussion of the idea that "capital rules"—especially corporate capitalism—see Korten (2001), Kelly (2001), and Derber (1998).

9. A fascinating slant on this process is described as the "McDonaldization" of American society. This has been defined as "the process by which the principles of the fast-food restaurant are coming to dominate more and more sectors of American society as well as of the rest of the world" (see Ritzer (1996: 1)).

10. A great deal has been written about corporate welfare. See, for instance, Zepezauer and Naiman (1996); Albeda et al. (1996: 20–21); Derber (1998: Chapter 8).

11. The Holland study was done by Ruigrok van Tulder (1995); reference to this study was made in Chomsky (1998). For documentation of the claim that there has never been free market capitalism in this country, see Zinn (2005) and Chomsky (1993).

12. See United for a Fair Economy, "CEO Pay Charts." http://www.faireconomy.org/research/CEO_Pay_charts.html.

13. Of all American-based multinationals with assets over $100 million, more than one-third (37%) paid *no* federal taxes in 1991, while the average tax for those who did pay was around 1% (Zepezauer and Naiman, 1996: 70).

14. See an article appearing on the Internet called "Illegal Immigrants Returning to Mexico for American Jobs." *The Onion.* http://www.theonion.com/content/node/47978. See also the following: Economist (1998), Greider (2001).

15. Eitzen and Zinn (1998: 200). The manufacturing sector constitutes 17% of the U.S. gross domestic product, yet is responsible for funding 70% of all industrial research and development. A widely held belief that the U.S. economy is being driven by information technologies, the Internet, and the growing service sector is leading to an under-investment in manufacturing research and development—this could be a bad sign for an already depressed economy. Information technology industries continue to expand as does the services sector (however, the services are not those offered by low-skilled, uneducated workers,

but are services led by information technology as well: information retrieval, professional computer services, data processing, and accounting and management consulting services) (U.S. Department of Commerce, 2000).

16. Gosselin (2004a, 2004b, 2004c). Space does not permit a detailed summary of this excellent series of reports. Consult the following websites for access to these articles: http://www.latimes.com/business/la-fi-riskshift3oct10,1, 4792 299.story?coll=la-home-headlines; http://www.latimes.com/business/la-fi-poor12dec12, 1,5929236.story?coll=la-home-headlines; http://www.latimes.com/business/la-fi-newdeal30dec 30,0,515 7802.story?coll=la-home-headlines. If these cannot be accessed, feel free to contact the author of this book.

17. Ehrenreich (2001: 200). She was citing an Economic Policy Institute Study—see Bernstein et al. (2000: 14).

18. The reader is encouraged to do your own "drive-through" or "walk-through" where you live or attend college. We are certain you will find a similar area of town that has experienced this form of deindustrialization. Even in the boomtown of Las Vegas, Nevada, where the author lives, driving through the very segregated African-American community reveals that the tremendous growth and the enormous wealth of this city have not "trickled down" to this part of town. Compared to 1977, when I first arrived in Las Vegas, not too much has changed in this community, save for a few token businesses, which are primarily located at the outer fringes of the African-American community. Little wonder that most gangs are concentrated here.

19. On the Internet at http://www.city-data.com/city/East-St.-Louis-Illinois.html.

20. This is reported in Bartollas (2003: 354).

References

Abbott, G. 1938. *The Child and the State.* Chicago: University of Chicago Press.

Abt Associates. 2000. "What America's Users Spend on Illegal Drugs 1988–1998." Washington, DC: ONDCP, December.

Ares, C. E., A. Rankin, and H. Sturz. 1963. "The Manhattan Bail Project: An Interim Report on the Use of Pre-Trial Parole." *New York University Law Review* 38: 71–92.

Addams, J. 1909. *Spirit of Youth and the City Streets.* New York: Macmillan.

———. 1910. *Twenty Years at Hull-House.* New York: Macmillan.

Adamson, C. R. 1984a. "Toward a Marxian Penology: Criminal Populations as Economic Threats and Resources." *Social Problems* 31: 435–458.

———. 1984b. "Hard Labor and Solitary Confinement: Effects of Business Cycle and Labor Supply on Prison Discipline in the United States, 1790–1835." *Research in Law, Deviance and Social Control* 6: 19–56.

———. 1999. "Punishment After Slavery: Southern State Penal Systems, 1865–1890." In R. P. Weiss (ed.), *Social History of Crime, Policing and Punishment.* Brookfield, VT: Ashgate.

Adler, J. S. 1986. "Vagging the Demons and Scoundrels: Vagrancy and the Growth of St. Louis, 1830–1861." *Journal of Urban History* 13: 3–30.

———. 1989a. "A Historical Analysis of the Law of Vagrancy." *Criminology* 27: 209–229.

———. 1989b. "Rejoinder to Chambliss." *Criminology* 27: 239–250.

Agee, P. 1975. *Inside the Company: CIA Diary.* New York: Bantam Books.

Albeda, R., N. Folbre, and the Center for Popular Economics. 1996. *The War on the Poor.* New York: The New Press.

Allen, H. E. and C. E. Simonsen. 1998. *Corrections in America* (8th ed.). Upper Saddle River, NJ: Prentice-Hall.

American Correctional Association. 1990. *The Female Offender.* College Park, MD: American Correctional Association.

———. 2005. *2005 Directory.* Lanham, MD: American Correctional Association.

Amsterdam, A. 1988. "Race and the Death Penalty." *Criminal Justice Ethics* 7: 84–86.

Anderson, D. 1995. *Crime and the Politics of Hysteria.* New York: Times Books.

Andrews, R. H. and A. H. Cohn. 1974. "Ungovernability: The Unjustifiable Jurisdiction." *Yale Law Journal* (June): 1383–1409.

Ares, C. E., A. Rankin, and H. Sturz. 1963. "The Manhattan Bail Project: An Interim Report on the Use of Pre-Trial Parole." *New York University Law Review* 38: 71–92.

Ariès, P. 1962. *Centuries of Childhood.* New York: Knopf.

Arrigo, B. A. 1999. "Marital Metaphors and Medical Justice: Implications for Law, Crime, and Deviance." *Journal of Political and Military Sociology* 27: 307–322.

Associated Press. 2003. "In Illinois, Pennsylvania and Wisconsin, Newly Built Prisons Remain Shut, As States Face Budget Crunch." January 8.

Association of Trial Lawyers of America. 2005. "No Evidence of a Malpractice Crisis."

http://www.atla.org/ConsumerMediaRes ources/Tier3/press_room/FACTS/health/ Researc/UTMar2005.aspx.

Austin, J. and J. Irwin. 2001. *It's About Time: America's Incarceration Binge* (3rd ed.). Belmont, CA: Wadsworth.

Ayres, E. L. 1984. *Vengeance and Justice: Crime and Punishment in the 19th Century American South.* New York: Oxford University Press.

Bacon, S. 1939. "The Early Development of American Municipal Police." Ph.D. dissertation, Yale University.

Baldus, D. C., G. Woodworth, and C. A. Pulaski. 1990. *Equal Justice and the Death Penalty: A Legal and Empirical Analysis.* Boston: Northeastern University Press.

Barak, G. 1975. "In Defense of the Rich: The Emergency of the Public Defender." *Crime and Social Justice* 3: 2–14.

———. (ed.). 1991. *Crimes by the Capitalist State.* Albany, NY: SUNY Press.

Barkan, S. E. 1977. "Political Trials and the Pro Se Defendant in the Adversary System." *Social Problems* 24: 324–336.

Barnes, H. E. 1972. *The Story of Punishment.* Montclair, NJ: Patterson Smith (originally published in 1930).

Barnes, H. E. and N. K. Teeters. 1951. *New Horizons in Criminology.* Englewood Cliffs, NJ: Prentice-Hall.

Bartlett, D. L. and J. B. Steele. 1992. *America: What Went Wrong?* Kansas City: Andrews and McMeel.

Bartollas, C. 2003. *Juvenile Delinquency* (6th ed.). Boston: Allyn and Bacon.

Bartollas, C. and S. J. Miller. 1998. *Juvenile Justice in America* (3rd ed.). Upper Saddle River, NJ: Prentice-Hall.

Bates, E. 1999. "CCA, the Sequel." *The Nation,* June 7: 22–23.

Baum, D. 1997. *Smoke and Mirrors: The War on Drugs and the Politics of Failure.* Boston: Little Brown/Back Bay Books.

Baum, N. and B. Bedrick. 1994. *Trading Books for Bars: The Lopsided Funding Battle Between Prisons and Universities.* San Francisco: Center on Juvenile and Criminal Justice.

Baumer, E. 1994. "Poverty, Crack, and Crime: A Cross City Analysis." *Journal of Research in Crime and Delinquency,* 31: 311–327.

Beard, C. 1935. *An Economic Interpretation of the Constitution.* New York: Macmillan.

Beccaria, C. 1963. *On Crimes and Punishment.* New York: Bobbs-Merrill.

Beck, A. J. and P. M. Brien. 1995. "Trends in the U.S. Correctional Populations: Recent Findings from the Bureau of Justice Statistics." In K. C. Haas and G. P. Alpert (eds.), *The Dilemmas of Corrections* (3rd ed.). Prospect Heights, IL: Waveland Press.

Beck, A. J., J. C. Karberg, and P. M. Harrison. 2002. "Prison and Jail Inmates at Mid-Year, 2001." Washington, DC: Bureau of Justice Statistics.

Beck, A. J. and C. J. Mumola. 1999. "Prisoners in 1998." Washington DC: U.S. Department of Justice, August.

Becker, H. S. 1963. *Outsiders: Studies in the Sociology of Deviance.* New York: Free Press.

Bedau, H. (ed.) 1964. *The Death Penalty in America.* Garden City, NY: Doubleday.

Belenko, S. R. 1993. *Crack and the Evolution of the Anti-Drug Policy.* Gulfport, CT: Greenwood Press.

Belknap, J. 2001. *The Invisible Woman: Gender, Crime, and Justice* (2nd ed.) Belmont, CA: Thomson/Wadsworth.

Benekos, P. and A. V. Merlo. 1995. "Three Strikes and You're Out!: The Political Sentencing Game." *Federal Probation* 59: 3–9.

Benner, L. A., B. Neary, and R. M. Gutman. 1973. *The Other Face of Justice: A Report of the National Defender Survey.* Chicago: National Legal Aid and Defender Association.

Bennett, W. L. 1994. *Inside the System: Culture, Institutions, and Power in American Politics.* New York: Harcourt Brace.

Berkowitz, B. 2002. "Smart ALEC's." Working for Change (www.workingforchange.com).

Bernard, T. J. 1992. *The Cycle of Juvenile Justice.* New York: Oxford University Press.

Bernstein, J. and E. Gould. 2006. "Working Families Fall Behind." *Economic Policy Institute,* August 29. http://www.epi.org/ content.cfm/webfeatures_econindicators_ income20060829.

Berrigan, P. 1970. *Prison Journals of a Priest Revolutionary.* New York: Holt, Rinehart & Winston.

Besser, T. 2003. "The Development of Last Resort." Paper presented at the Rural Sociological Society Meeting, August.

Blackstock, N. 1975. *COINTELPRO: The FBI's Secret War on Political Freedom*. New York: Vintage Books.

Blackstone, W. 1796. *Commentaries on the Laws of England*. Oxford: Clarendon Press.

Blakely, E. J. and M. G. Snyder. 1997. *Fortress America: Gated Communities in the United States*. Washington, DC: Brookings Institution Press.

Blauner, R. 1972. *Racial Oppression in America*. New York: Harper & Row.

Blomberg, T. G. and K. Lucken. 2000. *American Penology: A History of Control*. New York: Aldine De Gruyter.

Bluestone, B. and B. Harrison. 1982. *The Deindustrialization of America*. New York: Basic Books.

Blum, W. 1995. *Killing Hope: U.S. Military and CIA Intervention Since World War II*. Monroe, ME: Common Courage Press.

———. 2000. *Rogue State: A Guide to the World's Only Superpower*. Monroe, ME: Common Courage Press.

Bordua, D. (ed.). 1967. *The Police: Six Sociological Essays*. New York: John Wiley.

Boris, E. 1991. "Reconstructing the 'Family': Women, Progressive Reform, and the Problem of Social Control," in N. Frankel and N. S. Dye (eds.), *Gender, Class, Race, and Reform in the Progressive Era*. Louisville, KY: University of Kentucky Press.

Borosage, R. and J. Marks. 1976. *The CIA File*. New York: Grossman.

Bortner, M. A. 1982 *Inside a Juvenile Court: The Tarnished Idea of Individualized Justice*. New York: New York University Press, 1982.

Bottomore, T., L. Harris, V. G. Kiernan, and R. Miliband (eds.). 1983. *A Dictionary of Marxist Thought*. Cambridge, MA: Harvard University Press.

Bowers, W. J. 1974. *Executions in America*. Lexington, MA: D. C. Heath.

Bowles, S. 1975. "Unequal Education and the Reproduction of the Social Division of Labor. "In M. Carnoy (ed.). *Schooling in a Corporate Society*. New York: David McKay.

Brace, C. L. 1872. *The Dangerous Classes of New York*. New York: Wynkoop and Hallenbeck.

Brayson, C. 1996. "Crime Pays for Those in the Prison Business." *The National Times* (September): 28–35.

Breggin, P. R. and G. R. Breggin. 1998. *The War Against Children of Color*. Monroe, ME: Common Courage Press.

Bremner, R. H. (ed.). 1970. *Children and Youth in America*. Cambridge: Harvard University Press.

Brenzel, B. 1975. "Lancaster Industrial School for Girls: A Social Portrait of a 19th Century Reform School for Girls." *Feminist Studies* 3:40–53.

———. 1983. *Daughters of the State*. Cambridge: MIT Press.

Brown, D. 1971. *Bury My Heart at Wounded Knee*. New York: Holt, Rinehart and Winston.

Brown, W. B. 1999. Personal communication with the author.

Brownstein, H. H. 1991. "The Media and the Construction of Random Drug Violence." *Social Justice* 18: 85–103.

———. 1996. *The Rise and Fall of a Violent Crime Wave: Crack Cocaine and the Social Construction of a Crime Problem*. Guilderland, NY: Harrow and Heston, 1996.

Bureau of Justice Statistics. 2005. "Number of Federal Tort Trials Fell by Almost 80 Percent from 1985 through 2003." http://www.ojp.usdoj.gov/bjs/pub/press/fttv03pr. htm.

Burns, H. 1974. "Racism and American Law." In R. Quinney (ed.), *Criminal Justice in America*. Boston: Little, Brown.

———. 1990. "Law and Race in Early America." In D. Kairys (ed.), *The Politics of Law*. New York: Pantheon Books.

Burton-Rose, D. and P. Wright (eds.). 1998. *The Celling of America: An Inside Look at the U.S. Prison Industry*. Monroe, ME: Common Courage Press.

Buss, D. 1996. "The Brave New World of Business Security." *Nation's Business*, May.

Butterfield, F. 2002. "Inmates Go Free to Reduce Deficits." *New York Times*, December 18.

Bynum, T. 1982. "Release on Recognizance: Substantive or Superficial Reform?" *Criminology* 20: 67–82.

Byrnes, M., D. Macallair, and A. D. Shorter. 2002. "Aftercare as Afterthought: Reentry and the California Youth Authority." San Francisco: Center on Juvenile and Criminal Justice.

Cable, G. 1962. *The Silent South*. Montclair, NJ: Patterson Smith (originally published 1888).

Cain, M. (ed.). 1989. *Growing Up Good: Policing the Behavior of Girls in Europe.* London: Sage.

Calavita, K. and Pontell, H. N. 1994. "The State and White Collar Crime: Saving the Savings and Loans." *Law and Society Review* 28: 297–324.

Camp, C. G. and G. M. Camp. 2000. *The Corrections Yearbook 2000: Adult Corrections.* Middletown, CT: Criminal Justice Institute.

Campaign for an Effective Crime Policy. 1998. *"Three Strikes": Five Years Later.* Washington, DC: The Sentencing Project.

Cannon, A. 2004. "Special Report: Juvenile Injustice," *US News and World Report,* August 3.

Carey, A. 1995. *Taking the Risk Out of Democracy.* Chicago: University of Illinois Press.

Carlson, T. 1995. "Safety Inc.: Private Cops Are There When You Need Them." *Policy Review* 73 (Summer): 66–72.

Caufield, S. 1999. "Transforming the Criminological Dialogue: A Feminist Perspective on the Impact of Militarism." *Journal of Political and Military Sociology* 27: 291–306.

Center for Research on Criminal Justice. 1977. *The Iron Fist and the Velvet Glove* (2nd ed.) Berkeley: Center for Research on Criminal Justice.

Center on Budget and Policy Priorities. 2004. "Census Data Show Poverty Increased, Income Stagnated, and the Number of Uninsured Rose to a Record Level in 2003." http://www.cbpp.org/8-26-04pov.htm, August 27.

Center on Juvenile and Criminal Justice (CJCJ). 2006. "About the CCPOA." http://www.cjcj.org/cpp/growth_CCPOA.php.

Chambliss, W. J. (ed.). 1969. *Crime and the Legal Process.* New York: McGraw-Hill.

———. 1975a. "The Law of Vagrancy." In W. S. Chambliss (ed.), *Criminal Law in Action.* New York: John Wiley.

———. 1975b. "Vice, Corruption, Bureaucracy and Power." In W. S. Chambliss (ed.), *Criminal Law in Action.* New York: John Wiley.

———. 1976. "Functional and Conflict Theories of Crime: The Heritage of Emile Durkheim and Karl Marx." In W. J. Chambliss and M. Mankoff (eds.). 1976. *Whose Law, What Order?* New York: John Wiley.

———. 1977. "Markets, Profits, Labor and Smack." *Contemporary Crises* 1: 53–76.

———. 1989. "On Trashing Marxist Criminology." *Criminology* 27: 231–238.

———. 1993. "On Lawmaking" and "The Creation of American Law and Crime Control in Britain and America." In W. J. Chambliss and M. S. Zatz (eds.), *Making Law: The State, the Law, and Structural Contradictions.* Bloomington, IN: Indiana University Press.

———. 1995. "Crime Control and Ethnic Minorities: Legitimizing Racial Oppression by Creating Moral Panics." In D. F. Hawkins (ed.), *Ethnicity, Race, and Crime.* Albany, NY: SUNY Press.

———. 1999. *Power, Politics, and Crime.* Boulder, CO: Westview.

Chambliss, W. J. and T. F. Courtless. 1992. *Criminal Law, Criminology, and Criminal Justice.* Belmont, CA: Wadsworth.

Chambliss, W. J. and T. E. Ryther. 1975. *Sociology: The Discipline and Its Direction.* New York: McGraw-Hill.

Chambliss, W. J. and R. Seidman. 1982. *Law, Order and Power* (2nd ed.). Reading, MA: Addison-Wesley.

Chambliss, W. J. and M. S. Zatz (eds.). 1993. *Making Law: The State, the Law, and Structural Contradictions,* Bloomington, IN: Indiana University Press.

Champion, D. "Teenage Felons and Waiver Hearings: Some Recent Trends, 1980–1988." *Crime and Delinquency* 33, 1989.

———. 1996. *Provincial America: 1600–1763.* New York: Free Press.

Chapin, B. 1983. *Criminal Justice in Colonial America: 1600–1660.* Athens, GA: University of Georgia Press.

Chesney-Lind, M. 1973. "Judicial Enforcement of the Female Sex Role: The Family, Court and the Female Delinquent." *Issues in Criminology* (Fall): 51–59.

———. 1997. *The Female Offender.* Thousand Oaks, CA: Sage.

Chesney-Lind, M. and L. Pasko. 2004. *The Female Offender: Girls, Women and Crime* (2nd ed.). Thousand Oaks, CA: Sage.

Chesney-Lind, M. and R. G. Shelden. 2004. *Girls, Delinquency and Juvenile Justice* (3rd ed.). Belmont, CA: Thompson/Wadsworth.

Cheyney, E. P. 1913. *An Introduction to the Industrial and Social History of England.* New York: Macmillan.

Chomsky, N. 1987. "On the Responsibility of Intellectuals." In E. Peck (ed.), *The Chomsky Reader*. New York: Pantheon Books.

———. 1988. *The Culture of Terrorism*. Boston: South End Press.

———. 1989. *Necessary Illusions: Thought Control in Democratic Societies*. Boston: South End Press.

———. 1992. *Deterring Democracy*. New York: Hill and Wang.

———. 1993. *Year 501: The Conquest Continues*. Boston: South End Press.

———. 1994. *Keeping the Rabble in Line*. Monroe, ME: Common Courage Press.

———. 1996a. *Powers and Prospects*. Boston: South End Press.

———. 1996b. *Class Warfare*. Monroe, ME: Common Courage Press.

———. 1996c. "'Consent Without Consent': Reflections on the Theory and Practice of Democracy." *Cleveland State Law Review* 44: 415–437.

———. 1998. *The Common Good*. Monroe, ME: Odonian Press/Common Courage Press.

———. 1999a. *Profit Over People*. New York: Seven Stories Press.

———. 1999b. "Domestic Terrorism: Notes on the State System of Oppression." *New Political Science* 21: 303–324.

———. 2000. *Rogue States: The Rule of Force in World Affairs*. Boston: South End Press.

Chomsky, N. and E. S. Herman. 1979. *The Political Economy of Human Rights, Vol. I: The Washington Connection and Third World Fascism*. Boston: South End Press.

Chopra, D. 1994. *The Seven Spiritual Laws of Success*. San Rafael, CA: Amber-Allen.

Christianson, S. 1998. *With Liberty for Some: 500 Years of Imprisonment in America*. Boston: Northeastern University Press

Christie, N. 2000. *Crime Control As Industry: Towards Gulags, Western Style?* (3rd ed.). London: Routledge.

Chuang, S. C. 1998. "The Distribution of Texas State Prisons: Economic Impact Analysis of State Prison Sitting on Local Communities." Ph.D. dissertation, University of Texas, Arlington.

Churchill, W. and J. Vander Wall. 1988. *Agents of Repression*. Boston: South End Press.

———. 1990. *COINTELPRO Papers*. Boston: South End Press.

Clark, L. D. 1975. *The Grand Jury: The Use and Abuse of Political Power*. New York: Quadrangle.

Clarke, S. H. and G. G. Koch. 1976. "The Influence of Income and Other Factors on Whether Criminal Defendants Go to Prison." *Law and Society Review* 11: 57–92.

Clear, T. 2002. "Addition by Subtraction." In M. Mauer and M. Chesney-Lind (eds.), *Invisible Punishment: The Collateral Consequences of Mass Imprisonment*. New York: New Press.

Clear, T. and D. R. Rose. 1999. *When Neighbors Go to Jail: Impact on Attitudes about Formal and Informal Social Control*. Washington, DC: National Institute of Justice.

Cleeland, N. 1999. "Temps Become Full-Time Factor in Industry." *Los Angeles Times* (May 29).

Clement, D. 2002. "Big House on the Prairie." *Fedgazette* (Federal Reserve Bank of Minneapolis), January.www.minneapolisfed. org.pubs/fedgaz/02-01/house.cfm.

Clinard, M. B., R. Quinney and J. Wildeman. *Criminal Behavior Systems* (3rd ed.) Cincinnati: Anderson, 1994.

Cockburn, A. 1999. "With 'Gladiator Days,' Prisons Adopt the Gulag Paradigm." *Las Vegas Review-Journal*, November 12, p. 11B.

Cockburn, A. and J. St. Clair. 1999. *Whiteout: The CIA, Drugs and the Media*. New York: Verso.

Cohen, S. 1972. *Folk Devils and Moral Panics: The Creation of the Mods and Rockets*. London: MacGibbon and Kee.

Cohen, D. K. and M. Lazeron. 1972. "Education and the Corporate Order." In R. C. Edwards, M. Reich and T. E. Weisskopf (eds.). *The Capitalist System*. Englewood Cliffs, NJ: Prentice Hall.

Cohen, L. E. 1975. *Delinquency Dispositions: An Empirical Analysis of Processing Decisions in Three Juvenile Courts*. Washington, DC: U.S. Department of Justice.

Coight, C. C. 1998. "5.7 Million Under Correctional Supervision." *Overcrowded Times* 9 (October).

Cole, D. 1999. *No Equal Justice: Race and Class in the American Criminal Justice System*. New York: The New Press.

———. 2003. *Enemy Aliens: Double Standards and Constitutional Freedoms in the War on Terrorism*. New York: New Press.

Collins, C. F. 1997. *The Imprisonment of African-American Women*. Jefferson, NC: McFarland.

Collins, C. and J. L. Askin-Steve. 1996. "The Islamic Gulag: Slavery Makes a Comeback in Sudan." *Utne Reader* (March–April).

Collins, C., B. Leondar-Wright, and H. Sklar. 1999. *Shifting Fortunes: The Perils of the Growing American Wealth Gap*. Boston: United for a Fair Economy.

Collins, C. and F. Yeskel. 2005. *Economic Apartheid in America* (2nd ed.) New York: The New Press.

Common Cause. 1995. "The Anti-Crime Business." *Common Cause Magazine*, Spring.

Congressional Budget Office (CBO). 2004 "What Accounts for the Decline in Manufacturing Employment?" Washington, DC: Congressional Budget Office. http://www.cbo.gov/showdoc.cfm?index=5078&sequence=0.

Conquest, R. 1995. "Playing Down the Gulag." *Times Literary Supplement* (February 24).

Cook, F. 1974. "Setting Up the Vets." In S. Weissman (ed.), *Big Brother and Holding Company: The World Behind Watergate*. Palo Alto, CA: Ramparts Press.

Cooley, C. H. 1974. "Nature v. Nurture in the Making of Social Careers." In F. Faust and B. Brantingham (eds.), *Juvenile Justice Philosophy*. St. Paul, MN: West.

Crary, D. 2004. "States Export Inmates in Effort to Cut Costs" *Los Angeles Times*, February 1.

Cray, C. 2005. "Dodging Their Fare Share." Tom Paine Common Sense. July 6. http://www.tompaine.com/articles/2005/07/06/dodging_their_fare_share.php.

Critchley, T. A. 1972. *A History of Police in England and Wales*. Montclair, NJ: Patterson Smith.

———. 1975. "The New Police in London, 1750–1830." In J. Skolnick and T. Gray (eds.), *Police in America*. Boston: Little, Brown.

Cronin, M. 1992. "Gilded Cages." *Time*, May 25.

Cullen, L. 2002. *A Job to Die For*. Monroe, ME: Common Courage Press.

Currie, E. 1993 *Reckoning: Drugs, the Cities, and the American Future*. New York: Hill and Wang.

———. 1998. *Crime and Punishment in America*. New York: Metropolitan Books.

Dailey, B. R. 1991. "Ann Hutchison." In E. Forner and J. A. Garraty (eds.), *A Reader's Companion to American History*. Boston: Houghton Mifflin.

Daly, K. 1992. "Women's Pathways to Felony Court: Feminist Theories of Lawbreaking and Problems of Representation." *Southern California Review of Law and Women's Studies* 2: 11–52.

Daly, K. and M. Chesney-Lind. 1988. "Feminism and Criminology." *Justice Quarterly* 5: 497–538.

Datesman, S. and F. Scarpitti. 1977. "Unequal Protection for Males and Females in the Juvenile Court." In T. N. Ferdinand (ed.), *Juvenile Delinquency: Little Brother Grows Up*. Newbury Park: Sage.

Davis, M. 1992. *City of Quartz*. New York: Vintage Books.

de Beaumont, G. and A. de Tocqueville. 1964. *On the Penitentiary System in the United States and Its Application in France*. Carbondale, IL: Southern Illinois University Press (originally published 1833).

de Mause, L. (ed.). 1974. *The History of Childhood*. New York: Psychohistory Press.

de Tocqueville, A. 1961. *Democracy in America*. New York: Schoken.

de Yoanna, M. A. and T. Langeland. 2001. "Ground Zero for Columbus Day." *Z Magazine*, October (http://home.earthlink. net/~autonmsaim/id18.html).

Deloria, V. 1969. *Custer Died for Your Sins*. New York: Macmillan.

Derber, C. 1998. *Corporation Nation*. New York: St. Martin's Press.

Diamond, S. 1974. "The Rule of Law Versus the Order of Custom." In R. Quinney (ed.), *Criminal Justice in America: A Critical Understanding*. Boston: Little, Brown.

Dilulio, J. L. 1996. "Broken Bottles: Alcohol, Disorder, and Crime." *The Brookings Review* 14: 14–17.

Dinnerstein, L. and D. M. Reimers. 1975. *Ethnic Americans: A History of Immigration and Assimilation*. New York: Harper & Row.

Ditton, J. 1977. "Perks, Pilferage, and the Fiddle: The Historical Structure of Invisible Wages." *Theory and Society* 4: 39–71.

Dobash, R. E. and R. Dobash. 1979. *Violence Against Wives*. New York: Free Press.

Dobash, R. E., R. Dobash., and S. Gutteridge. 1986. *The Imprisonment of Women*. New York: Basil and Blackwell.

Domhoff, G. W. 1979. *The Powers That Be*. New York: Random House.

———. 1990. *The Power Elite and the State*. New York: Aldine De Gruyter.

———. 1998. *Who Rules America? Power and Politics in the Year 2000*. Mountain View, CA: Mayfield.

Donner, F. J. 1980. *The Age of Surveillance*. New York: Knopf.

Donziger, S. 1996. *The Real War on Crime*. New York: Harper/Collins.

Douglas, D. C. *William the Conqueror*. Berkeley, CA: University of California Press.

Dryfoos, J. 1991. *Adolescents at Risk*. New York: Oxford University Press.

Duke, L. 2000. "Prison Construction Boom Transforms Small Towns." *The Washington Post*, September 8.

Dumaine, B. 1991. "New Weapons in the Crime War." *Fortune* 123 (11): 180–185.

Durkheim, E. 1947. *The Division of Labor in Society*. Glencoe, IL: The Free Press.

Durose, M. R. and P. A. Langan. 2001. "State Court Sentencing of Convicted Felons, 1998 Statistical Tables." Washington, DC: U.S. Department of Justice, Bureau of Justice Statistics (December).

———. 2005. "State Court Sentencing of Convicted Felons, 2002. Statistical Tables." Washington, DC: U.S. Department of Justice, Bureau of Justice Statistics (May).

Duster, T. 1970. *The Legislation of Morality*. New York: Free Press.

Dyer, J. 2000. *The Perpetual Prisoner Machine: How America Profits from Crime*. Boulder, CO: Westview Press.

Eastman, M. (translator and editor). 1959. *Capital, The Communist Manifesto and Other Writings*. New York: The Modern Library.

Economist, The. 1998. "The World as a Single Machine." *The Economist*, June 18.

Eisenstein, E. 1979. *The Printing Press As an Agent of Change*. Cambridge, England: Cambridge University Press.

Eisenstein, Z. R. 1998. *The Female Body and the Law*. Berkeley: University of California Press.

Eitzen, D. S. and M. B. Zinn. 1998. *In Conflict and Order* (8th ed.). Boston: Allyn and Bacon.

Ekirch, A. R. 1987. *Bound for America*. New York: Oxford University Press.

Emerson, S. 2006. "Elusive Corporate Accountability and Weighted Social Responsibility." Graduate seminar paper, Department of Criminal Justice, UNLV, Fall.

Empey, L. T. 1982. *American Delinquency*. Homewood, IL: Dorsey Press.

Engles, F. 1972. *The Origin of the Family, Private Property and the State*. New York: International Publishers.

Erickson, K. T. 1966. *Wayward Puritans*. New York: John Wiley.

Eskridge, C. 1983. *Pre-Trial Release Programming*. New York: Clark Boardman.

Evans, S. M. *Born for Liberty: A History of Women in America*. New York: Free Press, 1989.

Ewen, S. 1976. *Captains of Consciousness: Advertising and the Social Roots of Consumer Culture*. New York: McGraw-Hill.

Ex Parte Crouse, 4 Wharton (Pa.) 9 (1938).

Faludi, S. 1991. *Backlash: The Undeclared War Against American Women*. New York: Anchor Books.

Farnham, A. 1992. "U.S. Suburbs Are Under Siege." *Fortune* 126 (14): 42–44.

Farrell, R. A. and V. L. Swigert. 1978. "Prior Offense Record as a Self-Fulfilling Prophecy." *Law and Society Review* 12: 437–453.

———. 1988. *Social Deviance* (3rd ed.). Belmont, CA: Wadsworth.

Feagin, J. R. and H. Vera. 1995. *White Racism*. New York: Routledge.

Federal Bureau of Investigation (FBI). 1998, 2005. *Uniform Crime Reports*. Washington, DC: U.S. Government Printing Office.

Federal Reserve Bank. 2002. "East St. Louis: One City's Story." http://www.stlouisfed.org.publications/br/2002/d/pages/2-article.

Feinman, C. 1980. *Women in the Criminal Justice System*. New York: Praeger.

Feld, B. 1999. "A Funny Thing Happened on the Way to the Centenary." *Punishment and Society* 1: 187–214.

Fellner, J. 1996. "Stark Racial Disparities Found in Georgia Drug Law Enforcement." *Overcrowded Times* 7, 5 (October).

Ferdinand, T. N. 1967. "The Criminal Patterns of Boston Since 1849." *American Journal of Sociology* 73: 84–99.

Finckenauer, J. O. 1984. *Juvenile Delinquency and Corrections*. New York: Academic Press.

Finder, A. 1999. "Jailed Until Found Not Guilty." *The New York Times*, June 6: 33–34.

Fisher, E. and P. C. Rupert (2005). "The Decline of Manufacturing Employment in the

United States." Cleveland, OH: Federal Reserve Bank. http://www.econ.ohio-state.edu/efisher/fr20050327.pdf.

Fitzgerald, K. 1994. "Gizmos Turn Home Protection into a Boom." *Advertising Age* 64: 51–52.

Flaherty, D. H. 1972. *Privacy in Colonial New England.* Charlottesville: University Press of Virginia.

———. 1984. "Criminal Practice in Provincial Massachusetts." In D. R. Coquillette (ed.), *Law in Colonial Massachusetts, 1630–1800.* Boston: The Colonial Society of Massachusetts, distributed by the University Press of Virginia.

Folbre, N. and the Center for Popular Economics. 1995. *The New Field Guide to the U.S. Economy.* New York: The New Press.

Foote, C. 1954. "Compelling Appearance in Court: Administration of Bail in Philadelphia." *University of Pennsylvania Law Review* 102: 1031–1079.

Foster, M. 2006. "La. Sheriff's Suggestion Upsets Blacks." *Associated Press*, October 27.

Foucault, M. 1979. *Discipline and Punish: The Birth of the Prison.* New York: Vintage Books.

Freedman, E. B. 1981. *Their Sisters' Keepers: Women's Prison Reform in America, 1830–1930.* Ann Arbor, MI: University of Michigan Press.

Friedman, L. J. 1970. *The White Savage: Racial Fantasies in the Postbellum South.* Englewood Cliffs, NJ: Prentice Hall.

Friedman, L. M. 1973. *A History of American Law.* New York: Simon and Schuster.

———. 1993. *Crime and Punishment in American History.* New York: Basic Books.

Friedrichs, D. O. 2004. *Trusted Criminals: White Collar Crime in Contemporary Society* (2nd ed.). Belmont, CA: Wadsworth.

Galliher, J. F. and J. L. McCartney (eds.). 1977. *Criminology: Power, Crime and Criminal Law.* Homewood, IL: Dorsey Press.

Galliher, J. F., J. L. McCartney, and B. E. Baum. 1977. "Nebraska's Marijuana Law: A Case of Unexpected Legislative Innovation." In J. F. Galliher and J. L. McCartney (eds.), *Criminology: Power, Crime and Criminal Law.* Homewood, IL: Dorsey Press.

Gardiner, J. 1969. "Wincanton: The Politics of Corruption." In W. J. Chambliss (ed.), *Crime and the Legal Process.* New York: McGraw-Hill.

Garfinkel, H. 1949. "Research Note on Inter- and Intra-Racial Homicides." *Social Forces* 27: 369–381.

Garland, D. 1990. *Punishment and Modern Society: A Study in Social Theory.* Chicago: University of Chicago Press.

Garrow, D. J. 1981. *The FBI and Martin Luther King, Jr.* New York: Penguin Books.

Geis, G. 1964. "Sociology and Jurisprudence: Admixture of Lore and Law." *Kentucky Law Journal* 52: 267–293.

———. 1996. "A Base on Balls for White Collar Criminals." In D. Shichor and D. K. Sechrest (eds.) *Three Strikes and You're Out: Vengeance as Public Policy.* Thousand Oaks, CA: Sage.

Genovese, E. 1976. *Roll, Jordan, Roll: The World the Slaves Made.* New York: Vintage Books.

Gest, T. 2001. *Crime and Politics: Big Government's Campaign for Law and Order.* New York: Oxford University Press.

Gibbons, D. and M. J. Griswold. 1957. "Sex Differences Among Juvenile Court Referrals." *Sociology and Social Research* 42: 106–110.

Giddens, A. 1971. *Capitalism and Modern Social Theory.* New York: Cambridge University Press.

Gilbert, D. 1998. *The American Class Structure* (5th ed.). Belmont, CA: Wadsworth.

Gilliard, D. K. 1999. *Prison and Jail Inmates at Midyear 1998.* Washington, DC: Bureau of Justice Statistics.

Gilliard, D. K. and A. J. Beck. 1996. *Prison and Jail Inmates, 1995.* Washington, DC: Bureau of Justice Statistics.

Glassner, B. 1999. *The Culture of Fear.* New York: Basic Books.

Glaze, L. E. and T. C. Bonczar. 2006. "Probation and Parole in the United States, 2005." Washington, DC: Bureau of Justice Statistics, November. http://www.ojp.us doj.gov/bjs/pub/pdf/ppus05.pdf.

Glaze, L. E. and S. Palla. 2005. "Probation and Parole in the United States, 2004." Washington, DC: Bureau of Justice Statistics, November. http://www.ojp.usdoj.gov/bjs/pub/pdf/ppus04.pdf.

Glick, H. R. 1983. *Courts, Politics, and Justice.* New York: McGraw-Hill.

Goffman, I. 1961. *Asylums.* New York: Doubleday.

Golden, R. 1997. *Disposable Youth: America's Child Welfare System.* Belmont, CA: Wadsworth.

Goldfarb, R. 1965. *Ransom: A Critique of the American Bail System.* New York: Harper and Row.

———.1975. *Jails: The Ultimate Ghetto of the Criminal Justice System.* New York: Doubleday.

Goldstein, P. J., H. H. Brownstein, P. J. Ryan and P. A. Bellucci. 1997. "Crack and Homicide in New York City: A Case Study in the Epidemiology of Violence." In C. Reinarman and H. G. Levine (eds.), *Crack in America: Demon Drugs and Social Justice.* Berkeley, CA: University of California Press.

Goode, E. and N. Ben-Yehuda. 1994. *Moral Panics: The Social Construction of Deviance.* Cambridge, MA: Blackwell.

Gordon, D. 1994. *The Return of the Dangerous Classes: Drug Prohibition and Policy Politics.* New York: W. W. Norton.

Gordon, L. 1988. *Heroes in Their Own Lives.* New York: Viking.

Gottfredson, D. M. 1974. "An Empirical Analysis of Pre-Trial Release Decisions." *Journal of Criminal Justice* 2: 287–304.

Gottfredson, M. R. and D. M. Gottfredson. 1988. *Decision-Making in Criminal Justice.* New York: Plenum.

Gottfredson, S. D. and G. R. Jarjoura. 1966. "Race, Gender, and Guidelines-Based Decision-Making." *Journal of Research in Crime and Delinquency* 33: 49–69.

Government Executive Magazine. 2004. "Analysts Predict Pentagon Budget Crunch in Years Ahead." http://goverexec.com.

Government Security. 2003. "Bush Releases Homeland Security Budget." http://govtsecurity.securitysolutions.com.

Graham, J. M. 1977. "Amphetamine Politics on Capitol Hill." In J. F. Galliher and J. L. McCartney (eds.). 1977. *Criminology: Power, Crime and Criminal Law.* Homewood, IL: Dorsey Press.

Gray, M. 2000. *Drug Crazy.* New York: Routledge.

Greenberg, D. F. (ed.) 1993. *Crime and Capitalism* (2nd ed.). Philadelphia: Temple University Press.

Greenberg, D. 1974. *Crime and Law Enforcement in the Colony of New York, 1691–1776.* Ithaca: Cornell University Press.

Greene, J. and T. Roche. 2003. "Cutting Correctly in Maryland." Washington, DC: Justice Policy Institute, February 20.

Greene, J. and V. Schiraldi. 2002. "Cutting Correctly: New Prison Policies for Times of Fiscal Crisis." Washington, DC: Justice Policy Institute, February 7. http://www.justicepolicy.org/article.php?list=type&type=24.

Greenfield, L. A. 1998. Alcohol and Crime: An Analysis of National Data on the Prevalence of Alcohol Involvement in Crime Washington, DC: U.S. Department of Justice, April.

Greider, W. 2001. "A New Giant Sucking Sound." *The Nation,* December 31.

Gross, S. R. and R. Mauro. 1989. *Death and Discrimination: Racial Disparities in Capital Sentencing.* Boston: Northeastern University Press.

Gruley, B. 2001. "Prison Building Spree Creates Glut of Lockups." CorpWatch, September 6, 2001. http://www.corpwatch.org/article.php?ld=22.

Haber, S. 1964. *Efficiency and Uplift: Scientific Management in the Progressive Era, 1890–1920.* Chicago: University of Chicago Press.

Haggerty, K. D. and R. V. Ericson. 1999. "The Militarization of Policing in the Information Age." *Journal of Political and Military Sociology* 27: 233–256.

Hall, J. 1969. "The Law of Theft: The Carrier's Case." In W. J. Chambliss (ed.), *Crime and the Legal Process.* New York: McGraw-Hill.

Hallett, M. 2006. *Race, Crime and For-Profit Prisons.* Champaign, IL: University of Illinois Press.

Hancock, L. 1981. "The Myth That Females Are Treated More Leniently Than Males in the Juvenile Justice System." *Australian and New Zealand Journal of Sociology* 16: 4–14.

Hanh, T. N. 1991. *Peace Is Every Step.* New York: Bantam Books.

Hanson, R. and J. Chapper. 1991. *Indigent Defense Systems: Report to the State Justice Institute.* Williamsburg, VA: National Center for State Courts.

Harring, S. 1976. "The Development of the Police Institution in the U.S." *Crime and Social Justice* 5: 54–59.

———. 1977. "Class Conflict and the Suppression of Tramps in Buffalo, 1892–1894." *Law and Society Review* 11, 5 (Summer).

———. 1978. "The 'Most Orderly City in America': Class Conflict and the Development of the Police Institution in Milwaukee, 1880–1914." Paper presented at the American Sociological Association annual meeting, September.

Harring, S. and L. McMullen. 1975. "The Buffalo Police: Labor Unrest, Political Power and the Creation of the Police Institution." *Crime and Social Justice* 4: 5–14.

Harris, J. R. 1997. "The Growth of the Gulag: Forced Labor in the Urals Region, 1929–1931." *The Russian Review* 56: 265–281.

Harris, M. 1978. *Cows, Pigs, Wars, and Witches: The Riddles of Culture.* New York: Vintage Books.

———. 2002. "Prisoners in 2001." Washington, DC: U.S. Department of Justice, Bureau of Justice Statistics, July.

———. 2003. "Prisoners in 2002." Washington, DC: U.S. Department of Justice, Bureau of Justice Statistics, July.

Harrison, P. M. and A. Beck. 2006. "Prisoners in 2005." Washington, DC: U.S. Department of Justice, Bureau of Justice Statistics, July. http://www.ojp.usdoj.gov/bjs/pub/pdf/p05.pdf.

Harrison, P. M., A. Beck, and J. C. Karberg 2003. "Prison and Jail Inmates at Mid-Year 2002." Washington, DC: Bureau of Justice Statistics, April.

Haskins, G. L. 1960. *Law and Authority in Early Massachusetts.* New York: Macmillan.

———. 1969. "A Rule to Walk By." In R. Quinney (ed.), *Crime and Justice in Society.* Boston: Little Brown.

Hawes, J. 1971. *Children in Urban Society.* New York: Oxford University Press.

Hawkins, D. F. (ed.). 1995. *Ethnicity, Race, and Crime.* New York: SUNY Press.

Hay, D. 1975. "Property, Authority and the Criminal Law." In D. Hay, P. Linebaugh, J. G. Rule, E. P. Thompson, and C. Wilslow (eds.), *Albion's Fatal Tree: Crime and Society in 18th Century England.* New York: Pantheon.

Hays, S. P. 1959. *The Response to Industrialism, 1885–1914.* Chicago: University of Chicago Press.

Heilbroner, R. L. 1985. *The Nature and Logic of Capitalism.* New York: W.W. Norton.

Heintz, J., N. Folbre, and the Center for Popular Economics. 2000. *The Ultimate Field Guide to the U.S. Economy.* New York: The New Press.

Helmer, J. 1975. *Drugs and Minority Oppression.* New York: Seabury Press.

Henderson, C. R. 1974. "Relation of Philanthropy to Social Order and Progress." In F. Faust and B. Brantingham (eds.), *Juvenile Justice Philosophy.* St. Paul, MN: West.

Hepburn, J. 1977. "Social Control and the Legal Order. Legitimate Repression in a Capitalist State." *Contemporary Crises* 1: 77–90.

Herman, E. 1997. Privatization: Downsizing Government for Principle and Profit." *Dollars and Sense* (March/April).

Herman, E. and N. Chomsky. 2002. *Manufacturing Consent* (2nd ed.). New York: Pantheon.

Higginbotham, A. L. 1996. *Shades of Freedom: Racial Politics and Presumptions of American Legal Process.* New York: Oxford University Press.

Hill, P. G. 2001. "Public Education and Moral Monsters: A Conversation with Noam Chomsky." Canadian Centre for Policy Alternatives, January 1. http://policy-alternatives.ca/index.cfm?act=news&do=Article&call=794&pA=E053430B&type=6.

Hindus, M. S. 1980. *Prison and Plantation: Crime, Justice and Authority in Massachusetts and South Carolina, 1767–1878.* Chapel Hill, NC: University of North Carolina Press.

Hoebel, E. A. 1973. *The Law of Primitive Man.* New York: Atheneum Press.

Hofstadter, R. 1955. *Social Darwinism in American Thought.* Boston: Beacon Press.

Hogg, R. 1979. "Imprisonment and Society Under Early British Capitalism." *Crime and Social Justice* 12.

Holmes, S. A. 1994. "Ranks of Inmates Reach One Million in a 2 Decade Rise." *New York Times*, October 28, p. A1.

Holt, M. I. 1992. *The Orphan Trains.* Lincoln, NE: University of Nebraska Press.

Hope, T. and R. Sparks (eds.). 2000. *Crime, Risk and Insecurity.* London: Routledge.

Huberman, L. 1963. *Man's Worldly Goods.* New York: Monthly Review Press.

Huling, T. (2002). "Building a Prison Economy in Rural America." In M. Mauer and M. Chesney-Lind (eds.), *Invisible Punishment: The Collateral Consequences of Mass Imprisonment.* New York: New Press.

Human Rights Watch. 2000. *Punishment and Prejudice: Racial Disparities in the War on Drugs.* http://www.hrw.org/reports/2000/usa/.

Humphries, D. and D. F. Greenberg. 1993. "The Dialectics of Crime Control." In Greenberg,

D. F. (ed.), *Crime and Capitalism* (2nd ed.). Philadelphia: Temple University Press.

Ichniowski, T. 1994. "Construction Industry Finds Crime Does Pay." *ENR News: McGraw-Hill Construction Weekly*, August 8.

Ignatieff, M. 1978. *A Just Measure of Pain*. New York: Pantheon.

Inciardi, J. A. 1975. *Careers in Crime*. Chicago: Rand McNally.

———. 2002. *The War on Drugs III*. Boston: Allyn and Bacon.

Institute of Governmental Studies. 2005. "California Correctional Peace Officers Association." Berkeley: University of California. http://www.igs.berkeley.edu/library/htCaliforniaPrisonUnion.htm.

Irwin, J. 1980. *Prisons in Turmoil*. Boston: Little Brown.

———. 1985. *The Jail: Managing the Underclass in American Society*. Berkeley: University of California Press.

———. 2005. *The Warehouse Prison: Disposal of the New Dangerous Class*. Los Angeles: Roxbury Press.

Ives, G. 1914. *History of Penal Methods*. London: Stanley Paul.

Jablon, R. 2000. "L.A. Prepares for Worst as Police Scandal Grows." *Associated Press*, February 19.

Jackson, B. (ed.) 1984. *Law and Order: Criminal Justice in America*. Chicago: University of Illinois Press.

Jankowski, M. S. 1991. *Islands in the Street: Gangs and American Urban Society*. Berkeley, CA: University of California Press.

Jeffery, C. R. 1969. "The Development of Crime in Early English Society." In W. J. Chambliss, (ed.), *Crime and the Legal Process*. New York: McGraw-Hill.

Jenkins, P. 1994. "'The Ice Age': the Social Construction of a Drug Panic." *Justice Quarterly* 11: 7–31.

Johnson, B. D., A. Golub, and J. Fagan. 1995. "Careers in Crack, Drug Use, Drug Distribution, and Non-Drug Criminality." *Crime and Delinquency* 41: 275–295.

Johnson, C. 2001. *Blowback: The Costs and Consequences of American Empire*. New York: Metropolitan/Owl Books

———. 2004. *Sorrows of Empire: Militarism, Secrecy, and the End of the Republic*. New York: Metropolitan Books

Johnson, C. S. 1930. *The Negro in American Civilization*. New York: Henry Holt.

Johnson, E. H. 1957. "Selective Factors in Capital Punishment." *Social Forces* 36: 165–169.

Johnson, G. B. 1941. "The Negro and Crime." *The Annals* 217: 93–104.

Johnson, H. A. and N. T. Wolfe. 1996. *History of Criminal Justice* (2nd ed.). Cincinnati, OH: Anderson Publishing.

Johnson, K. 2003. "Federal Prisons Packed with Almost 165,000." *USA TODAY*, January 22.

Josephson, M. 1962. *The Robber Barons*. New York: Harcourt Brace Jovanovich.

Justice Policy Institute. 2003. "Race and Incarceration in Maryland: Executive Summary." October 20. http://www.justicepolicy.org/article.php?id=342.

Kalmanoff, A. 1976. *Criminal Justice: Enforcement and Administration*. Boston: Little, Brown.

Karlsen, C. F. 1987. *The Devil in the Shape of a Woman*. New York: W. W. Norton.

Kelly, M. 1975. "The First Urban Policeman." In G. F. Killinger and P. Cromwell (eds.), *Issues in Law Enforcement*. Boston: Holbrook Press.

Kelly, M. 2001. *The Devine Right of Capital*. San Francisco: Berrett-Koehler.

Kelly, R. M. 1976. "Increasing Community Influence Over the Police." In A. W. Cohn and E. C. Viano (eds.), *Police Community Relations*. Philadelphia: Lippincott.

Kempf, K. 1992. *The Role of Race in Juvenile Justice Processing in Pennsylvania*. Harrisburg, PA: Pennsylvania Commission on Crime and Delinquency.

Kennedy, R. 1997. *Race, Crime and the Law*. New York: Vintage Books.

Kett, J. F. 1977. *Rites of Passage: Adolescence in America, 1790 to the Present*. New York: Basic Books.

Kilborn, T. 2001. "Rural Towns Turn to Prisons to Reignite Their Economies." *New York Times*, August 1.

Killinger, G. F. and P. Cromwell (eds.). 1973. *Penology*. St. Paul, MN: West.

———. (eds.). 1975. *Issues in Law Enforcement*. Boston: Holbrook Press.

King, R., M. Mauer, and T. Huling. 2003. "Big Prisons, Small Towns: Prison Economics in Rural America." Washington, DC: The Sentencing Project.

Kinzer, S. 2006. *Overthrow: America's Century of Regime Change from Hawaii to Iraq*. New York: Times Books, Henry Holt and Company.

Knapp Commission. 1975. "Police Corruption in New York." In J. Skolnick and T. Gray (eds.), *Police in America*. Boston: Little, Brown.

Knappman, E. W. 1994. *Great American Trials: From Salem Witchcraft to Rodney King*. Detroit, MI: Visible Ink Press.

Klein, M. 1995. *The American Street Gang*. New York: Oxford University Press.

Klein, M., C. Maxson, and L. Cunningham. 1991. "Crack, Street Gangs, and Violence." *Criminology* 29: 623–650.

Kolko, G. 1963. *The Triumph of Conservatism: A Reinterpretation of American History, 1900–1916*. New York: Free Press.

Komp, C. 2005. "Civil Disobedience Against War Gets Day in Federal Court." *The New Standard*, September 21. http://new standardnews.net/content/index.cfm/items/2384.

Kopp, P. 2006. "Stereotypes of Law Enforcement in Television." MA thesis, Department of Criminal Justice, University of Nevada-Las Vegas.

Korten, D. C. 2001. *When Corporations Rule the World* (2nd ed.). San Francisco: Berrett-Koehler.

Kraska, P. B. 1999. "Militarizing Criminal Justice: Exploring the Possibilities." *Journal of Political and Military Sociology* 27. 205–216.

Krisberg, B. and J. Austin. 1978. *The Children of Ishmael: Critical Perspectives on Juvenile Justice*. Palo Alto, CA: Mayfield.

———. 1993. *Reinventing Juvenile Justice*. Newbury Park, CA: Sage.

Kuhn, A. 2001. "Incarcerations Rates Across the World." In M. Tonry (ed.), *Penal Reform in Overcrowded Times*. New York: Oxford University Press.

Kulish, N. 2001. "Annexing the Penitentiary." *The Wall Street Journal*. August 8.

Kunzel, R. 1993. *Fallen Women, Problem Girls: Unmarried Mothers and the Professionalization of Social Work, 1890–1945*. New Haven, CT: Yale University Press.

Landis, T. 2002. "Hard Time." *Illinois Issues*, June.

Lane, R. 1967. *Policing the City: Boston, 1822–1885*. Cambridge: Harvard University Press.

Langbein, J. H. 1983. "Albion's Fatal Flaws." *Past and Present* 98: 96–120.

Laursen, E. 1996. "A Tale of Two Communities." *Z Magazine* (October): 45–50.

Lawrence, S. and J. Travis. 2004. *The New Landscape of Imprisonment: Mapping America's Prison Expansion*. Washington, DC: Urban Institute. http://www.urban.org/Uploaded PDF/410994_mapping_prisons.pdf.

Leong, A. 1998. "From Bruce Lee to Vincent Chin: Stereotyping in Anti-Asian Violence." Paper presented at the Northeastern Association of Criminal Justice, Newport, Rhode Island, June.

Leovy, J. and J. Chong. 2004. "Youth Authority to Review Use of Cages." *Los Angeles Times*, February 6.

Lerner, G. 1986. *The Creation of Patriarchy*. New York: Oxford University Press.

Lerner, S. 1986. *Bodily Harm: The Pattern of Fear and Violence at the California Youth Authority*. Bolinas, CA: Common Knowledge Press.

Leslie, R. J. 1977. "The Alliances of the CIA to Political and Underworld Figures." Seminar paper, Department of Sociology-Anthropology, SUNY-Cortland.

Levin, D. J., P. A. Langan, and J. M. Brown. 2000. "State Court Sentencing of Convicted Felons, 1996." Washington, DC: Bureau of Justice Statistics, February.

Levinthal, C. 1996. *Drugs, Behavior, and Modern Society*. Boston: Allyn & Bacon.

Lewis, A. 1964. *Gideon's Trumpet*. New York: Harper & Row.

Liazos, A. 1974. "Class Oppression: The Functions of Juvenile Justice." *Insurgent Sociologist* (Fall).

Lilly, J. 1993. "Great Leader's Gulag: Siberian Timber Camps Are Relics of the Cold War." *Far Eastern Economic Review* (September 9): 21–22.

Lilly, J. R. and P. Knepper. 1993. "The Correctional-Commercial Complex." *Crime and Delinquency* 39: 150–166.

Lindesmith, A. R. 1965. *The Addict and the Law*. New York: Vintage Books.

Linebaugh, P. 1975. "The Tyburn Riot Against the Surgeons." In D. Hay et al. (eds.), *Albion's Fatal Tree*.

———. 1976. "Karl Marx, the Theft of Wood, and Working Class Composition: A Contribution to the Current Debate." *Crime and Social Justice* 6: 5–16.

———. 1985. "(Marxist) Social History and (Conservative) Legal History: A Reply to Professor Langbein." *New York University Law Review* 60: 212–243.

Link, A. 1967. *American Epoch: A History of the U.S. Since the 1890s*. (3rd ed.) New York: Alfred A. Knopf.

Lipsitz, G. 1982. *Class and Culture in Cold War America*. South Hadley, MA: J. F. Bergin.

Litvan, L. M. 1995. "Security for Success." *Nation's Business* 83 (6), June, p. 15.

Lockwood, D., A. E. Pottieger, and J. A. Inciardi. 1995. "Crack Use, Crime by Crack Users, and Ethnicity." In D. F. Hawkins (ed.), *Ethnicity, Race, and Crime*. Albany, NY: SUNY Press.

Logan, C. nd. "Private Prisons" (http://www.ucc.uconn.edu/~logan/).

Lorde, A. 1988. "Age, Race, Class, and Sex: Women Redefining Difference." In P. S. Rothenberg (ed.), *Racism and Sexism: An Integrated Study*. New York: St. Martin's Press.

Los Angeles Times. 1984. "South Central Sales Explode into $25 'Rocks'." November 25.

———. 1999a. "LAPD Corruption Probe Grows to 7 Shootings." October 22.

———. 1999b. "Crime, Poverty Test Rampart Officers' Skill." November 10.

———. 1999c. "Latest Rampart Case Focuses on Third Officer." December 2.

———. 1999d. "Rampart Probe May Now Affect over 3,000 Cases." December 15.

———. 2000. "Outside Probe Sought in LAPD Scandal." February 11.

Low, S. 2003. *Behind the Gates: Life, Security, and the Pursuit of Happiness in Fortress America*. New York: Routledge.

Lubove, R. 1965. *The Professional Altruist: The Emergence of Social Work as a Career, 1880–1930*. Cambridge. MA: Harvard University Press.

Lyman. J. L. 1975. "The Metropolitan Police Act of 1829." In G. F. Killinger and P. Cromwell (eds.), *Issues in Law Enforcement*. Boston: Holbrook Press.

Lynch, M. J. and R. Michalowski. 2006. *Primer in Radical Criminology* (4th ed.). Monsey, NY: Criminal Justice Press, 2006.

Maas, P. 1975. "Serpico: The Cop Who Defied the System." In J. Skolnick and T. Gray (eds.), *Police in America*. Boston: Little, Brown.

Mackey, P. E. 1982. *Hanging in the Balance: The Anti-Capital Punishment Movement in New York State, 1776–1861*. New York: Garland Press.

MacKinnon, C. 1989. *Toward a Feminist Theory of the State*. Cambridge: Harvard University Press.

Madison, J. 1961. "No. 10: Madison." In A. Hamilton, J. Madison, and J. Jay (eds.), *The Federalist Papers*. New York: Mentor.

Mager, A. 2005. "St. Pat's Four Acquitted on Heaviest Charge." October. http://www.dhafirtrial.net/?p=155.

Maguire, K. and A. L. Pastore (eds.). 1995. *Sourcebook on Criminal Justice Statistics—1994*. Washington, DC: Department of Justice, Bureau of Justice Statistics.

———. 1996. *Sourcebook on Criminal Justice Statistics—1995*. Washington, DC: Department of Justice, Bureau of Justice Statistics.

———. 1997. *Sourcebook on Criminal Justice Statistics—1996*. Washington, DC: Department of Justice, Bureau of Justice Statistics.

———. 1998. *Sourcebook of Criminal Justice Statistics—1997*. Washington, DC: U.S. Department of Justice.

———. 1999. *Sourcebook of Criminal Justice Statistics—1998*. Washington, DC: U.S. Department of Justice.

Mancini, M. J. 1978. "Race, Economics, and the Abandonment of Convict Leasing." *Journal of Negro History* 63.

———. 1996. *One Dies, Get Another: Convict Leasing in the American South, 1866–1928*. Columbia: University of South Carolina Press.

Mann, A. (ed.). 1963. *The Progressive Era: Renaissance or Liberal Failure*. New York: Holt, Rinehart and Winston.

Mann, C. R. 1995. *Unequal Justice: A Question of Color*. Bloomington, IN: Indiana University Press.

Marchetti, V. and J. D. Marks. 1974. *The CIA and the Cult of Intelligence*. New York: Dell.

Marks, A. 2003. "Strapped for Cash, States Set Some Felons Free." *The Christian Science Monitor*, January 21;

Marx, K. 1975. "Debates on the Law of the Theft of Wood." In K. Marx and F. Engels. *Collected Works*. (Vol. 1). New York: International Publishers.

———. 1977. *Capital* (Vol. 1). 1977. New York: Vintage Books.

———. 1988. *The Economic and Philosophic Manuscripts of 1844*. Buffalo, NY: Prometheus Books.

———. 1993. "The Usefulness of Crime." In D. F. Greenberg (ed.), *Crime and Capitalism* (2nd ed.). Philadelphia: Temple University Press.

Marx, K. and F. Engels. 1955. *The Communist Manifesto*. Arlington Heights, IL: Crofts Classics.

———. 1975. *Collected Works* (Vol. 1). New York: International Publishers.

Massey, D. S. and N. A. Denton. 1993. *American Apartheid: Segregation and the Making of the Underclass*. Cambridge: Harvard University Press.

Mattera, P. and M. Khan. 2001. *Jail Breaks: Economic Development Subsidies Given to Private Prisons*. Washington, DC: Good Jobs First (October).

Mauer, M. 1994. *Americans Behind Bars: The International Use of Incarceration, 1992–1993*. Washington, DC: The Sentencing Project.

———. 1995. *Young Black Americans and the Criminal Justice System: Five Years Later*. Washington, DC: The Sentencing Project.

———. 2006. *Race to Incarcerate* (2nd ed.). New York: The New Press.

Mauer, M. and M. Chesney-Lind (eds.). 2002. *Invisible Punishment: The Collateral Consequences of Mass Imprisonment*. New York: New Press.

May, D. 1977. "Delinquent Girls Before the Court." *Medical Science Law Review* 17: 203–210.

Maynard, M. 2000. "Prison Math." *City Beat* 21. www.citypages.com/databank/21/1039/.

Mays, G. L. and L. T. Winfree, Jr. 1998. *Contemporary Corrections*. Belmont, CA: Wadsworth.

McConville, S. 1998. "Local Justice: The Jail." In N. Morris and D. J. Rothman (eds.), *The Oxford History of the Prison*. New York: Oxford University Press.

McCorkle, R. C. and T. D. Miethe. 2001. *Panic: The Social Construction of the Street Gang Problem*. Upper Saddle River, NJ: Prentice-Hall.

McCoy, A. W. 1973. *The Politics of Heroin in Southeast Asia*. New York: Harper & Row.

McDonald, W. F. (ed.). 1979. *The Prosecutor*. Beverly Hills, CA: Sage.

McGarrell, E. 1993. "Trends in Racial Disproportionality in Juvenile Court Processing: 1985–1989." *Crime and Delinquency* 39: 29–48.

McGarrell, E. F. and T. J. Flanagan (eds.). 1986. *Sourcebook of Criminal Justice Statistics—1985*. Washington, DC: U.S. Department of Justice.

McHenry, R. (ed.). 1983. *Famous American Women: A Biographical Dictionary from Colonial Times to the Present*. New York: Dover Publications, 1983.

McKelvey, B. 1968. *American Prisons*. Montclair, NJ: Patterson Smith (originally published 1936).

McKirdy, C. R.. 1984. "Massachusetts Lawyers on the Eve of the American Revolution: The State of the Profession." In D. R. Coquilette (ed.), *Law in Colonial Massachusetts, 1630–1800*. Boston: The Colonial Society of Massachusetts, distributed by the University Press of Virginia.

Meddis, S. V. and D. Sharp. 1994. "Prison Business Is a Blockbuster." *USA Today*, December 13.

Meier, A. and E. Rudwick. 1970. *From Plantation to Ghetto*. New York: Hill & Wang.

Meierhoefer, B. S. 1992. "The General Effect of Mandatory Minimum Prison Terms: A Longitudinal Study of Federal Sentences Imposed." Washington, DC: Federal Judicial Center.

Melossi, D. 1978. Review of *Punishment and Social Structure* by G. Rusche and O. Kirchheimer, *Crime and Social Justice* 9.

Melossi, D. and M. Lettiere. 1998. "Punishment in the American Democracy: The Paradoxes of Good Intentions." In W. P. Weiss and N. South (eds.), *Comparing Prison Systems: Toward a Comparative and International Penology*. Australia: Gordon and Breach.

Mennel, R. 1973. *Thorns and Thistles: Juvenile Delinquents in the U.S., 1820–1940*. Hanover, NH: University Press of New England.

Mergenbagen, P. 1996. "The Prison Population Bomb." *American Demographics* 18: 6–42.

Merry, S. E. 1990. *Getting Justice and Getting Even: Legal Consciousness Among Working Class Americans*. Chicago: University of Chicago Press.

Messerschmidt, J. W. 1987. "Feminism, Criminology, and the Rise of the Female Sex Delinquent, 1880–1930." *Contemporary Crises* 11: 243–263.

———. 1997. *Crime as Structured Action: Gender, Race, Class, and Crime in the Making*. Thousand Oaks, CA: Sage.

Michalowski, R. 1985. *Order, Law and Crime*. New York: Macmillan.

Michalowski, R. and R. Kramer (eds.). 2006. *State-Corporate Crime.* New Brunswick, NJ: Rutgers University Press.

Miliband, R. 1969. *The State in Capitalist Society.* New York: Basic Books.

Miller, E. 1986. *Street Woman.* Philadelphia: Temple University Press.

Miller, J. G. 1996. *Search and Destroy: African-Americans Males in the Criminal Justice System.* Cambridge University Press.

———. 1998. *Last One Over the Wall* (2nd ed.). Columbus: Ohio State University Press.

Miller, M. B. 1974. "At Hard Labor: Rediscovering the 19th Century Prison." *Issues in Criminology* 9: 91–114.

Miller, W. R. 1999. *Cops and Bobbies: Police Authority in New York and London, 1830–1870* (2nd ed.). Columbus: Ohio State University Press.

Millman, J. 1991. "Captive Market." *Forbes* 148, 6, p. 190.

Mills, C. W. 1959. *The Sociological Imagination.* New York: Oxford University Press.

Milovanovic, D. 1994. *A Primer in the Sociology of Law.* New York: Harrow and Heston.

Miringoff, M. and M. Miringoff. 1999. *The Social Health of the Nation.* New York: Oxford University Press.

Mokhiber, R. 1996 "Corporate Crime: Underworld U.S.A." In K. Danaher (ed.), *Corporations Are Gonna Get You're Mama: Globalization and the Downsizing of the American Dream.* Monroe, ME: Common Courage Press.

Monkkonen, E. 1975. *The Dangerous Class: Crime and Poverty in Columbus, Ohio, 1860–1885.* Columbus: Ohio State University Press.

Moore, J. 1991. *Going Down to the Barrio.* Philadelphia: Temple University Press.

Morain, D. 2003. "Leaves for Prison Guards Criticized." *Los Angeles Times,* May 9.

Morash, M. A. and E. A. Anderson. 1978. "Liberal Thinking on Rehabilitation: A Work-Able Solution to Crime." *Social Problems* 25: 556–563.

Morgan, E. S. 1958. *The Puritan Dilemma: The Story of John Winthrop.* Boston: Little, Brown.

Morris, N. and D. J. Rothman (eds.) 1995. *The Oxford History of the Prison.* New York: Oxford University Press.

Moyer, I. L. 1992. "Police/Citizen Encounters: Issues of Chivalry, Gender and Race." In I. L. Moyer (ed.), *The Changing Roles of Women in the Criminal Justice System.* (2nd ed.). Prospect Heights, IL: Waveland Press.

Munk, N. 1994. "Rent-A-Cops." *Forbes* 154 (8): 104–105.

Murray, C. 1994. *Losing Ground: American Social Policy, 1950–1980.* New York: Basic Books.

Murray, J. B. 1986. "An Overview of Cocaine Use and Abuse." *Psychological Reports* 243–264.

Murton, T. and J. Hyams. 1969. *Accomplices to the Crime: The Arkansas Prison Scandal.* New York: Grove Press.

Musto, D. F. 1999. *The American Disease: Origins of Narcotic Control* (3rd ed.). New Haven, CT: Yale University Press.

Myers, M. A. and J. L. Massey. 1999. "Race, Labor, and Punishment in Postbellum Georgia." In R. P. Weiss (ed.), *Social History of Crime, Policing and Punishment.* Brookfield, VT: Ashgate.

Nadel, B. 1995. "Putting a Lock on Prison Costs." *American City and County* 110 (1).

Naffine, N. 1987. *Female Crime: The Construction of Women in Criminology.* Sydney, Australia: Allen and Unwin.

National Commission on Law Observance and Enforcement. 1931. *Lawlessness in Law Enforcement.* Washington, DC: U.S. Government Printing Office.

National Poverty Center. 2006. "Poverty in the United States: Frequently Asked Questions." http://www.npc.umich.edu/poverty/.

Nelson, W. E. 1974. "Emerging Nations of Modern Criminal Law in the Revolutionary Era: An Historical Perspective." In R. Quinney (ed.), *Criminal Justice in America: A Critical Understanding.* Boston: Little, Brown.

———. 1975. *The Americanization of Common Law.* Cambridge, MA: Harvard University Press.

Neubauer, D. W. 2005. *America's Courts and the Criminal Justice System* (8th ed.). Belmont, CA: Thompson/Wadsworth.

New York Times. 1989a. "Crack—A Disaster of Historic Dimensions." May 28.

New York Times. 1989b. "The Spreading Web of Crack." October 2.

New York Times. 1989c. "Crack, Bane of Inner City Is Now Gripping Suburbs." October 1.

Newsweek. 1988. "Crack, the Drug Crisis: Hour by Hour Crack." November 28.

Nohn, H. 1976. "The Hughes, Nixon, Lansky Connection." *Rolling Stone,* May 20.

Nye, R. 1951. *Midwestern Progressive Politics.* East Lansing: Michigan State University Press.

O'Connor, J. 1973. *The Fiscal Crisis of the State.* New York: St. Martin's Press.

Odem, M. 1995. *Delinquent Daughters: Protecting and Policing Adolescent Female Sexuality in the United States, 1885–1920.* Chapel Hill: University of North Carolina Press.

Odem, M. and S. Schlossman. 1991. "Guardians of Virtue: The Juvenile Court and Female Delinquency in Early 20th Century Los Angeles." *Crime and Delinquency* 37: 186–203.

Office of National Drug Control Policy. 2004. "The Price and Purity of Illicit Drugs: 1981 Through the Second Quarter of 2003." Washington, DC: Executive Office of the President, Publication Number NCJ 207768.

Osgood, R. K. 1984. "John Clark, Esq., Justice of the Peace, 1667–1728." In D. R. Coquillette (ed.), *Law in Colonial Massachusetts, 1630–1800.* Boston: The Colonial Society of Massachusetts, distributed by the University Press of Virginia.

Oshinsky, D. M. 1996. *Worse than Slavery: Parchman and the Ordeal of Jim Crow Justice.* New York: Free Press.

Parenti, C. 1995. "Inside Jobs: Use of Prison Labor in the U.S." *New Statesman and Society* 8: 20–21.

———. 1996. "Pay Now, Pay Later: States Impose Prison Peonage." *The Progressive* 60 (7): 26–29.

———. 1999. *Lockdown America: Police and Prisons in the Age of Crisis.* New York: Verso.

Parenti, M. 1993. *Against Empire.* San Francisco: City Light Books.

———. 1994. *Land of Idols: Political Mythology in America.* New York: St. Martin's Press.

———. 2002. *Democracy for the Few* (7th ed.). Boston: Bedford/St. Martin's.

Parks, E. L. 1977. "From Constabulary to Police Society: Implications for Social Control." In J. F. Galliher and J. L. McCartney (eds.), *Criminology: Power, Crime and Criminal Law.* Homewood, IL: Dorsey Press.

Pasqualini, J. 1993. "Glimpses Inside China's Gulag." *The China Quarterly* 134: 352–358.

Patterson, E. B. and M. J. Lynch. 1991. "Biases in Formalized Bail Procedures." In M. J. Lynch and E. B. Patterson (eds.), *Race and Criminal Justice.* New York: Harrow and Heston.

"People v. Turner." 1974. In F. Faust and B. Brantingham (eds.), *Juvenile Justice Philosophy.* St. Paul, MN: West.

Perrucci, R. and E. Wysong. 2003. *The New Class Society* (2nd ed.). New York: Roman and Littlefield.

Peterson, R. D. "Youthful Offender Designations and Sentencing in the New York Criminal Courts." *Social Problems* 35 (April, 1988).

Pfohl, S. 1994. *Images of Deviance and Social Control: A Sociological History.* New York: McGraw-Hill.

Phillips, K. 1990. *The Politics of the Rich and the Poor.* New York: Random House.

———. 2002. *Wealth and Democracy.* New York: Broadway Books.

Pickett, R. 1969. *House of Refuge.* Syracuse: Syracuse University Press.

Piliavin, I. and S. Briar. "Police Encounters with Juveniles." *American Journal of Sociology* 70: 206–214.

Pisciotta, A. 1982. "Saving the Children: The Promise and Practice of *Parens Patriae,* 1838–98." *Crime and Delinquency* 28: 410–425.

———. 1983. "Race, Sex and Rehabilitation: A Study of Differential Treatment in the Juvenile Reformatory, 1825–1900." *Crime and Delinquency* 29: 254–268.

———. 1994. *Benevolent Repression: Social Control and the American Reformatory-Prison Movement.* New York: New York University Press.

Piven, F. F. and R. Cloward. 1972. *Regulating the Poor: The Functions of Social Welfare.* New York: Vintage Books.

Platt, A. 1974. "The Triumph of Benevolence: Origins of Juvenile Justice in the U.S." In R. Quinney (ed.), *Criminal Justice in America: A Critical Understanding.* Boston: Little, Brown.

———. 1977. *The Child Savers* (rev. ed.). Chicago: University of Chicago Press.

———. 2006. "The Child Savers Revisited: Revising the Canon." Keynote address at the annual meeting of the Justice Studies Association, Berkeley, CA, June.

Poggi, G. 1978. *The Development of the Modern State.* Palo Alto, CA: Stanford University Press.

Pollock, J. M. 1996. "Gender, Justice, and Social Control: A Historical Perspective."

In A. V. Merlo and J. M. Pollock (eds.), *Women, Law, and Social Control*. New York: Allyn and Bacon.

Pope, C. and W. Feyerherm. 1990. "Minority Status and Juvenile Justice Processing: An Assessment of the Research Literature," (Parts I and II). *Criminal Justice Abstracts* 22 (2, 3).

Postman, N. 1994. *The Disappearance of Childhood*. New York: Vintage Books.

Pound, R. 1922. *An Introduction to the Philosophy of Law*. New Haven: Yale University Press

————. 1942. *Social Control Through Law*. New Haven: Yale University Press.

Poveda, T. G. 1994. *Rethinking White Collar Crime*. Westport, CT: Praeger.

Powell, J. C. 1891. *The American Siberia*. Chicago: H.J. Smith.

Powers, E. 1966. *Crime and Punishment in Early Massachusetts*. Boston: Beacon Press.

President's Commission on Law Enforcement and Administration of Justice. 1967a. *Task Force Report: Science and Technology*. Washington, DC: U.S. Government Printing Office.

————. 1967b. *Task Force Report: The Police*. Washington, DC: U.S. Government Printing Office.

Prison Policy Initiative. 2003. "Diluting Democracy: Census Quirk Fuels Prison Expansion." Springfield, MA:. http://www.prisonpolicy.org.

Proband, S. C. 1997a. "Black Men Face 29 Percent Lifetime Chance of Prison." *Overcrowded Times* 8, 1.

————. 1997b. "Jail and Prison Populations Continue to Grow in 1996." *Overcrowded Times* 8, 4.

————. 1998a. "Corrections Populations Near 6 Million." *Overcrowded Times* 9 (June).

————. 1998b. "Prison Populations Up 5.2 Percent in U.S. in 1997." *Overcrowded Times* 9, 4.

Quigley, B. 2005. "The St. Patrick's Four and Resistance to the War in Iraq." March 17. http://www.commondreams.org/views05/0317-32.htm.

Quinney, R. (ed.) 1969. *Crime and Justice in Society*. Boston: Little Brown.

————. 1979. *Criminology*. Boston: Little Brown.

————. 1980. *Class, State and Crime* (2nd ed.). New York: Longman.

————. 1998. *For the Time Being*. New York. SUNY Press.

————. 2001. *The Social Reality of Crime*. New Brunswick, NJ: Transaction Books (originally published by Little Brown in 1970).

————. 2002a. *Critique of Legal Order: Crime Control in Capitalist Society*. New Brunswick, NJ: Transaction Books, 2002 (originally published by Little Brown in 1974).

————. 2002b. "Socialist Humanism and the Problem of Crime: Thinking About Erich Fromm in the Development of Critical/Peacemaking Criminology." In K. Anderson and R. Quinney (eds.), *Erich Fromm and Critical Criminology*. Chicago: University of Illinois Press.

Quinney, R. and J. Wildeman. 1991. *The Problem of Crime: A Peace and Social Justice Perspective* (3rd ed.). Mountain View, CA: Mayfield.

Radelet, L. A. 1977. *The Police and the Community* (2nd ed.). Beverly Hills, CA: Glencoe Press.

Radelet, M. L. 1981. "Racial Characteristics and the Imposition of the Death Penalty." *American Sociological Review* 46: 918–927.

Radelet, M. L., H. A. Bedau, and C. E. Putnam. 1992. *In Spite of Innocence*. Boston: Northeastern University Press.

Rafter, N. H. (ed.). 1988. *White Trash: The Eugenic Family Studies, 1899–1919*. Boston: Northeastern University Press.

————. 1990. *Partial Justice: Women, Prisons, and Social Control* (2nd ed.). New Brunswick, NJ: Transaction Books.

————. 1997. *Creating Born Criminals*. Chicago: University of Illinois Press.

Rafter, N. H. and E. A. Stanko (eds.). 1982. *Judge, Lawyer, Victim, Thief: Women, Gender Roles and Criminal Justice*. Boston: Northeastern University Press.

Rawson R. A. 1990. "Cut the Crack: The Policy Maker's Guide to Cocaine Treatment." *Policy Review* 11 (Winter).

Reaves, B. A. 1998. *Felony Defendants in Large Urban Counties, 1994*. Washington, DC: U.S. Department of Justice, Bureau of Justice Statistics.

Reaves, B. A. and J. Perez. 1994 "Pretrial Release of Felony Defendants, 1992." *Bureau of Justice Statistics Bulletin* (November): 1–16.

Redfield, J. 1993. *The Celestine Prophecy*. New York: Warner Books.

Reiman, J. H. 2007. *The Rich Get Richer and the Poor Get Prison* (8th ed.). Boston: Allyn and Bacon.

Reinarman, C. and H. G. Levine. 1997a. "Crack in Context." In C. Reinarman and H. G. Levine (eds.), *Crack in America: Demon Drugs and Social Justice*. Berkeley, CA: University of California Press, 1997.

———. 1997b. "The Crack Attack: Politics and Media in America's Latest Drug Scare." In C. Reinarman and H. G. Levine (eds.), *Crack in America: Demon Drugs and Social Justice*. Berkeley, CA: University of California Press, 1997.

Reith, C. 1975. *The Blind Eye of History: A Study of the Origins of the Present Police Era*. Montclair, NJ: Patterson Smith (originally published 1952).

Rendleman, D. 1974. "Parens Patriae: From Chancery to Juvenile Court." In F. Faust and B. Brantingham (eds.), *Juvenile Justice Philosophy*. St. Paul, MN: West.

Rhode, D. 2001. "A Growth Industry Cools as New York Prisons Thin." *New York Times*, August 21.

Richards, S. 1990. "Commentary: Sociological Penetration of the American Gulag." *Wisconsin Sociologist* 27: 18–28.

Richardson, J. F. 1974. *Urban Police in the U.S.* Port Washington, NY: Kennikat Press.

———. 1975. "The Early Years of the New York Police Department." In J. Skolnick and T. Gray (eds.), *Police in America*. Boston: Little, Brown.

Ritzer, G. 1996. *The McDonalization of Society* (rev. ed.). Thousand Oaks, CA: Pine Forge Press.

Rogers, K. 1972. "'For Her Own Protection': Conditions of Incarceration for Female Juvenile Offenders in the State of Connecticut." *Law and Society Review*: 223–246.

Rossides, D. W. 1997. *Social Stratification: The Interplay of Class, Race, and Gender* (2nd ed.). Upper Saddle River, NJ: Prentice-Hall.

Rothman, D. 1971. *The Discovery of the Asylum*. Boston: Little, Brown.

———. 1980. *Conscience and Convenience: The Asylum and Its Alternatives in Progressive America*. Boston: Little Brown.

———. 1998. "Perfecting the Prison." In N. Morris and D. J. Rothman (eds.), *The Oxford History of the Prison*. New York: Oxford University Press.

Rothman, R. 1998. *Social Inequality* (2nd ed.). Upper Saddle River, NJ: Prentice-Hall.

Rothman, S. 1978. *Woman's Proper Place: A History of Changing Ideals and Practices, 1870 to the Present*. New York: Basic Books.

Rotman, E. 1998. "The Failure of Reform: United States, 1865–1965." In N. Morris and D. J. Rothman (eds.), *The Oxford History of the Prison*. New York: Oxford University Press.

Ruigrok, W. and R. van Tulder. 1995. *The Logic of International Restructuring*. London: Rutledge.

Rusche, G. and O. Kirchheimer. 1968. *Punishment and Social Structure*. New York: Russell and Russell (originally published 1938).

Rush, G. 1997. *Inside American Prisons and Jails*. Incline Village, NV: Copperhouse Publishing.

Rush, G. E. 1994. *The Dictionary of Criminal Justice*. Chicago: Duskin Publishing Group.

Sabol, W. J. 1989. "Racially Disproportionate Prison Population in the United States." *Contemporary Crises* 13: 405–432.

Samaha, J. 1999. *Criminal Procedure* (4th ed.). Belmont, CA: Wadsworth.

Sampson, R. J. 1986. "SES and Official Reaction to Delinquency." *American Sociological Review* 51: 876–885.

Saxaki Magazine. 1997. "At the Bottom of The Global Narcotics Economy: Minority women couriers." (Vol. 3, No. 1). http://saxakali.com/ saxakali-magazine/saxmag31g2.htm.

Schiraldi, V. 1994. *The Undue Influence of California's Prison Guards' Union: California's Correctional-Industrial Complex*. San Francisco, CA: Center on Juvenile and Criminal Justice.

Schiraldi, V. and J. Zeidenberg. 1999. *The Punishing Decade: Prison and Jail Estimates at the Millennium*. Washington, DC: Justice Policy Institute.

Schlosser, E. 1998. "The Prison-Industrial Complex." *The Atlantic Monthly* (December).

Schlossman, S. 1977. *Love and the American Delinquent: The Theory and Practice of "Progressive" Juvenile Justice, 1825–1920*. Chicago: University of Chicago Press.

Schlossman, S. and S. Wallach. 1978. "The Crime of Precocious Sexuality: Female Delinquency in the Progressive Era." *Harvard Educational Review* 8: 65–94.

Schmidhauser, J. R. 1960. *The Supreme Court: Its Politics, Personalities and Procedures.* New York: Holt, Rinehart and Winston.

Schmidt, S. 2006. "Prison Guards Lock Up Bundle in Overtime Pay—2,400 Officers Made More Than $100,000." *San Diego Union-Tribune*, February 27.

Schorr, L. 1989. *Within Our Reach: Breaking the Cycle of Disadvantage.* New York: Anchor.

Schwartz, B. 1993. *A History of the Supreme Court.* New York: Oxford University Press.

Schwendinger, H. and J. Schwendinger. 1976. "Delinquency and the Collective Varieties of Youth." *Crime and Social Justice* 5 (Spring–Summer).

Seagal, D. 1993. "Tales from the Cutting-Room Floor: The Reality of 'Reality-Based' Television." *Harper's Magazine*, November.

Sellin, J. T. 1944. *Pioneering in Penology: The Amsterdam Houses of Correction in the Sixteenth and Seventeenth Centuries.* Philadelphia: University of Pennsylvania Press.

———. (ed.) 1967. *Capital Punishment.* New York: Harper and Row.

———. 1976. *Slavery and the Penal System.* New York: Elsevier.

Semmes, R. *Crime and Punishment in Early Maryland.* Montclair, NJ: Patterson Smith, 1970.

Server, A. 1994. "Crime Stoppers Making a Killing." *Fortune* 129 (7): 109–111.

Shank, G. 1978. Review of "Pioneering in Penology" and "Slavery and the Penal System" by J. T. Sellin, *Crime and Social Justice* 10: 36–52.

Shannon, R. T. (ed.). 1896. *Code of Tennessee.* Nashville: Marshall and Bruce.

Shapiro, I., and R. Greenstein. 1997. "Trends in the Distribution of After-Tax Income: An Analysis of Congressional Budget Office Data." Center on Budget and Policy Priorities, Washington, DC, August 14.

Shaw, A. G. L. 1966. *Convicts and the Colonies.* London: Faber and Faber.

Shearing, C. D. and P. C. Stenning. 1987. "Reframing Policing." In C. D. Shearing and P. C. Stenning (eds.), *Private Policing.* Newbury Park: Sage.

Shelden, R. G. 1976. "Rescued from Evil; Origins of the Juvenile Justice System in Memphis, Tennessee, 1900–1917." Ph.D. dissertation, Southern Illinois University, Carbondale.

———. 1980. "From Slave to Caste Society: Penal Changes in Tennessee, 1840–1915." *Tennessee Historical Quarterly* 38: 462–478.

———. 1981. "Sex Discrimination in the Juvenile Justice System: Memphis, Tennessee, 1900–1917." In M. Q. Warren (ed.), *Comparing Male and Female Offenders.* Newbury Park, CA: Sage.

———. 1982. *Criminal Justice in America: A Sociological Approach.* Boston: Little Brown.

———. 1992. "A History of the Shelby County Industrial and Training School." *Tennessee Historical Quarterly* (Summer): 96–106.

———. 1993a. "Origins of the Memphis Juvenile Court." *Tennessee Historical Quarterly* 52: 33–43.

———. 1993b. "Convict Leasing." In D. F. Greenberg, D. F. (ed.), *Crime and Capitalism* (2nd ed.). Philadelphia: Temple University Press.

———. 1998. "Confronting the Ghost of Mary Ann Crouse: Gender Bias in the Juvenile Justice System." *Juvenile and Family Court Journal* 49: 11–26.

———. 2004. "Why Are We So Punitive? Some Observations on Recent Incarceration Trends." http://cjcj.org/pdf/punitive.pdf.

Shelden, R. G. and W. Brown. 2000. "The Crime Control Industry and the Management of the Surplus Population." *Critical Criminology* 8: 39–62.

Shelden, R. G. and L. T. Osborne. 1989. " 'For Their Own Good': Class Interests and the Child Saving Movement in Memphis, Tennessee, 1900–1917." *Criminology* 27: 801–821.

Shelden, R. G., S. Tracy, and W. Brown. 2004. *Youth Gangs in American Society* (3rd ed.). Belmont, CA: Thompson/Wadsworth.

Sherman, L. W., L. Steele, D. Lauferweiler, N. Hoffer, and S. A. Julian. 1989. "Stray Bullets and Mushroom, Random Shooting of Bystanders in Four cities, 1987–1988." *Journal of Quantitative Criminology* 5: 297–316

Shichor, D. and D. K. Sechrest (eds.). 1996. *Three Strikes and You're Out: Vengeance as Public Policy.* Thousand Oaks, CA: Sage.

Sickmund, M. 2002. *Juvenile Offenders in Residential Placement, 1997–1999.* Washington, DC: U.S Department of Justice, Office of Juvenile Justice and Delinquency Prevention.

———. 2004. "Census of Juveniles in Residential Placement Data Book." Washington, DC: Office of Juvenile Justice and Delinquency Prevention.

———. 2006. "Juvenile Residential Facility Census, 2002: Selected Findings." Washington, DC: U.S Department of Justice, Office of Juvenile Justice and Delinquency Prevention, June.

Sickmund, M., T. J. Sladky, and W. Kang. 2004. "Census of Juveniles in Residential Placement Databook." http://www.ojjdp. ncjrs.org/ojstatbb/cjrp/asp/Offense_Comm itted.asp?state=0&topic=Offense_Commit ted&year=2001&percent=rate.

Sidel R. 1992. *Keeping Women and Children Last*. New York: Penguin.

Siegel, L. 1997. "The Pregnancy Police Fight the War on Drugs." In C. Reinarman and H. G. Levine (eds.), *Crack in America: Demon Drugs and Social Justice*. Berkeley, CA: University of California Press, 1997, pp 249-259.

Silver, A. 1967. "The Demand for Order in Civil Society." In D. Bordua (ed.), *The Police: Six Sociological Essays*. New York: John Wiley.

Simon, J. 1993. *Poor Discipline: Parole and the Social Control of the Underclass, 1890–1990*. Chicago: University of Chicago Press.

Sklar, H. 1998. "Let Them Eat Cake." *Z Magazine* (November).

———. 1999. "For CEO's, a Minimum Wage in the Millions." *Z Magazine* (July/August).

Skolnick, J. 1994. *Justice Without Trial* (3rd ed.). New York: Macmillan.

Skolnick, J. and T. Gray (eds.). 1975. *Police in America*. Boston: Little, Brown.

Smart, C. 1976. *Women, Crime and Criminology: A Feminist Critique*. London: Routledge and Kegan Paul.

Smelser, N. J. 1973. *Karl Marx on Society and Social Change*. Chicago: University of Chicago Press.

Sokoloff, N. J. and B. R. Price (eds.). 1995. *The Criminal Justice System and Women* (2nd ed.). New York: McGraw-Hill.

Solzhenitsyn, A. 1970. *The Gulag Archipelago*. New York: Bantam Books.

Soss, J. (2002). "TANF Reauthorization: Where Is the Language of Racial Justice? Race and Welfare in the U.S." Presentation to the CHN Welfare Advocates Meeting, American University, January 15.

Spitzer, S. 1975. "Toward a Marxian Theory of Deviance." *Social Problems* 22: 638–651.

———. 1993. "The Political Economy of Policing." In D. F. Greenberg (ed.), *Crime and Capitalism* (2nd ed.). Philadelphia: Temple University Press.

Spitzer, S. and A. T. Scull. 1977. "Privatization and Capitalist Development: The Case of Private Police." *Social Problems* 25.

Spring, J. 1972. *Education and the Rise of the Corporate State* Boston, Little, Brown.

Stabile, C. A. 1995. "Feminism Without Guarantees: The Misalliances and Missed Alliances of Postmodernist Social Theory." In A. Callari, S. Cullenberg, and C. Biewener (eds.), *Marxism in the Postmodern Age*. New York: Guilford Press.

Staples, W. G. 1997. *The Culture of Surveillance: Discipline and Social Control in the United States*. New York: St. Martin's Press.

Starkey, M. L. 1949. *The Devil in Massachusetts: A Modern Inquiry into the Salem Witch Trials*. Garden City, NJ: Doubleday and Company.

Sternberg, D. 1974. "The New Radical-Criminal Trials: A Step Toward a Class-for-Itself in the American Proletariat." In R. Quinney (ed.), *Criminal Justice in America*. Boston: Little, Brown.

Stoddard, E. R. 1975. "The Informal 'Code' of Police Deviancy." In J. Skolnick and T. Gray (eds.), *Police in America*. Boston: Little, Brown.

Stone, L. 1969. "Literacy and Education in England, 1640–1900." *Past and Present* 42: February.

Street, P. 2002. "Class, Color, and the Hidden Injuries of Race." *Z Magazine*, June, p. 40.

———. 2005. "Race, Place, and the Perils of Prisonomics." *Z Magazine* online, July/August, 2005. http://zmagsite.zmag.org/JulAug2005/street0705.html.

Streitfeld, D. 2004. "A Town's Future Is Leaving the Country." *Los Angeles Times*, March 28.

Substance Abuse and Mental Health Services Administration (1998). "National Household Survey on Drug Abuse: Summary Report." Rockville, MD: Substance Abuse and Mental Health Services Administration

Sudnow, D. 1965. "Normal Crimes: Sociological Features of the Penal Code in a Public Defender Office." *Social Problems* 12: 255–276.

Sutton, J. R. 1988. *Stubborn Children: Controlling Delinquency in the United*

States, 1640–1981. Berkeley: University of California Press.

Swisher, K., C. Wekesser, and W. Barbour (eds.). 1994. *Violence Against Women*. San Diego, CA: Greenhaven Press.

Tabb, W. 1970. *The Political Economy of the Black Ghetto*. New York: W.W. Norton.

Takagi, P. 1975. "The Walnut Street Jail: A Penal Reform to Centralize the Powers of the State." *Federal Probation* (December): 18–26.

Tanenhaus, D. 2004. *Juvenile Justice in the Making*. New York: Oxford University Press.

Tannenbaum, F. 1933. *Osborne of Sing Sing*. Chapel, NC: University of North Carolina Press.

Tappan, P. 1947. *Delinquent Girls in Court*. New York: Columbia University Press.

Taylor, A. A. 1941. *The Negro in Tennessee, 1865–1880*. Washington, DC: Associated Publishers.

Teitelbaum, L. E. and Harris, L. J. 1977. "Some Historical Perspectives on Governmental Regulation of Children and Parents." In L. E. Teitelbaum and A. R. Gough (eds.), *Beyond Control: Status Offenders in the Juvenile Court*. Cambridge, MA: Ballinger.

Tennessee Board of Prison Commissioners, *Report to the Governor* (annual and biennial reports). Nashville, 1896–1914.

Terkel, G. 1996. *Law and Society: Critical Approaches*. Boston: Allyn and Bacon, 1996.

Thomas, P. 1994. "Making Crime Pay: Triangle of Interests Creates Infrastructure to Fight Lawlessness." *Wall Street Journal*, May 12.

Thornberry, T. P. 1973. "Race, Socioeconomic Status and Sentencing in the Juvenile Justice System." *Journal of Criminal Law and Criminology* 64: 90–98.

Thrasher, F. 1927. *The Gang*. Chicago: University of Chicago Press.

Tigar, M. E. and M. R. Levy. 1977. *Law and the Rise of Capitalism*. New York: Monthly Review Press.

Time. 1988. "Where the War Is Being Lost," March 14.

Tipple, J. 1970. *The Capitalist Revolution*. New York: Pegasus.

Tolles, F. B. 1971. "Mary Dyer." In James, E. T., J. W. James, and P. S. Boyer (eds.), *Notable American Women, 1906–1950*. Cambridge, MA: Belknap Press of Harvard University Press.

Tonry, M. 1995. *Malign Neglect: Race, Crime, and Punishment in America*. New York: Oxford University Press.

———. 1998. "Crime and Punishment in America, 1971–1996." *Overcrowded Times* 9: 2 (April).

Travis, J. 2002. "Invisible Punishment: An Instrument of Social Exclusion." In M. Mauer and M. Chesney-Lind (eds.), *Invisible Punishment: The Collateral Consequences of Mass Imprisonment*. New York: New Press.

Trueblood, D. 1998. "Crack Cocaine and Social Control: The History of Cocaine Legislation." Masters thesis, Department of Criminal Justice, UNLV.

United Nations Office on Drugs and Crime (UNODC). 2005. *World Drug Report 2005*. Vienna, Austria: UNODC, June.

United States Census Bureau. 1918. *Prisoners and Juvenile Delinquents in the U.S., 1910*. Washington, DC: U.S. Government Printing Office.

United States Department of Commerce, Bureau of the Census. 1995. *Statistical Abstract of the United States, 1995*. Washington, DC: U.S. Government Printing Office.

U.S. Department of Justice. 1998. *Alcohol and Crime: An Analysis of National Data on the Prevalence of Alcohol Involvement in Crime*. Washington, DC: U.S. Department of Justice.

United States Sentencing Commission. 1995. *Cocaine and Federal Sentencing Policy, Special Report to Congress*. Washington, DC: U.S. Government Printing Office.

Vago, S. 1997. *Law and Society* (5th ed.). Upper Saddle River, NJ: Prentice Hall, 1997.

Vedder, C. B. and D. B. Sommerville. 1970. *The Delinquent Girl*. Springfield, IL: Charles C. Thomas.

Visher, C. A. 1983. "Gender, Police Arrest Decisions, and Notions of Chivalry." *Criminology* 21: 5–28.

Wagenaar, T. C. (1987). "What Do We Know About Dropping Out of High School?" *Research in Sociology of Education and Socialization*, 7: 161–90.

Wagner, D. 2005. *The Poorhouse America's Forgotten Institution*. New York: Rowman and Littlefield.

Walker, S. 1980. *Popular Justice: A History of American Criminal Justice*. New York: Oxford University Press.

———. 1998. *Popular Justice: A History of American Criminal Justice* (2nd ed.). New York: Oxford University Press.

———. 2006. *Sense and Nonsense About Crime and Drugs* (6th ed.). Belmont, CA: Thompson/Wadsworth.

Walker, S., C. Spohn, and M. DeLone. 2007. *The Color of Justice: Race, Ethnicity, and Crime in America*, (4th ed.). Belmont, CA: Wadsworth.

Wallace, L. H. and W. Pullman. 2004. "Socialization or Prisonization: Examining Deprivations in the School Setting." Paper presented at the Academy of Criminal Justice Sciences annual meeting, Las Vegas, NV, March 10.

Wambaugh, J. 1972. *The Blue Knight*. New York: Dell.

Ward, G. 2000. "Two Executives to Share $1.3 Million Upon Leaving Prison Realty Trust," www.tennessean.com/sii/oo/02/18/prison.shtml. February 17.

Warren, J. 2002. "Inmates' Families Pay Heavy Price for Staying in Touch." *Los Angeles Times*, February 16.

———. 2003. "Prison Guards Union Targets College Program for Inmates." *Los Angeles Times*, May 10.

———. 2004. "Shut Down State Youth Prisons, Experts Say." *Los Angeles Times*, September 22.

Washington Post. 1989. "Drug Buy Setup for Bush Speech: DEA Lured Seller to Lafayette Park." September 22.

———. 2000. "LAPD Corruption Case Keeps Growing. February 13.

Watterson, K. 1996. *Women in Prison: Inside the Concrete Womb.* Boston: Northeastern University Press.

Weber, M. 1946. *From Max Weber: Essays in Sociology* (Translated by H. H. Gerth and C. W. Mills). New York: Oxford University Press.

Webb, G. 1998. *Dark Alliance.* New York: Seven Stories Press.

Weinberg, D. H. 1996. "A Brief Look at Postwar U.S. Income Inequality." *Current Population Reports: Household Economic Studies, U.S. Census Bureau* (P60–191, June).

Weinstein, J. 1968. *The Corporate Ideal in the Liberal State, 1900–1918.* Boston: Little Brown.

Weiss, R. P. 1978. "The Emergence and Transformation of Private Detective Industrial Policing in the United States, 1850–1940." *Crime and Social Justice* 9: 35–48.

———. 1983. "Radical Criminology: A Recent Development." In E. H. Johnson (ed.). *International Handbook of Contemporary Developments in Criminology*, Vol. 1. Westport, CT: Guilford Press.

———. 1987a. "Humanitarianism, Labour Exploitation, or Social Control? A Critical Survey of Theory and Research on the Origin and Development of Prisons." *Social History* 12: 331–350. ·

———. 1987b. "From 'Slugging Detectives' to 'Labor Relations': Policing Labor at Ford, 1930–1947." In C. D. Shearing and P. C. Stenning (eds.), *Private Policing.* Newbury Park: Sage.

———. (ed.) 1999a. *Social History of Crime, Policing and Punishment.* Brookfield, VT: Ashgate.

———. 1999b. "Conclusion: Imprisonment at the Millennium 2000—Its Variety and Patterns Throughout the World." In R. P. Weiss and N. South (eds.), *Comparing Prison Systems: Toward a Comparative and International Penology.* Amsterdam: Gordon and Breach.

Western, B. and K. Beckett. 1999. "How Unregulated Is the U.S. Labor Market? The Penal System as a Labor Market." *American Journal of Sociology* 104: 1030–1060.

Whitt, J. A. 1993. "Toward a Class-Dialectical Model of Power: An Empirical Assessment of Three Competing Models of Political Power." In W. J. Chambliss and M. S. Zatz (eds.), *Making Law: the State, the Law, and Structural Contradictions.* Bloomington, IN: Indiana University Press.

Wice, P. B. 1985. *Chaos in the Courthouse: The Inner Workings of the Urban Criminal Courts.* New York: Praeger.

Wiebe, R. 1967. *The Search for Order, 1877–1920.* New York: Hill and Wang.

Wilbanks, W. 1986. "Are Female Felons Treated More Leniently by the Criminal Justice System?" *Justice Quarterly* 3: 517–529.

Williams, W. A. 1988. *The Contours of American History.* New York: W. W. Norton.

Wilson, V. Jr. 1974. *The Book of the Founding Fathers.* Brookeville, MD: American Historical Research Associates.

Wilson, W. J. 1987. *The Truly Disadvantaged.* Chicago: University of Chicago Press.

———. 1996. *When Work Disappears: The World of the New Urban Poor*. New York: Vintage Books.

Wines, E. C. and T. Dwight. 1973. *Report on the Prisons and Reformatories of the United States and Canada*. New York: AMS Press (originally published in 1867).

Wolfe, S. M. 1999. "Milton, Matthew and Managed Care." *Health Letter* 15, 12. Washington, DC: Public Citizen Health Research Group.

Wolff, E. 1994. "Trends in Household Wealth in the United States, 1962–83 and 1983–98." *Review of Income and Wealth* (Series 40, no. 2), June.

———. 1995. *Top Heavy: A Study of Increasing Inequality of Wealth in America*. New York: The Twentieth Century Fund Press.

Wolfgang, M. and M. Riedel. 1975. "Race, Judicial Discretion, and the Death Penalty." In W. J. Chambliss (ed.), *Criminal Law in Action*. New York: John Wiley.

Wolfgang, M., A. Kelly, and H. C. Nolde. 1962. "Comparisons of the Executed and the Commuted Among Admissions to Death Row." In M. E. Wolfgang, L. Savitz, and N. Johnston (eds.), *The Sociology of Punishment and Correction*. New York: John Wiley.

Woodward, C. V. 1955. *The Strange Career of Jim Crow*. New York: Oxford University Press.

———. 1969. *Origins of the New South, 1877–1913*. Baton Rouge: Louisiana State University Press.

Worden, A. P. 1991. "Privatizing Due Process: Issues in the Comparison of Assigned Counsel, Public Defender and Contracted Indigent Defense System." *Justice System Journal* 14: 390–419.

———.1993. "Counsel for the Poor: An Evaluation of Contracting for Indigent Criminal Defense." *Justice Quarterly* 10: 613–637.

Wray, L. R. 2000. "New Economic Reality: Penal Keynesianism." *Challenge* 43, 5: 39–59.

Wright, E. O. 1998. *Class Counts*. New York: Cambridge University Press.

Wright, P. 1997. "Profiting from Punishment." *Prison Labor News* (March). Reprinted in *CorpWatch: Holding Corporations Accountable*, online (www.corpwatch.org).

Wu, C. (ed.). 1972. *Chink: Anti-Chinese Prejudice in America*. New York: World.

Wu, H. 1996. "The Need to Restrain China." *Journal of International Affairs* 49: 355–360.

Zalman, M. and L. Siegel. 1994. *Cases and Comments on Criminal Procedure*. St. Paul: West.

Zawerucha, C. 2005. "SP4 Trial." *Z Magazine*. http://www.zmag.org/content/showarticle.cfm?ItemID=8644. September 03.

Zepezauer, M. 1994. *The CIA's Greatest Hits*. Tucson, AZ: Odonian Press.

Zepezauer, M. and A. Naiman. *Take the Rich Off Welfare*. Tucson, AZ: Odonian Press.

Ziedenberg, J. and V. Schiraldi. 2000. *Poor Prescription: The Costs of Imprisoning Drug Offenders in the United States*. Washington, DC: Justice Policy Institute.

Zimring, F. E. and G. Hawkins. 1991. "What Kind of Drug War?" *Social Justice* 18: 104–121.

Zinn, H. 1990. *The Politics of History* (2nd ed.). Urbana, IL: University of Illinois Press.

———. 1994. *You Can't Be Neutral on a Moving Train: A Personal History of Our Times*. Boston: Beacon Press.

———. 1997. *The Zinn Reader: Writings on Disobedience and Democracy*. New York: Seven Stories Press.

———. 2005. *A People's History of the United States* (6th ed.). New York: Harper Collins.

Name Index

Note: Page numbers followed by n *indicate notes.*

Abbott, G., 201, 210
Abt Associates, 58
Adamson, C. R., 39
Addams, J., 218
Adler, J. S., 32, 33, 63n
Albeda, R., 325n
Alinsky, Saul, 324
Allen, H. E., 172, 174–175
Altgeld, John, 78
American Correctional Association, 267, 268
Amsterdam, A., 140
Anderson, D., 54
Anderson, E. A., 163
Andrews, R. H., 252–253
Anslinger, Harry J., 45–47
Anthony, Susan B., 247
Ares, C. E., 143n
Ariès, P., 190
Arrigo, B. A., 275
Askin-Steve, J. L., 183
Associated Press, 290
Association of Trial Lawyers of America, 143n
Atwater, Bert, 296
Austin, J., 197, 218, 219, 305n
Ayres, E. L., 164, 165

Bacon, S., 67, 75
Baldus, D. C., 140
Barkan, S. E., 123, 124
Barnes, H. E., 152, 157, 159, 161, 162
Bartlett, D. L., 12, 19n

Bartollas, C., 326n
Barton, Clara, 238
Baum, B. E., 47–48
Baum, D., 52, 55, 129, 144n, 179, 304n
Baumer, E., 56
Beard, C., 36, 41
Beaumont, G. de, 159, 160, 161
Beccaria, C., 63n
Beck, A., 172, 184, 262, 276, 281, 293, 320
Beck, A. J., 101n, 275–276
Becker, H. S., 10, 46, 47
Beckett, K., 293
Bedau, H., 138
Bedau, H. A., 142
Belenko, S. R., 49, 50, 51, 53, 54, 55, 65n
Belknap, J., 19n
Bellucci, P. A., 44–45, 46, 56
Bender, Edwin, 282–283
Benekos, P., 137
Benner, L. A., 120
Bennett, William, 55
Bennett, W. L., 21
Ben-Yehuda, N., 63n
Berkowitz, B., 282
Bernard, T. J., 196, 199, 206, 212
Bernstein, J., 314
Berrigan, P., 123
Besser, T., 291
Bias, Len, 50–51
Blackstock, N., 95, 96
Blackstone, W., 195
Blakely, E. J., 272, 302
Blauner, R., 88–89

Blomberg, T. G., 149
Bluestone, B., 316
Blum, W., 95
Bonczar, T. C., 277
Borosage, R., 101n
Bottomore, T., 25
Bowers, W. J., 140
Bowles, S., 208, 209
Brace, Charles Loring, 14, 209, 210, 215
Bramhall, William, 109
Breggin, G. R., 59
Breggin, P. R., 59
Bremner, R. H., 196, 202, 203, 207, 210,
    211, 215, 230n
Brenzel, B., 210, 249, 250
Brewer, David J., 113–114
Brockway, Zebolun, 161, 162–163
Brown, D., 37
Brown, Henry B., 39
Brown, Joseph E., 167
Brown, W., 5, 272, 304n
Brownstein, H. H., 44–45, 46, 49, 50, 56
Buchanan, Michael, 94
Bureau of Justice Statistics, 134, 143n, 180,
    181, 187n, 255
Burns, Daniel, 126–127
Burns, H., 37, 38, 40
Burton-Rose, D., 284–285
Bush, George H. W., 54, 55, 129
Buss, D., 301
Butterfield, F., 290
Bynum, T., 143n

Cable, G., 165
Cain, M., 253
Calavita, K., 19n
Camp, C. G., 279, 281
Camp, G. M., 279, 281
Campaign for an Effective Crime
    Policy, 137
Cannon, A., 227, 230n
Carey, A., 86, 101n, 325n
Carlson, T., 302
Castro, Fidel, 94
Catchpole, Judith, 109
Cate, Matthew, 229
Caufield, S., 275
Center for Popular Economics, 3, 12, 316,
    317, 325n

Center for Research on Criminal Justice,
    74, 75, 79, 81–82, 86
Center on Budget and Policy
    Priorities, 314
Center on Juvenile and Criminal Justice,
    222, 285
Chambliss, W. J., 11, 19n, 24, 25, 30, 32,
    33, 35, 42–43, 44, 45, 54, 59, 60, 63n,
    66, 91–92, 92, 98, 150, 234
Chapin, B., 105, 108
Chapper, J., 120
Chesney-Lind, M., 19n, 219, 247–248, 254,
    255, 264, 267, 269n, 313
Cheyney, E. P., 27, 32
Chomsky, N., 15, 18, 19n, 37, 54, 60, 62n,
    63n, 64n, 65n, 84, 95, 96, 101, 101n,
    157, 186n, 325n
Christianson, S., 147, 148–149
Christie, N., 178, 312
Church, Frank, 95
Churchill, W., 101n
Clark, L. D., 114, 115
Clarke, S. H., 143n
Clear, T., 294
Clemens, Russell, 300
Clement, D., 287–288, 290–291, 305n
Clinton, Bill, 12, 63n
Cloward, R., 15, 19n, 83, 211
Cockburn, A., 64n, 95n, 101n, 285
Cohen, D. K., 209
Cohen, S., 63n
Cohen, Sidney, 48
Cohn, A. H., 252–253
Cole, D., 3, 17, 19n, 40, 51, 92, 93, 120,
    121, 141, 142, 143n, 325n
Collins, C., 3, 12, 13, 183, 317
Collins, C. F., 237, 242
Colquhoun, Patrick, 70–71,
    148–149
Common Cause, 301
Congressional Budget Office, 314
Conquest, R., 183
Cook, F., 123
Cooley, C. H., 214
Courtless, T. F., 234
Crary, D., 149, 150
Cray, C., 5
Critchley, T. A., 70, 71
Crofton, Walter, 161

Cromwell, P., 173
Cubberly, Ellwood, 209
Cullen, L., 60
Cunningham, L., 50, 56
Cuomo, Mario, 288
Currie, E., 19n, 98, 131, 178, 179, 221

Daile, B. R., 109
Daly, K., 248, 254, 255
Datesman, S., 253
Davis, M., 302
DeLone, M., 19n, 141, 222, 224
Deloria, V., 37
Denton, N. A., 187n
Derber, C., 79–80, 325n
Dewey, Thomas, 95
Diamond, S., 23, 27
Dilulio, J. L., 58
Dinnerstein, L., 39, 40
Ditton, J., 63n
Dix, Dorothea, 238, 240
Dobash, R. E., 198, 234
Dobbs, Dorothy, 48
Dole, Bob, 54
Domhoff, G. W., 3, 13, 21
Donner, F. J., 101n
Donziger, S., 255, 256, 258, 263, 287
Douglas, D. C., 26
Dryfoos, J., 267
Duke, L., 288, 289, 291, 293, 304
Dulles, John and Allen, 95
Durkheim, E., 7
Durkheim, Emile, 185
Durose, M. R., 99
Duster, T., 45
Dwight, T., 162
Dyer, J., 281, 284, 288, 298, 300
Dyer, Mary, 110, 235–236

Eastmen, M., 14
Economist, The, 325n
Eisenstein, E., 193
Eisenstein, Z. R., 234
Eitzen, D. S., 313, 314, 325n
Ekrich, A. R., 152
Ellsworth, Elizabeth, 111
Emerson, S., 113
Engels, F., 10, 14
Erickson, K. T., 34, 35, 63n

Ericson, R. V., 275
Evans, S. M., 109

Fagan, J., 51, 52, 53
Fair, Barbara, 150
Faludi, S., 236
Farnham, A., 302
Farrell, R. A., 143n
Feagin, J. R., 126
Feinman, C., 245–246
Feld, B., 214
Fellner, J., 99–100, 221–222
Ferdinand, T. N., 76
Feyerherm, W., 219
Fielding, Henry, 70
Finckenauer, J. O., 214
Finder, A., 118
Fisher, E., 314
Fisher, Frank, 206
Fitzgerald, K., 301
Flaherty, D. H., 106, 108
Folbre, N., 3, 12, 316, 317, 325n
Foote, C., 143n
Ford, Henry, 86–87
Fortus, Abe, 231n
Forward, Jonathan, 148
Foster, M., 66
Foucault, M., 146, 154
France, Anatole, 61–62
Freedman, E. B., 237, 238, 239, 240,
    245–246, 255
Freud, Sigmund, 43
Friedman, L. J., 165
Friedman, L. M., 34, 35, 36, 38, 39, 61,
    64n, 74, 105, 106, 108, 109, 110,
    112–113
Friedrichs, D. O., 5, 17, 19n, 60
Fry, Elizabeth, 238, 240
Furman, William, 138

Galliher, J. F., 47–48
Gardiner, J., 90
Garfinkel, H., 140
Garrow, D. J., 101n
Geis, G., 7, 19n
Genovese, E., 39, 68
Gerard, James W., 200
Gest, T., 50
Gibbons, D., 253

Giddens, A., 14, 311
Gilbert, D., 3
Gillaspy, Tom, 293–294
Gingrich, Newt, 63n
Glassner, B., 64n, 272
Glaze, L. E., 277
Glick, H. R., 106
Goffman, I., 153, 176, 186n
Gold, Steven, 150
Golden, R., 231n
Goldfarb, R., 117
Goldstein, P. J., 44–45,
    46, 56
Golub, A., 51, 52, 53
Goode, E., 63n
Gordon, D., 4, 15, 304n
Gordon, L., 245–246
Gould, E., 314
*Governmental Executive
    Magazine*, 276
Grady, Claire, 128
Grady, Theresa, 128
Graham, J. M., 48, 49
Gray, M., 45, 46, 47, 129
Greenberg, D., 109
Greenberg, D. F., 70, 73
Greene, J., 290, 305n
Greenfield, L. A., 58
Greenstein, R., 12
Greider, W., 325n
Griswold, M. J., 253
Gross, S. R., 140
Gutman, R. M., 120
Gutteridge, S., 234

Haber, S., 85
Haggerty, K. D., 275
Hall, J., 30, 31
Hallett, M., 147, 148, 153, 164, 165,
    167, 296
Hancock, L., 253
Hanh, T. N., 323–324
Hanson, R., 120
Harlan, John Marshall, 39
Harring, S., 41, 76, 77, 78, 79
Harris, J. R., 183
Harris, L., 25
Harris, L. J., 198, 244, 245
Harris, M., 63n

Harrison, B., 316
Harrison, P. M., 172, 184, 262, 275–276,
    281, 293, 320
Haskins, G. L., 34, 108
Hatch, Orin, 142
Hawes, J., 195, 197, 200–201, 203, 204,
    210, 230n
Hawkins, D. F., 19n
Hawkins, G., 49, 55
Hay, D., 28–29
Hays, S. P., 83
Healey, Kerry, 304n
Heilbroner, R. L., 63n, 269n, 278–279, 309,
    310, 311, 325n
Heintz, J., 3, 12, 317
Helmer, J., 43
Henderson, C. R., 214
Hepburn, J., 59
Herman, E., 65n, 101n,
    297–298, 325n
Herman, E. S., 65n
Hill, P. G., 158
Hindus, M. S., 109, 186n
Hoag, E., 169
Hobbes, Thomas, 7–8
Hoebel, E. A., 24
Hoffman, Abbie, 96
Hofstadter, R., 83
Hogg, R., 153, 155, 156
Holt, M. I., 210
Hoover, J. Edgar, 95, 97
Hope, T., 272
Horton, Scott, 127
Horton, Willie, 54
Howard, John, 158
Huberman, L., 32
Huling, T., 285–286, 287, 290, 291, 292,
    293, 294, 305n
Human Rights Watch, 100–101, 128, 132,
    133–134
Humphries, D., 70, 73
Hutchinson, Ann, 109
Hutchinson, Anne, 35, 235
Hyams, J., 170

Ignatieff, M., 72, 151, 152, 153, 154,
    155, 186n
Inciardi, J. A., 31, 44, 46, 98, 221
Ingersoll, John, 48

Irwin, J., 15, 116, 173, 175, 176, 177, 186n, 305n
Ives, G., 153

Jablon, R., 94
Jackson, B., 104
Jefferson, Thomas, 106
Jeffery, C. R., 29
Jenkins, P., 49, 55
Jiminez, Juan, 94
Johnson, B. D., 51, 52, 53
Johnson, C., 304n
Johnson, C. S., 165
Johnson, G. B., 140
Johnson, H. A., 21, 24, 25
Josephson, M., 40, 63n, 79, 143n
Justice Policy Institute, 133

Kalmanoff, A., 75, 85
Karberg, J. C., 262, 275–276, 293
Karlsen, C. F., 236
Kelly, A., 140
Kelly, M., 113, 143n, 325n
Kelly, R. M., 88
Kennedy, John F., 47, 94
Kennedy, R., 141, 142
Kennedy, Robert, 2, 94
Kett, J. F., 196–197
Kevorkian, Jack, 6
Keynes, John Maynard, 304n
Khan, M., 300
Kiernan, V. G., 25
Kilborn, T., 286
Killinger, G. F., 173
King, Martin Luther Jr., 95
King, R., 291, 292
King, Rodney, 1, 4, 93, 126
Kinzer, S., 65n, 95
Kirchheimer, O., 145–146, 151, 152, 155
Klass, Polly, 137
Klein, M., 50, 56, 93, 304n
Knapp Commission, 89, 90, 91
Knappman, E. W., 105, 109
Koch, G. G., 143n
Kolko, C., 83, 84
Komp, C., 126
Kopp, P., 270
Korten, D. C., 325n

Kramer, R., 97
Kraska, P. B., 275
Krisberg, B., 197, 218, 219
Kuhn, A., 178
Kulish, N., 292–293
Kunzel, R., 218

Landis, T., 286–287, 290
Lane, R., 75, 76
Langan, P. A., 99
Langeland, T., 37
Lansky, Meyer, 94–95
Laursen, E., 297
Lawrence, S., 274, 291–292
Lazeron, M., 209
Leondar-Wright, B., 3, 12, 13
Leong, A., 64n
Lerner, G., 233
Lerner, S., 269n
Leslie, R. J., 95
Lettiere, M., 156, 158, 160, 180, 185, 187n
Levine, H. G., 17, 49, 51, 65n
Levinthal, C., 43, 44, 45–46, 47
Levy, M. R., 23, 24, 25, 30
Lewis, A., 119
Lewis, Cora, 247
Liazos, A., 218
Lilly, J., 183
Lindesmith, A. R., 45
Linebaugh, P., 62n, 63n, 152
Link, A., 82, 84
Lipsitz, G., 87
Litvan, L. M., 302
Lockwood, D., 98, 221
Long, Terry, 51
Lorde, A., 234
Los Angeles Times, 50, 93, 94
Low, S., 303
Lowell, Josephine Shaw, 238, 239
Lubove, R., 218
Luciano, Lucky, 94–95
Lucken, K., 149
Lyman, J. L., 70, 72, 73
Lynch, M. J., 19n, 73, 121, 125, 126, 143n

Maas, P., 90
MacCormick, Austin, 171
Mackey, P. E., 109

MacKinnon, C., 236
Maconochie, Alexander, 161
Madison, J., 157
Mager, A., 127–128
Maguire, K., 65n, 101n, 121, 131, 178, 180
Mancini, M. J., 166, 167
Mann, A., 82, 101n
Mann, C. R., 98
Marchetti, V., 101n
Marcus, James, 90
Marks, A., 290
Marks, J., 101n
Marks, J, D., 101n
Marshall, John, 111–112
Marshall, Thurgood, 141
Marx, K., 10, 14, 63n, 70, 150, 151
Massey, D. S., 187n
Massey, J. L., 39
Mattera, P., 300
Mauer, M., 65n, 101n, 131, 183, 185–186, 291, 292, 313
Mauro, R., 140
Mause, L. de, 194
Maxson, C., 50, 56
Maynard, M., 294
McAvoy, Thomas J., 127
McCarthy, Joseph R., 45
McCartney, J. L., 47–48
McConville, S., 116–117, 118
McCoy, A. W., 64n
McDonald, W. F., 115
McGarrell, E., 99, 221
McHenry, R., 110, 235
McKelvey, B., 167
McKirdy, C. R., 106, 107
Meier, A., 165
Meierhoefer, B. S., 99
Melossi, D., 147, 155, 156, 158, 160, 180, 185, 187n
Mennel, R., 202, 203, 209, 230n
Merlo, A. V., 137
Merry, S. E., 103
Messerschmidt, J. W., 17, 245–246
Michalowski, R., 2, 8, 19n, 23, 24, 30, 60, 73, 97, 121, 125, 126
Miliband, R., 25, 62n
Miller, E., 254
Miller, J. G., 51, 52, 93, 98, 99, 179, 185–186, 219, 221, 224, 230n, 307n

Miller, M. B., 163, 170
Miller, W. R., 70, 71, 72–73, 101n
Millman, J., 302
Mills, C. W., 2
Milovanovic, D., 62
Miringoff, M., 12
Mitchell, John, 48
Mokhiber, R., 5, 60
Monkkonen, E., 15
Morain, D., 305n
Morash, M. A., 163
Morgan, E. S., 109
Mumola, C. J., 101n
Munk, N., 302
Murton, T., 170
Musto, D. F., 43, 44, 47
Myers, Gustavus, 60
Myers, M. A., 39

Naffine, N., 252
Naiman, A., 325n
National Commission on Law Obervance and Enforcement, 89
National Poverty Center, 319
Neary, B., 120
Nelson, W. E., 34, 35
Neubauer, D. W., 103, 104, 111, 114, 116, 120, 121
Newsweek, 55
New York Times, 56
Nixon, Richard, 48, 95
Nohn, H., 101n
Nolde, H. C., 140
Nye, R., 83

O'Connor, J., 11
Odem, M., 245–246, 247, 250, 251, 252
Office of National Drug Control Policy, 58
Oglethorpe, James Edward, 149
Osborne, L. T., 215, 230n
Osborne, Thomas Mott, 168
Osgood, R. K., 107, 108
Oshinksy, D. M., 165
Ovando, Francisco, 93

Parenti, C., 51, 65n, 93, 101n, 278, 288, 295
Parenti, M., 9, 21, 233–234
Parks, E. L., 69, 74, 81

Pasko, L., 19n, 254, 264, 267, 269n
Pasqualini, J., 183
Patrick, Deval, 304n
Patterson, E. B., 143n
Peel, Robert, 72–74
Penn, William, 156
Pepper, Claude, 48
Perrucci, R., 3, 12
Pfohl, S., 63n
Phillips, K., 3, 12
Pickett, R., 201, 202, 230n
Pina, Al, 94
Pisciotta, A., 161, 162, 203,
    230n, 248
Piven, F. F., 15, 19n, 83, 211
Platt, A., 162, 196, 197, 209, 213, 217,
    230n, 231n, 238, 245
Poggi, G., 63n
Pollock, J. M., 232, 236
Pontell, H. N., 19n
Pope, C., 219
Postman, N., 147, 189–195, 197, 207
Pottieger, A. E., 98, 221
Pound, R., 7
Poveda, T. G., 19n
Powell, J. C., 172
Powers, E., 34, 156
President's Commission, 89, 273
Price, B. R., 236
Prison Policy Initiative, 289, 292, 294
Proband, S. C., 179, 184
Pulaski, C. A., 140
Pullman, W., 305n
Putnam, C. E., 142

Quayle, Dan, 4
Quigley, B., 126–127
Quinney, R., 3, 6, 7, 8–10, 19n, 22, 25, 34,
    36, 59, 90, 97, 151, 273, 275

Radelet, L. A., 81
Radelet, M. L., 140, 142
Rafter, N. H., 232, 237, 238, 240,
    241–243, 244, 245, 249, 255
Rankin, A., 143n
Reagan, Ronald, 51, 96
Reaves, B. A., 99, 135, 136
Reiman, J. H., 3–5, 325n
Reimers, D. M., 39, 40

Reinarman, C., 17, 49, 51, 65n
Reith, C., 67, 69, 70
Rhode, D., 296
Richards, S., 178, 183
Richardson, J. F., 71, 74, 75, 76, 86
Riedel, M., 140
Rioting, 126
Ritzer, G., 325n
Rivas, Walter, 94
Roche, T., 290, 305n
Rogers, Don, 50
Rogers, K., 252
Romero, Gloria, 227
Rose, D. R., 294
Rossides, D. W., 19n
Rothman, D., 156, 158, 163, 168, 169,
    170, 171, 173, 197, 200, 202–203,
    204, 211
Rothman, R., 3, 153
Rotman, E., 173, 174, 175–177
Rudwick, E., 165
Ruigrok, W., 325n
Rupert, P. C., 314
Rusche, G., 145–146, 151, 152, 155
Rush, Benjamin, 160
Rush, G. E., 104
Ryan, George, 290
Ryan, P. J., 44–45, 46, 56
Ryther, T. E., 25, 150

Sabol, W. J., 187n
St. Clair, J., 95n, 101n
Samaha, J., 120
Scarpitti, F., 253
Schiraldi, V., 65n, 101n, 284, 290
Schlosser, E., 187n, 283, 288, 289
Schlossman, S., 214, 245, 247, 248, 249,
    250, 251, 252
Schmidhauser, J. R., 111
Schmidt, S., 304n
Schorr, L., 316
Schwartz, B., 111, 112
Schwendinger, H., 212
Schwendinger, J., 212
Scull, A. T., 297
Seagal, D., 4
Seale, Bobby, 123
Sechrest, D. K., 144n
Seidman, R., 11, 24, 66, 92

Sellin, J. T., 138, 144n, 151, 164, 166, 167, 187n, 237
Semmes, R., 109, 110, 235
Serpico, Frank, 89–90
Server, A., 301–302
Shank, G., 151
Shannon, R. T., 213
Shapiro, I., 12
Shaw, A. G. L., 152
Shearing, C. D., 79
Shelden, R. G., 5, 19n, 39, 164, 186n, 209, 215, 217, 219, 230n, 245, 247, 249, 255, 267, 269n, 272, 304n, 306
Shichor, D., 144n
Sickmund, M., 274, 277
Siegel, L., 20, 258, 259
Silver, A., 8, 73, 75
Simon, J., 15–16, 161, 275
Sklar, H., 3, 12, 13, 314
Smart, C., 253
Smyth, Dennis, 51
Snyder, M. G., 272, 302
Sokoloff, N. J., 236
Solis, David, 94
Sominsen, C. E., 172, 174–175
Sommerville, D. B., 252
Soss, J., 320
Sparks, R., 272
Spitzer, S., 15, 71, 297
Spohn, C., 19n, 141, 222, 224
Spring, J., 64n, 192, 207–208
Stabile, C. A., 4
Stanko, E. A., 232
Staples, M. L., 110
Steele, J. B., 12, 19n
Stenning, P. C., 79
Stern, Irv, 90
Sternberg, D., 122, 123–124, 125
Stoddard, E. R., 90
Stone, L., 207
Street, P., 287, 292
Streitfeld, D., 295
Sturgis, Frank, 95
Sturz, H., 143n
Substance Abuse and Mental Health Services Administration, 58, 101n
Sudnow, D., 6
Sutton, J. R., 197, 198
Swigert, V. L., 143n

Tabb, W., 88
Takagi, P., 35, 157
Tanenhaus, D., 217
Tannenbaum, F., 187n
Tappan, P., 250
Taylor, Chrissy, 257
Taylor, Frederick, 50
Teitelbaum, L. E., 198, 244, 245
Tennessee Board of Prison Commissioners, 166
Terkel, G., 20, 104, 233, 236
Thompson, Tommy, 282
Thrasher, F., 218
Tigar, M. E., 23, 24, 25, 30
Time, 55
Tipple, J., 84
Tocqueville, A. de, 159, 160, 161
Tolles, F. B., 110, 235
Tolman, William H., 208
Tonry, M., 98, 186, 221
Tracy, S., 5, 304n
Travis, J., 274, 277, 291–292
Tribble, Brian, 51
Trott, Nicholas, 106
Trueblood, D., 43, 44, 45, 46, 47, 50, 52, 53

United Nations Office on Drugs and Crime, 57
United States Department of Commerce, 224, 316, 318, 321, 326n
United States Sentencing Commission, 44, 45, 47, 49, 50, 51, 52, 53, 54, 55
U.S. Department of Justice, 58, 255

Vago, S., 103, 104
Vander Wall, J., 101n
van Tulder, R., 325n
Vedder, C. B., 252
Vera, H., 126

Wagner, D., 186n
Walker, S., 18n, 19n, 83, 85, 89, 108, 109, 137, 141, 163, 168–169, 172, 174, 222, 224
Wallace, L. H., 305n
Wallach, S., 245, 247, 248, 249
Ward, G., 299
Warren, Earl, 118

Warren, J., 227–228, 231n, 283, 285
Washington Post, 55, 94
Watterson, K., 237, 238, 239
Webb, G., 64n
Weber, M., 27, 28–29, 85
Weinstein, J., 84
Weiss, R. P., 15, 63n, 79, 80, 86–87,
    154–155, 163, 164, 167, 186n, 187n
Welch, Rachel, 238
Wells, Alice Stebbins, 246–247
Western, B., 293
Whitt, J. A., 19n
Wice, P. B., 120
Wiebe, R., 83
Wild, Jonathan, 148
Wildeman, J., 3
Williams, E., 169
Williams, W. A., 83
William the Conqueror, 25–26, 27
Wilson, James, 106
Wilson, V. Jr., 106
Wilson, W. J., 312
Wines, E. C., 162
Winthrop, John, 34
Wolfe, N. T., 21, 24, 25

Wolfe, S. M., 299–300
Wolfgang, M., 140
Woodward, C. V., 39, 165
Woodworth, G., 140
Worden, A. P., 121
Wray, L. R., 289
Wright, E. O., 3
Wright, P., 284–285, 295–296
Wu, C., 39–40
Wu, H., 183
Wysong, E., 3, 12

Yeskel, F., 12, 13, 317
Yoanna, M. A. de, 37

Zalman, M., 20
Zatz, M. S., 19n
Zawerucha, C., 127
Zepezauer, M., 101n, 325n
Ziedenberg, J., 65n, 101n
Zimring, F. E., 49, 55
Zinn, H., 1–3, 13, 19n, 36, 38, 41–42,
    60, 61, 62, 62n, 63n, 64n, 78, 84,
    101n, 112, 113–114, 122, 143n, 157,
    186n, 325n

Subject Index

Abuse
  in houses of refuge, 203, 205
  women in prisons and, 265, 267
Acephalous (non-state) societies, law and,
  23–24
Adolescence (*see also* Childhood)
  history of, 190–192
African Americans
  arrest rates for drug offenders, 100
  cocaine and, 44–45, 49, 50–51
  colonization of, 88–89
  convict leasing and, 164–166
  executions and, 140
  illegal drug use and, 99
  incarceration of, 1
  incarceration rates for women, 262–263
  juvenile institution populations and,
    224–225
  juvenile justice and, 219–229
  laws targeting, 129–137
  poverty and, 254–255, 317–318, 320
  prison populations and, 180–183
  in prisons, 165–166
  slavery, 37–39
  women prisoners and, 237, 238, 240–242,
    264–265
Alcatraz, 174
Alcohol, public drunkenness, 81
Alcohol abuse, 58
Alfred Binet Intelligence Test, 209
American Civil Liberties Union (ACLU)
  on pregnant women and drugs, 259–260
  on silencing dissent, 127

  women, drugs, and, 257–258
American Correctional Association (ACA),
  162, 175, 280
American Legislative Exchange Council
  (ALEC), 282–283
American Prison Association, 175
Anomie theory, 308
Anti-Coolie Act (1862), 64n
Anti-Drug Abuse Acts (1986, 1988), 49, 51,
  52–55
Apartheid (American), 177–184
Appeals, 139
Appellate Courts, 103–104
Arawaks, 37
Argersinger v. Hamlin, 119
Ashurst-Summers Act (1935), 172
Atkins v. Virginia, 142
Auburn Penitentiary, 238
Auburn State Prison, 237
Auburn system of penal discipline, 158–160

Bail, 116
Baltimore House of Refuge, 211
Bed brokers, 283–284
Bellevue Penitentiary, 237
Betts v. Brady, 118
Bias, 1–2, 19n, 223–224
Bible, references to women in, 233
Bifurcated trial, 139
"Big House," 172–173
Bill of Rights, 13, 36, 93
Black Codes, 39, 237
Black Death (England, 1348), 31, 32

Black Panther Party (BPP), 95, 96
Boggs Act (1951), 47
Bow Street Runners, 70
Buffalo, NY, police in, 76–79
Bureau of Immigration and Customs
    Enforcement, 277
Bureau of Narcotics and Dangerous Drugs,
    46, 48

California, prisons in, 184
California Correctional Peace Officer's
    Union, 284–285
California Youth Authority (CYA), 226–229
Capital flight, 313–314
Capitalism
    Auburn system and, 159–160
    children and, 193, 194
    convict labor and, 163
    criminal justice and, 309–313
    developmental effect of, 1
    kidnapping and, 148
    nature of, 16, 308
    negative effects of, 311
    onset of, 31–32
    prisoners and, 149
    prisons and, 278–281
    public relations for, 84, 86
    triumph of, 112
    women and, 233–234, 238
    workhouses and, 150–152
Capital punishment, 138–143
Carrier case (1473), 30–31
Case study method, 169
Central Intelligence Agency (CIA), 94–95
Chain gangs, 167, 172
Chicago Area Project, 218
Chicago House of Refuge, 205–206
Chicago Seven Trial, 123–124
Chief pledge, 69
Child abuse, charges against pregnant
    women, 258–261
Childhood
    in 17th century, 192–197
    history of, 190–192
    invention of, 189–190
    parens patriae and stubbornness, 197–199
Children
    criminal offenses by, 195–196
    discipline of, 195

    education for, 192, 193, 194
Child-saving movement, 212–217, 244–248
Chinese-Americans, 39–40
Chisholm v. Georgia, 112
Civil service system, 86
Class, social
    18th century divisions of, 157
    drug laws and, 42–58
    law and, 10–18
    in Supreme Court, 111
Class-dialectical model, 19n
Classification, in prisons, 170, 174,
    175, 176
Cocaine
    forms and uses of, 43
    legislation for, 44–45, 49–56
    "War on Drugs" and, 100
    women addicted to, 258
COINTELPRO, 95–97
Coleman v. Alabama, 119
Colonial model, 88–89
Commodification, 234
Common Law principle, 195
Compassionate release law, 263–264
Comprehensive Drug Abuse and Prevention
    Act (1970), 48
Congregate system, 159
Consensus/pluralist model of law, 7–8
Constabulary system, 69
Contract Labor Law (1864), 42
Contract system
    for attorneys, 121
    on convict labor, 163–164
Convict labor, in prisons, 163–164
Convict leasing, 163, 164–167, 237
Corn Laws of 1815, 71
Corporate crime, costs of, 5, 60
Correctional Services Corporation, 226
Corrections Corporation of America
    (CCA), 286
Corrections Today, 279–281
Courts, U.S.
    1960s, 118–121
    colonial, 105–110
    death penalty, 138–143
    defined, 104
    jails, 116–118
    modern, 128–138
    overview, 102–105

post-Revolutionary, 111–116
trials, 122–128
Crack babies, 259
Crack cocaine, legislation for, 49–56
CRASH (Community Resources Against
    Street Hoodlums), 93
Crime
    business profits from, 272–274
    concept of, 29–30
    dangers of, 5
    social reality of, 8–9
Crime control
    ALEC, 282–283
    globalization of, 275–276
    industry of, 272–278
    overview, 270–272
    prison-industrial complex, 278–304
    prison labor, 295–299
    private security, 301–303
Crime rate, 277–278
Criminal law
    in America, 34–42
    in ancient times, 21–21
    in Athens, Greece, 22
    in England, 25–34
    as ideological system of legitimate
        control, 28–29
    in Medieval times, 24–25
    nature and functions of, 20–21
    perspectives on, 6–14
    in Rome, 22–23
Criminal offenses, by children,
    195–196
Critical/Marxist model of law, 10–14
Critical perspective, history of, 1–19
Custodial prisons, 239–240, 244

Dangerous classes, 1, 14–17 (*see also*
    Surplus population)
    "War on Drugs" for control
        of, 98–101
Death penalty, 138–143
Debtor's prison, 116, 117
Delinquency
    conceptions of, 214–215
    by girls, 248
    statutes for, 201
Department of Homeland Security, 276
Determinate sentencing, 50

District courts, 103
District of Columbia Reformatory for
    Women, 239
Dobbs v. Zant, 141
Double-jeopardy, 127
Double-standard, 219, 239, 250–253
Drug Enforcement Administration, 47
Drug laws (*see also* Law)
    cocaine, 49–56
    impact of, 56–58
    juvenile courts and, 220–224
    overview, 42–49
    "War on Drugs," 98–101
Drug Policy Alliance, 260
Drugs
    prison populations and, 179–180
    women and, 255–258
Dyer Act (1919), 174

Eastern Penitentiary (Pennsylvania), 158
Economic Policy Institute, 317–318
Economy, criminal justice and, 307–309
Edifices, 188, 307
Education
    criminal justice programs, 303
    in England, 192, 193, 194
    public schooling, 208–209
Eighteenth Amendment, 17
Elizabethan Poor Law (1572), 117
Elmira Reformatory, 161, 162–163
Employment, within the crime control
    industry, 272–273, 274, 276
Exclusion Law (1882), 40
Executions, 138–143
Executive branch of U.S. government, 20
Ex Parte Crouse, 204–205, 244

Federal Bureau of Investigations (FBI),
    95–97
Federal Bureau of Narcotics, 45
Federal courts, 103
Federal prison system, 173–175
Feminization, of poverty, 319
Feminization of poverty, 255
Ferguson v. City of Charleston, 259–260
Fetal Alcohol Syndrome, 260
Feudalism, 24–25
Field of Dreams syndrome, 188
Fifteenth Amendment, 236

Fifth Amendment, 114, 116
Florence, AZ, 292–293
Fourteenth Amendment, 113, 125, 236
Furman v. Georgia, 138

Gainesville Eight Trial, 123
Gated communities, 302–303
Gendannerie, 67
Ghettos, policing in, 88–89
Gideon v. Wainwright, 118–119
Gini Index of Inequality, 12
Girls, juvenile justice system and, 244–253
Globalization
    of crime control, 275–276
    of the economy, 313
Golden rule, 18
Good roads system, 172
Grandfather clause, 39
Grand jury, 114–115
Gregg v. Georgia, 138
Group counseling, 176
Gulags, 183–184

Habeas corpus, 206
Habitual offender laws, 137
Hard labor penalty, 157
Harrison Act (1914), 242
Harrison Narcotic Act (1914), 45, 174
Hawes-Cooper Act (1929), 172
Hegemony, defined, 62n
Heroin, 44, 45
Homestead Act (1862), 41–42
Homicide, laws for, 59–60
House of Refuge movement, 200–204

Illinois Juvenile Court Act (1899), 212, 213
Immigrants, 201, 207
Incarceration rates, 178–182
Indeterminate sentence, 161, 169–170, 175
Indiana Women's Prison, 238
Indigents, lawyers for, 120–121
Individualized treatment model, 169–171
Inmate self-government, 168–169
In re Gault, 219
Instrumentalist perspective, 10–11
Intelligence testing, 209
Interagency Policy on Cocaine Abuse in
    Pregnancy (IPCAP), 260
Interest group/conflict model of law, 8–10

Intervention, for delinquents, 214–215
Iran-Contra Affair, 97
Irish system, 161

Jails
    history of, 115–118
        Walnut Street Jail, 156–158
Japanese-Americans, 40
Jim Crow laws, 39
Johnson-Reed Immigration Act (1924), 40
Johnson v. Macintosh, 37
Judicial branch of U.S. government, 20–21
Judiciary Act (1789), 111
Jurek v. Texas, 139
Jus gentium, 23
Justice of the peace, 27, 107–108
Juvenile court, establishment of, 212–217
Juvenile delinquents, 199–200, 201
Juvenile justice system
    20th century, 218–219
    child-saving movement and, 212–217
    defining *juvenile delinquent*, 199–200
    drug laws and, 220–224
    emergence of, 84
    Ex Parte Crouse, 204–205
    girls and, 244–253
    House of Refuge movement, 200–204
    mid-19th century reforms, 206–212
    O'Connell case, 205–206
    overview, 188–189
    parens patriae and stubborn children,
        197–199
    pre-19th century, 189–197
    social work and, 218
Juvenile Protective League, 218
Juveniles, executing, 142

Kent v. United States, 219
Khadi justice, 28–29
Kidnapping, 148
Knapp Commission, 89, 90, 91

Labor force, 314–316
Labor unions, 86–88
Law (*see also* Criminal law; Drug laws;
        specific laws)
    customary, 27
    for delinquency and predelinquent
        behavior, 213

drug laws, 42–58
interests served by, 58–62
perspectives of, 7–14
racism and, 36–40
as reflection of society, 6–7
"War on Drugs," 98–101
women and (*see* Women)
Law of Theft, 30–32
Law of the Twelve Tables, 22–23
Law of Vagrancy, 32–33
Legislative branch of U.S. government, 20–21
Less eligibility, 155
Literacy, in children, 192–193
Little Hoover Commission, 265–267
Lock-step, 159
Lone Wolf v. Hitchcock, 37
Low-wage society, United States as, 314, 315
Luddite Riots, 71
Lumpenproletariat, 14
Lynching, 164–166

Magistrates, 103
Mandatory sentencing, 136–137
Mann Act (1910), 174
Marbury v. Madison, 112
Marijuana Tax Act (1937), 46, 47
Married Women's Property Acts, 236
Massachusetts Prison at Framington, 239
Massachusetts State Reform School for Boys, 210
McCleskey v. Kemp, 141
Medical crime, 5
Medical model of treatment, 169–171
Mens rea, 29
Mental health issues, women prisoners and, 268
Mental retardation, 142
Metropolitan Police of London, 70–72
Mexican-Americans, 40
Michigan, prisons in, 184, 187n
Militarization, of criminal justice, 275
Milwaukee Twelve Trial, 123
Miranda v. Arizona, 119
Mistretta v. United States, 53
Mockery of justice standard, 120
Mollen Commission, 92

Moral boundaries, 7
Morality, 108–109
Moral panics, 63n
Mutual pledge system, 68
Mutual Welfare League, 168

Narcotic Drug Control Act (1956), 47
National Congress of Penitentiary and Reformatory Discipline, 162, 238
National Drug Control Policy, 54–55
National Household Survey on Drug Abuse (NHSDA), 130
National Institute of Drug Abuse, 52
National Survey on Drug Use and Health (NSDUH), 130
Native Americans, laws and, 36–37
Nebraska, drug laws in, 47–48
Negro Courts, 237
New American Apartheid, 177–184
Newgate Prison, 159, 237
New Jersey Reformatory for Women at Clinton, 239
"New penology," 217
New York Children's Aid Society, 207, 210
New York House of Refuge, 200–201, 203, 204, 248
New York Juvenile Asylum, 207
New York Reformatory for Women, 239
Non-state societies, law and, 23–24
Norman law, 25
North Fork Correctional Facility, 286

Occupational crime, 5
O'Connell case, 205–206, 212
Office of Strategic Services (OSS), 94
Omnibus Crime Bill (1994), 142
Opium, 42–45
Orphan trains, 210
Overcrowding, 155

Panopticon prisons, 153
Parens patriae, 197–199, 205, 206, 244
Parole system, 15–16, 161
Patria protestas, 232
Patriarchy, images of women and, 232–234
Penal colonies, 287–289
Penal discipline, 146–147, 158–160
Penitentiaries, republicanism and, 160
Penitentiary Act (1779), 155

Pennsylvania system of penal discipline, 158–160
Penry v. Lynaugh, 142
People v. Turner, 205–206
Personal troubles, 2
Philadelphia House of Refuge, 204–205, 213
Pinkertons, 80–81
Plantation prison, 62n
Plessy v. Ferguson, 39, 112
Police
  in 20th century, 81–89
  corruption in, 89–98
  early systems, 66–68
  in England, 68–74
  female, 246–247
  "pregnancy police," 258–261
  private, 79–81, 86–88
  in the United States, 74–81
Political trials, 122–126
Poorhouses, 151, 156–157
Poverty
  Americans living in, 317–318
  feminization of, 255, 319
  women and, 254–255
Powder cocaine, legislation for, 49–56
Powell v. Alabama, 118
Power
  capitalism and, 309–310
  class structure and, 19n
  public policy and, 9–10
Pregnancy police, 258–261
President's Crime Commission, 89
Prison, negative aspects of, 289–292
Prisoners, exploitation of, 292–295
Prison-industrial complex
  ALEC, 282–283
  bed brokers, 283–284
  California Correctional Officer's Union, 284–285
  capitalism and, 278–281
  negative aspects of prison expansion, 289–292
  phone companies, 283
  prisoner exploitation, 292–295
  prison labor, 295–297
  private security, 301–303
  privatization of prisons, 297–301
  rural prisons, 285–289

Prison labor, 295–297
Prison Policy Initiative, 294
Prison reform
  in late 18th century, 152–156
  during Progressive Era, 168–173
Prisons
  1600-1900, 145–167
  20th century American, 168–184
  American, development of, 156–167
  American gulag, 183–184
  background characteristics of women in, 264–269
  birth of prison systems, 152–156
  capitalism, the workhouse, and, 150–152
  construction of, 281
  federal system, 173–175
  industries in, 171–172
  inmate trafficking, 147–150
  late 18th century reforms, 152–156
  panopticon, 153
  populations in, 178–182
  privatization of, 297–301
  Progressive Era reforms, 168–173
  rural, 285–289, 292–295
  system of corrections, 175–177
  warehousing, 177–183
  for women, 236–239
  women in, 261–264
Private policing, 79–81, 86–88
Private security, 301–303
Privatazation of prisons, 297–301
Probation, origins of, 230n
Probation officers, 214
Proffit v. Florida, 139
Profits, from crime, 272–274
Progressive Era, 82–86, 168–173
Prohibition, 17, 45, 81, 242
Prosecutor, role of, 115
Public issues, 2
Pure Food and Drug Act (1906), 44
Pyrrhic defeat theory, 3

Quakers
  in 17th century America, 34–35
  child discipline and, 195

Race/racism
  arrest rates for drug offenders, 100
  colonial model and, 88–89

death penalty and, 140–142
drugs and, 46
illegal drug use and, 99
incarceration rates for women, 262–263
juvenile institution populations and, 224–225
juvenile justice and, 219–229
law and, 36–40
poverty and, 317–318, 320
prison populations and, 180–182
"War on Drugs" and, 128–138
women prisoners and, 240–242, 264–265
Racial Justice Act, 142
Radical-criminal trials, 122–126
Rampart scandal, 93–94
Rape, death penalty and, 140
Reasonably competent attorney standard, 120
Recidivism, 225–229
Reed v. Reed, 236
Reformation
in mid-19th century, 211–212
women's prisons and, 239
Reformatories
for girls, 248, 249–250
rise of, 161–163
for women, 239–244
Reform Darwinism, 214
Reformers, 203
Refuge movement, 203–204
Rehabilitative ideal, 175
Relative surplus population, 14–15
Renaissance, 193
Reorganization Act (1801), 111
Republicanism, penitentiaries and, 160
Reserve army, 14–15, 311–312
Right to Counsel, 118–121
Rioting, 70, 75, 77, 300
Rockefeller Drug Laws (1974), 256
Roman Law, 22–23, 24–25
Roper v. Simmons, 142
Ruling class
capitalism, 309–310
in England, 32–33
law and, 10–13, 23
lawyers in, 106
women prisoners and, 243
Rural prisons, 285–289, 292–295

Schools
in England, 192, 193, 194
public, 208–209
Sedition Act (1798), 13, 35–36
Sentencing, "War on Drugs," women, and, 255–258
Sentencing guidelines, 50
Sentencing Reform Act (1984), 50
Sexuality
women prisoners and, 242–244
of young women, 251
Sharecropping system, 62n
Shay's Rebellion, 157
Shelby County Industrial and Training School, 216
Sheriffs, 26, 69
Sherman Anti-Trust Act, 97, 112–113
Silent system, 159
Sing Sing Prison, 237
Sixth Amendment, 118, 120, 125
Slavery
the law and, 37–39
prisoners and, 147
Smith v. State, 121
Social class
children and, 194
defined, 309
importance of, 3
Social Darwinism, 214
Social justice, defined, 3
Social justice movement, 84
Social purity movement, 242, 246
Social reformers, 203
Social work, juvenile justice system and, 218
Society for the Reformation of Juvenile Delinquents (SRJD), 200–201, 203, 204
Sociological imagination, 2
Solitary confinement, 158, 163, 168, 175
Spectators, at trials, 124–125
Stanford v. Kentucky, 142
State-corporate crime, 97
State courts, 103
State Industrial School for Girls, 249
State law, 29
State system, defined, 62n–63n
State-use system, of convict labor, 164
State v. Aaron, 196

Statutes of Laborers (1349), 32
Statutory rape, 246
St. Patrick's Four, 126–128
Strain theory, 308
Strictland v. Washington, 120
Structuralist perspective, 11
Stubborn Child Law, 198, 244
Substance Abuse and Mental Health
    Services (SAMHSA), 130
Summit View Correctional Center, 226
Supreme Court
    1960s rulings, 118–120
    on the death penalty, 138–139, 141–142
    position in court structure, 103
    post-Revolutionary, 111–116
    on public trials, 125
Surplus, use of term, 309
Surplus population, 14–15, 311–323
Symbolic politics, 4
System of corrections, 175–177

Taft-Hartley Act (1947), 86
Temperance Movement, 81
Texas, prisons in, 184
Theft, law of, 30–32
Thirteenth Amendment, 236
Thompson v. Oklahoma, 142
Three-Strikes and You're Out laws, 137
Total institutions, 176
Totalitarian police force, 67
Tracking system, in schools, 209
Traditional criminal trial, 122
Tramp Acts, 41–42
Transportation, as punishment, 148–150
Treadwheel, 155
Treatment programs, 175, 176
Trial courts, 103–104
Trials, traditional vs. radical-criminal,
    122–126
Tribal law, 29
Truth in sentencing, 50
Tythings, 68–69

United States Sentencing Commission and
    Determinate Sentencing, 50
United States v. Wade, 119
U.S. Constitution
    for creation of laws, 20
    discrimination in, 39

    law enforcement and, 93
    purpose of, 13
    women and, 236
U.S. Courts of Appeals, 103
U.S. Department of Health and Human
    Services, 260
U.S. magistrates, 103
U.S. Office of Drug Control Policy, 57–58

Vagrancy, law of, 32–33
Venereal disease, 251
Vigilantism, 1, 18n
Volstead Act (1918), 174
Volstead Act (1919), 242

Wabash Railway v. Illinois, 113
Wagner Act (National Labor Relations Act)
    (1935), 86
Walnut Street Jail, 156–158
Warehousing, 177–184
War of 1812, 71
"War on Drugs"
    to control dangerous classes, 98–101
    impact of, 128–138
    juvenile courts and, 220–224
    women, sentencing, and, 255–258
Warren Court, 118–121
Watergate, 94, 96–97
Water torture, 167
Wayward Minor Court, 250
Welfare reform movement, 320
Western Penitentiary (Pennsylvania), 158
White collar crime, costs of, 5, 60
White House Seven Trial, 124
Wickersham Commission (1931), 89
Witchcraft, 35, 109–110
Witch hunts, 63n, 236
Women
    double-standard, 219
    girls and juvenile justice, 244–253
    juvenile institution populations and,
        224–225
    in labor force, 316
    living in poverty, 319
    patriarchy and images of, 232–234
    pregnancy police, 258–261
    present-day criminal justice and,
        254–269
    prison populations and, 181, 182

prisons and, 236–239, 261–269
punishing and controlling, 234–236
racism and, 240–242
reformatories for, 239–244
sentencing and, 255–258
sexuality and, 242–244
"War on Drugs" and, 255–258

witchcraft and, 35, 109–110
Women's Prison Association of New York,
    242–243
Workhouses
    capitalism and, 150–152
    for the poor, 156–157
World Drug Report 2005, 57